Student Edition

History Alive!®
The Medieval World and Beyond

Chief Executive Officer
Bert Bower

Chief Operating Officer
Amy Larson

Director of Product Development
Maria Favata

Director of Operations
Marsha Ifurung

Strategic Product Manager
Nathan Wellborne

Social Studies Team Manager
Ginger Wu

Senior Editor
Mikaila Garfinkel

Program Editors and Writers
Sally Isaacs
Lauren Kent
Beth Lasser
Tylar Pendgraft
Alex White

Production Manager
Jodi Forrest

Senior Production Designer
Sarah Osentowski

Art Direction
Julia Foug

Teachers' Curriculum Institute
PO Box 1327
Rancho Cordova, CA 95741

Customer Service: 800-497-6138
www.teachtci.com

ISBN 978-1-58371-238-2
4 5 6 7 8 9 10 11 WC 23 22 21 20 19

Manufactured by Webcrafters, Inc., Madison, WI
United States of America, July 2019, Job# WC1904987

Program Author

Wendy Frey

Contributing Writers

Lillian Duggan

Marisa A. Howard

Barbara Johnson

Christopher Johnson

Rena Korb

Joan Kane Nichols

Joy Nolan

Curriculum Developers

Joyce Bartky

April Bennett

Nicole Boylan

Terry Coburn

Sarah Cook

Julie Cremin

Mary Elizabeth

Erin Fry

Amy George

Jake Kerman

Beth Lasser

Anne Maloney

Steve Seely

Kelly Shafsky

Nathan Wellborne

Alex White

Ginger Wu

Reading Specialist

Kate Kinsella, Ed.D

Reading and TESOL Specialist

San Francisco State University

Teacher Consultants

Terry Coburn

Brookside School

Stockton, California

Randi Gibson

Stanford Middle School

Long Beach, California

Jana Kreger

Hanover Middle School

Hanover, Massachusetts

Dawn Lavond

SC Rogers Middle School

San Jose, California

Michal Lim

Borel Middle School

San Mateo, California

Alana D. Murray

Parkland Middle School

Rockville, Maryland

Stevie Wheeler

Rincon Middle School

San Diego, California

How to Use This Program

The components of this program provide the tools needed for a complete learning cycle.

1 The teacher begins each lesson with a **Lesson Presentation** preview activity that engages inquiry and sets a foundation for the lesson's content.

2 Guided by the Presentation, students participate in an interactive **activity** that connects to both the C3 Framework and English Language Arts literacy. In these activities, students use the tools of social studies inquiry: asking questions, using sources and other evidence to develop claims, and communicating conclusions.

3 In their online **Student Subscription,** students expand their knowledge through reading the **Student Text** and working through an **Interactive Tutorial**. They then process what they have learned in their online **Interactive Student Notebook**. Students can also test their knowledge by playing a game-like online **Reading Challenge**. Alternatively, students can read from the hardcover **Student Edition** and complete a consumable Interactive Student Notebook.

4 The lesson concludes with students demonstrating their knowledge of the lesson's core ideas and of the inquiry process though a variety of paper and online **assessments**.

How to Read the Table of Contents

The table of contents is your guide to *History Alive! The Medieval World and Beyond*. It lists all the lessons in your text, as well as additional resources, such as *Investigating Primary Sources* sections, maps, and diagrams.

Each unit begins with **Setting the Stage**, which provides historical and geographic background for the unit.

The **lesson title** tells you the overall topic of the lesson.

In a **Site of Encounter**, explore artifacts and narratives to better understand cultural exchanges in the medieval world.

Every lesson begins with an **essential question** to prepare you for inquiry—asking your own questions and proposing supported answers and solutions.

Reading Further and **Investigating Primary Sources** are in-depth explorations of relevant topics that promote literacy and help you explore the inquiry process even further.

A **Timeline** at the end of each unit serves as a visual recap of the content discussed in that unit.

UNIT 1

Europe During Medieval Times

UNIT 2

Islam in Medieval Times

UNIT 3

South Asia, 300–1200

UNIT 4

The Culture and Kingdoms of West Africa

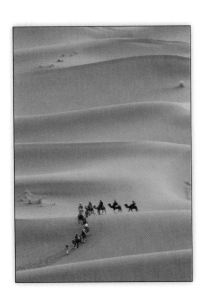

UNIT 5

Imperial China

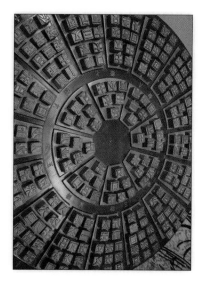

UNIT 6

Japan During Medieval Times

UNIT 7

Civilizations of the Americas

UNIT 8

The Medieval World, 1200–1490

UNIT 9

Europe's Renaissance and Reformation

UNIT 10

Europe Enters the Modern Age

Maps

Diagrams and Tables

Selected Primary Sources: Text

Stephen, Count of Blois and Chartres, To His Wife, Adele

Count Stephen to Adele, his sweetest and most amiable wife, to his dear children, and to all his vassals of all ranks—his greeting and blessing.

You may be very sure, dearest, that the messenger whom I sent to give you pleasure, left me before Antioch safe and unharmed, and through God's grace in the greatest prosperity. And already at that time, together with all the chosen army of Christ, endowed with great valor by Him, we had been continuously advancing for twenty-three weeks toward the home of our Lord Jesus. You may know for certain, my beloved, that of gold, silver and many other kind of riches I now have twice as much as your love had assigned to me when I left you. For all our princes, with the common consent of the whole army, against my own wishes, have made me up to the present time the leader, chief and director of their whole expedition.

You have certainly heard that after the capture of the city of Nicaea we fought a great battle with the perfidious Turks and by God's aid conquered them. Next we conquered for the Lord all Romania and afterwards Cappadocia. And we learned that there was a certain Turkish prince Assam, dwelling in Cappadocia . . . thither we directed our course. All his castles we conquered by force and compelled him to flee to a certain very strong castle situated on a high rock. We also gave the land of that Assam to one of our chiefs and in order that he might conquer the above-mentioned Assam, we left there with him many soldiers of Christ. Thence, continually following the wicked Turks, we drove them through the midst of Armenia, as far as the great river Euphrates. Having left all their baggage and beasts of burden on the bank, they fled across the river into Arabia.

—Stephen, Count of Blois, 1098

The C3 Framework

The four Dimensions identified by the National Council for Social Studies in *The College, Career, and Civic Life (C3) Framework for Social Studies State Standards* help prepare students to be engaged and thoughtful citizens as they explore social studies using the Inquiry Arc. *History Alive!* integrates each of these Dimensions.

Dimension 1

Developing Questions and Planning Inquiries

The inquiry process begins with the use of compelling and supporting questions that are developed by both teachers and students. The story-like Student Text in *History Alive!* inspires questioning. The Preview activities in each Presentation connect to prior knowledge and encourage students to ask questions and plan inquiries.

Dimension 2

Applying Disciplinary Concepts and Tools

Together, students and teachers create a base for inquiry and research by determining the background and content needed to answer their questions. *History Alive!* 's Student Text scaffolds disciplinary concepts in civics, economics, geography, and history throughout each grade.

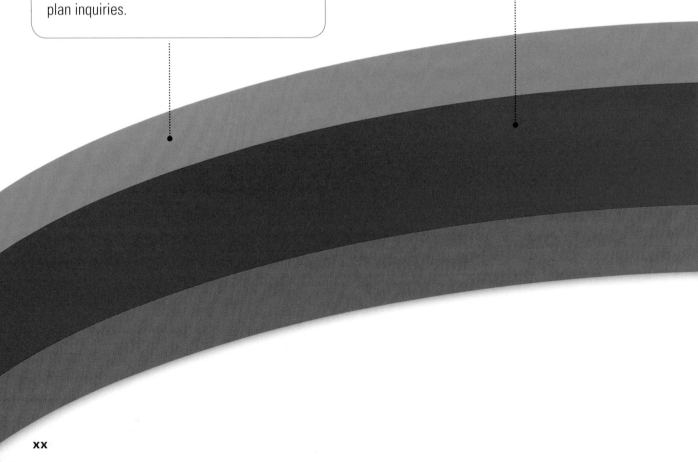

Dimension 3

Evaluating Sources and Using Evidence

Compelling questions call for students to obtain and evaluate evidence from primary and secondary sources to help support their claims. In *History Alive!*, students pursue research and make evidence-supported claims during class discussions and in their Interactive Student Notebooks.

Dimension 4

Communicating Conclusions and Taking Informed Action

Students have the opportunity to build their claims both independently and collaboratively, to receive critiques, and to present their claims in public settings. Both individually and in groups, students of *History Alive!* construct and critique historical explanations and arguments. Throughout activities, students present their claims in a variety of formats.

Investigating Primary Sources

Each unit in *History Alive!* has a four-page *Investigating Primary Sources* feature that engages and challenges students to analyze a variety of sources. Each feature incorporates a set of style and content elements that guides students into building strong arguments supported with evidence. Here are some highlights that show how *Investigating Primary Sources* engages students' curiosities.

The title frames an engaging, compelling question that guides the entire piece. Students later build a claim that answers this question.

A bold introduction paragraph sets up the compelling question and the sources that students will explore.

What Kind of Ruler Was Justinian I?

He was called Justinian the Great, but did he live up to his name? He is both praised and criticized in history books. Justinian I ruled the Byzantine Empire from 527 to 565. You will read two primary sources about Justinian that will help you understand and explain what kind of ruler he was.

Justinian I was the emperor of the Byzantine Empire, previously the Eastern Roman Empire, at a time of great turmoil. While he brought about several positive changes, many people considered him a tyrant.

One of his achievements was expanding the Byzantine Empire to its greatest size in history. By the time of his reign, most of the Western Roman Empire had collapsed, and Justinian was determined to regain that territory. He retrieved areas in Italy, the southeastern coast of Spain, and much of North Africa that had previously been lost by enemy invasion.

Justinian was also responsible for restoring much of the beauty of the empire, which had suffered devastation from earthquakes, wars, and attacks by rebellious citizens. He rebuilt the city of Constantinople with new harbors, bridges, aqueducts (water supply systems), public buildings, and churches. One of these churches, the Hagia Sophia with its breathtaking dome and magnificent marble art, is one of the most famous buildings in the world today.

Along with supporting the development of beautiful architecture, Justinian supported artists who created paintings and carvings of great beauty and value. This picture is an example of such art. It is a page from the *Codex Justinianus*, the set of law books created for Justinian. How are the people interacting with Justinian in this piece of art? Can you tell how the artist felt about Justinian?

Justinian may be best known for the set of legal codes he helped create. Soon after he became emperor, Justinian assigned a committee of ten lawyers to review all the laws and rules of previous emperors. He wanted outdated laws removed or updated and new laws added. The result was a set of four books called the *Codex Justinianus*, which translates from Latin to Justinian's Code. It remains the foundation for laws in many nations today.

This picture from the 6th century depicts Justinian I on the throne and his subjects around him. This image could be one piece of evidence about the kind of ruler Justinian was.

The following primary source includes excerpts from a book from this set called the *Institutes of Justinian*. This book was compiled and published in 533 and became a textbook for law students and lawyers. This passage is just a small section of the book that describes the rights of people.

After you read the passage, consider these questions: What do these laws tell you about the rights of a person in Justinian's empire? Why might it have been important to Justinian to have these laws? Why is Justinian's Code considered historically significant?

The Institutes of Justinian

I. *Justice and Law*
    JUSTICE is the constant and perpetual wish to render every one his due.

    1. *Jurisprudence is the knowledge of things divine and human; the science of the just and the unjust.*

    3. *The maxims of law are these: to live honestly, to hurt no one, to give every one his due.*

III. *The Law of Persons*
    All our law relates either to persons, or to things, or to actions. Let us first speak of persons; as it is of little purpose to know the law, if we do not know the persons for whose sake the law was made. The chief division in the rights of persons is this: men are all either free or slaves.

    1. *Freedom, from which men are said to be free, is the natural power of doing what we each please, unless prevented by force or by law.*

    5. *In the condition of slaves there is no distinction; but there are many distinctions among free persons; for they are either born free, or have been set free.*

IX. *The Power of Parents*
    Our children, begotten in lawful marriage, are in our power.

    2. *The power which we have over our children is peculiar to the citizens of Rome; for no other people have a power over their children, such as we have over ours.*

    3. *The child born to you and your wife is in your power. And so is the child born to your son of his wife, that is, your grandson or granddaughter; so are your great-grandchildren, and all your other descendants. But a child born of your daughter is not in your power, but in the power of its own father.*

    —*Institutes of Justinian, Book 1: "Of Persons," 527-565 C.E.*

Each section provides well-researched background related to the primary sources and their historical contexts. This content can be used to help support students' claims.

Textual primary sources are easily identifiable. Students are challenged and asked to analyze these primary sources, and use their analysis in a supported claim.

Students are invited to observe images of artifacts, portraits, and more to better understand the content. Captions highlight important details of the accompanying image.

Each page concludes with a set of supporting questions that help students pursue the main question.

Every feature ends with an activity that requires students to think critically and answer the compelling question.

This drawing shows Justinian and his wife, Empress Theodora. The artist helps us imagine the kind of ruler Justinian was.

Books and Pictures About Justinian

Despite Justinian's numerous accomplishments, he faced strong criticism. Both his biggest fan and his biggest critic might have been the military advisor and historian, Procopius.

Procopius was an ambitious writer of history. He wrote eight books about the wars fought by Justinian. Procopius also wrote six books on the buildings that were constructed during Justinian's reign. These books are filled with praise for Justinian's achievements. About the reconstruction of the Hagia Sophia, Procopius wrote,

It is indeed a proof of the esteem with which God regarded the emperor, that he furnished him with men who would be so useful in effecting his designs, and we are compelled to admire the wisdom of the emperor, in being able to choose the most suitable of mankind to execute the noblest of his works . . .

What does this quote tell you about the kind of ruler Justinian was? How might all of Procopius's books help you understand the kind of ruler Justinian was? How might Procopius's role as Justinian's military advisor have affected what he wrote about the wars?

Empress Theodora

This drawing shows Justinian with his wife Empress Theodora. She often influenced her husband's decisions with her advice and persuasion. Theodora played a big role during Justinian's reign and noted that he made few significant accomplishments after her death. What does this picture tell you about Justinian that you may not know from books? How are Justinian and Theodora portrayed here? What details do you notice? What does this picture tell us about the relationship between Justinian and Theodora?

Criticism of Justinian

Though much of Procopius's writing praised Justinian, he wrote a final book that did just the opposite. This book, titled *The Secret History*, attacks the way Justinian conducted war and ruled his empire with an iron fist. The book was not published until after Procopius's death, and probably after the deaths of Justinian and Theodora. What reasons might explain why this last book, and not the earlier ones, contains so much criticism of Justinian and Theodora?

Read this excerpt from *The Secret History*. What does Procopius say were Justinian's main goals? What other criticisms does Procopius claim? What does it mean that Justinian "abolished all existing institutions"? How does Procopius's attitude toward Justinian differ in these two excerpts? Which source do you think is more reliable and why? What other sources could give you more information so that you can explain what kind of ruler Justinian was?

The Secret History of the Court of Justinian

Chapter XI

When Justinian came to the throne, he straightway succeeded in upsetting everything. What had previously been forbidden by the laws he introduced, while he abolished all existing institutions, as though he had assumed the imperial robe for no other purpose than to alter completely the form of government. He did away with existing offices, and established other new ones for the management of affairs. He acted in the same manner in regard to the laws and the army; not that he was led to do so by any love of justice or the public advantage, but merely in order that all institutions might be new and might bear his name; if there was any institution that he was unable to abolish at once, he gave it his name, that at least it might appear new. He could never satisfy his insatiable desire, either of money or blood; but after he had plundered one wealthy house, he would seek for another to rob, and straightway squander the plunder upon subsidies to barbarians, or senseless extravagance in building . . .

—Procopius, mid-6th century

Compare the text excerpts you've just read and think about the pictures. Consider what they say about Justinian as a ruler. Then use these sources and what you know to make an argument about the kind of ruler Justinian was and if his impact on the empire was more positive or more negative.

Supporting Literacy in History and Social Studies

History Alive! has literacy instruction built into the Student Text, Interactive Student Notebook, and Lesson Presentations. The following six key points emphasizes integration of literacy and language arts practices. They are particularly important in social studies instruction.

Key Points in 6–8 Social Studies and History Literacy: Reading	History Alive!
Main Ideas and Details Identifying key ideas and details applies to reading primary and secondary text and the ability to use evidence and to create accurate summaries. Students should also identify the steps in relevant processes.	When students read *History Alive!* texts online, they have the option to see the main idea of each section highlighted. In the Presentation activities, students carry out inquiries and use their Interactive Student Notebooks to develop supported claims.
Craft and Structure Students determine the meaning of social studies vocabulary in context and can describe text structure and point of view.	*History Alive!* scaffolds the learning of social studies and history vocabulary by presenting the words and phrases in context but offering succinct definitions in the margins and glossary. Students record information based on text structure and historical perspective in their Reading Notes.
Integration of Knowledge and Ideas Students should be able to integrate their learning on a topic from observing visuals and from reading the text in primary and secondary sources.	Each lesson in *History Alive!* concludes with a Processing task that requires students to demonstrate their understanding of main ideas and core concepts, as a result of carrying out investigations, reading the text, and researching a variety of sources.

Key Points in 6–8 Social Studies and History Literacy: Writing	History Alive!
Purposes for Writing Students write supported arguments that use organization, accurate evidence, and counterclaims. They are written in a formal style and include a strong conclusion.	*History Alive!* requires students to write for different purposes, including to develop claims that are supported with evidence. In inquiry activities, students are often asked to construct written arguments to persuade others to accept a conclusion or proposal. They construct their claims using precise language and social studies vocabulary.
Learning Through Research Short research projects, using a variety of print and digital sources appropriately, should be carried out to answer broad questions that generate more specific questions.	*History Alive!* provides opportunities for building research skills using print sources and digital sources. In the Presentation activities and Processing assignments, students gather and assess relevant information, and integrate this information with what they learn during hands-on activities to answer the compelling question.
Producing and Publishing Writing Clear, coherent, and routine writing appropriate to its purpose and audience is central throughout the writing standards.	*History Alive!* provides many writing opportunities, including to explain main ideas and proposals to compelling questions. Students engage in various writing exercises in their Interactive Student Notebooks.

Considerate Text

History Alive! is both engaging and helps students read text that is more complex and at a higher level. That's because our writers wrote it as "considerate text," which is another way to say that it makes readers want to read it. Considerate text it is well-written and well-organized. Here are some ways this Student Text is considerate of all levels of readers.

Short sections, each with an informative title, create an organized structure that help readers understand and remember the main ideas.

Important new social studies words are in bold and blue type. These words are defined in the margin and in the glossary.

Captions for photos, illustrations, tables, and maps reinforce the main idea of the section and provide details that guide students' interpretation of the graphics.

Academic vocabulary words are bolded in black and presented with a clear context.

Prince Shotoku a Japanese ruler who encouraged cultural diffusion from countries on the Asian mainland

The cultures of China, India, and Korea were major influences on the culture of medieval Japan.

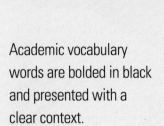

1. Cultural Influences on Japan

By the time Empress Suiko and **Prince Shotoku** came to power in 593, cultural influences from the Asian mainland had been reaching Japan for hundreds of years. For example, craftspeople from the Korean Peninsula had brought knowledge of bronze casting and advanced ironworking to Japan. Immigrants and visitors from Korea had also introduced Japan to Confucianism and Buddhism. However, as Suiko, Shotoku, and later rulers sought out contact with the mainland, the pace of cultural diffusion quickened.

Japan in Empress Suiko's and Prince Shotoku's day was a **rural,** agricultural society. People grew rice and other crops. The upper classes owned slaves and lived in houses with wooden floors and roofs of wood or thatch. The common people lived in huts with dirt floors and thatched roofs. Family life centered on the mother, who raised the children, while fathers often lived apart from their families. Compared to later eras, women enjoyed relatively high status.

Japan at this time was far from being a unified country. Power was divided among chiefs of a number of clans called *uji* (OOH-jee). But one ruling family in the region of Yamato, on the island of Honshu, had grown powerful enough to loosely control much of Japan. Empress Suiko came from this line of rulers, as did Prince Shotoku, who ruled as regent under the empress.

Under Suiko, Shotoku, and later rulers, the government of Japan took an active interest in Korean and Chinese culture. Sometimes, knowledge of mainland culture came from Japanese who traveled to China. Sometimes, it came in the form of gifts, such as books and art objects, sent from the mainland to Japan. Sometimes, it came from Korean workers who settled in Japan, bringing their knowledge and skills with them.

During the next three centuries, Japan sent officials, students, translators, and monks on ships across the sea to China. These people often remained in China for years before returning home with what they had learned. They also brought many examples of mainland culture, including paintings, religious statues, and musical instruments. As a result of these contacts, the Japanese **acquired** new ideas in government, the arts, architecture, and writing.

The Japanese did not just change their old ways for new ways, however. Instead, they blended new ideas with their own traditions to create a unique culture. Let's look at several areas in which this happened, beginning with government.

322 Lesson 23

Section introductions help link the new section to the last section.

2. Government: Imitating the Chinese System

Starting with Prince Shotuku, Japanese rulers adopted new ideas about government from China. China's form of government was both like and unlike Japan's. For example, the emperors in China and Japan had quite different powers. The emperor in China was the sole ruler, whereas in Japan, the emperor had only loose control over the semi-independent uji. Uji controlled their own land, and their leaders struggled among themselves for the right to select the emperor and influence his decisions.

While Japanese emperors depended on local leaders, the Chinese emperor ruled with the help of a bureaucracy of government officials. At least in theory, appointments to government jobs were based on merit. Any man who did well on an examination could become an official.

During the 7th and 8th centuries, Japanese rulers adopted a Chinese style of government. Japanese tradition credits Prince Shotoku with starting this development. Borrowing Confucian ideas, the prince created ranks for government officials. In 604, he issued a set of guidelines called the Seventeen Article Constitution, which stated that the emperor was the supreme ruler: "In a country there are not two lords; the people have not two masters. The sovereign is the master of the people of the whole country."

Later rulers went much further in bringing Chinese-style changes to Japan. In the late 7th century, Emperor Tenmu and his wife and successor Empress Jitō reformed and strengthened the central government. Control of the land was taken away from clan leaders and given to the emperor. The emperor then redistributed the land to all free men and women, and in return, people paid heavy taxes to support the imperial government.

By the 700s, Japan's imperial government looked much like China's. It was strongly centralized and supported by a large bureaucracy. Over time, however, one key difference emerged. Although Prince Shotoku had called for government officials to be chosen on the basis of their ability, as in China, a powerful aristocracy developed in Japan during the 9th century. As a result, members of noble families held all the high positions in the government.

Thoughtfully selected large images illustrate the main ideas and support visual learners.

Prince Shotoku was the first Japanese ruler to borrow ideas about government from China. Shotoku is shown here between his two sons.

The text is written in clear and engaging way without figurative language. Each section ends with a conclusion that wraps up the main ideas.

Single-column text makes it easier to read. Paragraphs end at the bottom of the page instead of continuing onto the next page.

The Influence of Neighboring Cultures on Japan **323**

The World in 300 C.E.

How did the distant regions of the world become more interconnected through medieval and early modern times?

Introduction

In *History Alive! The Medieval World and Beyond*, you will learn about various peoples, cultures, and civilizations that existed thousands of years ago and in unique locations all across the globe. Each of these groups arose in different places and at different times. But there are many common themes among them.

These similarities include the settlement of people based on geography and climate as well as the development of social structures. Also, you'll learn about the development of arts, architecture, writing, government, politics, and religion within these regions. You will also read about how webs of trade routes connected these peoples and brought them new ideas and products. Finally, you'll discover how huge kingdoms and empires rose from rural and urban societies as well as why they failed.

Throughout this program, you'll learn about various groups based on their location in the world. But first, let's explore them based on their common themes. Keep these patterns in mind as you explore the wonders of the medieval world.

Social Studies Vocabulary

empire

gender roles

kinship

pastoral nomad

site of encounter

◀ One group that thrived around 300 C.E. was the Maya in Mesoamerica. The Maya created this stone carving to honor their gods.

The development of new ideas is part of a theme of world history. Here, scientist Galileo (center) is on trial for suggesting the idea that Earth revolves around the sun.

1. Thematic Approach

Historians use themes to identify patterns in history. Many possible themes can apply to historical events. Two broad themes are continuity and change, that is, the way things have stayed the same or changed over time. Two other broad themes are integration and difference. *Integration* refers to ways in which the peoples of the world have been drawn together by historical factors. *Difference* concerns how they have remained distinct and diverse.

History Alive! The Medieval World and Beyond highlights six themes in world history: human-environment interaction, rise of empires, growth and changes in societies, development of political institutions and ideas, belief systems, and interconnectedness of societies. Studying history with these themes in mind will help you make connections among events and interpret the past.

Human-Environment Interaction The interaction between humans and the environment is the first theme. The environment has been a key factor in human activity throughout history. The fact that people have to operate within the limits of the natural world has helped shape their actions. It has affected how and where people live and how they support themselves. At the same time, human actions have also changed the environment in many ways.

This theme covers topics such as:
- disease
- population growth
- migration
- patterns of human settlement

These factors can reflect or influence conditions in the environment. Another topic is the environmental impact of technology, a major concern today because of energy use and climate change. Throughout history, however—from the birth of farming to the creation of factories—the use of technology has affected the environment. By changing how we interact with the natural world, technology has had a major impact on the course of history. As humans created new and more advanced technologies, they should become aware of how they will affect the environment.

Rise of Empires The way in which empires arose is another important theme. As humans learned the advantages of cooperating with one another, civilizations arose across the globe. Many of these civilizations developed from early cities called city-states. Kingdoms and even larger empires eventually formed from these civilizations. Sometimes empires conquered other neighboring kingdoms or states in hopes of expanding their power. Today, evidence of the success of these powerful kingdoms and empires still remains.

This theme covers a wide range of topics. Some examples are:

- the development of trade networks
- artistic and architectural advancements
- the unification of smaller states into kingdoms and empires
- the prominence of patriarchal societies

Growth and Changes in Societies The organization of societies is also a key theme. Throughout history, each society has developed its own rules and customs to govern behavior and help it function. Although these structures varied from culture to culture, they also had many things in common. By examining and comparing social structures throughout history, we can get a better understanding of human life.

Among the topics covered by this theme are:

- **gender roles** and relations, including the place of women in society
- customs relating to family and **kinship**
- racial and ethnic differences and their impact on society
- division of society into social and economic classes

The cultures of Mexico, Central, and South America produced great art work, such as this gold ornament. Which themes do you see in this image?

Development of Political Institutions and Ideas Another key theme is the creation of political systems and forms of government. World history has often been presented as a series of one ruler or government after another. It is much more than that. Nevertheless, political structures are an important aspect of history. The way in which people have organized and governed themselves says a great deal about human society.

gender roles customs relating to the position of men and women in society

kinship family relationship, either by birth, marriage, or adoption

Various topics fall under the theme of development of political institutions and ideas. Here are some examples:

- forms of government
- the nature and growth of kingdoms and empires, large territories controlled by a single ruler or state
- the development of nations
- the Renaissance
- the Enlightenment
- political revolts and revolutions

Belief Systems An additional key theme is the creation and development of belief systems. As ideas continued to develop throughout the medieval world, new philosophies and religions began to emerge. These belief systems often brought great social and political change to both the regions they originated in as well as those they eventually spread to.

Various topics fall under the theme of belief systems. Here are some examples:

- the perseverance of Jews during the Crusades
- the impact of Christianity on empirical motivations
- the spread of Islam and its affect on the world

Interconnectedness of Societies The last theme you'll learn about is the interconnectedness of societies. All of the new ideas, products, and advancements that were developed in the medieval world eventually reached other parts of it. Large networks of trade routes throughout the world connected the societies you'll learn about, resulting in the combining of cultures.

The Chinese held exams for hiring scholar-officials to help the emperor rule. Many themes of world history are present in this image, but which can you find?

Various topics fall under the theme of interconnectedness of societies. Some examples are:

- the exchange of inventions and products
- the spread of religions, arts, and ideas
- the migration of people to new locations
- the practice of diplomacy among societies

Keep these themes in mind as you read through the rest of this lesson and the rest of *History Alive! The Medieval World and Beyond.*

2. Teaching the World's History

Major Historical Changes The historical themes you just read about relate to many major changes that happened throughout medieval and early modern times. The first is the increase in the world's population as agricultural lifestyles led to more prosperity. Another great change of this time is the advancement of technologies that enabled the production of more food and items, which catered to the world's rising population. Additionally, global trade routes emerged that allowed those within this large population to interact and exchange products as well as ideas with one another. A third major change during this time was the rise of powerful kingdoms, empires, and patriarchal societies to rule over the world's people. The final major change was the increased human impact on the environment, including the distribution of plants and animals to parts of the world they were not native to.

Zheng He was a Chinese explorer of the lands around the Indian Ocean during medieval times. His expeditions led to the development of trade routes and connections among multiple civilizations and empires.

Sites of Encounter While the historical themes and major changes all offer a lot of insight into studying world history, you will also need to investigate historical sources in depth. One way to do this is through studying sites of encounter.

A **site of encounter** is a specific place where people from different cultures meet and exchange products, ideas, and technologies. The places you'll be studying in this program are:

- Rome (From Republic to Empire)
- Cairo (Muslim Innovations and Adaptations)
- Norman Sicily (From the Crusades to New Muslim Empires)
- Calicut (Evolution of Religions in South Asia)
- Mali (The Influence of Islam in West Africa)
- Quanzhou (China's Contacts with the Outside World)
- Tenochtitlán (Daily Life in Tenochtitlán)

site of encounter a specific place where people from different cultures meet and exchange products, ideas, and technologies

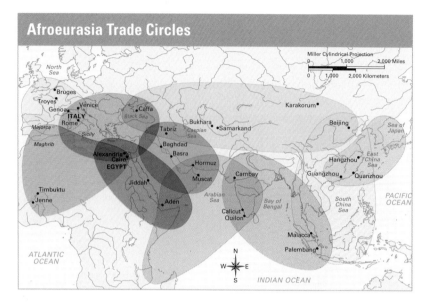

Afroeurasia Trade Circles

These trade circles demonstrate how interconnected societies across Afroeurasia were throughout history. Although not pictured here, the Americas also had valuable trade networks.

The Great Market in the city of Tenochtitlán was a center of daily life for the Aztecs, another civilization that thrived in Mesoamerica.

By exploring the historical happenings of these locations, you can gain an understanding of multiple cultures and perspectives at once. Additionally, you'll learn to consider how these cultures influenced each other. Studying these sites of encounter will also give you a better sense of world geography.

The final benefit to exploring these specific locations is that you will gain a more global understanding of medieval history. Many mistakenly learn about medieval and early modern times by focusing on Western Europe. However, as you have already learned, there is much more history to learn than Europe's. In fact, throughout this program, you'll learn about Africa, China, Japan, Mexico, Central and South America, and the Middle East.

3. The Americas and Afroeurasia in 300 c.e.

In 300 C.E., the world's people were divided roughly into two regions: the Americas in the Western Hemisphere and Afroeurasia in the Eastern Hemisphere. Both of these regions were home to various unique cultures that you will explore more in-depth as you read *History Alive! The Medieval World and Beyond*.

The Americas By the year 300 C.E., there were two developing areas within the Americas. The first was Mesoamerica where the Maya thrived. They built large cities, states, and empires that were all supported by agriculture and local trade. Also in Mesoamerica was the city of Teotihuacán in central Mexico. At the time, Teotihuacán was the largest city in the world. The people from central Mexico often traded with the Maya.

The second developing area within the Americas was along the Andean mountain spine in South America. Here, large civilizations also rose to power and made many agricultural advancements. This area was also active in trade, with routes running from present-day Peru to Chile. The notable Andes state that controlled those trade routes was the state of Tiahuanaco.

Both Mesoamerica and the areas of the Andes mountain range were home to thriving cultures around 300 C.E. However, these separate regions likely did not have contact with each other.

Afroeurasia Although there were many isolated cultures within Afroeurasia that had their own languages and customs, many cultures in the center of Afroeurasia were connected by a large network of trade routes. The Silk Road and the Silk Road on the Sea, which originally developed around 140 B.C.E., are examples of these interconnecting trade routes.

Many luxury goods such as silk from China and frankincense from Africa traveled across Afroeurasia. Merchants often brought these goods to a group of elites who would purchase the luxury products and take them back to their homelands. Although the goods traveled between merchants all across Afroeurasia from Atlantic to Pacific coasts, the merchants themselves did not travel that far.

In addition to the exchange of products, ideas and technologies were also exchanged along these trade routes. For example, many Buddhist and Christian missionaries spread their religions via these routes.

Even though the regions of Afroeurasia became very interconnected around 300 C.E., they are even more intertwined today. Despite the important influence of other cultures, the most significant influences of each culture thriving in 300 C.E. came from within its own culture.

The land routes of the Silk Road crossed more than 4,000 miles of the continent of Asia. The water routes followed the coastlines of China, India, and Arabia. As many traders discovered, both routes presented substantial challenges.

The Silk Road on the Sea

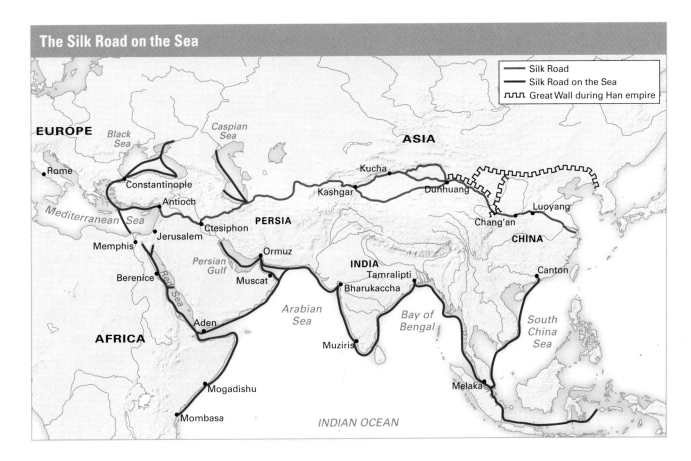

Legend:
— Silk Road
— Silk Road on the Sea
⊓⊔⊓⊔ Great Wall during Han empire

empire a large territory controlled by a single ruler or state

pastoral nomad a person who migrates and depends on the livestock they raise

4. Empires, Migrations, and Turbulent Times

In Afroeurasia, four dominant empires thrived. **Empires** are large territories controlled by a single ruler or state. One was the Roman Empire in the Mediterranean region and Europe. In Southwestern Asia, the Sasanian Persian Empire arose. The others were the Gupta Empire in South Asia and China in East Asia.

As the power of these empires increased, many farmers called pastoral nomads migrated east and west along the northern edges of China, India, Persia, and Rome. **Pastoral nomads** are people who migrate and depend on the livestock they raise. Some of these nomads formed mounted armies to attack those to the south, such as the empires of China, India, Persia, and Rome. These attacks often interrupted exchanges along the Silk Road and other Eurasian trade routes.

Between 300 and 600 C.E., these Silk Road disruptions led to the decline of some empires including the Han, Parthian, and Western Roman empires. They also triggered many turbulent times for people all across the globe. The number of cities declined from around 75 in 100 C.E. to about 47 by 500 C.E.

In 410 C.E., a northern Germanic tribe attacked Rome, which was by then the capital of only the western part of the Roman Empire. Rome is one of the sites of encounter you'll learn about.

However, African societies managed to flourish during this period. Trade across the Sahara Desert expanded, allowing new commercial kingdoms to emerge such as Ghana in the southern end of the desert and Aksum in East Africa. Aksum became a prominent center of trade for Indian Ocean commerce. This expanded trade route led to an increase in the spread of religious ideas among Afroeurasian societies as well as other forms of cultural exchanges.

Additionally, many Bantu-speaking farmers from sub-Saharan Africa migrated southward and founded more urban communities that added to the expanding trade networks. These farmers mixed with and displaced many older cattle-herding and foraging populations. Also, many Polynesian explorers added to these trade routes when they used canoes and their navigational expertise to expand their settlement to new islands across the Pacific Ocean.

The Kingdom of Aksum was a center of trade for Indian Ocean commerce. This picture shows the ruins of an Aksum palace that once stood in modern-day Ethiopia during the 6th century.

Lesson Summary

In this lesson, you learned about the world in 300 C.E.

Thematic Approach The six themes for analyzing medieval history are as follows: human-environment interaction, rise of empires, growth and changes in societies, development of political institutions and ideas, belief systems, and interconnectedness of societies.

Teaching the World's History Many great changes occurred during medieval times. One way to understand these changes as well as other aspects of history is to investigate primary sources from sites of encounter.

The Americas and Afroeurasia in 300 C.E. The Americas had civilizations that thrived during this time, but those in Mesoamerica stayed separate from those in the Andes mountain area. In Afroeurasia, large networks of trade routes contributed to the interconnectedness among the cultures in this region.

Empires, Migrations, and Turbulent Times As empires gained more power, conflicts among empires increased during this time. This lead to much human migration and often deadly wars.

Europe During Medieval Times

Castles built by medieval monarchs still stand in Europe today, like this one on the northern coast of Ireland. Thick castle walls gave protection against invaders. Castles were also homes for royalty and people of high rank, although they were built for defense rather than for comfort.

Unit 1 Setting the Stage

Physical Features of Europe

ICELAND

Arctic Circle

80°N
10°W
0°
10°E 20°E 30°E 40°E 50°E 60°E 70°E 80°E
20°W
30°W
40°W
70°N
60°N
50°N
40°N

Norwegian Sea

FAROE ISLANDS
(Den.)

SHETLAND ISLANDS
(U.K.)

ATLANTIC
OCEAN

Ben Nevis
(4,406 ft., 1,343 m)

North
Sea

Baltic Sea

S C A N D I N A V I A

N O R T H E R N   E U R O P E A N   P L A I N

BRITISH
ISLES

*Celtic
Sea*

*Thames
River*

English Channel

Seine River

Loire River

Elbe River

Danube River

CARPATHIAN MOUNTAINS

*Bay of
Biscay*

Mont Blanc
(15,781ft., 4,810 m)
A L P S
Po River

PYRENEES

IBERIAN
PENINSULA

Corsica

40°N

Sardinia

BALEARIC
ISLANDS

Strait of Gibraltar

APENNINES

*Tiber
River*

ITALIAN
PENINSULA

Tyrrhenian Sea

Adriatic Sea

BALKAN MTS.

BALKAN
PENINSULA

Black Sea

Bosporus

Aegean Sea

PELOPONNESUS

Sicily

*Ionian
Sea*

Crete

ASIA

M e d i t e r r a n e a n   S e a

AFRICA

Elevation

Feet	Meters
Over 10,000	Over 3,050
5,001–10,000	1,526–3,050
2,001–5,000	611–1,525
1,001–2,000	306–610
0–1,000	0–305
Below sea level	Below sea level

▲ Mountain peak

Present-day
boundary

0   250   500 miles
0   250   500 kilometers
Lambert Azimuthal Equal-Area

N
W   E
S

Europe During Medieval Times

The title of this unit includes two key words—*Europe* and *medieval*. You probably recognize Europe as the continent east of North America across the Atlantic Ocean. But what does *medieval* mean, and why is it important?

The period of time called medieval began with the fall of the Roman Empire and lasted until about 1450. This long period of time, also known as the Middle Ages, is the period between ancient and modern times.

Historians divide the Middle Ages into three parts—early, high, and late. The Early Middle Ages lasted from about the year 476 to 1000 C.E., the High Middle Ages lasted from about 1000 to 1300, and the Late Middle Ages lasted from about 1300 to 1450.

You will begin your study of the medieval world with Europe. Although the physical geography of Europe has remained largely unchanged since medieval times, the political geography of this region—such as place names and boundaries—has changed a great deal.

Europe is a giant peninsula attached to the huge landmass called Eurasia. Look at the map *Physical Features of Europe*. Water borders this continent to the north, south, and west. Much of Europe's land lies on the Northern European Plain, one of the largest expanses of flat land on Earth. Additionally, several mountain ranges extend across Europe, separating different regions. The Alps, for example, form a barrier between central and southern Europe.

Now look at the map *Medieval Europe, About 1300*. Some place names, such as England and France, will be familiar to you. Other names refer to political features that no longer exist but live on as present-day names. For example, Castile, Leon, and Navarre were kingdoms in medieval Spain. Now they designate regions in present-day Spain.

It is beneficial to study the medieval period because events in the past have helped to shape the present. Studying the past helps us understand the government, economy, and culture we have today. For example, in the year 1295 an English king created a governing body that centuries later influenced the creation of modern democratic institutions—including our own Congress.

Medieval Europe, About 1300

Lesson 1

From Republic to Empire

Did the benefits of Roman expansion outweigh the costs?

Introduction

As the ancient republic of Rome grew, its power expanded. By the early 1st century C.E., it had become a mighty empire that ruled the entire Mediterranean world.

The expansion of Roman power occurred over **approximately** five hundred years, from 509 B.C.E. to 14 C.E. At the beginning of this period, Rome was a tiny republic in central Italy. However, five hundred years later, it was the thriving center of a vast empire. At its height, the Roman Empire included most of Europe, together with North Africa, Egypt, much of the present-day Middle East, and Asia Minor.

The increase of Rome's power happened gradually and came at a price. Romans had to fight countless wars to defend their developing territory and to conquer new lands. Along the way, Rome itself transfomed. The Romans had once been proud to be governed under a republic of elected leaders. Their heroes were men who had helped to preserve the republic. Leaders in different parts of the world would later be inspired by this structure of government.

However, by 14 C.E., the republic was just a memory. Power was in the hands of a single supreme ruler, the emperor. Some Romans even worshipped old emperors as gods, an act that shows how powerful these rulers could be.

In this lesson, you'll see how this dramatic change occurred. You'll trace the gradual expansion of Roman power. You will also explore the costs of this expansion, both for Romans and for the people they conquered.

Social Studies Vocabulary

Caesar Augustus

civil war

dictator

Julius Caesar

Pax Romana

Punic Wars

◀ As Rome grew, power flooded into the hands of one supreme ruler.

1. From Republic to Empire: An Overview

The growth of Rome from a republic to an empire happened over 500 years. The story has four major periods.

The First Period of Expansion The first period of expansion, or becoming larger, began in 509 B.C.E. At this time, the Romans drove the last Etruscan king out of power, and Rome became a republic.

The Romans wanted to protect their borders and to gain more land, which led to a series of wars. During the next 245 years, the Romans combatted one enemy after another. They conquered their Latin neighbors in central Italy and also defeated their old rulers, the Etruscans.

Wisely, the Romans eventually made allies, or friends, of their former enemies. By 264 B.C.E., Rome and its allies controlled the entire Italian peninsula.

The Second Period of Expansion Rome's growth threatened two great powers—the Persian Empire and the city of Carthage (KAR-thidge) in North Africa. During the second period of expansion, from 264 to 146 B.C.E., Rome and Carthage fought three major wars. Through these wars, Rome gained control of North Africa, much of Spain, and the island of Sicily. Roman armies also conquered Macedonia and Greece.

Rome gained power over new lands through three savage wars with Carthage, across the Mediterranean Sea. This victory granted Rome control over North Africa.

Roman general Julius Caesar helped expand Roman power by conquering Gaul and by invading Britain. Many later leaders went on to further increase Rome's strength.

The Third Period of Expansion   During the third period of expansion, from 145 to 44 B.C.E., Rome came to rule the entire Mediterranean world. In the east, Rome took control of Asia Minor, Syria, and Egypt. In the west, the Roman general Julius Caesar conquered much of Gaul (modern-day France).

Proud Romans now called the Mediterranean "our sea." However, the republic was in trouble because **civil wars** divided the city. Roman generals were becoming **dictators** and setting their armies against the power of the Senate. Caesar himself ruled as a dictator for life until he was assassinated in 44 B.C.E.

The men who murdered Caesar thought they were saving the power of the Senate. However, several more years of civil war followed. Then Caesar's grandnephew, Octavian, seized total power. The Senate named him Augustus, or "honored one." Rome was now an empire governed by one supreme ruler.

civil war a war between groups in the same country

dictator a ruler with absolute power

Julius Caesar's grandnephew, Octavian, became Caesar Augustus, the supreme ruler of the Roman Empire.

The Fourth Period of Expansion   The fourth period of expansion began with the start of the empire and lasted until 14 C.E. The first emperor, Augustus, added an enormous amount of new territory by pushing the borders of the empire all the way to natural boundaries, like rivers, to more easily defend it. Later emperors continued to add more territory so that, at its height, the Roman Empire stretched from the island of Britain in the northwest to the Black Sea in the east.

Each period of expansion involved cost and sacrifice. The next four sections provide more details about each expansion. As you read, ask yourself how Romans of the time might have perceived these events.

2. Rome's Conquest of the Italian Peninsula, 509 B.C.E to 264 B.C.E.

Rome's first period of expansion included more than 200 years of almost constant warfare. During this time, Rome gradually took control of the entire Italian peninsula.

After the last Etruscan king was overthrown in 509 B.C.E., the Romans began to expand their territory and influence. In 493 B.C.E., Roman leaders signed a treaty, or agreement, with their Latin neighbors to the south. The treaty stated, "There shall be peace between the Romans and all the communities of Latins as long as heaven and earth endure." These new allies agreed to band together against their common enemies. During the next 100 years, the Romans fought a number of wars against the Etruscans, as well as against tribes living in hills surrounding Rome.

Then, in 390 B.C.E., Rome nearly came to an end. A band of Gauls (gawlz), a warlike people from the north, crushed a Roman army and surged into the city. Most of Rome's people fled into the countryside, and the Gauls looted the city, burning most of it down.

In 458 B.C.E., the Roman Senate named Lucius Quinctius Cincinnatus dictator, or supreme ruler, to lead the defense of the city during an attack. After defeating the enemy, Cincinnatus willingly sacrificed power and returned to his farm. His sense of duty and respect for the republic made Cincinnatus one of Rome's notable heroes.

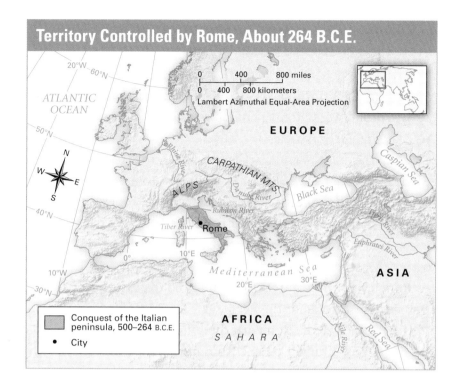

Territory Controlled by Rome, About 264 B.C.E.

0 400 800 miles
0 400 800 kilometers
Lambert Azimuthal Equal-Area Projection

EUROPE

ATLANTIC OCEAN

Rhine River
CARPATHIAN MTS.
ALPS
Danube River
Black Sea
Caspian Sea
Rubicon River
Tiger River
Tiber River • Rome
Euphrates River
Mediterranean Sea
ASIA

AFRICA
SAHARA
Nile River
Red Sea

Legend:
Conquest of the Italian peninsula, 500–264 B.C.E.
• City

By 264 B.C.E., the Romans had taken over the entire Italian peninsula. All those under Roman rule paid a cost for the territory's expansion.

With the city in ruins, the Romans considered fleeing. Instead, they bravely decided to start over by rebuilding their city and surrounding it with walls. They also developed their army, and, before long, Roman soldiers were on the march again.

During the 300s B.C.E., Rome conquered the Etruscans and many neighboring tribes. To the south, they battled a people called the Samnites and several Greek city-states. By 275 B.C.E., Rome's conquest of the Italian peninsula was complete. However, expansion came at great cost. Romans had been fighting for two centuries, and the Gauls had once destroyed their capital city.

As Rome's territory expanded, the city had to maintain a large, permanent army to defend it and the conquered lands. As a result, more and more Romans were forced to serve in the army. Many soldiers were plebeians who resented this fact, leading to civil unrest.

Roman citizens were not the only ones who sacrificed for Rome's expansion. Rome allowed the people of some defeated cities to become Roman citizens. Unfortunately, other cities were not treated so well. Many received more limited privileges, such as the ability to trade with Rome. And Roman allies were required to pay Roman taxes and supply soldiers for Roman armies.

By 264 B.C.E., Rome had more citizens and well-trained soldiers than any other power in the Mediterranean world. But very soon, the Romans would face their greatest challenge yet.

Punic Wars a series of wars
fought between Rome and
Carthage for control of the
Mediterranean

3. Expansion During the Punic Wars, 264 B.C.E. to 146 B.C.E.

During Rome's second period of expansion, it fought three savage wars for control of the Mediterranean region. In each of these brutal wars, Rome's enemy was Carthage, a powerful city-state in North Africa.

When the wars began, Carthage held North Africa, most of Spain, and part of the island of Sicily. It also controlled most of the trade in the western Mediterranean. The Greek cities in southern Italy had frequently clashed with Carthage over trading rights. When Rome conquered these cities, it was drawn into the fight with Carthage.

Rome's wars with Carthage are referred to as the **Punic Wars,** after the Latin name for the people of Carthage. The First Punic War began in 264 B.C.E. and was fought mostly at sea. Carthage had a very powerful navy, but the Romans developed their own navy by copying and improving on the Carthaginians' ship designs. A decisive victory at sea in 241 B.C.E. won the war for the Romans. The triumphant Romans took over Sicily, as well as other islands in the area.

The Second Punic War started 23 years later when the Carthaginians decided to attack Italy itself. In 218 B.C.E., Hannibal, a brilliant Carthaginian general, surprised the Romans by marching his army from Spain across the Alps (a high mountain range) and into Italy. His troops rode elephants and braved snowstorms, landslides, and attacks by local tribes. For 15 years, Hannibal's men fought the Romans in Italy.

In 202 B.C.E., Hannibal needed to return home to defend Carthage against an attack by a Roman army. There he was defeated in the battle that ended the Second Punic War. Carthage was forced to give up Spain to Rome, along with huge sums of money.

In 218 B.C.E., the Carthaginian general Hannibal led his troops across the Alps to attack Rome. In this image, he endures the journey across the Rhone River atop an elephant.

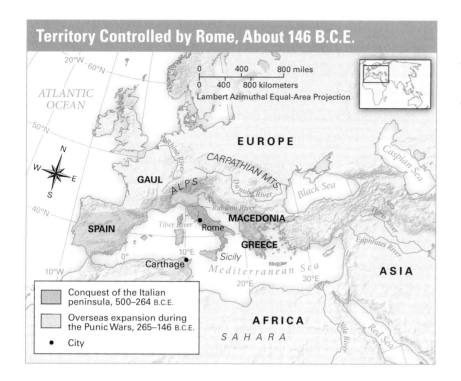

Territory Controlled by Rome, About 146 B.C.E.

Conquest of the Italian peninsula, 500–264 B.C.E.

Overseas expansion during the Punic Wars, 265–146 B.C.E.

● City

By 146 B.C.E., Roman power had spread across much of the northern Mediterranean. However, this expansion came with great sacrifice.

For about 50 years, there was peace between Rome and Carthage. Then, encouraged by Cato (KAY-toh), a senator who demanded the complete destruction of Carthage, the Romans attacked once more.

The Third Punic War lasted three years. In 146 B.C.E., the Romans burned Carthage to the ground. They killed many people and sold others into slavery. Rome was now the greatest power in the Mediterranean region, controlling North Africa, much of Spain, Macedonia, and Greece.

The Punic Wars expanded Roman power and territory, but Rome's victories came at a price. Countless young men had died in the long wars. Additionally, people living outside Rome suffered huge losses in population and property. Hannibal's army had destroyed thousands of farms, and others had been neglected while farmers went off to fight in Rome's armies. By the time the soldiers returned home, Rome had been forced to import grain from Sicily and other places. Small farms were being replaced by large estates, where the wealthy planted vineyards and raised livestock. Unable to compete with the wealthy landowners, many poor farmers were forced to sell their land.

While riches and slaves flowed into Rome from the conquered lands, so did new customs, many of which came from Greece. Wealthy Romans competed with one another to build Greek-style homes and beautiful temples.

Julius Caesar a Roman general who ended the Roman Republic when he seized power and became dictator for life

Despite being warned that harm would come to him if he went to the Senate that day, Julius Caesar attended the meeting where he was stabbed 23 times and bled to death at the door of the Senate. This day is famously referred to as the "Ides of March."

4. Expansion During the Final Years of the Republic, 145 B.C.E. to 44 B.C.E.

By 145 B.C.E., Roman conquests had brought considerable wealth to the city of Rome, but they had also put the ideals of the republic under great strain. By the end of Rome's third period of expansion, the republic **collapsed**.

The final years of the republic were marked by still more wars. Many of Rome's allies resented having to pay Roman taxes and fight in Roman armies without enjoying the rights of citizenship. In 90 B.C.E., some rebelled, and, to end the revolt, Rome agreed to let all free Italians become Roman citizens.

Rome also had to fight to subdue slave revolts. As Romans conquered new territory, they brought hundreds of thousands of prisoners to Roman lands and turned them into slaves who labored on farms and in the city. Although some slaves were respected, Romans often treated their slaves very harshly. A slave named Spartacus led a famous revolt in 73 B.C.E. After crushing his army and killing Spartacus in battle, the Romans sentenced thousands of the surviving rebels to death on crosses.

There was trouble brewing in the city, too. With so many slaves to do the work, thousands of farmers and laborers had no jobs. They crowded into Rome, becoming a mob that an ambitious leader could turn into an army.

Rome's army was producing many such leaders. Generals used their armies to gain fame and power in distant lands and then to fight for influence in Rome. In one such civil war in the 80s B.C.E., a Roman leader named Sulla commanded an army to put down a revolt by Italian allies to obtain Roman citizenship.

Forty years later, another civil war erupted between two ambitious generals, Pompey (POM-pee) and **Julius Caesar** (SEE-zer). Pompey had expanded Roman rule in such eastern lands as Syria and the island of Cyprus, while Caesar had conquered much of Gaul.

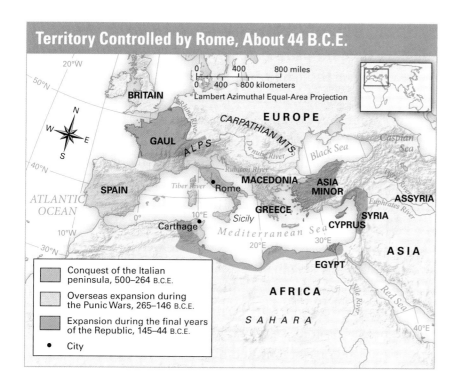

Territory Controlled by Rome, About 44 B.C.E.

0   400   800 miles
0 400   800 kilometers
Lambert Azimuthal Equal-Area Projection

BRITAIN

EUROPE

CARPATHIAN MTS.

GAUL

ALPS

Danube River

Black Sea

Caspian Sea

Rhine River

Rubicon River

SPAIN

Tiber River · Rome

MACEDONIA

ASIA MINOR

Euphrates River

ASSYRIA

ATLANTIC OCEAN

GREECE

SYRIA

CYPRUS

Carthage

Sicily

Mediterranean Sea

ASIA

EGYPT

AFRICA

Nile River

Red Sea

SAHARA

Conquest of the Italian peninsula, 500–264 B.C.E.

Overseas expansion during the Punic Wars, 265–146 B.C.E.

Expansion during the final years of the Republic, 145–44 B.C.E.

· City

By the time Julius Caesar seized power in the 40s B.C.E., Rome ruled most of the Mediterranean and much of Europe. Uniting the diverse environments of Egypt, North Africa, Syria, Asia Minor (or Anatolia), Greece, and Europe increased Roman access to trade routes and other needed resources.

By 49 B.C.E., Pompey was back in Rome, while Caesar commanded an army to the north of Italy, across the Rubicon River. Both men wanted to control Rome, but Pompey had the support of the Roman Senate.

Encouraged by Pompey, the Senate forbade Caesar to enter Italy with his army. Caesar disobeyed in January of 49 B.C.E. and crossed the Rubicon with his army. After three years of fighting, he defeated Pompey. The frightened Senate named Caesar dictator for life. With Caesar in control, and after nearly 500 years, the republic came to an end.

As dictator, Julius Caesar introduced many reforms. He provided work to thousands of Romans by starting projects to create new roads and public buildings. To keep the poor satisfied, he staged gladiator contests that they could watch for free. He also adopted a new calendar that is still used today.

Caesar had a **vision** of Rome as a great empire. He started new colonies and granted citizenship to the people of cities in Gaul and Spain. However, he did not live to see his vision come true. On March 15, 44 B.C.E., a group of enemies stabbed Caesar to death as he was entering the Senate.

The men who killed Caesar thought they were saving the republic, but were wrong. Instead, real power would never return to the Senate, as an emperor eventually emerged to replace Caesar.

As emperor, Augustus encouraged education and literature. He was also known for the harsh punishments that he enforced upon the Romans. Augustus ruled for 41 years, until his death in 14 C.E.

Caesar Augustus Julius Caesar's grandnephew and adopted son, Octavian; Rome's first emperor

Pax Romana a 200-year period of peace and stability established and maintained by the Roman Empire

5. Rome Becomes an Empire, 44 B.C.E. to 14 C.E.

Caesar's murder plunged Rome into civil wars that lasted over ten years. When the fighting ended, Caesar's grandnephew and adopted son Octavian was the sole ruler of Rome. So began the Roman Empire, and Rome's fourth period of expansion.

To gain power, Octavian had to defeat jealous rivals, one of whom was Marc Antony, a popular general. Antony had married Queen Cleopatra of Egypt. In 31 B.C.E., Octavian defeated Antony and Cleopatra in a sea battle near Actium, Greece. His army chased the couple to Egypt, where they killed themselves. Octavian was now the supreme ruler of the Mediterranean region.

Octavian knew that the Romans prized their republic. He told them he was restoring the authority of the Senate, but in fact, he was in complete control. The Senate gave him the title *Augustus*, which means "revered" or "honored." He ruled for life as **Caesar Augustus,** and historians call him Rome's first emperor.

Augustus encouraged education, art, and literature. He completed grand construction projects, repairing more than eighty temples. "I found Rome brick and left it marble," he boasted. He also gave Rome its first police force and firefighters.

Augustus ruled over more than 50 million people. He turned eastern kingdoms, such as Judea and Armenia, into Roman provinces. To better defend the empire, he pushed its borders to natural boundaries: the Rhine and Danube rivers in the north, the Sahara in the south, and the Atlantic in the west.

The empire needed a strong economy, so the Roman government implemented taxation in order to fund the building of harbors, canals, and roads to improve trade. Romans also established a single system of currency, which made it easier for goods to flow across the empire and into foreign lands, as far away as China.

But Rome's final expansion brought new problems. To reform Roman morals, Augustus harshly punished people for being unfaithful to their husbands or wives. To protect himself and his family, he established a private army, the Praetorian (pray-TOR-ee-uhn) Guard. Later, this same Guard sometimes participated in murder **plots** against the emperors it was supposed to protect.

Under Rome, the Mediterranean world was mostly at peace for 200 years, a period which is called the *Pax Romana,* or Roman Peace. But keeping the peace cost the Romans a great deal. During Augustus's reign, one rebellion in the east took three years and thousands of soldiers to subdue.

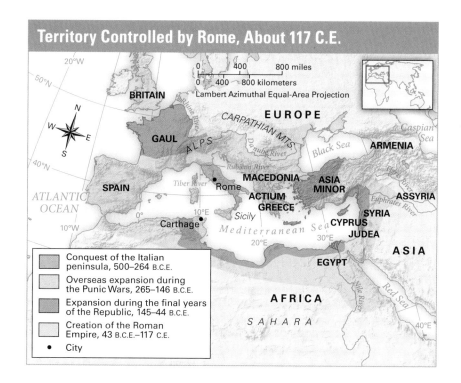

Territory Controlled by Rome, About 117 C.E.

0 400 800 miles
0 400 800 kilometers
Lambert Azimuthal Equal-Area Projection

BRITAIN
EUROPE
CARPATHIAN MTS.
GAUL
ALPS
Rhine River
Danube River
Black Sea
Caspian Sea
ARMENIA
SPAIN
Tiber River
Rubicon River
Rome
MACEDONIA
ACTIUM
GREECE
ASIA MINOR
ASSYRIA
Euphrates River
ATLANTIC OCEAN
Carthage
Sicily
Mediterranean Sea
CYPRUS
SYRIA
JUDEA
ASIA
EGYPT
AFRICA
SAHARA
Nile River
Red Sea

Legend:
- Conquest of the Italian peninsula, 500–264 B.C.E.
- Overseas expansion during the Punic Wars, 265–146 B.C.E.
- Expansion during the final years of the Republic, 145–44 B.C.E.
- Creation of the Roman Empire, 43 B.C.E.–117 C.E.
- • City

At its largest, Rome was a mighty empire that ruled over the entire Mediterranean, large parts of the Middle East, and most of Europe. Many emperors contributed to this territory's countless achievements.

Later emperors added to the territory controlled by Rome. From Britain to the Red Sea, a single power ruled over the greatest empire the world had ever known.

Lesson Summary

In this lesson, you read about four main periods of Roman expansion. In each period, the costs of expansion were great. Yet, the Roman Empire lasted 500 years.

Conquest of the Italian Peninsula The first period of expansion began in 509 B.C.E. The Romans rebelled against the Etruscans, and Rome became a republic. The Romans then conquered central Italy, which they controlled entirely by 264 B.C.E.

The Punic Wars During the second period of expansion, from 264 to 146 B.C.E., Rome fought Carthage in the three Punic Wars. As a result, Rome gained North Africa, much of Spain, and Sicily. Rome also conquered Macedonia and Greece.

The Final Years of the Republic During the third period of expansion, from 145 to 44 B.C.E., Rome took control of Asia Minor, Syria, Egypt, and Gaul. However, civil wars divided the republic. Julius Caesar made himself dictator for life. Then Octavian seized power, becoming the first emperor, Caesar Augustus.

Rome Becomes an Empire The fourth period of expansion began with the start of the empire and lasted until 14 C.E. The emperors continued to add a great deal of new territory. At its height, around 117 C.E., the Roman Empire stretched from Britain to the present-day Middle East.

Rome (27 B.C.E.–476 C.E.)

Rome was the capital of a very large republic and an enormous empire. Through Rome's extensive trade networks, products from across the eastern hemisphere flowed into the city. The emperors worked to bring the best of everything the empire offered to the capital city. People from the provinces came to Rome, as freeman or slaves, and became citizens. As a result, the city ceased to be what it originally had been: a group of culturally similar people, most of whom had been born within the city borders.

Merchants from across the world, other people who had business in Rome, and those who came to see the sights mingled with the native people. Rome went from a city where people were very similar to a site of encounter. A site of encounter is a location in which products, ideas, and technologies from different cultures come together. Encounters happen both when people pass through a location, as well as when people move from their birthplace and settle in new areas, creating multicultural societies. The interactions and exchanges between peoples and cultures often leads to new creations, such as new products, technologies, and ideas.

Without the influence of Roman architecture, religion, and literature, the world would be a much different place. In studying Rome as a site of encounter, you will examine the nature and contributions that the Roman Empire made to the world.

Rome was the capital of the Roman Empire. It is still a major influential city today.

This is the Arch of Titus, a triumphal arch located in Rome that was built in the 1st century.

Architecture and Engineering

Ancient Rome's construction demonstrates the skill of Roman architects and engineers. Some buildings and structures, like aqueducts and public baths, served the daily needs of the people. Others, like triumphal arches, temples, and buildings such as the famed Colosseum, were built for military, religious, or sporting reasons.

An aqueduct is a complex series of connected tunnels and pipes. Water can be brought from faraway distances using aqueducts. Public baths were places in Rome where water was always needed. Here, both the rich and poor often relaxed while they bathed, swam, exercised, and enjoyed a steam bath or a massage. The baths also had gardens, libraries, shops, and art galleries.

Triumphal arches were grand structures that had as many as three entrances. However, they served no practical purpose other than to glorify Roman military victories.

Roman temples combined Greek and Etruscan architectural influences. They sat on a raised platform, had entrances with steps, and were surrounded by columns. Most Roman temples were built to face the sun as it rose in the east.

Gladiators were often slaves or prisoners of war who fought in the Colosseum, another architectural success in Rome. Crowds would shout as the gladiators fought each other and wild animals to the death. Although some won or bought their freedom eventually, many thousands of gladiators died bloody and painful deaths for the entertainment of the spectators.

The ruins of Trajan's Market, known in Italian as *Mercati di Traiano*, are pictured. Some historians consider Trajan's Market to be the world's oldest shopping mall.

Cultural and Religious Influences

The wealthy residents of Rome could only maintain their lifestyle thanks to both those who lived in the city and those who lived in the country. Specialized city markets sold a variety of goods from other nations. Exotic goods like oil, spices, and wine could be found at the city's Trajan's Market.

Silk from China was also a very popular item in Rome even though it had its critics. Some Romans thought men who wore silk seemed too feminine. These people also believed that it was immoral for women to wear the fabric.

The empire's farms provided much of the food for Rome and other cities. Grain was produced for bread, grapes for wine, and olives for oil. Goats and sheep provided cheese, and their skins and wool were made into clothing. Cattle and pigs were raised for their meat. Farmers also kept bees for making honey, the sweetener used by the Romans. Slaves did much of the actual work of farming. Others who were not slaves labored on estates, tended animals, helped with crops, or worked as servants.

Rome was a multicultural empire, so its peoples believed in a variety of spiritual beings. The early Romans believed that spirits lived in everything around them. Many thought their ancestors watched over them. Therefore, people wanted to please these spirits. Over time, the Romans built temples and shrines where people made offerings and promises to gods like Jupiter, the supreme god, and Mars, the god of war. These practices became the state religion of Rome. People often left gifts of food, such as honey cakes and fruit. They also sacrificed animals, including bulls, sheep, and oxen.

Sometimes the exchange of religious ideas challenged the beliefs of the government in Rome. Cults existed in the ancient empire. Some were considered to be acceptable in Roman society while others were feared because officials viewed them as a threat to their power. One such cult honored Bacchus, a god who was related to both a Greek god and an early Roman god. Festivals celebrating Bacchus often left people entranced and excited, and the Roman Senate became concerned as the cult's influence spread. The group began to worship in secret when the government restricted its actions in the late 100s B.C.E.

Romans believed that young boys would become men on March 17, the day of the festival honoring Bacchus.

Lesson 2

The Origins and Spread of Christianity

How did Christianity originate and spread?

Introduction

In this lesson, you will discover how a new religion, Christianity, spread throughout the Roman Empire. Christianity is based on the life and teachings of Jesus, a man who lived from about 6 B.C.E. to about 30 C.E. The New Testament of the Christian Bible tells that Jesus was sentenced to death by crucifixion, a form of execution in which a person is tied or nailed to a cross. Christians believe that Jesus was the Son of God and refer to him as Jesus Christ.

As time passed and Christianity gained followers, many Romans perceived the faith as a threat to Roman order and tradition. Several emperors attempted to cease the spread of the new religion through violent persecutions. Then, in 312 C.E., the day before going into battle against a rival, the emperor Constantine reported having a vision of a cross hanging in the sky. Around the cross were the words "In this sign, you will conquer." That night he had a dream about Jesus. The emperor interpreted the vision and dream as a sign that he would win the battle if he accepted Christian beliefs.

Constantine's soldiers went into battle with the first two letters of the word *Christ* on their shields. At the Battle of Milvian Bridge, near Rome, they won a great victory. From that moment on, Constantine favored the Christian God over all others. His mother became a leader in the faith. By 380 C.E., Christianity was the official religion of the Roman Empire.

How did this happen? Where did Christianity begin? How did it gradually spread throughout the Roman Empire? Read on to discover the answers to these questions.

Social Studies Vocabulary

Christianity

Constantine

disciple

Gospel

Jesus

Messiah

missionary

parable

Resurrection

◀ The Church of the Holy Sepulchre in Jerusalem is sacred to Christians.

1. Judea: The Birthplace of Christianity

The birthplace of **Christianity** was a remote territory at the eastern end of the Mediterranean Sea. According to the New Testament, **Jesus** was born in this region. Referred to as Judea by the Romans, this area had once been ruled by King David and King Solomon when it was part of the ancient kingdom of Israel.

The Jews of the region were devoted to their homeland and to their belief in a single God. This belief, combined with their religious customs, distinguished them from their neighbors in the ancient world.

Once an independent kingdom, Judea came under Roman rule in 63 B.C.E. The Romans attempted to govern the country by appointing Jewish rulers who agreed with Roman rule. However, groups of Jews rebelled against Roman control several times.

In 37 B.C.E., Rome appointed a man named Herod to be the king of Judea. Although Herod was not Jewish by birth, he practiced the Jewish religion and rebuilt the Temple of Jerusalem. However, many Jews distrusted him because they viewed him as a puppet of the Romans.

When Herod died in 4 B.C.E., his kingdom was divided among his three sons. Once again, unrest erupted. Finally, Rome sent soldiers to Judea to regain control, and they replaced Herod's sons with a military governor.

The military governor maintained order and ensured that Judeans paid taxes to Rome, but he usually left local affairs to the Jews themselves. For example, a council of Jewish leaders ruled the holy city of Jerusalem. The council was headed by a high, or chief, priest.

Judea was outwardly peaceful, but many Jews despised the Romans. In their sacred writings, the Jews read prophecies that one day God would send a savior to restore the glorious kingdom of David. This savior was called the **Messiah,** or "anointed one." *Anointed* means "blessed with oil." More generally, it means specially chosen by God.

Christianity the religion based on the life and teachings of Jesus

Jesus a man whose life and teachings would later become the foundation of Christianity

Messiah a savior who many Jews believe had been promised to them by God

Judea, where the New Testament says Jesus was born, was located in the present-day Middle East.

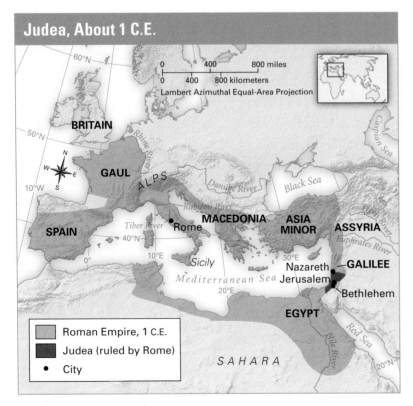

Judea, About 1 C.E.

0 400 800 miles
0 400 800 kilometers
Lambert Azimuthal Equal-Area Projection

60°N
50°N
10°W
0°
10°E
40°N
30°E
20°E
20°N

BRITAIN
GAUL
SPAIN
ALPS
Rhine River
Danube River
Rubicon River
Tiber River
Rome
MACEDONIA
Sicily
Mediterranean Sea
Black Sea
ASIA MINOR
ASSYRIA
Euphrates River
Caspian Sea
Nazareth
Jerusalem
GALILEE
Bethlehem
EGYPT
Nile River
Red Sea
SAHARA

Roman Empire, 1 C.E.
Judea (ruled by Rome)
• City

2. The Birth of Jesus

No one knows exactly when Jesus was born. Our modern calendar dates the start of the Common Era from the supposed year of Jesus's birth. However, after careful study, historians now believe that Jesus's birth occurred around 6 B.C.E., during the reign of King Herod.

Historical records supply great descriptions of the days of the Roman Empire. The lives of the emperors, for example, were recorded in detail. However, few historians of the time wrote about Jesus. Instead, most of the information about him comes from the writings of his followers.

These writings comprise the New Testament of the Christian Bible. Among them are four **Gospels,** which are accounts of Jesus's life that were written in Greek some years after his death. The followers' names have come down to us as Matthew, Mark, Luke, and John.

According to many interpretations of the Gospel of Luke, Jesus was born in a stable where his parents had taken shelter because the inn could not accommodate them. There, humble shepherds and three kings came to see him.

Gospel an account of the life and teachings of Jesus; four of them are included in the New Testament of the Christian Bible

In this mosaic, Mary holds baby Jesus. When he was older, Jesus began to preach in Galilee near present-day Israel.

The Gospel of Luke describes the story of Jesus's birth. According to Luke, Jesus's mother, Mary, lived in a town called Nazareth in the Roman territory of Galilee. There, the Gospels claim, an angel appeared to Mary and told her she would have a child and that she should name him Jesus.

Luke's gospel says that around this time, the Roman emperor Augustus ordered a census, or head count, of all the people in the Empire. Each man was supposed to return to the town of his birth to be counted. Mary's husband, a carpenter named Joseph, set out from Nazareth to his hometown of Bethlehem (BETH-lih-hem), in the territory of Judea. Mary traveled with him and gave birth to Jesus in Bethlehem.

According to the Gospel of Luke, Jesus's family returned to Nazareth after his birth. The New Testament gospels mention little about Jesus's childhood, but it is likely that he grew up in Nazareth and learned carpentry. According to Luke, at age 12, Jesus astonished the rabbis, or teachers, in the great Temple of Jerusalem with his wisdom and his knowledge of Jewish law.

When Jesus was about 30, a teacher known as John the Baptist identified Jesus as the Messiah—the savior the Jews had been waiting for. After 40 days of praying in the wilderness, Jesus began to preach in Galilee.

3. The Life and Death of Jesus

According to the Gospels, Jesus began preaching in Galilee, an area in present-day Israel. Initially, he preached in synagogues, or Jewish places of worship. The crowds that gathered to hear him grew larger, so Jesus began teaching in open areas—in the street, on hillsides, and by the Sea of Galilee.

Jesus called a small number to be his followers, or **disciples**. His disciples were mostly commoners such as laborers and fishermen. Throughout his life, Jesus spent time with the poor and the sick, rather than those who were wealthy and powerful.

The Teachings of Jesus   Jesus based his teachings on traditional Jewish beliefs. However, the Gospels claim he put special **emphasis** on love and mercy. Of all the Jewish laws, he said, two were the most important. The first was, "You shall love the LORD your God with all your heart and all your soul." The second was, "You shall love your neighbor as yourself."

disciple a person who helps spread the religious teachings of another

According to the Gospels, Jesus informed his followers that the kingdom of God was coming soon. To Jesus, however, God's kingdom was not an earthly kingdom of power and riches. Instead, the kingdom of God described a time when people would live according to God's will. Then, Jesus said, everyone would know God's love for all people, even those who suffer or who are looked down upon by others.

One of Jesus's favorite ways of teaching was through **parables,** simple stories with moral or religious messages. Jewish law states that you should love your neighbor as yourself. When asked, "Who is my neighbor?" Jesus replied with the Parable of the Good Samaritan. In this parable, a traveler was wounded and robbed on the road. Two local people passed by and ignored him, but then an outsider called a Samaritan stopped and helped the injured traveler. In this parable it is the outsider, and not the neighbors, who shows compassion and stops to help the traveler in trouble. Because of the Samaritan's good deed, Jesus considered him a neighbor, worthy of love.

Some Judeans worried that Jesus's growing following would cause trouble with the Romans. Although it was easy for some people to view him as a troublemaker, Jesus did not directly preach revolt against the Romans.

The Crucifixion and Resurrection According to the Gospels, after a year or two of traveling and preaching, Jesus went to Jerusalem for the Jewish festival of Passover, which celebrated God's rescue of the Jews from Egypt more than a thousand years before his time. Every year, thousands of Jews traveled to Jerusalem to celebrate Passover. Roman soldiers remained on watch for anyone who might start a demonstration against Rome.

The Gospels mention crowds that gathered to hear Jesus preach and to ask him to cure the sick. This painting illustrates the Christian belief that Jesus could heal the ill.

parable a simple story that explains a moral or religious lesson

This 19th-century stained glass window stands in a church in Stockholm, Germany. It is an interpretation of the Christian belief that Jesus rose from the dead and appeared to his disciples.

According to the Gospels, Jesus explained that his enemies would come together to destroy him and that he would be killed. The Gospels then tell that one of Jesus's disciples, Judas, had decided to betray him. After a final meal with his disciples, Jesus went to pray in a garden. Judas then reported where Jesus could be found. As Jesus was led away under guard, the other disciples fled. Christians call Jesus's final meal with his disciples "the Last Supper."

Jesus had gained a large following in Jerusalem. The city's Roman rulers feared that his supporters might create trouble, and they worried that Jesus might lead a revolt. To eliminate this threat, they decided that he must die. According to the Christian Bible, Pontius Pilate, the Roman governor of Judea, ordered that Jesus be executed. In Roman times, a common form of execution was to be crucified, or tied or nailed to a cross until dead.

According to the New Testament, the Romans took Jesus to a hill outside the city walls. There, they nailed him to a cross and left him to die between two other condemned men who were also crucified. A few faithful followers later removed his body and buried it in a tomb carved out of rock.

The Gospels say that three days later Jesus rose from the dead and then appeared to his disciples, an event Christians refer to as the **Resurrection**. Belief in the Resurrection convinced Jesus's disciples that he was the Son of God. According to the Gospels, Jesus left them again sometime later to join his Father, God, in heaven. His disciples then began spreading the news of his life and teachings.

4. The Missionary Work of Paul

The early **converts** to Christianity were Jews, just as Jesus and his disciples had been. One such convert was Paul, one of the most important people in Christianity. He devoted his life to spreading the teachings of Jesus. After his death, he was declared a saint in the Christian churches.

Resurrection in Christian belief, Jesus's rise from the dead

Paul came from Tarsus, a town in present-day Turkey. Initially, he opposed Christianity and helped to persecute Christians. According to the New Testament, one day Paul was traveling to Damascus in present-day Syria. He saw a blinding light and heard the voice of Jesus, a vision that changed his life. Paul adopted the Christian faith and became a **missionary**.

As an educated man with Roman citizenship who spoke Greek, Paul made it his special mission to convert non-Jews, called Gentiles, to the new religion. He spent several years visiting cities throughout the Greek-speaking world. Wherever he went, he made new converts and started new churches.

In his preaching and letters, Paul **stressed** the need to believe in Jesus as the Son of God. He taught that all people, Jews and Gentiles alike, were God's children. Jesus, he said, was the Christ, God's chosen one. He was a Messiah for everyone, not just his fellow Jews.

Paul's journeys took him through much of the empire. He preached throughout Asia Minor, in Greece, and in Rome. Occasionally, his visits caused riots when angry people protested what they considered blasphemous, or unholy, teaching.

For a time, Paul was imprisoned, or jailed, in Rome, where he continued to write letters to other Christians. Tradition says that he was beheaded by the Romans around 65 C.E., a time when Romans were beginning to persecute Christian believers.

missionary someone who tries to convert others to believe in a particular religion or set of beliefs

This painting of Paul stands in a Roman Catholic Church in Paris, France. It depicts Paul and the letters he wrote to Christian communities describing the life, death, and Resurrection of Jesus. These letters became part of the Christian Bible.

As illustrated in this painting, the emperor Constantine supported Christianity and was baptized before he died. Baptism is a ritual Christians participate in to signify their acceptance of the Christian faith.

5. Christianity Spreads

By the 60s C.E., Christians were beginning to attract the notice of the Romans. Christian preachers traveled along the roads of the empire, winning converts to their new religion. Both Paul and Peter, a close friend of Jesus, preached in Rome. Initially, Rome was not unfriendly to Christians. What was another god, among so many?

However, Christians refused to worship the other Roman gods. Worse, they would not accept that the emperor was a god. Their way of life seemed to be an insult to Roman customs. Instead of wealth and luxury, they preached about simplicity. Recalling Jesus's message of peace and love, many refused to serve in the army.

As the number of Christians increased, many Romans viewed them as a threat to Roman order and patriotism. Eventually, the Christian religion was declared illegal.

Some emperors were determined to make an example of these disloyal citizens. For refusing to honor the Roman gods, Christians were sentenced to die in cruel and painful ways. Some were crucified, and some were burned to death. Others were brought into arenas, where they were devoured by wild animals in front of cheering crowds.

Instead of destroying the new religion, the Christians won new followers by facing death bravely. Christianity offered many people in the empire a sense of purpose and hope. It taught that even the poor and enslaved could look forward to a better life after death if they followed the teachings of Jesus.

Gradually, people of all classes began to adopt the new faith. By 300 C.E., millions of Christians resided in the Roman lands of Europe, North Africa, and western Asia.

At the beginning of the lesson, you read about the emperor **Constantine** and how a victory in battle made him favor the Christian religion. In 313 C.E., Constantine announced the Edict of Milan in which he gave Christians the freedom to practice their religion openly. Future emperors also accepted the new faith. Emperor Theodosius I banned all pagan sacrifices. By 380, Christianity was the official religion of the Roman Empire.

Constantine Roman emperor from about 312 to 337 C.E.; the first Roman emperor to become a Christian

Lesson Summary

In this lesson, you learned how Christianity began and how it spread across the Roman Empire.

Judea: The Birthplace of Christianity Christianity began in Judea in the present-day Middle East. Jews there told prophecies about a Messiah who would remove the Romans and restore the kingdom of David.

The Birth of Jesus What is known about Jesus's life and his birth around 6 B.C.E. comes from the four Gospels. Not much is known about his childhood, but when Jesus was about 30, John the Baptist presented him as the Messiah.

The Life and Death of Jesus Jesus preached with his disciples in present-day Israel, emphasizing love and mercy and often teaching in parables. His teachings angered some. In his early 30s, the Romans executed Jesus by crucifixion. According to the Christian Bible, three days later, he arose from the dead and appeared to his disciples, who began to spread his teachings.

The Missionary Work of Paul According to the New Testament, Paul of Tarsus persecuted Christians. But after Paul reported a vision, he became an important Christian missionary, spreading the religion around the empire. His letters to early churches remain part of the Christian Bible.

Christianity Spreads The new religion survived harsh persecution and spread across the Roman Empire. In 313 C.E., the emperor Constantine gave Christians freedom of religion in the Edict of Milan. It was the official Roman religion by 380.

Lesson 3

The Legacy of the Roman Empire

To what extent have the contributions of ancient Rome influenced modern society?

Introduction

"All roads lead to Rome," boasted the ancient Romans. For 500 years, from about 27 B.C.E. to 476 C.E., the city of Rome was the capital of the greatest empire the world had ever seen. Road markers that stretched thousands of miles showed the distance to Rome, but the empire's 50 million people were connected by more than roads. They were also connected by Roman law, Roman customs, and Roman military might.

At its height, around 200 C.E., the Roman Empire spanned the whole of the Mediterranean world, from northern Africa to the Scottish border, from Spain to Syria. During this time, the Roman world was generally peaceful and prosperous. There was one official language and one code of law. Roman soldiers guarded the frontiers and kept order within the empire's boundaries. Proud Romans believed that the empire would last forever, an idea that would eventually be challenged.

But the empire did not last. By the year 500 C.E., the western half of this great empire had **collapsed**. For historians, the fall of Rome marks the end of the ancient world and the beginning of the Middle Ages.

As one historian wrote, "Rome perished, yet it lived on." The medieval world would pass on many aspects of Roman culture that still affect us today.

What contributed to the decline of this powerful empire? In this lesson, you will discover how and why the Roman Empire fell. Then you will learn how Rome's influence continues to live on in so many ways today—in art, architecture and engineering, language and writing, and philosophy, law, and citizenship.

Social Studies Vocabulary

aqueduct

corruption

decline

empire

mosaic

philosophy

proverb

Roman Empire

scribe

◀ The oldest of ancient Rome's great roads, the Appian Way, ran from Rome to southern Italy.

In 410 C.E., a Germanic tribe attacked Rome, which was by then the capital of only the western part of the Roman Empire.

Roman Empire an empire that, at its height, around 200 C.E., spanned the Mediterranean world and most of Europe

empire a large territory in which several groups of people are ruled by a single leader or government

corruption a pattern of illegal or immoral activities by government officials

decline a slow breakdown or failure

1. The End of the Roman Empire in the West

Rome's first emperor, Caesar Augustus, ended 100 years of civil war and expanded the boundaries of the **Roman Empire**. When he died in 14 C.E., few Romans could imagine that their **empire** would ever end. Yet by the year 500, the western half of the empire had collapsed. What caused the fall of the mighty Roman Empire?

Problems in the Late Empire There was no single reason for the end of the Roman Empire. Instead, historians point to a number of problems that combined to bring about its fall.

Political Instability Rome never solved the problem of how to peacefully transfer political power to a new leader. When an emperor died, ambitious rivals with independent armies often fought each other for control of the empire.

Even when the transfer of power happened without **conflict,** there was no good system for selecting the next emperor. Many times, the Praetorian Guard, the emperor's private army, chose the new ruler. But they frequently chose leaders who would reward them rather than those who were best prepared to be emperor.

Economic and Social Problems Besides political instability, the empire suffered from economic and social problems. To finance Rome's huge armies, its citizens had to pay heavy taxes. These taxes weakened the economy and drove many people into poverty. Trade also suffered.

Unemployment was a serious problem for the economy. Additionally, wealthy families used slaves and cheap labor to work their large estates. Small farmers could not compete with the large landowners. Even though they fled to the cities looking for work, there were not enough jobs for everyone.

Other social problems plagued the empire, including growing **corruption** and a **decline** in the spirit of citizenship. Notorious emperors like Nero and Caligula wasted large amounts of money. A rise in crime made the empire's cities and roads unsafe.

Weakening Frontiers A final problem was the weakening of the empire's frontiers. The huge size of the empire made it hard to defend, and it sometimes took weeks for leaders in Rome to communicate with generals. By the 300s C.E., Germanic tribes were pressing hard on the western borders of the empire. Many of these peoples went on to settle inside the empire and were recruited into the army. But often these soldiers had little loyalty to Rome.

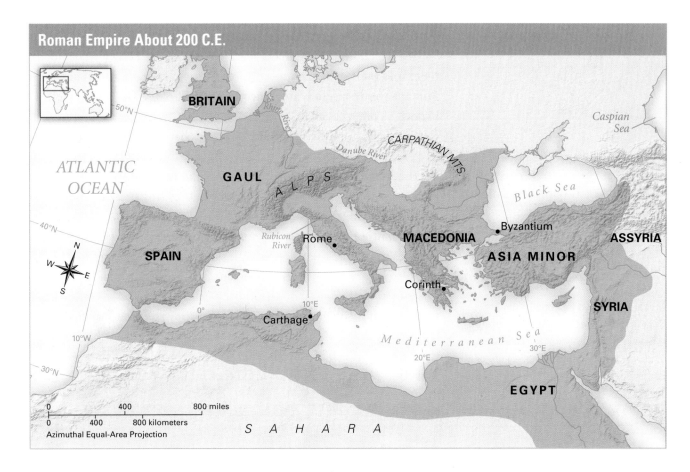

Roman Empire About 200 C.E.

BRITAIN

Rhine River

CARPATHIAN MTS.

Danube River

ATLANTIC
OCEAN

GAUL

A L P S

Caspian
Sea

Black Sea

Byzantium

MACEDONIA

ASIA MINOR

ASSYRIA

SPAIN

Rubicon
River

Rome

Corinth

Carthage

Mediterranean Sea

SYRIA

EGYPT

S A H A R A

0   400   800 miles
0   400   800 kilometers
Azimuthal Equal-Area Projection

The Fall of Rome In 330 C.E., the emperor Constantine took a step that changed the future of the Roman Empire. He moved his capital 850 miles east, to the ancient city of Byzantium. He renamed the city New Rome. Later, it was called Constantinople. In modern times, it was renamed yet again, and today, it is known as Istanbul, Turkey.

After Constantine's reign, the vast empire was usually ruled by two emperors, one based in Rome and one based in Constantinople. Rome became the capital of just the western part of the empire. Constantinople was the capital of the eastern part of the empire.

The emperors in Rome soon found themselves threatened by invading Germanic tribes. In 410 C.E., one of these tribes attacked and looted Rome itself. Finally, in 476, the last emperor in the west was driven from his throne. The western half of the empire began to dissolve into separate kingdoms.

In the east, the empire continued for another 1,000 years. Today, we refer to this eastern empire as the Byzantine Empire, after Byzantium, the original name of its capital city.

In western Europe, Rome's fall did not mean the end of Roman civilization. The influence of Rome lived on through the medieval period and all the way to our time. As you read about the legacy of the Romans, think about how ideas and events from the distant past still affect us today.

At its height, the Roman Empire controlled territory all around the coast of the Mediterranean, most of Europe, and large parts of the Middle East. Can you find the cities of Rome and Byzantium on this map?

2. The Legacy of Roman Art

The Romans adopted many features of other cultures and blended them into their own, **unique** culture. This was true of Roman art. The Romans were especially influenced by the art of the Greeks. In fact, historians often speak of "Greco-Roman" art. Rome played a vital role in passing on this tradition, which has had a major influence on western art.

The Romans added their own talents and tastes to what they learned from other cultures. For example, they imitated Greek sculpture and were particularly good at making lifelike busts and statues.

Romans were also great patrons, or sponsors, of art. Wealthy families decorated their homes with statues and colorful murals and mosaics. Roman artists were especially skilled in painting frescoes, scenes painted on the moist plaster of walls or ceilings with water-based paints. Roman frescoes often showed three-dimensional landscapes, so looking at one of these frescoes was almost like looking through the wall at a view outside. You've probably seen similar murals in restaurants, banks, and other modern public buildings.

mosaic a picture made up of small pieces of tile, glass, or colored stone

Mosaics, such as this one from the Roman city of Herculaneum, decorated the walls in wealthy homes. This art form often showed scenes of Roman life or landscapes, as with this hunting scene.

The Romans also brought a sense of style and luxury to everyday objects. For example, they made highly decorative bottles of blown glass. A wine bottle might be shaped as a cluster of grapes. The Romans also developed the arts of gem cutting and metalworking.

One popular art form was the cameo, which is a carved decoration showing a portrait or a scene. The Romans wore cameos as jewelry and used them to decorate vases and other objects. You can find examples of all these art forms today.

About a thousand years after the fall of the empire, during the period called the Renaissance, Roman art was rediscovered. During the Renaissance, great artists, such as Michelangelo, revived the Greco-Roman style in their paintings and sculptures.

A good example is the famous ceiling of the Sistine Chapel in Rome. Painted by Michelangelo in the 1500s, the ceiling shows scenes from the Bible. A Roman would feel right at home looking up at this amazing creation. Tourists still flock to Rome to see it.

Roman art has continued to influence painters and sculptors. Roman styles were especially popular during the early days of the United States. Americans frequently imitated these styles to give their art dignity and nobility. Today, you can see a number of statues in Washington, D.C., that reflect a strong Roman influence.

American artists often adopted a Roman style to add nobility to sculptures and paintings of heroes. Here you see a Roman statue of the emperor Augustus (left) and an American statue of general and first president George Washington (right). How are the statues alike?

3. The Legacy of Roman Architecture and Engineering

The Romans were skilled and clever builders. In their architecture and engineering, they borrowed ideas from the Greeks and other peoples. But the Romans improved on these ideas in ways that future engineers and architects would imitate.

Architecture The Romans learned how to use the arch, the vault, and the dome to build huge structures. A vault is an arch used for a ceiling or to support a ceiling or roof. A dome is a vault in the shape of a half-circle that rests on a circular wall.

Roman baths and other public buildings often had great arched vaults. The Pantheon, a magnificent temple that still stands in Rome, is famous for its huge dome. The Romans used concrete to help them build much bigger arches than anyone had attempted before. Concrete is made by mixing broken stone with sand, cement, and water and allowing the mixture to harden. The Romans did not invent the material, but they were the first to make widespread use of it.

The Romans also invented a new kind of stadium, large, open-air structures that could seat thousands of spectators. The Romans used concrete to build tunnels into the famous stadium in Rome, the Colosseum. The tunnels made it easy for spectators to reach their seats. Modern football stadiums still use this feature.

With its large concrete dome, the Pantheon is an example of Roman architecture. It still stands in Rome as an immense tribute to the legacies of Roman architecture.

The grand style of Roman buildings has inspired many architects through the centuries. Early medieval architects, for example, frequently imitated Roman designs, especially in building great churches and cathedrals. You can also see a Roman influence in the design of many modern churches, banks, and government buildings. A fine example is the Capitol building, the home of the U.S. Congress in Washington, D.C.

Another Roman innovation that has been widely copied is the triumphal arch. This is a huge monument built to celebrate great victories or achievements. A famous example is the Arc de Triomphe (Arch of Triumph) in Paris, France, which celebrates the victories of the French emperor Napoleon in the early 1800s. Today, it is the national war memorial of France.

Engineering In addition to architecture, the Romans also improved engineering. They were the greatest builders of roads, bridges, and **aqueducts** in the ancient world.

More than 50,000 miles of road connected Rome with the frontiers of the empire. The Romans built their roads with layers of stone, sand, and gravel. Their **techniques** set the standard of road building for 2,000 years. People in some parts of Europe still drive on highways built over old Roman roads.

The Romans also set a new standard for building aqueducts. They created a system of aqueducts for Rome that brought water from about 60 miles away to the homes of the city's wealthiest citizens, as well as to its public baths and fountains. The Romans built aqueducts in other parts of the empire as well. The water system in Segovia, Spain, still uses part of an ancient Roman aqueduct. Roman arches from aqueducts can still be found in Europe, North Africa, and Southwest Asia.

The ruins of the Roman Colosseum (left), where gladiators fought for the entertainment of spectators, still stand in Rome today. What features of Roman architecture can you spot in the U.S. Capitol building (right)?

aqueduct a pipe or raised channel built to carry water over a long distance

Latin uses all capital letters, as seen on this ancient ruin from a Roman temple. As the base of several modern languages, including English, Latin remains hugely influential.

scribe a person trained to write or copy documents by hand

4. The Legacy of Roman Language and Writing

An especially important legacy of Rome for people in medieval times was the Romans' language, Latin. After the fall of the empire, Latin continued to be used by scholars and the Roman Catholic Church. Church **scribes** used Latin to create important **documents**. Educated European nobles learned Latin so they could communicate with their peers in other countries.

Latin remains extremely influential. Several modern European languages developed from Latin, including Italian, Spanish, and French. English is a Germanic language, but it was strongly influenced by the French-speaking Normans, who conquered England in 1066 C.E. English has borrowed heavily from Latin, both directly and by way of French. In fact, we still use the Latin alphabet, although Latin has 23 letters and English has 26.

You can see the influence of Latin in many of the words we use today. For example, our calendar comes from the one adopted by the Roman ruler Julius Caesar. The names of several months come from Latin. August honors Caesar Augustus, and September comes from Latin words meaning "the seventh month." (The Roman year started in March, so September was the seventh month.) October means "the eighth month." Can you guess the meanings of the words *November* and *December*? Latin also remains very important in the subjects of the law, medicine, and religion, as well.

Latin Prefixes Used in English Words

Latin Prefix	Meaning	English Word(s)
in, im, il	not	inactive, impossible, illogical
inter	among, between	international
com, co	together, with	communicate, cooperate
pre	before	precede
post	after, behind	postpone
re	back, again	recount
semi	half	semicircle
sub	under, less than, inferior to	submarine
trans	across, through	transportation

Many English words start with Latin prefixes. A prefix is a word part placed at the beginning of a word that carries its own meaning. Attaching a prefix to a root word creates a new word with a new meaning. In fact, the word *prefix* was formed this way. It comes from *pre-* ("in front of") and *-fix* ("fasten" or "attach").

As this chart shows, other English words come from Latin root words. For instance, the words *manual* and *manipulate* are derived from the Latin word *manus*, meaning "hand."

Roman influence is still important today. For example, this public clock was designed with Roman numerals and is still used today.

Even Latin **proverbs** are still in use. For example, if you look at the reverse side of a U.S. penny, you'll see the U.S. motto *E pluribus unum* ("Out of many, one").

Finally, we still use Roman numerals, which is a system that uses letters to write numbers. In the Roman numeral system, the letters I, V, X, L, C, D, and M represent 1, 5, 10, 50, 100, 500, and 1,000. You may have seen Roman numerals used on clocks, sundials, and the first pages of books. You might also spot Roman numerals on buildings and in some movie and television credits to show the year in which they were made.

proverb a popular saying meant to express something wise or true

Latin Roots Used in English Words

Latin Root	Meaning	English
anima	life, breath, soul	animal, animate
civil	citizen, community	civic
lex, legalis	law, legal	legislature
manus	hand	manual, manipulate
militare	to serve as a soldier	military
portare	to carry	portable
unus	one	united
urbs	city	urban, suburb
verbum	word	verbal

5. The Legacy of Roman Philosophy, Law, and Citizenship

Roman **philosophy**, law, and ideas about citizenship were greatly influenced by the Greeks. But the Romans made contributions of their own that they passed on to future generations.

A Philosophy Called Stoicism A Greek school of thought that was especially popular in Rome was Stoicism (STOH-ihk-ism). Many upper-class Romans adopted this philosophy and made it their own. Stoics believed that a divine (godly) intelligence ruled all of nature and that a person's soul was a spark of that divine intelligence. "Living rightly" meant living in a way that agreed with nature.

To the Stoics, the one truly good thing in life was to have a good character, which meant having virtues such as self-control and courage. Stoics prized duty and the welfare of their community over personal comfort. Roman Stoics were famous for bearing pain and suffering bravely and quietly. To this day, we call someone who behaves in this way "stoic."

The emperor Marcus Aurelius was a devoted Stoic. He wrote about this philosophy of life in his *Meditations*, and many people are still inspired by the ideas in this book.

Law and Justice Roman law covered marriages, inheritances, and contracts (agreements) between people, as well as countless other areas of daily life. Modern legal codes in European countries like France and Italy are based in part on ancient Roman laws.

Another legacy of the Romans was the Roman idea of justice. The Romans believed that there was a universal law of justice that came from nature and that, by this natural law, every person had rights. Judges in Roman courts tried to make just, or fair, decisions that respected people's rights.

Like people everywhere, the Romans did not always live up to their ideals. Their courts did not treat the poor or slaves equally with the rich, and emperors often made laws simply because they had the power to do so. But the ideals of Roman law and justice live on. For example, the ideas of natural law and natural rights are echoed in the Declaration of Independence. Modern-day judges, like judges in Roman courts, often make decisions based on ideals of justice as well as on written law. Similarly, many people around the world believe that all humans have basic rights that no written law can take away.

Citizenship When Rome first began expanding its power in Italy, to be a "Roman" was to be a citizen of the city-state of Rome. Over time, however, Rome's leaders gradually extended citizenship to all free people in the empire. Even someone born in Syria, in Southwest Asia, or in Gaul (modern-day France) could claim to be Roman. All citizens were subject to and protected by Roman law, enjoyed the same rights, and owed allegiance (loyalty) to the emperor.

U.S. citizens enjoy the right to vote for government leaders, thanks to the ideas of citizenship that began in Roman times. It is one of many ways that Roman culture has influenced our own.

The idea of citizenship as both a privilege and a responsibility has descended from Roman times to our own. While most people in the United States are citizens by birth, many immigrants become citizens by solemnly promising loyalty to the United States. Regardless of where they were born, all citizens have the same responsibilities. For example, they must obey the law. And all enjoy the same basic rights spelled out in the Constitution and its amendments, including the Bill of Rights.

Lesson Summary

In this lesson, you explored the rich legacy of ancient Rome. The Roman Empire fell more than 1,500 years ago. But it left a lasting influence throughout Western culture that you experience nearly every day.

Art, Architecture, and Engineering Artists still follow Roman styles in sculpture, mosaics, glass, and other art forms. Roman influences are seen in the arches, domes, and vaults of many modern churches, banks, and government buildings. The Romans also were talented engineers, whose construction methods and standards lasted thousands of years.

Language and Writing Many words and word parts in modern languages, including English, French, and Spanish, developed from the Roman language, Latin. Roman numerals appear today on clocks, in books, and in TV and movie credits.

Philosophy, Law, and Citizenship Roman ideals, such as the philosophy of Stoicism, rule of law, and justice, shaped the law codes and government structures of many nations today. Examples of the continuing influence of Roman ideas include today's law courts, written law, such as the U.S. Constitution, and our representative government.

Lesson 4

The Development of Feudalism in Western Europe

How well did feudalism establish order in Europe in the Middle Ages?

Introduction

The collapse of the Roman Empire in 476 C.E. marks the beginning of the period in Europe known as the Middle Ages. During this time period, a complex political and economic system developed that largely shaped people's lives.

Historians divide the Middle Ages into three periods. The Early Middle Ages lasted from about 476 to 1000 C.E. The High Middle Ages lasted from about 1000 to 1300. The Late Middle Ages lasted from about 1300 to 1450.

The Middle Ages began with the fall of the Roman Empire, which had unified much of Europe for about 500 years. After its collapse, life became dangerous and difficult in Western Europe. People worked hard simply to survive and to have enough to eat. They also needed to protect themselves from conquest by invading barbarians and neighboring kingdoms.

These challenges gave rise to the economic and political system historians call feudalism (FEWD-ahl-ism) in which people had clearly defined roles and relationships with each other. In the feudal system, people pledged loyalty to a lord—a ruler or powerful landholder. In return, they received protection from that lord. Warriors fought on behalf of their lords, and peasants worked the land. At the bottom of the system were serfs, or peasants who were not free to leave the lord's land without permission.

In this lesson, you will discover more about the difficulties people faced during the Early Middle Ages. Then you will learn about the rise of feudalism and how it helped to establish order and security after the fall of Rome. Finally, you will explore what daily life was like for people living under feudalism.

Social Studies Vocabulary

Charlemagne

chivalry

feudalism

fief

serf

◀ This page from an illuminated manuscript shows peasants working on a feudal manor.

1. Western Europe During the Early Middle Ages

For 500 years, much of Europe was part of the Roman Empire. The rest of the continent was controlled by groups of people the Romans called "barbarians" because they did not follow Roman ways. When Rome fell to invading barbarians in 476 C.E., Europe was left with no central government or system of defense. Throughout Western Europe, many invading groups set up kingdoms that were often at war with one another. The most powerful rulers were those who controlled the most land and had the greatest warriors.

In 800 C.E., Charlemagne was crowned Holy Roman emperor by Pope Leo III, as shown in this 16th-century fresco. His success at unifying most Christian land into a single empire made him a well-respected and effective ruler.

Charlemagne the leader of the Franks from 768 to 814 C.E., who unified most of the Christian lands of Europe into a single empire

Charlemagne's Empire One powerful group during this time was the Franks (from whom modern-day France takes its name). The Franks were successful because they had developed a new style of warfare that depended on troops of knights, heavily armed warriors who fought on horseback. To achieve and hold power, a ruler needed the services and loyalty of many knights. In return for their loyalty and service, the ruler rewarded knights with land and privileges.

One of the early leaders of the Franks was an ambitious young warrior named Clovis. In 481 C.E., at the age of 15, Clovis became leader of the Franks. Five years later, he defeated the last great Roman army in Gaul at Soissons. During his 30-year **reign,** he led the Franks in wars that largely extended the boundaries of the Frankish kingdom.

Clovis also helped convert the Franks to Christianity. Clovis married a Christian woman, Clotilda, and eventually was baptized into the Roman Catholic Church. Many of his followers became Christians, as well.

The most important leader of the Franks was **Charlemagne** (SHAR-luh-main), which means "Charles the Great." This impressive king ruled for over 40 years, from 768 to 814. Writings from that period say that he was six feet four inches tall—extremely tall for his time—and "always stately and dignified." Legend has it that he read very little and couldn't write, yet he loved to have scholarly works read to him. He encouraged education and scholarship, making his court a center of culture. Most important, he unified nearly all the Christian lands of Europe into a single empire. One of the poets at his court called him the "King Father of Europe."

Charlemagne built his empire with the help of a pope—Leo III, the leader of the Roman Catholic Church. The Church was a central part of society during this time, and for Charlemagne, the blessings of the Church sent the message, "God is on my side." The Church also valued support from the empire, and Leo needed the backing of someone with an army. In return for Charlemagne's help, the pope crowned him Holy Roman emperor in 800 C.E.

Charlemagne's empire survived many attacks. After his death in 814, however, it quickly fell apart. The weak rulers who followed him could not defend the empire against new waves of invasions. Still, these kings helped prepare the way for the system of **feudalism** by following Charlemagne's example of rewarding knights with land and privileges in return for military service.

feudalism the economic and political system of medieval Europe in which people exchanged loyalty and labor for a lord's protection

A Need for Order and Protection In the 9th and 10th centuries, Western Europe was threatened by three main groups. Muslims, or the followers of the religion of Islam, advanced from the Middle East and northern Africa into what is now Spain. The Magyars, a central Asian people, pressed in from the east. Vikings swept down from present-day Norway and Denmark.

The Vikings were fierce warriors who instilled fear in the people of Europe. At times, the Vikings' intent was to set up colonies, but they were best known for their terrifying raids on towns and religious centers.

Picture a Viking attack. The people of the town are at early morning church services when an alarm bell starts to clang. Vikings! Long, shallow wooden boats have brought the Vikings close to shore. Now they leave their boats and run toward the town with swords and axes raised over their heads. People are running in all directions, while several villagers who attempt to resist are killed. Others are seized by the Viking raiders and taken back to the ships.

Clearly, the people of Western Europe needed to figure out new methods of defense. To protect themselves and their property, they gradually developed the system we call feudalism.

The Vikings were known for carrying out attacks and capturing villagers in Western Europe. A raiding party of fierce Vikings attacked the walled city of Paris in 885 C.E.

In the system of feudalism, the monarch was at the top, followed by the nobles, and then knights. Here, a lord gives orders to peasants, who were at the bottom of the social system.

This pyramid shows the basic social structure in the system of feudalism.

fief land grated by a lord to a vassal in exchange for loyalty and service

serf a peasant who could not leave the lord's land on which he or she was born and worked

2. Feudalism: Establishing Order

By the High Middle Ages (about 1000 C.E.), Europeans had developed the system of feudalism. Feudalism provided people with protection and safety by establishing a stable social order.

Under this system, people were bound to one another by promises of loyalty. In theory, all the land in the kingdom belonged to the monarch (usually a king, but sometimes a queen). A large amount of land was also owned by the Church. The king kept some land for himself and gave **fiefs** (FEEFS), or land grants, to his most important lords, who became his vassals. In return, each lord promised to supply the king with knights in times of war. A lord then enlisted lesser lords and knights as his vassals. At times, these arrangements were written down, and some of these contracts even **survive** to this day in museums.

At the bottom of the social system were peasants. Lords rented some of their land to the peasants who worked for them. However, some peasants, called **serfs,** were "tied" to the land they worked, which meant that they could not leave the lord's land without permission and had to farm his fields in exchange for a small plot of their own.

Most lords and wealthier knights lived on manors, or large estates. A manor included a castle or manor house, one or more villages, and the surrounding farmland. Manors were in the country, far from towns, which required peasants to produce everything the people on the manor needed. Only a few goods came from outside the manor, such as salt for preserving meat and iron for making tools.

During the Middle Ages, people were born into a social class for life. They had the same social position, and often the same job, as their parents. Let's take a closer look at the social classes in feudal society.

3. Monarchs During Feudal Times

At the very top of feudal society were the monarchs, or kings and queens. As you have learned, medieval monarchs were also feudal lords. They were expected to keep order and to provide protection for their vassals.

Most medieval monarchs believed in the divine right of kings, the idea that God had given them the right to rule. In reality, the power of monarchs varied greatly. Some had to work hard to **maintain** control of their kingdoms, and few had enough wealth to keep their own armies. They had to rely on their vassals, especially nobles, to provide enough knights and soldiers. In some places, especially during the Early Middle Ages, great lords grew very powerful and governed their fiefs as independent states. In these cases, the monarch was little more than a figurehead, a symbolic ruler who had little real power.

In England, monarchs became quite strong during the Middle Ages. Since the Roman period, a number of groups from the continent, including Vikings, had invaded and settled England. By the mid-11th century, it was ruled by a Germanic tribe called the Saxons. The king at that time was descended from both Saxon and Norman (French) families. When he died without an adult heir, there was confusion over who should become king.

William, the powerful Duke of Normandy (a part of present-day France), believed he had the right to the English throne. However, the English crowned his cousin, Harold. In 1066, William and his army invaded England. William defeated Harold at the Battle of Hastings and established a line of Norman kings in England. His triumph earned him the nickname "William the Conqueror."

When William of Normandy conquered England, he brought feudal institutions from Europe with him. Supported by feudalism, strong rulers brought order to England. In fact, by the start of the High Middle Ages, around 1000 c.e., the feudal system had brought stability to much of Europe.

William, Duke of Normandy, became known as "William the Conqueror" after he seized the English throne. This scene is on the famous Bayeux Tapestry and shows William of Normandy and his men conquering England.

Lords and ladies, both members of the nobility, were served elaborate meals at feasts or banquets in the manor house. Often, musicians and jesters entertained them while they ate.

4. Lords and Ladies During Feudal Times

Like monarchs, lords and ladies were members of the nobility, the highest-ranking class in medieval society. Most of them lived on manors. Some lords had one manor, while others had several. Those who had more than one manor usually lived in one for a few months and then traveled with their families to another.

Manor Houses and Castles Many of the people on a manor lived with the lord's family in the manor house. Built of wood or stone, manor houses were surrounded by gardens and outbuildings, such as kitchens and stables. They were protected by high walls.

The manor house was the center of the community, and in times of trouble, villagers entered its walls for protection. Its great hall served as the lord's court, but it also offered a place for special celebrations and feasts, such as those given at Christmas or after a harvest.

Kings and queens, high-ranking nobles, and wealthy lords lived in even grander structures: castles. Castles were built for many purposes, but one of their main **functions** was to serve as a home. Castles were also one of the most important forms of military technology. With their moats, strong walls, and gates, they were built for defense. Finally, their large size and central locations made castles visual reminders of the social hierarchy and the power of the ruling classes.

The earliest medieval castles were built of wood and surrounded by high wooden fences. The strongest part, the *motte*, was built on a hilltop. A walled path linked the motte to a lower enclosed court, the *bailey*, where most people lived. After about 1100 C.E., most castles were built of stone to resist attacks by more powerful siege weapons.

Castles gradually became more elaborate. Many had tall towers for looking out across the land. The main castle building had a variety of rooms, including storerooms, kitchens, a dining hall, sleeping quarters for distinguished guests, and the lord and lady's quarters.

The Responsibilities and Daily Life of Lords and Ladies It was the lord's responsibility to manage and defend his land and its laborers. The lord appointed officials to make sure villagers fulfilled their duties, which included farming the lord's land and paying rent in the form of crops, meat, and other foods. Lords also acted as judges in manor courts and had the power to fine and punish those who broke the law. Some lords held posts in the king's government. In times of war, lords fought for their own higher-ranking lords, or at least supplied them with a well-trained fighting force.

In theory, only men were part of the feudal relationship between lord and vassal. However, it was quite common in the Middle Ages for noblewomen to hold fiefs and inherit land. Except for fighting, these women had all the duties that lords had. They ran their estates, sat as judges in manor courts, and sent their knights to serve in times of war.

Both lords and ladies had many responsibilities when it came to running their land. However, they also made time for fun. Playing board games, such as chess, was one recreational activity they enjoyed.

Noblewomen who were not landowners were still extremely busy. They were responsible for raising and training their own children and, often, the children of other noble families. Ladies were also responsible for overseeing their household or households. Some households had hundreds of people, including priests, master hunters, and knights-in-training called *pages* and *squires*, who assisted the knights. There were also cooks, servants, artists, craftspeople, and grooms. Entertainment was provided by musicians and jesters who performed amusing jokes and stunts.

When they weren't hard at work, lords and ladies enjoyed hunting and hawking (hunting with birds), feasting and dancing, board games such as chess, and reading. Ladies also did fine stitching and embroidery, or decorative sewing.

Although nobles and monarchs had the most privileged lives in medieval times, they were not always easy or comfortable by modern standards. Lit only by candles and warmed only by open fires, manor homes and castles could be gloomy and cold. There was little or no privacy. Fleas and lice infected all medieval buildings, and people generally bathed only once a week, if that. Clothes were not washed daily either. Diseases affected the rich as well as the poor. And, of course, warfare was a great and ever-present danger.

5. Knights During Feudal Times

Knights were the mounted soldiers of the medieval world. In general, knights needed to have a good deal of wealth, since a full suit of armor and a horse cost a small fortune. Knights were usually vassals of more powerful lords.

Before a joust or tournament, knights received gifts, or tokens of support, from the ladies of the manor. A squire would assist the knight by dressing him in armor and caring for his horse.

Becoming a Knight The path to becoming a knight involved many years of training. A boy started as a page, or servant. At the age of seven, he left home and went to live at the castle of a lord, who was often a relative. Nearly all wealthy lords had several pages living in their castles and manors. A page learned how to ride a horse and received religious instruction from the local priest or friar.

During this first stage of training, a page spent much of his time with the ladies of the castle and was expected to help them in every way possible. During this period, the ladies taught pages how to sing, dance, compose music, and play the harp—skills that were valued in knights.

After about seven years as a page, a young boy became a squire. During this part of his training, he spent most of his time with the knight who was his lord. The squire helped care for his horse and polished the knight's armor, sword, shield, and lance. He even waited on his lord at mealtime, carrying water for hand washing, carving meat, and filling his cup when it was empty.

Most importantly, squires trained to become warriors. They learned how to fight with a sword and a lance, a kind of spear that measured up to 15 feet long. They also learned how to use a battle-axe and a mace (a club with a heavy metal head). Squires practiced by fighting in make-believe battles, but they also went into real battles. A squire was expected to help dress his lord in armor, care for his weapons and horses, follow him into battle, and look after him if he was wounded.

In his early 20s, if deserving of the honor, a squire became a knight, a **process** that at times was a complex religious event. A squire often spent the night before his knighting ceremony in prayer. The next morning, he bathed and put on a white tunic, or long shirt, to show his purity. During the ceremony, he knelt before his lord and said his vows. The lord drew his sword, touched the knight-to-be lightly on each shoulder with the flat side of the blade, and knighted him. Sometimes, if a squire did particularly well in battle, he was knighted on the spot.

The Responsibilities and Daily Life of Knights Being a knight was more than a profession. It was a way of life. Knights lived by a strong code of behavior called **chivalry**. (*Chivalry* comes from the French word *cheval*, meaning "horse.") Knights were expected to be loyal to the Church and to their lord, to be just and fair, and to protect the helpless. They performed acts of gallantry, or respect paid to women. From these acts, we get the modern idea of chivalry as traditional forms of courtesy and kindness toward women.

Jousts and tournaments were a major part of a knight's life. In a joust, two armed knights on horseback galloped at each other with their lances extended, aiming to unseat the opponent from his horse. Jousts were held as sporting events, for exercise, or as serious battles between rival knights. A tournament involved a team of knights in one-on-one battle.

Knights fought wearing heavy suits of armor. In the 11th century, armor was made of linked metal rings, called chain mail. By the 14th century, plate armor was more common and offered better protection.

The medieval style of knighthood lasted until about the 17th century, when warfare changed with the growing use of gunpowder and cannons. Knights, who fought one-to-one on horseback, were no longer effective against such weapons.

But knights were only a small group in medieval society. Next, let's turn to daily life for the vast majority of the population: the peasants.

Done for both sport and for battles, jousts involved knights trying to knock each other off their horses. Knights wore heavy suits of armor, which were made of metal.

chivalry the medieval knight's code of ideal behavior, including bravery, loyalty, and respect for women

6. Peasants During Feudal Times

Most people during the Middle Ages were peasants. They were not included in the feudal relationship of vassal and lord, but they supported the entire feudal structure by working the land. Their labor freed lords and knights to spend their time preparing for war or fighting.

During medieval times, peasants were legally classified as free or unfree. These categories had to do with the amount of service owed to the lord. Free peasants rented land to farm and owed only their rent to the lord. Unfree peasants, or serfs, farmed the lord's fields and could not leave the lord's manor. In return for their labor, they received their own small plot of land to farm.

The daily life of peasants revolved around work. Most peasants raised crops and tended livestock (farm animals), but every manor also had carpenters, shoemakers, smiths (metalworkers), and other skilled workers. Peasant women worked in the fields when needed, while also caring for their children, their homes, and livestock.

Along with the work they performed, peasants and serfs might owe the lord numerous taxes. There was a yearly payment called "head money," at a fixed amount per person. In addition, the lord could demand a tax, known as *tallage*, whenever he needed money. When a woman married, she, her father, or her husband had to pay a fee called a *merchet*.

At the bottom of the system, peasants supported their lords by laboring the land. They also were required to pay yearly taxes and provide their lord with money whenever requested.

Peasants were also required to grind their grain at the lord's mill (the only mill on the manor). As payment, the miller kept portions of the grain for the lord and for himself, with lords keeping any amount they wanted. Peasants found this practice so hateful that some of them hid small handmills in their houses.

Most peasants lived in small, simple houses composed of one or two rooms. A typical house was made of woven strips of wood covered with straw or mud, usually with little furniture or other possessions inside. There was a hearth fire in the middle of the main room, but often there was no chimney, making the room dark and smoky. An entire family might eat and sleep in one room that sometimes also housed their farm animals.

Peasants ate vegetables, meat such as pork, and dark, coarse bread made of wheat mixed with rye or oatmeal. Almost no one ate beef or chicken. During the winter, they ate pork, mutton, or fish that had been preserved in salt. Herbs were used widely, to improve flavor and reduce saltiness, or to disguise the taste of meat that was no longer fresh.

Their homes were small and crowded with people and animals.

Lesson Summary

In this lesson, you learned about life during feudal times. The fall of the Roman Empire led to a period of uncertainty and danger. Europeans developed the system of feudalism to help provide economic and social stability and safety.

Feudalism The feudal system arose as a way of protecting property and creating stability. It was based on loyalty and personal relationships. Monarchs gave fiefs to lords, their most important vassals. In exchange, vassals promised to supply monarchs with soldiers in war.

Monarchs and Lords At the top of the feudal social structure was the monarch. Below the monarch were his vassals, the lords, or nobles. Monarchs and nobles oversaw their lands and the people who worked them. They lived in manor houses or castles.

Knights and Peasants Below the lords were the knights, heavily armored warriors on horseback who provided service in war in return for land and protection. At the bottom of the social hierarchy were free peasants, followed by serfs. Peasants farmed the land and made most of the necessary articles of life. Serfs were peasants bound to the land.

Lesson 5

The Roman Catholic Church in Medieval Europe

How influential was the Roman Catholic Church in medieval Europe?

Introduction

The Catholic Church in Europe had a heavy influence during the High Middle Ages, the period from about 1000 to 1300 C.E. The Church was the center of life in medieval western Europe. Almost every community had a church building, and larger towns and cities had a cathedral. Church bells rang out the hours, called people to worship, and warned of danger.

The church building was the center of community activity and many parts of daily life. Religious services were held several times a day. Town meetings, plays, and concerts were also held in churches. Merchants had shops around the square in front of the church. Farmers sold their produce in the square, and markets, festivals, and fairs were held there, as well.

During the Middle Ages, the Church was a daily presence from birth to death. It provided education and helped the poor and sick. In fact, religion was so much a part of daily life, that people even said prayers to decide how long to cook an egg!

Christian belief was so **widespread** during this time that historians sometimes call the Middle Ages the "Age of Faith." People looked to the Church to explain world events. Storms, disease, and famine were believed to be punishments sent by God. People hoped prayer and religious devotion would prevent such disasters. They were even more concerned about the fate of their souls after death. The Church claimed that salvation, or the saving of one's soul, would come to those who followed its teachings.

In this lesson, you will learn how the Church began and how it expanded. You will also discover how much the Church influenced people's daily lives during the High Middle Ages.

Social Studies Vocabulary

clergy

natural law

persecute

pilgrimage

religion

religious order

Roman Catholic Church

sacrament

◄ England's Tewkesbury Abbey used to be a Benedictine Monastery.

The pope is the most powerful official of the Roman Catholic Church. This painting of the procession of Pope Lucius III was created in the year 1183 and shows the pope, cardinals, archbishops, bishops, and priests in their various garments and finery.

religion a set of spiritual beliefs, values, and practices

persecute to cause a person to suffer because of his or her beliefs

Roman Catholic Church the Christian church headed by the pope in Rome

clergy the body of people, such as priests, who perform the sacred functions of a church

1. The Christian Church Takes Shape

The Christian **religion** is one of ancient Rome's most important legacies. Christians are followers of Jesus, who, according to Christian scripture, was put to death on a Roman cross in the 1st century C.E. Christians believe that Jesus was the son of God, that God sent him to Earth to save people from their sins, and that he rose from the dead after his death by crucifixion.

Initially, the Romans **persecuted** Christians for their beliefs. Yet the new religion continued to spread. In 313 C.E., the Roman emperor Constantine issued a decree allowing Christians to practice their religion freely. In 395 C.E., Christianity became the official religion of the Roman Empire.

At the start of the Middle Ages, all Christians in western Europe belonged to a single church, which became known as the **Roman Catholic Church**. After the collapse of Rome, the Church played a vital role in society. In part, it was one of the few ties that people had to a more stable time. The Church provided leadership and, at times, even organized the distribution of food. Monasteries, or communities of monks, provided hospitality to refugees and travelers. Monks also copied and preserved old texts, and in this way helped keep both new and ancient learning alive. The spread of monasteries and the preaching of missionaries helped bring new converts to the Christian faith.

The Organization of the Roman Catholic Church Over time, Church leaders developed an organization that was modeled on the structure of the old Roman government. By the High Middle Ages, they had created a system in which all **clergy** members had a rank.

The pope, who was the bishop of Rome, was the supreme head of the Roman Catholic Church. He appointed high-ranking clergy men, called cardinals, to assist and counsel him. These cardinals ranked just below the pope in the Church **hierarchy**.

Archbishops came next. They oversaw large or important areas called archdioceses. Below them were bishops, who governed areas called dioceses from great cathedrals. Within each diocese, priests served local communities, called parishes, each of which had its own church building.

The Increasing Power of the Church During the Middle Ages, the Church acquired great economic power. By the year 1050, it was the largest landholder in Europe. Some land was gifted to the church by monarchs and wealthy lords, while other land was taken by force. The medieval Church added to its wealth by collecting a tithe, or tax. Each member was expected to give one-tenth of his money, produce, or labor to help support the Church.

In the winter of 1077, the Holy Roman emperor, Henry IV, traveled to Italy to the castle of Canossa to beg forgiveness from Pope Gregory. Legend has it that the pope made Henry stand barefoot in the snow for three days before he forgave him.

The Church also came to wield great political power. Latin, the language of the Church, was the only common language throughout Europe. Church officials were often the only people who could read. As a result, they kept records for monarchs and became trusted scribes and advisers.

At times, the Church's power lead to conflict with European monarchs. One key struggle involved Pope Gregory VII and Henry IV, the Holy Roman emperor.

Gregory was elected pope in 1073. An ambitious leader, he undertook several reforms, such as forbidding priests to marry and outlawing the selling of Church offices (official positions). He also banned the practice whereby kings could appoint priests, bishops, and the heads of monasteries. Only the pope, announced Gregory, had this right.

Gregory's ruling angered Henry IV. Like rulers before him, Henry considered it his duty (and privilege) to appoint Church officials. He called a council of bishops and declared that Gregory was no longer pope. Gregory responded by excommunicating Henry. This action meant that Henry was thrown out of the Church and, therefore, could not gain salvation. Gregory also said that Henry's subjects were no longer obliged to obey him.

The pope's influence was so great that Henry begged forgiveness and was readmitted to the Church. For the moment, his action revealed the pope's **authority,** even over an emperor. But future rulers and popes would resume the fight over the rights of the Church versus those of the state.

The sacrament of baptism welcomes a person into a Christian church. Baptism is the first sacrament of a Christian's life. It is required to receive the other sacraments.

2. Sacraments and Salvation in the Middle Ages

Most people in medieval Europe believed in God and an afterlife, the idea that the soul lives on after the body's death. The Church taught that people gained salvation, or entry into heaven and eternal life, by following the Church's teachings and living a moral life. Failing to do so condemned the soul to eternal suffering in hell.

To believers, hell was a real and terrifying place. Its torments, such as fire and demons, were pictured in vivid detail in many paintings. The Church asserted that receiving the **sacraments** was an essential part of gaining salvation. Sacraments were sacred rites that Christians believed brought them grace, or a special blessing from God. The sacraments marked the most important occasions in a person's life, such as baptism and marriage.

sacrament a sacred rite of the Christian religion

The Seven Catholic Sacraments

Baptism	Entry into the Church; to cleanse a person of sin, a priest pours water gently over the person's head at the baptismal font, the basin that holds the baptismal water.
Confirmation	Formal declaration of belief in God and the Church
Eucharist	A central part of the mass, the Church service in which the priest consecrates (blesses) bread and wine. In Catholic belief, the consecrated bread and wine become the body and blood of Jesus.
Matrimony (marriage)	A formal union blessed by the Church; after being married by a priest, a couple signs their names in a registry, or book of records.
Holy Orders	The sacrament in which a man becomes a priest
Penance	Confession of sins to a priest in order to receive God's forgiveness; today, Catholics call this sacrament *reconciliation.*
Extreme Unction	A blessing in which a person in danger of death is anointed (blessed with holy oil) by a priest; today, this rite is known as the sacrament (or anointing) of the sick.

3. Pilgrimages and Crusades

During the Middle Ages, religious faith led many people to perform extraordinary acts of devotion. For instance, most Christians hoped to go on a **pilgrimage** at some point in their lives. Pilgrims traveled long distances to visit holy sites, such as Jerusalem (the place where Jesus was killed) and Rome. They also visited churches that housed relics, or the body parts or belongings of saints. Canterbury Cathedral in England was another major destination for pilgrims.

Pilgrims went on these journeys to demonstrate their devotion to God, to perform penance for their sins, or to attempt to cure an illness. A pilgrimage **required** true dedication since travel at the time was difficult and often dangerous. Most pilgrims traveled on foot. Because robbers were a constant threat, pilgrims often banded together for safety, and sometimes even hired an armed escort. Along the routes of popular pilgrimages, local rulers built roads and bridges. Monks and nuns set up hostels, or special guest houses, spaced a day's journey apart.

Geoffrey Chaucer, who lived in England from about 1342 to 1400, wrote a popular narrative poem about pilgrims called *The Canterbury Tales*. His amusing "tales" are stories that a group of pilgrims tell to entertain each other as they travel to the shrine of Saint Thomas Becket at Canterbury. Among Chaucer's pilgrims are a knight, a miller (someone who helps grind crops into flour), a cook, and a prioress (the head of a convent, or community of nuns).

A second type of extraordinary service that dedicated people carried out involved fighting in the Crusades. The Crusades were a series of military expeditions to the land where Jesus had lived, which Christians called the Holy Land. During the 7th century, this part of the Middle East had come under the control of Muslims. Jerusalem, which was a holy city to Jews, Christians, and Muslims alike, became a Muslim-controlled city. Between 1095 and 1270, Christians in western Europe organized several Crusades to recover Jerusalem and other sites of pilgrimage in that region.

Some people went on Crusade to seek wealth, and others to seek adventure. Others went with the belief that doing so would guarantee their salvation. Many Crusaders acted from deep religious belief.

pilgrimage a journey to a holy site

Pilgrims believed that their journeys of devotion earned them grace in the eyes of God. This image shows a page of Geoffrey Chaucer's *The Canterbury Tales*, a collection of humorous stories that described a pilgrimage.

The construction of Chartres Cathedral in France began in 1194 and took 66 years to complete. Further additions spanned 300 years.

4. Art and Architecture

During the Middle Ages, most art was created for a religious purpose. Paintings and sculptures portrayed Jesus and Christian saints and were placed in churches to support worship. Since most people could not read, art helped tell the story of Jesus's life in a way that everyone could understand.

Medieval art and architecture found their most glorious expression in cathedrals, the large churches headed by bishops. (The word *cathedral* comes from the Latin word *cathedra,* meaning "the throne upon which a bishop sits.") Cathedrals were built to inspire awe, or wonder. For centuries, they were the tallest buildings in any community, often taller than a 30-story building of today. Most were built in the shape of a cross, with a long central section called the nave and shorter side sections called *transepts.*

The cathedrals constructed between 1150 and 1400 were designed in the Gothic style and built to appear as if they are rising to heaven. On the outside are stone arches called *flying buttresses*. The arches spread the massive weight of the soaring roof and walls more evenly, a building **technique** that allowed for taller, thinner walls and more windows.

Gargoyles are a unique feature of Gothic cathedrals. Gargoyles are decorative stone sculptures projecting from the rain gutters or edges of a cathedral roof. They were usually carved in the form of mythical beasts. In medieval times, some people believed gargoyles were placed as a reminder that devils and evil spirits would catch them if they did not obey the Church's teachings.

The immense space inside a Gothic cathedral was lined with pillars and decorated with religious images. Beautiful stained-glass windows (windows made from pieces of colored glass arranged in a design) let in colorful light. The pictures on medieval stained-glass windows often depicted stories from the Bible.

Cathedrals were visible expressions of Christian devotion. Hundreds of workers and craftsmen constructed cathedrals by hand over many years. On average, it took from 50 to 100 years to complete a cathedral, but the work took more than 200 years in some cases.

Gothic cathedrals often had elaborate details such as gargoyles.

With the inside displaying artwork that showed stories from the Bible, Gothic-style cathedrals had both purpose and beauty. Sculpted gargoyles and decorative flying buttresses made the outside of a cathedral equally appealing as the inside.

5. Education

During the Middle Ages, most schooling took place in monasteries, convents, and cathedrals. This pattern was established under Charlemagne, who encouraged the Church to teach people to read and write. During his reign, scholars developed a new form of writing that helped make reading easier. Instead of writing in all capital letters, as the Romans did, scholars began to use lowercase letters, too. We still use this system today.

In medieval times, the clergy were the people most likely to be educated. Most of the students in Church schools were sons of nobles who were studying for careers in the clergy. They spent much of their time memorizing prayers and passages from the Bible in Latin.

Beginning in the 1200s, cathedral schools gave rise to universities. Students in universities studied Latin grammar and rhetoric (the art of argument), logic, geometry, arithmetic, astronomy, and music. Books at that time were hand copied and very rare, so teachers often read to students.

Ancient texts were greatly respected in the universities, but the Church was sometimes uneasy about them. The Church taught people to be guided by faith. In contrast, ancient writers like the Greek philosopher Aristotle taught that reason, or logical thinking, was the path to knowledge. The clergy feared that studying such writers might lead people to question the Church's teachings.

During the Middle Ages, the Church created universities, such as the University of Paris, pictured here. This illustration from 1400 shows teachers and students, both of whom wore caps and gowns.

natural law the concept that there is a universal order built into nature that can guide moral thinking

Thomas Aquinas (uh-KWINE-iss), an Italian scholar of philosophy and theology, tried to bridge the gap between reason and faith. Aquinas greatly admired Aristotle. He saw no conflict between faith and reason, arguing that both were gifts from God. Reason, he believed, helped people discover important truths about God's creation, while faith revealed its own truths about God.

Aquinas wrote logical arguments in support of his faith to show how reason and religious belief worked together. For example, his concept of **natural law** stated that there was an order built into nature that could guide people's thinking about right and wrong. Natural law, he said, could be discovered through reason alone. Since God had created nature, natural law agreed with the moral teachings of the Bible.

Aquinas's teachings unified ancient philosophy and Christian theology. His teachings were later accepted and promoted by the Church.

6. Holidays

Medieval Europeans enjoyed many festivals and fairs that marked important days of the year. Most of these celebrations were connected in some way to the Church. Almost every day of the year was dedicated to a Christian saint, an event in the life of Jesus, or an important religious idea. In fact, our word *holiday* comes from "holy day."

Two of the main medieval holidays were Christmas and Easter. Christmas is the day when Christians celebrate the birth of Jesus. During the Middle Ages, Christmas celebrations lasted for 12 days. On Christmas day, Christians attended church before enjoying a great feast, which was often held for everyone on the manor by its lord.

Easter is the day when Christians celebrate the Resurrection. In Christian belief, the Resurrection is Christ's rising from the dead. For medieval Christians, Easter was a day of church services, feasting, and games. Often the games involved eggs, a symbol of new life.

Music, dancing, and food were all part of major medieval holidays and festivals. People sang folk songs and danced. They drank their favorite beverages and ate baked and fried foods.

Other favorite holiday entertainments included bonfires, acrobats and jugglers, and dancing bears. Plays were also popular. During religious services on special days, priests sometimes acted out Bible stories. By the 13th century, plays were often held outdoors in front of the church so more people could watch. In some English villages, mummers (traveling groups of actors) performed with masks, drums and bells, dances, and make-believe sword fights.

In the Middle Ages, most holidays were connected to the Church. Christmas was celebrated for 12 days and included excitement such as feasting and dancing. This illustration shows a Christmas celebration at a manor in the 1500s.

Work was especially important to Saint Benedict, who once wrote, "To work is to pray." He developed the monastic way of life that many men dedicated their lives to during the Middle Ages.

7. Monks, Nuns, and Friars

Religion was important to all Christians in the Middle Ages. Some men and women, however, solemnly promised to devote their lives to God and the Church.

The Monastic Way of Life Monks were men who joined monasteries, or communities devoted to prayer and service to fellow Christians. This way of life is called monasticism.

Men became monks for many reasons. Some were seeking refuge from war, sickness, or sinfulness. Some came to study, and others were attracted to the quiet life of prayer and service it offered.

The man who developed the monastic lifestyle in western Europe was Saint Benedict. In the 6th century, he founded a monastery in Italy. His followers, known as the Benedictines, followed Benedict's "Rule," or instructions. Benedictines made three solemn vows, or promises: poverty (to own no property), chastity (never to marry), and obedience (to obey their leaders).

Monks spent their lives in prayer, study, and work, and even attended eight church services every day. Other duties included caring for the poor and sick, teaching, and copying religious texts. Since most monasteries were self-sufficient, monks spent much of their time working. They farmed their land, tended their gardens, raised livestock, and sewed clothing.

Most monasteries were laid out around a *cloister*, a covered walkway surrounding an open square. On the north side was the church, and the kitchen and dining hall were on the south side. On the third side was the *dormitory*, or sleeping quarters, where monks slept in small cells, often on beds of wood.

The library writing room, called the *scriptorium*, on fourth side of the cloister, provided monks a place to copy books by hand and create beautiful illuminated manuscripts. By copying rare documents, monks kept knowledge of the past alive. Much of what we know today, about both the Middle Ages and ancient times, comes from their important work.

Both monks and nuns joined **religious orders**. Each order had its own distinctive rules and forms of service. The Benedictines were only one such group.

religious order a brotherhood or sisterhood of monks, nuns, or friars

Monastic life was one of the few opportunities open to medieval women who did not wish to marry. Women who became nuns lived in convents, which were communities run in the same way as monasteries. Nuns did most of the same types of work that monks performed.

Many nuns became important reformers and thinkers. For example, in Germany, Hildegard of Bingen founded a convent and was an adviser to popes and other Church officials. She also wrote books in which she criticized some of the practices of the Church.

Friars Some people wanted to live a religious life without the seclusion of the monastery. A famous example is Saint Francis of Assisi who was born to a wealthy Italian family but gave up his money to serve the poor. He founded the Franciscans, an order that is also called the Little Brothers of the Poor.

Instead of living in monasteries, Franciscan friars traveled among ordinary people to preach and to care for the poor and sick. They lived in complete poverty and had to work or beg for food for themselves and the poor. For this reason, they were also called *mendicants*, a word that means "beggars." With his friend Clare, Francis founded a similar order for women called the Poor Clares.

Francis, who loved nature, believed that all living things deserved respect. For this reason, he is often pictured with animals. To many, his example of faith, charity, and love of God represents an ideal of Christian living.

St. Francis of Assisi lived a simple life, with great love and respect for all living things, as reflected in his teachings. Here, he is portrayed preaching to the birds.

Lesson Summary

The Roman Catholic Church emerged from the fall of Rome to play a central role in daily life in medieval western Europe.

The Church Takes Shape More than just a religious institution, the Catholic Church was the center of community life and acquired great political and economic power. All clergy had a rank in the hierarchy, from priests to bishops, archbishops, to the pope.

Sacraments, Pilgrimages, and Crusades The Church's sacraments marked all the most important occasions of life, from birth to death. Many people expressed their faith by going on pilgrimages or fighting in the Crusades.

Art, Architecture, Education, and Holidays The importance of the Church to medieval people was seen in the art and architecture of churches, in education, and in holidays.

Monks, Nuns, and Friars During the Middle Ages, Saint Benedict developed his "Rule" for religious communities of monks and nuns. Other religious orders were founded, too, including groups of friars, such as the Franciscans, and the nuns called the Poor Clares.

Lesson 6

Life in Medieval Towns

What was life like in medieval European towns?

Introduction

The Late Middle Ages lasted from about 1300 to 1450 C.E., a time in which people experienced a shift in daily life. At the start of the Middle Ages, most lived in the countryside, either on feudal manors or in religious communities. Many owned or worked on farms where they produced their own food. But by the 12th century, towns were emerging around castles and monasteries and along trade routes. These bustling towns became centers of trade and industry.

Almost all medieval towns were protected by thick stone walls and required visitors to enter through gates. Inside, homes and businesses lined unpaved streets. Since few people could read, signs with colorful pictures hung over the doorways of shops and businesses. Open squares in front of public buildings, such as churches, served as gathering places. People in the town might shop at the local market place or watch religious plays.

Most streets were very narrow. The second stories of houses jutted out, blocking the sunlight from reaching the street. With few sources of indoor light, houses were often dark, too. Squares and streets were crowded with people, horses, and carts—as well as cats, dogs, geese, and chickens. There was no garbage collection, so residents threw their garbage into nearby canals and ditches or simply out the window. As you can imagine, most medieval towns were filled with unpleasant smells.

In this lesson, you will first learn about the growth of medieval towns. Then you will look at several aspects of daily life. You will explore trade and commerce, homes and households, disease and medical treatment, crime and punishment, and leisure and entertainment.

Social Studies Vocabulary

apprentice

charter

common law

guild

◀ Towns during the Late Middle Ages bustled with activity.

charter a written grant of rights and privileges by a ruler or government to a community, class of people, or organization

1. The Growth of Medieval Towns

In the ancient world, town life was well established, particularly in Greece and Rome. Ancient towns were busy trading centers. But after the collapse of the Roman Empire in the west, trade with the east suffered, and town life declined. In the Early Middle Ages, most people in western Europe lived in scattered communities in the countryside.

By the High Middle Ages, towns were growing again. One reason for their growth was improvements in agriculture. Farmers were clearing forests and adopting better farming methods, which resulted in a **surplus** of crops for them to sell in town markets. And because of these surpluses, not everyone had to farm to feed themselves. Another reason for the growth of towns was the revival of trade. Seaport towns, such as Venice and Genoa in Italy, served as trading centers for goods from the Middle East and Asia. Within Europe, merchants often transported goods by river, and many towns grew up near these waterways.

Many merchants who sold their wares in towns became permanent **residents**. So did people practicing various trades. Some towns grew wealthier because local people specialized in making specific types of goods. For example, towns in Flanders (present-day Belgium and the Netherlands) were known for their fine woolen cloth. Meanwhile, workers in the Italian city of Venice produced glass. Other towns built their wealth on the banking industry that grew up to help people trade more easily.

At the beginning of the Middle Ages, towns were generally part of the domain of a feudal lord—whether a monarch, a noble, or a high-ranking Church official. As towns grew wealthier, town dwellers began to resent the lord's feudal rights and his demands for taxes. They felt they no longer needed the lord's protection—or his interference.

In some places, such as northern France and Italy, violence erupted as towns struggled to become independent. In other places, such as England and parts of France, the change was more peaceful. Many towns became independent by purchasing a royal **charter,** which granted them the right to govern themselves, make laws, and raise taxes. Free towns were often governed by a mayor and a town council. Power gradually shifted from feudal lords to the rising class of merchants and craftspeople.

The trade routes shown on this map carried a constant flow of goods among European cities and from distant Asia and Africa. Towns of the Hanseatic League cooperated to form a powerful trade group in northern Europe.

Medieval European Towns and Trade Routes, About 1500 C.E.

Land routes
Water routes
Hanseatic League
• City

0 200 400 miles
0 200 400 kilometers
Azimuthal Equal-Area Projection

Riga
Danzig
London
Cologne
Paris
Venice
Genoa
Marseille
Constantinople
Lisbon
Toledo
Tunis

2. Guilds

Medieval towns began as centers for trade, but they soon developed into places where many goods were produced, as well. Both trade and production were overseen by organizations called **guilds**.

There were two main kinds of guilds: merchant guilds and craft guilds. All types of craftspeople had their own guilds, from cloth makers to cobblers (who fixed shoes, belts, and other leather goods), to the stonemasons who built the great cathedrals.

Guilds provided help and protection for the people doing a certain kind of work, and they maintained high standards. Guilds controlled the hours of work and set prices. They also handled complaints from the public. If, for example, a coal merchant cheated a customer, it might reflect poorly on all coal merchants. The guilds, therefore, punished members who had bad practices.

Guild members paid dues to their organization, which paid for the construction of guildhalls and for guild fairs and festivals. Guilds also used the money to take care of members and their families who were sick and unable to work.

It was not easy to become a member of a guild. Starting around age 12, a boy, and sometimes a girl, became an **apprentice**. An apprentice's parents signed an agreement with a master of the trade. The master agreed to shelter, feed, and train the apprentice. In some cases, the parents paid the master a sum of money, but apprentices rarely got paid for their work.

At the end of seven years, apprentices had to prove to the guild that they had mastered their trade. To do this, an apprentice produced a piece of work called a "master piece." If the guild approved of the work, the apprentice was given the right to become a master and set up his or her own business. Setting up a business was expensive, however, and few people could afford to do it right away. Often they became journeymen instead. The word *journeyman* does not refer to a journey, but comes from the French word *journée*, for "day." A journeyman was a craftsperson who found work "by the day," instead of becoming a master who employed other workers.

Craftsmen like the ones pictured here joined guilds to oversee the production and trade of their goods. Guilds provided many benefits to members, though joining them was not an easy process.

guild an organization of people in the same craft or trade

apprentice a person who works for a master in a trade or craft in return for training

During the Late Middle Ages, marketplaces provided townspeople with food and goods from local farmers and faraway lands. The emergence of markets in the middle ages meant that people no longer had to always produce their own food and daily goods.

3. Trade and Commerce

What brought most people to towns was business—meaning trade and commerce. As trade and commerce grew, so did towns.

At the beginning of the Middle Ages, most trade was in luxury goods, which only the wealthy could afford. People made everyday necessities for themselves. By the High Middle Ages, more local people were buying and selling more kinds of products, including everyday goods like food, clothing, and household items. Different towns also began specializing in producing certain goods, such as woolen cloth, glass, and silk.

Most towns had a market, where food and local goods were bought and sold. Much larger were the great merchant fairs, which a town might hold a couple times a year. These fairs could attract merchants from many countries who sold goods from all over Europe, the Middle East, and beyond.

With the growth of trade and commerce, merchants grew increasingly powerful and wealthy. They ran sizable businesses and looked for trading opportunities far from home. Merchant guilds came to **dominate** the business life of towns and cities. In towns that had become independent, members of merchant guilds often sat on town councils or were elected mayor.

Not everyone prospered, however. Medieval towns commonly had sizable Jewish communities, but in Christian Europe, they often faced deep prejudice. The hostility of Christians, sometimes backed up by laws, made it difficult for Jews to earn their living. They were not allowed to own land, and their lords sometimes took their property and belongings at will. Jews could also be the targets of violence.

One opportunity that was open to Jews was to become bankers and moneylenders. This work was generally forbidden to Christians because the Church taught that charging money for loans was sinful. Jewish bankers and moneylenders performed an essential service for the economy. Still, they were often looked down upon and abused for practicing this "wicked" trade.

4. Homes and Households

Medieval towns were typically small and crowded. They were narrow and could be up to four stories high. Most of the houses were made of wood, and they tended to lean over time. Sometimes two facing houses would lean so much, they touched across the street!

Rich and poor lived in quite different households. In poorer neighborhoods, several families might occupy a single house with only one room in which they cooked, ate, and slept. In general, people worked where they lived. If a father or mother was a weaver, for example, the loom would be in their home.

Wealthy merchants often had splendid homes. The first level might be given over to a business, including offices and storerooms. The family's living quarters might be on the second level, complete with a solar, a space where the family gathered to eat and talk. An upper level might house servants and apprentices.

Even for wealthy families, life was not always comfortable compared to life today. With fireplaces as the main source of heat and light, rooms were cold, smoky, and dim. Most windows were small and covered with oiled parchment instead of glass, so little sunlight came through.

As with many medieval families, this family in Italy probably conducted most of their indoor activities in this one main room. Here, two women are preparing tripe, while the men at the table enjoy a meal.

Growing up in a medieval town wasn't easy, either. About half of all children died before they became adults, and those who did survive began preparing for their adult roles around the age of seven. Some boys and a few girls attended school, where they learned to read and write. Children from wealthier families might learn to paint and to play music on a lute (a stringed instrument). Other children soon began work as apprentices.

In general, people of the Middle Ages believed in an orderly society in which everyone knew their place. Most boys grew up to do the same work as their fathers. Some girls trained for a craft, but most married young, usually around the age of 15, and were soon raising children of their own. For many girls, their education was at home, where they learned cooking, cloth making, and other skills necessary to care for a home and family.

5. Disease and Medical Treatment

Unhealthy living conditions in medieval towns led to the spread of disease. Towns were very dirty places. There was no running water in homes, and instead of bathrooms, people used outdoor privies (shelters used as toilets) or chamber pots that they emptied into nearby streams and canals. Garbage, too, was tossed into streams and canals or onto the streets. People lived crowded together in small spaces and usually bathed only once a week, if that. Rats and fleas were common and often carried diseases. It's no wonder people were frequently ill.

Many illnesses that can be prevented or cured today had no cures in medieval times. One example is leprosy, a disease of the skin and nerves that causes open sores. Because leprosy can spread from one person to another and can cause death, lepers were ordered to live by themselves in **isolated** houses, usually far from towns. Some towns even passed laws to keep out lepers.

Common diseases for which there was no cure at this time included measles, cholera, smallpox, and scarlet fever. The most feared disease was bubonic plague, known as the Black Death.

No one knew exactly how diseases were spread. Unfortunately, this made many people look for someone to blame. For example, after an outbreak of illness, Jews—often a target of unjust anger and suspicion—were sometimes accused of poisoning wells.

This doctor is treating a patient by "bleeding," which was believed to remove contaminated blood from the body and restore health. Doctors often practiced treatments, such as this one, based on tradition rather than science.

Although hospitals were invented during the Middle Ages, there were few of them. When sickness struck, most people were treated in their homes by family members or, sometimes, a doctor. Medieval doctors believed in a combination of prayer and medical treatment, many involving herbs. Using herbs as medicine had a long history based on traditional folk wisdom and knowledge handed down from ancient Greece and Rome. Other treatments were based on less scientific methods. For example, medieval doctors sometimes consulted the positions of the planets and relied on magic charms to heal people.

Another common technique was to "bleed" patients by opening a vein or applying leeches (a type of worm) to the skin to suck out blood. Medieval doctors believed that this "bloodletting" helped restore balance to the body and spirit. Unfortunately, such treatments often weakened a patient further.

6. Crime and Punishment

Besides being unhealthy, medieval towns were noisy, smelly, crowded, and often unsafe. Pickpockets and thieves were always on the lookout for vulnerable travelers with money in their pouches. Towns were especially dangerous at night because there were no streetlights. In some cities, night watchmen patrolled the streets with candle lanterns to deter, or discourage, criminals.

People accused of crimes were held in dirty, crowded jails. Prisoners relied on friends and family to bring them food or money, or else they risked starving or being ill-treated. Wealthy people sometimes left money in their wills to help prisoners buy food.

In the Early Middle Ages, trial by ordeal or combat was often used to establish an accused person's guilt or innocence. In a trial by ordeal, the accused had to pass a dangerous test, such as being thrown into a deep well. Unfortunately, a person who floated instead of drowning was declared guilty because he or she had been "rejected" by the water.

In a trial by combat, the accused person had to fight to prove his or her innocence. People believed that God would ensure the right party won. Clergy, women, children, and disabled people could name a champion to fight on their behalf.

Punishments for crimes were very harsh. For lesser crimes, people were fined or put in the stocks (a wooden frame with holes for the person's arms and sometimes legs). Being left in the stocks publicly for hours or days was both painful and humiliating.

People found guilty of crimes, such as highway robbery, stealing livestock, treason, or murder, could be hanged or burned at the stake. Executions were carried out in public, often in front of large crowds.

In most parts of Europe, important nobles shared with monarchs the power to prosecute major crimes. In England, kings in the early 1100s began creating a nationwide system of royal courts. The decisions of royal judges contributed to a growing body of **common law**. Along with an independent judiciary, or court system, English common law would become an important safeguard of individual rights. Throughout Europe, court trials based on written and oral evidence eventually replaced trials by ordeal or combat.

The introduction of a court system to judge crimes and decide punishments was a great improvement over trials by ordeals and combat. The emergence of the court system contributed to the body of common law.

common law a body of rulings made by judges or very old traditional laws that become part of a nation's legal system

7. Leisure and Entertainment

Many aspects of town life were challenging and people worked hard, but they also participated in leisure activities. They enjoyed quite a few days off from work, too. In medieval times, people engaged in many of the same activities we enjoy today. Children played with dolls and toys, such as wooden swords, balls, and hobbyhorses. They rolled hoops and played games like badminton, lawn bowling, and blind man's bluff. Adults also liked games, such as chess, checkers, and backgammon. They might gather to play card games, go dancing, or enjoy other social activities.

Townspeople also took time off from work to celebrate special days, such as religious feasts. On Sundays and holidays, animal baiting was a popular, though cruel, amusement. First, a bull or bear was fastened to a stake by a chain around its neck or a back leg, and sometimes by a nose ring. Then, specially trained dogs were set loose to torment the captive animal.

Fair days were especially festive, as jugglers, dancers, and clowns entertained the fairgoers. Minstrels performed songs, recited poetry, and played instruments such as harps, while guild members paraded through the streets dressed in special costumes and carrying banners.

Guilds also staged mystery plays in which they acted out Bible stories. Often they performed stories that were appropriate to their guild. In some towns, for instance, the boat builders acted out the story of Noah, which describes how Noah had to build an ark (a large boat) to survive a flood that God sent to "cleanse" the world of sinful people. In other towns, the coopers (barrel makers) acted out this story, too. The coopers put hundreds of water-filled barrels on the rooftops. Then they released the water to represent the 40 days of rain described in the story.

Mystery plays gave rise to another type of religious drama, the miracle play. These plays dramatized the lives of saints, often showing the saints performing miracles, or wonders. For example, in England it was popular to portray the story of St. George, who slew a dragon that was about to eat the king's daughter.

Mystery and miracle plays were put on by guild members to entertain townspeople with dramatizations of stories from the Bible or from the lives of saints. In many cases, the guild members selected topics that were relevant to their own line of work.

In the Late Middle Ages, towns such as Paris in France grew around castles and monasteries and along trade routes. Most were protected by walls, with only a few entry gates.

At the beginning of the Middle Ages, most Europeans lived in the countryside. By about 1200, however, towns were growing.

Guilds, Trade, and Commerce Many towns were wealthy enough to purchase a charter that made them independent from feudal lords. An economy based on trade and commerce significantly changed daily life. Guilds became leading forces in their communities. Farmers brought crops, and merchants brought many goods to sell in town marketplaces.

Homes and Households Homes varied, depending on how wealthy or poor a family was. Most families had small, crowded homes with only a fireplace for heat. Few children were educated. Girls married relatively early and boys began work as early as age seven.

Disease and Treatment Medieval towns were crowded, noisy, and dirty. Diseases spread rapidly, and many people could not be cured with the medical knowledge of the time.

Crime and Punishment Crime was a problem in medieval towns, and it was punished harshly. Prisons were filthy, dark places, and many prisoners had to buy their own food.

Leisure and Entertainment Despite the hardships in a medieval town, many types of leisure activities made life more enjoyable for town dwellers, including games, fairs, festivals, and religious plays put on by guilds.

Lesson 7

The Decline of Feudalism

How did events in Europe contribute to the decline of feudalism and the rise of democratic thought?

Introduction

Several key events contributed to the decline of feudalism in Europe from the 12th through the 15th centuries. There were many causes for the breakdown of the feudal system. You will explore three of these causes: political changes in England, a terrible disease, and a long series of wars.

In England, several political changes in the 12th and 13th centuries helped to weaken feudalism. A famous document known as *Magna Carta*, or Great Charter, dates from this time. Magna Carta was a written legal agreement that limited the king's power and strengthened the rights of nobles. As feudalism declined, Magna Carta took on a much broader meaning and contributed to ideas about individual rights and liberties in England.

In the 1300s, a terrible disease called the bubonic plague, or Black Death, swept across Asia and reached Europe in the late 1340s. Over the next two centuries, this terrifying disease killed millions in Europe. It struck all kinds of people—rich and poor, young and old, town dwellers and country folk. Almost everyone who caught the plague died within days. In some places, whole communities were wiped out. The deaths of so many people led to sweeping economic and social changes.

Lastly, between 1337 and 1453, France and England fought a series of battles known as the Hundred Years' War. This conflict changed the way wars were fought and shifted power away from feudal lords to monarchs and the common people.

How did such different events contribute to the decline of feudalism? What social and political changes occurred as feudalism weakened? In this lesson, you will find out.

Social Studies Vocabulary

bubonic plague

habeas corpus

heretic

Hundred Years' War

Magna Carta

Model Parliament

◀ The Hundred Years' War, shown here, is one reason feudalism declined in the Middle Ages.

Magna Carta a written legal agreement signed in 1215 that limited the English monarch's power

1. Political Developments in England

Political development was rampant during the Middle Ages, and in one country, England, developments during the 12th and 13th centuries helped to weaken feudalism. The story begins with King Henry II, who reigned from 1154 to 1189.

Henry II's Legal Reforms Henry made legal reform a central concern of his reign. For example, he insisted that a jury formally accuse a person of a serious crime. Cases were then tried before a royal judge. In theory, people could no longer simply be jailed or executed for no legal reason, but had to go through a court trial as well. These reforms strengthened the power of royal courts at the expense of feudal lords.

Henry's effort to strengthen royal authority led to a serious conflict with the Catholic Church. In the year 1164, Henry issued the Constitutions of Clarendon, a document that he claimed spelled out the king's **traditional** rights. Among them was the right to try clergy accused of serious crimes in royal courts, rather than in Church courts.

Henry's action led to a long, bitter quarrel with his friend, Thomas Becket, the archbishop of Canterbury. In 1170, four knights, perhaps seeking the king's favor, killed Becket in front of the main altar of Canterbury Cathedral. The cathedral and Becket's tomb soon became a popular destination for pilgrimages. In 1173, the Catholic Church proclaimed him a saint. Still, most of the Constitutions of Clarendon remained in force.

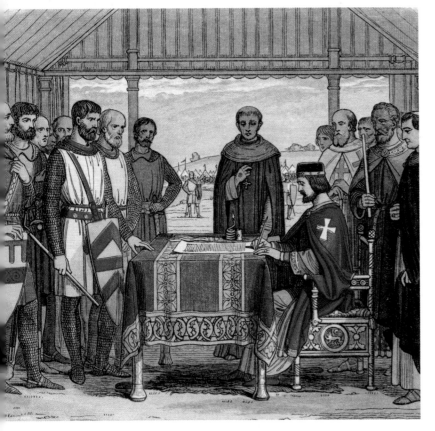

King John's acceptance of Magna Carta has been illustrated and painted many times. He is often, as he is here, incorrectly shown signing his name with a pen. In fact, he stamped his royal seal on the document to show his agreement.

King John and Magna Carta
In 1199, Henry's youngest son, John, became king of England. John soon made powerful enemies by losing most of the lands the English had controlled in France. He also taxed his barons heavily and ignored their traditional rights, arresting opponents at will. In addition, John quarreled with the Catholic Church and collected large amounts of money from its properties.

In June 1215, angry nobles forced a meeting with King John in a meadow called Runnymede, beside the River Thames, outside of London. There, they insisted that John put his seal on a document called **Magna Carta,** which means "Great Charter" in Latin.

Magna Carta was an agreement between the nobles and the monarch. The nobles concurred that the monarch could continue to rule. For his part, King John agreed to observe common law and the traditional rights of the nobles and the Church. For example, he promised to consult the nobles and the Church archbishops and bishops before imposing special taxes. He also agreed that "no free man" could be jailed except by the lawful judgment of his peers or by the law of the land. This idea eventually developed into a key part of English common law known as **habeas corpus** (HAY-be-us KOR-pus).

In many ways, Magna Carta only protected the rights and privileges of nobles. However, as time passed, the English people came to regard it as one of the **foundations** of their rights and liberties.

King Edward I made significant efforts to include more people in the government. He set up Model Parliament, which included Church officials and nobles, as well as commoners.

King Edward I and the Model Parliament In 1295, Edward I, King John's grandson, took a major step toward including more people in government. Edward called together a governing body called the Model Parliament that included commoners and lower-ranking clergy, as well as high-level Church officials and nobles.

The Impact of Political Developments in England These political changes contributed to the decline of feudalism in two ways. Some of the changes strengthened royal authority at the expense of the nobles. Others eventually shifted some power to the common people.

Magna Carta established the idea of rights and liberties that even a monarch cannot violate. This document also affirmed that monarchs should rule with the advice of the governed. Henry II's legal reforms strengthened English common law and the role of judges and juries. Finally, Edward I's Model Parliament gave a voice in government to common people, as well as to nobles. All these ideas formed the basis for the development of modern **democratic** institutions.

habeas corpus the legal concept that an accused person cannot be jailed indefinitely without being charged with a crime

Model Parliament a governing body created by King Edward I of England that included some commoners, Church officials, and nobles

2. The Bubonic Plague

In addition to political developments in England, another reason for the decline of feudalism was the **bubonic plague,** which affected all of Europe. The bubonic plague first struck Europe from 1346 to 1351. It returned in waves that occurred about every decade into the 15th century, leaving major changes in its wake.

Historians suspect that the plague began in Central Asia, possibly in China, and spread throughout China, India, the Middle East, and eventually to Europe. The disease traveled from Central Asia to the Black Sea along the Silk Road (the main trade route between Asia and the Mediterranean Sea). It probably was carried to Italy on a ship, causing it to spread north and west, throughout the continent of Europe and to England.

The Black Death Symptoms, or signs, of the plague included fever, vomiting, fierce coughing and sneezing fits, and egg-sized swellings or bumps, called *buboes.* The term "Black Death" probably came from these black-and-blue swellings that appeared on the skin of victims.

The dirty conditions in which people lived contributed significantly to the spread of the bubonic plague. The bacteria that cause the disease are carried by fleas that feed on the blood of infected rodents. When the animal dies, the fleas jump to other animals and people. During the Middle Ages, it was not unusual for people to go for many months without a change of clothing or a bath. Rodents, covered with fleas, often roamed the floors of homes looking for food. City streets were filled with human waste, dead animals, and trash.

At the time, though, no one knew where the disease came from or how it spread. Terrified people falsely blamed the plague on everything from the positions of the planets to lepers and to Jews.

> **bubonic plague** a deadly contagious disease caused by bacteria and spread by fleas; also called the Black Death

The bubonic plague, or Black Death, most likely originated in Asia. In the 14th century, this disease killed about one-third of the population of Europe and brought about major political and social change.

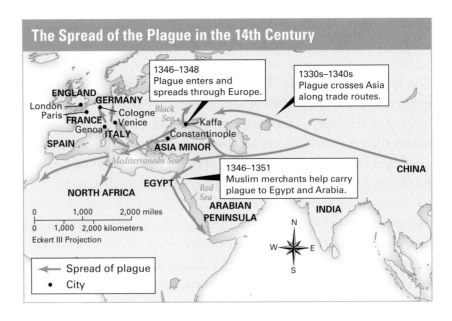

The Spread of the Plague in the 14th Century

1346–1348
Plague enters and spreads through Europe.

1330s–1340s
Plague crosses Asia along trade routes.

ENGLAND
London
Paris
FRANCE
GERMANY
Cologne
Venice
Genoa
ITALY
SPAIN
Black Sea
Kaffa
Constantinople
ASIA MINOR
Mediterranean Sea
EGYPT
Red Sea
NORTH AFRICA
ARABIAN PENINSULA
CHINA
INDIA

1346–1351
Muslim merchants help carry plague to Egypt and Arabia.

0   1,000   2,000 miles
0 1,000 2,000 kilometers
Eckert III Projection

N
W   E
S

→ Spread of plague
• City

Persecution of the Jews did not begin with the plague. Prejudice against Jews provoked the English government to order all Jews to leave the country in 1290. In France, the same thing happened in 1306 and again in 1394. But fear of the plague made matters worse, and during the Black Death, many German cities ordered Jews to leave.

The Impact of the Plague The plague took a terrible toll on Asian and European populations. China's population was reduced by nearly half between 1200 and 1393, probably because of the plague and famine. Travelers reported that dead bodies covered the ground in Central Asia and India.

Some historians **estimate** that 24 million Europeans died of the plague—about a third of the entire population. The deaths of so many people accelerated, or sped up, changes in Europe's economic and social structure, which contributed to the decline of feudalism.

The Black Plague took an estimated 24 million lives, about a third of Europe's population. As Europe recovered, new social and economic systems replaced the once strong feudalistic society.

Trade and commerce slowed almost to a halt during the plague years. As Europe began to recover, the economy needed to be rebuilt. But it wouldn't be rebuilt in the same way, as feudal lords no longer held most of the power.

After the plague, there was a shift in power from nobles to the common people. One reason for this change was a desperate need for workers because so many people had died. The workers who did survive could, therefore, demand more money and more rights. In addition, many peasants and some serfs abandoned feudal manors and moved to towns and cities, seeking better opportunities. This led to a weakening of the manor system and a loss of power for feudal lords.

After the plague, a number of peasant rebellions broke out. When nobles tried to return to the system from before the plague, resentment exploded across Europe. There were peasant revolts throughout Europe in France, Flanders, England, Germany, Spain, and Italy.

The most famous of these revolts was the English Peasants' War in 1381. The English rebels succeeded in entering London and presenting their demands to the king, Richard II. The leader of the rebellion was killed, however, and after his death, the revolt lost **momentum**. Still, in most of Europe, the time was coming when serfdom would end.

3. The Hundred Years' War

Between 1337 and 1453, England and France fought a series of battles for control over lands in France. Known as the **Hundred Years' War,** this long conflict contributed to the erosion of feudalism in England and in France.

English monarchs had long claimed lands in France. This was because earlier English kings had actually been feudal lords over these French fiefs. French kings now disputed these claims. When Philip VI of France declared that the French fiefs of Edward III, King of England, were part of Philip's own realm, war broke out in France.

Early English Successes Despite often being outnumbered, the English won most of the early battles of the war. What happened at the Battle of Crécy (KRAY-see) demonstrates why.

Two quite different armies faced each other at the French village of Crécy in 1346. The French had a feudal army that relied on horse-mounted knights. French knights wore heavy armor that made it difficult to move when not on horseback. Their weapons were swords and lances. Some of the infantry, or foot soldiers, used crossbows, which were effective only at short ranges.

In contrast, the English army was composed of lightly armored knights, foot soldiers, and archers armed with longbows. Some soldiers were recruited from the common people and paid to fight.

The longbow had many advantages over the crossbow. Larger arrows could be fired more quickly. The arrows flew farther, faster, and more accurately, and could pierce the armor of the time. At Crécy, the longbow helped the English defeat the much larger French force.

The French Fight Back The French slowly chipped away at the territory that the English had won in the early years of the war. In 1415, after a long truce, English King Henry V again invaded France. This time, the English met with stronger resistance, partly because the French were now using more modern tactics. The French king was recruiting his army from commoners and paying them with money collected by taxes, just as the English did.

Another reason for increased French resistance was a new sense of national identity and unity. In part, the French were inspired by a 17-year-old peasant girl, known today as Joan of Arc. Joan claimed that she heard the voices of saints urging her to save France. Disguised as a boy, she put on a suit of armor and set out to fight.

In 1429, Joan led a French army to victory in the Battle of Orléans (OR-lay-uhn). The following year, the "Maid of Orléans" was captured by English allies. The English pushed certain Church leaders to accuse Joan of being a witch and a **heretic** and to burn her at the stake.

Joan of Arc inspired the people of France to fight. To this day, she is honored for her heroism. A late 19th-century artist painted this scene of Joan of Arc, in which she is looking up victoriously up at heaven.

Hundred Years' War a series of battles fought between France and England from 1337 to 1453

heretic a person who holds beliefs that are contrary to a set of religious teachings

Joan of Arc's heroism changed the way many French men and women felt about their king and nation. Twenty-two years after Joan's death, the French finally drove the English out of France. Almost 500 years later, the Roman Catholic Church made Joan a saint.

The Impact of the Hundred Years' War The Hundred Years' War contributed to the decline of feudalism by helping to shift power from feudal lords to monarchs and to common people. During the struggle, monarchs on both sides had collected taxes and raised large professional armies. As a result, kings no longer relied extensively on nobles to supply knights for the army.

In addition, changes in military technology reduced the need for nobles' knights and castles. The longbow proved to be an effective weapon against mounted knights. Castles also became less effective as armies began using gunpowder to shoot iron balls from cannons and blast holes in castle walls.

The new feeling of nationalism also shifted power away from lords. Previously, many English and French peasants felt more loyalty to their local lords than to their monarch. The war created a new sense of national unity and patriotism on both sides.

In both France and England, commoners and peasants bore the heaviest burden of the war. They were forced to fight and to pay higher and more frequent taxes. Those who survived the war, however, were needed as soldiers and workers. For this reason, the common people emerged from the conflict with greater influence and power.

At the Battle of Crécy, the English army's lighter armor and longbows triumphed over the French knights' heavy armor and crossbows. The war brought major shifts to medieval Europe, as the decline of feudalism was met with a new sense of unity and more benefits for the commoners.

Lesson Summary

In this lesson, you have explored three key events that contributed to the decline of feudalism in Europe in the Late Middle Ages.

Political Developments in England Henry II's legal reforms strengthened English common law and the role of judges and juries. Magna Carta established the idea of rights and liberties that even a monarch cannot violate. It also affirmed that monarchs should rule with the advice of the governed. Edward I's Model Parliament gave a voice in government to common people, as well as to nobles.

The Bubonic Plague The bubonic plague killed about one-third of the people of Europe. After the plague, the need for workers to rebuild Europe led to a slight shift in power from feudal lords to the common people.

The Hundred Years' War This series of battles between England and France caused a rise in national pride and identity in both countries. It strengthened the monarchs and began to reduce the importance of nobles and knights on the battlefield.

Artists all over the world have depicted Joan of Arc as a brave heroine. This stained-glass window from a church in New Zealand shows Joan dressed in armor.

The Trials of Joan of Arc

In 1429, during the weakening of Europe's feudal system, a teenage girl named Joan of Arc bravely helped a prince become the king of France. How did Joan's extraordinary life demonstrate the new ways that were about to replace old traditions in Europe?

The visions and the voices came without warning, like a flash of lighting. In 1425, Joan of Arc, the daughter of northern French peasants, had just turned 13. Until then, she had had a normal childhood, attending mass and praying frequently to God.

Then the voices and visions started when Saints Michael, Catherine, and Margaret suddenly came to her. "I was terrified," Joan remembered later. "There was a great light all about." But soon she was reassured by the sweet, kind voices and stopped being afraid.

Joan lived in a religious time, and it wasn't unheard of for people to report that saints spoke to them. But Joan's voices gave her a daunting task of helping Charles, the dauphin (DOE-fehn), or French heir to the throne, to become king. They also wanted her to free France from the English, who had conquered portions of the country.

France in Chaos

The year when Joan's voices began, France was in chaos. Since 1337, the English and French had been fighting the Hundred Years' War, and, in 1420, English king Henry V obtained the French throne. Upon Henry's death in 1422, the dauphin Charles insisted that he, and not Henry's infant son, was the rightful king. His claim led to even bloodier fighting between the English and French.

Tensions within the borders were also high, as France itself was deeply divided. The feudal lords of the powerful province of Burgundy helped the English seize northern France. Those loyal to Charles controlled the southern half of the country. Even though Charles was the dauphin, he hadn't been crowned.

Since the 11th century, all French kings had been crowned in Reims (RAHNZ), but the English controlled land around the city. However, Joan's voices informed her that she should lead Charles to Reims and see that he was crowned king.

A Journey to Find a King

At the age of 17, Joan set out to find Charles. It was dangerous for a female to travel alone, so she disguised herself by cutting her hair and putting on men's clothing. Without telling her parents, she rode to a nearby fort to ask the commander for soldiers to protect her.

When she reached the fort, the commander merely laughed at her request. But Joan soon convinced him, and he ordered a group of soldiers to accompany her. On February 13, 1429, they set out for Charles' court at Chinon (shee-NOHN).

Charles heard she was on her way. He had heard prophecies, or predictions, that this young peasant woman would rescue France from the English. When she arrived at Chinon, Charles tested Joan's claims by disguising himself and had court officials introduce another man to Joan as the dauphin. However, Joan immediately picked out Charles from the crowd. She knelt before him, announcing, "Very noble Dauphin, I am come and sent by God to bring succor [help] to you and your kingdom." Charles agreed that God had sent Joan to save France.

After picking Charles out of a crowd, Joan knelt before him and announced that she was sent to help save France.

The Battle to Free Orléans

Joan's first challenge on the way north to Reims was to free the city of Orléans (OR-lay-uhn). Charles had a suit of armor made for her, but she still needed a sword. She predicted that priests would find one for her in a nearby church, and sure enough, they dug behind the altar and discovered a sword. Armed with her sword and carrying a banner that she had made, Joan filled the French with hope.

In the spring of 1429, Joan guided Charles's troops toward Orléans, which the English had had under siege for six months. The French feared that if they lost that city, they would lose all of France. On May 4, Joan led the French troops into battle for the first time.

At a monastery near Orléans held by the English, French soldiers attacked. They were on the verge of defeat when Joan suddenly galloped into the battle, carrying her banner and flashing her sword, and the French soldiers soon overwhelmed the English.

In this 19th-century engraving, you can see Joan of Arc entering Orléans. She then led her army in a battle against British troops to free the city from the English.

Three days later, the French attacked Orléans itself. Joan was hit by an arrow in the middle of the battle, but, grimacing in pain, she pulled it out and threw herself back into the fight. She then led French troops across a moat and stormed the city's walls, where the French soon poured into Orléans, and the English beat a rapid retreat.

After the victory, thirty thousand grateful residents of Orléans cheered Joan as she rode with her soldiers through the streets. Forever after, she would be known as the "Maid of Orléans." In the following weeks, Joan's forces freed more surrounding towns from the English.

Crowning King Charles VII

After these victories, Joan returned to Charles and persuaded him to travel to Reims to be crowned. At last, on July 17, 1429, with Joan at his side, the dauphin became King Charles VII. After the coronation, Joan burst into tears of joy.

Joan was captured by French soldiers under the command of the Duke of Burgundy and turned over to the English, who put her on trial for witchcraft. This engraving from 1882 depicts Joan after she had been captured and imprisoned.

Unfortunately, the coronation proved to be the high point for Joan. Charles started to distance himself from her, perhaps fearing her enormous popularity. In the fall of 1429, Charles and Joan led troops toward Paris, which the English and their allies controlled. But without Joan's knowledge or input, Charles reached a ceasefire agreement with the Duke of Burgundy. When Joan learned about the agreement, she was outraged, for she wanted to fight to free Paris. "I am not satisfied with this manner of truce," she fumed.

Joan's Capture

Meanwhile, French troops, now with a king to follow and tired of fighting, were deserting Joan's army. In May 1430, Burgundy's army of 6,000 soldiers prepared to attack Compiègne (komp-YANE), a French-held town near Paris. Joan's army had only 300 soldiers. At five in the evening, she launched a surprise attack.

At first, the French held their own, but thousands of English soldiers soon joined the battle. The French were forced to retreat to Compiègne. When the town's mayor saw English troops approaching, he closed the drawbridge, trapping Joan outside. The Burgundian leaders captured her and threw her into prison, and Charles made no effort to rescue or ransom the woman to whom he owed so much. After several months, the English paid the Burgundians an enormous ransom for her.

On Trial for Her Life

The English and the Catholic Church put Joan on trial in Rouen (ROO-ahn) for witchcraft and for heresy, or spreading beliefs that violate accepted religious teachings. They hoped that, by proving that God did not guide Joan, they could undermine Charles VII's right to the French throne. Bishop Pierre Cauchon, an ally of the English, led the proceedings. When the trial started in February 1431, Joan boldly warned the bishop, "You say that you are my judge. Take thought over what you are doing. For, truly, I am sent from God, and you are putting yourself in great danger."

The warning did not prevent Bishop Cauchon from drilling Joan with questions, such as, "Did God command you to put on men's clothing?" Joan responded, "I did not put on this clothing, or do anything else, except at the bidding of God and the angels." Ordinary people watching the trial loved Joan's courageous answers. She was following her conscience and standing up to the bishop and to the English.

The court made 70 accusations against Joan, and in May, to save her life, she signed a confession. But after several days, she took it back, saying, "What I said, I said for fear of the fire." She had made the brave decision to stay true to her beliefs—even though she faced execution as punishment.

A huge crowd gathered in Rouen on May 30, 1431, to watch Joan be burned at the stake, a common death sentence for heretics and witches. Through her horrible ordeal, she showed great courage.

Charles VII remained king for 40 years, forced the English out of France, and united the country. During that time, Joan's life became a legend.

In 1455, Joan's family requested that the pope reopen her case, and Joan was found innocent of all charges. In 1920, Joan was recognized as a Catholic saint. Today, Saint Joan is one of the most beloved of French heroes, the patron saint of the nation and of its soldiers. She inspired her country and helped to restore the throne to a French king. She also proved that women could be brave and effective leaders. Finally, her remarkable life shows that with faith, courage, and determination, someone from ordinary beginnings can make history.

At her execution, Joan asked a priest to hold a crucifix high for her to see and to pray loud enough so that she could hear him over the roar of the flames.

Lesson 8

The Byzantine Empire

How did the Byzantine Empire develop and form its own distinctive church?

Introduction

At its peak, the great Byzantine Empire controlled land in three continents, Europe, Asia, and Africa. This vast empire lasted from about 500 to 1453 C.E., when it was conquered by the Ottoman Turks.

At first, the Byzantine Empire was the continuation of the Roman Empire in the east. In 330 C.E., the Roman emperor Constantine moved his capital from Rome to the city of Byzantium, an old Greek trading colony on the eastern edge of Europe. Constantine called his capital New Rome, but it soon became known as Constantinople, which is Greek for "Constantine's City."

Later, control of the huge original empire was divided between two emperors—one based in Rome and one based in Constantinople. After the fall of Rome, the eastern empire continued for another 1,000 years. We call this the Byzantine Empire, after Byzantium, the original name of its capital city.

The eastern and western parts of the original empire remained connected for a time through a shared Christian faith. However, the Church in the east developed in its own unique ways. It became known as the Eastern Orthodox Church. Over time, Byzantine emperors and Church officials came into conflict with the pope in Rome, which eventually led to a permanent split between the Eastern Orthodox Church and the Roman Catholic Church.

In this lesson, you will learn about the Byzantine Empire, one of its greatest emperors, its **distinctive** church, and rising conflict between the east and the west. Let's begin by exploring the empire's capital—the fabulous city of Constantinople.

Social Studies Vocabulary

Byzantine Empire

Constantinople

Eastern Orthodox Church

patriarch

◀ In 330 C.E., the emperor Constantine moved his capital from Rome to the city of Byzantium.

1. Constantinople

Constantinople the city on the eastern edge of Europe, which Constantine made the capital of the Roman Empire in 330 C.E.

Byzantine Empire the name for the eastern Roman Empire, located at the crossroads of Europe and Asia; it lasted from about 500 to 1453 C.E.

Constantinople was more than 800 miles to the east of Rome. Why did Constantine choose this site to be the capital of the Roman Empire?

One reason was that the site was surrounded by water on three sides, making it easy to defend. The Byzantines fashioned a chain across the city's harbor to guard against seafaring intruders. Miles of walls, fortified by watchtowers, and gates discouraged invasion by land and by sea.

Constantinople also stood at the crossroads of Europe and Asia, and the many sea and overland trade routes linking east and west. During the **Byzantine Empire,** this ideal location helped to make the city, and some of its citizens, very wealthy. For more than 700 years, Constantinople was the richest and the most elegant city in the Mediterranean region. Ivory, silk, furs, perfumes, and other luxury items flowed through its markets. A French soldier who saw the city in 1204 exclaimed, "One could not believe there was so rich a city in all the world."

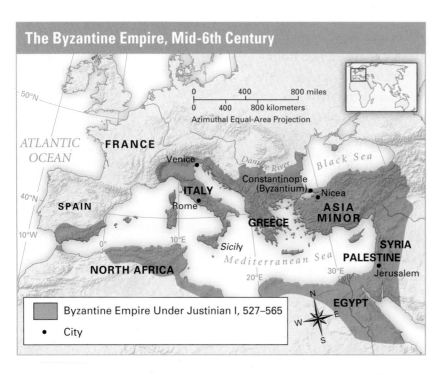

The Byzantine Empire, Mid-6th Century

Byzantine Empire Under Justinian I, 527–565
• City

The eastern Roman Empire, later called the Byzantine Empire, ruled much of the Mediterranean world for several hundred years. Constantinople served as a rich and flourishing city for over 700 years.

At its height, Constantinople was home to around one million people. The city's language and culture were Greek, but traders and visitors spoke many languages. Ships crowded the city's harbor, loaded with goods. The city streets, some narrow and twisting, some grand and broad, teemed with camel and mule trains.

Life in Constantinople was more comfortable than in western Europe. The city boasted a sewer system, which was quite rare in medieval times. Social services were provided by hospitals, homes for the elderly, and orphanages.

Despite the luxuries enjoyed by the rich, many people lived in poverty. The emperor gave bread to those who could not find work, but in exchange, the unemployed performed tasks such as sweeping the streets and weeding public gardens.

Almost everyone attended the exciting chariot races at a stadium called the Hippodrome. Two chariot teams, one wearing blue and the other green, were fierce rivals. In Constantinople and other cities, many people belonged to opposing groups called the Blues and Greens after the chariot teams. At times the rivalry between the Blues and Greens erupted in deadly street fighting. But in 532, the two groups united in a rebellion that destroyed much of Constantinople. You will find out what happened in the next section.

2. The Reign of Justinian I

One of the greatest Byzantine emperors was Justinian I, whose long reign lasted from 527 to 565. But Justinian's reign nearly came to an abrupt end much sooner. In January 532, the emperor and his beautiful wife, Theodora, were attending chariot races at the Hippodrome. In the past, Blues and Greens among the spectators often battled each other. This time, however, both groups were dismayed over the recent arrests of some of their members. To Justinian's horror, they united in denouncing him. Fighting broke out, spilled into the streets, and escalated into a full-scale rebellion.

The rioting continued for a week while Justinian and Theodora hid in the palace. Much of the city was in flames, and Justinian's advisors wanted him to flee. Theodora, however, urged him to stay and fight. With her encouragement, Justinian put down the **revolt**. According to the official court historian, Procopius (pro-KOH-pee-us), 30,000 people were killed in the fighting, which ended with the city of Constantinople laying in ruins.

Justinian was determined to rebuild the city on a grand scale and put huge sums of money into public works. Soon, Constantinople had new bridges, public baths, parks, roads, and hospitals. The emperor also built many grand churches, including the magnificent Hagia Sophia (AH-ee-yah SOH-fee-uh), which is Greek for "Holy Wisdom." Today, this great structure is one of the most famous buildings in the world.

During a revolt in Constantinople, the empress Theodora (third from the left) encouraged her husband, Justinian I, to stay and fight for his city. After the rebellion, Justinian I worked to rebuild the city and create a systematic body of law, which became the basis for many other legal codes.

Besides rebuilding Constantinople, Justinian tried to reclaim some of the Roman Empire's lost territory. He launched military campaigns that, for a time, took back parts of North Africa, Italy, and Spain.

Justinian is most famous, however, for creating a systematic body of law. Under his direction, a committee studied the thousands of laws the Byzantines had inherited from the Roman Empire. They revised outdated and confusing laws. They also made improvements, such as extending women's property rights. The result of their work is known as Justinian's Code, which became the basis for many legal codes in the western world.

Procopius, the court historian, wrote glowing accounts of Justinian's achievements. But he also wrote the *Secret History*, in which he called the emperor "a treacherous enemy, insane for murder and plunder." Throughout Byzantine history, distrust and divisions often plagued the imperial court, and Justinian's court was no exception.

Hagia Sophia was built between the years 532 and 537. Its architectural features inspired the design of many later Orthodox churches.

Eastern Orthodox Church a Christian religion that developed out of early Christianity in the Byzantine Empire

3. The Eastern Orthodox Church

To the Byzantines, Christianity was more than a religion. It was the very foundation of their empire.

When Constantine built his new capital, he intended it to be the religious center of the empire, as well as the seat of government. Constantine himself tried to settle religious disputes by assembling a council of bishops.

Over time, the Byzantine Church separated from the Church in Rome and became known as the **Eastern Orthodox Church**. The word *orthodox* means "in agreement with right belief." The leaders of the medieval Eastern Orthodox Church thought that their church was based on a set of beliefs that they could trace back to Jesus Christ and to the work of bishops in early Christian councils.

The Role of the Eastern Orthodox Church in the Empire

Religion and government were more closely linked in the Byzantine Empire than in the west. The Byzantines viewed the emperor not just as the head of the government but as the living representative of God and Jesus Christ. This meant that church and state were combined into one all-powerful body.

The state religion also united people in a common belief. The Eastern Orthodox Church played a central role in daily life. Most people attended church regularly. Religious sacraments gave shape to every stage of the journey from birth to death. Monasteries and convents cared for the poor and the sick. These institutions were supported by wealthy people and became quite powerful.

Church Hierarchy Like Roman Catholic clergy, Orthodox clergy were ranked in order of importance. In Byzantine times, the emperor had supreme authority in the Church. He selected the **patriarch** of Constantinople, who ranked just below him in matters of religion.

Unlike the pope in the west, the patriarch did not claim strong authority over other patriarchs and bishops. Instead, he was "first among equals." The patriarch of Constantinople (modern Istanbul, Turkey) still holds this honor.

Orthodox priests served under patriarchs and other bishops. Unlike Roman Catholic priests, many Orthodox priests were allowed to marry. Bishops, however, could rise only from the ranks of unmarried clergy.

patriarch in the Eastern Orthodox Church, the bishop of an important city

Liturgy and Prayer The Orthodox Church service corresponding to the Roman Catholic mass was the Divine Liturgy. Both the clergy and worshippers sang or chanted the liturgy, or form of public worship. The liturgy was conducted in Greek or in the local language.

Orthodox Christians also prayed to saints, two of whom were particularly important. Saint Basil promoted charity and reformed the liturgy. Saint Cyril helped create the Cyrillic (sih-RIL-ik) alphabet, which allowed scholars to translate the Bible for people in eastern Europe.

Architecture and Art Christian faith inspired magnificent architecture and artwork in the Byzantine Empire. With its square base and high dome, the cathedral Hagia Sophia served as a model for many Orthodox churches. The architecture of the church also reflects Orthodox views. The simple base represents the earthly world, and the "dome of heaven" rests on top of it. Rich decorations on the inside were meant to remind worshippers of what it would be like to enter God's kingdom.

A feature of Eastern Orthodox churches is an image of Christ the Pantocrator, like this one, watching over Orthodox worshippers from the dome above. Images such as this one demonstrate the importance of art and beauty in Orthodox Church practices.

Building on the Greek love of art, the Orthodox Church used many images in its services and prayers. Byzantine artists created beautiful icons, which were usually painted on small wooden panels. Artists also fashioned sacred images as mosaics and painted them in murals.

An image of Christ as the *Pantocrator*, or ruler of all, gazed down from the domes of all Orthodox churches. Most churches also displayed an icon of Jesus's mother, Mary (called the *Theotokos*, or god-bearer) and the Christ child over the altar.

Many Byzantines believed that sacred pictures brought them closer to God. But later, icons also became a source of violent disagreement.

4. Conflict Between East and West

Medieval Europe and the Byzantine Empire were united in a single faith, Christianity. Over the centuries, however, cultural, political, and religious differences led to conflict between the two parts of the old Roman Empire.

The two regions had been quite different even in the days of the early Roman emperors. The eastern half of the empire had many cities, much trade, and great wealth. The western half was mostly rural and agricultural, and not nearly as wealthy.

Other differences became more pronounced after the fall of Rome. Byzantine culture was largely shaped by its Greek heritage, whereas the west was influenced by Frankish and Germanic cultures. In the city of Constantinople, people spoke Greek. In the west, Latin was the language of scholars, diplomats, and the Church.

Perhaps most important was the conflict that developed between the churches of east and west. After the fall of Rome, popes gradually **emerged** as powerful figures in western Europe. The popes claimed supreme religious authority over all Christians. The emperors and patriarchs of the east did not claim that power.

Other differences added to the conflict. Three major disagreements in particular led to a split in the Christian Church.

Iconoclasm The first major disagreement concerned religious icons. Many Christians in medieval times used images of Jesus, Mary, and the saints in worship and prayer. Some Christians in the east, however, believed that people were wrongly worshipping the icons as if they were divine, so in 730 C.E., Byzantine emperor Leo III banned the use of religious images in all Christian churches and homes.

This policy of *iconoclasm* ("icon smashing") led to the destruction of much religious art. Throughout Christian lands, people cried out in protest. In Rome, Roman Church leaders were angry because Leo's order applied to parts of Italy that were under Byzantine control. Pope Gregory III even excommunicated the emperor.

The Byzantine Empire lifted its ban on icons in 843, but the dispute over iconoclasm had caused a major split between the east and west. It also helped motivate popes in Rome to look for support and protection against enemies.

Byzantine emperor Leo III banned the use of religious images, or icons, in 730 C.E. The ban was lifted in 843. This mosaic of Jesus in Hagia Sophia escaped destruction because it was created after the ban was lifted.

The Crowning of a Holy Roman Emperor Another major disagreement occurred in 800 C.E., a time when Empress Irene ruled the Byzantine Empire. Because she was a woman, Pope Leo III did not view her as honorable or strong enough to govern. He wanted the protection of a strong male leader to help defend the Church in the west.

Instead, Leo decided to crown Charlemagne, the king of the Franks, as Holy Roman emperor. The pope's action outraged the Byzantines, who acknowledged their empress as the rightful ruler of the remains of the Roman Empire.

The Final Break Matters between east and west came to a head in 1054 when Cerularius, the patriarch of Constantinople, wanted to reassert Byzantine control of the Church. He closed all churches that worshipped with western rites. Pope Leo IX was furious. He sent Cardinal Humbert to Constantinople. The cardinal marched up to the altar of Hagia Sophia. In front of everyone, he laid down a bull (a proclamation by the pope) excommunicating Cerularius.

Cerularius responded by excommunicating the cardinal. This was purely a symbolic act, for the patriarch did not have that power. But it showed that the schism, or split, between east and west was complete. Despite future attempts to heal the division, the Eastern Orthodox Church and the Roman Catholic Church were now separate churches.

The division between the Eastern Orthodox and Roman Catholic churches lasted until 1964. In that year, Patriarch Athenagoras (left) and Pope Paul VI (right) met in Jerusalem and made a formal statement that undid the excommunications of 1054.

Lesson Summary

In this lesson, you learned about the founding of the Byzantine Empire and the Eastern Orthodox Church.

Constantinople and the Byzantine Empire In 330 C.E., the Roman emperor Constantine moved his capital to Byzantium, later called Constantinople. After the fall of Rome, the eastern half of the empire continued on there. Today, it is referred to as the Byzantine Empire.

The Reign of Justinian I One of the greatest Byzantine emperors was Justinian I. He rebuilt Constantinople after it was destroyed by rioting in 532 and worked to reclaim some of Rome's lost territory. His most lasting contribution is probably the Justinian Code, which became the basis for many other, later legal codes in the western world.

The Eastern Orthodox Church The Byzantine Empire was a Christian state. The Eastern Orthodox Church was at the center of daily life and inspired distinctive and magnificent art and architecture.

Conflict Between East and West Byzantine emperors and patriarchs in Constantinople clashed with popes in Rome over a number of issues. These disagreements led to a schism between the Roman Catholic Church and the Eastern Orthodox Church in 1054.

What Kind of Ruler Was Justinian I?

He was called Justinian the Great, but did he live up to his name? He is both praised and criticized in history books. Justinian I ruled the Byzantine Empire from 527 to 565. You will read two primary sources about Justinian that will help you understand and explain what kind of ruler he was.

Justinian I was the emperor of the Byzantine Empire, previously the Eastern Roman Empire, at a time of great turmoil. While he brought about several positive changes, many people considered him a tyrant.

One of his achievements was expanding the Byzantine Empire to its greatest size in history. By the time of his reign, most of the Western Roman Empire had collapsed, and Justinian was determined to regain that territory. He retrieved areas in Italy, the southeastern coast of Spain, and much of North Africa that had previously been lost by enemy invasion.

Justinian was also responsible for restoring much of the beauty of the empire, which had suffered devastation from earthquakes, wars, and attacks by rebellious citizens. He rebuilt the city of Constantinople with new harbors, bridges, aqueducts (water supply systems), public buildings, and churches. One of these churches, the Hagia Sophia with its breathtaking dome and magnificent marble art, is one of the most famous buildings in the world today.

Along with supporting the development of beautiful architecture, Justinian supported artists who created paintings and carvings of great beauty and value. This picture is an example of such art. It is a page from the *Codex Justinianus*, the set of law books created for Justinian. How are the people interacting with Justinian in this piece of art? Can you tell how the artist felt about Justinian?

Justinian may be best known for the set of legal codes he helped create. Soon after he became emperor, Justinian assigned a committee of ten lawyers to review all the laws and rules of previous emperors. He wanted outdated laws removed or updated and new laws added. The result was a set of four books called the *Codex Justinianus*, which translates from Latin to Justinian's Code. It remains the foundation for laws in many nations today.

This picture from the 6th century depicts Justinian I on the throne and his subjects around him. This image could be one piece of evidence about the kind of ruler Justinian was.

The following primary source includes excerpts from a book from this set called the *Institutes of Justinian*. This book was compiled and published in 533 and became a textbook for law students and lawyers. This passage is just a small section of the book that describes the rights of people.

After you read the passage, consider these questions: What do these laws tell you about the rights of a person in Justinian's empire? Why might it have been important to Justinian to have these laws? Why is Justinian's Code considered historically significant?

The Institutes of Justinian

I. *Justice and Law*
   JUSTICE is the constant and perpetual wish to render every one his due.

   1. *Jurisprudence is the knowledge of things divine and human; the science of the just and the unjust.*

   3. *The maxims of law are these: to live honesty, to hurt no one, to give every one his due.*

III. *The Law of Persons*
   All our law relates either to persons, or to things, or to actions. Let us first speak of persons; as it is of little purpose to know the law, if we do not know the persons for whose sake the law was made. The chief division in the rights of persons is this: men are all either free or slaves.

   1. *Freedom, from which men are said to be free, is the natural power of doing what we each please, unless prevented by force or by law.*

   5. *In the condition of slaves there is no distinction; but there are many distinctions among free persons; for they are either born free, or have been set free.*

IX. *The Power of Parents*
   Our children, begotten in lawful marriage, are in our power.

   2. *The power which we have over our children is peculiar to the citizens of Rome; for no other people have a power over their children, such as we have over ours.*

   3. *The child born to you and your wife is in your power. And so is the child born to your son of his wife, that is, your grandson or granddaughter; so are your great-grandchildren, and all your other descendants. But a child born of your daughter is not in your power, but in the power of its own father.*

   —*Institutes of Justinian, Book 1: "Of Persons," 527-565 C.E.*

Books and Pictures About Justinian

Despite Justinian's numerous accomplishments, he faced strong criticism. Both his biggest fan and his biggest critic might have been the military advisor and historian, Procopius.

Procopius was an ambitious writer of history. He wrote eight books about the wars fought by Justinian. Procopius also wrote six books on the buildings that were constructed during Justinian's reign. These books are filled with praise for Justinian's achievements. About the reconstruction of the Hagia Sophia, Procopius wrote,

> It is indeed a proof of the esteem with which God regarded the emperor, that he furnished him with men who would be so useful in effecting his designs, and we are compelled to admire the wisdom of the emperor, in being able to choose the most suitable of mankind to execute the noblest of his works . . .

What does this quote tell you about the kind of ruler Justinian was? How might all of Procopius's books help you understand the kind of ruler Justinian was? How might Procopius's role as Justinian's military advisor have affected what he wrote about the wars?

Empress Theodora

This drawing shows Justinian with his wife Empress Theodora. She often influenced her husband's decisions with her advice and persuasion. Theodora played a big role during Justinian's reign and noted that he made few significant accomplishments after her death. What does this picture tell you about Justinian that you may not know from books? How are Justinian and Theodora portrayed here? What details do you notice? What does this picture tell us about the relationship between Justinian and Theodora?

This drawing shows Justinian and his wife, Empress Theodora. The artist helps us imagine the kind of ruler Justinian was.

Criticism of Justinian

Though much of Procopius's writing praised Justinian, he wrote a final book that did just the opposite. This book, titled *The Secret History*, attacks the way Justinian conducted war and ruled his empire with an iron fist. The book was not published until after Procopius's death, and probably after the deaths of Justinian and Theodora. What reasons might explain why this last book, and not the earlier ones, contains so much criticism of Justinian and Theodora?

Read this excerpt from *The Secret History*. What does Procopius say were Justinian's main goals? What other criticisms does Procopius claim? What does it mean that Justinian "abolished all existing institutions"? How does Procopius's attitude toward Justinian differ in these two excerpts? Which source do you think is more reliable and why? What other sources could give you more information so that you can explain what kind of ruler Justinian was?

The Secret History of the Court of Justinian

Chapter XI

When Justinian came to the throne, he straightway succeeded in upsetting everything. What had previously been forbidden by the laws he introduced, while he abolished all existing institutions, as though he had assumed the imperial robe for no other purpose than to alter completely the form of government. He did away with existing offices, and established other new ones for the management of affairs. He acted in the same manner in regard to the laws and the army; not that he was led to do so by any love of justice or the public advantage, but merely in order that all institutions might be new and might bear his name; if there was any institution that he was unable to abolish at once, he gave it his name, that at least it might appear new. He could never satisfy his insatiable desire, either of money or blood; but after he had plundered one wealthy house, he would seek for another to rob, and straightway squander the plunder upon subsidies to barbarians, or senseless extravagance in building . . .

—Procopius, mid-6th century

Compare the text excerpts you've just read and think about the pictures. Consider what they say about Justinian as a ruler. Then use these sources and what you know to make an argument about the kind of ruler Justinian was and if his impact on the empire was more positive or more negative.

Europe During Medieval Times

313
Constantine's Decree
Roman emperor Constantine issues a decree allowing Christians to worship freely, leading to the recognition of Christianity as the official religion of the Roman Empire.

476
Fall of Rome
The last Roman emperor in the west is driven from his throne, and the western half of the empire dissolves into separate kingdoms.

About 500–1453
Byzantine Empire
Straddling two continents, Europe and Asia, the Byzantine Empire gives rise to a new church in the east called the Eastern Orthodox Church.

1 C.E.   200 C.E.   400 C.E.   600 C.E.   800 C.E

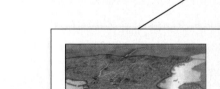

330
New Capital of the Roman Empire
Constantine moves the capital of the Roman Empire from Rome to Byzantium. The city is renamed Constantinople.

About 476–1450
Middle Ages
The Middle Ages begin after the fall of Rome, continue through the rise and decline of feudalism, and end with the fall of the Byzantine Empire.

527–565
Rule of Justinian I
During his reign over the Byzantine Empire, Justinian I rebuilds the city of Constantinople and creates a systematic body of law known as Justinian's Code.

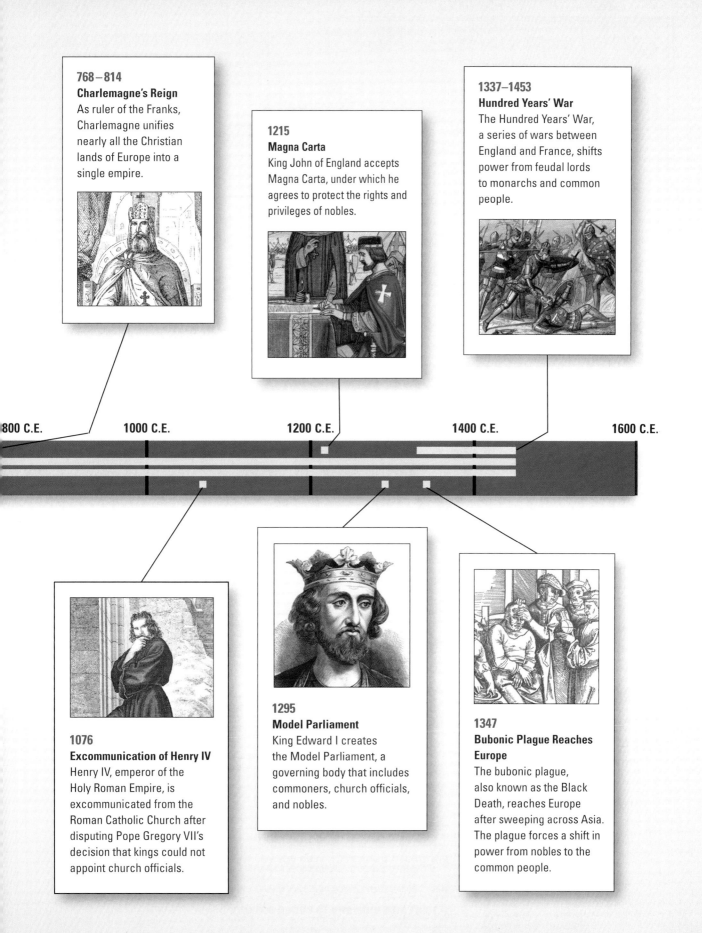

768–814
Charlemagne's Reign
As ruler of the Franks, Charlemagne unifies nearly all the Christian lands of Europe into a single empire.

1215
Magna Carta
King John of England accepts Magna Carta, under which he agrees to protect the rights and privileges of nobles.

1337–1453
Hundred Years' War
The Hundred Years' War, a series of wars between England and France, shifts power from feudal lords to monarchs and common people.

800 C.E.   1000 C.E.   1200 C.E.   1400 C.E.   1600 C.E.

1076
Excommunication of Henry IV
Henry IV, emperor of the Holy Roman Empire, is excommunicated from the Roman Catholic Church after disputing Pope Gregory VII's decision that kings could not appoint church officials.

1295
Model Parliament
King Edward I creates the Model Parliament, a governing body that includes commoners, church officials, and nobles.

1347
Bubonic Plague Reaches Europe
The bubonic plague, also known as the Black Death, reaches Europe after sweeping across Asia. The plague forces a shift in power from nobles to the common people.

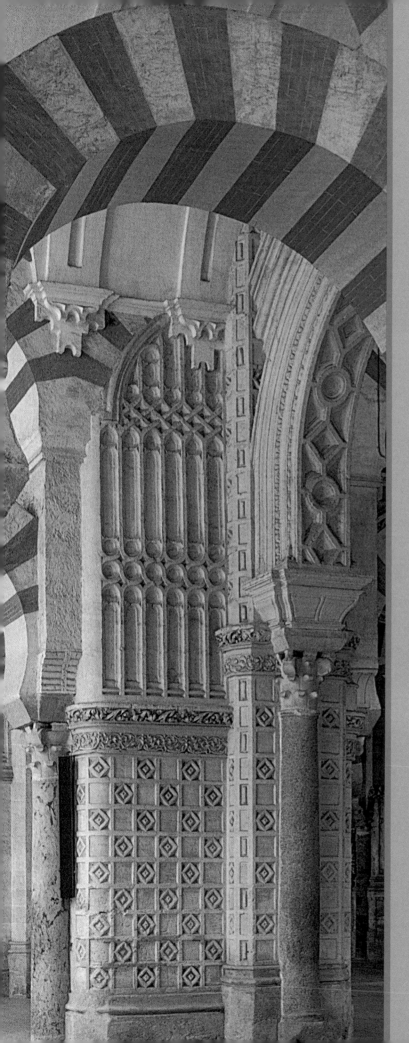

Unit 2

Islam in Medieval Times

Muslims built the Great Mosque of Cordoba in Spain around the late 700s. Shown here is its prayer room. The mosque was converted into a Christian church in the late 1200s.

Physical Features of the Arabian Peninsula and Surrounding Lands

EUROPE

Black Sea

ANATOLIAN PLATEAU

TAURUS MOUNTAINS

Caspian Sea

Amu Darya

ASIA

Mediterranean Sea

Tigris River

ZAGROS MOUNTAINS

Sea of Galilee

SYRIAN DESERT

Euphrates River

Dead Sea

SINAI PENINSULA

Persian Gulf

Strait of Hormuz

Gulf of Suez

Nile River

Gulf of Oman

Tropic of Cancer

Red Sea

ARABIAN PENINSULA

AFRICA

SAHARA

RUB AL KHALI (EMPTY QUARTER)

20°E

30°E

40°E

50°E

60°

20°

20

10°

Arabian Sea

Gulf of Aden

0   200   400 miles

0   200   400 kilometers

Albers Conic Equal-Area Projection

Elevation

Feet	Meters
Over 10,000	Over 3,050
5,001–10,000	1,526–3,050
2,001–5,000	611–1,525
1,001–2,000	306–610
0–1,000	0–305
Below sea level	Below sea level

Present-day boundary

N W E S

Islam in Medieval Times

If you could zoom out a satellite picture of the Arabian Peninsula to see the surrounding land, you would find that it borders on the continents of Africa, Asia, and Europe. Satellite imagery also shows that most of the Arabian Peninsula is brown, dry land. These two geographic facts about the Arabian Peninsula—its location and its dry climate—have shaped and defined its people and their history. That history centers on trade with northern Africa, Asia, and Europe. It also centers on the religion of Islam.

The people of the Arabian Peninsula learned how to survive in the desert. They raised sheep, goats, and camels and learned to keep moving in search of food and water. Over time, they also learned to earn a living through trade. These skills proved valuable as merchants came to the Arabian Peninsula from surrounding countries, buying and selling. Trade between Africa and Asia passed through the peninsula,

as did trade between Asia and Europe. The Arabian Peninsula became a major trading hub for all three continents.

Traders carried silk, jewels, cotton, spices, and other goods from one region to another. But more than merchandise passed between merchants and traders. Ideas, knowledge, and beliefs also passed along trade routes.

One belief that spread quickly was the religion of Islam, which began on the Arabian Peninsula and spread outward. Islamic traders from the Arabian Peninsula who traveled to Persia, Egypt, Spain, and elsewhere brought their religion with them. The followers of Islam also won people to their religion through war and conquest. The map *Islamic World by 750* shows the extent of Islamic lands by the year 750.

Today, more than a billion people around the world practice Islam, and the Middle East, which includes the Arabian Peninsula, is one of the most important regions in the world. In this unit, you will take a closer look at this region.

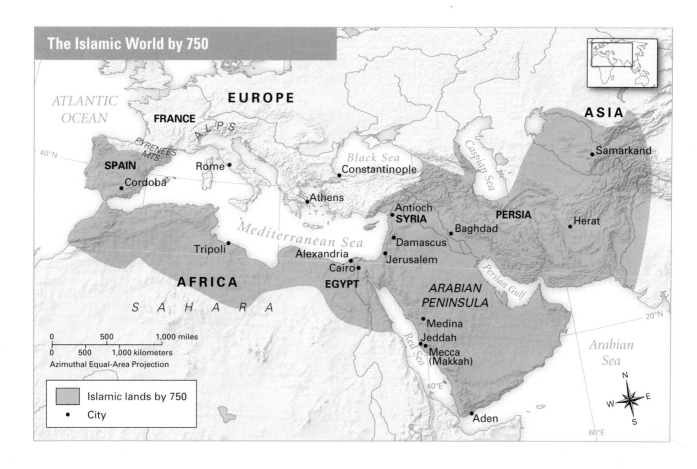

The Islamic World by 750

Lesson 9

The Origins and Spread of Islam

How did Islam originate and spread?

Introduction

In *History Alive! The Ancient World*, you learned about several major religions, including Judaism and Christianity. In this lesson, you will explore Islam, a religion that emerged in the Middle Ages.

Muhammad, born around 570 C.E., founded and taught the faith called Islam, which became one of the major religions of the world. In the centuries after his death in 632 C.E., Islam spread throughout the Arabian Peninsula and beyond.

Muhammad's birthplace, Mecca (Makkah), was an ancient place of worship. According to tradition, many centuries before Muhammad was born, God tested the prophet Abraham's faith by ordering him to leave Hagar and their infant son Ishmael in a desolate valley. As Hagar desperately searched for water, a miracle occurred. A spring, which became known as Zamzam, bubbled up at her son's feet. According to Islamic beliefs, Abraham built a house of worship at the site, called the Ka'bah. Over time, people settled near it.

By the time of Muhammad's birth, this settlement, or Mecca, was a **prosperous** city at the crossroads of great trade routes. Many people came to worship at the Ka'bah. However, instead of honoring one God as Abraham had preached, the worshippers at the Ka'bah honored the many traditional gods whose shrines were there.

According to Islamic teachings, Muhammad was living in Mecca when he experienced his own call to faith. Just as Abraham did, Muhammad **proclaimed** belief in a single God. At first, Islam was met with resistance in Mecca. But Muhammad and his followers, called Muslims, eventually attracted a great number of followers. Mecca became Islam's most sacred city, and the Ka'bah became a center of Islamic worship. You will learn more about the vast Muslim empire.

Social Studies Vocabulary

boycott

Islam

monotheism

Muhammad

Muslim

polytheism

prophet

siege

◀ The ancient Ka'bah shrine in Mecca is one of the holiest sites of Islam.

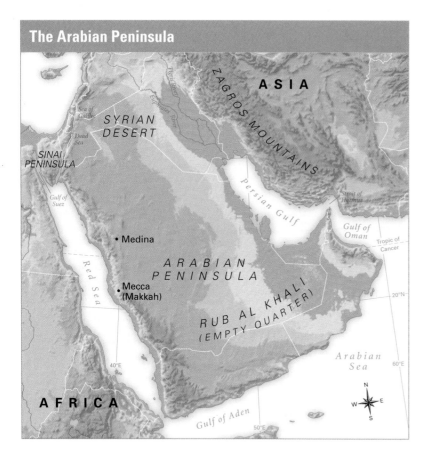

The Arabian Peninsula

The holy city of Mecca is located on the Arabian Peninsula and is the birthplace of Muhammad, the founder of Islam. The Qur'an describes Mecca as a flourishing settlement that also served as a religious center.

Islam the religion of Muslims

Muhammad a man born around 570 C.E. who taught the faith of Islam

polytheism belief in more than one god

1. Arabia in the 6th Century

Islam has its roots in Arabia, where **Muhammad** was born. To understand Islam's beginnings, it is important to first look at the time period in which Muhammad grew up.

The town of Mecca, Muhammad's birthplace, was located in a dry, rocky valley in western Arabia. Mecca did not have agriculture, but instead gained wealth as a center of trade. Merchants traveling along caravan routes stopped at the city's market, where they bought spices, sheepskins, dates, and other wares from towns-people and nomads.

By the time Muhammad was born, Mecca was a prosperous city. Merchant families brought goods into Mecca from faraway places, growing wealthy through trade with Yemen (southern Arabia), Syria, and king-doms in Africa. Over time, a handful of clans, or families, had come to rule the city. These families refused to share their fortune with the weaker, poorer clans who lived there.

Mecca was also a religious center. According to the Qur'an (koor-AHN), the holy book of Islam, Abraham had built the cube-shaped shrine, the Ka'bah, centuries before to honor God. In Muhammad's day, according to Islamic teaching, most Arabs followed **polytheism,** and the Ka'bah housed hundreds of statues of different gods. Pilgrims from all over Arabia came to worship at Mecca.

Many Arabs lived a nomadic life in the desert environment. But some Arabs led a more urban and sedentary lifestyle in towns like Medina. However, there was no central government in Arabia. Instead, Arabs pledged loyalty to their clans and to larger tribes. These tribes sometimes fought each other to capture territory, animals, goods, watering places, and even wives. When someone from one tribe was killed during a raid, his family was honor-bound to avenge that death. This led to long periods of fighting among tribes.

Although Arabs on the peninsula were not united as a nation, they shared cultural ties, especially language. Arabic poetry celebrated the history of the Arab people, the beauty of their land, and their way of life. Poets and singers from different tribes competed at gatherings held at the markets and during pilgrimages. This was the culture into which Muhammad was born.

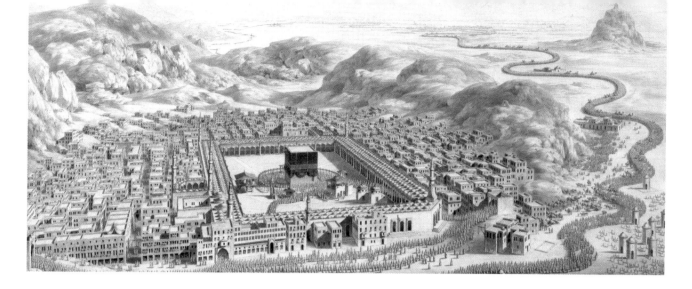

2. Muhammad's Early Life

As you have learned, around 570 C.E., an infant named Muhammad was born in Mecca. According to Muslim tradition, Muhammad's early life was ordinary. Few people who were not members of his clan, the Hashim, noted his birth. His father had died before his birth, and his clan was not very wealthy. However, the Hashim had some prestige, as they belonged to the leading tribe in Mecca.

Following custom, Muhammad's mother sent her baby to live with a family of nomads in the desert. There, the young boy learned about traditional Arab values, such as being kind to strangers and helping orphans, widows, and other needy members of society.

When Muhammad was about six, he returned to the city and to his mother. They had little time together, because she soon died, so Muhammad was left in the care of his grandfather, a highly regarded leader of the Hashim clan. Upon the grandfather's death, Muhammad's uncle, Abu Talib, a respected merchant, became head of the clan and took charge of the orphan.

As a boy, Muhammad tended his family's flocks of sheep and goats. When he was about 12 years old, he accompanied his uncle on a trading journey far north to Syria, where Muhammad gained his first experiences outside Arabia.

As Muhammad grew up, he took on more duties and made more trading journeys. He became a merchant who enjoyed a reputation throughout Mecca for his honesty. People called him *al-Amin*, which means "the Trustworthy."

According to Muslim teachings, Muhammad was still a young man when he began managing caravans for a widow named Khadijah, who ran a trading business. Muhammad earned her great profits. Impressed with his abilities and honesty, Khadijah proposed marriage. Muhammad accepted her offer, and when he was about 25, they married. Muhammad and Khadijah had several children, but only their daughter Fatima had children of her own. She continued the bloodline of Muhammad.

In Muhammad's time, Mecca was a center of caravan trade and the home of the Ka'bah. People came from all over Arabia to worship many gods at Mecca.

3. The Call to Prophethood

For the next 15 years, Muhammad made his living as a merchant. In addition to enjoying success in business, he also cared about spiritual matters, often spending time at prayer and meditation in the mountains around Mecca. He was concerned about the effects of wealth and the worship of idols on his city.

In about 610 C.E., Muhammad went to one of his spiritual retreats in a cave in the mountains. There, according to Islamic teachings, Muhammad received the call to be a **prophet,** or messenger of Allah. *Allah* is the Arabic word for God. The same word for God, Allah, is used by Arab Jews and Arab Christians.

Muhammad later described the remarkable events of that night. He told of being visited by the angel Gabriel who brought revelations, or revealed teachings, from God. Gabriel also told Muhammad, "You are the messenger of God."

prophet a person who speaks or interprets the words of God

monotheism the belief in a single God

Muslim a follower of the Islamic faith

In the Hira Cave, according to Islamic teachings, the angel Gabriel first visited Muhammad. Today, people still visit the cave, which is located in present-day Saudi Arabia.

According to Islamic tradition, at first Muhammad feared that he might be going mad. But Khadijah consoled Muhammad and expressed her faith that God had chosen him as a prophet to spread his words to the people. Khadijah became one of the first converts to Islam.

Islam is based on **monotheism,** or the belief in a single God. This God, Muhammad taught, was the same God of Abraham, Moses, and Jesus. Through Gabriel, God instructed Muhammad to teach others to practice compassion, honesty, and justice.

Muslim tradition teaches that the angel Gabriel continued to bring God's messages for about the next 20 years. At first, Muhammad confided these messages only to family and friends, including his cousin Ali and his close friend, Abu Bakr (ah-BOOH BAHK-uhr). Gradually, a small group of followers developed at Mecca. They were called **Muslims,** which means "those who surrender to God." For Muslims, Islam was a way of life and the basis for creating a just society.

Though Muhammad apparently could neither read nor write, he said that the messages from Gabriel were imprinted on his mind and heart. His followers also memorized them, and eventually some even wrote down these words and collected them in the Qur'an (also spelled *Koran*), the holy book of Islam. The poetic style of this book helped lend **credibility** to Muhammad's claim that it contained the words of God. It also attracted new believers to Islam.

boycott a refusal to do business with an organization or group

4. Muhammad's Teachings Meet with Rejection

Around 613 C.E., Muhammad began to preach to other Meccans. He taught that people must worship the one God, that all believers in God were equal, and that the rich should share their wealth. He urged Meccans to care for orphans and the poor and to improve the status of women.

Although some members of different clans, including Muhammad's, and social classes converted to Islam, most Meccans rejected Muhammad's teachings. Some Meccans did not want to share their wealth and feared that if Muhammad grew stronger, he would seize political power. Merchants worried that their businesses would be hurt if people stopped coming to Mecca to trade while visiting the shrines of their gods. Muhammad's monotheistic teachings also disturbed Arabs who did not want to give up their gods.

To prevent the spread of the prophet's message, some Arabs called Muhammad a liar, and some persecuted his followers. Despite this treatment, the Muslims refused to give up their faith. Muhammad was also protected by Abu Talib, the head of the Hashim clan, so anyone who harmed a member of the clan would face Abu Talib's vengeance.

As the number of Muslims increased, the powerful clans of Mecca started a boycott to pressure Muhammad's followers into giving up Islam. For three years, the Hashim clan suffered as Meccans refused to do business with them. Although they were threatened with starvation, the boycott failed to break their will. These difficult years, however, took their toll on Abu Talib and Khadijah. In 619, these trusted family members died.

While these losses were terrible for Muhammad, that same year, he reported a miraculous event. Muslim tradition tells the story of the Night Journey in which a winged horse-like creature took Muhammad to Jerusalem, the city toward which early Muslims had directed their prayers. Jerusalem was already holy to Jews and Christians. According to Muslim teachings, Muhammad met with earlier prophets, such as Abraham, Moses, and Jesus. Then the creature guided Muhammad through the seven levels of heaven, and Muhammad met God. To this day, Jerusalem is a holy city for Muslims.

This eight-sided domed monument, called the Dome of the Rock, marks where Muhammad is believed to have ended his Night Journey to Jerusalem and was led to heaven. Built in the 7th century C.E., it is one of the oldest surviving Islamic monuments.

The Prophet's Mosque in Medina contains Muhammad's tomb. During his lifetime, Muhammad stayed in Medina, where he helped develop a strong Muslim community.

5. From the Migration to Medina to the End of His Life

With Abu Talib's death, Muhammad lost his protector. As Muslims came under more attacks, Muhammad sought a new home. A group of Arab pilgrims from a town called Yathrib visited Mecca and converted to Islam. They asked Muhammad to move to Yathrib to bring peace between feuding tribes and, in return, they pledged to protect him.

In 622, Muhammad and his followers left Mecca on a journey known as the *hijrah* (HEEJ-rah). Yathrib was renamed Medina (also spelled *Madinah*), short for "City of the Prophet." The year of the hijrah later became the first year of the Muslim calendar.

Over the next several years in Medina, Muhammad developed a new Muslim community as more Arabs converted to Islam. Muslims pledged to be loyal and helpful to each other. They emphasized the brotherhood of faith over the ties of family, clan, and tribe. Even though Muhammad and the Qur'an criticized Jews and Christians on some aspects of their beliefs, Muhammad asked his followers to respect Christians and Jews. Like Muslims, these "People of the Book" believe in one God, and Muhammad asked that they be treated as lawful members of society.

As the community in Medina grew and became stronger, the Meccans felt increasingly threatened. In 624, fighting broke out between the Muslims and Meccans, and the Muslims won that battle. A few years later, the Meccans staged a **siege** of Medina, but failed to capture the city.

siege a military action in which a place is surrounded and cut off to force those inside to surrender

Victories against the Meccan troops—and the ideas of charity, generosity, and forgiveness that Muhammad preached—convinced other tribes to convert to Islam. With Muhammad gaining more land and followers in Arabia, the Meccans agreed to a truce that would allow the Muslims to make their pilgrimage to Mecca. Around 630, however, they broke the truce. In response, Muhammad's army marched on Mecca, and the city's leaders surrendered without a battle. Muhammad and his followers entered the city, destroyed the idols (statues of gods) at the Ka'bah, and rededicated the shrine solely to one God. Muhammad then forgave his former enemies. The war had ended.

In March 632, Muhammad led his final pilgrimage to Mecca. In the town of his birth, he delivered his final sermon. He reminded Muslims to treat each other well and to be faithful. Shortly after his return to Medina, Muhammad died.

6. The Four Caliphs

By the time of Muhammad's death, most of central and southwestern Arabia was under the control of Muslims. Now, his followers had to choose a new leader to preserve the community. After much debate, Abu Bakr, Muhammad's friend and father-in-law, was selected.

Abu Bakr became the first *caliph* (KAY-lif), or Muslim ruler. He and the three leaders who followed him came to be known to a large group of Muslims as the "rightly guided" caliphs. These caliphs were said to have followed the Qur'an and the example of Muhammad. The Muslim government led by the caliphs was called the *caliphate*.

When some tribes tried to break away, Abu Bakr used military force to reunite the community. He also completed the **unification** of Arabia. Then Muslims began to carry the teachings of Islam beyond the Arabian Peninsula.

After Abu Bakr died in 634, Caliph Umar (ooh-MAR) continued to expand the Muslim empire by conquest, which allowed Muslims to gain new lands and resources. By 643, the Muslim empire included lands in Iraq, Persia, the eastern Mediterranean, and North Africa. Umar established governments and tax systems in all these provinces. Among the taxes was one levied on Jews and Christians and other non-Muslims. Umar often let Jews and Christians practice their beliefs as they liked within their own homes and places of worship, but more often forced other religions to convert. In Egypt, treaties allowed for freedom of worship in exchange for the payment of tribute. Later, Muslims completed similar treaties with the Nubians, a people who lived to the south of Egypt.

The four Muslim leaders, or caliphs, who ruled after Muhammad were known as the "rightly guided" caliphs. These leaders oversaw the expansion of the Muslim empire.

The Expansion of Islam, 632–750

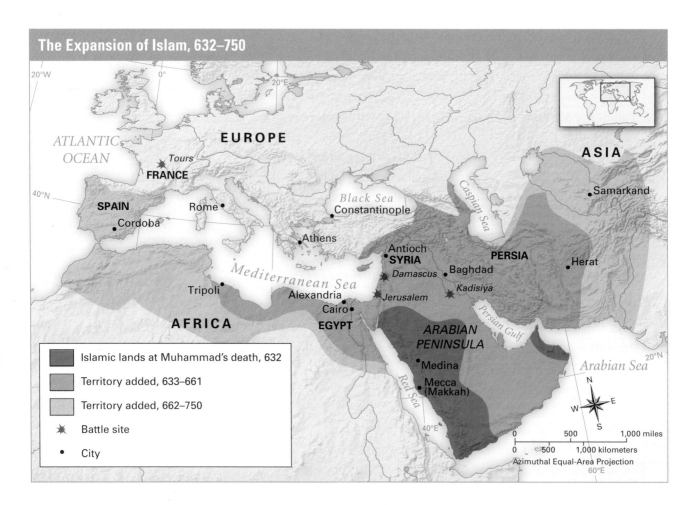

Early Muslims spread Islam and Muslim rule across the entire Middle East and as far west as Spain and North Africa. At times, the caliphs used military force and conquest to expand the Muslim empire.

Upon Umar's death in 644, Uthman, who was a member of the Umayyad (ooh-MY-ed) clan, became the third caliph. He attempted to unite Muslims by overseeing the creation of an official edition of the Qur'an. But he also awarded high posts to relatives, and people in the provinces complained that he ruled unfairly. Discontent spread, and rebels killed Uthman in 656.

Ali ibn Abi Talib (AH-lee i-ben ah-bee TAH-lib), Muhammad's cousin, and his daughter Fatima's husband, agreed to become the fourth caliph. Some important Muslims challenged his rule, which led to civil war. Ali sent forces against them, fought two major battles, and won one. But when he ended the other through negotiation, he lost supporters. In 661, one of these former supporters murdered Ali.

7. The Umayyad Dynasty

Soon after Ali's death, Mu'awiyah (mooh-AH-wee-YAH), the leader of the Umayyads, claimed the caliphate. Most Muslims, called the Sunnis (SOOH-neez), came to accept him. But a minority of Muslims, known as the Shi'ite (SHEE-eyt), or "party" of Ali, refused to do so because they believed that only people directly descended from Muhammad through his daughter Fatima and son-in-law Ali should be caliph. The schism between the Sunnis and Shi'ite lasts to this day.

Mu'awiyah put down a revolt by Ali's supporters and held on to the caliphate. He also founded the Umayyad dynasty. In 661, the Umayyads moved their capital to Damascus, Syria, from where the caliphs ruled the huge Muslim empire for close to 100 years.

Slowly, the lands of the Muslim empire took on more elements of Arab culture. Muslims introduced the Arabic language. Along with Islam, acceptance of Arabic helped unite the diverse people of the empire. In addition, Arabs took over as top officials, and people bought goods with new Arab coins. While it was not policy to force conversion to Islam, some non-Muslims began to embrace the new faith for a variety of reasons, including personal belief in the message of Islam and social pressure to join the people of the ruling group.

The Muslim empire continued to expand. The Umayyad caliphs sent armies into central Asia and northwestern India. In 711, Muslim armies began their conquests of present-day Spain. However, at the Battle of Tours in 732, forces under the Frankish king Charles Martel turned the Muslims back in France. This battle marked the farthest extent of Muslim advances into Europe, outside of Spain.

Muslims held on to land in Spain, where Islamic states lasted for almost 800 years. Muslims in Spain built some of the greatest cities of medieval Europe. Their capital city, Cordoba, became an intellectual center where Muslim, Jewish, and Christian scholars collectively lived and interacted. Through their work, Muslim culture made important advances in arts, science, technology, and literature.

Muslims followed Muhammad's teachings as Islam spread throughout the Middle East and beyond.

Lesson Summary

In this lesson, you learned about the life of Muhammad and the early spread of Islam. Muhammad and his followers unified Arabia and created a great empire.

Arabia in the 6th Century When Muhammad was born, Arabia was not politically united. But Arabs did share ties through trade, as well as the Arabic language and culture.

The Life of Muhammad Born in Mecca, Muhammad became the prophet of Islam after he received revelations from the angel Gabriel, which were recorded in the Qur'an, the holy book of Islam. However, many in Mecca opposed Islam. In the year 622, Muhammad and his followers moved to Medina, where they established a Muslim community. By the time Muhammad died in 632, people throughout Arabia had accepted the teachings of Islam and the Qur'an as the words of God.

The Four Caliphs and the Umayyad Dynasty The caliphs who followed Muhammad greatly expanded the lands under Islamic rule, despite struggles over leadership and civil war. In 661, the Umayyad caliphs moved their capital to Syria. By the mid-700s, the Muslim empire included Spain, North Africa, the Middle East, and parts of Asia and India. Along with the Arabic language, the acceptance of Islam helped unify this vast empire.

Lesson 10

Learning About World Religions: Islam

How do the beliefs and practices of Islam shape Muslims' lives?

Introduction

If you visited a city in a Muslim country today, you may notice things that reflect the teachings of Islam. In some cities, you would hear a call to prayer five times a day. While some people hurry to houses of worship, others simply remain where they are to pray, such as their homes or even in the street. You might see people dressed modestly and many women wearing head scarves. You would discover that many people there do not drink alcohol or eat pork. You might learn how Muslims donate money to support their houses of worship and many charities. Soon, you would come to understand the ways in which Islam, one of the world's major religions, is practiced as a complete way of life.

This lesson explores the basic beliefs and practices of Islam, the religion founded by the prophet Muhammad in the 7th century. Like both Christianity and Judaism, Islam has a holy book that followers use in their practice. The holy book of Islam is called the Qur'an. Muslims rely on the Qur'an and Sunnah (SOON-ah)—the example of Muhammad—for guidance in their religious belief.

Central to Muslim practice are the Five Pillars of Islam: declaration of faith, prayer, charity, fasting, and making a pilgrimage to Mecca. Both the Qur'an and the Sunnah lay out the foundation for these practices. You will also study the idea of jihad (jee-HAHD). Jihad represents Muslims' struggle with internal and external challenges as they strive to please God. Finally, you will examine shari'ah (sha-REE-uh), or Islamic law, which covers practices toward God and toward other people. This lesson will help you understand how the beliefs and practices of Islam shape the daily lives of Muslims across the world.

> ### Social Studies Vocabulary
>
> Five Pillars of Islam
> jihad
> mosque
> Qur'an
> Ramadan
> shari'ah
> Sunnah

◀ These Muslims are praying at a mosque in Pakistan.

Islam is a fast-growing religion that is practiced by people across the world. These Muslims are praying at a mosque in Yazd, Iran.

1. Background on Islam

Since the time of Muhammad, Islam has had an impact on world history. Islam spread rapidly throughout the Middle East, across North Africa to Spain, and across Central Asia nearly to China. In addition to sharing a common faith, Muslims also belonged to a single Islamic community, called the *ummah* (UH-mah), that blended many peoples and cultures.

Islam is the world's second largest religion, after Christianity. One out of four people in the world is Muslim. Most people in the Middle East and North Africa are Muslim, but Muslims live in nearly every country of the world. In fact, the majority of Muslims live in Asia, in nations such as Pakistan, Afghanistan, and the southeast Asian country of Indonesia. Islam is also one of the fastest-growing religions in the United States.

Islam, Judaism, and Christianity have much in common. For instance, members of all three faiths are monotheists (they believe in one God) and trace their origins to Abraham. Their scriptures, or sacred writings, all include such figures as Adam, Noah, and Moses. Muslims also believe that all three religions worship the same God.

Muslims consider Jews and Christians to be "People of the Book." Muslims believe that God **revealed** messages to Moses, Jesus, and others that were compiled into holy books, just as the Qur'an came from God to Muhammad. The Qur'an states that God earlier revealed the Torah (Judaism) and the Gospel (Christianity) as a source of guidance for people.

For Muslims, however, the Qur'an contains God's final revelations to humanity. They believe that its messages reveal how God wants his followers to act and worship.

2. The Qur'an and the Sunnah

Two foundations of Islam are the **Qur'an** and the **Sunnah**. According to Muslim teachings, God describes his laws and moral teachings, or the "straight path," through the Qur'an. Regarded as the direct word of God, the book holds a central position for Muslims everywhere, and even inspires Muslim art, poetry, and literature.

The Qur'an contains passages that Muslims believe Muhammad received from the angel Gabriel. Muhammad and his followers recited and memorized these verses. Because Muhammad apparently could not read or write, scribes wrote down these passages. The Arabic of the Qur'an is notable for its beauty.

In about 651 C.E., Caliph Uthman established an official edition of the Qur'an. He asked those with different versions of the Qur'an to destroy them so that there would be no confusion between those and the official **edition**. The Qur'an used today has remained largely unchanged since then.

Muhammad described the Qur'an as God's "standing miracle." Muslims honor the spoken and written Qur'an. Most Muslims today do not let copies of the sacred book touch the ground, and they handle the Qur'an in special ways. Most Muslims memorize at least certain parts of the Qur'an in Arabic, and some even memorize the entire book. The memorized parts may be recited in daily prayer or during special occasions. Its verses accompany Muslims throughout their lives, from birth to death.

The Sunnah ("practice") is the example that Muhammad set for Muslims during his lifetime. What Muhammad did or said in a certain situation has set a precedent, or guideline, for all Muslims. For instance, Muhammad told his followers to make sure that their guests never left the table hungry, underscoring the importance of hospitality. He also reminded children to honor their parents when he said, "God forbids all of you to disobey your mothers." For Muslims, the Sunnah is second only to the Qur'an in religious authority.

About 300 years after Muhammad's death, thousands of reports about the prophet had spread throughout Muslim lands. Called *hadith* ("reports" or "tradition"), these accounts provided written evidence of Muhammad's Sunnah through his own words and deeds. Scholars looked into each story and organized the ones that they could verify into collections. These collections remain important sources for Muslim beliefs, laws, and history.

The most basic acts of worship for Muslims are called the **Five Pillars of Islam**. The Qur'an provides general commands to perform these five duties, whereas the Sunnah explains how to perform them, based on Muhammad's example. Let's look next at each of the Five Pillars.

Qur'an the holy book of the religion of Islam

Sunnah the example that Muhammad set for Muslims about how to live

Five Pillars of Islam the most basic acts of worship for Muslims: declaration of faith, prayer, charity, fasting, and making a pilgrimage to Mecca

These children are reading the Qur'an, which is considered by Muslims to be the word of God. This book is central to Muslim belief and practice.

3. The First Pillar: Shahadah

The first Pillar of Islam is *shahadah* (shah-HAH-dah), the profession or declaration of faith. To show belief in one God and in Muhammad's prophethood, a Muslim testifies, "I bear witness that there is no god but God, and that Muhammad is the messenger of God."

The first part of the shahadah affirms monotheism—"There is no god but God." Like Christians and Jews, Muslims believe that one all-powerful God—called *Allah* in Arabic—created the universe. They believe that the truth of that God was revealed to humankind through many prophets, including Adam, Abraham, Moses, and Jesus, who appear in either the Jewish or Christian scriptures. The Qur'an honors all of these prophets.

The second part of the shahadah **identifies** Muhammad as God's messenger—"and Muhammad is the messenger of God." According to this statement, Muhammad announced the message of Islam, which Muslims believe to be God's final word to humankind.

The meaning of shahadah is that people not only believe in God, but also pledge their submission to him. For Muslims, God is the center of life. To enter into the religion of Islam, a person must pronounce the shahadah aloud in the presence of two Muslim witnesses. It is also part of the call to prayer, which is regularly recited in **mosques** (MOSKS) and part of certain traditions.

Beyond the shahadah, some Muslims also believe in the idea of an unseen world of angels and other beings. According to their faith, God created angels to do his work throughout the universe. Some angels reveal themselves to prophets, as Gabriel did to Muhammad. Other angels observe and record the deeds of each human being. Belief in angels is found in Christianity and Judaism, as well.

Muslims also believe that all souls will face a day of judgment. On that day, God will weigh each person's actions. Those who have believed in God and lived according to his rules will be rewarded with paradise.

A muezzin calls Muslim people to prayer from a mosque's tower, or minaret. This muezzin is calling from a tower in Xinjiang, China.

4. The Second Pillar: Salat

The second Pillar of Islam is *salat* (SAH-laht), daily ritual prayer. Muhammad said that "prayer is the proof" of Islam. Salat emphasizes religious discipline, spirituality, and closeness to God.

Throughout Muslim communities, people are called to prayer five times a day: at dawn, noon, mid-afternoon, sunset, and after nightfall. A crier, called a *muezzin* (moo-EHZ-en), chants the call to prayer, sometimes through a loudspeaker, from the tall minaret (tower) of the community's mosque.

Before praying, Muslims must perform ritual washings. All mosques have fresh, flowing water in which worshipers wash their hands, face, arms, and feet. With a sense of being purified, Muslims enter the prayer area where they form lines behind a prayer leader called an imam. The worshipers face the *qiblah* (KIB-lah), the direction of the Ka'bah, which is marked by a niche in a wall. People of all classes stand shoulder to shoulder, but men stand in separate rows from women.

The imam begins the prayer cycle by proclaiming "Allahu akbar!" ("God is most great!"). The worshipers then recite verses from the Qur'an and kneel before God.

This mosque in Dubai has two minarets. Some muezzins climb to the top of the tall towers to chant their calls to prayer out over the city. In present day, many mosques have loudspeakers to broadcast calls to prayer.

While praying at a mosque is preferable, Muslims may worship anywhere. In groups or by themselves, they may perform their prayers at home, at work, in airports, in parks, or on sidewalks. A qiblah compass may help them locate the direction of the Ka'bah. Some Muslims carry a prayer rug to have a clean spot on which pray. Some use prayer beads for additional worship and recite words describing what they believe to be God's many characteristics.

Unlike Christians and Jews, Muslims do not observe a sabbath, or day of rest. On Fridays, however, Muslims gather at a mosque for midday congregational prayer. The worshipers listen to a Qur'an reading and the sermon. After saying prayers together, some return to their regular business. For others, Friday is a special day when people meet with family and friends.

Through zakat, the third Pillar of Islam, Muslims give to the poor or needy. This person is collecting donations at a mosque in Paris, France.

5. The Third Pillar: Zakat

The third Pillar of Islam is *zakat*, or charity. The Qur'an says wealthy people should share their riches with the less fortunate, a practice that remains a basic part of Islam.

The word *zakat* means "purification." Muslims believe that wealth becomes pure by giving some of it away, and that sharing wealth helps control greed. Zakat also reminds people of God's great gifts to them.

According to the teachings of Islam, Muslims must share about one-fortieth (2.5 percent) of their surplus wealth each year with their poorer neighbors. They are encouraged to give even more. Individuals decide the proper amount to pay. Then they may either give this sum to a religious official or **distribute** it themselves.

Zakat helps provide for many needs. In medieval times, zakat often went to constructing public fountains, so everyone had clean water to drink, or to inns so that pilgrims and travelers had a place to sleep. If you walk down a busy street in any Muslim town today, you will see the effects of zakat everywhere. Zakat pays for soup kitchens, clothing, and shelter for the poor. It supports the building and running of orphanages and hospitals. Poorer Muslims may receive funds to pay off their debts. Zakat provides aid to stranded travelers.

Zakat also helps other good causes that serve the Muslim community. For instance, it can cover the school fees of children whose parents cannot afford to send them to schools. It can be used to pay teachers.

Zakat is similar to charitable giving in other religions. For instance, Jews ask for charitable giving and actions to help the needy and the community, a concept called tzedakah (TZE-DAH-KAH), meaning justice and fairness. Christians also ask for donations, called tithes (TYTHZ), to support their houses of worship and charitable activities.

6. The Fourth Pillar: Siyam

Ramadan the ninth month of the Islamic calendar, during which Muslims are required to fast

The fourth Pillar of Islam is *siyam* (see-YAM), or fasting (going without food). Muslims were not the first people to fast as a way of worshipping God. The Bible praises the act. But the Qur'an instructs Muslims to fast for an entire month during **Ramadan,** the ninth month of the Islamic calendar.

During Ramadan, Muslims fast from daybreak to the setting of the sun. Pregnant women, travelers, the sick, the elderly, and young children do not have to fast.

According to Islamic teachings, Ramadan was the month when God first revealed his message to Muhammad. Muslims use a lunar calendar (one based on the phases of the moon). A year on this calendar is shorter than a 365-day year. As a result, over time, Ramadan cycles through all the seasons of a standard year.

During the daylight hours of each day during the month of Ramadan, Muslims do not eat any food or drink any liquid, including water. At sunset, Muslims then break their fast, often with dates—as Muhammad usually did—and other food and beverages. They then perform the sunset prayer. After a meal shared with family or friends, Muslims attend special prayer services in which a portion of the Qur'an is read aloud each night. By the end of Ramadan, devout Muslims who attended mosque regularly would have heard the entire holy book.

The holy month of Ramadan encourages generosity, equality, and charity within the Muslim community. Fasting teaches Muslims self-control and leads them to a deeper understanding of hunger and poverty. Well-to-do Muslims and mosques often provide food for others. During Ramadan, Muslims also strive to forgive people, give thanks, and avoid gossip, arguments, and bad deeds.

Toward the end of Ramadan, Muslims remember Gabriel's first visit to Muhammad. It is supposed to have occurred during one of the last ten odd-numbered nights of the month. Worshippers seek out this night because, according to the Qur'an, prayer during this "night of power" is equal to a thousand months of devotion. A celebration called Eid al-Fitr (eed-AL-fitter) takes place when Ramadan ends. People attend prayers, wear new clothes, decorate their homes, and prepare special foods. They visit friends and family, exchange gifts, and give to the poor.

Muslims fast from sunrise to sunset during the month of Ramadan. Here, a crowd in Indonesia prepares to eat a meal on the last day of Ramadan.

7. The Fifth Pillar: Hajj

The fifth Pillar of Islam is *hajj* (HAJZH), the pilgrimage to the holy city of Mecca. In the twelfth month of the Islamic year, millions of believers from all over the world come together at Mecca. All adult Muslims who are financially and physically able to make the journey are expected to perform the hajj at least once during their lifetime. By bringing Muslims from many places and cultures together, the hajj promotes fellowship and equality.

In Mecca, pilgrims follow what Muslims believe are the footsteps of Abraham and Muhammad, and so draw closer to God. For five days, they dress in simple white clothing and perform a series of rituals, moving from one sacred site to another.

Upon arrival, Muslims announce their presence with these words: "Here I am, O God, at Thy command!" They go to the Great Mosque, which houses the Ka'bah. Muslims believe that Abraham built the Ka'bah as a shrine to honor God. The pilgrims circle the Ka'bah seven times, which is a ritual mentioned in the Qur'an. Next, they run along a passage between two small hills, as Hagar did when she searched for water for her baby Ishmael. The pilgrims drink from the Zamzam spring, which is believed to have appeared miraculously at Ishmael's feet.

Pilgrims to the holy city of Mecca circle the Ka'bah seven times as directed in the Qur'an and the Sunnah. Muslims who are able to do so are expected to make the pilgrimage at least once in their lifetime.

Later, pilgrims leave Mecca to sleep in tents at a place called Mina. In the morning, they move to the Plain of Arafat to pray until sunset, asking God's forgiveness. Some climb Mount Arafat, where Muhammad preached his Last Sermon. After spending another night camped in the desert, they reject evil by casting stones at pillars representing Satan.

Afterward, pilgrims may celebrate with a four-day feast. In honor of Abraham's ancient sacrifice, as recounted in religious scriptures, Muslims sacrifice animals, typically sheep or goats, and share the meat with family, friends, and the poor. Then, having completed the hajj, they dress again in their own clothes. Before leaving Mecca, each pilgrim circles the Ka'bah seven more times. Muslims around the world celebrate this "farewell" day as Eid al-Adha (eed-AL-adh-hah).

8. Jihad

The word **jihad** means "to strive." There are multiple ways to fulfill the duty of jihad, and different groups emphasize different methods. Some people interpret the duty to mean a "physical struggle with spiritual significance." The Qur'an tells Muslims to fight to protect themselves from those who would harm them or to right a terrible wrong. Early Muslims considered efforts to protect their territory and conquests to extend their empire as forms of jihad. However, the Qur'an forbids Muslims to force others to convert to Islam. So, non-Muslims under Muslim rule were usually allowed to practice their faiths.

In another interpretation, jihad represents the human struggle to overcome difficulties and do things that would be pleasing to God. Muslims strive to respond positively to personal difficulties as well as to worldly challenges. For instance, they might work to become better people, reform society, or correct injustice.

Jihad has always been an important Islamic concept. One hadith tells about the prophet's return from a battle. He declared that the prophet and his men had carried out the "lesser jihad," the external struggle against oppression. The "greater jihad," he said, was the fight against evil within oneself. Examples of the greater jihad include working hard for a goal, giving up a bad habit, getting an education, or obeying your parents when you may not want to.

> **jihad** an Arabic term that describes the struggle, usually an internal, spiritual one, that Muslims undergo to get closer to God. A small percentage of Muslims interpret jihad to justify acts of violence and terrorism.

The term "Jihad" can have different meanings for Muslims. It can mean a physical struggle against those who fight against Muslims or it can mean an inner spiritual struggle against personal weaknesses.

Another hadith says that Muslims should fulfill jihad with the heart, tongue, and hand. Muslims use the heart in their struggle to resist evil, while the tongue may convince others to take up worthy causes. Hands may perform good works and correct misdeeds.

Today, some have used jihad to try to make their government more Islamic or to resist perceived aggression from non-Muslims with acts of violence and terrorism. However, most Muslims reject such actions and believe that to deliberately harm civilians, including non-Muslims, is forbidden in Islam. They agree that although the Qur'an allows war, it sets specific terms for fighting. Muhammad told his followers to honor agreements made with foes and for fighters to not mutilate (remove or destroy) the dead bodies of enemies. He also forbade harming certain people, such as children or the elderly, and destroying property and sacred objects.

This illuminated manuscript from 1334 shows a shari'ah court. Muslims use the Qur'an and Sunnah as guides for interpreting shari'ah.

9. Islamic Law: Shari'ah

The search to understand God's law is called **shari'ah** (sha-REE-ah). Muslims use the Qur'an and the Sunnah as important sources to try to understand shari'ah. Shari'ah covers Muslims' duties toward God and others. It guides them in their personal behavior and relationships with others. Shari'ah promotes obedience to the Qur'an and respect for others.

In the Muslim community that Muhammad first established, Muhammad explained the Qur'an and decided how to resolve disputes. After his death, the leaders in the community used different methods to answer questions that came up about how to practice Islam. They often referred to the Qur'an and the Sunnah for guidance. As the Muslim empire expanded, leaders faced new situations. Gradually, scholars developed various approaches to understand Islamic law, and several schools of Islamic law had emerged by the 12th century.

Islamic law guides Muslim life by placing actions into one of five categories: forbidden, discouraged, allowed, recommended, and obligatory (required). Sometimes the law is quite specific. Muslims, for instance, are forbidden to eat pork or drink alcohol. But other matters are mentioned in general terms. For example, the Qur'an tells women "not to display their beauty" to strangers. For this reason, Muslim women usually wear various forms of modest dress, with most women covering their arms and legs. Many also wear scarves over their hair. Others cover themselves from head to toe.

Shari'ah also outlines Muslims' duties toward other people. These duties can be broadly grouped into criminal, commercial, family, and inheritance law.

shari'ah the search to understand God's law, which relies heavily on the Qur'an and the Sunnah

In a shari'ah court, a *qadi* (KAH-dee), or judge, hears a case, which includes witnesses and evidence. Then the qadi makes a ruling. Sometimes the qadi consults a *mufti*, or scholar of law, for an opinion.

Shari'ah helped Muslims to develop laws that relied on the Qur'an and Sunnah and that applied to different situations. By the 19th century, however, many Muslim regions had come under European rule, and Western codes of law soon replaced the shari'ah except in matters of family law. Today, most Muslim countries apply some parts of Islamic law, but shari'ah continues to develop in response to modern ways of life and its challenges.

For the past century, one of the major questions the Muslim world faces is how Islamic law can be made to relate to modern society and government. Turkey has chosen a non-religious legal model. However, Saudi Arabia and Iran have chosen to follow Islamic law in their governance, each nation according to its own ideas. Some countries, such as Egypt and Pakistan, have both strong Islamist parties and strong non-Islamist parties. Many Muslims feel that democracy and freedom do not **contradict** the teachings and law of Islam. But others feel that the two cannot go hand in hand. The debate continues.

Lesson Summary

In this lesson, you learned about the basic beliefs and practices of Islam. One of the world's major religions, Islam has more followers than any faith except Christianity.

Background on Islam Islam, Judaism, and Christianity share many similarities. People of these faiths believe in one God and have holy books. Muslims accept the Jewish and Christian scriptures as earlier revelations by God.

The Qur'an and the Sunnah The Qur'an is the Muslim scripture. It contains God's final messages to humanity and guides Muslims on how to live their lives. Additional guidance comes from the Sunnah (practice), the example of Muhammad. The hadith (tradition) provides a written record of sayings and deeds of the prophet.

The Five Pillars of Islam Islam is a way of life, as well as a set of beliefs. Muslims follow the Five Pillars of Islam. The five pillars are: shahadah (declaration of faith), salat (daily worship), zakat (charity), siyam (fasting), and hajj (the pilgrimage to Mecca).

Jihad The term "jihad" refers to the effort that Muslims perform to become closer to God. A vast majority of Muslims emphasize a spiritual, inner struggle. But a minority of individuals and groups claim to fulfill this duty through acts of violence.

Islamic Law: Shari'ah Shari'ah, a large body of guidelines, helps Muslims live by the teachings of the Qur'an. Islamic law covers practices of daily life, as well as conduct with others.

Muslim Innovations and Adaptations

What important innovations and adaptations did medieval Muslims make?

Introduction

In the Middle Ages, Muslims developed a rich culture. By 750 C.E., Muslims ruled Spain, North Africa, the Middle East, and much of central Asia. Over the next 500 years, many cultural influences blended in this vast region, and Arabs, Persians, Turks, and others all helped to build Islamic civilization.

The Islamic world was rich, **diverse,** and creative. Great cities flourished as centers of culture. Jewish, Christian, and Muslim scholars worked to translate ancient texts from Greece, India, and Persia into Arabic. They preserved old learning and made significant advancements in fields such as medicine, math, astronomy, biology, and physics. This progress impacted the Scientific Revolution in Europe centuries later.

Today, Muslim contributions are still visible in societies around the world. For instance, Muslims introduced many foods to other parts of the world, such as sugar (*al-sukkar*, in Arabic), rice (*al-ruzz*), and oranges (*naranj*). The English words *mattress* and *sofa* are both from Arabic. *Pajamas* and *tambourine* are derived from Persian words. The Arabic numerals (1, 2, 3, and so on) used today were brought to Europe by Muslims.

In this lesson, you will explore Muslim contributions to world civilization. You will study Muslim achievements in city building and architecture, scholarship and learning, science and technology, geography and navigation, mathematics, medicine, literature and bookmaking, art and music, and recreation. Let's begin by looking more closely at the flowering of Islamic civilization following the Arab conquests of the 7th and 8th centuries.

Social Studies Vocabulary

adaptation

cultural diffusion

evolution

immortal

innovation

philosopher

◄ In the 14th century, Muslim rulers built the magnificent palace complex called the Alhambra in Granada, Spain.

adaption a change made to an existing object or way of doing things

innovation something new; an improvement

cultural diffusion the spread of cultural elements from one society to another

Over many connecting trade routes, goods and ideas moved from Asia through Muslim lands, where they were adapted. They then spread as far as North Africa and Europe.

1. The Flowering of Islamic Civilization

Islam began on the Arabian Peninsula. By the middle of the 8th century, Arab conquests had created a vast Muslim empire. Spain, North Africa, and much of western and central Asia came under Muslim rule. Over the next 500 years, Islamic civilization flowered over this huge area.

Although the empire did not last as a political unit, Islamic civilization flourished. Muslim rulers built great cities where scholars and artists made **adaptations** and **innovations** in many fields.

Muslims learned from other cultures and helped spread their own cultural influences to other places. The spreading of ideas and ways of life is called **cultural diffusion**. Cultural diffusion occurs as different societies interact through trade, travel, or even conflict. Often, these cultural elements are changed, or adapted, in the regions to which they spread.

The Islamic lands were ideally located for cultural diffusion. As shown on this map of medieval trade routes, several important trade routes linking Asia, Europe, and Africa met in the Middle East. Muslim traders carried ideas, as well as goods, along these routes, spreading learning to and from Asia, Europe, and Africa.

For instance, Muslims learned paper making from the Chinese and then passed this knowledge on to Europeans. Muslims also produced new scientific, medical, and philosophical texts based on earlier Greek works. Many of these Muslim texts were translated into Latin in the 12th century and became available to western Europeans for the first time.

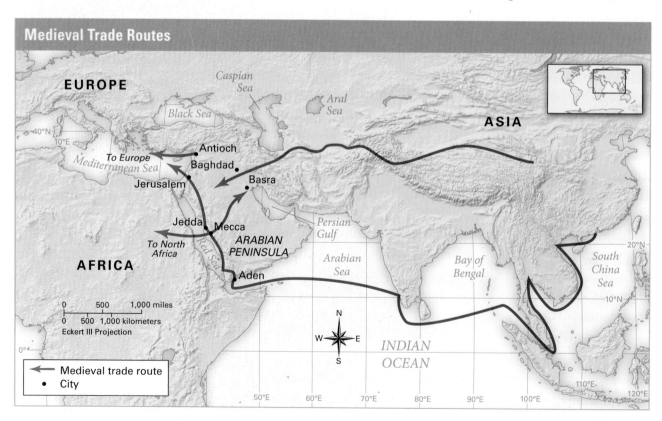

Medieval Trade Routes

EUROPE · Caspian Sea · Black Sea · Aral Sea · ASIA · Antioch · To Europe · Mediterranean Sea · Baghdad · Jerusalem · Basra · Jedda · Mecca · Persian Gulf · To North Africa · ARABIAN PENINSULA · Red Sea · AFRICA · Aden · Arabian Sea · Bay of Bengal · South China Sea · INDIAN OCEAN

0 500 1,000 miles
0 500 1,000 kilometers
Eckert III Projection

→ Medieval trade route
• City

Muslim mathematicians were also able to translate and study the works of Babylonian, Indian, Chinese, Greek, and Jewish math scholars. They were able to develop innovations in that field, too.

With only a minority of Muslims from the Arabian Peninsula, the Islamic world exhibited great diversity. Persians, Egyptians, North Africans, Turks, and others all contributed to the cultural blending we associate with Islamic civilization.

2. City Building and Architecture

Many large cities developed in Muslim lands, and this growth encouraged new kinds of architecture. Thousands of workers labored to build palaces, schools, orphanages, hospitals, mosques, and other buildings.

The City of Baghdad After the Muslim Abbasid dynasty (758–1258 C.E.) rose to power in the Middle East, Caliph al-Mansur decided to move his capital from Damascus to a site that was more central to his far-flung empire. The site he chose was Baghdad, a village between the Tigris and Euphrates rivers, in present-day Iraq. This location was a crossroads of trade routes connecting distant parts of the empire.

Baghdad was one of the most glorious Muslim cities. It took 100,000 architects, workers, and craftspeople four years to build the new capital. Because of its shape, people called the capital complex the "round city." At its center were the caliph's palace and the grand mosque. Around them were offices and the houses of court officials and army officers. A double wall with four guarded gates surrounded the inner city. Shops, markets, and residences grew up outside the wall. Soon, Baghdad was one of the world's largest cities. Bridges, palaces, and gardens all added to its splendor. One Arab historian of the 11th century called Baghdad "a city with no equal in the world."

The Mosque Muslims created distinctive forms of architecture. A particularly important type of building was the mosque, the Muslim house of worship.

Mosques usually have at least one minaret (tower) with a small balcony where the muezzin chants the call to prayer. In a courtyard, stands a fountain for washing before prayers. Inside the mosque is the prayer room where worshippers sit on mats and carpets on the floor. The imam gives the sermon from a raised pulpit called the minbar. Next to the minbar is a niche in the wall that indicates the direction of prayer towards Mecca.

Many design styles and materials went into building mosques, reflecting the great diversity of Muslim lands. Like the cathedrals of Europe, mosques express the religious faith and the artistic heritage of their builders.

The minaret of the Great Mosque of Samarra has a spiral design. Muezzins climb spiral steps around the outside of the tower to the balcony at the top.

Students in Muslim schools discussed and debated philosophical ideas with their teachers, as shown in this 13th-century manuscript. Muslim philosophers were influenced by Greek thinkers in their writings on reason and logic.

philosopher a scholar, teacher, or thinker who seeks knowledge

immortal able to live forever

3. Scholarship and Learning

Scholarship and learning were very highly valued in Islamic culture. Muhammad is reported to have said, "The ink of scholars is more precious than the blood of martyrs."

Acceptance of the Arabic language helped promote learning. Beginning in the 8th century, Arabic became the language of scholarship and science throughout Islamic lands. A shared language and love of learning allowed scholars in Europe, North Africa, and the Middle East to exchange ideas and build on one another's work.

Muslim rulers built schools, colleges, libraries, and other centers of learning. From a small village, Baghdad grew into one of the world's largest cities. It became a major center of learning, where Persian influences combined with the Arabic heritage of Islam. There, Caliph al-Ma'mun founded the House of Wisdom in 830, where scholars from many lands gathered to do research and to translate texts from Greece, Persia, and India.

Other cities also became great centers of learning. For example, in the 10th century, the Fatimid dynasty in Egypt built a capital, Cairo, which rivaled Baghdad. Its university became the most advanced in the Muslim world. In Cairo, the Hall of Wisdom opened in the 10th century, where scholars and ordinary people visited its library to read books. In Spain, the Muslim capital, Cordoba, flourished and became a large and wealthy city. Jews, Christians, and Muslims worked and studied there together. That city's huge library held as many as 400,000 volumes, and buyers traveled far and wide to purchase books for its shelves.

Among the texts studied were the works of ancient Greek thinkers, such as the **philosophers** Plato (PLAY-toh) and Aristotle. Following the example of the Greeks, Muslim philosophers used reason and **logic** to try to prove important truths.

Like thinkers in Europe, thinkers in the Islamic world sometimes wondered how to make reason and logical proof agree with their faith. Al-Kindi, a 9th-century Arab philosopher, tried to resolve this issue. Humans, he said, had two sources of knowledge: reason and revelation by God. People could use reason to better understand the teachings of faith. Some truths, however, could be known only through God's word. For example, no one could prove that there would be a resurrection, or rising from the dead, on the day of judgment.

Ibn Sina (i-ben SEE-na), a Persian, is among the most famous of Muslim philosophers. Known as Avicenna in Europe, he wrote in the early 11th century. He believed that all knowledge could be known through revelation and reason. For example, he presented an argument that the soul was **immortal**. His writings were widely translated and influenced many thinkers in medieval Europe.

4. Science and Technology

Muslims demonstrated an endless curiosity about the world. In fact, the Qur'an instructed them to learn more about the world God had made:

> *Have they not looked at the camels—how they are created?*
> *And at the sky—how it is raised up?*
> —Qur'an, Chapter 88, Verses 17–18

As a result, Muslims made advances in science and technology. They were particularly interested to learn about how things worked.

Zoology A number of Muslim scholars became interested in zoology, the scientific study of animals. Some wrote books describing the structure of animals' bodies, while others explained how to make medicines from animal parts. In the 800s, a scholar named al-Jahiz (AHL-jay-HEEZ) even presented theories about the **evolution** of animals. Muslims also established zoological gardens, or zoos.

evolution the slow process of change in plants and animals from simpler forms to more complex forms

Astronomy Muslim scholars did much work in the field of **astronomy,** the study of objects in the universe. Astronomy had many practical uses for Muslims. For example, navigational tools were improved to locate the direction of Mecca. These instruments allowed worshippers far from the holy city to pray facing in the correct direction. Astronomers also figured out exact times for prayer and the length of the month of Ramadan.

Beyond such practical matters, Muslim astronomers simply wanted to learn about the universe. Some realized that Earth rotates, or turns, like a spinning top. Muslims also continued to improve upon models of the universe that had been proposed by Greek and Roman astronomers.

The town of Hama, Syria, has 17 wooden waterwheels from medieval times. These waterwheels scoop water from the Orontes River into aqueducts, bringing it to homes and farms.

Irrigation and Underground Wells Muslims made technological advances to make the most of scarce water resources, since much of the land under Muslim rule was hot and dry. Muslims restored old irrigation systems and designed new ones. They built dams and aqueducts to provide water for households, mills, and fields. They improved existing systems of canals and underground wells. Muslims also used water wheels to bring water up from canals and reservoirs.

5. Geography and Navigation

Another subject of study for Muslim scholars was geography. Muslim geographers examined plants and animals in different regions, as well as divided the world into climate zones.

Most educated people in medieval times believed that Earth was round, but they disagreed about Earth's size. Muslim scientists improved on calculations made by the ancient Greeks to reach a measure of Earth's circumference that was close to the correct value.

As with all scholarship, some Muslims studied geography simply out of curiosity, but it had practical uses, too. For example, Muslims were able to create extremely accurate maps due to the study of geography. A scholar in Muslim Spain even produced a world atlas, with dozens of maps of lands in Europe, Africa, and Asia.

A work called *The Book of Roads and Provinces* provided maps and descriptions of the major Muslim trade routes. *The Book of Countries* listed useful facts about the lands under Muslim rule. From this book, travelers could get information about a region's location, physical features, and natural resources.

Travelers were another source of knowledge. Some travelers wrote guidebooks to help pilgrims make the journey to Mecca to fulfill the hajj. Others explored and described foreign lands, such as China and Scandinavia.

As aids to travel, Muslims used navigational instruments. Muslim scientists adapted and perfected the compass and astrolabe. Muslims probably learned about the compass, a device that allows people to identify the direction in which they are traveling, from the Chinese.

The astrolabe is a navigation device for computing time based on the location of the sun or the stars. It was probably invented much earlier by the Greeks. With this instrument, sailors at sea could use the position of objects in the sky, such as the sun or stars, to pinpoint their location by knowing how far they had traveled.

The astrolabe was a navigational tool widely used in the Islamic world and in Europe. Islamic sailors used an astrolabe to determine their location based on the position of objects in the sky.

6. Mathematics

Muslims greatly advanced the study of mathematics. They based their work in part on ideas from ancient Babylon, India, and Greece. For example, scholars in Baghdad's House of Wisdom translated the works of the Greek mathematician Euclid (YOO-klid), as well as important texts from India. Then they adapted what they learned and added their own contributions.

One of these Muslim scholars was the astronomer and mathematician al-Khwarizmi (ahl KWAR-iz-mee), who worked in the House of Wisdom in Baghdad in the 9th century. Al-Khwarizmi is best known as "the father of algebra." In fact, the word *algebra* comes from the title of one of his books. It originated in an Arabic phrase, al-jabr, meaning "the reunion of broken parts."

Algebra is used to solve problems involving unknown numbers. An example is the **equation** $7x + 4 = 25$. Using algebra, we can figure out that in this equation, x represents 3. Al-Khwarizmi's famous book on algebra was translated into Latin in the 12th century and became one of the most important mathematics textbooks used in the universities of Europe.

The translation of another one of al-Khwarizmi's books helped to popularize Arabic numerals in Europe. Actually, Muslims learned this way of writing numerals, along with fractions and decimals, from Indian scholars. Arabic numerals were a big help to business and trade since, compared to earlier systems like Roman numerals, they made it easier for people to do calculations and check their work. We still use Arabic numerals today.

Muslims also spread the Indian concept of zero. In fact, the word *zero* comes from an Arabic word meaning "something empty." Ancient peoples used written symbols for numbers long before anyone thought of using a symbol for zero. However, zero is very important in calculations. (Try subtracting 2 from 2. Without using zero, how would you express the answer?) Zero also made it easier to write large numbers. For example, zero allows people to distinguish between 123 and 1,230.

The geometric designs in Muslim art and architecture are based on knowledge about advanced mathematical principles. Muslim scholars greatly influenced the field of mathematics.

7. Medicine

Muslims made some of their most important innovations in the field of medicine. They learned a great deal from the work of ancient Greeks and Indians. Then, as in other fields of study, they improved upon this earlier knowledge.

Muslim doctors established hospitals that were open to all people. By the 10th century, Baghdad had at least five hospitals. Many hospitals served as teaching centers for doctors in training. Anyone who needed treatment could get it at these centers, but there were also hospital caravans that brought medical care to people in remote villages.

Muslim hospitals had separate wards for men and women, surgical patients, and people with diseases that others could catch. Doctors treated ailments with drugs, diet, and exercise. They gave patients remedies made from herbs and other plants, animals, and minerals. Pharmacists made hundreds of medications, such as drugs that dulled patients' pain. Antiseptics (medications that fight infection) cleaned wounds, and ointments helped to heal them.

For some problems, surgeons performed delicate operations as a last resort. Drugs, such as opium and hemlock, put patients to sleep before operations. Muslim surgeons removed limbs, took out tumors, and cleared cataracts (cloudy spots) from the eye. After surgery, doctors used thread made from animal gut to stitch the wounds.

Muslim doctors treated patients with herbal remedies, as well as drugs, diet, and exercise. This illustration of a lily plant is from an Arabic herbal encyclopedia of the 10th century.

Muslim doctors made many discoveries and helped spread medical knowledge. For example, al-Razi, a Persian doctor, realized that infections were caused by bacteria. He also studied smallpox and measles. His work helped other doctors diagnose and treat these deadly diseases.

The Persian philosopher Ibn Sina (Avicenna), whom you read about earlier in this lesson, was also a great doctor. In fact, he has been called "the prince of physicians." His most important medical book, *The Canon of Medicine,* explored the treatment of diseases and became one of the classics in the history of medical scholarship.

Europeans later translated Ibn Sina's book and many other Muslim works into Latin. Medical schools then used these texts to teach their students. In this way, Muslim doctors had a major impact on European medicine.

8. Bookmaking and Literature

In the 8th century, Muslims learned the art of making paper from the Chinese and soon were creating bound books of their own. Bookmaking, in turn, encouraged the growth of Muslim literature.

Craftspeople used their talents to produce beautiful books. Bookmakers gathered the sheets of paper and often sewed them into leather bindings. They **illuminated** the bindings and pages with designs in gold, as well as with miniature paintings.

Books became a big business in the Muslim world. In Baghdad, more than 100 bookshops lined Papersellers' Street. In addition to copies of the Qur'an, booksellers there sold many volumes of poetry and prose.

Arabs had a rich heritage of storytelling and poetry. Arab poetry often honored love, praised rulers, or celebrated wit. They often wrote epic poems, or long poems that tell a story. Prose eventually replaced poetry for recording history, special events, and traditions. Writers also composed stories in prose.

One famous collection of stories is called *A Thousand and One Nights*. Also known as *Arabian Nights*, this book gathered stories that originally came from many places, including India and Persia, as well as elsewhere in the Middle East. In the book, a wife tells her husband a new tale each night. The stories take place in Muslim cities and in places such as China, Egypt, and India. Later, a European translator added tales that were not part of the medieval Arabic collection. Among these added tales are those about Aladdin's magic lamp, Ali Baba, and Sinbad the Sailor, which remain well-known today.

As in medieval Europe, bookmaking was an art in the Muslim world. This Qur'an from around the 13th century shows the elaborate letters and gold decorations that were placed on the Muslim's holy book.

Muslim literature was enriched by Sufism, or Islamic mysticism. This type of religious practice involves intense personal experiences of God, in addition to the regular performance of rituals. Sufis longed to draw close to God in their everyday lives and inspired commoners on the frontier of the Muslim world to convert. One way to express their love and devotion was through poetry filled with vivid images and beautiful language. Rabi'a, a poet of the 8th century, shared her feelings in this verse: "But your door is open to those who call upon you. My Lord, each lover is now alone with his beloved. And I am alone with Thee."

A 13th-century Sufi poet, Rumi, had an enormous influence on Islamic mysticism. Rumi wrote a long religious poem in Persian that filled six volumes. Pilgrims still travel to his tomb in Turkey.

9. Art and Music

Muslims created many forms of art and music. In this section, you'll look at four types of artistic expression in the medieval Islamic world.

Geometric and Floral Design Muslims earned fame for their decorative arts. Early in the history of Islam, Muslims did not favor the use of images of humans or animals in religious art. Instead, artists referenced shapes and patterns found in nature and geometry to create marvelous designs and decorations.

Art sometimes was religious, as in the elaborately illuminated manuscripts of the Qur'an. But artists and craftspeople also applied their talents to everyday items like plates, candlesticks, glassware, and clothing. They decorated the walls and other features of mosques and palaces with intricate designs.

Arabic calligraphy and arabesque designs are featured in the decoration on the inside of the Selimiye Mosque, built in 1575. The script on the walls, geometric shapes, and intricate nature-inspired details are all elements of medieval Muslim art.

A type of design called *arabesque* took its beauty from the natural world. In arabesque, artists crafted stems, leaves, flowers, and tendrils (threadlike parts of plants) into elegant patterns that were repeated over and over. Artists carved, painted, and wove intricate arabesque designs into objects both large and small, including metal boxes, ceramic bowls, tiles, carpets, and even entire walls.

Artists also used geometric shapes in their designs, as circles, triangles, squares, and hexagons had special meaning to Muslims. Artists used simple tools—rulers and compasses—to create abstract designs from these shapes. This basic design was then repeated and combined to create a complex pattern.

Calligraphy For Muslims, the highest form of decorative art was calligraphy, the art of beautiful handwriting. When Muslims began copying the Qur'an, they used calligraphy to artistically record the words of God. Skilled calligraphers have been honored as great artists in different periods of Islamic history.

Calligraphers used sharpened reeds or bamboo dipped in ink to write on parchment and paper. Some forms of calligraphy had letters with angles. Most featured round letters and cursive writing, in which the script flowed, and letters within words were connected.

In addition to copying the Qur'an, artists used calligraphy to decorate everyday items. They put elegantly written lines of poetry on pottery, tiles, and swords, while bands of calligraphy trimmed the borders of fabric. Calligraphy even adorned coins, which sometimes featured verses from the Qur'an.

Verses of the Qur'an also decorated mosques. Sometimes, the holy verses were engraved along the tops of exterior walls, or they circled the inside dome of the mosque.

Textiles Manufactured fabrics, or textiles, had long been important to Arab people as practical items and as trade goods. Muslims in medieval times brought great artistry to making textiles. Weavers wove wool, linen, silk, and cotton into cloth, and then dyed it in vivid colors. Valuable cloths sometimes featured long bands of inscriptions or designs showing important events. Fabrics were also embroidered, often with gold thread.

As is still often the case today, clothes showed rank, and served as status symbols in the Muslim world. The caliph and his court wore robes made of the most valuable materials. Fine textiles served as awnings and carpets in the royal palace.

Music in Muslim Spain There were several centers of music in the Islamic world, including Baghdad and Damascus. Persian musical styles were very influential. But in Cordoba, Spain, a unique style developed that blended elements of Arab and native Spanish cultures.

A key figure in this cultural innovation was Ziryab, a talented musician and singer from Baghdad. In 822, Ziryab re-settled in Cordoba where he established Europe's first conservatory, or music school. Musicians from many different social classes came to Cordoba to learn from the great Ziryab. Many of his students were then hired as entertainers at royal courts in other parts of the world.

Singing was an essential part of Muslim Spain's musical culture. Musicians and poets worked together to create songs about love, nature, and the glory of the empire. Vocalists performed the songs accompanied by such instruments as drums, flutes, and lutes. Although this music is lost today, it undoubtedly influenced later musical forms in Europe and North Africa.

Calligraphy was one form of art that was prominent throughout the medieval Muslim world. Here, calligraphy decorates a column from the Alhambra palace, located in Granada, Spain.

10. Recreation

Recreation was also part of medieval Islamic culture. Two favorite pastimes that Muslims helped popularize were polo and chess.

Polo Muslims first learned about the game of polo from the Persians. Polo is a sport in which teams on horseback use mallets (long wooden hammers) to strike a ball through a goal. Muslims looked at horses as status symbols, and polo quickly became popular among the wealthy. Muslims adapted and refined the game of polo, and today, the game is enjoyed all over the world.

Chess The game of chess was probably invented in India. Persians introduced the game to the Muslim world in the 600s. It quickly became popular at all levels of society. Caliphs invited chess champions to their palaces to play in matches. Players enjoyed the **intellectual** challenge that chess presented.

Chess is a battle of wits in which players move pieces on a board according to a set of complex rules. Each player commands a small army of pieces, one of which is the king. The goal is to checkmate the opponent's king. *Checkmate* means that the king cannot move without being captured.

As with polo, Muslims adapted and improved the game of chess. They spread it across Muslim lands and introduced it to Europe. Chess remains one of the world's most popular board games.

This illustration shows two men playing chess. The board is shown flipped up so that readers could analyze the players' positions in the game.

Muslim people greatly influenced the course of history as they traveled from place to place, carrying cultural influences and goods between Asia and Europe.

In this lesson, you learned about many contributions Muslims have made to world civilization. In a variety of fields, Islamic culture has left a lasting mark.

The Flowering of Islamic Civilization Arab conquests created a vast Muslim empire. Although the empire did not last as a political unit, Islamic civilization thrived. Muslim rulers built great cities. Cultural diffusion occurred due to the location of Muslim lands where trade routes connected Asia and Europe. This allowed a flow of new ideas.

Architecture, Scholarship, Learning, Science, and Technology Muslims made a number of advances in city building, architecture, technology, and the sciences. Muslim cities became important centers of culture and scholarship, where ancient learning could be preserved and shared. Scientists very accurately measured the circumference of Earth and studied subjects such as logic, zoology, and astronomy.

Geography, Navigation, Mathematics, and Medicine Muslim scientists built on the work of Indians and Greeks, adapting and improving devices such as the compass and astrolabe. Muslim mathematicians developed a new type of math called algebra. Doctors, too, improved on ancient knowledge. Many of these advances had a major influence on Europe.

Bookmaking, Literature, Art, Music, and Recreation Having learned paper making from the Chinese, Muslims created beautiful books. Writers composed works of both poetry and prose. The religious poetry of Sufis celebrated the love of God. Muslim artists and crafts- people created distinctive forms of decorative art. A unique style of music developed that combined Arabic and Spanish influences. Two of medieval Muslims' favorite pastimes, polo and chess, are still enjoyed around the world.

History at the Dinner Table

Books, movies, and even computer games can reveal a lot about past cultures and civilizations. You can also learn from what is on the dinner table. Both the foods we eat and the ways that we eat them have roots in the past. Nearly every culture has contributed to world cuisine, or cooking. What are some of the foods and related traditions that can be found in Middle Eastern cultures?

Many of the foods we eat today, as well as spices such as these, originally came from or through the Middle East. This area was connected to many trade routes, which allowed Middle Eastern chefs to cook with a variety of foreign ingredients.

Al-Mahdi was a famous Muslim poet and singer who lived in the 800s. He was the uncle of Caliph al-Ma'mun who ruled the Abbasid Empire from the capital city of Baghdad. Al-Ma'mun invited his uncle to live at his court. As a gourmet, or a person who loves fine food, al-Mahdi took charge of planning the caliph's feasts.

The chefs of the court had an amazing variety of meats, grains, fruits, and vegetables in their kitchens and storerooms. The geography of the Middle East was ideal for growing certain kinds of food. The climate was temperate and the growing season was long. Fig and date trees thrived. Their fruits appealed to people because they were naturally sweet and kept relatively well. Watermelons, oranges, limes, lemons, bananas, mangoes, apricots, plantains, and apples were abundant. Vegetables, such as eggplants, artichokes, and spinach, were also plentiful.

Foods from Other Lands

The Middle East was at the crossroads of several major trade routes that connected Asia and the Mediterranean world. Because of its location, al-Mahdi and the caliph's chefs were able to serve many dishes from other lands. They had melons shipped from Europe in metal boxes filled with snow, like modern coolers, to preserve the fresh fruit. They served jams and fruit preserves from around Southern Asia. They ate eggplant and sweetened recipes with sugar, both of which came from India.

Many of the foods they served at the royal court in Baghdad had arrived there as a result of cultural diffusion. This is the process by which foods, songs, stories, poems, plants, animals, and other cultural features move from one region to another. Cultural diffusion enriches civilizations all over the world.

Middle Easterners were exposed to Persian food, and eventually began using some the same spices and ingredients. This influence has carried on to present day, as shown by this meal in Sanna, Yemen.

Caliph al-Ma'mun's table was so varied because, for many years, Muslim merchants imported foods from Africa and Asia. When Muslims conquered Persia, they discovered that the Persians had many delicious recipes. Bit by bit, Muslims adopted them. By the time of Caliph al-Ma'mun, people in Muslim lands ate Persian dishes all the time. They cooked stews that combined lamb with vegetables, herbs, and spices. They baked using a tandoor oven, which is cylinder-shaped and creates a steady, high, even heat.

One imported food that became very important to the Middle Eastern diet was sugar. Originally, Muslim merchants brought it from India, but farmers quickly mastered the art of growing sugar cane. By the 13th century, Middle Easterners improved methods of refining sugar cane, and sugar became an essential ingredient in Middle Eastern cooking.

In addition to sugar, Muslim merchants brought home from their travels foods such as eggplants, bananas, spinach, and watermelons. Chefs then included these foods in recipes they developed.

Incorporating different cultures' food was often a process, such was the case with eggplant. During the 9th century, Muslim merchants brought eggplants from India. People hated them at first and claimed that the odd-looking vegetable had "the color of a scorpion's belly and the taste of a scorpion's sting." However, people in Muslim lands gradually developed a taste for eggplant, and it is among the main vegetables used in the region's cuisine today.

Muslim culture often requires people to eat "halal" meat that has been prepared according to a specific set of rules. Halal meat is prepared in a specific way that aligns with Islamic law.

Arab and Muslim Traditions in Food

In addition to the food of a culture, the way people eat can also reveal a lot about history. A long-standing tradition in the Muslim world, for instance, is for people to eat with their right hands. In the caliphs' time, people held food between their thumbs and first and second fingers. It was very rude to eat with the left hand. Another common custom was that people washed the food down with water flavored with mint, roses, or lemon since the Qur'an forbids drinking beer or wine.

Religion played an important role in deciding how and what Muslims ate. The Qur'an does not allow Muslims to eat pork. As a result, the most common meat during the middle ages was lamb, though people also ate some veal and chicken. Muslim butchers had to cut the meats in certain ways to ensure cleanliness. Meats prepared according to these rules were called halal, or "allowed." Halal foods are still important in Muslim culture today.

Caliph al-Ma'mun enjoyed feasts, but he was also wise enough to know that most people in Baghdad could not afford the types of food served at court. He took seriously the third Pillar of Islam, zakat, which calls for Muslims to share their wealth. One evening, al-Ma'mun went to al-Mahdi's house for dinner. Al-Mahdi served a dish made with the tongues of hundreds of small fish. The dish was delicious, but the caliph thought it was terribly wasteful. He remembered the prophet Muhammad's words that the wealthy should share with the poor. So, he ordered al-Mahdi's servants to hand out 1,000 silver pieces to needy people in Baghdad. He also gave away the expensive plate on which the dish was served.

Al-Ma'mun was not the only Muslim leader to incorporate the third Pillar of Islam into food and eating. A later caliph named al-Mutawakkil, who died in 861, also practiced this tradition. He lived in a palace next to a canal, where he one day smelled a wonderful aroma. The caliph looked out and saw that a sailor and his cook were preparing a stew on the sailor's small boat. The caliph ordered the sailor to bring the stew to him. He ate it and exclaimed that it was the best meal he had ever eaten, even though it had simple ingredients. To thank the sailor and cook, he directed his servants to fill their stewpot with silver coins.

Cuisine for the World

Stories like the one of al-Mutawakkil show that food and cooking have been central to Muslim culture for more than 1,000 years. Throughout this timespan, Middle Easterners participated in another kind of cultural diffusion. In addition to importing foods, they sent their own food to other parts of the world. For instance, when Muslims conquered Spain and Portugal during the 8th century, they introduced sugar to Europe. The word *sugar* even comes from the Arab word *al-sukkar*. Other words related to *sugar* also have an Arabic origin, including *syrup, caramel, sherbet,* and *candy*. Muslims also introduced eggplants, watermelons, rice, lemons, and other vegetables and fruits to Europe.

Another food that peoples of the Middle East introduced was pita bread, which is common in the United States today. Pita bread is baked without yeast so that it doesn't rise, remaining flat. In an American restaurant today, you also might eat falafel, which is a fried ball or patty made of chickpeas and flavored with various spices. A popular dip is the Middle Eastern hummus, also made from chickpeas.

The Cultural Diffusion Continues

Today, Middle Easterners still exchange foods with the rest of the world. In 2004, a Jordanian man named Fadi Jaber visited the United States. While there, he ate a cupcake. In 2007, he started selling cupcakes in Jordan, his native country in the Middle East. Fadi had to educate some of his customers, who thought that the cupcakes were muffins. But no matter what people called them, they flew off the shelves. Soon, Jaber opened shops in Dubai in the United Arab Emirates and in Beirut, the capital and largest city in Lebanon. Shops that sell only cupcakes first became popular in the United States and spread to Australia, South Korea, Italy, Germany—and also to the Middle East. Jaber brought a sweet treat back to his homeland, completing a cycle of cultural diffusion that began many centuries ago.

After Middle Easterners were introduced to sugar by the Persians, they eventually introduced it to parts of Europe. This French manuscript from the 15th century shows someone baking "sugar bread."

Cairo (1300–1500)

Cairo was one of the major cities in medieval Afroeurasia. It was at the center of a network of roads, sea routes, and cities that supported trade and pilgrimages in the Islamic world and beyond. Although it was not on the sea, it was on the Nile River, which flowed to the Mediterranean Sea. Also, it was connected to the Red Sea by canal. Cairo's location placed it at the heart of multiple trade networks.

Trade and Exchange

Being in the center of Afroeurasia made Cairo an important center of exchange, a point from which goods, ideas, technologies, and even diseases spread. For example, paper-making technologies arrived in Cairo from China in the 700s and then moved on to Europe in the following centuries. Similarly, foods that passed through Cairo, such as oranges, eggplants, spinach, and melons, were traded and spread along exchange routes. Additionally, Cairo was the source of some products. Local merchants exported goods such as textiles and sugar.

Merchants from across the Islamic world traveled through Cairo as they moved between the great cities of the world, such as Córdoba, Damascus, and Quanzhou. Although most people in the city and region were Muslim, the area was also home to Jews and Christians. Both groups participated in trade, but they had to pay a special tax to the government. Jewish merchants traded freely in the Islamic world. They set up communities throughout Afroeurasia that supported trade connections.

Cairo was known as the point of exchange for items desired throughout Afroeurasia, including silk and porcelain from China, spices from Southwest Asia, and gold from West Africa. However, it was also the point of exchange for something far less luxurious: the bubonic plague. In the 1300s, the bubonic plague, or the Black Death, killed millions. It spread across Asia along trade routes and then to Europe and the Muslim world, which each lost about one-third of their populations.

Goods, such as spices from Southwest Asia, passed through Cairo on their way to their final destination in Europe, Africa, or the Middle East.

The Black Death was a bacterial infection spread by infected fleas from small animals. Agnolo di Tura, who chronicled life in Siena, Italy, wrote about the outbreak that began there in May 1348.

It was a cruel and horrible thing . . . It seemed to almost everyone that one became stupefied by seeing the pain. . . . one who did not see such horribleness can be called blessed. And the victims died almost immediately. They would swell beneath their armpits and in their groins, and fall over dead while talking. . . . this illness seemed to strike through the breath and sight. . . . And none could be found to bury the dead . . . in many places in Siena great pits were dug and piled deep with the multitude of dead. And they died by the hundreds both day and night, and all were thrown in those ditches and covered over with earth. And as soon as those ditches were filled more were dug.

. . .

There was no one who wept for any death, for all awaited death. And so many died that all believed that it was the end of the world. And no medicine or any other defense availed. . . . so that in all it is found that in the city and suburbs of Siena 80,000 persons died. . . . and there remained in Siena (alone) less than 10,000 men.

Traders passed through this gateway in Cairo to meet with others and exchange their wares.

In his journal, Ibn Battuta, the Moroccan traveler and scholar, recounted a three-day period in which all of Damascus was told to avoid food prepared in the market to prevent the spread of plague. This was a three-day fast for many. During these days, fewer than 2,000 people died per day in Damascus, but in Cairo, around 24,000 people died each day.

Al-Maqrizi, an Egyptian historian, described the effects of the death and destruction he saw in Cairo. Many neighborhoods were filled with vacant homes, but the belongings of the dead remained untouched. There was no one left to take them. Similarly, there were no farmers to harvest the crops. Al-Maqrizi wrote:

> . . . the time of the harvest came when most of the farmers had died, and . . . soldiers and their young men went for the harvest, and called whoever [could] harvest [to] take what they harvest[ed]. . . . they used their horses and their hands, and in most cases they were unable to harvest a lot of the crops so they left [them].

During this period, the markets of Egypt were disrupted. There was no one to buy clothes and perfume. Like humans, livestock were sickened and killed by the plague. Those who survived experienced reduced earnings and an economic recession. The goods that were most in demand were wrapping materials for the dead and coffins.

In the 14th century, Ibn Battuta spent 30 years traveling through the Middle East, West and North Africa, and Asia. He chronicled his adventures in *The Travels of Ibn Battuta A.D. 1325–1354, Vol. 1.*

The Influence of Islam

The Islamic world was a network of cities that was tied together not only by trade but by a common religion. One aspect of Islam that brought many to Cairo was the hajj, one of the Five Pillars of Islam. The hajj is the yearly pilgrimage to the holy city of Mecca that Muslims are supposed to perform once during their life. Many Muslims traveled through Cairo on their way to Mecca.

Pilgrims and merchants followed the same routes through the region. To prevent robberies and attacks, they would often travel together because it was safer to travel in large groups known as caravans.

On journeys to Mecca and elsewhere in the Islamic world, religious institutions assisted travelers. These institutions, such as funduqs (FUHN-duhks—hotels and business centers), caravanserais (kair-uh-VAN-tsuh-rize—hotels on the road), souqs (SOOOKS—markets), and madrassas (muh-DRASS-uhz—Islamic colleges), were a common link throughout the Islamic world. Moreover, favorable government policies helped travelers and merchants and enabled these institutions to succeed. For example, souqs were initially temporary. Merchants set up their goods for display and sale. Later, rulers created permanent markets and rented space to merchants. Similarly, rulers established caravanserais so that there would be shelters for people and their animals and goods on the road. (Caravanserais were built a day's travel apart so that caravans would have a place to stop each night.)

Although Cairo was located near major waterways in the middle of Afroeurasia, these Islamic institutions helped Cairo become a major center of exchange. They created an environment that welcomed travelers, helped merchants conduct business, and protected the safety of travelers on the road.

Pilgrims and merchants traveled together, often on camels, in caravans. People traveling in large groups were less likely to be attacked or robbed on their journey.

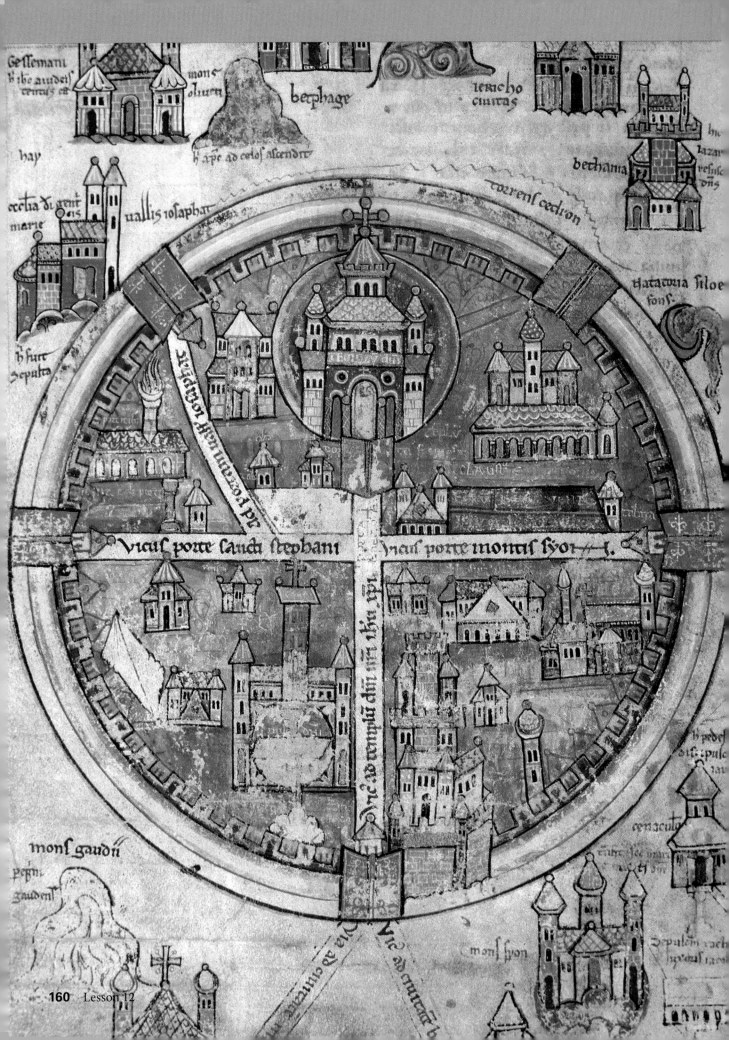

Lesson 12

From the Crusades to New Muslim Empires

How did the Crusades affect the lives of Christians, Muslims, and Jews?

Introduction

During the Middle Ages, a series of religious wars, called the Crusades, took place. The Crusades were launched by European Christian nations to reclaim Jerusalem and other holy sites in the Middle East from Muslims.

Christians mounted these religious wars beginning in 1096. A major purpose was to gain control of Palestine, the ancient homeland of Jews and the place where Jesus was crucified. The spiritual heart of Palestine was the city of Jerusalem, a city that was, and is, sacred to Jews, Christians, and Muslims alike.

In the 11th century, Palestine came under the rule of a rising Muslim power, the Seljuk Turks. The advances of the Seljuk Turks into Byzantine territory, and their ill treatment of Christians, alarmed the Byzantine emperors. In 1076, the Seljuks took Jerusalem. For several years, emperors sought help from Pope Urban II. In 1095, the pope called on Christians to go on a religious war to turn back the Seljuks and win control of Jerusalem and the surrounding area. The next year, the first armies set out from Europe.

Muslims were not the only targets of these religious wars. Europeans also mounted violence against Jews and Christian heretics. Religious wars were waged in Europe and North Africa, as well as the Middle East.

In this lesson, you will read the story of these religious wars and explore their effects on Christians, Muslims, and Jews. You will also learn how new Muslim empires arose after the wars, and how Islam continued to spread to new parts of the world.

Social Studies Vocabulary

anti-Semitism

Crusades

Holy Land

Inquisition

segregation

shah

sultan

◀ This 12th-century map shows the city of Jerusalem, which is holy to Jews, Christians, and Muslims.

Jerusalem is still considered a sacred place to Christians, Jews, and Muslims alike. Threat over this city paved the way for the Crusades.

Crusades a series of religious and political wars launched by European Christians to reclaim Jerusalem and other holy sites from Muslims

sultan the supreme ruler of a Muslim state

Holy Land the area between Egypt and Syria that was the ancient homeland of Jews and the place where Jesus Christ had lived; also called Palestine

1. Events Leading Up to the Crusades

Why did European Christians begin the religious wars, or Crusades, at the end of the 11th century? To answer this question, we need to look at what was happening in Muslim lands at the time.

During the 10th century, the Seljuk Turks established a new Muslim dynasty. The Turks were a Central Asian people who had been migrating into Muslim lands for centuries. The Seljuks were named for a Turkish chieftain who converted to Islam in the mid-10th century. In 1055, his descendants took control of the Abbasid dynasty's capital of Baghdad in what was then Persia, meaning that a Seljuk sultan now ruled the old Abbasid Empire. The Seljuks were eager to expand their territory. Moving westward, they took Syria and Palestine from the Fatimid dynasty. They also overran much of Anatolia (also called Asia Minor), which was part of the Byzantine Empire. In 1071, the Seljuks defeated a large Byzantine army at Manzikert in present-day Turkey. The Seljuk advance alarmed Christians in Europe, who feared for the safety and property of Christians living to the east, as well as the control they held over western lands. The Seljuks' power seemed to threaten the Byzantine Empire itself. Christians also worried about the Holy Land, especially the city of Jerusalem, where the Seljuks sometimes treated Christians and their holy sites with intolerance.

Jerusalem was, and still is, a sacred city to Jews, Christians, and Muslims. It was the spiritual capital of the Jews, where their great Temple had once stood, and had been their political capital in ancient times. For Christians, it was the city where Jesus was crucified and arose from the dead. For Muslims, it was where Muhammad ascended to heaven during his Night Journey.

Jerusalem and the rest of Palestine first came under Muslim rule during the Arab conquests of the 7th century. Muslims built a shrine in Jerusalem, the Dome of the Rock, to mark where they believed that the Night Journey had occurred. Under Muslim rule, Jews, Christians, and Muslims all lived together. People of all three faiths made pilgrimages to Jerusalem and built houses of worship there. But, depending on the policies of various Muslim rulers, non-Muslims' rights and freedoms varied from time to time, and some Muslim rulers allowed the destruction of important Christian churches.

After the Seljuks took control of Palestine, political turmoil made travel unsafe. Tales began reaching Europe of highway robbers attacking and even killing Christian pilgrims. Christians feared they would no longer be able to visit Jerusalem and other sacred sites in the Holy Land. More and more, Christians began to carry weapons and travel in groups when they made the journey to Jerusalem. Together, with concern over the Seljuk threat to Christian lands in Europe, this fear helped pave the way for the Crusades.

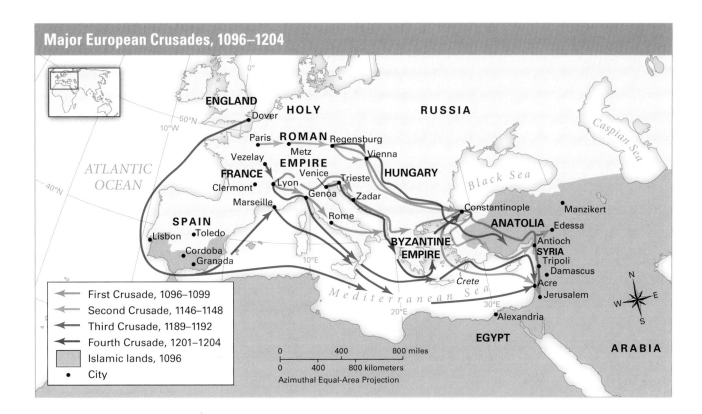

Major European Crusades, 1096–1204

Legend:
- First Crusade, 1096–1099
- Second Crusade, 1146–1148
- Third Crusade, 1189–1192
- Fourth Crusade, 1201–1204
- Islamic lands, 1096
- City

0   400   800 miles
0 400 800 kilometers
Azimuthal Equal-Area Projection

2. The Story of the Crusades

The Crusades began as a **response** to the threat posed by the Seljuks. Many emperors appealed to Pope Urban II for help. By 1095, the Seljuks had advanced to within 100 miles of the Byzantine capital, Constantinople.

In response, the pope invited nobles and Church leaders to attend a council in Clermont, France where he called for a crusade to drive out the Muslims and reclaim Jerusalem. He promised a forgiveness of sins to all who joined the fight. French-speaking nobles quickly organized armies to fight in the Holy Land. In addition to trained knights, thousands of townspeople, craftsmen, and peasants joined in the crusade.

Throughout the Crusades, the Christian faith inspired many to put on the red cross, worn by Crusaders as a symbol of their mission, and join the fight. Many viewed crusading as an act of love and devotion to God. Others believed that by joining the Crusades, their sins would be forgotten. Noble families often spent their own money to embark on the Crusades, without hope of regaining their losses.

The First Crusade (1096–1099) Several European nobles led the First Crusade. Around 100,000 Crusaders fought their way through Anatolia and headed south toward Palestine. In June of 1098, the Crusaders laid siege to the city of Antioch, in Syria, which was protected by a ring of walls. Soon the Crusaders found a way over the walls, and Antioch fell to the Christians.

For more than 200 years, in four major Crusades, Europeans and Muslims clashed over control of the Holy Land and the nearby territory. In the end, Muslims retained control of the area.

In 1099, the Crusaders surrounded Jerusalem and scaled the city walls. After a month of fighting, the city surrendered. The victorious Crusaders killed most of the people who had fought against them. With Jerusalem taken, most of the Crusaders returned home. Some, however, stayed behind. They established four Crusader kingdoms in Palestine, Syria, and modern-day Lebanon and Turkey.

The Second Crusade (1146–1148) The Crusaders owed their early victories, in part, to a lack of unity among Muslim groups. When the Crusades began, the Seljuk Empire was already crumbling into a number of smaller states. Muslims had trouble joining together to fight the invaders.

When Muslims started to band together, they were able to fight back more effectively. In 1144, they captured Edessa, the capital of the northernmost crusader kingdom. Christians responded by mounting the Second Crusade.

That Crusade ended in failure. An army from Germany was badly defeated in Anatolia. A second army, led by the king of France, arrived in Jerusalem in 1148. About 50,000 Crusaders marched on the city of Damascus, which was on the way to Edessa. Muslims from Edessa came to the city's aid and beat back the Crusaders. Soon after this defeat, the French army went home, ending the Second Crusade.

Richard I, king of England, led the Third Crusade to try to regain Christian control of Jerusalem from Muslims. He later signed a peace treaty with Salah al-Din over the Jerusalem territory.

The Third Crusade (1189–1192) Over the next few decades, Muslims in the Middle East increasingly came under common leadership. By the 1180s, the great sultan Salah al-Din (SAL-eh ahl-DEEN), called Saladin by Europeans, had formed the largest Muslim empire since the Seljuks. Salah al-Din united Egypt, Syria, and other lands to the east. He led a renewed fight against the Crusaders in the Holy Land and quickly recovered most of Palestine. In 1187, his armies captured Jerusalem.

The loss of Jerusalem shocked Europeans and sparked the Third Crusade. King Richard I of England, known as "the Lionheart," was one of the European leaders who led the fight against Salah al-Din.

In 1191, Richard's army forced the surrender of the Palestinian town of Acre (AH-kreh). Afterward, arrangements were made between the two sides to exchange prisoners. Salah al-Din tried to stall the completion of the exchange, and Richard, who grew impatient, ordered the deaths of all 2,700 of his Muslim prisoners.

Richard then fought his way toward Jerusalem, but his army was not strong enough to take the city. Salah al-Din's forces had also grown weaker. In September 1192, the two leaders signed a peace treaty. The Crusaders kept a chain of cities along the coast of Palestine, and Muslims agreed to let Christian pilgrims enter Jerusalem.

Later Crusades The Crusades continued for centuries. Some Crusades were popular movements of poor people, rather than organized military campaigns. In 1212, for example, thousands of young peasants from France and Germany marched in a Children's Crusade. Few, if any, ever reached the Holy Land. Some made it to European port cities, only to be sold into slavery by merchants. Some returned home. Many disappeared without a trace.

None of the later Crusades succeeded in recapturing Jerusalem. Muslims, meanwhile, were gaining back the land they had lost and took Acre, the last Crusader city, in 1291. This victory ended some 200 years of Christian kingdoms in the Holy Land.

The Reconquista Crusaders fought against Muslims in Europe and North Africa, as well as in the Middle East. One important series of wars was called the *Reconquista* (ree-con-KEE-stah), which means "reconquest" in Spanish. For several decades, Christian kingdoms launched these wars to retake the Iberian Peninsula from Muslims. The Iberian Peninsula is a region in southwestern Europe that contains Spain and Portugal.

The Umayyads had established a Muslim dynasty in Spain in the 8th century, where Muslims, Jews, and Christians lived together. However, non-Muslims were treated differently, including having to pay a special tax.

Over time, Christian rulers in northern Iberia chipped away at Muslim lands. The pace of reconquest quickened after the Umayyad caliphate in Cordoba broke up into rival kingdoms around 1002. In 1085, Christians gained a key victory by capturing Toledo, in central Spain.

Muslims gradually gave up more and more territory. In 1039, Portugal became an independent Christian kingdom. By 1248, only the kingdom of Granada, in southern Spain, remained in Muslim hands.

Many Jews and Muslims remained in areas ruled by Christians. In the late 1400s, Queen Isabella and King Ferdinand wanted to unite Spain as a Catholic country. They used the **Inquisition,** a Roman Catholic court, against Muslims and Jews, as well as those who claimed to have converted to Christianity. Judges, called inquisitors, sometimes used torture to find out whether supposed converts were practicing their old religion. Thousands of people were burned at the stake.

In 1492, Granada fell to Ferdinand and Isabella, ending Muslim rule in Spain. In the same year, Jews were ordered to become Catholics or leave the country. Roughly 170,000 Jews left their homes forever. Many found refuge in Muslim lands, including in Constantinople, now called Istanbul, the capital of the Ottoman Empire. Muslims remained in Spain, but many were forced to become Catholics. Spain expelled remaining Muslims beginning in 1609, ending any **cooperation** among these groups and Christians in Spain.

Later Crusades, such as the Children's Crusade, were movements by poor people, rather than organized military events led by monarchs or nobles. None of these later crusades, however, were successful in reclaiming Jerusalem.

Inquisition a judicial body established by the Roman Catholic Church to combat forms of religious error

3. Christians and the Crusades

The religious wars were a costly ordeal, although Crusaders who participated were promised rewards in the afterlife. But European Christians also reaped many benefits from the Crusades.

Impact on Christians as a Group Crusaders suffered all the terrible effects of war. Many were wounded or killed in battle, and those that were not often died of disease and the hardships of travel.

The impact of the Crusades reached far beyond those who fought, however. The Crusades brought many **economic** changes to Europe. For instance, Crusaders needed a way to pay for supplies, a need that increased the use of money in Europe. As a result, some knights began performing banking functions, such as making loans or investments. Monarchs established tax systems to raise funds for Crusades.

The Crusades changed society, as well. Monarchs grew more powerful, as nobles and knights left home to fight in the Middle East. The increasing power of monarchs weakened feudalism.

Contact with Middle Eastern cultures had an impact on Christians' way of life. In the Holy Land, Christians learned about new foods and other goods. They dressed in clothing made of muslin, a cotton fabric from Persia. They developed a taste for melons, apricots, sesame seeds, and carob beans, and used spices like pepper. After Crusaders returned home with these goods, European merchants earned enormous profits by trading in them.

New foods and fabrics from Arabian seaports were introduced to Europe through the travels and trading of the Christian Crusaders. Bringing in new imports to Europe is one way that the Crusades influenced Christian life.

The Experiences of Individuals Recall that Richard I of England led the Third Crusade. Richard was devoted to the Christian cause and to knightly ideals of courage and honor. Both ruthless and brave, Richard spent most of his reign fighting in the Crusades and taxed his people heavily to pay for his armies.

Anna Comnena, the daughter of a Byzantine emperor, wrote about her experiences during the First Crusade. She expressed mixed feelings about the Crusaders, for although she respected them as Christians, she also realized that many were dangerous. Comnena questioned whether all of the Crusaders were truly fighting for God, or if some were merely seeking wealth, land, and glory in battle. Her suspicions proved to be justified. During the Fourth Crusade, a force of Crusaders invaded and looted Constantinople, then under Christian control.

4. Muslims and the Crusades

The Crusades brought fewer benefits to Muslims than they did to Christians. While Muslims succeeded in driving the Crusaders from the Middle East, they also lost lands on the Iberian Peninsula. In addition, Muslim societies were among the most advanced in the world, so Muslims had less to gain from contact with Christians.

Impact on Muslims as a Group The Crusades were a terrible ordeal for many Muslims. Many lost their lives in battles and the conquests of Middle Eastern cities. Crusaders also destroyed Muslim property in Jerusalem and other communities.

Muslims did gain exposure to some new weapons and military ideas during the Crusades. Like Europeans, they began to adopt standing, or permanent, armies. Muslim merchants, especially in Syria and Egypt, earned riches from trade with Europe. This money helped to fund building projects, such as new mosques and religious schools. The Crusades also brought political changes, as Muslims united to fight their common foe. The Ayyubid dynasty founded by Salah al-Din ruled Egypt and parts of Syria and Arabia until 1250.

The Experiences of Individuals Salah al-Din was the greatest Muslim leader during the Crusades. His experiences taught him many valuable lessons. As a boy in Damascus during the Second Crusade, he saw that Muslims needed to defend themselves and Islam. As a soldier, he realized that Muslims had to be organized and to cooperate with one another. He unified Muslim groups under his strong leadership. Along with his military skills, Salah al-Din also was famed in the west for his courtesy.

Usamah ibn-Munqidh also grew up during the time of the Crusades. Believing it was the will of God, Usamah fought against the Crusaders. Usamah wrote a valuable account of the Crusades from a Muslim viewpoint that told how Muslims and Christians observed, and sometimes admired, one another. He also described how the Muslims were willing to give their lives to protect their families, lands, and property from the Crusaders.

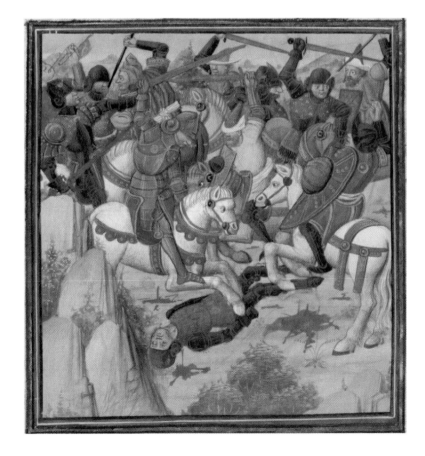

Salah al-Din, who many considered to be the greatest Muslim leader during the Crusades, founded the Ayyubid dynasty and ruled as the sultan of Egypt. This 15th-century manuscript shows a battle between the Christians and Muslims under Salah al-Din's rule.

5. Jews and the Crusades

Violence and intolerance during the Crusades made targets, not only of Christians who did not strictly follow Church teachings, but especially of non-Christians. In this climate, Jews suffered enormously. Some Church leaders spoke out strongly against ill treatment of Jews and warned Christians that the only aim of the Crusades was to reclaim the Holy Land. However, the Crusades also led to **dramatically** worsened lives for Jews in Europe.

Impact on Jews as a Group During the First Crusade, European Jews suffered a series of violent persecutions. As Crusaders crossed northern France and Germany, some of them murdered whole communities of Jews. They destroyed synagogues and holy books. They looted homes and businesses. Some Crusaders tortured Jews to make them accept Christianity.

In Europe, anti-Semitism, or hostility to or discrimination against Jews, spread among noncrusaders, as well. Religious prejudice was mixed with resentment of Jews who were wealthy bankers and traders. Violent riots and massacres broke out in a number of European cities.

By the end of the Crusades, the Jews' place in European society had deteriorated. Jews could not hold public office, and Christians took over trading businesses that had been run by Jews. In 1290, England expelled all Jews, and France followed suit in 1394. Many Jews relocated to Eastern Europe.

The segregation of Jews spread throughout Europe during the 14th and 15th centuries. Jews were forced to live in crowded neighborhoods called ghettos, which were typically separated from the rest of the town or city by walls and gates.

The Experiences of Individuals A German Jew named Eliezer ben Nathan lived during the First Crusade. He wrote about the violent destruction of his community by Christians. Eliezer told of Jews who killed their families and themselves rather than give up their religion. He admired their intense devotion but wondered how God could let so many Jews die. He also expressed his hatred for the Crusaders.

Eleazar ben Judah, a Jewish scholar, also lived in Germany. During the Second Crusade, he and other Jews were forced to flee their town and leave behind their belongings, including their holy books.

Several years later, two Crusaders attacked Eleazar's home and killed his wife and children. This horrible event led him to wonder if his people would be able to survive in Europe. As a Jewish leader in the city of Worms, he continued to preach love for all humanity, despite his suffering.

During the Crusades, there was violence against Jews in Europe and elsewhere. Many Jews relocated to avoid these ruthless persecutions.

anti-Semitism hostility or discrimination against Jews

segregation the forced separation of one group from the rest of a community

6. The Mongol Invasion

As you have learned, Muslims succeeded in driving the Crusaders from the Holy Land. Even as the Crusades were taking place, other changes were happening in Muslim lands. By the mid-1200s, Muslims were facing a greater threat than the European Crusaders—the Mongols.

The Mongols were a nomadic people whose homeland was north of China. In the 13th century, Mongols began wars of conquest under their leader, Genghis Khan (JENG-giss KAHN). After attacking northern China, Genghis Khan turned his sights westward, and the Mongols swept across Central Asia, destroying cities and farmland. Hundreds of thousands of Muslims were killed, and those who survived were often carried off to Mongolia as slaves.

Under Genghis Khan's successors, the Mongols built an empire that stretched across much of Asia. They defeated the Seljuk Turks in Anatolia and seized parts of Persia. In 1258, they destroyed Baghdad and killed the sultan.

This contemporary statue of Genghis Khan is located in Ulaanbaatar, the modern capital of Mongolia. Khan ruled the Mongols and led wars intending to conquer the entire world.

Farther west, Muslims were able to stop the Mongol advance. The Mamluks, whose capital was at Cairo, Egypt, led the resistance. In the mid-1200s, they had overthrown the dynasty begun by Salah al-Din. In 1260, they defeated the Mongols in an important battle in Palestine. The Mamluks continued to rule Palestine, Egypt, Syria, Arabia, and parts of Anatolia until 1517.

The Mongols still ruled a huge empire in Asia, including China. Toward the end of the 1200s, in some places they began converting to Islam, which helped bring unity to their empire. The Mongols made Persian the language of government. They rebuilt the cities they had destroyed and encouraged learning, the arts, and trade.

However, the empire suffered from in-fighting among rival local rulers who controlled different regions, leaving it badly weakened by the mid-1300s.

Mongol leader Timur Lang led an invasion of Anatolia in 1402. His armies prevented the Ottoman Turks from advancing eastward.

7. New Muslim Empires and the Expansion of Islam

New empires arose in Muslim lands after the decline of the Mongols' power. Islam also continued its spread to new lands.

The Ottoman Empire In 1299, a Turk named Osman I started the Ottoman dynasty in northern Anatolia. The Ottomans quickly conquered new lands in Anatolia and southeastern Europe.

The Ottomans' advance to the east was stopped for a time by a new enemy—Timur (TEE-moor) Lang, known to Europeans as Tamerlane. Timur came from a Mongol tribe in Central Asia, and he claimed descent from Genghis Khan.

Timur began building his own empire in the late 1300s. His armies overran much of Central Asia, including present-day Iraq, and then proceeded to invade India, Syria, and Anatolia. In 1402, Timur defeated an Ottoman army at Ankara in Anatolia. Ottoman rule was on the brink of collapse, but after Timur's death in 1405, the Ottomans regained control of their lands.

Turning back toward Europe, the Ottomans set out to expand their empire. In 1453, they captured Constantinople, bringing an end to the once powerful Byzantine Empire. The city was renamed Istanbul and became the Ottoman capital.

In the 1500s, the Ottomans destroyed the Mamluk Empire. They conquered Syria, Palestine, Egypt, and Arabia. At its height, the Ottoman Empire also took in parts of southeastern Europe, North Africa, and Persia, as well as Turkey.

The Ottomans allowed their subjects considerable freedom. Jews, Christians, and Muslims had their own local communities, called *millets*, that were allowed to govern themselves. A ruling class collected taxes and protected the sultan and the empire. In the empire's European provinces, some young Christian men were taken and then raised in the sultan's palace. After most of them were forced to convert to Islam, they joined an elite corps of soldiers and government officials known as Janissaries.

The Ottoman Empire slowly declined after about 1700. It finally came to an official end, after World War I, in 1922.

The Safavid Empire Later Ottoman expansion to the east was stopped by another Muslim power. In 1501, Muslims in Persia founded the Safavid dynasty. Their **shahs,** or rulers, soon controlled the heartlands of ancient Persia, which included modern-day Iran and parts of Iraq. Unlike the Ottomans, who were Sunni Muslims, the Safavids were Shi'ah. The two groups fought a number of wars.

The Safavids became a great power that promoted trade, the arts, and learning. Their dynasty lasted until the mid-1700s.

shah a ruler in certain Middle East lands, especially Persia (modern-day Iran)

The Mughal Empire A third Muslim empire was founded by Babur, a descendant of both Genghis Khan and Timur Lang. In 1526, Babur invaded India and founded the powerful Mughal [MOOG-uhl] Empire. The word *Mughal* is Arabic for "Mongol." Mughal emperors ruled most of India until sometime after 1700. Muslims make up the largest minority population in India today.

The Further Spread of Islam
Muslim dynasties grew up in other places, as well. For instance, Muslims in North Africa carried Islam into the region of West Africa. Pilgrims and merchants also spread Islam among peoples living around the Sahara.

Traders brought Islam across the Indian Ocean to Southeast Asia. By the late 1200s, there were Muslim kingdoms on the islands of Indonesia. Today, Indonesia has more Muslims than any other country in the world.

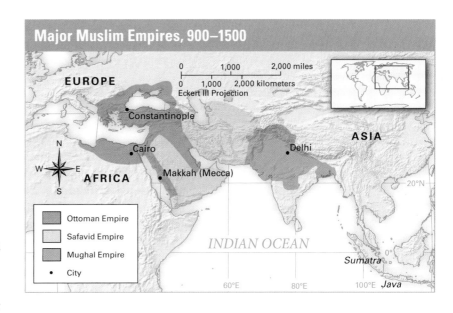

Major Muslim Empires, 900–1500

Legend:
- Ottoman Empire
- Safavid Empire
- Mughal Empire
- • City

Three Muslim empires dominated eastern and central Asia and the eastern Mediterranean for over 600 years. The Ottoman Empire lasted longest of all—until the early 20th century.

Lesson Summary

In this lesson, you learned about the series of medieval wars between European Christians and Middle Eastern Muslims over the Holy Land, known as the Crusades.

The Crusades European Christian nations began the Crusades to repel the Muslims and re-take the Holy Land. Between 1096 and 1291, a number of Crusades were fought in the Middle East. Crusaders won control of Jerusalem and set up Christian kingdoms in the region. In 1187, Muslims won back Jerusalem. By 1291, Muslims had recaptured all the Crusader cities.

Effects of the Crusades on Christians, Muslims, and Jews As a result of the Crusades, European monarchs gained power, weakening feudalism. Jews suffered great hardship, with many killed or forced to give up their homes and properties. Crusaders also waged war against Muslims in North Africa and Europe. During the Reconquista, Christians drove Muslims out of much of Europe.

The Mongol Invasion In the 13th century, the nomadic Mongols under Genghis Khan and his descendants conquered vast areas of Muslim lands and ruled much of Asia.

New Muslim Empires and the Expansion of Islam After the Crusades and Mongol invasion, the Ottoman Turks built a great Muslim empire in the Middle East and southeastern Europe. The Safavid Empire arose in what is now Iran and Iraq. The Mughals brought Muslim rule to most of India. Islam also spread to West Africa and Indonesia.

What Motivated People to Participate in the Crusades?

The Holy Land was at stake. In 1095, the Seljuk Turks were taking control of Jerusalem as well as the rest of Palestine. Acts of conquest to expand the Muslim empire had been happening for centuries. In response, European Christians stormed across Europe and Asia, causing Muslims, Jews, and Christians to react in terror. Tens of thousands of people died during the set of religious wars called the Crusades. But why did rulers, soldiers, and everyday townspeople engage in these bloody battles? You will examine a variety of primary source writings from the time and construct a claim about what motivated people to participate in the Crusades.

Many illustrations have been created of the meeting of the Council of Clermont in 1095. This is a reproduction of a medieval illustration showing Pope Urban II, on his elaborate chair, calling for knights to fight in the First Crusade. Church officials are standing by the pope.

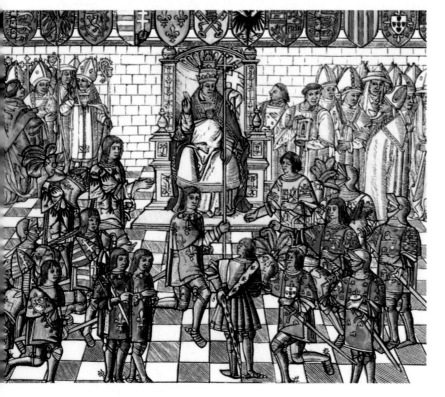

As the Seljuks advanced toward the Byzantine capital of Constantinople in 1095, the emperor of the Byzantine Empire pleaded for military assistance, a message that reached Pope Urban II. As the leader of the Roman Catholic Church, the pope called together knights and nobles to persuade them to fight in the crusade to reclaim the Holy Land.

Historical records tell us about this meeting that was held in Clermont, France, and was called the Council of Clermont. The words of Pope Urban's speech spread throughout the land and provoked thousands to join the Crusades. Here is an excerpt from an account of the speech that was written later:

> On this account I, or rather the Lord, beseech you as Christ's heralds to publish this everywhere and to persuade all people of whatever rank, foot-soldiers and knights, poor and rich, to carry aid promptly to those Christians and to destroy that vile race from the lands of our friends. I say this to those who are present, it meant also for those who are absent. Moreover, Christ commands it.

What is the pope's message in this section of the speech? What words does he use to motivate his audience to agree with his mission?

People from all walks of life ventured from home to join the Crusade armies. This letter is from a leader in the First Crusade, Stephen, Count of Blois and Chartres. A count is someone from the noble class, and legend says that this count was wealthy enough to own 365 castles. Stephen wrote letters during the Crusades that describe the conflict and his experiences.

Stephen wrote this letter to his wife, Adele, on March 29, 1098. In the letter, he describes the army of Crusaders before they successfully attacked Antioch, an ancient city in what was then Syria. What is Stephen telling his wife in this correspondence? What role does Christianity play in the situation he is describing? Based on this piece of correspondence, what are some of the reasons Stephen might feel inspired to become part of this crusade?

Stephen, Count of Blois and Chartres, To His Wife, Adele

Count Stephen to Adele, his sweetest and most amiable wife, to his dear children, and to all his vassals of all ranks—his greeting and blessing.

You may be very sure, dearest, that the messenger whom I sent to give you pleasure, left me before Antioch safe and unharmed, and through God's grace in the greatest prosperity. And already at that time, together with all the chosen army of Christ, endowed with great valor by Him, we had been continuously advancing for twenty-three weeks toward the home of our Lord Jesus. You may know for certain, my beloved, that of gold, silver and many other kind of riches I now have twice as much as your love had assigned to me when I left you. For all our princes, with the common consent of the whole army, against my own wishes, have made me up to the present time the leader, chief and director of their whole expedition.

You have certainly heard that after the capture of the city of Nicaea we fought a great battle with the perfidious Turks and by God's aid conquered them. Next we conquered for the Lord all Romania and afterwards Cappadocia. And we learned that there was a certain Turkish prince Assam, dwelling in Cappadocia . . . thither we directed our course. All his castles we conquered by force and compelled him to flee to a certain very strong castle situated on a high rock. We also gave the land of that Assam to one of our chiefs and in order that he might conquer the above-mentioned Assam, we left there with him many soldiers of Christ. Thence, continually following the wicked Turks, we drove them through the midst of Armenia, as far as the great river Euphrates. Having left all their baggage and beasts of burden on the bank, they fled across the river into Arabia.

—Stephen, Count of Blois, 1098

The First Crusade

Letters, such as the one Stephen of Blois wrote to his wife, are one type of primary source that describes details of events from the past. Historians also learn from written reports such as this one by Fulcher of Chartres in the 1100s.

Fulcher was a French chaplain who wrote reports about the First Crusade after participating in it first-hand. He accompanied Stephen of Blois into battles in southern Italy, Bulgaria, and Constantinople in 1096. A year earlier, Fulcher attended the Council of Clermont and wrote down Pope Urban II's speech to share with the public. The pope's message, that the wars were "God's will," became the emotional battle cry of the crusaders.

This excerpt from Fulcher's report tells how people responded to Pope Urban's speech at Clermont. Other eyewitnesses of the event also wrote a chronicle of the speech. However, like Fulcher's reports, these reports were written much later. How might historians use these different sources to learn about the Council of Clermont?

According to Fulcher's report, who was inspired to join the Crusade? What was the reason that people decided to engage in these battles?

The Response to Pope Urban II's Plea

. . . When these tidings were proclaimed throughout the provinces, they agreed under oath that the peace which was called the Truce should be kept mutually by all. Finally, then, many persons of every class vowed, after confession, that they were going with a pure intent whither they were ordered to go . . .

It is evident that a good intention brings about the achievement of a good work, and that good work earns the soul's salvation. For if it is good to intend well, it is still better to accomplish a good work which has been planned. Therefore the best thing one can do is to provide for the salvation of his soul by a worthy action. Let each one then plan good deeds, which by still more worthy action he will fulfil, so that he shall at length receive the never ending reward which he has earned. So Urban, a man prudent and revered, conceived a work by which later the whole universe prospered. For he restored peace and re-established the rights of the church in their pristine condition. And with a lively determination he also made an effort to drive out the pagans from the Christian lands. Therefore, since he endeavored in every way to glorify everything which was God's, almost all voluntarily submitted themselves to his paternal direction.

—Fulcher of Chartres, 1100s

Hierosolymita

Another important primary source from the Crusades comes from a German historian named Ekkehard of Aurach. He undertook the notable task of writing a history of the world, which he completed in 1101.

Then he decided to travel to Jerusalem where he learned more about the First Crusade. When he returned, he entirely rewrote the section of his book that described the Crusades and published this small section in a separate volume entitled *Hierosolymita*. This excerpt tells how the Crusaders arrived in Germany and attempted to encourage Germans, including a tribe called the Teutons, to join the cause. According to this source, how did the Germans respond to the Crusaders? What types of people joined the Crusades? What were their reasons for following other Europeans into these wars?

The Germans at first regard of the crusaders as madmen.

. . . *So it came about that almost the whole German people were, at the beginning of the expedition, quite unacquainted with the reasons for it. Consequently the many legions of horsemen who passed through their land, the hosts of people on foot, the crowds of country people, women and children, were viewed by them with contempt as persons who had altogether lost their wits.*

Those bound for the Holy Land seemed to them to be leaving the land of their birth and sacrificing what they already had for a vain hope. The promised land offered no certainty but danger, yet they deserted their own possessions in a greedy struggle for those of others. Nevertheless, although our people are far more arrogant than others, the fury of the Teutons finally gave way in view of the divine mercy, and after they had thoroughly discussed the matter with the multitude of pilgrims, they too inclined their hearts.

—Ekkehard of Aurach, early 1100s

Compare the primary sources, and describe how they are similar to one another. Then describe what is uniquely different about each one. Do you think these sources provide a complete picture of the motivations for joining the Crusades? What other information would be helpful? Write an argument that describes what motivated people to participate in the Crusades. Support your argument with these primary sources, and also include a discussion of the limitations of these sources.

Norman Sicily (1100–1200)

In the 1100s, Europe began to feel the impact of the Crusades, a series of religious conflicts between Christians and Muslims. However, these battles did not only affect the faiths that people practiced. They also influenced the demand for goods and the way different groups of people interacted with one another to buy and sell those goods. The Crusades brought conflict with them, but some cooperation came along as well because the amount of long-distance trade to Europe began to increase.

A Busy Place

The people of Sicily were already used to a life that included those who came from different cultures and religious backgrounds. When Muslims from North Africa ruled the region in the 800s, Sicily's Greek Christians and Jews were allowed to practice their religions as long as they paid a special tax.

As the Crusades continued, Sicily became a busy place where different cultural groups interacted with one another. Europeans were discovering the ideas, customs, and cultures found in the Islamic World. They desired products from abroad, such as spices and cotton cloth from India and silk from China. Sicily's location connected Europe with Islamic trade routes that were to the south and east. Latin Christian merchants would arrive in Sicily to buy goods from Muslim and Jewish merchants who had access to Asian products.

The Book of Roger

Sicily continued to be a welcoming place for different faiths under the rule of the Normans, who were descendants of the Vikings. The first Norman ruler arrived in Sicily in the middle of the 11th century, but the kingdom particularly thrived during the reign of Roger II.

He was an intelligent man who loved to learn. Roger II had been raised by tutors and other adults who were Greek and Muslim. By the time he became king in 1112, Roger was quite comfortable in Sicily's multicultural setting of people of other cultures and faiths. He loved to talk to all types of scholars, such as philosophers, mathematicians, doctors, and geographers.

The ambitious and curious leader wanted to know more about the world, so Roger directed the Muslim geographer al-Idrisi to create a book of maps and information. The goal was to document and illustrate all that was then known about the physical world.

Al-Idrisi used several different sources in his research. These included his own knowledge of trade routes, ideas from other Muslim

The Book of Roger begins with the following words: "The earth is round like a sphere..."

geographers, and studies the Normans had already done about northern Europe. Ship captains and merchants who came to Sicily were also interviewed, and al-Idrisi sent travelers to distant lands to gather more facts and details. It took 15 years to accomplish the entire task. The completed work is now known as *The Book of Roger*. One historian describes it as "the greatest geographical work of the Middle Ages."

Sophisticated Diplomacy

Some believe that Roger II was more sophisticated than his Norman ancestors when it came to expanding his kingdom and dealing with other cultures. At times, he could be extremely aggressive. For example, he outmaneuvered his cousins to take over two territories in southern Italy. His navy also captured Corfu and parts of Tunisia.

Roger had no problem using his navy's skill to fulfill his personal pleasures. He kept a strict count of the money that he spent, but he also liked to live in luxury. During a voyage to Thebes, Roger's navy kidnapped the best female silk workers from the area. They brought them to Sicily's capital so that the women could work in the royal court's silk factory.

There were times when Roger chose to avoid conflict. In fact, he intentionally kept Sicily out of the Second Crusade. Jerusalem was then controlled by Frankish rulers. Roger's mother had remarried a Frankish king many years earlier, and the marriage had been a disaster. Because of this, Roger hated the Franks and was uninterested in coming to their aid.

He also wanted to maintain cultural and religious tolerance in Sicily. One of Roger's chief admirals spoke both Arabic and Greek. Several bishops had come from nations such as England, France, and Italy. Many of the kingdom's officials were Muslim, and they kept records in Arabic. Other Muslims worked in Sicily as translators. Their job was to take information that was from the Islamic World written in Arabic and copy those words in other languages. Most works were translated from Arabic to Latin, but there was also one Muslim translator who used languages like Greek, Hebrew, and Turkish in his translation of a book about the study of plants.

The Kingdom Declines

After Roger II died in 1154, Sicily's multicultural society began to break apart. Roger's son William I ruled the kingdom. William's son, William II, then followed, but neither had the power and influence that Roger II had held. During their reigns, rebellion took place, a government minister was assassinated, and attacks on Muslims began. When William II died without an heir, control of the kingdom passed to Roger's daughter Constance. Eventually, her husband, Emperor Henry VI made Sicily part of the Holy Roman Empire.

This is a statue of Roger II in the wall of the Royal Palace of Naples, Italy. Like the Byzantine monarchs, Roger II believed that his status as king placed him between his subjects on Earth and God in heaven.

Islam in Medieval Times

About 570 C.E.
Muhammad's Birth
Muhammad is born in Mecca, an ancient place of worship on the Arabian Peninsula.

About 613 C.E.
Beginnings of Islam
Muhammad begins to preach Islam, a religion based on monotheism, but he meets much resistance, including a boycott and violence in Mecca.

632 C.E.
The Last Sermon
Muhammad dies shortly after leading his final pilgrimage to Mecca, where he delivers his Last Sermon.

500 C.E.   600 C.E.   700 C.E.   800 C.E.   900 C.E.   1000 C.E.

About 610 C.E.
Call to Prophethood
According to Islamic teachings, Muhammad is praying in the Hira Cave when the angel Gabriel calls him to be a prophet, or messenger of God.

622 C.E.
Migration to Medina
Muhammad and his followers, known as Muslims, move to Medina and establish a Muslim community.

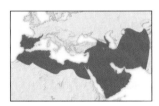

632–750 C.E.
Expansion of Islam
Islam expands as Muslims conquer lands in the Middle East, central Asia, the eastern Mediterranean, North Africa, and Spain.

About 651 C.E.
Official Version of Qur'an
Caliph Uthman establishes an official version of the Qur'an, the holy book of Islam.

About 825 C.E.
Al-Khwarizmi Invents Algebra
Arab scholar al-Khwarizmi invents algebra. His textbook is translated into Latin and becomes the most important mathematics textbook in European universities.

If $\gamma = 6$
Solve for x:
$x + 2\gamma = 20$

1192 C.E.
Peace Treaty Ends Third Crusade
Richard the Lionheart, King of England and leader of the Crusaders, and Salah al-Din, leader of the Muslim forces, sign a peace treaty ending the Third Crusade.

1000 C.E.	1100 C.E.	1200 C.E.	1300 C.E.	1400 C.E.	1500 C.E.

750–1250 C.E.
Flourishing of Islamic Civilization
Islamic civilization flourishes as Muslims build great cities and spread knowledge and ideas to new lands through cultural diffusion.

1096–1291 C.E.
Christians Launch Crusades
European Christians launch a series of Crusades to recapture the Holy Land from Muslims.

1478 C.E.
Spanish Inquisition Begins
Queen Isabella and King Ferdinand begin the Spanish Inquisition, a church court intended to rid Spain of Muslims and Jews who have not fully converted to Christianity.

The Kailasa temple is one of the 32 caves temples known collectively as the Ellora Caves. These rock-cut temples date back to the 600s and feature Hindu, Buddhist, and Jain monuments.

Physical Features of South Asia and Surrounding Areas

ALTAY MTS.

MANCHURIAN PLAIN

GOBI DESERT

TAKLIMAKAN DESERT

Huang He (Yellow River)

LOESS PLATEAU

NORTH CHINA PLAIN

HINDU-KUSH

KUNLUN MTS.

PLATEAU OF TIBET

Chang Jiang (Yangtze River)

Indus River

H I M A L A Y A

Brahmaputra River

Mt. Everest (8,850 m, 29,035 ft.)

Thar Desert

Ganges River

pic of Cancer

INDIAN PENINSULA

DECCAN PLATEAU

WESTERN GHATS

EASTERN GHATS

Irrawaddy River

DAWNA RANGE

Mekong River

INDOCHINESE PENINSULA

South China Sea

Arabian Sea

Bay of Bengal

Andaman Sea

Gulf of Thailand

Sri Lanka

Equator

Indonesia

Elevation

Feet	Meters
Over 10,000	Over 3,050
5,001–10,000	1,526–3,050
2,001–5,000	611–1,525
1,001–2,000	306–610
501–1,000	153–305
0–500	0–152

▲ Mountain peak

☐ Present-day boundary

INDIAN OCEAN

N
W   E
S

0   300   600 miles
0   300   600 kilometers
Lambert Azimuthal Equal-Area Projection

70°E   80°E   90°E   100°E   110°E

South Asia, 300–1200

In the southern region of the Asian continent lies South Asia, which covers about 2 million square miles of land. This region is home to the modern-day countries of India, Afghanistan, Pakistan, Bangladesh, Bhutan, Maldives, Nepal, and Sri Lanka.

The ancient civilizations that developed in South Asia were influenced by the physical geography of the region. The Himalayan Mountain Range form a barrier between India and the rest of Asia. The Ganges River flows through India and Bangladesh and contribute to the fertile farmland in this area. The river empties into the Bay of Bengal and the Indian Ocean, these bodies of water preventing contact with other people. Because of the physical environment, early civilizations developed in South Asia with little outside influence.

In the third century C.E., the Gupta Empire arose in India. The Gupta Empire brought great stability and relative peace to India, as well as a strong education system. Many universities were built throughout the empire, with classes taught on Buddhist and Hindu philosophy, as well as math, astronomy, and chemistry. Gupta writers crafted literary works, painting, and sculpture. Metalworking and the creation of coins to honor Gupta rulers was also a major accomplishment of the empire. The Gupta Empire also successfully constructed a system of hard-packed dirt roads. These roads facilitated trade and connected South Asia with China and lands in Africa and the Middle East.

These roads also led to the spread of culture and ideas. For instance, Buddhism, which began in South Asia, spread as Buddhist merchants traveled between regions to trade. These merchants would often build temples alongside these roads. Priests and monks would then preach at these temples, spreading Buddhist ideas to the local people and other travelers. This helped spread Buddhist ideas throughout the rest of Asia.

Hinduism also grew and developed throughout South Asia during this period. As you study this unit, you will learn about the successes of the the Gupta Empire. You will also explore how several different religions grew, changed, and influenced South Asia.

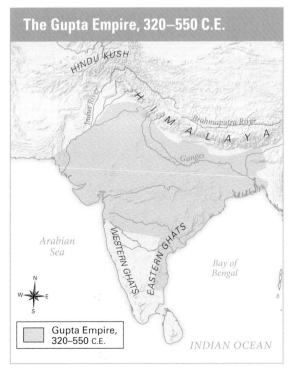

The Gupta Empire, 320–550 C.E.

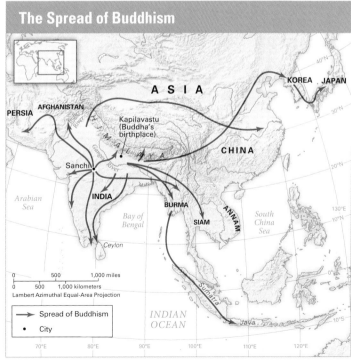

The Spread of Buddhism

Lesson 13

The Achievements of the Gupta Empire

Why is the period during the Gupta Empire known as a "golden age"?

Introduction

Under the Mauryan Empire, India was unified for the first time and Buddhist beliefs became widespread. The next great empire to unite India was called the Gupta (GOOP-tuh) Empire.

The Guptas were a line of rulers, beginning in the mid-200s, who controlled much of India from 320 to 550 C.E. Many historians have called this period a golden age, which is a time of great **prosperity** and **achievement**. In unstable times, people are likely to be busy meeting their immediate needs for food, shelter, and safety.

However, in times of peace and prosperity, people can turn their attention to more creative activities. For this reason, a number of advances in the arts and sciences occurred during the peaceful golden age of the Gupta Empire. Many of these achievements have left a lasting mark on the world.

Archaeologists have made some notable discoveries that have helped us learn about the accomplishments of the Gupta Empire. For example, they have unearthed palm-leaf books that were created about 550 C.E. Sacred texts often appeared in palm-leaf books. These sacred texts are just one of many kinds of literature that Indians created during the Guptas' reign.

Literature was one of several areas of major accomplishment during India's golden age. In this lesson, you will learn more about the rise of the Gupta Empire. Then you will take a close look at seven achievements that came out of this rich period in India's history and how these achievements affected the people of India.

Social Studies Vocabulary

alliance

golden age

Gupta Empire

province

◀ A Gupta artist painted this mural, which can be found within the Ajanta caves.

This is the entrance to one of the Ajanta caves, which contain many art forms created during the Gupta Empire.

Gupta Empire the empire covering much of northern India that was ruled by the Guptas from about 320 C.E. to about 550 C.E.

alliance a bond between families, states, or other groups to further their common interests

province a territory that is part of a country or an empire

golden age a period of great happiness, prosperity, and achievement

1. The Rise of the Gupta Empire

After the Mauryan Empire fell around 187 B.C.E., India broke apart into separate kingdoms. For about 500 years, these smaller kingdoms fought each other for land and power. Beginning around 320 C.E., a second great empire arose in India: the Gupta Empire.

The empire began under a ruler named Chandragupta I. He and his family, the Guptas, conquered and united the northern kingdoms. Arranged marriages between members of the Gupta family and the sons and daughters of other rulers helped this new kingdom form alliances.

The Gupta line of kings lasted until about 550 C.E. At the height of their power, the Guptas ruled most of northern India. Their empire was the largest that India had known since the days of the Mauryas.

In some ways, the Gupta Empire was similar to the Mauryan Empire. The Guptas set up a central government to oversee the empire. A council, made up of advisers and members of the royal family, helped the king make decisions.

Unlike the Mauryas, the Guptas gave local areas a great deal of independence. They divided the empire into large sections called provinces. Each of these provinces was ruled by a royal governor. Within the provinces, town leaders could make many of their own decisions.

The Guptas' ruling strategy helped them stay in power for nearly 230 years. The relatively peaceful times, as well as the empire's stability, encouraged growth in both the arts and the sciences. The result was a golden age that produced some of the greatest advances in Indian history. Let's look at seven areas of achievement for the Gupta Empire.

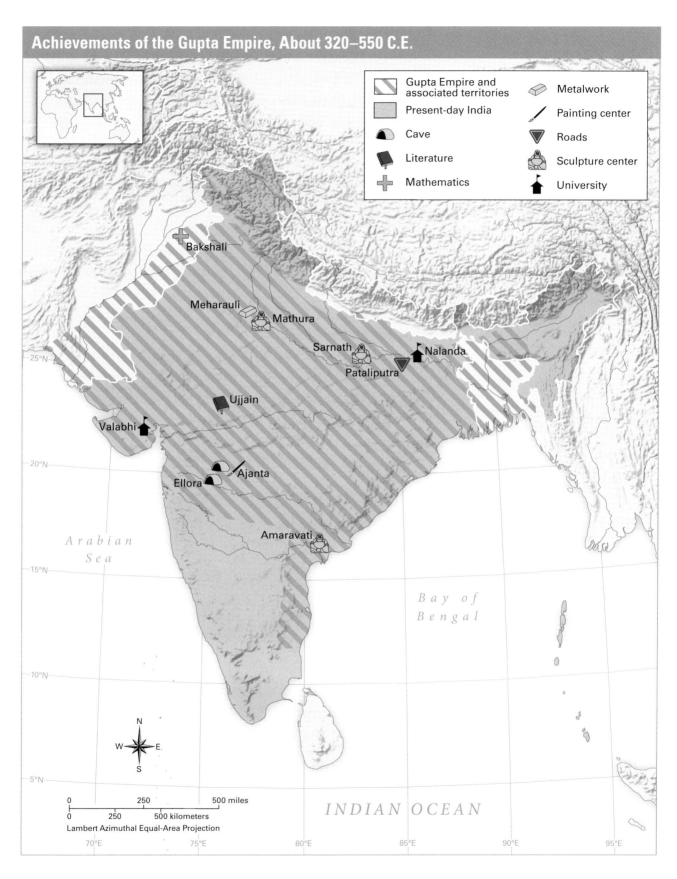

Achievements of the Gupta Empire, About 320–550 C.E.

Legend:
- Gupta Empire and associated territories
- Present-day India
- Cave
- Literature
- Mathematics
- Metalwork
- Painting center
- Roads
- Sculpture center
- University

Bakshali

Meharauli
Mathura

Sarnath
Pataliputra
Nalanda

Ujjain

Valabhi

Ajanta
Ellora

Amaravati

Arabian Sea

Bay of Bengal

0   250   500 miles
0   250   500 kilometers
Lambert Azimuthal Equal-Area Projection

INDIAN OCEAN

Under the rule of the Guptas, India made great advances in many
areas, including the arts, education, and the building of roads.

2. Universities

The period of the Gupta Empire was a time of learning. The Guptas built many colleges and universities throughout the empire. Some universities were Hindu; others were Buddhist. The schools were open primarily to males. However, teachers' daughters were allowed to attend.

These universities provided upper classes with religious training. Students attended classes in religion, **mathematics, astronomy,** chemistry, and Sanskrit. They could also study sculpture, painting, music, and dancing.

The most famous university was the school at Nalanda, in northern India. The school had eight colleges and three libraries. It also had a hospital and a monastery. Students were instructed in Buddhist and Hindu philosophy. They also studied logic, grammar, and medicine.

Students of medicine learned the practices and treatments of the time and were trained in how to question patients about their physical problems. Students were taught how to make cures from bark, roots, leaves, and minerals. They also learned how to use the front claws of giant ants to stitch up wounds. Hindu doctors were especially skilled at performing surgery.

The ruins of the university at Nalanda are impressive in size. Notice how well-preserved this ancient building is.

3. Literature

Gupta writers crafted many kinds of literary works. They wrote poetry, fables, and folktales. They also created plays, including both comedies and dramas. Some of the plays were about historical and political subjects. Large audiences gathered to watch the performances.

There were other forms of writing as well. Scholars and lawyers wrote about Hindu law and religion, while some of the great Sanskrit literature also took shape. The *Puranas* ("Ancient Lore") was a collection of Hindu legends that taught the lessons of the Vedas, or sacred Hindu texts, through tales of sages and kings. These stories had been passed down orally for generations. The Guptas were the first to gather these stories together and record them as a collection. The *Mahabharata* ("Great Work"), a poem composed over hundreds of years, reached its final form during the Gupta era. Its themes relate to Hindu values and the battle between good and evil.

The *Bhagavad Gita* (BAH-guh-vahd GHEE-tuh) is part of the *Mahabharata*. Its name means "Song of the Lord." The *Bhagavad Gita* is one of the most beloved works of Hinduism. In this poem, Prince Arjuna is taught basic truths of Hinduism by Krishna, an earthly form of the deity Vishnu.

Some Gupta literature spread beyond India, influencing cultures of countries as far away as Greece and Persia (present-day Iran). The famous Arabian tale about Aladdin and his magic lamp was inspired by a Gupta folktale.

Manuscripts were written in Sanskrit and often illustrated. This page is from the Bhagavata Purana, a sacred Hindu literary text. This work's 18,000 verses about the Hindu god Vishnu have greatly influenced Indian culture.

This part of an Ajanta cave mural depicts the Jataka tales of Buddhism. These stories describe the Buddha's different stages of life.

4. Painting

In the Gupta Empire, painting was an important art form and part of life for noble families, who were wealthy people of high birth. No home was complete without a painting board or an easel. Popular subjects included deities and other religious topics. Nobles and members of the royalty also hired artists to create works of art, including pieces made on long scrolls that highlighted the luxury of noble life.

Perhaps the greatest ancient Indian paintings are those known as the Ajanta (uh-JUHN-tuh) cave murals, which cover the walls of the 30 caves that make up an ancient Buddhist monastery in central India. The paintings are done in rich, bright colors including red, purple, and green paints made from minerals and clay.

Some of the Ajanta murals show scenes from the Buddha's life. Some murals portray stories that reflect Buddhist values, such as love and understanding. Many of the scenes include graceful images of kings, queens, musicians, and dancers. Other scenes show animals and hunters in the forest. These woodland scenes are decorated with flowers, trees, and complex patterns. Gupta artists were skilled painters.

5. Sculpture

Another art form in the Gupta Empire was sculpture. Sculptors created statues out of stone, wood, bronze, and terra-cotta clay. Many of these statues portrayed the Buddha or Hindu deities. Some sculptures showed scenes from important people's lives. Many sculptures were created to stand on their own foundations. Others were carved into the walls of temples and caves.

Gupta sculptures portrayed the human form simply and gracefully. One example is the sculpture of the river deity, Ganga, shown here. The statue's lines are curved and elegant, and curved details form her dress, hair, and jewelry.

The temple statue of the Buddha's head shown here demonstrates the same attention to clean lines and detail. Notice the defined curls in his hair, as well as the detail in his lips. His expression is calm and peaceful. The sculptor used lowered eyes and a calm face to portray the Buddha's wisdom.

These sculptures of the Buddha's head, and the river deity, Ganga, are typical of Gupta sculptures. Artists from the Gupta Empire put great effort and detail into their works.

Gupta metalworkers made gold coins to honor the kings who owned the mines. The coin on the far left depicts a king riding an elephant into battle.

6. Metalwork

One remarkable accomplishment of the Gupta Empire was its metalwork. Gupta kings controlled huge mines of gold, copper, and iron. Metalworkers made gold and copper coins, engraving them with pictures honoring Gupta rulers. The coins often highlighted the rulers' wealth and their achievements in art, politics, and war.

Gupta metalworkers were also famous for their ironwork. An iron pillar at a place called Meharauli is one example of these artisans' unusual skill. The pillar is made of solid iron, stands 25 feet tall, and weighs about 13,000 pounds. The sides are engraved with a story that describes the achievements of a Gupta emperor. The iron is nearly rust free after 1,600 years in the rain and sun. No one knows how Gupta ironworkers acquired such advanced metalworking skills.

7. Mathematics

Earlier Hindu mathematicians had created a way of writing whole numbers using the numerals 1 through 9. Some Gupta mathematicians made further advances, one of which was developing the decimal system. The decimal system uses ten basic numerals that have different values depending on their "place." In the number 105, for instance, 1 is in the "hundreds place" and means 100. The system also works for fractions. In the decimal 0.10, 1 means one-tenth. Note the zeros in these examples. Hindu mathematicians were the first to treat zero as a number. Many calculations are impossible without the zero.

In later centuries, Arab peoples learned the Indian system of numbers and spread it to Europe. As a result, Europeans called this way of writing numbers "Arabic numerals." A more accurate name would be "Hindu-Arabic numerals," because the system actually originated with the ancient Indians. We still use this system today.

The use of mathematics allowed ancient Indians to build complex structures such as this temple. This beautiful structure is called the Great Mahabodhi Temple, or the Great Awakening Temple.

One of the most famous Gupta mathematicians was a man named Aryabhata (AR-ee-ah-bah-tah), who combined mathematics and astronomy to make important discoveries. He figured out that a year was exactly 365.258 days long. He also calculated the approximate size of Earth and proposed that planets were spheres. Aryabhata was one of the earliest scientists to suggest that Earth spins on its **axis**, an imaginary line through Earth's center.

Mathematics had immediate practical uses as well. For example, Gupta builders applied their knowledge of mathematics to design complex structures like the one shown here.

8. Roads

Gupta rulers encouraged trade by creating a system of well-built roads. Care and precision were used to build these roads. First, engineers cleared the roadway of plants, trees, and rocks. Then, holes were filled in. Finally, workers smoothed the ground until it was level. The finished roads were made of hard-packed dirt.

Designed for safety and comfort, the roadways were lifted a few feet off the ground. Ditches, or canals, ran along either side, which helped prevent flooding during the rainy monsoon season since water would run off the road and into the ditches.

Signs along the roadway told travelers where they were and indicated the distances so that people could calculate how far they had traveled. Rest houses provided travelers with a place to relax or spend the night. Wells provided them with water for drinking and cooking.

The network of roads the Gupta rulers created encouraged trade throughout the empire and beyond it. This trade contributed to the empire's prosperity.

The empire's roads greatly benefited trade since busy traders could move easily from city to city within the large empire. Traders could also move goods from the middle of the country to important waterways. From there, traders could ship their goods and sell them in other countries. The roads also connected India to China and the lands east of the Mediterranean Sea.

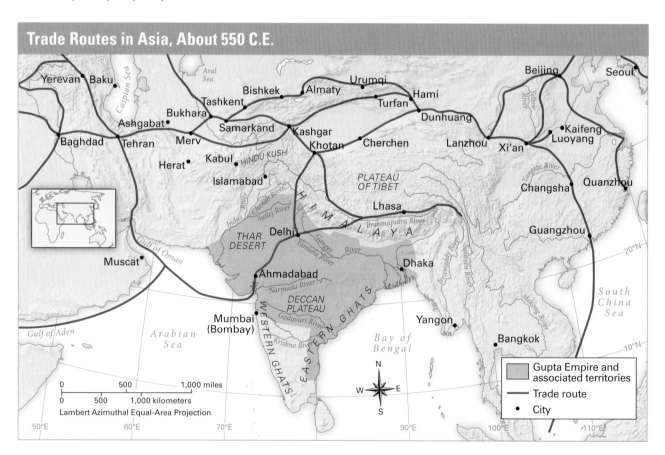

Trade Routes in Asia, About 550 C.E.

Gupta Empire and associated territories
Trade route
City

These roads also influenced the exchange of ideas and goods throughout India. The network of roads created during this period allowed people from many different regions across the Indian subcontinent to interact in all aspects of their lives. The roads also facilitated commercial, cultural, and religious exchanges more than in any earlier period.

This Ajanta cave mural depicts Buddha with several attendants.

Lesson Summary

In this lesson, you learned about the many advances made in ancient India during a golden age under the rule of the Gupta Empire.

The Rise of the Gupta Empire The Gupta Empire arose around 320 C.E. under Chandragupta I. Like the Mauryas, the Guptas created a strong central government, while also giving significant independence to local leaders. This strategy helped create an era of stability and prosperity. India experienced a surge of learning and artistic growth in many areas.

Universities The Guptas built many Hindu and Buddhist universities attended by students from the upper classes. Nalanda was the most famous school.

Literature Writers created poetry, fables, folktales, and plays. Scholars wrote about law and religion. Great works of Sanskrit literature, including the *Puranas* and the *Mahabharata*, were recorded. Some of this work spread beyond India and continues to be influential today.

Painting and Sculpture Artists and members of noble families created paintings depicting religious values and noble life. The Ajanta cave murals are among the greatest ancient Indian paintings. Sculptors worked in stone, wood, bronze, and terra-cotta clay. Their work showed Hindu deities, the Buddha, and scenes from important people's lives.

Metalwork Skilled metalworkers engraved gold and copper coins. Artisans were famous for their ironwork, including engravings on iron pillars.

Mathematics Gupta mathematicians developed a decimal system and were the first to treat zero as a number. One astronomer, named Aryabhata, calculated the length of a year and estimated the size of Earth. We still use their advances today.

Roads Engineers designed and built a system of roads that helped improve trade and prosperity.

Evolution of Religion in South Asia

How did the spread of Hinduism, Buddhism, and Islam throughout Asia affect each religion?

Introduction

During the medieval period, South Asia's interaction with the rest of the world changed. The Silk Road, the network of trade routes between China and the Mediterranean, led to new ideas flowing into and out of India and the rest of South Asia.

Because of its location, parts of South Asia became important trading posts in the silk trade. India began trading cotton cloth, textiles, jewelry, gemstones, pearls, finished silk products, food grains, and spice along the trade network as well. This network also allowed Indian monks, nuns, merchants, and travelers to spread their religious beliefs, practices, and cultural styles to other places. These ideas spread to the Srivijaya, Java, and Khmer Empires of Southeast Asia. They also spread to China and countries in East Asia.

As these religious beliefs spread, they began to change. They affected how people in India and throughout the rest of Asia lived.

In this lesson, you will learn how the people of South Asia exchanged ideas with people around the world. You will study the changes that Indian religions underwent as they came in contact with other cultures. You will also learn about how Islam spread into South Asia.

Social Studies Vocabulary

Bhakti movement

Mahayana Buddhism

◀ This statue of the Hindu God Hanuman is located near the Red Fort built by the Islamic Mughal Empire in New Delhi, India.

1. Evolution of Hinduism

Hinduism began to change during the medieval period. During this time, new types of devotional worship (called bhakti) focused on specific Hindu deities began to emerge. Separate religious sects, such as Vaishnavism (devotion to Vishnu), Shaivism (devotion to Shiva), and Shaktism (devotion to Shakti, the Mother Goddess), all appeared during this period.

Under the Gupta Empire, this new type of devotional worship flourished. One reason that devotional worship grew was because of the rise of temple worship. Early Hindu temples made from wood were replaced by temples made from stone and brick devoted to specific gods. Devotional writing, such as poetic literature, also emerged as different sects wrote about their chosen deity. Since many of these texts were written in Sanskrit, the shared language of Indian intellectual life, devotional worship became an important force in creating a shared culture throughout India.

When the Gupta empire collapsed, India split apart into smaller regional kingdoms. These regional kingdoms were often devoted to a specific sect of Hinduism. The Chola Empire, for example, was a regional kingdom that ruled much of southern India from about 800 C.E. to about 1300 C.E. The Chola established sea trading routes throughout the Indian Ocean. They also made significant contributions to literature and art, such as remarkable sculptures and bronzes, in India. The Chola Empire also primarily followed the ideas of Shaivism. They built temples to honor the god Shiva throughout their kingdom.

Great regional temples, like the Jagganatha in Puri, were also created in these regional kingdoms. These temples soon became centers of both religious and political power throughout India.

The Jagannatha Temple of Puri is dedicated to the god Vishnu. The temple holds daily worship services, as well as festivals that millions of people attend.

These devotional forms of Hinduism also changed how people experienced religious texts. Religious literature written in vernacular languages, such as Tamil (one of the languages of southern India), began to appear alongside Sanskrit texts. These writers, called poet-saints, wrote hymns and songs dedicated to specific Hindu gods. These hymns, along with the use of the vernacular, reflected a change in Hinduism toward personal devotion. The work of poet-saints, like Ramananda, Ravidas, and Tukaram, are still followed by many in India today.

This movement toward personal devotion to God was called the **Bhakti movement**. The Bhakti movement changed how people experienced Hinduism and worshiped God, who has three aspects in Hinduism: Brahma, the creator; Vishnu, the protector; and Shiva, the transformer. One aspect of the movement was an emphasis on social and religious equality throughout Indian society. This challenged the class system that had existed in Indian society for generations. The Bhakti movement also addressed the level of power that priests had in society. Instead, people of all social groups were encouraged to worship song, dance, and through temple visits.

Meera Bai's devotional songs were sung throughout northern India. Much of her work can still be read today.

Women also played an important role in the Bhakti movement. Female poet-saints sometimes wrote about the struggles they faced in their own lives. Some wrote about the restrictions they felt in married life or about their status in society. Others rejected the traditional roles of women and left their homes behind. Poet-saints, like Meera Bai, were acknowledged for their work. Many of their teachings are still widely remembered today.

Bhakti movement a movement within Hinduism that emphasized personal devotion and social and religious equality

2. Spread of Buddhism

Buddhism also changed during this time. While the network of trade routes known as the Silk Road allowed goods to flow between countries, it also allowed for the exchange of ideas and knowledge from one culture to another. Christians and Muslims used the Silk Road to help spread their beliefs to the people in the East. Buddhist missionaries and travelers from the Indian subcontinent also spread their religion to other places around the world using the Silk Road.

As Buddhist merchants traveled to foreign countries to trade, they would sometimes build shrines and temples along the Silk Road. Over time, larger temples, such as the Cave Temples of Dunhuang, the Yungang Grottoes, and the Buddhas of Bamiyan, were created. Soon, Buddhist temples could be found in Southeast Asia, China, and the Middle East. Many of these larger temples can still be visited today.

Buddhist priests and monks preached at these temples and spread the ideas of Buddhism to local people and passing travelers alike. To many, the ideas of equality taught in Buddhism were appealing, and the religion spread quickly throughout Asia.

In China, many of these Buddhist missionaries began translating sacred Buddhist texts into Chinese. People from China also began making pilgrimages into India to learn more about Buddhism. In the late 620s, Xuan Zang, a man from a prominent Chinese family, made a pilgrimage throughout Afghanistan, Pakistan, India, and Nepal to learn more about Buddhism. Over the course of his journey, Xuan Zang collected over 600 Buddhist texts, which he brought back to China.

As Buddhism spread into China, it came in contact with the philosophies of Daoism and Confucianism. In Daoism, people are taught to discover truth for themselves. The goal of Confucianism, on the other hand, is to create a just and peaceful society. The interactions of these philosophies with Buddhism allowed the religion to spread quickly throughout China. For example, Buddhist missionaries in China borrowed from the Daoist vocabulary. This allowed the people of China to more clearly understand Buddhist teachings.

The Cave Temples of Dunhuang (top), the Yungang Grottoes (middle), and the Buddhas of Bamiyan (bottom) were all created along the Silk Road. Temples like these helped spread Buddhism throughout much of Asia.

Buddhism's interaction with Daoism and Confucianism led to the formation of a popular form of Buddhism that incorporated ideas from all three. Chinese Buddhism focused on moral living, rituals, and a dedication to one's family and community. Several concepts of Buddhism changed in this new popular religion. For example, the concept of nirvana, or true happiness and peace, came from the idea that one could break free, after many lifetimes of effort, from the cycle of life and death and thereby escape all suffering. However, in China, the concept of nirvana changed to become a sudden and spontaneous realization. Buddha himself, who is first viewed as a wise man in the earliest forms of Buddhism, became a god-like figure in Buddhist texts that spread throughout China.

Another aspect of Buddhism that took root in China was the concept of Mahayana. In **Mahayana Buddhism,** divine beings, called bodhisattvas, delayed their entry into nirvana and instead chose to help people on Earth. Some forms of Mahayana Buddhism taught that people could attain salvation through faith in Amita or Amida, the Buddha of Infinite Light, a very powerful and compassionate bodhisattva.

Thousands of monasteries were built in China during this period. At Buddhism's height in the 9th century, there were nearly 50,000 monasteries in China. Buddhism's popularity in China caused it to quickly spread to Korea and Japan.

Confucian scholar-officials and Daoist priests, however, were concerned about the growth of this "foreign religion." Tang emperors stopped accepting Buddhism and began to persecute it. They also prevented Buddhism from becoming the official religion of China. Despite this, many parts of Asia had already incorporated Buddhist teachings into their cultures.

Mahayana Buddhism a branch of Buddhism that became popular in China and focused on salvation through personal faith

Xuanzang collected and translated hundreds of Buddhist texts that he brought back from India. He also helped establish Buddhist schools throughout China.

3. Introduction of Islam

In the 11th century, a new religion appeared in India. Turks from Central Asia, who had recently converted to Islam, conquered territory in the northern parts of India. By the mid-13th century these conquests spread as far as Bengal in the eastern portion of India.

One result of these conquests was the formation of Muslim kingdoms within India. The most prominent of these Muslim Kingdoms was the Delhi Sultanate. From the 13th century to the 16th century, the Delhi Sultanate ruled over northern India. Islam also spread to some coastal regions and to parts of the Deccan Plateau in southern India.

While much of India remained Hindu, Islam was able to spread throughout other parts of India. This spread of Islam caused tension with Hindus and Buddhists who lived in India. These missionaries would sometimes destroy temples before rededicating them. Muslim missionaries also adapted Hindu and Buddhist stories to reflect different Islamic beliefs.

Over time, India's interaction with Islam led to new cultural developments. The blending of Islamic and Indian ideas formed new styles of music, architecture, literature, and painting. Indo-Islamic architecture, for example, began to incorporate minarets and other Islamic architecture features into building designs. One of the most famous Indo-Islamic buildings in India is the Taj Mahal, which includes a dome and the four minarets in its design.

The Taj Mahal was built in the Indian city of Agra. Its architectural features are a mix of Indian and Islamic designs.

Another effect of India's interaction with Islam was the trade of innovations. Under the Gupta Empire, the people of India had made major advancements in the fields of science and mathematics. These innovations were shared with the new Islamic Empires. For example, the system of numbers used by Indians in the Gupta Empire, which would become known as the Hindu-Arabic numeral system, was used by the Persian mathematician, al-Khwarizmi, to create the study of algebra. An Indian astronomer named Aryabhatta theorized that the earth was round and that it spun in space. These theories were later explored by Islamic astronomers.

This statue found in Khiva, Uzbekistan, honors al-Khwarizmi, the founder of algebra.

Today, the effects of Indo-Islamic influence can still be seen throughout India. These ideas have also been shared around the world.

Lesson Summary

In this lesson, you learned about how religion changed as it flowed out of and into India.

Hinduism Hinduism changed around the time of the Gupta Empire. Religious sects emerged that were dedicated to individual gods, like Shiva or Vishnu. The Bhakti movement also led to changes in how people viewed social order, and refocused religion on personal access.

Buddhism Buddhism spread throughout much of Asia because of the Silk Road. Shrines and temples were built along the Silk Road, and people from China made pilgrimages to India to learn more about the religion. As it came in contact with new cultures, the religion began to change.

Islam Following the Turkish conquest, Islam became a prominent religion in many areas around India. The close interaction of Islam and India allowed for the creation of new types of architecture, art, and music. It also led to new innovations in science and mathematics.

Calicut (1400)

Beginning in the 13th century, the city-state of Calicut became a major trading port on the Malabar Coast. Calicut connected the people of South and Southeast Asia with places around the world, including the Middle East, China, and Europe.

Along the Indian Ocean, trade continually grew. In time, India would become a major producer of cotton, spices, and other commodities for export. The volume of commodities that India produced made it second only to China in trade. Merchants visiting Calicut bought and sold these Indian exports for silk and porcelain from China; metals, armor, weapons, and perfume from Egypt and Persia; horses and glassware from the Mediterranean; and slaves from the Mongol lands and East Africa.

Calicut's role as a trading post led to people from many different cultures living together. This led to the spread of Chinese, Hindu, Buddhist, and Muslim cultures in addition to trade goods. Famous travelers like Zheng He and Ibn Battuta wrote about the city. What made Calicut an economic and cultural center? Why was it such an important site of encounter?

How Calicut's Location Supported Trade

During the 13th through the 15th centuries, India and Southeast Asia were made up of a few large states, many small states, and some city-states. Since the smaller communities, such as city-states, could not produce everything they needed, trade became incredibly important. The Zamorin Dynasty, which ruled over Calicut during this period, made laws that helped merchants. They also protected merchants from theft, lowered their taxes, and treated all people as equals.

While Calicut's laws provided a place for people to trade without trouble, this wasn't the only reason it became an important trading post. Since all ships were powered by wind during this period, seasonal monsoons determined where and when people could sail in India. Calicut's location allowed people to utilize the monsoon seasons from all around India to trade goods with one another.

Calicut is in the modern-day state of Kerala in India. Its location near the coast helped make it a major trading port in the 13th century.

Monsoon Direction and Season	Itinerary	Dates Given	Source
Sailing west to east (Arabia to Malacca) **Two seasons** 1) Long monsoon season (Feb. – May)	Hormuz to Calicut	2/20 – 4/11	Ibn Majid
	Hormuz to Calicut	Leave before 5/1	Ibn Majid
	Cambay to Malacca	Leave by 3/18 – 4/27	Sulayman
	Calicut to Malacca	Leave by 4/16	Celebi
2) Short monsoon season (Aug. 15 – Sept. 30)	Aden to Calicut	8/29 – 9/18	Ibn Majid
	Aden to Malacca	Leave 8/19	Ibn Majid
	Calicut to Malacca	Leave 9/23	Ibn Majid
Sailing east to west (China to Arabia) One long season (Oct. 15 – Apr. 15)	Quanzhou to Malacca	11/23 – 3/2	Ibn Majid
	Malacca to Aden	12/28 – 2/16	Sulayman
	Sumatra to Aden	12/7 – 2/5	Celebi
	Calicut to Cambay	October – April	Ibn Majid
	Cambay to Aden	10/14 – 3/28	Sulayman
	Cambay to Aden	10/18 – 4/11	Ibn Majid

Examine this table. It includes navigational data about monsoon winds from three separate travelers. The first of these travelers was Ahmad Ibn Majid. Ibn Majid was a 15th-century Arab navigator, cartographer, and writer. Known as the "Lion of the Seas," Ibn Majid compiled seafaring manuals that listed sea currents and winds that travelers would use. The second traveler is Sulayman al-Mahri. Al-Mahri was a 16th-century Arab navigator who studied as a philosopher and scientist under Ibn Majid. He compiled the *Book of the Mahri Masterpiece on Exact Maritime Sciences*, which included both theories and practices on traveling the Indian Ocean. The third traveler is Sidi Ali Celebi, a 16th-century Egyptian admiral. In his book, *The Ocean*, Celebi described winds, weather, and ocean currents that affected sailors. What do these monsoon wind patterns tell us about sailors and how they might have had to plan their voyages across the Indian Ocean?

This chart table shows navigational data from the works of Ahmad Ibn Majid, Sulayman al-Mahri, and Sidi Ali Celebi.

Using these monsoon winds, ships from many different places traveled to Calicut. The most popular of these ships was the Chinese *junk*. The junk had many features that made it popular. First, it had a rudder that allowed sailors to easily steer the ship. Second, it had internal walls that prevented the ship from flooding after hull breaks.

Finally, the junk had sails made from bamboo sticks and cloth that made it strong against the powerful monsoon winds. Before long, Southeast Asian shipbuilders began building junks as well. As a result, by the 14th century, the junk would become the most widely used ship in the Indian Ocean.

During the Ming Dynasty, Chinese naval expeditions, under the command of Zheng He, sent hundreds of ships around the Indian Ocean. First setting sail in 1405, Zheng He embarked on seven separate voyages. These voyages led to the spread of Chinese commercial influence throughout South Asia. Zheng He would eventually die in Calicut.

The Spice Trade

Spices had many different uses for the people of the medieval period. Some used spices to create incenses and perfumes. Often, spices were used to flavor foods. Several 14th- and 15th-century manuscripts have recipes that include spices. However, due to their price, spices were only used in food and perfumes for the wealthiest Europeans.

Spices were also used as medicines. During the medieval period, many doctors believed that there were four elements that controlled illness and medicines—hot, cold, dry, and wet. They would then treat the illness with its elemental opposite. For example, doctors would treat a disease they labeled as "hot" (such as a fever) with medicine they labeled as "cold" (such as mandrake). Doctors used spices like mandrake and sugar to make different medicines to treat illnesses.

The spice trade brought traders from across Afroeurasia to Calicut.

Spread of Culture

Calicut's unique location also led to the diffusion of cultural and religious ideas. Arab and Chinese merchants influenced many aspects of culture throughout Asia and Southeast Asia. With so many different ideas flowing into the city, Calicut merged many types of cultural and religious ideas together.

These ideas also extended beyond Calicut. Places in Southeast Asia became influenced by Indian ideas of religion and culture. Some Southeast Asian kings adopted these cultural, religious, and artistic styles from the more powerful Indian kingdoms and empires in order to support their own power and legitimacy.

One way Southeast Asian kings adopted Indian culture, religion, and art was through the construction of temples. In many early cultures, temples were seen as displays of power. Similar styles of temples found in different regions of Asia show the shared culture or rulership between these areas. Over time, Southeast Asian architecture and art began to more closely resemble Indian works and structures.

Angkor Wat in Cambodia was originally built in the 12th century as a Hindu temple.

South Asia, 300–1200

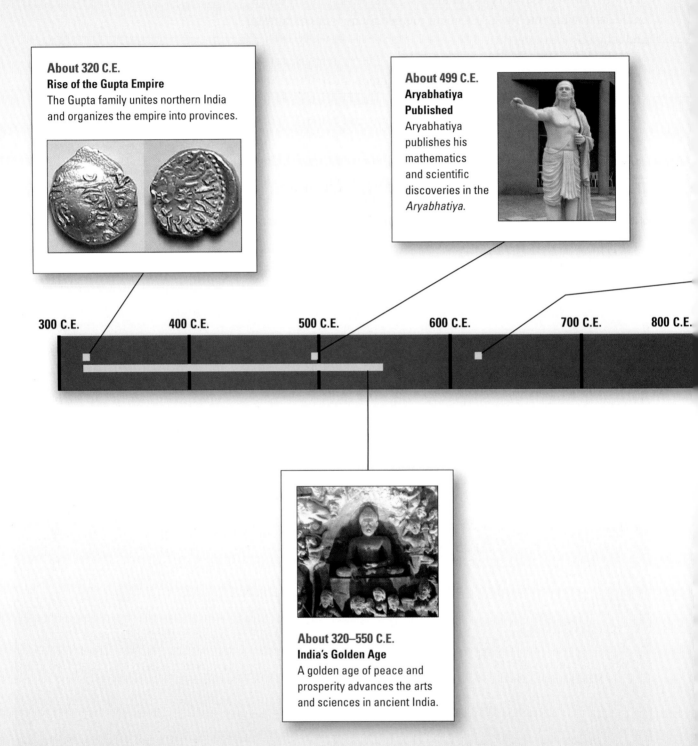

About 320 C.E.
Rise of the Gupta Empire
The Gupta family unites northern India and organizes the empire into provinces.

About 499 C.E.
Aryabhatiya Published
Aryabhatiya publishes his mathematics and scientific discoveries in the *Aryabhatiya*.

300 C.E.   400 C.E.   500 C.E.   600 C.E.   700 C.E.   800 C.E.

About 320–550 C.E.
India's Golden Age
A golden age of peace and prosperity advances the arts and sciences in ancient India.

About 620 C.E.
Pilgrimage of Xuan Zang
Xuan Zang travels through South Asia and collects Buddhist texts to bring back to China.

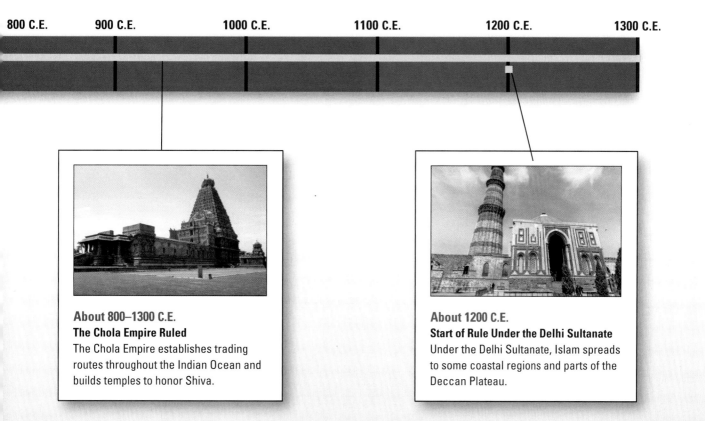

800 C.E.　　900 C.E.　　1000 C.E.　　1100 C.E.　　1200 C.E.　　1300 C.E.

About 800–1300 C.E.
The Chola Empire Ruled
The Chola Empire establishes trading routes throughout the Indian Ocean and builds temples to honor Shiva.

About 1200 C.E.
Start of Rule Under the Delhi Sultanate
Under the Delhi Sultanate, Islam spreads to some coastal regions and parts of the Deccan Plateau.

The Culture and Kingdoms of West Africa

West Africans dressed in traditional clothing stand in front of the Great Mosque of Djenne in present-day Mali. The mosque dates to the 13th century and is the largest mud brick building in the world.

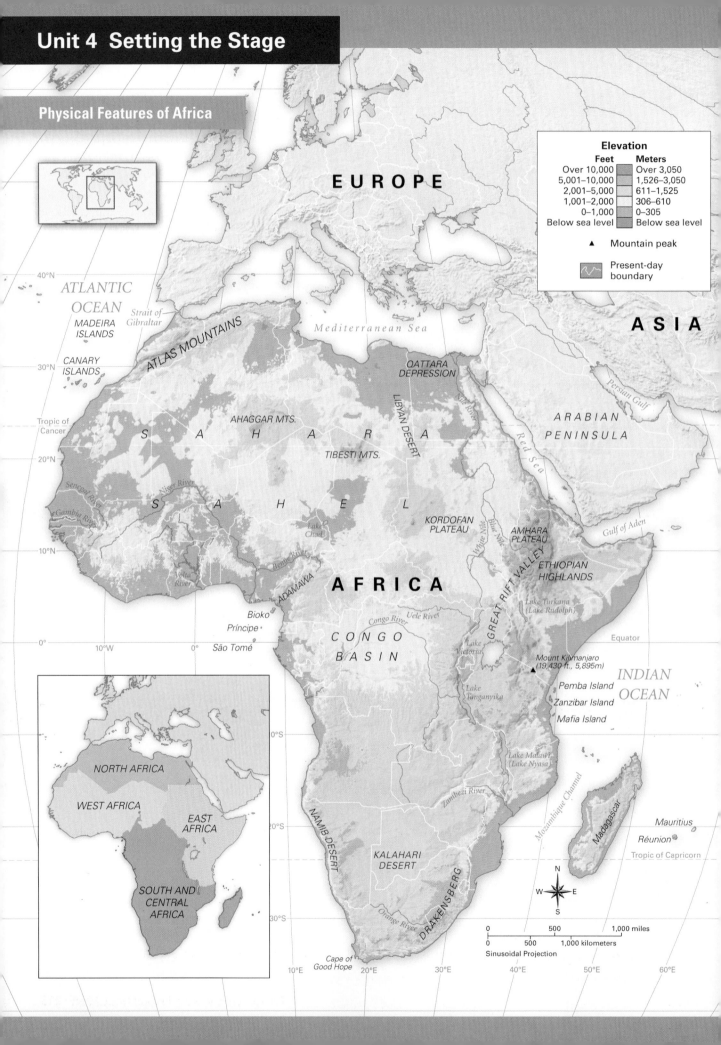

EUROPE

ASIA

AFRICA

ATLANTIC OCEAN

INDIAN OCEAN

MADEIRA ISLANDS

CANARY ISLANDS

Strait of Gibraltar

Mediterranean Sea

ATLAS MOUNTAINS

QATTARA DEPRESSION

LIBYAN DESERT

Nile River

Red Sea

Persian Gulf

ARABIAN PENINSULA

S A H A R A

AHAGGAR MTS.

TIBESTI MTS.

S A H E L

Senegal River

Niger River

Gambia River

Lake Chad

Benue River

Volta River

KORDOFAN PLATEAU

White Nile

Blue Nile

AMHARA PLATEAU

Gulf of Aden

ETHIOPIAN HIGHLANDS

ADAMAWA

Bioko

Príncipe

São Tomé

CONGO BASIN

Congo River

Uele River

GREAT RIFT VALLEY

Lake Turkana (Lake Rudolph)

Lake Victoria

Equator

Mount Kilimanjaro (19,430 ft., 5,895m)

Pemba Island

Zanzibar Island

Mafia Island

Lake Tanganyika

Lake Malawi (Lake Nyasa)

Mozambique Channel

Madagascar

Mauritius

Réunion

Tropic of Capricorn

Zambezi River

NAMIB DESERT

KALAHARI DESERT

Orange River

DRAKENSBERG

Cape of Good Hope

Tropic of Cancer

40°N

30°N

20°N

10°N

0°

10°W

0°

10°S

20°S

30°S

10°E

20°E

30°E

40°E

50°E

60°E

Elevation

Feet	Meters
Over 10,000	Over 3,050
5,001–10,000	1,526–3,050
2,001–5,000	611–1,525
1,001–2,000	306–610
0–1,000	0–305
Below sea level	Below sea level

▲ Mountain peak

Present-day boundary

NORTH AFRICA

WEST AFRICA

EAST AFRICA

SOUTH AND CENTRAL AFRICA

0 500 1,000 miles

0 500 1,000 kilometers

Sinusoidal Projection

N W E S

The Culture and Kingdoms of West Africa

In this unit, you will explore the history of one of the regions to which Islam spread: the region of West Africa. West Africa is part of the continent of Africa, which is the second largest continent on Earth. As you can see on the map *Physical Features of Africa*, Africa is located south of Europe. The Atlantic Ocean borders Africa on the west, and the Indian Ocean lies to the east.

Several vegetation zones form belts across Africa. Four zones in West Africa are especially important because of their influence on developing civilizations. These vegetation zones are desert, desert scrub, temperate grassland, and tropical grassland (or savanna). Find them on the map *Vegetation Zones of Africa*, and read the definitions of these four vegetation zones.

In ancient times, farming communities developed in the grasslands south of the Sahara, an area called the Sahel. Rivers, such as the Senegal and the Niger, helped make the land fertile, provided fish, and served as trade routes within the region.

For centuries, West Africans had limited contact with lands to the north because travel across the Sahara was very difficult. By the late 700s, however, Arab Muslim traders from North Africa were crossing the Sahara. Trans-Saharan trade played a key role in the growth of the three great medieval kingdoms: Ghana, Mali, and Songhai.

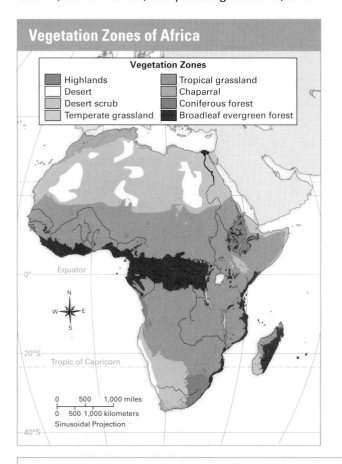

Vegetation Zones of Africa

Vegetation Zones
- Highlands
- Desert
- Desert scrub
- Temperate grassland
- Tropical grassland
- Chaparral
- Coniferous forest
- Broadleaf evergreen forest

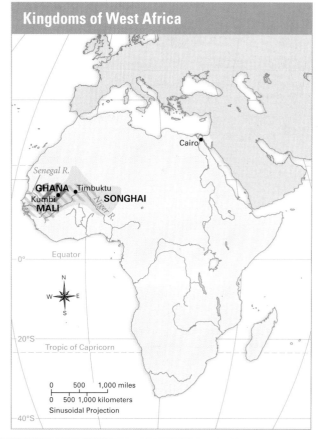

Kingdoms of West Africa

West African Vegetation Zones

Desert: dry region with few plants
Desert scrub: small trees, bushes, and other plants adapted to a dry climate
Temperate grassland: short and tall grasses
Tropical grassland: grasses and scattered trees adapted to a tropical wet and dry climate

Lesson 15

Early Societies in West Africa

What was the most significant factor in the development of early societies in West Africa?

Introduction

People have lived in West Africa for tens of thousands of years. For most of this time, historians do not have written records to study. Muslim scholars first began writing about the kingdom of Ghana in the 800s. By then, Ghana was perhaps 300 years old, and possibly much older. How did the first kingdoms arise? Why did they develop where they did?

To answer questions like these, historians and archaeologists study many kinds of clues. For example, they look closely at geography. Natural features, such as rivers and vegetation, help explain why people chose to settle where they did and what kind of life they created for themselves.

Additionally, scholars try to understand evidence from ancient settlements. How were villages and towns laid out? What can this reveal about life there?

Items left by earlier cultures also provide helpful clues about the past. Iron farming tools, for example, show that agricultural methods improved in West Africa. Scholars have worked to understand how more **efficient** farming affected the growth of towns and cities. Gradually, scholars have pieced together a picture of how complex societies developed in West Africa.

Between about 500 and 1600 c.e., three kingdoms arose in West Africa: Ghana, Songhai, and Mali. In this lesson, you will explore current thinking about the origins of West African kingdoms. You will discover how early family-based communities developed into villages. You will also learn how some villages were able to expand into towns and cities. Finally, you will see how some cities became great kingdoms.

Social Studies Vocabulary

artifact

Jenne-jeno

Niger River

Nok

Sahara

Sahel

savanna

smelting

tribute

◀ Behind the caravan is Timbuktu, a city in the early West African kingdom of Mali.

1. Geography and Trade

Geography offers many clues about why people settle where they do and how they live. It also helps to explain patterns of trade. As you will see throughout this lesson, trade played a critical role in the growth and advancement of West African societies. Let's examine the geography of West Africa and its influence on trade.

Sahara a large, hot desert in North Africa that covers about 3.5 million square miles

Sahel a zone of semidesert, south of the Sahara, where short grasses, small bushes, and a few trees grow

savanna a vegetation zone of tall grasses and scattered trees, with a long rainy season

Niger River the longest river in West Africa, which was a kind of trading highway in early times

Geography In the north, West Africa begins in the **Sahara**. To the west and south, the region is bordered by the Atlantic Ocean. To the east, it is bordered by the mountains of the present-day country of Cameroon. West Africa includes varied vegetation zones of desert, semidesert, savanna, and forest.

The Sahara spreads across approximately 3.5 million square miles in North Africa and the northern part of West Africa. Although sand dunes cover one-quarter of the Sahara, this desert also has bare, rocky plains, and even mountains. The Sahara is very dry except for some scattered oases, or water sources with some vegetation, so it was not a suitable location for large settlements.

South of the Sahara is a zone of semidesert called the **Sahel**. The Sahel is not as dry as the Sahara, and it has enough water for short grasses, some small bushes, and trees to survive.

The southern part of the Sahel merges into the **savanna,** an area of tall grasses and scattered trees. The savanna has a long rainy season, so grains such as millet, sorghum, and rice can thrive there. Grasses provide food for cattle, camels, goats, and sheep. Rivers, such as the long **Niger River,** help fertilize nearby land and also provide fish for eating.

The Niger River extends into the forest zone, a much wetter area than the savanna, located in the southern part of West Africa. Its northern part is a woodland forest of trees and shrubs. Oil palms, yams, and kola trees grow here. The southern part of the zone is lush rainforest, where rain falls year-round. In the rainforest, tall trees—such as mahogany and teak—rise above swamps and lagoons.

As they did in the past, people still use canoes to travel along the Niger River. This portion of the river is in the forest zone in the southern part of West Africa.

Trade The geography of West Africa influenced the patterns of trade that developed there. Different resources are found in each of the vegetation zones. As a result, people living in different zones had to trade to acquire items they could not provide for themselves. For example, people on the savanna may have traded grains for yams or mahogany from forest dwellers.

While several major rivers served as trading routes in West Africa, the region's longest river, the Niger, became a kind of trading highway. People in ancient times traveled the Niger and other rivers by canoe to trade goods. Some traders also crossed the Sahara from North Africa, but most early trade was among West African settlements.

Early West African villages might have had homes, such as these, built close together for protection. These early communities traded with one another to get resources they could not produce on their own.

2. Early Communities and Villages

By about 4000 B.C.E., some people had settled to farm south of the Sahara. The earliest farming communities were comprised of extended families, which included close relatives, such as grandparents, as well as aunts, uncles, and cousins.

An extended-family community might have had about 15 to 20 members. Each community produced most of the things it required. Family members worked together to clear the fields, plant seeds, and harvest crops. These small communities traded with one another for additional goods. Very likely, one of the male elders made decisions for the family community.

Eventually, family-based communities joined together to form villages that might contain one- to two-hundred people. The village leader was probably selected for his wisdom and strength.

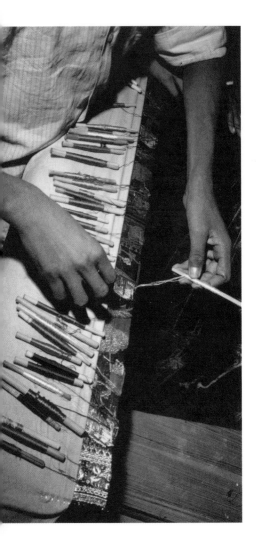

Iron tools made farming more efficient and productive. This allowed people to devote more time to weaving, still practiced today, as well as other crafts.

Nok a people living in West Africa in the 500s B.C.E. who mastered ironworking

artifact an item left behind by an earlier culture

smelting the process of melting ore to produce iron or other metals from it

Extended families usually banded together in villages to get needed help. For example, people might need to collaborate to control a flooding river or to mine for iron or gold. They may also have united for protection. Archaeologists have discovered ruins of high walls and gates at the ancient West African village of Dhar Tichitt, in the present-day country of Mauritania. These structures suggest that the villagers united to defend themselves from outside attacks.

3. The Development of Towns and Cities

Some West African villages gradually developed into towns and cities. Although some had thousands of residents, ancient cities in West Africa were not as large as modern cities. Why did villages grow into cities in West Africa? Two important reasons were the growth of ironworking and the expansion of trade.

Ironworking and Trade The Hittites of present-day Turkey mastered ironworking as long ago as 1500 B.C.E. Gradually, the knowledge of ironworking spread and eventually reached West Africa, perhaps by way of traders who crossed the Sahara. However, some scholars think that ironworking flourished independently among people in the northern part of West Africa.

By the 500s B.C.E., a people called the **Nok,** who resided in what is now central Nigeria, made iron tools. Archaeologists have found some important **artifacts** of the Nok culture, such as their iron tools and iron-smelting furnaces.

Smelting is the process of melting ore to extract iron or other metals. The Nok used enormous amounts of charcoal to fuel their iron-smelting furnaces. Skilled workers called blacksmiths hammered and bent the red-hot iron into useful tools like axes, hoes, and weapons, such as spears.

The valuable craft of ironworking spread rapidly throughout West Africa. The ability to make tools out of iron brought major changes. With iron tools, farmers could clear land and cultivate crops more efficiently than with stone tools. The greater abundance of food supported larger villages, where more people were free to pursue other trades, such as weaving, metalworking, and pottery making.

More and more, villages produced surplus food and handcrafted goods. They could then trade their surpluses for goods they could not produce themselves.

As goods traveled across West Africa, villages located along rivers or other easily traveled routes became important trading sites. Villages that controlled the trade routes became market centers, and the inhabitants became wealthy by charging fees for trading activity. Additionally, these villages drew many people to work at new jobs, such as supervising trade, learning crafts, and helping to construct public buildings.

Some villages expanded into sizable towns and cities. Other large settlements were able to grow because of nearby natural resources, such as iron ore and good farmland.

The Ancient City of Jenne-Jeno

In 1977, archaeologists began excavating the ancient West African city of **Jenne-jeno** (jen-NAH jen-OH). Built in the 3rd century B.C.E., Jenne-jeno existed for more than 1,600 years. Before its rediscovery, historians believed that cities did not exist in West Africa until outsiders arrived and helped local people build them. However, the discovery of Jenne-jeno proved this theory wrong.

Jenne-jeno was built where the Niger River intersects the Bani River,

This is an artist's depiction of the ancient city of Jenne-jeno. Its location along the Niger River was less than two miles from the modern city of Jenne. What signs of trade can you find in this illustration?

an ideal location for farming, fishing, and trade. The people of Jenne-jeno traded their surplus goods—such as catfish, fish oil, onions, and rice—for salt, iron ore, copper, and gold. The iron ore came from 50 miles away and the copper from 600 miles away.

Jenne-jeno grew into a busy city of about 20,000 people. It was surrounded by a wall 10 feet wide and 13 feet high. The wall may have been built to give the city more status and to make it easier to control the arrival and departure of traders.

The people of Jenne-jeno lived in circular houses. Initially, they built the houses from bent poles and woven mats, but they later used mud blocks.

The city's people participated in many crafts. Besides farmers and fishers, there were potters, metalsmiths, weavers, leatherworkers, bead makers, and ivory carvers.

The most respected people in Jenne-jeno were blacksmiths because the people of West Africa prized iron more than gold. They were amazed by blacksmiths' ability to make tools from iron. As in many other early cultures, early West Africans thought blacksmiths had supernatural (magical or godlike) powers. For this reason, blacksmiths had authority and many responsibilities including the ability to act as political leaders, judges, and doctors. Some even believed they could **predict** the future.

In recent years, scientists have **analyzed** the sites of other ancient cities in West Africa. They have found evidence of trade, craftsmanship, and great wealth.

Jenne-jeno an ancient West African city built along the Niger River, which existed for 1600 years

4. The Rise of Kingdoms and Empires

Trade was a major factor in the rise of West African kingdoms. Because Ghana, Mali, and Songhai were all trading powers that ruled over large areas, historians often refer to them as empires, as well as kingdoms.

How did these first kingdoms develop? The rulers of some trading cities in West Africa became wealthy by collecting taxes from the goods that were purchased and sold. With their wealth, they could afford to raise large armies to conquer other trading areas nearby. Then the ruler could take over the trade of those areas and become even wealthier.

Rulers also collected **tribute** from the people they conquered. The payment of tribute was an indication that the conquered people accepted the king's authority. Tribute could also pay for the king's protection from outside attackers.

West African kings were both the political and the religious leaders of their kingdoms. People believed that the gods gave them special powers. The kings performed religious ceremonies to please the gods.

As a king conquered more territory, the kingdom became an empire. Occasionally, a king sent a governor to rule a conquered area, while other times he allowed conquered people to rule themselves.

Becoming part of a kingdom or an empire had disadvantages such as the obligation to pay tribute. Another was that men had to serve in the king's army. However, there were also advantages. Kings provided protection for the conquered territory. Armies ensured that trade routes remained safe, and they kept out raiders and foreign armies. Wars between small cities ended. Kings collected luxury goods from their subjects and distributed them fairly throughout the kingdom. They also gave expensive presents to their governors.

tribute payment made by one ruler or country to another for protection or as a sign of submission

These modern horsemen from West Africa are a reminder of the armies that rulers were able to raise with the wealth they received from trade. Rulers also acquired wealth from tributes.

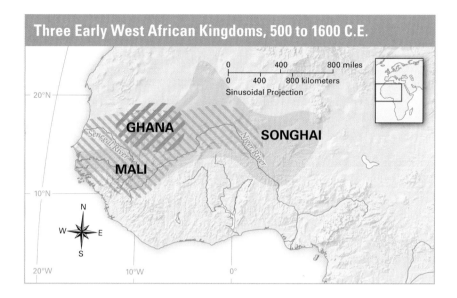

Three Early West African Kingdoms, 500 to 1600 C.E.

GHANA

MALI

SONGHAI

Senegal River

Niger River

0   400   800 miles
0   400   800 kilometers
Sinusoidal Projection

20°N

10°N

20°W   10°W   0°

N W E S

Three major kingdoms—Ghana, Songhai, and Mali—arose in West Africa between 500 and 1600 C.E. Each of these kingdoms benefitted from trade.

The great kingdoms of West Africa did not rely only on local trade. By the time Ghana became a significant power, trans-Saharan trade was directing new wealth to West Africa from other regions, such as the present-day Middle East. Control of trade, particularly in West African gold, was also crucial to the power of Mali. Songhai, too, relied on trade with distant lands.

Lesson Summary

In this lesson, you learned how kingdoms and empires grew out of early societies in West Africa.

Geography and Trade Geography was a major factor in the development of West African societies. Settled communities flourished south of the Sahara, where the land permitted farming. Geography also influenced trading patterns. Communities traded with one another for items they could not produce locally. Rivers, such as the Niger, served as trade routes.

Early Communities Early societies in West Africa were family-based communities. Some of these communities combined to form villages, which allowed them to take advantage of natural resources and to defend themselves from attack.

Towns and Cities Ironworking and trade helped some villages grow into sizable towns and cities. Iron tools allowed farmers to cultivate food more efficiently. As a result, more people could engage in other crafts. Villages traded their surplus goods for items they could not make themselves. Some villages became important trading sites and expanded into cities. Others developed into large communities near important resources, such as iron ore or gold.

Kingdoms and Empires Trade brought some cities great wealth. The rulers of the wealthiest cities conquered neighboring areas, leading to the rise of kingdoms and empires. Rulers gained even more wealth through tribute, as well as by controlling trade.

Lesson 16

Ghana: A West African Trading Empire

To what extent did trans-Saharan trade lead to Ghana's wealth and success?

Introduction

The early West African societies of Ghana, Mali, and Songhai all created empires that gained much of their wealth from trade. As you explore Ghana, you will learn more about the role of trade in the first of West Africa's empires.

The kingdom of Ghana lasted from sometime before 500 C.E. until its final collapse in the 1200s. It arose in the semidesert Sahel and eventually spread over the valley between the Senegal and Niger rivers. To the south was forest, and to the north lay the Sahara. Today, this region is part of modern nations Mali and Mauritania (maw-reh-TAIN-ee-uh). The modern country of Ghana takes its name from the old kingdom, but it is located far to the south.

The earliest writings about the kingdom of Ghana come from Arab scholars. These scholars recorded information they had gathered from travelers to the kingdom. By the time they began writing about Ghana in the 9th century, it was already a flourishing empire.

Historians are unsure of exactly how Ghana developed into an empire. Possibly, a group of warriors used iron weapons to defeat their neighbors. In fact, the word *ghana* means "war chief." However, archaeologists have concluded that control of trade, particularly the gold trade, made the king of Ghana and his people very wealthy. West Africans still sing songs about the majesty of ancient Ghana.

In this lesson, you will first learn about Ghana's government and military. Then you will learn how Ghana's people acquired wealth by participating in trans-Saharan trade, as well as how this trade led to Ghana's wealth and success. Finally, you will discover how Ghana declined and a new empire, Mali, arose in West Africa.

Social Studies Vocabulary

Ghana

matrilineal

trans-Saharan trade

◄ Camel caravans carried goods across the Sahara to and from medieval Ghana.

Ghana's kings wore caps like this one, decorated with gold. In medieval Ghana, after the king's death, his nephew replaced him on the throne.

1. Ghana's Government and Military

Arab scholars described **Ghana** as a fabled "land of gold." Their accounts paint a picture of a rich kingdom with a strong government and a large, powerful army.

The King and His Government Ghana was ruled by a powerful king. The king was the head of the army, made the final decisions in matters of justice, and led the people in religious worship.

Ghana's king acquired great wealth through control of the gold trade. Gold was especially plentiful in areas to the south of Ghana. As you will see, Ghana's government collected taxes on the gold that passed through the kingdom.

To preserve his wealth, the king tightly controlled the supply of gold. All the gold nuggets, or chunks, found in the kingdom had to be given to the king. Ordinary people could have only gold dust. One of the king's gold nuggets is said to have weighed almost forty pounds. According to legend, another was large enough to be used as a hitching post for his horse.

Each day, the king held court with his people. The king, splendidly dressed in colorful robes, gold jewelry, and a cap decorated with gold, arrived at court to the beating of royal drums. His people demonstrated their respect for him by kneeling and throwing dust on their heads as he approached.

Once at court, the king conducted the business of his empire and heard the people's concerns. One Arab historian described the scene at the court like this:

> *Behind the king stand ten pages [young servants] holding shields and swords decorated with gold and on his right are the sons of the vassal kings of his empire wearing splendid garments and their hair plaited [braided] with gold. The governor of the city sits on the ground before the king and around are ministers seated likewise. At the door . . . are dogs of excellent pedigree [ancestry] who hardly ever leave the place where the king is, guarding him. Round their necks, they wear collars of gold and silver.*

A large hierarchy of officials, some Muslim, helped the king govern. These officials were probably in charge of different parts of Ghana's society, such as the armed forces, industry, tax collection, and foreigners. The king appointed governors to rule some parts of his empire, such as the capital city and some conquered areas.

When the king died, his son did not inherit the throne because the royal inheritance was **matrilineal,** which means that it was traced through women's bloodlines rather than men's. Therefore, in Ghana, the son of the king's sister was the heir to the throne.

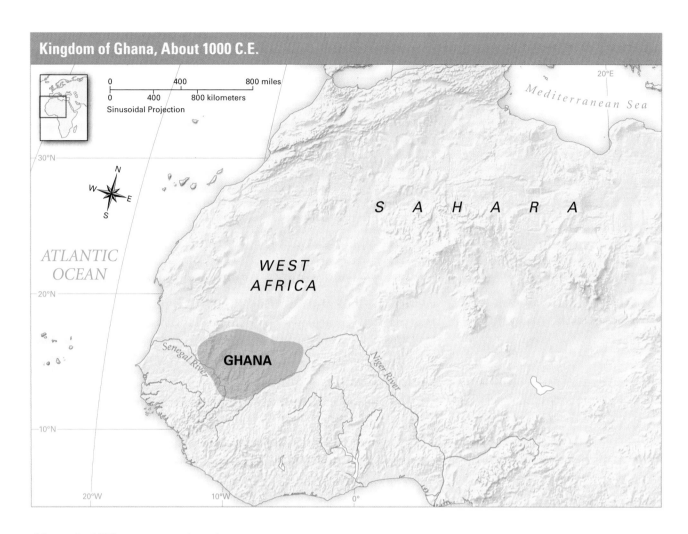

Kingdom of Ghana, About 1000 C.E.

0   400   800 miles
0 400   800 kilometers
Sinusoidal Projection

Mediterranean Sea

20°E

30°N

N
W   E
S

SAHARA

ATLANTIC
OCEAN

20°N

WEST
AFRICA

Senegal River

GHANA

Niger River

10°N

20°W   10°W   0°

Ghana's Military Ghana's military included a regular army, reserve forces, and elite soldiers. The regular army was comprised of several thousand career soldiers who kept the borders secure, suppressed minor revolts, and maintained peace and order. These soldiers wore knee-length cotton pants, sleeveless tunics (long shirts), sandals, and headdresses adorned with feathers. Both the color of a soldier's tunic and the number of feathers in his headdress indicated his rank. The soldiers used weapons such as spears, daggers, swords, battle clubs, and bows and arrows. They were well paid and highly respected.

During wartime, the king called up additional reserve forces and the troops of other governors under his rule. Every man in the empire was required to complete military training so that he would be prepared to serve when called. Stories describe a king who could call up an army of 200,000 warriors. This number no doubt grew as the story was passed on, but the king certainly could summon a sizable army, including infantry archers.

Special groups of soldiers were selected for their courage, honesty, and intelligence. These soldiers served the king as bodyguards, escorts, and military advisors.

Its location at the crossroads of major trade routes south of the Sahara and along the rivers brought medieval Ghana great wealth and power. The king built up large armies to maintain order across his land.

This brass weight in the shape of a horse and rider was made by the Ashanti people of Ghana. Trans-Saharan traders used this artifact to weigh gold dust .

trans-Saharan trade trade between peoples north and south of the Sahara

2. Trade: The Source of Ghana's Wealth

Ghana was located between two areas that wanted to trade—North Africa and West Africa. Traders from North Africa crossed the Sahara with salt, copper, and cowrie shells—a type of seashell that was used as money. The merchants traded these and other goods for kola nuts, hides, leather goods, ivory, slaves, and gold from the southern forests of West Africa. Then they returned to North Africa, bringing the goods from the south to markets at home.

Ghana's location enabled it to control this **trans-Saharan trade**. Traders traveling to and from the south had to pass through Ghana, paying heavy taxes on their goods each time. These taxes helped make Ghana rich.

The History of Trans-Saharan Trade Trans-Saharan trade has a long history. Archaeologists have found evidence that North Africans brought back gold from the southern forests of West Africa as long ago as 400 to 500 B.C.E. Travel across the Sahara, however, was especially challenging for these early peoples.

Centuries later, two factors contributed to the growth of trans-Saharan trade. The first was the introduction of the camel to the Sahara, and the second was the spread of Islam.

Arab traders first brought camels to the Sahara around 300 C.E. These animals are well suited for desert travel. A camel can drink up to 25 gallons of water at a time, allowing it to travel several days in the desert without stopping. Additionally, camels have double rows of eyelashes and hairy ear openings that help keep out blowing sand.

The introduction of camels allowed traders to establish caravan routes across the Sahara. By the 4th century C.E., large amounts of gold were being made into Roman coins in North Africa. It is likely that that gold came from West Africa.

Trade continued to expand because of the spread of Islam. In the 7th century, Muslims invaded Ghana's empire. Besides wanting to convert West Africans to Islam, Muslims hoped to control trade in West Africa. Although Ghana turned back the invaders, many Muslims settled in West African towns and became merchants.

Control of the trans-Saharan trade made Ghana wealthy and powerful. By the year 1000, Ghana's empire dominated the trade routes between North and West Africa.

The Journey South The traders who traveled to West Africa faced a long, difficult journey. The trans-Saharan caravan routes began in North Africa along the northwestern border of the Sahara. From there they stretched across the desert, passed through Ghana, and continued south to the Gulf of Guinea and east to present-day Chad.

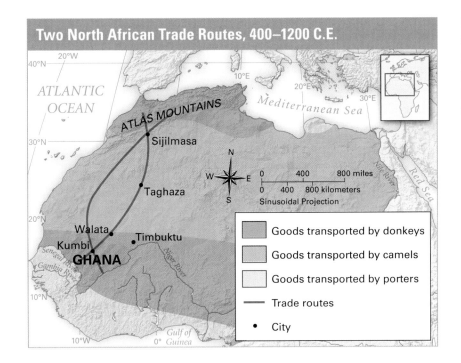

Two North African Trade Routes, 400–1200 C.E.

Goods transported by donkeys
Goods transported by camels
Goods transported by porters
— Trade routes
• City

Differences in geography led to different methods of transportation along the trade routes between North and West Africa. Camels, donkeys, and porters all contributed to the transport of the traded goods.

In 1352, a Muslim historian and traveler named Ibn Battuta (ib-ehn bat-TOO-tah) crossed the Sahara with a trade caravan. Battuta's account of his trip describes what the traders' journeys were like.

Battuta's caravan started at the oasis city of Sijilmasa (see-jeel-MAH-sah), on the northern edge of the Sahara, in the foothills of the Atlas Mountains. Donkeys carried goods from Europe, Arabia, and Egypt to Sijilmasa from the Mediterranean coast. Then camel caravans took the goods south.

Battuta and his caravan stayed in Sijilmasa for a few months, waiting for the rainy season to end. When the watering places were full and there was grass for the animals to eat, the traders embarked on their journey and traveled from oasis to oasis. Each day, the traders walked until the afternoon, when the sun was high in the sky. Then they rested until sunset.

Walking across the Sahara was challenging and dangerous. Caravans sometimes lost their way, and some traders died in the desert. During one stretch of Battuta's trip, the travelers could not find water, so they slaughtered some of their camels and drank the water stored in the animals' stomachs.

On its way through the desert, the caravan stopped at Taghaza, a village where salt mines were located, and took on a load of salt. When the traders reached the town of Walata, at the edge of the desert, they transferred their salt and other goods from the camels to donkeys and to porters, people who carry goods for a living. Then they continued south, passing through Ghana on their way to markets on the Gulf of Guinea, near the southern forests. The entire journey took about two months.

The Romans and people in Muslim lands used West African gold to make their coins. They likely acquired this gold from the Wangarans, who never revealed the locations of their gold mines.

3. The Gold-Salt Trade

Although many items were traded between North Africa and West Africa, the two goods that were most in demand were gold and salt. The North Africans wanted gold, which came from the forest region south of Ghana. The people in the forests wanted salt, which came from the Sahara. Ghana made most of its money from the taxes it enforced on the gold-salt trade that passed through its lands.

Wangara: The Secret Source of Gold Gold has long been a source of wealth in much of the world. In the time of Ghana's empire, people in Muslim lands and in Italy created coins from gold. Muslims also needed gold to purchase silk and porcelain from China, which would accept only gold in exchange.

In an area known as Wangara, gold was plentiful. Wangara was located near the forests south of Ghana, but no one except the people of Wangara knew its exact location. The Wangarans kept the locations of their gold mines secret. According to ancient stories, merchants occasionally captured a gold miner and tried to force him to reveal the location of Wangara. The miners would sacrifice their lives rather than reveal the secret.

In one tale, after the capture of a miner, the Wangarans stopped trading for three years in order to ensure no one had discovered Wangara's location. To this day, no one knows for certain exactly where Wangara's mines were located.

Taghaza: A Village Built with Salt To West Africans, salt was more precious than gold. Their culture had little use for gold, except as an item for trade. However, they craved salt, and for good reason. Salt is an important aspect of a person's diet because when people and animals perspire, or sweat, they lose salt in their perspiration. People who reside in hot climates, like West Africa, perspire a lot and must replace the salt they lose. West Africans also needed salt to prevent their food from spoiling and to give to their cattle. In addition, people enjoyed the taste.

West Africans had no local source of salt. Instead, they had to obtain it from Taghaza and other places in the Sahara.

Salt was produced in two ways in the Sahara. One method was through **evaporation**. Water was poured into holes in the salty earth. The water slowly drew out the salt and then evaporated in the sun. The salt that remained was collected and packed into blocks. The second way to acquire salt was through mining. At Taghaza, salt deposits were found about three feet below the surface of the earth. Miners, enslaved by Arab merchants, reached the salt by digging trenches and tunnels. Then they cut it out in large blocks.

Since it was a dismal place lacking crops or vegetation, Taghaza would not have existed without salt. People lived there for one purpose only: to mine and sell salt. Even the houses and mosques were built of salt blocks. Trade caravans passed through Taghaza on their way through the Sahara. There, they obtained salt to sell in Ghana and the southern forests. Because no food was produced in Taghaza, the miners had to rely on caravans to bring food, such as camel meat, dates, and a type of grain called millet. If the caravans did not arrive, the miners starved.

Ghana's System of Taxes Traders paid taxes to Ghana on all the goods they carried through the empire. Goods were taxed both when traders entered and left Ghana. Ghana charged one-sixth of an ounce of gold for each load of salt that came into the kingdom from the north. It then charged one-third of an ounce of gold for each load the traders exported out of the kingdom to the south. The traders also paid taxes for carrying other types of goods. For every load of copper, they were charged five-eighths of an ounce of gold. They paid slightly more than one ounce of gold per load of general merchandise.

The taxes enriched Ghana's treasury and helped finance armies that protected the kingdom, which allowed the king to conquer other territories. Additionally, traders benefited, because Ghana secured the trade routes against bandits who might rob the caravans.

In some parts of Africa, salt is made by the evaporation of water in areas called salt flats, such as this one. The salt is then dug out in large blocks.

4. The Exchange of Goods

When trade caravans entered Ghana, they brought their goods to the great marketplace in the capital city of Kumbi. From there, they headed to the southern forests to trade with the Wangarans.

Kumbi had the busiest market in West Africa. Many local crafts-people sold their goods there. Ironsmiths sold weapons and tools, while goldsmiths and coppersmiths sold jewelry. Weavers sold cloth, and leatherworkers sold leather goods. There were blue blouses from Spain and robes from Morocco, in North Africa. People could also purchase cattle, sheep, honey, wheat, raisins, dried fruit, ivory, pearls, and slaves. All goods, including slaves, were paid for with gold dust.

Kumbi had one of the largest slave markets in West Africa. Raiders captured the slaves along the southern border of Ghana. Many were bought at Kumbi by Arab merchants, who took them across the Sahara and sold them to North Africans or Europeans.

Even today, salt remains an important trade item in West Africa. Marketplaces still exist along the Niger River, a major transportation route through West Africa.

Trade with the Wangarans occurred along a river in the southern forests. Traders conducted their business using a system of silent barter, or trade. The caravans arrived bringing wool, silk, cotton, dates, figs, grains, leather, and salt. They distributed their goods along the river. The traders beat on a drum to announce that they were making an offer to trade and then walked several miles away from the location.

When the Wangarans heard the drum, they traveled to the site by boat. They put some gold dust next to the goods, beat a drum, and left. Later, the traders returned. If the amount of gold dust was acceptable, they took it and left. If not, they retreated again and waited for the Wangarans to return and leave more gold dust. The groups bargained back and forth in this way without ever meeting in person.

This system of silent barter had two advantages. First, it enabled people who spoke different languages to trade. Second, it allowed the Wangarans to protect the secret location of their gold mines.

5. The Decline of Ghana and the Rise of Mali

Ghana's empire reached its height around the year 1000 C.E. However, war and the loss of natural resources led to the West African empire's downfall, and the rise of a new power.

In the second half of the 11th century, Muslim warriors known as Almoravids began attacking Ghana's empire. In 1076, they captured the capital city of Kumbi. Although Ghana's king regained power in 1087, the old empire had already broken apart.

The loss of natural resources further weakened Ghana. The increasing population added great stress on scarce resources, such as trees and water. Trees were cut down to provide charcoal for iron-smelting furnaces. Water became so scarce that farmers could no longer cultivate crops and keep flocks. People were forced to leave in search of better conditions. The empire came to an end in 1203, when a rival kingdom conquered Kumbi.

The end of Ghana's empire opened the way to the rise of a new power, Mali. Around 1240, a group of West Africans called the Mande conquered Kumbi. Their homeland of Mali was south of Kumbi, closer to the Niger River. The Mande built an empire that reached from the Atlantic Ocean to beyond the Niger River, and from the southern forest to the salt and copper mines of the Sahara.

Similar to Ghana, Mali gained much of its wealth from the control of trade, particularly in gold. Its leaders had accepted Islam, and under their rule, the Muslim faith continued to become even more influential in West Africa.

Natural resources, such as water and trees, are still scarce in areas like the Sahel. The loss of resources led to the decline of Ghana and allowed Mali to become a new power in West Africa.

Lesson Summary

Trade played a key role in the growth of kingdoms and empires in West Africa. The first of these was Ghana.

Ghana's Government and Military Ghana was ideally located to control the trans-Saharan trade. It used the wealth from trade to develop a strong army, which allowed it to conquer other peoples and build an empire.

Trade: Gold and Salt Ghana became wealthy by charging taxes on goods, especially gold and salt. Gold was mined in secret locations in forests south of Ghana and carried north to trade, while salt was produced in the Sahara and transported south.

The Exchange of Goods The Wangarans used a system of silent barter to trade goods.

The Decline of Ghana and Rise of Mali Years of war and the loss of natural resources led to Ghana's downfall in the 13th century. The next powerful West African empire, Mali, also built its wealth on trade.

The Influence of Islam on West Africa

In what ways did Islam influence West African society?

Introduction

The Islamic faith and culture had a great impact on the early empires that developed in West Africa, such as Ghana. Islam also influenced the West African people and culture in many different areas of life.

During the 7th century, the religion of Islam spread quickly through the Middle East and North Africa. In the 8th century, trans-Saharan trade brought Muslim merchants and traders to West Africa. Over the next few hundred years, Islam spread throughout the region—first to Ghana, and then to other areas. The new faith left a lasting impression on the culture of West Africa. It changed the way people there lived, worked, and communicated. For example, many West Africans learned Arabic to study the Qu'ran.

The people of West Africa often blended Islamic culture with their own local traditions. For example, West Africans who became Muslims began praying to God in Arabic and building mosques as places of worship. However, they also continued to pray to the spirits of their ancestors, upholding a tradition that had been in place for centuries.

Islamic beliefs and customs affected many areas of life besides religious faith. In this lesson, you will learn about what brought Islam to West Africa and how it spread. Then you will take a detailed look at Islam's influence on several aspects of West African culture. Additionally, you will explore changes in religious practices, government and law, education, language, architecture, and decorative arts. The effects and influences of these changes in West Africa are still visible throughout this region today.

Social Studies Vocabulary

Mali

Mansa Musa

patrilineal

Songhai

textile

◀ Bricks and mud were used to construct the Grand Mosque in Mali. The beams projecting from its walls are used as scaffolding when it needs repairs.

Muslim traders and the missionaries who accompanied them spread Islam to Ghana and beyond. Trans-Saharan travel was a great platform for exchanging goods and ideas.

1. The Spread of Islam in West Africa

Trans-Saharan trade brought Islam to West Africa in the 8th century. Initially, Muslim traders and merchants lived alongside the non-Muslims of West Africa. Over time, however, Islam played a growing role in West African society.

Traders Bring Islam to Ghana Between the years 639 and 708 C.E., Arab Muslims conquered North Africa, and before long, they wanted to bring West Africa into the Islamic world. But sending armies to conquer Ghana was not practical since Ghana was too far away and protected by the Sahara.

Islam first reached Ghana through Muslim traders and missionaries. The king of Ghana did not **convert** to Islam, nor did the majority of the people. However, the king did allow Muslims to establish settlements within his empire.

Many Muslim merchants and traders settled in Kumbi, the great market city of Ghana. Over time, a thriving Muslim community developed around the trans-Saharan trade with North Africa. The Muslims in Kumbi had 12 mosques and their own imam (spiritual leader). Scholars studied the Qur'an.

In the 11th century, Muslims from the north, the Almoravids, invaded West Africa. In 1076, they captured Kumbi. The Almoravids did not retain power for long in Ghana, but under their rule Islam became more widespread.

Islam in Mali To the south of Ghana, the Mande also accepted Islam. Muslims showed **tolerance** toward traditional religious practices, which helped Islam to spread. For example, West Africans continued to pray to the spirits of their ancestors.

In about 1240, the Mande conquered Kumbi. They took control of the trade routes to North Africa and built the empire of **Mali**.

As in many other cultures, the early leaders of Mali accepted Islam in their own way and chose to follow specific teachings. In 1312, a new leader, **Mansa Musa,** took over in Mali and became the first West African ruler to practice Islam devoutly.

Under Mansa Musa's rule, Mali became a major crossroads of the Islamic world. Muslim merchants, traders, and scholars from Egypt and North Africa came to Mali to conduct business or to settle.

Like other Muslims, Musa made a hajj, or pilgrimage, to the sacred city of Mecca in Arabia. The hajj was an enormous undertaking, covering some 3,000 miles. Officials and servants started preparing for the trip months before Musa left. As many as 80,000 people may have accompanied Musa on the hajj.

Musa reached Cairo, Egypt, in July 1324, after eight months of travel. A writer from Cairo described Musa's caravan as "a lavish display of power, wealth, and unprecedented by its size and pageantry." Ahead of Musa arrived 500 slaves, each carrying a gold staff. He was followed by a caravan of up to 100 camels carrying 30,000 pounds of gold, along with food, clothing, and supplies.

In Cairo, Musa met the local sultan, or ruler. When Musa was asked to kneel before the sultan, he felt insulted since he was very proud of being the ruler of Mali. After Musa finally agreed to kneel, the sultan invited him to sit beside him as his equal.

Mali a West African empire ruled by the Mande that became a major crossroads of the Islamic world

Mansa Musa the first West African ruler to practice Islam devoutly

The pilgrimage of Mansa Musa to Mecca was so impressive that when news of it reached Europe, mapmakers there produced this map of West Africa with Musa's image prominently displayed. Many Muslims still make the hajj to the city of Mecca.

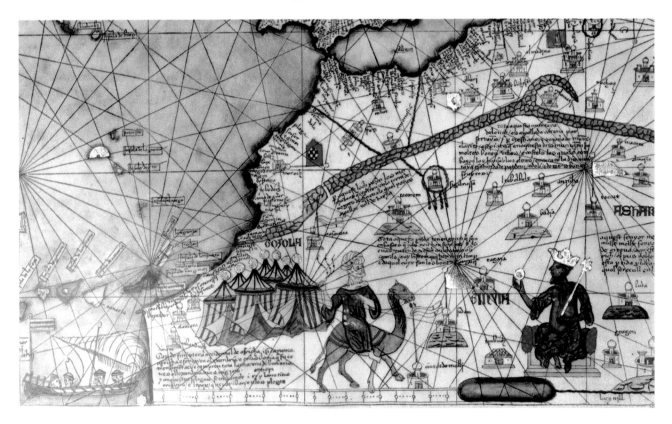

After leaving Cairo, Musa traveled to Arabia to visit Mecca and Medina. When word spread that the king of Mali was visiting, people lined the streets to see him. Musa's wealth impressed the people and rulers of Arabia. He paid in gold for all the goods and services he received and gave expensive gifts to his hosts.

Because of Musa's hajj, Mali became known as an important kingdom. By 1375, Mali appeared on a European map of West Africa.

Islam in Songhai One of the groups within Mali's empire was the Songhai people. In the 1460s, the great warrior Sunni Ali became the new ruler of the Songhai. He created a powerful army that enabled the Songhai to break away from Mali and, eventually, to conquer it.

The early Songhai rulers did not practice Islam as strictly. In the 1490s, Muslims in the Songhai empire rebelled. They placed Askia Mohammed Toure, a devout Muslim, on the throne. Toure established and enforced rigid controls to make sure Islam was practiced as he felt was proper. Additionally, he led a series of wars to convert non-Muslims to Islam. Under his rule, the Songhai empire covered a territory about as large as western Europe.

2. Religious Practices

As Islam spread in West Africa, the people adopted new religious practices in addition to ethical values, and learned the Five Pillars of Islam. They prayed in Arabic, fasted, worshipped in mosques, made pilgrimages, and gave alms. They were taught to regard themselves and all other Muslims as part of a single community.

West Africans also began to celebrate Muslim religious festivals. The festival of Eid al-Fitr marks the end of the holy month called Ramadan. A second festival called Eid al-Adha commemorates a significant event in the story of the prophet Abraham. According to the story, God asked Abraham to sacrifice his son as a test of faith, and after Abraham proved his faith through his willingness to offer his son to God, God spared the boy.

Alongside these new customs, West Africans preserved some of their old religious practices. Muslim leaders allowed them to continue religious traditions as long as they did not contradict the Five Pillars of Islam. So, for example, West African Muslims continued to demonstrate respect for the spirits of dead ancestors. They retained their belief in spirits who could help those who prayed to them or made sacrifices to them. They used amulets, or charms, that they believed helped people or protected them from harm.

Ibn Battuta was an Arab who traveled to Mali in the 14th century. Some local customs there upset Battuta. For instance, women, including the daughters of rulers, went unclothed in public. These customs disturbed him because they contradicted the teachings of Islam.

Songhai a people who broke away from the empire of Mali and eventually built their own vast empire in West Africa

With the introduction of Islam, West Africans began praying five times daily, as many still do today. During these prayers, Muslims face the direction of Mecca.

Regardless, Battuta was impressed by how **devoted** West Africans were to Islam and noted, "Anyone who is late at the mosque will find nowhere to pray, the crowd is so great. They zealously learn the Qur'an by heart. Those children who are neglectful in this, are put in chains until they have memorized the Qur'an."

3. Government and Law

The arrival of Islam and Arabic to Africa paved the way for other changes as well, especially to government and law. One major change concerned the line of succession, or inheritance of the right to rule. In West Africa, the succession had traditionally been matrilineal, meaning the right to rule was traced through the mother or female relative, rather than the father or a male relative. For example, in Ghana the son of the king's sister inherited the throne. After the arrival of Islam, succession became **patrilineal,** so the right to rule now passed from father to son.

A second change affected the structure of government. After West African kings converted to Islam, they started to exercise more control over local rulers. The kings also adopted titles used in Muslim lands. Often, the head of a region was called the sultan, the amir, or emir. *Amir* and *emir* are shortened forms of Amir al-Muminin, an Arabic expression meaning "Commander of the Faithful."

A third major change was the adoption of shari'ah. In many towns and cities, shari'ah replaced the customary law of West Africa, which was very different. Although laws were not written, everyone understood what they were and accepted them from long tradition. A chief or king usually enforced customary law but did not give physical punishments. Instead, the guilty party paid the injured party with gifts or services. The family or clan of the guilty person could also be punished.

One example of customary law was "trial by wood." Suppose a man was accused of not paying debts or of injuring another person. The accused man was forced to drink water that had been poured over sour, bitter wood. If the man became ill, he was believed to be innocent.

Unlike customary law, shari'ah is written law. Muslims believe that shari'ah came from God. Judges called *qadis* administered shari'ah. The qadis hear cases in a court, listen to witnesses, and rule on the basis of the law and the evidence.

With the arrival of Islam, the power of the central ruler increased and local chiefs grew less important. Pictured here is the emir of Kano, Nigeria, returning from his hajj.

patrilineal a family line traced through the father

The influence of Islam made the medieval city of Timbuktu a center for learning. Several universities were established there.

4. An Emphasis on Education

In West Africa, Muslims encouraged people to pursue an education. They built many schools and centers of learning.

One key center was the trading city of Timbuktu, on the Niger River. Under Mali and Songhai rule, Timbuktu became famous for its community of Islamic scholars and remained an important center of learning until the Songhai were conquered by Morocco in the 1500s.

Several universities were built in Timbuktu, the most famous of which was the University of Sankore. At that time, it was one of the world's great centers of learning.

Sankore was made up of several small, independent schools, each of which was run by an imam, or religious leader. The imams at Sankore were respected throughout the Islamic world.

Students at Sankore studied under a single imam. The basic course of learning included the Qur'an, Islamic studies, law, and literature. After mastering these subjects, students could continue their studies in a particular field. Many kinds of courses were available, including medicine, surgery, astronomy, mathematics, and other sciences. Additionally, they could take up philosophy, geography, art, or history.

The highest degree a student could earn at Sankore required roughly ten years of study. During graduation, students wore a cloth headdress called a turban, which was a symbol of divine light, wisdom, knowledge, and excellent moral character.

When travelers and traders passed through Timbuktu, they were encouraged to study at one of the universities. Trade associations also established their own colleges where students learned about the profession of trading, in addition to studying Islam.

Muslims also developed schools to educate children about the Qur'an. Timbuktu had about 150 Qur'anic schools, where children learned to read and interpret Islam's holy book.

With their love of education, Muslims treasured books. Muslims did not have printing presses, so books had to be copied by hand. Mosques and universities in West Africa constructed large libraries of these precious volumes. Additionally, some individuals created sizable collections including one Islamic scholar whose private library contained 700 volumes, some of which were extremely rare.

5. The Arabic Language

Islam is rooted in Arab culture, so as Islam spread throughout West Africa, the Arabic language did, as well. In West Africa, Arabic became the language of religion, learning, commerce, and government. However, West Africans continued to use their native languages in everyday speech.

For Muslims, Arabic was the language of religion. The Qur'an, of course, was written in Arabic. All Muslims were expected to read the Qur'an and memorize parts of it, so as West Africans converted to Islam, more and more of them learned Arabic.

Arabic also became the language of learning since the scholars who came to West Africa were mainly Arabic-speaking Muslims. Some of their students became scholars themselves and, like their teachers, they read and wrote Arabic.

Scholars used Arabic to write about the history and culture of West Africa, and they wrote about a wide variety of topics. They described how people used animal and plant parts and minerals to cure diseases. They discussed ethical behavior for business and government. They told how to use the stars to determine the seasons. They recorded the history of the Songhai. They also wrote about Islamic law. These writings are an invaluable source of knowledge about West Africa in this period.

Finally, Arabic became the language of trade and government. Arabic allowed West African traders who spoke different native languages to communicate more easily, and enabled rulers to keep records and to write to rulers in other countries.

Arabic, the language of the Qur'an, became the language of learning, government, and trade in West Africa. This language was very key for trading in West Africa, since it allowed those who spoke different native languages to still communicate and exchange goods.

Islamic architects built flat-roofed houses made of sun-dried bricks. The town of Timbuktu, pictured here, still maintains this architectural style in its buildings.

6. Islamic Architectural Styles

The influence of Islam brought new styles of architecture to West Africa as well. People designed mosques for worship. They also created a new design for homes.

Traditionally, West Africans had erected small shrines to honor the forces of nature. However, as they converted to Islam, they began to build mosques. The materials that were most available on the savanna were mud and wood, so West Africans used these materials to build mosques that blended Islamic architectural styles with their own traditional religious art. For example, the minaret (tower) of one mosque was designed to resemble the symbol of a Songhai ancestor.

After his pilgrimage to Mecca, the Mali ruler Mansa Musa wanted to construct more mosques. He convinced Al-Saheli, an architect from Spain, to return to Mali with him. Al-Saheli built several structures in Mali, one of which is the most famous mosque in West Africa, Djingareyber (jin-gar-AY-ber). Located in the city of Timbuktu, Djingareyber was built out of limestone and earth mixed with straw and wood. Projecting from the walls of the mosque are beams, which workers used as scaffolding when the building needed to be repaired.

Additionally, it is believed Al-Saheli introduced a new design for houses. Most traditional houses in West Africa were round with cone-shaped, thatched roofs. Using what may have been Al-Saheli's design, architects created rectangular houses out of brick with flat roofs, very plain outside walls, and no windows. Only a single wooden door, decorated with a **geometric** design, interrupted the rows of bricks.

textile a woven cloth

7. Islamic Decorative Arts

Muslims used calligraphy (artistic writing) and geometric patterns in their decorative arts. West Africans adopted these intricate designs for their own art and textiles.

Muslims used calligraphy to decorate objects with words or verses from the Qur'an. West Africans adopted this practice and began using the Arabic word for God to decorate costumes, fans, and even weapons. They wrote verses from the Qur'an on amulets as well.

Geometric patterns are an important element in Islamic art. Geometric designs were also popular in traditional West African art, and they were used to decorate **textiles** and everyday objects, such as stools and ceramic containers. The arrival of Islam reinforced this practice.

Muslims also influenced the way people dressed in West Africa. Arab Muslims commonly wore an Arab robe as an outer layer. An Arabic robe has wide, long sleeves and a long skirt. Muslims used calligraphy to personalize and decorate their robes. West Africans adopted the Arabic robe and, like Arabs, still wear it today.

Islam reinforced the West African tradition of using geometric designs in arts and crafts, such as weaving. Today, these designs remain prevalent in West African fashion and art.

Lesson Summary

In this lesson, you learned about the influence of Islam in medieval West Africa. Islam left a deep imprint on West African culture.

The Spread of Islam in West Africa Traders and missionaries first brought Islam to Ghana in the 8th century. The influence of Islam increased under the rulers of Mali and Songhai.

Religious Practices Islam changed West African religion. Although many continued to show respect for the spirits of ancestors and to follow other traditional beliefs, they learned to adhere to the Five Pillars of Islam and to celebrate Muslim religious festivals.

Government, Law, and Education Islam contributed to different ideas about government and law. The royal succession became patrilineal, government became more centralized, and shari'ah replaced customary law in some places. There was a new emphasis on learning, so people studied at Qur'anic schools and Islamic universities. Timbuktu became a center of Islamic and academic study.

Arabic Language and Islamic Architecture and Decorative Arts Arabic became the language of religion, learning, commerce, and government. New styles of architecture developed as West Africans constructed mosques and changed the designs of their homes. They also adopted new, geometric styles in their decorative arts.

What Does Ibn Battuta's Writing Reveal About Islam in Medieval Mali?

Ibn Battuta is considered one of the greatest medieval Arab travelers. For almost 30 years, he traveled some 75,000 miles through the equivalent of over 40 modern countries, most of which were under the government of Muslim leaders. While in Mali in West Africa, he wrote his observations about the Mali people, who interwove their traditional customs with Muslim practices. You will read Battuta's writings and construct a claim about what his writings reveal about Islam in Mali at the time.

When historians try to understand how Islam spread through West Africa, they study the writings and records of medieval travelers, such as Ibn Battuta. At the age of 21, in 1325, Battuta set out to visit Mecca and fell in love with travel. Over the next 30 years, he traveled about 75,000 miles through the Middle East, North and West Africa, and Asia. His adventures included a shipwreck, a war, and being hosted by wealthy kings. His books mention more than 2,000 people that he either personally met or whose tombs he visited.

Merchants, traders, and other travelers introduced their Muslim customs and beliefs to Mali where the people had been practicing their traditional rituals. By 1300, many West African kings practiced Islam. Over the years, the West African people blended Muslim practices with their own native ways.

Battuta himself was a Muslim with strong Islamic beliefs. While traveling in West Africa, he observed how the people practiced their native customs and rituals and also how they practiced Islam. The following texts were written by Battuta about the people in the empire of Mali. As you read, think about the unique perspective from which Battuta writes. How might his faith have influenced how he wrote about his observations of the people? How can historians verify that what Battuta reported is true?

Between the years 1325 and 1353, Ibn Battuta traveled through most of the Muslim world on the routes shown here. His reports about the people he observed reveal how the practices of Islam were integrated with the traditional customs and beliefs.

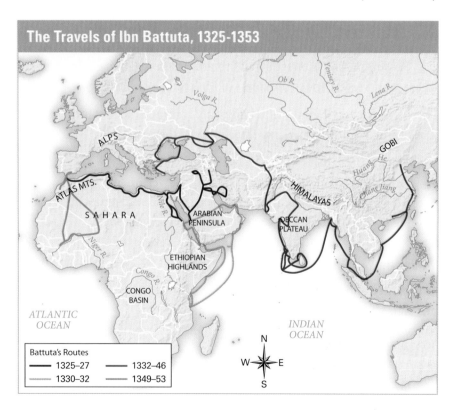

The Travels of Ibn Battuta, 1325-1353

Battuta's Routes
— 1325–27   — 1332–46
— 1330–32   — 1349–53

Travels in Asia and Africa

The negroes possess some admirable qualities. They are seldom unjust, and have a greater abhorrence of injustice than any other people. Their sultan shows no mercy to anyone who is guilty of the least act of it. There is complete security in their country. Neither traveller nor inhabitant in it has anything to fear from robbers or men of violence. They do not confiscate the property of any white man who dies in their country, even if it be uncounted wealth. On the contrary, they give it into the charge of some trustworthy person among the whites, until the rightful heir takes possession of it. They are careful to observe the hours of prayer, and assiduous in attending them in congregations, and in bringing up their children to them. On Fridays, if a man does not go early to the mosque, he cannot find a corner to pray in, on account of the crowd. It is a custom of theirs to send each man his boy [to the mosque] with his prayer-mat; the boy spreads it out for his master in a place befitting him [and remains on it] until he comes to the mosque. Their prayer-mats are made of the leaves of a tree resembling a date-palm, but without fruit.

Another of their good qualities is their habit of wearing clean white garments on Fridays. Even if a man has nothing but an old worn shirt, he washes it and cleans it, and wears it to the Friday service. Yet another is their zeal for learning the Koran by heart. They put their children in chains if they show any backwardness in memorizing it, and they are not set free until they have it by heart. I visited the qádí in his house on the day of the festival. His children were chained up, so I said to him "Will you not let them loose?" He replied "I shall not do so until they learn the Koran by heart."

—Ibn Buttata, 1325-1354

This text was written by Battuta and published in a book titled *The Travels of Ibn Battuta A.D. 1325-1354. Vol I.* Historians value Battuta's focus on his detailed observations of daily life and how people interact with one another. This excerpt describes Battuta's visit in Mali and discusses how the native people practice Islam. Note that the word *qadi* means "judge" and *Koran* is another way to spell "Qur'an," the holy book of the religion of Islam.

Read this excerpt, and consider the following questions: What characteristics about the Mali people is Battuta describing in these two sections? How is Islam practiced in Mali, and how is it a part of the lives of the Mali people? How does Battuta portray their attitude toward religion? What kind of detail does Battuta choose to incorporate into his observations? Why do you think this excerpt would still be valuable to historians today?

Travels in Asia and Africa

I was at Málli during the two festivals of the sacrifice and the fast-breaking. On these days the sultan takes his seat on the pempi after the midafternoon prayer. The armour-bearers bring in magnificent arms--quivers of gold and silver, swords ornamented with gold and with golden scabbards, gold and silver lances, and crystal maces. At his head stand four amirs driving off the flies, having in their hands silver ornaments resembling saddle-stirrups. The commanders, qádi, and preacher sit in their usual places. The interpreter Dúghá comes with his four wives and his slave-girls, who are about a hundred in number. They are wearing beautiful robes, and on their heads they have gold and silver fillets, with gold and silver balls attached. A chair is placed for Dúghá to sit on. He plays on an instrument made of reeds, with some small calabashes at its lower end, and chants a poem in praise of the sultan, recalling his battles and deeds of valour. The women and girls sing along with him and play with bows. Accompanying them are about thirty youths, wearing red woollen tunics and white skull-caps; each of them has his drum slung from his shoulder and beats it. Afterwards come his boy pupils who play and turn wheels in the air, like the natives of Sind. They show a marvellous nimbleness and agility in these exercises and play most cleverly with swords. Dúghá also makes a fine play with the sword. Thereupon the sultan orders a gift to be presented to Dúghá and he is given a purse containing two hundred mithqáls of gold dust, and is informed of the contents of the purse before all the people. The commanders rise and twang their bows in thanks to the sultan. The next day each one of them gives Dúghá a gift, every man according to his rank. Every Friday after the ʿasr prayer, Dúghá carries out a similar ceremony to this that we have described.

On feast-days, after Dúghá has finished his display, the poets come in. Each of them is inside a figure resembling a thrush, made of feathers, and provided with a wooden head with a red beak, to look like a thrush's head. They stand in front of the sultan in this ridiculous make-up and recite their poems. I was told that their poetry is a kind of sermonizing in which they say to the sultan: "This pempi which you occupy was that whereon sat this king and that king, and such and such were this one's noble actions and such and such the other's. So do you too do good deeds whose memory will outlive you." After that, the chief of the poets mounts the steps of the pempi and lays his head on the sultan's lap, then climbs to the top of the pempi and lays his head first on the sultan's right shoulder and then on his left, speaking all the while in their tongue, and finally he comes down again. I was told that this practice is a very old custom amongst them, prior to the introduction of Islám, and that they have kept it up.

—Ibn Buttata, 1325–1354

In the previous passage, Battuta describes a festival celebrated by the Mali people. The festival rituals developed prior to the introduction of Islam in Mali. Battuta mentions in the first sentence that the festival follows a period of fasting, or a voluntary abstinence from food, a practice many still participate in today. How are the Mali people portrayed in this passage? How do the practices of the Mali people compare to those described in the first excerpt? What differences and similarities do you notice?

In the next passage, Battuta talks about other rituals he experienced in Mali. What is Battuta's reaction to the Mali sultan's gift? Why do you think he reacted this way? What does Battuta's description of the gift reveal about his attitude toward Mali customs?

Travels in Asia and Africa

... When the ceremony was over I went forward and saluted Mansá Sulaymán. The qádí, the preacher, and Ibn al-Faqíh told him who I was, and he answered them in their tongue. They said to me "The sultan says to you 'Give thanks to God,'" so I said "Praise be to God and thanks under all circumstances."

When I withdrew the [sultan's] hospitality gift was sent to me. It was taken first to the qádí's house, and the qádí sent it on with his men to Ibn al-Faqíh's house. Ibn al-Faqíh came hurrying out of his house bare-footed, and entered my room saying "Stand up; here comes the sultan's stuff and gift to you." So I stood up thinking [since he had called it "stuff"] that it consisted of robes of honour and money, and lo! it was three cakes of bread, and a piece of beef fried in native oil, and a calabash of sour curds. When I saw this I burst out laughing, and thought it a most amazing thing that they could be so foolish and make so much of such a paltry matter.

—Ibn Buttata, 1325–1354

Think about all the examples of Battuta's writing. How does he portray Mali traditional customs and Islamic customs? For example, what adjectives does he use to describe traditional and Muslim clothing? Some historians say that Arab travelers such as Battuta may have exaggerated the importance of Islam in West Africa. With that in mind, write a claim that tells what Battuta's writing reveals about Islam in medieval Mali. Include your thoughts about how reliable Battuta is as an objective observer. What biases might he have? What might be the purpose of his writing?

Mali (1300–1400)

In the 14th century, the west African empire of Mali was larger than Western Europe. It was also one of the richest and most powerful states in the world. Through the trans-Saharan trade route, many items were exported to regions to the north and the south. Cultures, Muslim religion, and the Arabic language also spread. In time, the flowing trade made Mali's capital, Timbuktu, a hub of commerce and Islamic culture. Additionally, it led to the establishment and development of many **institutions**.

Trade and Exchange

Medieval Mali was landlocked so it did not border large bodies of water, making sea trade non-existent. However, caravan routes were used along the Niger River valley to reach other regions for almost 1,000 years. Timbuktu's close proximity to the river made it a crossroads for traders and travelers. Other cities like Djenné and Mopti also became bustling marketplaces.

Gold was the main export in Mali, and the region became known for its abundance of the precious mineral. In fact, it's been estimated that one ton of gold was exported per year. The trade of gold greatly boosted northern Africa and Europe's economy. In addition to gold, northbound caravans also shipped ivory, ostrich feathers, and slaves captured in raids and wars.

Although Medieval Mali was landlocked, routes along the Niger River helped traders reach places like Timbuktu.

Both men and women were traded for **commodities** like gold and salt, but the majority of Saharan slaves were women. Merchants would sell the slave women to the Mediterranean or Middle East to serve in Muslim households. Women were more expensive but they were seen as the best workers for household duties.

The southbound trade included the other major export second to gold: salt. The mineral was in huge demand from West Africa and was even used as money at one point. It was found from Saharan mines and taken by camel to the southern countries. Other southbound commodities included copper, horses, and Arabic books.

This is a present-day market in Djenné, Mali that's held right in front of the Great Mosque of Djenné. This mosque is an example of an institution.

The Influence of Muslim Culture

Arabic- and Berber-speaking merchants and, later, Arab clerics from North Africa likely introduced Islam to West Africa in the 8th century. They established bonds with Sudanic traders, many of whom converted to the new faith. A few rulers and courtiers followed shortly afterwards. Travelers and geographers al-Bakri and Ibn Battuta have written several accounts of their observations about the spread of Islam.

Even for those Africans who did not convert to Islam, Muslim culture had a significant impact. For example, West African architecture, education, and languages were all greatly influenced by Islam. The Arabic language played a large role in both trade and government in West Africa. Large mosques built in the cities of Gao, Djenne, and Timbuktu became centers for learning while Arabic became the language of Muslim religion, trade, and government.

Lesson 18

The Cultural Legacy of West Africa

In what ways do the cultural achievements of West Africa influence our culture today?

Introduction

The medieval cultures of West Africa are diverse and have a rich legacy. Many groups of people, each with its own language and way of life, have lived in the region of West Africa. From poems and stories to music and visual arts, their cultural achievements have left a lasting mark on the world.

Much of West African culture has been passed down through its oral traditions. Think for a moment of the oral traditions in your own culture. When you were younger, did you learn nursery rhymes from your family or friends? How about sayings such as "A penny saved is a penny earned"? Did you hear stories about your grandparents or more distant ancestors? You can probably think of many ideas that were passed down orally from one generation to the next.

Suppose that your community depends on you to remember its oral traditions so that they will never be forgotten. You memorize stories, sayings, and the history of your city or town. You know about the first people who lived there, how the community grew, and which teams have won sports championships. On special occasions, you share your knowledge through stories and songs. You are a living library of your community's history and traditions.

In parts of West Africa, there are people whose job it is to preserve oral traditions and history in this way. They are talented poet-musicians. For many centuries, they have helped to preserve West Africa's history and cultural legacy.

In this lesson, you will learn about the role of both oral traditions and written traditions in West Africa. You will also explore West African music and visual arts. Along the way, you will see how the cultural achievements of West Africans continue to influence our world.

Social Studies Vocabulary

appliqué
call-and-response
folktale
genealogy
griot
kente
oral tradition
terra-cotta

◀ Kente cloth and hand-carved furniture are traditional arts in West Africa.

1. West African Oral and Written Traditions

For centuries, the beliefs, values, and knowledge of West Africans were **transmitted** orally from one generation to the next. In medieval times, written traditions also became important. In this section, you will examine the oral traditions and written traditions of West Africa.

Griots: Record Keepers of the People A griot (GREE-oh) is a **verbal** artist of the Mande people. Griots are poet-musicians who tell stories, sing songs of praise, and recite poems, often while playing a drum or stringed instrument. Although they perform music, dance, and drama, griots are much more than skilled entertainers. They also educate their audiences with historical accounts and genealogies, or histories of people's ancestry. In many ways, they are the record keepers and historians of their people.

Long before the Mande had written histories, griots preserved the memory of the past. Every village had its own griot who memorized all the important events that occurred there. Griots could recite everything from births, deaths, and marriages, to battles, hunts, and the successions of kings. Some griots could tell the ancestry of every villager, going back centuries and were known to speak for hours and, sometimes, even for days.

This rich oral tradition passed from griot to griot. Rulers relied on griots as their trusted advisors because they used the griots' knowledge of history to shed light on their current problems.

oral tradition learning and cultural ideas passed down orally, from one generation to the next

griot a talented poet-musician of the Mande people, who tells stories, sings songs, and recites poems to share history

genealogy an account of the line of ancestry within a family

Muslim traders and the missionaries who accompanied them spread Islam to Ghana and beyond.

The most cherished information in griot history is the story of Sundjata Keita (soon-JAHT-ah KAY-tah). Sundjata was the king who founded Mali's empire in the 13th century. In fact, griot stories were told about him even in his own lifetime.

The art of the griots remains alive today. Some of the most famous artists in West African popular music are griots who changed traditional oral works into modern songs. Poets and storytellers make recordings and appear on radio broadcasts performing both old and new works.

Folktales West Africa's oral tradition includes hundreds of old stories called **folktales**. West Africans used folktales to pass along their history and to teach young people morals and values.

Many traditional folktales were brought to the Americas by West Africans who were sold into slavery beginning in the 1500s. The tales were spread orally among the enslaved Africans as well as their descendants, and became part of the culture of North and South America and the West Indies.

One example is a type of folktale known as a "trickster tale." These stories tell of a clever animal or human who outsmarts others. Trickster tales are popular in many cultures. In West Africa, one famous trickster was the hare. West Africans brought tales of the hare to America, where he became known as Brer Rabbit. In the 19th century, a writer named Joel Chandler Harris retold a number of African American stories about Brer Rabbit. These stories have since been woven into American culture.

Proverbs West African oral tradition includes proverbs, or popular sayings. Proverbs are found in all cultures. West African proverbs use images from everyday life to express ideas or give advice and reveal a great deal about the wisdom and values of West Africans.

One proverb illustrates how Africans valued their stories. The proverb states, "A good story is like a garden carried in the pocket." Another explains the importance of oral tradition. "Every time an old man dies," the proverb says, "it is as if a library has burnt down." Enslaved West Africans brought proverbs like these to the Americas.

Written Tradition After Islam spread to West Africa, written tradition became more important. Muslims published many works in Arabic. A number of these writings were preserved in mosques and Qur'anic schools. Today, they are a key source of information about West African history, legends, and culture.

Modern writers in West Africa are adding to the literary legacy of the region. Some of them have turned ancient oral traditions into novels and other works.

Griots, or storytellers, continue the oral traditions of West African culture, they also represent the importance of elders in West African society. Many of their stories were brought to the Americas.

folktale a story that is passed down orally and becomes part of a culture's tradition

2. West African Music

Music has always been an important aspect of life in West Africa and serves many functions in West African society. It **communicates** ideas, values, and feelings. It celebrates historic events and important occasions in people's lives. For instance, there are songs for weddings, funerals, and ceremonies honoring ancestors. Among the Yoruba of present-day Nigeria, mothers of twins have their own special songs. In Ghana, there are songs for celebrating the loss of a child's first tooth.

The musical traditions of West Africa continue to influence both African and world culture. Let's analyze some key characteristics of West African music.

Call-and-Response In a common West African style of music known as **call-and-response,** a leader plays or sings a short phrase referred to as a call. Then a group of people, the chorus, answer by playing or singing a short phrase, the response. The leader and chorus repeat this pattern continuously as they perform the song.

call-and-response a song style in which a singer or musician leads with a call, and a chorus responds

Enslaved Africans brought call-and-response songs to the Americas. Slaves used the songs to ease the burden of hard work, celebrate social occasions, and express outrage at their situation. This African tradition has influenced many American musical styles, including gospel, jazz, blues, rock and roll, and rap.

Musical Instruments Traditional musical instruments in West Africa include three that griots have used for centuries. They are called the *balafon* (BAH-la-fon), the *ngoni* (en-GOH-nee), and the *kora* (KOR-ah).

The balafon is a traditional musical instrument of West Africa made of wooden bars attached to a horizontal frame. The bars are struck with a hammer, much like with a xylophone.

The balafon probably was the original griot instrument. Like a xylophone or marimba, a balafon is made of wooden bars laid across a frame. The musician strikes the bars with a mallet, or hammer, to make melodies. The balafon is used today in popular music in modern Guinea.

The ngoni is a small stringed instrument made of hollowed-out wood carved in a shape similar to a canoe. The instrument's strings are made of thin fishing line. The ngoni is the most popular traditional stringed instrument in Mali today.

The kora is a harplike instrument with 21 strings. The body of the kora is made of a gourd that has been cut in half and covered with cow-hide. The kora's strings, like those of the ngoni, are made of fishing line.

West African musicians have introduced kora music to people around the world. Some modern musicians in West Africa combine the sounds of the kora with electronic music.

Drumming Drums play a significant role in West African culture. Drummers perform at parties, religious meetings, and ceremonies, such as weddings and funerals.

West African drums are made of hollowed-out logs or pieces of wood. The drums are covered with animal skins.

Drummers in West Africa play in ensembles, or groups, which include different types and sizes of drums, along with bells and rattles. Drumming, singing, and dancing take place together in a circle. Sometimes, drum ensembles use a call-and-response style.

West African slaves brought their drumming traditions to the Americas. Eventually, West African drum music **evolved** into new styles, particularly in Cuba. West African drum music and Afro-Cuban drumming are now popular elements of world music.

Drumming is an important element of West African music. Drums of different sizes and shapes often have bells and rattles attached to them.

Dance In West Africa, dance is as much a part of life as singing and drumming are. Traditional West African dances are still performed in Africa and around the world.

West Africans perform dances for all kinds of occasions including rituals and ceremonies that commemorate important events in people's lives. Dances can celebrate a success at work or help educate children. Additionally, West Africans perform dances to seek the help of spirits and to connect with dead ancestors.

Dance movements often reflect the conditions people live in. Among forest-dwelling people, for example, dancers move as if they are finding their way through forest undergrowth.

Some dancers wear elaborate masks that represent the spirits of traditional West African religion. For example, to ask the spirits for good hunting for their community, dancers may wear masks of wild animals and imitate their movements.

The Yoruba people of Ife, Nigeria, made brass sculptures of their royalty. Notice the crown on this brass head.

3. West African Visual Arts

West African culture includes many forms of visual art. The traditional art of West Africa served a number of functions. Some art objects, such as fabrics and baskets, satisfied everyday needs. Others, such as masks and sculptures, were used in rituals and ceremonies, or to honor ancestors, spirits, or royalty.

Sculpture West Africans of ancient and medieval times used religious sculptures to call upon the spirits to help them in every phase of life. They also used sculptures to honor their leaders.

A wealth of West African sculpture has been discovered in Nigeria. The oldest examples come from the Nok culture (500 B.C.E. to 200 C.E.), which made **terra-cotta** sculptures of human figures. The sculptures tended to have long, narrow heads, unusual hair styles, and dramatic expressions. Scholars believe that they represented ancestors or mythical figures.

The Yoruba people of Ife (EE-fay), Nigeria, also made sculptures of terra-cotta. Later, they used bronze and copper. By the 11th century C.E., they were making brass sculptures of royalty. Over time, they taught their neighbors in Benin (founded in 1100 C.E.) how to make brass sculptures. Benin artists produced sculptures in honor of the royal court. By the 16th century, they were creating elaborate plaques that showed the king's power and authority.

Masks Wooden masks have been a part of West African life for centuries. Masks were worn during ceremonies, in performances, and in sacred rites. Like sculptures, they were used to bring the spirits of gods and ancestors into the present.

Because West African masks are detailed and expressive, they have inspired a number of artists around the world. Among these artists is Pablo Picasso, a world-famous Spanish painter of the 20th century.

Textiles West Africans have a long tradition of making textiles that are both beautiful and symbolic. Three well-known types of West African textiles are stamped fabrics, story fabrics, and a particularly colorful kind called **kente** (KEN-tay) cloth.

West Africans create stamped fabric by drawing a grid on a piece of cloth, using a thick dye. They use stamps to fill in the squares with patterns. The stamps represent proverbs, historical figures, objects, plants, or animals.

terra-cotta a baked clay used to make pottery, tiles, and sculptures

kente a traditional form of cloth produced in West Africa

appliqué a technique in which shaped pieces of fabric are attached to a background fabric to form a design or picture

Story fabrics depict events. For example, they might show kings performing great feats, like hunting lions. Some West Africans make story fabrics using a technique called **appliqué** in which smaller pieces of fabric are attached to a larger, background piece to form designs or pictures.

Kente cloth is a famous West African textile created by sewing together narrow strips of silk or other fabrics. The designs of kente cloth have symbolic meanings that reflect the artists' life or family history, values and beliefs, or political or social circumstances.

The influence of West African textiles is evident in quilts made by African American slaves. Today, commercially manufactured kente cloth is worn around the world.

Everyday Objects West African visual arts also include the design and decoration of everyday objects. Skilled artists transform practical objects into beautiful products such as ceramic storage containers, utensils, furniture, and baskets.

In many parts of West Africa, baskets are made using the coil method. The basket maker winds fibers into coils and then uses strips of fiber to bind the coils together. Some of these baskets are so tightly constructed that they can hold water.

Enslaved West Africans brought their basket-making tradition to America and taught it to their descendants. This art is still practiced in the American South.

West Africans incorporate their artistic talents in everyday, ordinary objects like baskets.

Lesson Summary

In this lesson, you explored the cultural legacy of West Africa. You learned about written and oral traditions, music, and visual arts. The cultural achievements of West Africans are still influential today.

Oral and Written Traditions Storytellers called griots helped to preserve the history and culture of West Africa. Folktales and proverbs are also part of West Africa's rich oral tradition. In medieval times, Muslim scholars added a body of Arabic writings to this heritage, which were preserved in Qur'anic schools and mosques. Modern writers incorporate many elements from West African oral traditions in their novels and other works.

Music Important features of West African music include call-and-response, traditional instruments, drumming, and dance. West African influences are still heard in world music.

Visual Arts Visual arts include sculptures, masks, textiles, and the design of everyday objects. West African sculpture and mask-making, particularly, influenced many modern artists, one of whom was Pablo Picasso. Kente cloth is still worn today and its influence can be seen in fashions around the world.

Senegalese performer Youssou N'Dour is a best-selling musician and a modern-day griot. N'Dour has a special ability to use his music to expose the truth, and to promote global tolerance.

Youssou N'Dour: A Modern-Day Griot

Rolling Stone magazine celebrated him as "perhaps the most famous singer alive." Folk Roots magazine named him African artist of the century. For over 30 years, Senegalese singer Youssou N'Dour has made hit albums and performed around the world. N'Dour is a modern-day griot whose songs awaken the world to the problems African nations face.

As Youssou N'Dour, Senegal's greatest recording artist, sat in his studio in Dakar, he started picking out a series of notes on the keyboard. His guitar player grabbed his guitar and started strumming chords, while the drummer sat down behind his kit and laid down a rhythm.

N'Dour began to sing in his clear, strong tenor voice. He improvised the lyrics, making them up as he went along. Eventually, a song about the tough life of a fisherman developed. It told how he rose before dawn and went out to sea, but all he caught was a shark. He brought the shark to market, but no one would purchase it. The fisherman hoped his luck would change the next day. When N'Dour finished singing, he had just created his newest song. Like so many of his songs, it captured how ordinary people in his native country of Senegal struggle every day to make ends meet.

A Singer Who Tells the Truth

Youssou N'Dour was born in the African nation of Senegal in 1959. In addition to being a modern-day griot and the nation's most celebrated musician, he has been called one of the best African singers.

In traditional West African cultures, griots passed along the history of their people through stories and songs. In the past, griots also communicated messages from a king to his people and told stories of the king's triumphs. However, griots also told the truth and revealed royal mistakes, which would sometimes anger kings.

Exposing the truth is one way in which Youssou N'Dour is a modern griot. In one of his songs, titled "Africa," he criticizes the corruption of many of Africa's political leaders. In another song, "Donkaasi Gi," he calls for equality among the people of Senegal. When he sees people perform acts of kindness to one another, he celebrates them in song. As a devout Muslim, he has also sung about modern Islamic life.

N'Dour's albums have sold in the millions. He has collaborated with some of the most popular musicians in the world, including Peter Gabriel, Bruce Springsteen, Sting, Paul Simon, Tracy Chapman, and American jazz musician Branford Marsalis.

His songs have helped increase awareness of Africa's challenges. However, he also sings of Africa with hope and pride.

A Musical Background

N'Dour was born in Medina, a tough section of Dakar, the capital of Senegal. His mother was a *griotte*—a female griot. His grandparents were talented singers who were much in demand in Dakar.

Unfortunately, music caused some conflict in his family. His father did not come from the griot tradition and forbade N'Dour's mother to sing in public. He also opposed his son's ambitions to be a musician and urged him to attend school and prepare for a more stable career. Yet, when N'Dour showed extraordinary musical talent as a child, his mother and grandparents supported him.

N'Dour was fortunate to grow up in Dakar during the 1960s and 1970s because an amazing variety of music made its way there. He grew up listening not only to local and traditional musical styles but also to African American artists such as Marvin Gaye, James Brown, Michael Jackson, and Jimi Hendrix. He also loved Latin American music. All these styles influenced him.

In 1973, when he was 14 years old, he sang in a talent contest—and won. Brimming with confidence, he went to see the manager of The Miami, a successful nightclub in Dakar, and asked to be hired as a singer. The manager initially rejected the idea, but N'Dour kept asking relentlessly until the manager finally gave in. N'Dour became a singer for the Star Band, the most famous band in Dakar.

N'Dour performs his music in concerts around the world with his band Super Étoile de Dakar. In 2005, N'Dour won a Grammy Award for best contemporary world music album for an album called *Egypt*.

N'Dour frequently performs at benefit concerts. Here he appears with songwriter and rapper Neneh Cherry at a concert held to raise awareness about poverty around the world.

A New Style of Dance Music

The teenage N'Dour was a sensation, and the young people of Dakar crowded into the club to dance and listen to his songs. With his silky voice, he expressed what they were feeling. In 1977, in a bold move, Youssou hired away six members of the Star Band for his own group, which he called Étoile de Dakar, French for "Star of Dakar." In 1979, he formed the band Super Étoile de Dakar.

N'Dour and his band gradually developed a new style of dance music. Everybody called it *mbalax* (um-bah-lahks), which means "rhythm" in the Senegalese language *Wolof.* N'Dour and his band also added the sounds of hip-hop, rock, soul, and rhythm and blues to their music.

A Voice of Conscience

Soon N'Dour and Super Étoile de Dakar started to record albums, with N'Dour either writing the songs himself or co-writing them with his bandmates. From 1979 to 1988, they recorded an astonishing 14 albums, which merchants sold on the streets of Dakar. His popularity quickly exploded.

N'Dour was now famous throughout Senegal. Although he was making a lot of money for such a young man, N'dour always remained connected to his roots. In the lyrics of his songs, he expressed his concern for the problems facing Africa, such as hunger, poverty, and disease. For example, in his song "New Africa," which was released in the mid-1980s, he urged the people of the continent to work together. "Unity," he wrote, "was the traditional strength of Africa."

In other songs, he called for the people of Africa to care for one another, to choose good over evil, and to be honest in their dealings. One song encouraged the Senegalese to remember their roots and learn as much as they can about their country. In the album *Nelson Mandela*, N'Dour celebrated the courage of the South African civil rights leader who eventually became that nation's first black president.

Keeping the Griot Tradition Alive

By singing about Africa's issues, N'Dour keeps alive a griot tradition that has lasted for centuries. Griots are the voices of their communities and pass along their people's history from one generation to the next. They tell stories and sing songs that teach lessons so that young people can develop positive values. They make people feel as if they are part of a community.

Some griots have made extraordinary efforts to preserve West African traditions. In the nation of Gambia, the griot Alhaja Papa Susso founded a school where musicians, dancers, and poets can study griot traditions. They take lessons, rehearse, give concerts, make new friends, and exchange ideas. Scholars also visit the school to learn more about griots and their roles in African society.

In a way, N'Dour has also become a griot to the world. One night during the mid-1980s, the British rock musician Peter Gabriel went to listen to N'Dour perform. When Gabriel heard the young singer, he was amazed and asked N'Dour to sing on his album *So*, which became one of the best-selling albums of the 1980s. They also co-wrote the song "Shaking the Tree—Woman's Day," a remarkable song about women's rights in Africa. Since then, N'Dour has worked with many other musicians to raise money to improve conditions in Africa and around the world.

N'Dour uses his fame to bring attention to important causes. Here he attends a conference on African development with rock musician Bono (right) and pop singer Juanes (left).

In recent years, N'Dour has continued to sing about Africa. For example, until 2008 he organized the Great African Ball, which was an annual all-night concert and party in New York City and Paris. N'Dour and other modern-day griots are essential voices for the future of Africa. They reveal problems in order to help unify the continent and help Africans face the future with hope and pride.

The Culture and Kingdoms of West Africa

About 4,000 B.C.E.
Settlements in West Africa
Early farming communities, made up of extended families, farm the area south of the Sahara.

About 250 B.C.E.–1400 C.E.
Jenne-Jeno
Jenne-Jeno thrives on the Niger River, growing to a city of 20,000 people who farmed, fished, and made tools from iron.

| 1500 B.C.E. | 1000 B.C.E. | 500 B.C.E. | 1 C.E. |

About 500 B.C.E.
Trans-Saharan Trade
North Africans bring gold from the southern forests of Africa through the Sahara, a journey that would eventually be made easier by the use of camels.

About 500 B.C.E.–200 C.E.
The Nok
The Nok make iron tools in West Africa, fueling the spread of ironworking and helping to begin trade among West African villages.

About 300 C.E
Camels Arrive in West Africa
Camels are introduced to the Sahara region, spurring the growth of trans-Saharan trade.

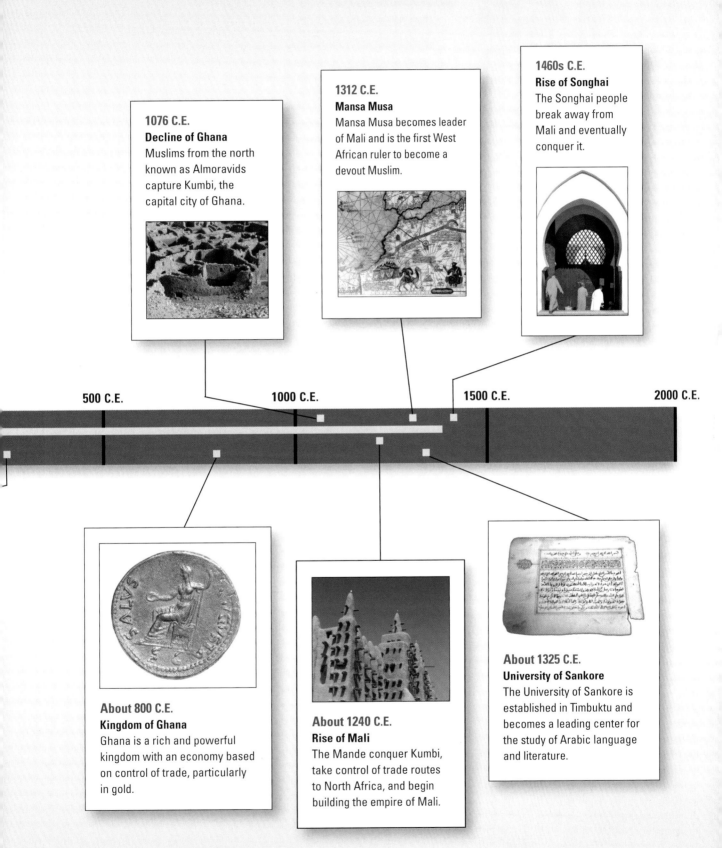

1076 C.E.
Decline of Ghana
Muslims from the north known as Almoravids capture Kumbi, the capital city of Ghana.

1312 C.E.
Mansa Musa
Mansa Musa becomes leader of Mali and is the first West African ruler to become a devout Muslim.

1460s C.E.
Rise of Songhai
The Songhai people break away from Mali and eventually conquer it.

500 C.E.   1000 C.E.   1500 C.E.   2000 C.E.

About 800 C.E.
Kingdom of Ghana
Ghana is a rich and powerful kingdom with an economy based on control of trade, particularly in gold.

About 1240 C.E.
Rise of Mali
The Mande conquer Kumbi, take control of trade routes to North Africa, and begin building the empire of Mali.

About 1325 C.E.
University of Sankore
The University of Sankore is established in Timbuktu and becomes a leading center for the study of Arabic language and literature.

Imperial China

A bronze lion stands guard at the Forbidden City in Beijing, China. A complex of palaces built in the early 1400s, the Forbidden City was the seat of Chinese power for five centuries.

Physical Features of Asia

ARCTIC OCEAN

EUROPE

East Siberian Sea

Laptev Sea

Bering Sea

Kara Sea

S I B E R I A

Lena River

KAMCHATKA PEN.

URAL MTS.

Ob River

Yenisey River

Sea of Okhotsk

Sakhalin

Mediterranean Sea

Black Sea

CAUCASUS MTS.

Caspian Sea

THE STEPPES

Ural River

Aral Sea

Lake Balkhash

ALTAY MTS.

Lake Baikal

GOBI DESERT

Sea of Japan (East Sea)

Hokkaido

KOREAN PEN.

Honshu

PACIFIC OCEAN

ZAGROS MTS.

Euphrates River

Tigris River

Persian Gulf

Red Sea

ARABIAN PENINSULA

TIAN SHAN

TAKLIMAKAN DESERT

KUNLUN SHAN

Huang He (Yellow R.)

Yellow R.

NORTH CHINA PLAIN

Yellow Sea

Shikoku

Kyushu

RYUKYU IS.

Tropic of Cancer

PLATEAU OF TIBET

Indus River

H I M A L A Y A

Brahmaputra River

▲ Mount Everest (29,035 ft., 8,850 m)

Ganges River

CHINA

Chang Jiang (Yangtze)

Xi R.

CHANG JIANG BASINS

East China Sea

Taiwan

Philippine Sea

Arabian Sea

INDIAN PENINSULA

DECCAN PLATEAU

WESTERN GHATS

EASTERN GHATS

Bay of Bengal

ANDAMAN ISLANDS

Mekong River

Hainan

PHILIPPINE ISLANDS

AFRICA

Equator

MALDIVE ISLANDS

NICOBAR ISLANDS

Malay Peninsula

Gulf of Thailand

South China Sea

Celebes Sea

Halmahera

Equator

New Guinea

BATU IS.

Sumatra

GREATER SUNDA

Borneo

Celebes

Ceram

INDIAN OCEAN

MENTAWAI ISLANDS

Java Sea

ISLANDS

Flores

Java

Sumbawa

Sumba

Timor

Tropic of Capricorn

AUSTRALIA

Elevation

Feet	Meters
Over 10,000	Over 3,050
5,001–10,000	1,526–3,050
2,001–5,000	611–1,525
1,001–2,000	306–610
0–1,000	0–305
Below sea level	Below sea level

▲ Mountain peak

Present-day boundary

N W E S

0   500   1,000 miles
0   500   1,000 kilometers
Lambert Azimuthal Equal-Area Projection

80°N

60°N

40°N

20°N

0°

20°S

40°S

60°E   80°E   100°E   120°E   140°E

Imperial China

In this unit, you will study imperial China during the period from about 221 B.C.E. to about 1644 C.E. The word *imperial* means "ruled by an emperor." During this time, China was under the control of a series of dynasties, or ruling families.

China is located on the continent of Asia—the largest continent on Earth. China has three distinct elevations: the highlands in western China, the slightly lower plateau in central China, and the lowlands along the eastern coast.

The land is rocky, and the climate is cold in the towering Himalaya and Tian Shan mountains of western China. The Gobi Desert in the northern plateau is very dry. As a result, few people settled in these places. Although the central and southern part of the plateau were more inviting, the coastal lands were the real population centers of imperial China because these plains were threaded with life-giving rivers and blanketed with rich soil.

Look at *Physical Features of Asia* to locate the North China Plain, the Huang He (Yellow River), and the Chang Jiang (Yangtze River). This is where Chinese civilization began since people could cultivate food here and the rivers made transportation easy. Because of these factors, trade flourished. The bustling market for goods led to the growth of cities. During these years of peace and prosperity, scholars and scientists were able to develop new technologies. Some of these led to new industries, while others helped the Chinese enlarge their trade empire.

The history of China is tied to its geography in other ways as well. Several strong emperors were able to expand China's borders to the west and south, while the Gobi Desert stopped Chinese expansion to the north. To the southwest, the cold, high Plateau of Tibet prevented the Chinese from enlarging their empire. At other times, and under other leaders, China was able to protect itself behind its oceans, mountains, and deserts, easily cutting itself off from the world.

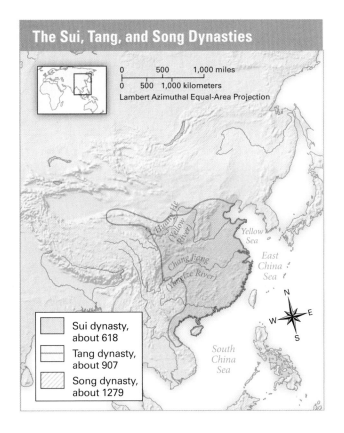

The Sui, Tang, and Song Dynasties

0   500   1,000 miles
0 500 1,000 kilometers
Lambert Azimuthal Equal-Area Projection

Huang He (Yellow River)
Chang Jiang (Yangtze River)
Yellow Sea
East China Sea
South China Sea

Sui dynasty, about 618
Tang dynasty, about 907
Song dynasty, about 1279

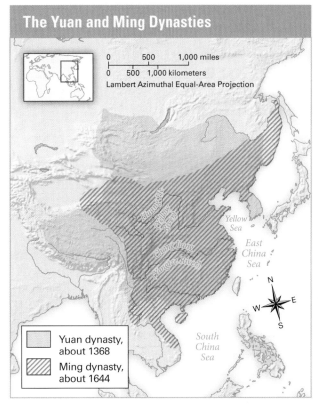

The Yuan and Ming Dynasties

0   500   1,000 miles
0 500 1,000 kilometers
Lambert Azimuthal Equal-Area Projection

Huang He (Yellow River)
Chang Jiang (Yangtze River)
Yellow Sea
East China Sea
South China Sea

Yuan dynasty, about 1368
Ming dynasty, about 1644

Lesson 19

The Political Development of Imperial China

Which method of selecting officials led to the best leaders for China?

Introduction

Welcome to imperial China. Historians divide Chinese history into periods ruled by dynasties, or ruling families. You will learn about China's political development under several dynasties from 220 to 1644 C.E.

China was first unified under an emperor in the 3rd century B.C.E. From the beginning, emperors needed help to rule. Emperor Han Wu Di, for example, once sent out this announcement:

Heroes Wanted! A Proclamation

Exceptional work demands exceptional men . . . We therefore command the various district officials to search for men of brilliant and exceptional talents, to be our generals, our ministers, and our envoys to distant states.

Over time, Chinese emperors tried several methods of finding qualified people to administer their government. One method was to rely on the class of wealthy families. Emperors like Han Wu Di, however, preferred to choose officials for their merit, or worth. During the Han dynasty, candidates for government jobs had to prove their knowledge and ability by passing strict tests. As a result, a class of scholar-officials evolved. Under later emperors, this system developed into a rule by officials of proven merit.

In the 13th century C.E., a nomadic people called the Mongols built a great empire in Asia. Toward the end of the century, the Mongols conquered China. Under Mongol emperors, government officials in China were foreigners.

In this lesson, you will explore how changes in the government affected medieval China. You will also learn which of these government methods were successful in improving medieval China.

Social Studies Vocabulary

aristocracy

bureaucracy

civil service examination

dynasty

emperor

imperial

meritocracy

warlord

◀ The Chinese held exams for hiring scholar-officials to help the emperor rule.

1. The Government of Imperial China

In 221 B.C.E., Prince Zheng (JUNG), the head of the state of Qin (CHIN), became the first Chinese ruler to claim the title of **emperor**, adopting the name Qin Shi Huangdi (chin SHEE hwahng-dee), which means "First Emperor of Qin." From that time on, China usually had an **imperial** form of government headed by an emperor or, sometimes, an empress.

China's Imperial Dynasties Chinese emperors named a relative, often a son, to become emperor after their deaths. In this way, they established a **dynasty**, or line of rulers from the same family.

From ancient times, Chinese rulers based their right to govern on the Mandate of Heaven, the idea that Heaven had chosen a particular dynasty to rule. The Chinese believed that Heaven supported the dynasty throughout the emperor's reign, as long as the emperor ruled well. Natural disasters such as floods, famines, plagues, and earthquakes were interpreted as signs that Heaven was displeased. If an emperor ruled poorly and lost the Mandate of Heaven, the people could overthrow him.

This table lists the imperial dynasties that ruled China between 221 B.C.E. and 1644 C.E. Each of these dynasties brought about change for the people of medieval China.

emperor the political leader of a territory containing several countries or groups of people

imperial belonging or related to an emperor

dynasty a line of rulers descended from one family

China's Imperial Dynasties

Dynasty	Time Period	Known for
Qin dynasty	221–206 B.C.E.	unification of China under an emperor
Han dynasty	206 B.C.E.–220 C.E.	a golden age for a united China
Six dynasties	220–581 C.E.	a period of chaos and division
Sui dynasty	589–618 C.E.	reunification of China
Tang dynasty	618–907 C.E.	economic development and growth; many inventions and discoveries
Five dynasties in the north Ten Kingdoms in the south	907–960 C.E. 907–970 C.E.	a period of chaos and division
Song dynasty	960–1279 C.E.	economic development and growth; many inventions and discoveries
Yuan dynasty (the Mongols)	1279–1368 C.E.	control of China by foreigners
Ming dynasty	1368–1644 C.E.	opening up of China to foreign influences at the start of the dynasty; closing down of China by the end of the dynasty

China's Breakup and Reunification The Han dynasty held power in ancient China for more than 400 years and ushered in a golden age of expansion and prosperity. In 220 C.E., however, the Han rulers lost their grip on power, resulting in a long period of disunity and conflict. This period ended when the Sui and Tang dynasties reunified China.

What happened to bring about the end of Han rule? Like earlier emperors, the Han governed China with the help of a large **bureaucracy** of government officials. As long as the bureaucracy was skilled, honest, and hardworking, China prospered. By 220, however, corrupt, or dishonest, relatives and servants of the emperor had seized control of the government.

The result was disastrous. High taxes plunged many families into poverty, and workers were forced to labor for long periods of time on public projects. Additionally, bandits attacked farmers in the countryside. All of this turmoil led **warlords** to oppose the emperor and fight against one another, causing the government to become weak and unable to protect farmers.

Warriors on horseback fought for the Han emperors as they struggled to maintain control of the empire against warlords and invaders. Eventually, the Han dynasty ended, and China broke apart.

Small farmers suffered because they were required to pay taxes and give half of everything they produced to their landlords. As they plunged into debt, they were forced to give up their own land to large landowners and work for them, instead.

Finally, the farmers rebelled because they believed that the Han dynasty had lost the Mandate of Heaven. No new dynasty took over from the Han, so China broke apart into separate kingdoms, just as Europe did after the fall of Rome. Nomadic invaders ruled the north, while several short-lived dynasties ruled the south.

In 589, the northern state of Sui (SWAY) conquered the south and reunified China. The Sui dynasty created a new central government and ruled for 29 years, but by 617, heavy taxes led to unrest and a struggle for power.

In 618, a general named Li Yuan declared himself emperor and established the Tang dynasty. Tang rulers built on the accomplishments of the Sui dynasty, strengthened the central government, and increased Tang influence over outlying areas.

Under the Tang, a unified China enjoyed a period of wealth and power that lasted nearly 300 years. Let's now examine how Tang rulers approached problems of government.

bureaucracy a highly complex body of workers with many levels of authority

warlord a military leader operating outside the control of the government

aristocracy a ruling class of
noble families

civil service examination a
test given to qualify candidates
for positions in the government

meritocracy rule by officials of
proven merit

2. Aristocracy: The Tang Dynasty

Like earlier emperors, Tang rulers relied on a large bureaucracy. Officials collected taxes, oversaw building and **irrigation** projects, managed the army, and enforced the laws. But how could emperors ensure that they selected the best people for these positions?

Earlier emperors answered this question in different ways. Before the Han dynasty, emperors chose members of the **aristocracy** to help them govern. These people were born into noble families of wealthy and powerful landowners. However, simply being wealthy did not guarantee an individual was talented or knowledgeable.

To improve the bureaucracy, Han emperors created **civil service examinations** in which candidates took long tests to qualify for office. The tests had questions on Chinese classics, poetry, and legal and administrative issues. Mainly, they were based on the works of Confucius (kon-FEW-shus), China's great philosopher and teacher. This began the system under which a class of scholar-officials ran the government.

Later, Tang emperors also used civil service exams to fill some government positions. Early in the dynasty, however, emperors chose aristocrats for most high-level jobs. Some officials were hired because their fathers or grandfathers had held high government rank, and some were hired because of personal recommendations. Often, aristocrats gained positions by marrying into the imperial family.

Even the civil service exams favored aristocrats. The tests were supposedly open to all except for certain groups, such as merchants, actors, and beggars. In theory, any man could attend the university where students prepared for the exams. In reality, however, only the wealthy could afford tutors, books, and time to study properly. As a result, aristocrats held almost all offices in the early part of the Tang dynasty.

After peasant rebellions and battles between generals ended the Tang dynasty in 907, China split apart once again. Five military dynasties followed one another to power in the north, while the south broke up into independent kingdoms.

Beginning in 960, the Song (SOONG) dynasty rose. Gradually, Song emperors reunified the country. As you will see, they built on the civil service system to reform how government officials were chosen.

3. Meritocracy: The Song Dynasty

Under Song emperors, the idea of scholar-officials reached its height. The Song relied on civil service exams and made them available to far more candidates, creating a **meritocracy**.

A new school of thought known as neo-Confucianism influenced the exams. This new teaching blended the teachings of Confucius with elements of Buddhism and Daoism (two traditional religions in China).

Civil service exams to choose China's government officials were based largely on the teachings of Confucius, a Chinese thinker and teacher who lived from 551 to 479 B.C.E. He is considered the most famous philosopher in Chinese history.

During the Song dynasty, scholar-officials performed many tasks. Here scholars organize ancient manuscripts.

A Confucian scholar, Zhu Xi (JU SHEE), commented on classic Chinese writings. In 1190, his work was published as the *Four Books,* which became the basis of study for all civil service exams.

Confucius taught that people must act properly in five important relationships: ruler and subject, father and son, older **sibling** and younger sibling, husband and wife, and friend and friend. Except for friends, one person in each relationship is above the other. Those above should be kind to those below, while those below should respect and obey those above. In particular, subjects must be loyal to their rulers. Song emperors and scholars believed that officials who had studied Confucius would be **rational,** moral, and able to maintain order.

Under the Song, people from lower classes gained the ability to become scholar-officials since they could attend the new state-supported schools and continue on to the university. If they passed a local test, they became eligible to take the imperial exam in the capital. On those exams, they wrote essays and poems in a certain style and answered questions about political and social problems based on Confucian ideas.

The exams were organized to prevent cheating. Candidates were locked in a small room for several days. A second person copied each paper so that the examiners would not know whose work they were reading.

Only a small proportion of candidates passed the difficult exams. Those who failed could take the tests again in the future. Those who passed had to wait a few years before their first appointment. When it came, it was for a job far from their hometown, so that they could not give unfair advantages to their family and friends. At the end of three years, officials could move up in rank.

Despite the challenges, people were happy to receive such respected positions. As government officials, they also enjoyed certain privileges, such as being excused from taxes and military service.

4. Government by Foreigners: The Period of Mongol Rule

In the 13th century, the Mongols conquered almost all of Asia. In 1276, they captured China's imperial capital. Three years later, the last Song emperor died fleeing from the invaders.

The Mongol leader, Kublai Khan (KOOH-bly KAHN), took the title of emperor of China and called his dynasty the Yuan dynasty. For nearly 100 years, from 1279 to 1368, China was under Mongol rule.

Under the Mongols, Chinese society was divided into four classes. The Mongols were at the top. Next came foreigners who were their friends, including Tibetans, Persians, Turks, and Central Asians. Many of them were Muslims. The third class was made up of the northern Chinese, who were more accustomed to the neighboring Mongols. The southern Chinese came last.

Kublai Khan ended the system of civil service exams because he did not believe that Confucian learning was needed for government jobs nor did he want to rely on Chinese people to run his government. To fill important positions, he chose other Mongols whom he felt he could trust. Some of these people were his relatives.

Unfortunately, there weren't enough Mongols to fill every job. Besides, many were illiterate, or unable to read and write. Kublai and later Mongol emperors needed people who could handle the paperwork of a complex government, so they were forced to appoint trusted foreigners to government positions, even some Europeans. Chinese scholars were appointed only as teachers and minor officials. Other Chinese worked as clerks, and some of them rose to important positions.

Without the examination system, however, there was a shortage of capable administrators. In 1315, the Mongols restored the exam system, although they set limits on who could take the exam, favoring Mongol and other non-Chinese candidates.

The Mongols were a dynamic group of nomads who conquered huge areas of Asia, including China. The fall of the Mongol dynasty gave way for the rise of the Ming dynasty.

As time passed, fighting among Mongol leaders weakened the government of China, as did the greed and corruption of officials. Additionally, the Mongols had made many enemies among the native Chinese. In the 1350s and 1360s, rebels rose up against them. In 1368, the Mongol dynasty collapsed, and the Chinese reestablished their own government under the Ming dynasty, which ruled China for nearly 300 years.

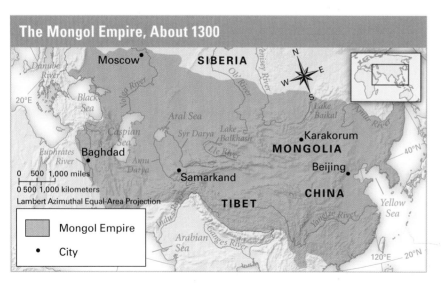

The Mongol Empire, About 1300

Moscow • SIBERIA
Danube River
20°E
Black Sea
Volga River
Ob' River
Yenisey River
N E W S
Aral Sea
Caspian Sea
Syr Darya
Lake Balkhash
Lake Baikal
Amur River
Ili River
• Karakorum
MONGOLIA
40°N
Euphrates River
Baghdad
Amu Darya
• Samarkand
Beijing •
0 500 1,000 miles
0 500 1,000 kilometers
Lambert Azimuthal Equal-Area Projection
CHINA
TIBET
Yellow Sea
Indus
Ganges River
Arabian Sea
Yangtze River
120°E
20°N

Mongol Empire
• City

5. The Revival of the Civil Service System

Under Ming emperors, civil service exams were again used to fill government positions. This system lasted into the 20th century.

In many ways, the exam system served China well. It provided a well-organized government. The education of its scholar-officials **emphasized** moral behavior, justice, kindness, loyalty to the emperor, proper conduct, and the importance of family. These values helped to unify Chinese culture.

The civil service system allowed poor men who were ambitious and hardworking the opportunity to be government officials. At the same time, it ensured that officials were trained and talented, not merely rich or related to the emperor.

Yet China's civil service system may also have stood in the way of progress. The exams did not test understanding of science, mathematics, or engineering. People with such knowledge were therefore kept out of the government. Confucian scholars also had little respect for merchants, business, and trade. Confucians had often considered merchants to be the lowest class in society because they purchased and sold things rather than producing useful items themselves. Under the Ming, this outlook dominated, and trade and business were not encouraged. Additionally, the bureaucracy became set in its ways, and its inability to adapt contributed to the fall of the Ming in 1644.

Civil service exams lasted for several days. In this Chinese scroll, scholars turn in their completed exams to be graded.

Lesson Summary

In this lesson, you have learned how China was governed between 220 and 1644 C.E. Chinese emperors relied on a bureaucracy to help them govern. At different times, they used various methods of selecting government officials.

Imperial Government In 221 B.C.E., a prince of Qin became the first Chinese emperor under the name Qin Shi Huangdi. For more than 1,500 years, China was ruled under an imperial government by a series of dynasties.

Aristocracy Early emperors chose officials from the aristocracy. The Han tried to improve government by creating a civil service examination system. Candidates for government jobs had to pass tests based mostly on Confucian learning. Under the Sui and Tang dynasties, civil service exams continued, but aristocrats filled most government jobs under the Tang.

Meritocracy Rulers of the Song dynasty used civil service exams to create a meritocracy of scholar-officials.

Government by Foreigners Mongol emperors from outside of China relied on family members, friends, and trusted foreigners to help run the government.

Civil Service System Restored Under the Ming, the Chinese restored their civil service system. Bureaucrats became set in their ways, and innovation was not encouraged.

What Was It Like to Take a Civil Service Examination?

The effectiveness of the Chinese government depended on the people who served as government officials. Through several dynasties of imperial China, painstaking civil service exams determined who was placed in these government jobs. You will examine four primary sources about these tests and write an argument about what it was like to take civil service examinations.

Rather than handing out government jobs to the emperor's family and friends, the Han dynasty began to award jobs to men who performed well on civil service examinations. Universities were set up to train students and then test their knowledge of Chinese literature, laws, poetry, and government administration. Many of the courses were based on the teachings of Confucius, a respected Chinese teacher.

This primary source was written in 1804 by an ambassador from England, Sir John Barrow. He was sent to China to record his observations about Chinese life. In this excerpt of his report, Barrow describes China's civil service examinations. How does Barrow's background affect the reliability of this source? What does this primary source tell you about the experience of the person taking the exam? Why might someone be motivated to take these examinations?

Travels in China

The examinations to be passed for the attainment of office are principally confined to the knowledge of the language; and as far as this goes, they are rigid to the utmost degree. The candidates are put into separate apartments, having previously been searched, in order to ascertain that they have no writing of any kind about them. They are allowed nothing but pencils, ink, and paper, and within a given time they are each to produce a theme on the subject that shall be proposed to them. The excellence of the composition, which is submitted to the examining officers, or men of letters, depends chiefly on the following points.

That every character be neatly and accurately made.

That each character be well chosen, and not in vulgar use.

That the same character do not occur twice in the same composition.

—John Barrow, 1804

The Chinese scholars who created the civil service exams agreed that successful students must have a solid understanding of texts called *The Four Books*. These included books, poems, and reports by Confucius and other Chinese philosophers. To prepare for the tests, which would require answering questions and writing essays, candidates memorized hundreds of classic passages.

This next primary source is an excerpt from one of *The Four Books* called *The Great Learning*. It is one of the first texts that students learned to repeat word for word. It is a numbered list of virtues that historians believe to be the words of Confucius. The other sections of the book were written by philosophers in response to Confucius's writing. What do you think the text means when it refers to the "cultivation of a person"? According to this primary source, why are education and knowledge important? Why would a Chinese emperor benefit from having civil servants in his government who understand this philosophy?

The Great Learning

1. What the Great Learning teaches, is—to illustrate illustrious virtue; to renovate the people; and to rest in the highest excellence . . .

3. Things have their root and their completion. Affairs have their end and their beginning. To know what is first and what is last will lead near to what is taught in the Great Learning.

4. The ancients who wished to illustrate illustrious virtue throughout the empire, first ordered well their own States. Wishing to order well their States, they first regulated their families. Wishing to regulate their families, they first cultivated their persons. Wishing to cultivate their persons, they first rectified their hearts. Wishing to rectify their hearts, they first sought to be sincere in their thoughts. Wishing to be sincere in their thoughts, they first extended to the utmost their knowledge. Such extension of knowledge lay in the investigation of things . . .

6. From the emperor down to the mass of the people, all must consider the cultivation of the person the root of every thing besides.

7. It cannot be, when the root is neglected, that what should spring from it will be well ordered. It never has been the case that what was of great importance has been slightly cared for, and, at the same time, that what was of slight importance has been greatly cared for.

—Confucius, date unknown

The civil service exams were highly competitive, and passing the test brought great prestige, as well as wages. Candidates learned their test results when names of those who passed were posted on a scroll in a public place. If a candidate failed, he had to wait for more than a year to prepare for and take the test again.

Pu Songling was one man who failed the test multiple times, as he describes in this account. He lived from 1640 to 1715, but the actual date he wrote this text is unknown. After repeatedly failing the civil service examination, Songling became a writer, often creating stories that mocked the testing system. This text is from his most famous story called *The Seven Likenesses of a Candidate*.

How does the author describe the candidate's reaction to the exam results? How might the author's experience and perspective affect the reliability of this source? How will answering these questions support your response to the larger question: What was it like to take a civil service examination?

The Seven Likenesses of a Candidate

A licentiate taking the provincial examination may be likened to seven things. When entering the examination hall, bare-footed and carrying a basket, he is like a beggar. At roll-call time, being shouted at by officials and abused by their subordinates, he is like a prisoner. When writing in his cell, with his head and feet sticking out of the booth, he is like a cold bee late in autumn. Upon leaving the examination hall, being in a daze and seeing a changed universe, he is like a sick bird out of a cage. When anticipating the results, he is on pins and needles; one moment he fantasizes success and magnificent mansions are instantly built; another moment he fears failure and his body is deducted to a corpse. At this point he is like a chimpanzee in captivity. Finally the messengers come on galloping horses and confirm the absence of his name on the list of successful candidates. His complexion becomes ashen and his body stiffens like a poisoned fly no longer able to move. Disappointed and discouraged, he vilifies the examiners for their blindness and blames the unfairness of the system. Thereupon he collects all his books and papers from his desk and sets them on fire; unsatisfied, he tramples over the ashes; still unsatisfied, he throws the ashes into a filthy gutter. He is determined to abandon the world by going into the mountains, and he is resolved to drive away any person who dares speak to him about examination essays. With the passage of time, his anger subsides and his aspiration rises. Like a turtle dove just hatched, he rebuilds his nest and starts the process once again.

—Pu Songling, date unknown

A Cultural History of Civil Examinations in Late Imperial China, by Benjamin A. Elman, © 2000 by the Regents of the University of California. Published by the University of California Press.

Test preparation schools were expensive, and men from the lower classes could not easily take time away from work to attend classes and study for the exam. In order to take the test, a man from a lower class needed to find a wealthy sponsor to support him during the training period. Many men hoped to move up in social class by passing the test and being hired for a government job.

Taking the examination was a grueling task that took 24 to 72 hours. Each candidate was locked in a small room with just a board for a desk and a bucket to use for a toilet so that they did not interact with anyone else. Candidates also had to bring and prepare their own food. Sometimes a candidate went mad or even died from exhaustion during the exam.

Because of the intense challenges of the test, a passing score was cause for great celebration, as shown in this painted scroll from the 14th or 15th century titled *The Festive Return of the Civil Servant*. The people at the top of the scroll have received the news that a member of their community has successfully passed the imperial civil service examination. They are coming together to prepare for his arrival. In the lower part of the painting, the candidate has been carried into his hometown in a box-like transporter called a palanquin. Armed men surround him. Why do you think a candidate's success was so lavishly celebrated? Why might a new civil servant receive an armed escort to his hometown?

Consider all the primary sources about China's civil service examinations. Write a claim to describe what it was like to take the exam. Support your claim with evidence from the primary sources, noting any limitations of a source.

This silk scroll portrays the celebration of a candidate who passed the civil service examination. It was painted in Vietnam in the 14th or 15th century and is called *The Festive Return of the Civil Servant*.

China Develops a New Economy

How did the Chinese improve their economy during the Tang and Song dynasties?

Introduction

The Song period from about 618 to 1279 C.E. was a time of great prosperity in China. Changes in agriculture, especially a boom in the production of rice, fueled the growth of the economy. Trade and business flourished. These developments had started during the Tang dynasty. China's economy grew rapidly during the Tang and the Song dynasties. Under the Song, these developments would help make China one of the most advanced economies in the world.

Along with prosperity came the development of cities. During this period, China's huge cities dwarfed those of medieval Europe. The cities were filled with merchants, who opened shops along the streets to sell goods to the wealthy. Farmers traded crops from their fields, and artisans sold silk and jade goods they had crafted.

An Italian traveler named Marco Polo first saw China toward the end of the Song dynasty. He marveled at China's crowded cities and bustling markets. Polo was especially impressed by the boat traffic on the Grand Canal, a great waterway that linked northern China with the Chang Jiang (Yangtze) river valley in the south. Farmers and merchants used the canal to ship their crops and goods. Polo wrote, "It is indeed surprising to observe the multitude [vast number] and the size of the vessels that are continually passing and repassing, laden [loaded] with merchandise of the greatest value."

In this lesson, you will learn how changes in agriculture, trade and commerce, and urbanization made China so prosperous that it had the highest standard of living in the world at the time. Let's begin by finding out how changes in agriculture improved China's economy during the Tang and Song dynasties.

Social Studies Vocabulary

commerce

currency

economy

urbanization

◀ The Grand Canal provided a waterway between northern and southern China.

1. Changes in Agriculture

economy a system of managing the wealth and resources of a community or region

Changes in agriculture were a major reason for the growth of China's **economy** during the Song dynasty. This period saw a huge increase in the production of rice, as well as new and better farming methods. Let's explore how and why these changes happened.

Reasons for Agricultural Changes There were several reasons for the changes in agriculture. The first was the movement of farmers to the fertile basins of the Chang Jiang in southern China.

During the Tang dynasty, northern China was the wealthiest and most populous part of the country, but wars and attacks from Mongolian tribes drove many landowners to move south. Under the Song, southern China continued to grow. By 1207, about 65 million people lived in the south, compared to 50 million in the north.

The move to the south changed what farmers grew. Northern farmers had cultivated wheat and millet since these crops thrived in the north's cold, dry climate. In contrast, the south's climate was warm and wet, so wetlands covered most of the Chang Jiang valley. These conditions were ideal for cultivating rice plants, which require a lot of water.

Rice farmers, though, did face challenges. Rice crops were frequently destroyed by periods of drought and violent storms, called typhoons. Even if a crop survived, it took five months for the rice to mature from planting to harvest.

During the 11th century, a new variety called champa rice was brought to China from Vietnam. It was resistant to drought, and it matured in two months instead of five. Now farmers could plant at least two crops of rice each year. As a result, rice production in China boomed.

Rice became the most important crop in China in the 13th century. Farmers often used harrows to prepare rice paddies for planting. Then they would plant rice seedlings in flooded paddies.

A chain pump provided water for the rice paddy. When it was ready, peasants would harvest the rice by hand.

Production increased even more with new and better farming techniques and tools. An improved plow and harrow, a tool used to level plowed ground, made it easier to prepare fields for planting. Additionally, farmers began using fertilizer to produce larger crops. A device called a chain pump, which used containers attached to a loop of chain to move water, helped farmers irrigate land at the edges of lakes, marshes, and rivers. To grow rice on hillsides, farmers created flat areas called terraces. More and more land was devoted to farming, and landowners became wealthier.

Characteristics of the New Agriculture

Anyone visiting a farming area in southern China during the 13th century would see small farms covering every bit of suitable land. Terraced hillsides spread as far as you can see, each covered in flooded fields called paddies where rice is grown. **Elaborate** irrigation systems crisscross the paddies, bringing water where it's needed.

Early in the growing season, you see water buffaloes pulling a plow and harrow to level the fields and prepare them for planting. The seeds have been growing in seedbeds for a month. Now, workers will transplant the young plants to the paddy.

Growing rice takes a lot of hard work done by many hands. In the fields, large numbers of workers walk backward as they transplant the rice plants in straight rows. Two months from now, the workers will harvest the rice by hand.

commerce the buying and selling of goods; business

currency the form of money used in a country

Before and during the growing season, the rice paddy has to be constantly watered and drained. Dams, dikes, gated channels, and chain pumps help to move water into and out of the paddies.

Although rice is the main crop, peasants grow tea, cotton, and sugar. They also grow mulberry trees, which produce the leaves that feed silkworms.

Results of Agricultural Changes The shift to growing rice was an important development for medieval China. It increased food production, which helped to support a larger population. For the first time, China's population grew to more than 100 million people.

Peasants could take time away from farming to weave silk, cotton cloth, and other products. Rice farmers could market their surplus rice. Landowners became rich enough from growing rice to buy luxury items. All these changes encouraged the growth of trade.

2. The Growth of Trade and Commerce

Trade and commerce were already underway during the Tang dynasty. Tang emperors eased **restrictions** on merchants, and they actively promoted trade. Products like rice, silk, tea, porcelain, and jade traveled along trade routes to India, Arabia, and Europe. Under the Song, business activity blossomed even more.

Reasons for Growth in Trade and Commerce One reason for the growth of trade and commerce was that wealthy landowners were eager to buy luxuries. The demand for luxuries encouraged an increase in trade, as well as an increase in the number of Chinese artisans, who made silk and other goods.

Water transportation also helped commerce. A vast network of rivers and canals connected different parts of China. Farmers in central China could ship their rice north along the Grand Canal. Boat owners had plenty of business, because moving goods by water was cheaper and faster than by road. A long boat with a flat bottom, called a barge, could travel 45 miles a day, compared to 25 miles a day for an oxcart.

Innovations in navigation helped increase foreign and overseas trade. Navigational charts and diagrams, along with the magnetic compass (a Chinese invention), made it easier for sailors to keep to their routes on long voyages.

With so much buying and selling, people needed **currency**. In the 11th century, the government minted huge numbers of copper coins—so many that there was a copper shortage. Therefore, moneylenders began issuing paper money to merchants. The idea caught on, and the government printed paper money in large quantities. The increase in currency further spurred the growth of commerce.

Chinese trade goods included objects of high value and beauty, such as this carved jade dragon cup from the Song dynasty.

Characteristics of China's Commercial Growth Let's take a trip on the waterways of China in the 13th century. Our first stop is a market town along a canal, which is crowded with barges loaded with rice and other goods. The barges are sailed, rowed, or pushed along with the help of long poles. Oxcarts and pack animals trudge along the roads and over the bridges that cross the canal. Peasants are coming to town to sell their surplus crops and animals, as well as items they have made at home, such as silk and charcoal.

On the streets and bridges, merchants have set up small shops to attract customers who are visiting the city. Street peddlers sell goods from the packs they carry.

You also see "deposit shops" where merchants trade long strings of copper coins for paper money. Paper money is much easier to carry around, but unlike copper, it has no value in itself. If there is too much paper money in **circulation,** it loses its value. For this reason, the government controls the amount of paper money that is available. It also threatens to decapitate counterfeiters who print fake money.

Let's continue our journey to a port city on the eastern coast where men in the harbor are loading silk, ceramics, sugar, and rice into large sailing vessels called junks. These ships are big enough to hold several hundred men. Their sails are made of bamboo matting. The junks depart for Korea, Japan, Southeast Asia, India, the East Indies, and even Africa. They are expected to return loaded with indigo for making blue dye, spices, silver, ivory, and coral.

Results of Growth in Trade and Commerce The increase in China's trade and commerce had several effects. First, it resulted in the growth of the merchant class. Second, business brought increased prosperity, giving China the highest living standard in the world at that time. Third, many commercial centers grew into big cities.

Commerce greatly expanded in China under the Song dynasty. This scene illustrates commercial life in the city of Kaifeng during the 13th century. Kaifeng was an important city, and the capital under both the Tang and the Song dynasties.

As population increased and commerce flourished, huge cities developed, such as Kaifeng. This scene is part of a 15-foot illustrated scroll called Ch'ing Ming Festival on the River.

urbanization the growth of cities

3. The Growth of Urbanization

Urbanization increased during the Song dynasty as cities sprouted up all over China. Chinese cities became the largest in the world. The city of Hangzhou had perhaps 2 million people within its walls. Since European cities of this period had no more than 50,000 residents, it's no wonder that Marco Polo was impressed with the cities he visited.

Reasons for Urbanization Why did the growth of cities increase under the Song? One answer is that the growth of commerce encouraged people to move to cities and towns. There, people could make a living as merchants, traders, peddlers, and shopkeepers. In addition, landowners left their farms because they preferred the shops and social life of the cities. More people brought still more opportunities for business and jobs, and cities grew even larger.

Characteristics of Cities China's cities at this time were crowded, exciting places. The crowds in Hangzhou astonished Marco Polo who wrote, "Anyone seeing such a multitude would believe it impossible that food could be found to feed them all, and yet on every market day all the market squares are filled with people and with merchants who bring food on carts and boats."

Let's stroll through a typical 13th-century city. The streets are filled with rich landowners, merchants, traders, moneylenders, and visiting peasants eager to sell their surplus crops. Signs in the market area identify the goods sold in each shop.

In the entertainment area musicians, jugglers, acrobats, and puppeteers perform outdoors. People are enjoying the theater. They are visiting with friends in restaurants and teahouses. Food vendors carrying trays of food on their heads provide plenty to eat.

Also in the cities, wealthy young girls tightly bound their feet with cloth so that their toes were bent under. These girls grew up to have tiny feet, which the Chinese considered beautiful. But they had great difficulty walking.

This custom of foot binding first became common during the Song dynasty. It marked a decline in the status of women. Some followers of Confucianism taught that women were **inferior** to men. In addition, women of the middle and upper classes in cities did not work. In the countryside, women enjoyed greater status because they did participate in work on farms.

Results of Urbanization The growth of cities changed the way many ordinary Chinese lived. Cities were vibrant centers of activity, from buying and selling, to hobbies and board games. Public-works projects provided employment for many city dwellers. Urbanization also **stimulated** culture, giving artists an audience of wealthy, leisured people. Paintings produced during the Song period are considered some of the finest in the world.

Lesson Summary

In this lesson, you learned about changes in agriculture, trade and commerce, and urbanization during the Tang and the Song dynasties.

Changes in Agriculture During this time, the center of Chinese civilization shifted from the north to the south. The south's climate was ideal for growing rice. Rice became China's most important crop. A new kind of rice seed and improvements in farming methods greatly increased rice production. This helped support a larger population. It also gave landowners money to buy luxuries, which stimulated the growth of commerce.

The Growth of Trade and Commerce Commerce was also helped by a network of rivers and canals. Improvements in navigation made overseas trade easier. Traders and merchants supplied the goods people wanted to buy. As China moved to a money economy, the increase in currency helped business to grow.

The Growth of Urbanization Increased commercial activity contributed to the growth of cities. Merchants, peasants, peddlers, and traders sold all kinds of goods. China enjoyed the highest living standard in the world at that time.

Lesson 21

Chinese Discoveries and Inventions

How have medieval Chinese discoveries and inventions influenced the modern world?

Introduction

Between about 200 and 1400 C.E., the Chinese made many discoveries and inventions. Many of these advances occurred during the Tang and Song dynasties, and the influence of these advancements is still evident today.

Over the centuries, Chinese scholars and scientists studied engineering, mathematics, science, and medicine, among other subjects. Their studies led to scientific and technological progress that was often far ahead of advances in the rest of the world.

To understand the importance of one Chinese innovation, suppose that you are a trader in the 10th century. You are far out at sea on a Chinese junk loaded with goods you are bringing to Korea. Without landmarks to guide you, how do you know in which direction you're headed? Normally, you might steer by the sun or the stars. But what if it's cloudy? Can you still figure out which way to travel?

In the past, you might have been lost. But thanks to the **magnetic** compass, you can find your way. Your compass is a magnetized needle that aligns itself with Earth's magnetic poles so that one end points north and the other south. By the Song dynasty, the Chinese were using this type of compass to help them navigate on long voyages. People still use the same kind of device today.

Like the compass, other Chinese inventions and discoveries made it possible for people to do things better than they had before. In this lesson, you will learn about Chinese advances in exploration and travel, industry, military technology, everyday objects, and disease prevention. You will see that the influence of many Chinese ideas reached far beyond China.

Social Studies Vocabulary

gunpowder

inoculate

mass-produce

movable type

◀ Scientific advances helped medieval Chinese sailors to make long sea voyages.

1. Exploration and Travel

Several Chinese inventions made exploration and travel safer and faster. Some innovations benefited traders and other voyagers who ventured out to sea, while others improved travel on rivers, lakes, canals, and bridges within China.

Paddlewheel boats were easy to maneuver, which made them effective warships, perhaps starting as early as the 6th century. They are still used today as recreational boats.

Improving Travel by Sea The Chinese developed the first compass as early as the 3rd century B.C.E. The first Chinese compasses were pieces of a magnetic mineral called lodestone. Earth itself is like a giant magnet with north and south poles. Because lodestone is magnetic, it is influenced by Earth's magnetic poles. If you put a piece of lodestone on wood and float it in a bowl of water, the lodestone will turn until it points in a north-south direction.

Europeans also developed a compass using lodestone. Eventually, the Chinese replaced the lodestone with a steel needle because they learned that rubbing a needle with lodestone made the needle act in the same way as the lodestone. However, a needle in a compass gave a more accurate reading than a piece of lodestone.

By the time of the Song dynasty, the Chinese were using magnetic compasses for navigation at sea. Compasses made long sea voyages possible because sailors could figure out directions even without a landmark or a point in the sky to steer by. The compass remains an important navigational tool today.

Additionally, the Chinese made sea travel safer by improving boat construction. By the 2nd century C.E., they started building ships with separate, watertight compartments. Builders divided the ships into sections and sealed each section with caulk, a sealant that repels water. If there were a leak, it would be isolated, and the other compartments would not fill with water, keeping the ship afloat. Modern shipbuilders still use this technique.

Improving Travel on Rivers, Lakes, Canals, and Bridges
Within China, people often traveled by boat on rivers or across lakes. An innovation of a vessel called a paddlewheel boat made this type of travel much faster.

Have you ever paddled a canoe or other small boat? As you push your paddle through the water, the boat moves forward. In the 5th century, the Chinese adapted this idea by arranging a series of paddles in a wheel. People walked on a treadmill to turn the paddlewheel, which in turn moved through the water, moving the boat forward. The Romans had also developed a paddlewheel-powered boat, but it was powered by oxen, which are not as easy to direct as people.

The people-powered paddlewheel boats allowed the Chinese to travel much faster on rivers and lakes, and were also much easier to maneuver than other types of watercraft. People still use this type of boat for recreational activities.

Another way the Chinese improved transportation was by developing a new type of canal lock, during the Song dynasty. The Chinese used canals extensively to connect the many rivers. As the surrounding land sloped up, parts of canals were at different levels. Before the improved locks were invented, the Chinese had to drag their boats up stone ramps to reach water at a higher level, a difficult task that could damage the boats.

The new canal locks solved this problem. When a boat entered the lock, a gate was lowered to hold in water. The water was then allowed to rise until it reached the level of the water up ahead, and the boat floated on. To go "downhill," water was released by the lock until it fell to the level of the water down below.

The innovative new type of locks made canal travel much easier. Locks could raise boats more than 100 feet above sea level.

The Chinese also found ways to improve bridges. For example, in 618 C.E., a Chinese engineer completed a new type of arched bridge. In Europe, Roman-designed bridges rested on arches that were half-circles. The new Chinese bridge used arches that were a smaller part, or **segment,** of a circle, making the bridges broader and flatter than semicircular arches could. Called a segmental arch bridge, the new type of bridge required less material to build and was stronger, as well.

Many cultures developed engineering technologies. However, the segmental arch bridge is one of China's most prized achievements. Bridges of that design stretch over expressways around the world.

The Great Stone Bridge, completed in 618, spans the river Chiao Shui in China. It was the world's first segmental arch bridge and has a span of 123 feet.

2. Industry

Some Chinese advances led to new industries. During this period, the medieval Chinese made advances and innovations in the way they produced paper, print, tea, porcelain, and steel.

Paper By the 2nd century C.E., the Chinese invented the art of papermaking. Historians believe the earliest Chinese paper was probably made from hemp and then the bark of the mulberry tree. Later, the Chinese used rags.

Papermaking became an important industry in China. For more than 500 years, the Chinese were the only people in the world who knew the secret of making paper. From China, knowledge of papermaking traveled to Japan and across Central Asia. Europeans probably first learned about this art after 1100. Considering how important it is for recording and transmitting information, few inventions have been more important in history than paper.

Printing The invention of paper made another key development possible: printing. In about the 7th century, the Chinese invented a technique called woodblock printing. The printer first drew characters (symbols) on paper and then glued the paper to a wooden block. When the glue was dry, the printer carved out the wood around the characters, leaving the characters raised on the wood.

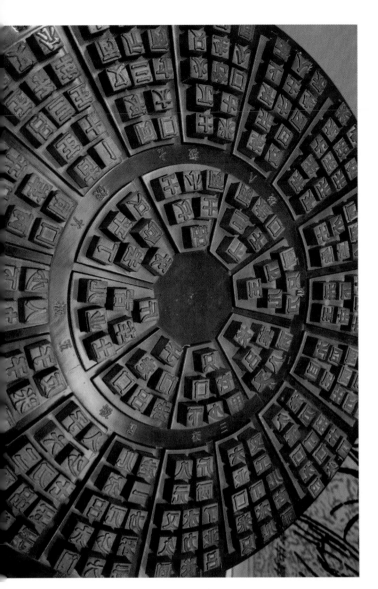

Movable type was placed on a revolving plate, each character on a separate block. Printers placed the characters in a frame to create a page. Movable type was used to print books and newspapers around the world.

movable type individual characters made of wood or metal that can be arranged to create a printing job and then be used over again

To print from the block, the printer covered the characters with black ink, spread paper over the block, and smoothed the paper with a brush. Some artists still use block printing today to create fine art prints.

By the 8th century, there was an entire woodblock printing industry in China. Printers created religious and other works on scrolls. In the 10th century, the Chinese started printing modern-style books with pages.

In the 11th century, during the Song dynasty, the Chinese invented **movable type,** which consists of separate blocks for each character. (Europeans developed movable type independently in the 1400s.) Printers made their type by carving characters out of clay and baking them. To print, they selected the characters they needed and placed them in an iron frame in the order they would appear on the page. When the printing job was complete, the type could be removed from the frame and rearranged to use again.

With the invention of movable type, printers no longer had to create a new set of woodblocks for each item they printed. This dramatically lowered the cost and labor of printing. Written materials became more widely available, and advances in printing helped spread learning throughout China. Until the last century, all newspapers, books, and magazines were printed using movable type.

The first woodblock prints were made in one color, usually with black ink. Then printers began making several versions of one scene and printed each with a different color. With this method, they could produce a colorful picture.

A printer used engraving tools such as these to carve the scene on the woodblock.

The woodblock was then covered with ink, and paper was pressed onto it to create the print.

Notice that the printed scene is a mirror image of the carved scene on the woodblock.

Tea Historians have discovered from written accounts that the Chinese have been drinking tea since at least 2700 B.C.E. For several thousand years, tea—made by steeping tea leaves in boiling water—was drunk mostly as medicine. However, by the 8th century C.E., tea had become a hugely popular everyday beverage that was enjoyed throughout China. Tea houses had sprung up throughout the country. A famous writer, Lu Yu, wrote a book, *Cha Jing* (*Tea Classic*), describing how to cultivate, prepare, and drink tea. The drink's popularity made tea-plant cultivation a major industry, often involving an entire community.

Basic tea cultivation and processing has not changed much since early times. Tea farmers grow small tea trees or shrubs on high ground, usually above 4,000 feet. When the trees are ready for harvest, only new-growth leaves are picked—by hand. Then the tree is pruned, or cut back, so it will grow new leaves for the next harvest, and the cycle repeats several times a year. Workers then dry the fresh leaves by leaving them out in sunlight for different numbers of days, depending on the variety of tea. The final drying process occurs in a dry wok or in a small oven.

During the Tang Dynasty, the first tea-plant seeds were brought to Japan where tea cultivation developed into an industry by about 1200. Europeans became involved in tea farming and trade by the 18th century. Dutch traders brought seeds from Japan and China to their colonies in Indonesia. Tea plants were found in the British territories of Burma (now Myanmar) and India. The Dutch and British produced and traded tea throughout their empires, spreading the beverage around the world and competing for the tea trade in the 13 American colonies. During the Boston Tea Party, colonists tossed British tea into Boston Harbor, helping to spark the American Revolution. Today, tea is one of the most popular beverages in the world, and, as in ancient China, people now often drink tea for their health.

The tea industry started in China and soon became a global market. In this 19th-century painting, tea farmers are transporting bags of tea on bamboo rafts.

Porcelain Another Chinese invention is a type of fine pottery called porcelain. Some historians believe that the Chinese produced the first porcelain as early as the 1st century C.E.

Porcelain is made by combining clay with the minerals quartz and feldspar, and it is then baked in a kiln, or pottery oven, at very high temperatures. The resulting pottery is white, hard, and waterproof. Despite its sturdiness, light can still pass through porcelain, creating an appearance that is quite delicate and beautiful.

By the 10th century, the Chinese were making porcelain of great artistry. Craftspeople learned how to paint pictures on porcelain and made colored glazes to decorate their work.

Porcelain making became a major industry in China. Hundreds of thousands of people worked to mass-produce dishes, bowls, and vases. Some workers washed the clay, while others applied the glaze or operated the kiln.

Since Europeans did not learn how to make fine porcelain until the 18th century, Chinese porcelain became a prized item for trade. Many people consider medieval Chinese porcelain to be the finest in the world, and people today still refer to fine porcelain dinnerware as "china."

The art of making porcelain was invented in China and became a major industry there. Works of fine Chinese porcelain, such as this vase from the Ming dynasty, are still prized around the world.

mass-produce to make quantities of an item by using standardized designs and dividing steps of production among the workers

Steel The Chinese first made steel, a very useful metal, before 200 B.C.E. Steel is made from iron, but it is less brittle than iron and easier to bend into different shapes.

The earliest Chinese steel was made from cast iron. The Chinese were the first to learn how to make cast iron by melting and molding iron ore. Later they learned that blowing air into molten, or melted, cast iron causes a chemical reaction that creates steel, which is a great deal stronger than iron.

These developments eventually made it possible to produce large amounts of steel cheaply. In the 1800s, the mass production of steel was crucial to the Industrial Revolution in the West. Today, iron and steel making are among China's most important industries.

3. Military Technology

During the Song and Mongol periods, the Chinese developed powerful weapons. The invention of **gunpowder**—one of the most significant inventions in history—made these weapons possible.

The Development of Gunpowder The Chinese who first made gunpowder were alchemists, people who practiced a blend of science and magic known as alchemy. Alchemists experimented with mixtures of natural ingredients in an attempt to locate a substance that might allow people to become immortal. They also searched for a way to make gold out of cheaper metals.

Chinese alchemists experimented with a mineral called saltpeter, which they may have believed could extend life. Perhaps by accident, they discovered that it could be used to make an explosive powder. In 850 C.E., during the Tang dynasty, alchemists recorded a formula for gunpowder but warned others to avoid it because it was extremely dangerous.

By the 10th century, the Chinese had developed the first weapon that used gunpowder: the flamethrower. Early flamethrowers contained gunpowder mixed with oil and were used to spray enemies with a stream of fire.

Between the 11th and 14th centuries, the Chinese created many other weapons using gunpowder. Artillery shells, for example, exploded after being hurled at enemies by a war machine called a catapult. The sound of the exploding shells confused the enemy and terrified their horses. Small bombs, or grenades, were lit and thrown by hand.

In the 13th century, the Chinese used large bombs that were as explosive as modern bombs. Around the same time, they developed weapons much like today's rifles and cannons.

By the early 1300s, travelers had brought the knowledge of gunpowder to Europe. Gunpowder forever changed the way people waged war and, eventually, weapons like crossbows, swords, and spears gave way to guns and cannons.

Rocket Technology Rocket technology was developed in China during the Song dynasty. Rockets were powered by a black powder made of saltpeter, charcoal, and sulfur. Initially, rockets were used only in fireworks, but later, the Chinese used them as weapons and even developed a two-stage rocket for their armies. The first stage propelled the rocket through the air, and the second stage dropped arrows down on the enemy.

By 1300, rockets had spread through much of Asia and into Europe. The rockets used to explore space today are based on principles discovered by the Chinese.

gunpowder an explosive powder made of saltpeter and other materials

This illustration depicts an early Chinese rocket launcher. A soldier could light the end of the string on fire, and then have time to run for safety before the rockets shot out towards the enemy.

4. Everyday Objects

Do you ever play games with a deck of cards? If so, you are using a Chinese invention. The Chinese invented a number of everyday objects people use today, including game cards, paper money, and mechanical clocks, all of which were developed during the Tang dynasty.

Cards were invented in about the 9th century in China. A typical pack had 30 cards and was used to play many different games.

Game Cards and Paper Money Game cards were invented in China in about the 9th century. Printers used woodblock printing to make the cards from thick paper, and famous artists drew the designs that appeared on the backs of the cards. Europeans were introduced to card games by the late 1300s. Today, card games are played throughout the world.

The Chinese invented paper money in the late 8th or early 9th century. Before that time, coins were the only form of currency. Like game cards, paper money was printed with wood blocks. By 1107, Song printers were using multiple wood blocks to print each bill. A single bill would include many colors. Paper money is the most common form of currency in the world today.

The Development of the Mechanical Clock The Chinese developed the first mechanical clock in about the 8th century. The new clock was more accurate than earlier timekeeping devices, such as sundials and hourglasses. The Chinese devised a wheel that made one complete turn every 24 hours. Dripping water made the wheel turn. Every quarter hour, drums would beat; and every hour, a bell would chime. The sounds let people know what time it was.

The Chinese improved the mechanical clock in 1092, during the Song dynasty. Although the new clock worked on the same principles as the earlier one, it was much more complex and accurate.

Europeans first developed mechanical clocks in the late 1200s. As with Chinese clocks, a bell rang to indicate the hour. Later, dials and hands were added. Modern-day mechanical clocks are based on the same **fundamental** principles as early Chinese clocks.

5. Disease Prevention

Chinese knowledge of medicine and disease prevention dates to ancient times. Before the 1st century C.E., the Chinese developed a way of fighting infectious diseases, which can spread from person to person. When an individual died from an infectious disease, the Chinese burned a chemical that released a poisonous smoke that they believed would destroy whatever was causing the illness.

Today, it is well known that many diseases are caused by germs and that people can prevent the spread of disease by using disinfectants—substances like chlorine bleach that kill germs. The poisonous smoke used by the Chinese was a type of disinfectant.

Doctors and patients in China during the medieval period benefited from new knowledge of medicine and treatment of diseases. Here, a medieval Chinese doctor examines one of his patients.

During the Song dynasty, the Chinese discovered another way to prevent the spread of disease. A Chinese monk recommended steaming the clothes of sick people because he believed that the steam would prevent others from becoming ill. The idea was sound, because hot temperatures kill many germs. Today, people boil medical instruments to kill disease-causing germs.

Sometime around the 10th century, the Chinese discovered how to **inoculate** people against smallpox, a dreaded infectious disease. Inoculation is a way of stimulating a person's immune system to fight a particular disease. It works by exposing the person to a disease-carrying substance. To inoculate people against smallpox, Chinese physicians took a small part of a scab from an infected person, crushed it into a powder, and then inserted the powder into the nose of the person they wanted to immunize, or protect against the disease.

The Chinese knew that they had to be careful when exposing people to smallpox. Sometimes the treatment itself caused people to become ill. To be as cautious as possible, the Chinese took the infectious material from people who had already been inoculated.

Chinese knowledge about smallpox inoculation eventually led to the development of drugs called vaccines. Modern medical professionals have developed vaccines for many diseases, including smallpox and the flu.

inoculate to protect against disease by transmitting a disease-causing agent to a person, stimulating the body's defensive reactions

Lesson Summary

In this lesson, you learned about Chinese inventions and discoveries between about 200 and 1400 C.E. The influence of many of these advances spread far beyond China. Many Chinese inventions and discoveries continue to affect our lives today.

Exploration and Travel Several Chinese ideas improved travel and exploration. They include the magnetic compass, paddlewheel boats, canal locks, and segmental arch bridges.

Industry Advances in papermaking and printing, including movable type, helped spread learning. Chinese porcelain became famous for its quality and beauty. The Chinese also discovered ways to make steel.

Military Technology The Chinese revolutionized military technology when they discovered how to use gunpowder to make powerful weapons. They also developed the first rockets.

Everyday Objects A number of Chinese inventions enriched people's everyday lives. Among them are game cards, paper money, and mechanical clocks.

Disease Prevention The Chinese also made great strides in medicine and disease prevention since they discovered how to stop the spread of disease by using disinfectants and steam. Inoculations were used to protect individuals from catching smallpox.

Lesson 22

China's Contacts with the Outside World

How did the foreign-contact policies of three medieval Chinese dynasties affect China?

Introduction

Medieval China had contact with foreign nations and peoples. However, policies toward these contacts varied with different dynasties, including the Tang dynasty (618–907), the Mongol, or Yuan (YOO-an), dynasty (1279–1368), and the Ming dynasty (1368–1644).

At times, the Chinese welcomed foreign contacts. Great cultural exchange resulted as new ideas and products flowed into and out of China through trade routes across Central Asia and on the sea. In this exchange, the Chinese were introduced to new ideas and goods, such as perfume, wine, and the game of polo.

Buddhism, which originally came from India, reached its height of influence during the Tang dynasty. A Chinese monk, Xuan Zang (zhwoo-AN ZANG), traveled to India at this time and brought back thousands of Buddhist scriptures. The Chinese honored him for making Buddhism more widely known. Although it was foreign in origin, Buddhism became very popular in China.

Many Chinese, however, resented foreign influence. Less than two centuries after Xuan Zang's trip to India, one scholar-official harshly criticized Buddhism. "Buddha," he said, "was a man of the barbarians who did not speak the language of China and wore clothes of a different fashion. His sayings did not concern the ways of our ancient kings, nor did his manner of dress conform to their laws." More than once, such feelings led rulers to try to limit the influence of foreigners.

In this lesson, you will learn how the Chinese both welcomed and rejected foreign contacts. You will find out how China's emperor Chengzu sent the explorer Zheng He to other countries to display China's power and to acquire tributes from new lands. You will also discover how Ming emperors tried to close China's doors to foreign influence entirely.

Social Studies Vocabulary

maritime

Ming

Mongols

tributary

◀ The gates of the imperial Forbidden City were open to foreigners at times.

1. Foreign Contacts Under the Tang Dynasty

During the Tang dynasty (618–907), China welcomed contact with foreigners. Traders and visitors brought new ideas, goods, fashions, and religions into the country.

The Influence of Traders and Visitors Beginning in the Han dynasty, traders and visitors came to China by a network of trade routes across Central Asia. From Chang'an, China's capital, camel caravans crossed the deserts of Central Asia between oases. The routes followed by the caravans are known collectively as the Silk Road, though many goods besides silk were traded.

For a time, travel along the Silk Road became unsafe because of fighting in Central Asia. The Tang dynasty made travel safe again by taking control of much of Central Asia, which allowed trade to flourish with Central Asian kingdoms, Persia (modern-day Iran), and the Byzantine Empire. Traders also traveled by sea between China and Korea, Japan, Indonesia, and India.

Merchants, missionaries, and other visitors also came to China. Thousands of Arabs, Turks, Persians, Tibetans, Indians, Jews, Koreans, Japanese, and other foreigners lived in seaports and in Chang'an.

All these foreign contacts brought about much cultural exchange. The Chinese sent their silk, porcelain, paper, iron, and jade along the trade routes, and in return, they **imported** ivory, cotton, perfumes, spices, and horses. From India, the Chinese learned to make sugar from sugarcane and wine from grapes. New medicines also came from India.

The rulers of the Tang dynasty were open to foreign contact, and their control over much of Central Asia made the Silk Road an important trade route again, as it had been in earlier times.

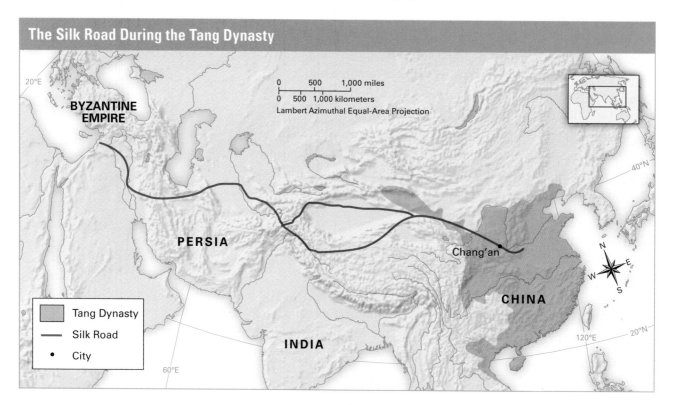

The Silk Road During the Tang Dynasty

0 500 1,000 miles
0 500 1,000 kilometers
Lambert Azimuthal Equal-Area Projection

20°E

BYZANTINE EMPIRE

40°N

PERSIA

Chang'an

CHINA

Tang Dynasty
Silk Road
City

INDIA

60°E

120°E

20°N

The Tang Chinese, especially the upper classes, welcomed new products and ideas from foreign cultures. They wore rubies, pearls, and other jewels, and they drank from goblets made of glass, a material that had previously been unknown in China. They ate new foods, such as spinach, garlic, mustard, and peas. They used cloves, a type of spice, to treat toothaches. Sitting in chairs from Central Asia instead of on floor cushions became a **status** symbol. The game of polo, a Persian sport played on horseback, became the rage among the upper-class.

Chinese music was greatly influenced by melodies and musical instruments from India, Persia, and Central Asia. Artists and artisans also imitated new foreign styles. Silversmiths, for example, began using Persian designs.

New religions also came to China, which the Tang dynasty tolerated. Jews, Christians, and Muslims built houses of worship in Chang'an and were even allowed to preach, although they converted few Chinese.

The Indian religion of Buddhism had come to China hundreds of years earlier, but it became a major part of Chinese life under the Tang dynasty. Many Chinese became Buddhists. Buddhist monks came from India to teach in China, and Chinese pilgrims went to study in India. Buddhist monks and nuns paid no taxes. They ran schools, public baths, hospitals, and lodgings for travelers. Monasteries **accumulated** great wealth. Buddhism influenced Chinese art by providing new subjects for painting and sculpture. Buddhist festivals became popular.

Foreign visitors, such as those from the west and Korea, were always welcome at the courts of the Tang emperors. This is a ceramic sculpture of an 8th century foreign wine merchant in China.

Changing Attitudes Toward the end of the Tang dynasty, foreigners and their beliefs became less welcome in China. The government placed restrictions on foreigners when a people called the Uighurs (WEE-gourz) began attacking China from across the border. In cities, violence broke out against foreign merchants, in part because many Chinese resented their prosperity.

The wealth of Buddhist monasteries also brought resentment, with some claiming that people became monks just to avoid paying taxes. In addition, influential Chinese began attacking Buddhism as a foreign religion. In 843, the Tang government, which needed money, began seizing Buddhist property and forcing thousands of Buddhist monks and nuns to give up their way of life. Monasteries, shrines, and temples were destroyed, and precious metals from statues were melted down and turned over to the treasury. The persecution of Buddhists lasted only a few years, but it greatly weakened the power of the monasteries.

Despite this distrust of foreigners, the Chinese continued to trade with other lands. By the end of the Tang dynasty, trade was being taxed and shifting from the Silk Road. A flourishing sea trade developed between China, India, and the coastal cities of Southeast Asia. Thanks to the compass and improved shipbuilding techniques, overseas trade continued to thrive during the Song dynasty (960–1279).

2. Foreign Contacts Under the Yuan Dynasty

As you have read, the Song dynasty came to an end when the **Mongols** conquered China. Recall that the Mongol leader Kublai Khan became emperor of China in 1279. He called his dynasty the Yuan dynasty. Under the Mongols, foreigners ruled China for nearly 100 years.

The vast Mongol empire stretched clear across Asia. Travel along the Silk Road became very safe because the entire region was now under the control of one government. The Mongols also developed a far-reaching **maritime** trade. Travel and trade expanded as never before, and more and more foreigners came to China.

The powerful ruler Kublai Khan (top, center) founded the Yuan dynasty, which ruled China for almost 100 years.

Thriving Trade and Cultural Exchange

By welcoming traders and other foreigners, the Yuan leaders encouraged cultural exchange. They respected merchants and actively promoted trade. They set up stations along the Silk Road every 20 miles where traders could find food and a place to sleep. Muslim merchant associations managed the Silk Road trade and traded Chinese silk and porcelain for medicines, perfumes, and ivory.

Some of the foreign visitors who traveled the Silk Road from Europe to China were Christian missionaries. They wanted to convert the Chinese to Christianity, and they also wanted Kublai Khan to form an alliance with Europeans against the Muslims. Both goals failed. Still, Christian missionaries did make some converts, and they helped bring new ideas to China.

Sea trade also flourished under the Yuan emperors. Ships from India brought diamonds and pearls. Ginger, cotton, and muslin came from Ceylon (now Sri Lanka). From Java came black pepper, white walnuts, and cloves.

Many foreigners who came to China brought special skills. Muslim architects, for example, built the Yuan capital of Dadu, today's Beijing. Persians brought their advanced knowledge of astronomy, mathematics, medicine, and water management. Jamal al-Din, a Persian astronomer, introduced new and better astronomical instruments, helped to develop a new calendar, and set up an observatory, which was a special building for the study of astronomy. Muslim and Persian doctors established new hospitals.

Foreign contacts also allowed skills and information to flow from China and spread to other parts of the world. Europeans, for example, learned about the Chinese inventions of gunpowder and printing.

The Role of Foreigners in China Foreigners enjoyed high status under the Yuan rulers, and foreign merchants, in particular, were given special privileges. Unlike Chinese merchants, they could travel freely and did not have to pay taxes. They also spoke other languages, which the Chinese were forbidden to learn.

Kublai Khan appointed many visiting foreigners to official positions in his government. The most famous was Marco Polo, a young Italian merchant and adventurer who traveled throughout China.

Polo first traveled to China as a teenager with his father and uncle, who were merchants from Venice in Italy. Their route took them across Persia and along the southern branch of the Silk Road. Throughout the long journey, Marco Polo paid attention to the interesting new things he saw.

After three and a half years and over 5,000 miles, the Polos reached the court of Kublai Khan. The khan liked Marco and enjoyed his accounts of his travels, so he sent Marco to represent him on inspection tours around China.

Although Marco Polo did not read or write Chinese, he observed carefully. He traveled around China for about 17 years before beginning his journey home. When he returned to Italy, he dictated an account of his experiences to an author who wrote a book about him. The tale of Polo's travels gave Europeans firsthand knowledge of China and further stimulated interest in trade.

Under Kublai Khan, life was more pleasant for Mongols and foreigners, such as Marco Polo, than it was for the native Chinese. The Chinese were at the bottom of the social order and resented the restrictions placed on them. They also disliked being ruled by foreigners, especially since a few foreign government officials were harsh and dishonest. The Chinese hated a Muslim finance minister named Ahmed so much that they assassinated him. The resentment that built up under Yuan rule helped make the Chinese suspicious of further contact with foreigners.

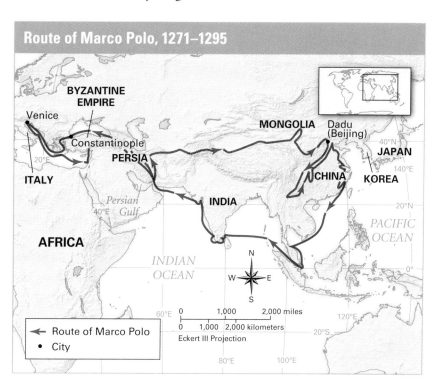

Route of Marco Polo, 1271–1295

Marco Polo followed a land route to reach China. He returned home by sea.

3. Foreign Contacts Under the Ming Dynasty

The Chinese eventually rebelled against the Yuan. From 1368 to 1644, the **Ming** dynasty ruled China. Although foreign contacts continued, later Ming rulers tried to isolate China from foreign influences.

Ming the dynasty that ruled China after the overthrow of the Yuan

tributary a conquered country or territory that pays tribute to the conqueror

Tributaries and Maritime Expeditions The Ming dynasty saw China as the oldest, largest, most civilized, and most important country in the world. Other nations, they felt, should acknowledge China's superiority by paying tribute.

Under the Ming, many other countries were China's **tributaries**. The Chinese emperors acknowledged their rulers, provided military help, and allowed them to trade with China. When ambassadors from the tributaries visited China, they had to kowtow before the emperor. This meant they had to kneel and touch their heads to the floor three times.

In return for bringing tribute, the ambassadors were given valuable gifts. They were also allowed to buy and sell goods at official markets. These exchanges benefited the foreigners as well as the Chinese.

Emperor Chengzu (sheng-ZOO), who came into power in 1402, wanted more tributaries. He gave a trusted adviser, Zheng He (JENG HAY), the title "Admiral of the Western Seas" and told him to sail to "the countries beyond the horizon . . . all the way to the end of the earth." Zheng He was to display China's power, to give gifts, and to collect tribute.

One of the great explorers of history, Zheng He made several long voyages. He even reached the east coast of Africa.

In 1405, Zheng He set off with a fleet of more than 300 ships, the largest fleet in the world at that time. It carried about 28,000 men, including sailors, soldiers, translators, merchants, and doctors. To feed this enormous force, ships carried huge loads of rice and other food. They had tubs of soil for growing vegetables and fruit onboard, as well as large watertight compartments that were converted into aquariums to hold fresh fish for the crew.

The largest ships had four decks, nine masts with twelve sails, and twelve watertight compartments. Cabins were provided so that merchants on long trading voyages could bring their wives.

Zheng He made seven expeditions between 1405 and 1433. At first, he traveled only as far as India.

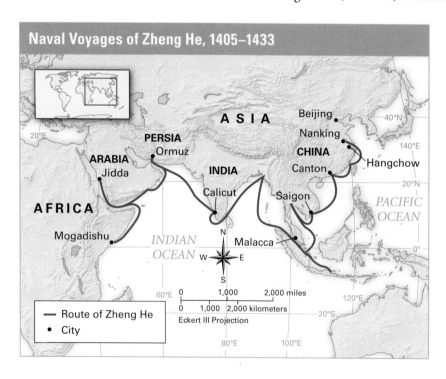

Naval Voyages of Zheng He, 1405–1433

Route of Zheng He
City

ASIA
Beijing
Nanking
CHINA
Canton
Hangchow
PERSIA
Ormuz
ARABIA
Jidda
INDIA
Calicut
Saigon
AFRICA
Mogadishu
INDIAN OCEAN
Malacca
PACIFIC OCEAN

0   1,000   2,000 miles
0 1,000 2,000 kilometers
Eckert III Projection

Later, he reached the Persian Gulf and even sailed to ports along the east coast of Africa. Thirty or more of the places he visited became tributaries of China.

Zheng He's ships returned laden with precious cargo. From India they brought sashes made of gold thread, decorated with pearls and gems. They also carried medicinal herbs, dyes, spices, gems, pearls, ivory, and even exotic animals such as zebras, ostriches, lions, leopards, and giraffes.

Turning Inward When Zheng He died, in about 1434, a new emperor ruled China. The government needed money to fight off attempts of the Mongols to retake control, and scholar-officials persuaded the emperor to stop the expensive expeditions.

From that time on, the dynasty turned inward. Ming rulers wanted to protect their people from foreign influences, so they forbade travel outside China. All contact between Chinese people and foreigners had to be approved by the government.

The Ming dynasty and its scholar-officials wanted a strongly unified state based on a single ruler and traditional values. The huge and complex government bureaucracy was staffed by scholar-officials chosen by examinations. The conservative outlook of these officials dominated Chinese thought and government into the 20th century.

The Ming desire for uniformity made it difficult for the government to change in response to new conditions. In the end, it became too rigid to adapt. Peasant rebellions helped to bring down the government in 1644, ending the Ming dynasty.

A statue of a scholar-official guards the Ming tombs near Nanjing, China.

Lesson Summary

In this lesson, you learned that medieval Chinese rulers welcomed or rejected foreign contacts at various times, depending on the policies of the particular dynasty.

Foreign Contacts Under the Tang During the Tang dynasty, ideas and goods from other places flowed into China. Buddhism, imported from India, became very popular. Eventually, however, many Chinese came to resent foreigners and foreign influences.

Foreign Contacts Under the Yuan Coming from outside China themselves, the Mongols of the Yuan dynasty promoted trade and gave foreigners important positions in the government. Cultural exchange flourished. At the same time, the Chinese began to resent their non-Chinese rulers. This attitude lasted long after the Yuan dynasty was overthrown.

Foreign Contacts Under the Ming Under the early Ming rulers, China collected tribute from other lands and undertook great maritime expeditions, such as those led by Zheng He. Later Ming emperors, however, tried to close China off from foreign influence, even forbidding Chinese people to travel abroad.

Chinese admiral Zheng He, shown here on a Chinese stamp from 2005, was one of the world's great early explorers.

The Explorations of Admiral Zheng He

Six hundred years ago, Admiral Zheng He led Chinese sailors on seven extraordinary expeditions to India, Arabia, and Africa. At the time, Chinese ships called junks were far more advanced than European vessels. Sailing those magnificent ships, Zheng He traded with countries on two continents. However, in the 1430s, the Chinese suddenly stopped trading and exploring. What happened?

The year was 1405, and Admiral Zheng He stood on the deck of his ship. At almost seven feet in height, Zheng He towered over everyone around him. People who knew him said, "His eyebrows were like swords and his forehead wide, like a tiger's." When he gave an order, his sailors obeyed immediately.

From his deck, Zheng saw his ships spread behind him as far as he could see. With pride, he looked at the vessels that followed his out of the harbor of Luijia, near Nanjing, China's capital. The entire fleet, which carried about 28,000 people, was heading toward the cities of India.

"Treat Distant People with Kindness"

Known as the "Admiral of the Western Seas," Zheng He led the greatest fleet of merchant vessels up to that time. The man who sent out the fleet was Emperor Chengzu, a bold and ambitious leader who wanted his people to explore the world and expand trade. In 1403, he ordered his royal carpenters to construct a huge fleet, and for the next three years, they tackled this vast job.

The emperor selected Zheng He, his friend since boyhood, to be the admiral of this powerful new fleet. Zheng came from a Muslim family in western China. When the Chinese defeated the Mongols in the region in 1382, they took Zheng prisoner and brought him to Chengzu's court. The two boys hunted and rode horses together, and soon became good friends.

Later, when Zheng He served in the Chinese army, he showed a talent for strategy and commanded the respect and obedience of others. He also won Chengzu's complete trust.

The emperor directed Zheng He to sail west to faraway lands, "confer presents," and "treat distant people with kindness." We know the emperor's exact words because Zheng He carved reports about the expeditions into stone tablets that still exist. Chengzu ordered merchants across China to supply trade goods for the expedition, including silk, cotton, wine, tea, silk robes, and porcelain.

The Greatest Fleet in the World

Zheng He's ships were far more technologically advanced than were European ships of that time. The largest vessels in his fleet were the enormous treasure ships, measuring about 400 feet long and 160 feet wide. In contrast, the *Santa Maria*, Christopher Columbus's flagship, measured about 85 feet in length. The treasure ships had 9 masts and 12 sails of red silk, and each vessel had more than 50 luxurious staterooms for officers and merchants.

As the fleet sailed out of Luijia Harbor, Zheng He set a course toward Calicut, a city-state on the west coast of India. The most advanced navigation tools in the world helped the fleet sail across the Indian Ocean. Ninety years later, Columbus would not have equipment as good as Zheng He's.

The key was the magnetic compass, an essential tool the Chinese invented in the 11th century. The compass allowed the Chinese to steer their ships even under cloud cover.

Chinese sailors could also determine their latitude, or distance from the equator. Each evening they took readings to find the North Star's position above the horizon. The closer the star's position to the horizon, the farther south they were. The farther the star's position from the horizon, the farther north they were.

Equipped with advanced navigation tools, Zheng He was able to steer his huge fleet across the Indian Ocean on his great expeditions.

During the first expedition, Zheng He's fleet traded for spices, such as these, with Indian merchants at the port of Calicut.

Success in India

Zheng He and his fleet reached the wealthy city-state of Calicut in late 1406. Calicut's merchants had fabulous goods, such as spices, to trade and eagerly boarded Zheng He's ships. The Indian merchants drove hard bargains, but the bargaining was always honest. One observer wrote that they "have all joined hands and sealed our agreement with a handclasp."

Zheng He returned in triumph from India in 1407. Along with trade goods, he brought ambassadors from Calicut and other Asian countries, all of whom paid tribute to Emperor Chengzu and gave him gifts. The Chinese celebrated Zheng He as a great hero for expanding China's influence all the way to India.

Sailing to Arabia and Africa

Zheng He made a total of seven voyages of discovery. His second and third expeditions, which occurred between 1407 and 1411, built on the success of the first. On the third voyage, Zheng He sailed to the South Asian kingdoms of Malacca and Ceylon (now Sri Lanka).

In 1412, the emperor started to plan the fourth expedition, which included 62 ships. In 1414, after two years of preparation, Zheng He launched his fleet. This time he sailed beyond India to Hormuz, a wealthy Arabian city. Chinese merchants on this expedition traded for pearls, rubies, sapphires, and beautiful carpets.

In addition, Zheng He wrote, "Hormuz presented lions, leopards with gold spots, and large western horses." On their return trip home to China, one of Zheng He's officers received another gift for the emperor—a giraffe. The Chinese marveled at the creature's long neck and believed that it was a *quilin*, or mythical creature.

When Zheng He returned to China, the emperor and the people again welcomed him as a hero. In 1416, he left on his fifth voyage, again to Arabia. However, this time the fleet continued to eastern Africa.

The expeditions of Zheng He were the earliest and largest of the medieval period.

Voyages of Discovery, 1405–1521

Explorer	Number of Ships	Number of Crew
Zheng He (1405–1433)	48–317	28,000
Christopher Columbus (1492)	3	90
Vasco da Gama (1498)	4	170
Ferdinand Magellan (1521)	5	265

When Zheng He reached the city of Mogadishu in Somalia, the city's leaders refused to welcome him. Angered, he launched explosives over the walls of the city until finally Mogadishu's doors opened to him. According to Zheng He, "Mogadishu presented . . . zebras as well as lions."

Zheng He made his sixth voyage in 1421. Partway through the expedition, however, he returned to China to help Emperor Chengzu celebrate the opening of Beijing, China's new capital. In 1424, Emperor Chengzu died, ending the men's nearly 50-year friendship.

Disagreements over Expeditions

The new emperor did not share Chengzu's adventurous spirit and put a stop to Zheng He's voyages. When that emperor died in 1426, however, his successor allowed Zheng He to resume exploring. The admiral, now over the age of 60, made his seventh and final voyage in 1431 to the southern coast of Arabia. He and his crew were also received by the sultan of Egypt. However, the years had caught up with Zheng He, and he died on the way home and was buried at sea.

By 1435, another new emperor was on the throne, and China began to turn inward. The new leadership was very traditional. They claimed that China already had the best of everything and had no need to trade. The royal government even destroyed some records of Zheng He's voyages because they feared that they might inspire others. In 1525, the emperor ordered all ships capable of ocean voyages to be destroyed.

China was increasingly isolated from the rest of the world and began a long decline. Only in recent decades has China, once again, begun to reach beyond its own borders. Now, it is a major trading partner with the United States and other nations. Today, the spirit of Zheng He is alive and well.

At the Arabian port of Hormuz, Zheng He acquired gems, as well as beautiful carpets, such as these.

Quanzhou (1100–1400)

During the 13th century, China was the largest state in the world. Many merchants flocked there seeking treasured goods such as silk and porcelain. One of the ports they went to was Quanzhou, a coastal city in southeast China.

Getting to Quanzhou by land was difficult, but its location on a bay between the estuaries of two large rivers provided easy access for ships coming in from the sea. During the Tang dynasty, the city began to develop into a major port, attracting merchants from many foreign places.

Over the next few centuries, Quanzhou's population grew and grew, with many Persians and Arabs settling there. In the 13th and 14th centuries, Quanzhou became China's largest and busiest port. Famous travelers like Marco Polo and Ibn Battuta wrote about the city. What made Quanzhou an economic and cultural center? Why was it such an important site of encounter?

Quanzhou's location by the estuaries of the Jinjiang and Louyang rivers provided access for merchant ships that arrived from across Asia.

Trade and Interconnectedness c. 1300

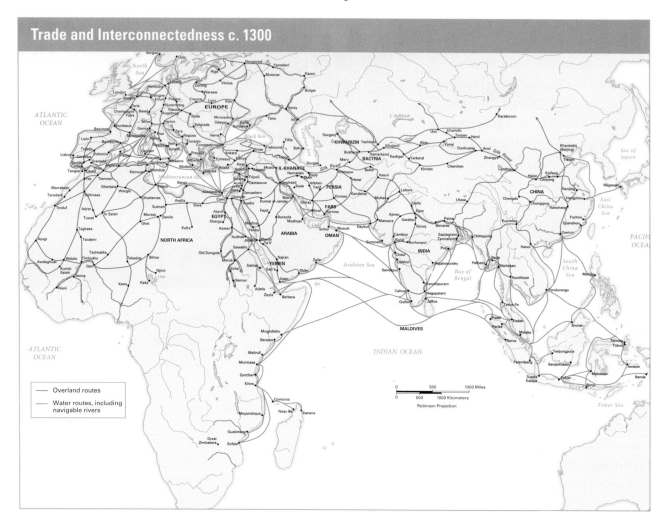

Overland routes
Water routes, including navigable rivers

Built in the 11th century, the Ashab Mosque is the oldest mosque in Quanzhou.

Communities in Quanzhou

Quanzhou's location made it ideal for trading with ports in Southeast Asia. Those ports were also connected to ports in India and Arab states, which were connected to ports in Europe. Many foreigners came to live in Quanzhou, usually in neighborhoods set aside for people of their own culture. The largest group was the Arab Muslims, who lived in a foreign quarter on the waterfront. Hindu, Persian, Southeast Asian, and Italian Christian merchants also built communities in Quanzhou.

The foreign communities established buildings in their quarters. In addition to establishing hotels and business centers for visitors from their homeland, foreigners also built religious buildings. A Buddhist shrine and mosque were built in Quanzhou in the early 11th century, and a Latin Christian church was built in the 13th century.

Chinese Regulation

The Chinese government was the most centralized state in the medieval world. It had the power to create and enforce strict regulations for merchants and foreigners. For example, the government regulated the foreign quarters. Each community had an official who settled problems between people in the community. The official also made sure that the people who lived there followed Chinese laws. The government set up Chinese schools for foreigners.

The Chinese government also had strict trade policies. These policies helped bolster trade in official trade cities, including Quanzhou. At these cities, foreign merchants had to pay import taxes on their goods. They also had to register in an official trade city before traveling elsewhere in China. The government also regulated trade by inspecting cargo and requiring traders to use paper money instead of traditional metal coins.

This 15th-century depiction of Quanzhou is found in a manuscript of Marco Polo. In his book, Polo calls Quanzhou "one of the two greatest havens in the world for commerce."

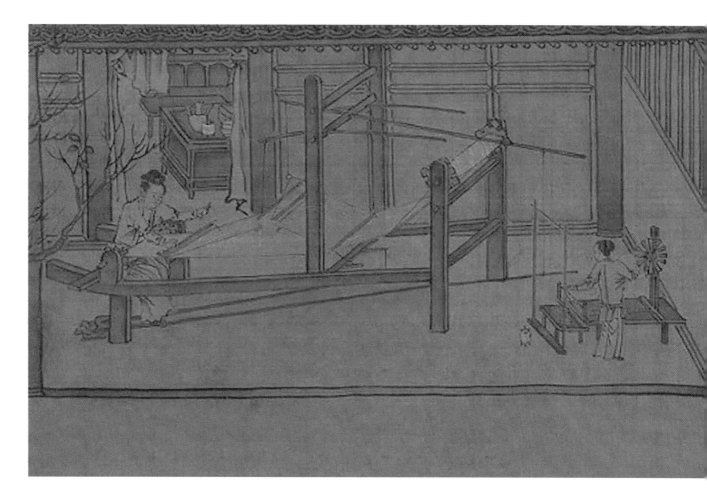

Chinese Technology and Innovations

China exported more goods than it imported in part because its products and technologies were highly valued by foreigners. One of Quanzhou's most important exports was porcelain. Porcelain, a thin and durable material used for dishware, was first developed in China during the Tang dynasty. The process for making porcelain involved mixing different types of clay and firing the items in a kiln at extremely high temperatures. Chinese porcelain makers kept the process secret, and foreigners were not able to make porcelain until the 18th century.

Like porcelain, silk was another highly valued Quanzhou export that originated in China. Silk production was very complicated and involved hatching and raising silkworms, drawing out silk, and using large machines to reel and weave silk into cloth. These machines were run by water power.

Other advances in technology also contributed to China's success in trade. Chinese inventors developed the junk, a ship designed to sail long distances. Compasses, clock towers, and smelting were other technologies used during that time.

Chinese silk production used large machines to weave silk into cloth.

Imperial China

About 960 C.E.
Merit-Based Exams Begin
During the Song dynasty, people of all classes become scholar-officials through a merit-based civil service exam based on the works of Confucius.

206 B.C.E.–220 C.E.
Han Dynasty
The Han dynasty rules over a golden age of expansion and prosperity for China.

About 850 C.E.
Gunpowder Invented
A formula for gunpowder is recorded in China and allows for the later development of weapons such as grenades, flamethrowers, artillery shells, and bombs.

| 300 B.C.E. | 100 B.C.E. | 100 C.E. | 300 C.E. | 500 C.E. | 700 C.E. |

618–907 C.E.
Tang Dynasty
During the Tang dynasty, Buddhism spreads from India to China and gains many Chinese followers.

960–1279 C.E.
Song Dynasty
During the Song dynasty, agricultural improvements increase food production, allowing for growth in areas other than farming, such as trade and commerce.

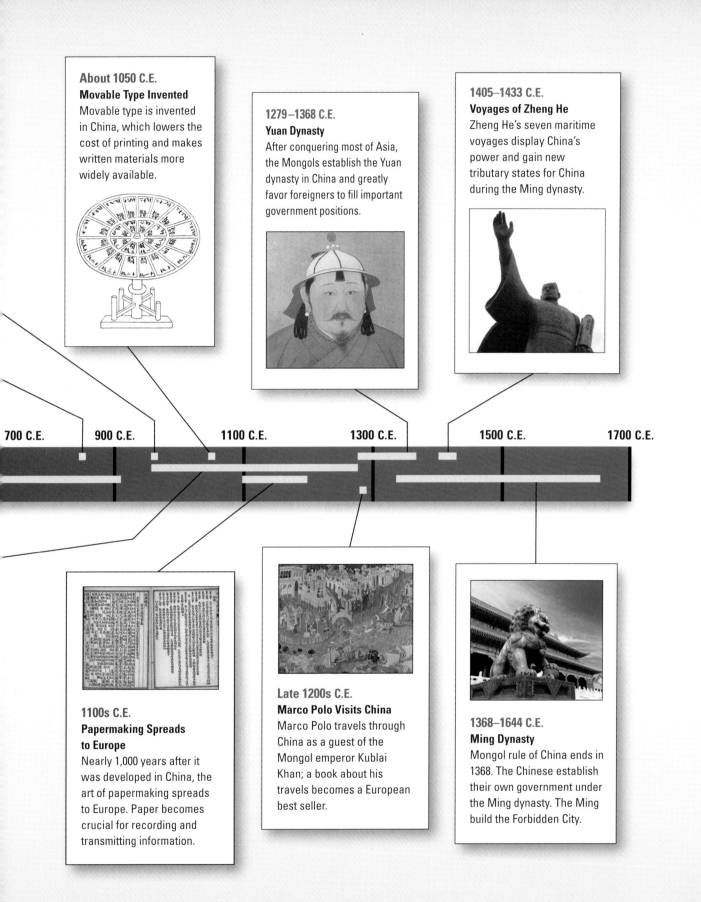

About 1050 C.E.
Movable Type Invented
Movable type is invented in China, which lowers the cost of printing and makes written materials more widely available.

1279–1368 C.E.
Yuan Dynasty
After conquering most of Asia, the Mongols establish the Yuan dynasty in China and greatly favor foreigners to fill important government positions.

1405–1433 C.E.
Voyages of Zheng He
Zheng He's seven maritime voyages display China's power and gain new tributary states for China during the Ming dynasty.

700 C.E.   900 C.E.   1100 C.E.   1300 C.E.   1500 C.E.   1700 C.E.

1100s C.E.
Papermaking Spreads to Europe
Nearly 1,000 years after it was developed in China, the art of papermaking spreads to Europe. Paper becomes crucial for recording and transmitting information.

Late 1200s C.E.
Marco Polo Visits China
Marco Polo travels through China as a guest of the Mongol emperor Kublai Khan; a book about his travels becomes a European best seller.

1368–1644 C.E.
Ming Dynasty
Mongol rule of China ends in 1368. The Chinese establish their own government under the Ming dynasty. The Ming build the Forbidden City.

Unit 6

Japan During Medieval Times

23 The Influence of Neighboring Cultures on Japan

24 Heian-kyo: The Heart of Japan's Golden Age

25 The Rise of the Warrior Class in Japan

This gate on Itsukushima Island forms the entrance to one of Japan's most famous Shinto shrines. Shinto is a traditional religion that shows respect for nature. The island is also called Miyajima, which means "shrine island" in Japanese.

RUSSIA

CHINA

ASIA

Hokkaido

HIDAKA RANGE

45°N

140°E

145°E

135°E

130°E

40°N

Sea of Japan
(East Sea)

KOREA

KOREAN
PENINSULA

Honshu

PACIFIC
OCEAN

JAPANESE
ALPS

KANTO
PLAIN

Mount Fuji
(12,388 ft., 3,776 m)

CHUGOKU RANGE

35°N

Strait

Korea

Shikoku

Kyushu

East
China
Sea

Philippine
Sea

N

W   E

S

30°N

Elevation		
Feet	**Meters**	
Over 10,000		Over 3,050
5,001–10,000		1,526–3,050
2,001–5,000		611–1,525
1,001–2,000		306–610
0–1,000		0–305
Below sea level		Below sea level

▲   Mountain peak

Present-day
boundary

0   100   200 miles

0   100   200 kilometers

Lambert Conformal Conic Projection

Japan During Medieval Times

In this unit, you will explore the civilization of Japan from about 500 to 1700 C.E. Japan is located off the coast of East Asia. The country consists of four large islands and about 3,900 smaller ones, which together form the shape of a crescent on a map.

Together, the Japanese islands make up an area about the size of Montana. Japan's four large islands are Hokkaido, Honshu, Shikoku, and Kyushu. Of these, Honshu is the largest and most centrally located. To the west, the Sea of Japan (East Sea) separates Japan from Korea and China, while to the east of Japan lies the Pacific Ocean.

In medieval times, being surrounded on all sides by water gave Japan an advantage because no enemy could approach without being seen. Additionally, the oceans were highways to other countries and provided an unlimited supply of food.

Mountains took up about three-quarters of Japan and made farming challenging in ancient and medieval times. The highest mountain in Japan at more than 12,000 feet is Mount Fuji on the Pacific coast in central Honshu. Mount Fuji is always covered with snow and looms above cities, lakes, and farms. On a clear day, Mount Fuji can even be seen from Tokyo, 60 miles away.

Volcanoes are common in Japan. Many of Japan's mountains are actually volcanoes, and occasionally one of them erupts. Mount Fuji is a volcanic mountain, but it has not had a major eruption since 1707.

Earthquakes are also quite common in Japan. They are usually minor, but at times major earthquakes have resulted in severe destruction and loss of life.

Japan is a land of beauty. Because of its mild temperatures and abundant rainfall, Japan has lush forests. Throughout the islands, rugged, tree-covered mountains meet cascading rivers and sparkling streams. In wintertime, snow-frosted trees surround crystalline lakes. Barren, rock-strewn shores rise above the blue waves of the sea. In medieval times, artists and poets found inspiration in the breathtaking scenery of their nation.

Japan's mild temperatures and heavy rainfall provide perfect conditions for growing crops such as rice and tea. The Japanese people learned to cut into the mountains to make level areas, or terraces, on which to grow food. They also cultivated crops in the low valleys between the mountains where the soil was enriched by nutrients that washed down into the valleys from the highlands.

Japan's location off the coast of Asia has been important throughout its history. Initially, Japan developed in isolation because it was surrounded by water. Later, however, cultural ideas traveled to Japan from China and India by way of the Korean Peninsula, which lies about 100 miles from the coast of Kyushu.

Medieval Japan

Lesson 23

The Influence of Neighboring Cultures on Japan

In what ways did neighboring cultures influence Japan?

Introduction

The island country of Japan lies just off the eastern coast of the Asian mainland. Japan's culture was enriched by borrowing from other places in Asia between the 6th and the 9th centuries C.E.

Many ideas traveled to Japan by way of the Korean Peninsula, but some of these ideas originally came from China and India. For example, in the mid-500s, Buddhist priests from Korea visited Japan. In this way, the Japanese were introduced to Buddhism, which had begun in India about one thousand years earlier. Similarly, the Japanese borrowed the style of their curved-roofed pagodas from China, which had adopted it from India's bell-shaped roofs.

In 593, a female ruler, Empress Suiko, came to power in Japan. Her nephew Prince Shotoku admired Chinese and Korean culture and encouraged contact with these mainland countries. In 607, he sent an official representative to the Chinese court. Upper-class Japanese began traveling to China and Korea, where they learned about Chinese literature, art, philosophy, and government. Groups of Koreans also came to Japan, bringing with them their extensive knowledge of Chinese culture.

Over the next 300 years, Japan absorbed elements of culture—objects, ideas, and customs—from the Asian mainland. As you may remember, the spread of cultural elements is called *cultural diffusion*. In this lesson, you will learn how cultural diffusion with India, China, and Korea helped to shape medieval Japanese culture including its language, art, architecture, and music. You will discover how the Japanese blended ideas from other cultures into their own unique civilization.

Social Studies Vocabulary

meditation

pagoda

Prince Shotoku

Shinto

◄ Prince Shotoku encouraged relations with China and sent official representatives to the Chinese court.

1. Cultural Influences on Japan

By the time Empress Suiko and **Prince Shotoku** came to power in 593, cultural influences from the Asian mainland had been reaching Japan for hundreds of years. For example, craftspeople from the Korean Peninsula had brought knowledge of bronze casting and advanced ironworking to Japan. Immigrants and visitors from Korea had also introduced Japan to Confucianism and Buddhism. However, as Suiko, Shotoku, and later rulers sought out contact with the mainland, the pace of cultural diffusion quickened.

Japan in Empress Suiko's and Prince Shotoku's day was a **rural,** agricultural society. People grew rice and other crops. The upper classes owned slaves and lived in houses with wooden floors and roofs of wood or thatch. The common people lived in huts with dirt floors and thatched roofs. Family life centered on the mother, who raised the children, while fathers often lived apart from their families. Compared to later eras, women enjoyed relatively high status.

Japan at this time was far from being a unified country. Power was divided among chiefs of a number of clans called *uji* (OOH-jee). But one ruling family in the region of Yamato, on the island of Honshu, had grown powerful enough to loosely control much of Japan. Empress Suiko came from this line of rulers, as did Prince Shotoku, who ruled as regent under the empress.

Under Suiko, Shotoku, and later rulers, the government of Japan took an active interest in Korean and Chinese culture. Sometimes, knowledge of mainland culture came from Japanese who traveled to China. Sometimes, it came in the form of gifts, such as books and art objects, sent from the mainland to Japan. Sometimes, it came from Korean workers who settled in Japan, bringing their knowledge and skills with them.

During the next three centuries, Japan sent officials, students, translators, and monks on ships across the sea to China. These people often remained in China for years before returning home with what they had learned. They also brought many examples of mainland culture, including paintings, religious statues, and musical instruments. As a result of these contacts, the Japanese **acquired** new ideas in government, the arts, architecture, and writing.

The Japanese did not just change their old ways for new ways, however. Instead, they blended new ideas with their own traditions to create a unique culture. Let's look at several areas in which this happened, beginning with government.

The cultures of China, India, and Korea were major influences on the culture of medieval Japan.

Asian Influences on Japanese Culture

0   500   1,000 miles
0   500   1,000 kilometers
Lambert Azimuthal Equal-Area Projection

JAPAN
KOREA
CHINA
INDIA

2. Government: Imitating the Chinese System

Starting with Prince Shotoku, Japanese rulers adopted new ideas about government from China. China's form of government was both like and unlike Japan's. For example, the emperors in China and Japan had quite different powers. The emperor in China was the sole ruler, whereas in Japan, the emperor had only loose control over the semi-independent uji. Uji controlled their own land, and their leaders struggled among themselves for the right to select the emperor and influence his decisions.

While Japanese emperors depended on local leaders, the Chinese emperor ruled with the help of a bureaucracy of government officials. At least in theory, appointments to government jobs were based on merit. Any man who did well on an examination could become an official.

During the 7th and 8th centuries, Japanese rulers adopted a Chinese style of government. Japanese tradition credits Prince Shotoku with starting this development. Borrowing Confucian ideas, the prince created ranks for government officials. In 604, he issued a set of guidelines called the Seventeen Article Constitution, which stated that the emperor was the supreme ruler: "In a country there are not two lords; the people have not two masters. The sovereign is the master of the people of the whole country."

Later rulers went much further in bringing Chinese-style changes to Japan. In the late 7th century, Emperor Tenmu and his wife and successor Empress Jitō reformed and strengthened the central government. Control of the land was taken away from clan leaders and given to the emperor. The emperor then redistributed the land to all free men and women, and in return, people paid heavy taxes to support the imperial government.

By the 700s, Japan's imperial government looked much like China's. It was strongly centralized and supported by a large bureaucracy. Over time, however, one key difference emerged. Although Prince Shotoku had called for government officials to be chosen on the basis of their ability, as in China, a powerful aristocracy developed in Japan during the 9th century. As a result, members of noble families held all the high positions in the government.

Prince Shotoku was the first Japanese ruler to borrow ideas about government from China. Shotoku is shown here between his two sons.

Shinto a Japanese religion that expresses love and respect for nature

meditation a spiritual discipline that involves deep relaxation and clearing the mind of distracting thoughts

3. City Design: Adapting Chinese Ideas for a Magnificent City

With a stronger central government and a large bureaucracy, Japan needed a new capital city. In 710, the imperial government built a Chinese-style capital on the site of the modern city of Nara.

The new city was a smaller version of Chang'an, China's capital. Chang'an had an area of 35 square miles and a population of 2 million people, whereas Nara, with about 8 square miles, had no more than 200,000 people. As in Chang'an, Nara's streets were laid out in an orderly checkerboard pattern, with a wide boulevard running down the center. In the northern section, Buddhist temples and monasteries clustered near the imperial palace.

There was one major difference between the two capitals. Chang'an was surrounded by a wall as protection against enemies. Nara did not have a wall.

4. Religion: Buddhism Comes to Japan

Nara's Buddhist temples were another result of cultural diffusion. Buddhism began in India in the 500s B.C.E., and about 1,000 years later, it came to Japan from China by way of Korea.

Japan's original religion was **Shinto**. This religion expresses the love and respect of the Japanese for nature. Its followers worship spirits called *kami,* which are impressive natural objects, such as wind, lightning, rivers, mountains, waterfalls, large trees, and unusual stones. The emperor and other special people are also considered kami.

Instead of emphasizing a code of morality, Shinto stresses purifying whatever is unclean, such as dirt, wounds, and disease. Touching the dead also makes one unclean. Most of all, however, Shintoists celebrate life and the beauty of nature.

The buildings at Nara, Japan, with their upturned roofs, reflect the influence of Chinese architecture and the religious influence of Indian Buddhism.

In contrast, Buddhists see life as full of pain and suffering. The founder of Buddhism, Siddhartha Gautama, taught that life is an endless cycle of birth, death, and rebirth. To escape this cycle, one must follow a moral code called the Eightfold Path, which emphasizes showing respect for others, acting rightly, and achieving wisdom through **meditation.** Following the path leads to **enlightenment,** or seeing the world as it really is. Those who achieve enlightenment can enter *nirvana,* a state of perfect peace, and will never be born again into a life of suffering.

Shinto expresses love and respect for nature. This is part of a Shinto temple in a forest.

By finding the path to enlightenment, Siddhartha became the *Buddha,* or "enlightened one." As Buddhism spread throughout India, a new form arose, called Mahayana, or "Greater Vehicle." This name symbolizes a core teaching of Mahayana: that all people can reach nirvana. Its followers believe in *bodhisattvas,* Buddhists who can enter nirvana but choose instead to help others reach enlightenment. These godlike spirits live in different paradises, and worshippers pray to them in hopes of being reborn into one of these paradises. It is this form of Buddhism that spread along trade routes to China. The influence of Chinese culture brought Buddhism to Korea.

Mahayana Buddhism arrived in Japan in 552 when a Korean king sent the Japanese emperor a statue of the Buddha and a recommendation for the new religion. The statue arrived at the emperor's court surrounded by chanting monks, books of prayer, gongs, and banners. The emperor was not quite sure what to make of it. "The countenance [expression] of this Buddha," he said, "is of a severe dignity such as we have never at all seen before. Ought it to be worshipped or not?" The members of an uji clan called the Soga, who were originally from Korea, were the main supporters of the new religion.

After a fierce controversy, the emperor and his court adopted the new religion. They admired its wisdom and rituals, and they considered the Buddha a protector of families and the nation. Later rulers, such as Prince Shotoku, learned more about Buddhism through Korean monks and teachers.

Buddhism did not replace Shinto. Instead, both religions thrived and even blended, with Buddhists building shrines to kami, and Shintoists enshrining bodhisattvas. Even today, ceremonies to celebrate birth and marriage often come from Shinto, the joyful religion, whereas funeral ceremonies are Buddhist, the religion that acknowledges suffering and pain.

The kana system of writing, shown here, was used by many women writers in medieval Japan.

5. Writing: Applying Chinese Characters to the Japanese Language

Ancient Japanese was only a spoken language. The Japanese had no writing system of their own, so written documents were in Chinese, a language the Japanese had learned from Korean scholars. Over time, however, the Japanese adapted Chinese characters, or written symbols, to write their own language.

First, Japanese scholars began using *kanji,* or "Chinese writing," to write Japanese words. Kanji allowed the Japanese to keep records, write legends, and develop their own literature. However, using Chinese characters to read and write Japanese was difficult because the two languages have different grammar, sounds, and pronunciations.

By 900, the Japanese invented *kana,* which means "borrowed letters" in Japanese. In kana, simplified Chinese characters represent Japanese syllables. Kana allowed the Japanese to spell out the sounds of their own language. As a result, they were able to write freely in Japanese. Both kanji and kana are still part of written Japanese.

6. Literature: Adapting Chinese Poetic Form

The earliest literary works in Japan were poems that date from the 7th and 8th centuries. Using Chinese characters, Japanese poets developed a form of poetry called *tanka,* which was created from songs from Japan's oral tradition.

Tanka is based on the number of syllables in each line. Each short poem contains 31 syllables, divided into five lines of 5, 7, 5, 7, and 7 syllables. The poems are often devoted to love and to the beauty of nature.

Try to count the syllables in this Japanese tanka, which appears in English on the right. Has the translator kept to the tanka form?

Haru tateba	*When spring comes*
Kiyuru koori no	*The melting ice*
Nokori naku	*Leaves no trace;*
Kimi ga kokoro mo	*Would that your heart too*
Ware ni tokenan	*Melted thus toward me.*

7. Sculpture: Carving Techniques Travel to Japan

Like Buddhism, new techniques and subjects of sculpture came to Japan from Korea and China. Similarly, these sculptural ideas began their journey in India and Central Asia, and spread through Korea and China to Japan.

Archaeologists have found examples of early Japanese sculpture around burial mounds that date to the 4th and 5th centuries. The sculptures are clay figures of armored warriors, saddled horses, robed ladies, and objects such as houses and boats. They were probably meant to accompany or protect the dead.

Meanwhile, Buddhism was inspiring new subjects for sculpture on the Asian mainland. As these ideas moved east, sculptors' techniques and materials gradually changed. You can see this in the work of three artists—from China, Korea, and Japan.

At the top with the gray background, from China, is a stone image of the Buddha. The Chinese began carving images like these on cave walls near the end of the 5th century. Notice the faint smile and the positions of the arms and legs. The figure's position and gestures identify him as the Buddha of the future, whose arrival will begin a golden age.

The statue with the red background was fashioned by a Korean artist. This time, the Buddha has been cast in bronze and covered in gold leaf. How is this Buddha statue similar to the stone carving from China? In what ways is it different?

The third Buddha statue is located near the Koryu-ji Temple in Kyoto. It was carved by a Japanese artist in the 7th century. Artistic styles change as artists travel from place to place, as do materials, depending on what is locally available. This sculpture is made of wood, which allowed the artist to make the figure look more natural, especially in the upper body and the folds of the clothing.

From the middle of the 6th century to the middle of the 7th century, Chinese and Korean immigrants created most of Japan's religious art. Japanese artists learned new techniques from them.

These Buddhas were created by a Chinese artist (top), a Korean artist (center), and a Japanese artist (bottom). How are they alike? How are they different?

The Heian-Jingu Shrine in Kyoto, Japan, is a fine example of the pagoda, an architectural form imported from China.

pagoda a tower-shaped structure with several stories and upturned, tiled roofs

8. Architecture: Adapting Temple Designs

New forms of temple design came to Japan from India by way of China. Like sculpture, temple architecture evolved as it moved east. In India, Buddhist monasteries featured shrines called *stupas* with roofs shaped like bells or inverted bowls. The Chinese replaced the bell shape with a series of stories and curved roofs, creating structures called **pagodas**. These tower-like buildings always had three, five, seven, or nine roofs.

When Buddhism arrived in Japan, the Japanese adopted the pagoda design. For Buddhist worship, Prince Shotoku founded the Horyuji, a magnificent temple in Nara with wooden buildings, including a hall for worship and a pagoda. Lofty pagodas soon appeared all around the capital city. They were intended to contain relics of the Buddha and of bodhisattvas, as well.

Buddhist pagodas may have inspired Shinto priests to build their own permanent shrines. Shinto shrines reflected Japan's agricultural society and the Japanese love of nature. Based on the idea of the raised storehouse, a symbol of plenty, these shrines had raised floors and thatched roofs. Unpainted and undecorated, they blended in with their natural surroundings.

9. Music: Adopting New Music and Instruments

Japan's native music consisted of chanted poems, war songs, folk songs, and Shinto prayers, all of which were recited using just a few notes. Sculpted clay figures from early Japan show musicians playing the cither (a stringed instrument), flute, and percussion instruments.

As contacts with the Asian mainland increased, the Japanese imported music from the region, especially from China. *Gagaku* (gah-GAH-koo), a form of Chinese court music, arrived in Japan in the 6th century. Gagaku is still sometimes played in Japan, much as it was in China 1,500 years ago.

These women, in traditional costume, are playing gagaku music with cithers.

New kinds of music required new musical instruments. One of the most interesting was a wind instrument the Chinese called a *sheng*, which the Japanese called a *sho*. The sho is a type of mouth organ that was designed to look like a phoenix, a **mythical** bird. Its sound was said to imitate the call of the phoenix.

Lesson Summary

In this lesson, you learned how, from the 6th to the 9th centuries, the Japanese acquired and adapted elements of other Asian cultures, creating a unique civilization.

Cultural Influences on Japan Objects, ideas, skills, and customs flowed to Japan from India, China, and Korea, encouraged by Prince Shotoku and other early Japanese rulers.

Government and Cities From China, the Japanese borrowed the idea of a strong central government supported by a bureaucracy. To house the imperial government, they built a new capital modeled after China's capital city.

Religion Buddhism, which began in India, came to Japan from China by way of Korea. Buddhism strongly influenced Japanese religion, art, and architecture.

Writing and Literature Koreans introduced Chinese writing to Japan. The Japanese invented kanji and kana to write Japanese words and sounds with Chinese characters. Poets used Chinese characters to write tanka, a type of poetry based on Chinese models.

Sculpture, Architecture, and Music Like Buddhism, ideas about sculpture traveled from India to Korea and China, and then to Japan. Similarly, India's stupas inspired Chinese pagodas. Japan then adapted this architectural style. New kinds of music, such as gagaku, and instruments came to Japan from China.

Heian-kyo: The Heart of Japan's Golden Age

What was life like for aristocrats during the Heian period?

Introduction

The culture of medieval Japan was rich and varied due to exchanges with other Asian peoples. These exchanges enabled a unique Japanese culture to blossom between the 9th and the 12th centuries.

As you may know, Japan is close enough to the mainland of Asia to be affected by cultural ideas from that region. At the same time, the waterways separating Japan from mainland Asia helped protect the Japanese from conquest by other Asian peoples. As a result, Japan remained politically independent and had the chance to develop its own civilization.

For most of the 8th century, the city of Nara was the imperial capital of Japan. During this time, contact with China brought many new cultural ideas to Japan. Then, in 794, Emperor Kammu moved the capital to Heian-kyo (hay-AHN-keeyo), an event that marked the start of the Heian period, which lasted until 1185.

The Heian period is often called Japan's golden age. During this time, **aristocrats** led a great flourishing of Japanese culture. The aristocrats prized beauty, elegance, and correct manners. Over time, they developed new forms of literature and art. Poets wrote delicately about feelings and the fragile beauties of nature. Court women composed diaries and other types of nonfiction, as well as fiction. Painters and sculptors invented new styles of art. Performers entertained the court with new kinds of music, dance, and drama.

The brilliant culture of the Heian period still influences Japanese art and life. In this lesson, you will learn more about Japan's golden age. You will examine how Heian aristocrats lived and how they created new kinds of Japanese art and literature.

Social Studies Vocabulary

courtier

Heian period

Tale of Genji

◄ This scene from the *Tale of Genji* illustrates the luxurious lifestyle of the aristocrats during the Heian period.

The Phoenix Hall was one of the most beautiful structures built in the new capital city of Heian-kyo.

Heian period the cultural flowering in Japan that took place between the late 8th and the late 12th centuries

In 794, the emperor Kammu moved the Japanese capital from Nara to Heian-kyo. This began the Heian period, a time of rich cultural development.

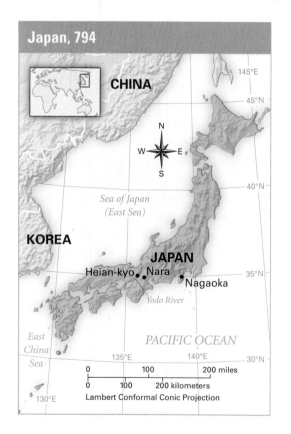

Japan, 794

CHINA

145°E

45°N

N
W   E
S

Sea of Japan
(East Sea)

40°N

KOREA

JAPAN

Heian-kyo Nara

Nagaoka

35°N

Yodo River

East
China
Sea

PACIFIC OCEAN

135°E   140°E   30°N

0   100   200 miles

0   100   200 kilometers

Lambert Conformal Conic Projection

130°E

1. A New Capital

During the 8th century, the Buddhist priests of Nara gained a great deal of influence over the Japanese court. In 784, Emperor Kammu decided to move his capital away from Nara, in part because he thought the priests' power was damaging to the government. The emperor also wanted a larger, grander city for his capital.

The first site Kammu chose was Nagaoka, about 30 miles from Nara, but the move was troubled from the beginning. As money poured in to build the new city, rumors of corruption, or dishonesty, spread. People said the land had been acquired through a deal with a rich Chinese family. The site also seemed to be unlucky, because the emperor's family suffered illnesses at this time. In 794, the emperor stopped work on the city and, once again, ordered that the capital be moved.

This time, Kammu chose a village on the Yodo River, a site that was both lovelier than Nagaoka and easier to defend. There, Kammu began building a new city he called Heian-kyo. *Kyo* means "city" in Japanese. *Heian-kyo* means, "The Capital of Peace and Tranquility." This event marks the beginning of the **Heian period**.

Heian-kyo, which is now the city of Kyoto, became the first truly Japanese city. As with Nara, Heian-kyo was laid out in a checkerboard pattern like the Chinese city of Chang'an. Built on a grand scale, the walled city was lovely and elegant, with wide, tree-lined streets. It was set in forested hills, amid streams, waterfalls, and lakes. Shrines and temples blended with the area's natural beauty.

Heian-kyo's crisscrossing streets were modeled after those of Chang'an, but the city's architecture was Japanese. In the center of the city were palaces and government offices. Wealthy Heian families lived in mansions surrounded by beautiful gardens with artificial lakes. The grounds of each home covered three to four acres and were enclosed by white stone walls.

Inside the mansions, large rooms were divided by screens or curtains and connected with open-air covered hallways. Simplicity was considered beautiful, so there were few objects on the wood floors other than straw mats and cushions. The Japanese did not use chairs.

Daily life was very formal, and correct manners were extremely important. For example, a Heian lady sat behind a portable screen that hid her from view while she talked and took part in life around the house. An unmarried lady would permit her suitor to see past the screen only after a romance had become serious.

2. The Rise of the Fujiwara Family

During much of the Heian period, which was a golden age, aristocrats were the political and cultural leaders of Japan. By the mid-9th century, the real power in the imperial court shifted from the emperor to aristocratic families. The most important of these noble families were the Fujiwara, who controlled Japan for nearly 300 years.

The Fujiwara were never actually rulers. The Japanese believed that the emperor's family was descended from Japan's sun goddess, giving the royal family a special right to govern. However, the Fujiwara had other ways of exercising power.

First, beginning in 858, the Fujiwara married many of their daughters into the royal family. They also made sure that sons of Fujiwara royal wives were chosen to be emperors. Second, the Fujiwara acted as advisers to the emperor, which, in reality, gave them more power than the rulers they guided. They often coaxed older emperors to retire so that a child or youth could take the throne, allowing the Fujiwara to rule as regents in the young emperor's name.

Fujiwara Michinaga, one of the most powerful leaders during Japan's golden age, was very wealthy. In this page from the diary of Lady Murasaki, Michinaga is entertained by watching boats on a lake at his home.

The most successful Fujiwara leader was Fujiwara Michinaga, who led Japan from 995 to 1028. He never had an official position in the government, but this smart, ambitious man had the respect of everyone around him. He was the father-in-law of four emperors and the grandfather of three more. He lived a life of great wealth and luxury. Michinaga rightly said, "This world, I think, is indeed my world."

Michinaga is one of the best-known figures in Japan's history. During his time in power, the Fujiwara family became even richer and built palaces, mansions, and temples. After Michinaga's death, his son built a famous temple that came to be called Phoenix Hall. It likely earned this name because it was shaped like a bird in flight. Part of the temple still stands as a gracious reminder of Japan's golden age.

The Fujiwara family used their power to better their own lives. However, they also kept peace in Japan for nearly three centuries, which helped Japanese culture blossom during the Heian period.

3. Social Position in the Heian Court

Rank, as determined almost completely by the position of a person's birth family, was very important during this period. Birth into a high-ranking family mattered more than personal qualities or skills.

There were nine main ranks in the Heian court hierarchy. High court nobles appointed by the emperor filled the top three ranks. Less important officials filled the fourth and fifth ranks. Nobles in all these ranks received profits from rice farms throughout the country, as well as money from taxes paid by peasant farmers. The sixth through the ninth ranks were filled by minor officials, clerks, and experts in such fields as law and medicine.

Noble women in higher ranks had servants to help them with their personal needs from morning to night.

The nine main ranks were divided into classes, such as senior and junior, upper and lower. In total, there were some 30 sub-ranks, each of which had specific privileges and detailed rules of **conduct**. Members of different ranks had different types of houses and carriages. Rank determined the number of servants people had and even the number of folds in the fans they carried. Men of the first, second, and third ranks carried fans with 25 folds, whereas men of the fourth and fifth ranks used fans with 23 folds. The fans of those in lower ranks had only 12 folds.

This precise ranking system also determined such matters as what color clothing a noble could wear and the height of the gatepost in front of his family's home. In addition, if a person was found guilty of a crime, rank determined the harshness of the sentence.

courtier a male member of a ruler's court

4. Beauty and Fashion During the Heian Period

Heian society prized beauty, elegance, and fashion. To be described as yoki (good), people had to come from an important family. They also had to look nice and be sensitive to beauty in nature, poetry, and art. Individuals were judged on whether they had good taste, and the ability to recognize beauty was valued over qualities like generosity and honesty.

Both men and women groomed themselves with great care. Small, pointed beards were considered attractive on male **courtiers**. For women, long hair was an important beauty feature. Ideally, a woman's hair would grow longer than she was tall.

The Japanese of this time considered white teeth unattractive, so both men and women carefully blackened their teeth with a dye made from iron and other ingredients soaked in tea or vinegar. Personal scent was also very **significant,** so both men and women wore perfume. Perfume competitions were frequent and popular, and people guarded their perfume recipes carefully.

For women, makeup was also important. Women used white face powder to make themselves look very pale. Over the chalky powder, a Heian woman put touches of red on her cheeks and then painted on a small red mouth. She also plucked out her eyebrows and painted on a set in just the right spot on her forehead.

A woman's clothing needed to be ornate and beautiful. An aristocratic woman might wear as many as 12 silk underrobes at one time. When she rode in a carriage, she might dangle a wrist so that people in the street would notice the lovely layers of colored silk.

The love of beauty also showed in Heian architecture, calligraphy, poetry, and artwork. Concern with form and beauty was so great that courtiers sometimes had to perform stylized dances as part of their official duties.

Long hair, eyebrows painted high on the forehead, and bright red lips were signs of beauty during the Heian period, and multiple layers of brightly colored silk robes reflected a woman's status.

Bugaku performances combine dance with music and drama. This traditional Japanese dance style started in the Heian period and continues to be performed today.

5. Entertainment at the Heian Court

Heian-kyo's aristocrats had plenty of leisure time for sporting events, games, and contests. Men enjoyed watching horse races, archery contests, and sumo wrestling. In sumo wrestling, which remains very popular in Japan, men of great weight try to throw each other to the ground or out of the ring. When the weather was warm, men and women alike enjoyed watching boat races along the river that flowed through the city.

Groups of courtiers played a game called *kemari*, in which they kicked a leather ball back and forth, keeping it in the air for as long as possible. They played in the same elegant robes they wore at court. Women used the stone pieces of the popular board game Go to play a game called *rango*, the object of which was to balance as many stones as possible on one finger.

Each of the many festivals and celebrations on the Heian calendar had its own customs. Many involved contests that tested athletic, poetic, or artistic skill. For example, in the Festival of the Snake, cups were floated in a stream. Guests took a cup, drank from it, and then had to compose and recite a poem. Other special days featured contests that judged the best-decorated fans, the most fragrant perfumes, the loveliest artwork, or the most graceful dancing.

Dancing was an important skill for Heian-kyo's nobles because dance was part of nearly every festival. *Bugaku* (boo-GAH-koo) performances, which combined dance with music and drama, were a popular form of entertainment. Bugaku dancers wore masks and acted out a simple story using memorized movements.

6. Sculpture and Painting During the Heian Period

During the Heian period, many artists continued to be influenced by Chinese art. Gradually, however, sculptors and painters created their own Japanese styles.

Early Heian sculptors commonly made an entire work from a single piece of wood. Later in this period, sculptors made statues by carving separate pieces from carefully selected wood and then joining them. With the help of assistants, sculptors could make the separate parts in large quantities, enabling them to create a group of similar statues quickly and precisely. Jocho, an artist who worked for Fujiwara Michinaga, probably developed this technique.

Jocho made perhaps the greatest masterpiece of Heian sculpture, the Amida Buddha. This beautifully carved Buddha, "The Lord of Boundless Light," expresses a sense of deep peace and strength.

In painting, Heian artists consciously developed a Japanese style, which they called *yamato-e*, or "Japanese painting." Painters drew their scenes with thin lines and then filled them in with bright colors. Lines were made quickly to suggest movement, but they were drawn more deliberately in restful scenes.

At first, artists used the new style to paint Buddhist subjects, but over time they focused on nonreligious scenes. There were four main types of yamato-e: landscapes showing the four seasons, places of natural beauty, people doing seasonal tasks, and scenes from literature (called "story paintings").

The new style of painting was used to decorate walls, screens, and the sliding doors of houses and temples. Some of the most famous examples of yamato-e, however, are scroll paintings. A scroll painting shows a series of scenes from right to left so that viewers see events chronologically as they unroll the scroll. Scroll painting had been invented in China, but Heian painters added their own distinctive touches. For example, they often showed scenes inside buildings from above, as if the viewer were peering down though an invisible roof.

The sculptor Jocho developed the technique called yosegi-zukuri, in which blocks of wood were hollowed out, carved, and then assembled. This Amida Buddha is a replica of Jocho's work.

7. Writing and Literature During the Heian Period

Writing was the most valued form of expression in Heian Japan. Everyone was expected to show skill in using words well. Early Heian writers composed artful poems in Chinese but, as time passed, distinctly Japanese ways of writing developed both in daily life and in the creation of works of literature.

Writing in Daily Life Poetry was part of daily life in Heian-kyo, and people were expected to compose poetry in public. If they could not think up a few clever lines to fit an occasion, others noticed the failure. Men and women carefully created poems to charm each other. When someone received a poem from a friend, family member, or acquaintance, he or she was expected to write one in response. The responding poem was supposed to be written in the same style and mood, and have the same imagery, as the original.

This is a statue of Murasaki Shikibu, a leading writer during the Heian period, in Kyoto. She wrote the *Tale of Genji,* considered by many to be the world's first novel.

In earlier times, the Japanese had used *kana,* which was based on simplified Chinese characters, to write the syllables of their language. In Heian times, there were two ways of writing, much like we have cursive and print letters in English. One, *katakana,* was more formal. Men used katakana when they wrote anything important. The second form of writing was *hiragana.* Characters in hiragana are formed with simple strokes that make writing and reading easier and faster. Hiragana was mostly seen as "women's writing." Court women favored hiragana for personal writing, such as diaries, and some of them used it to create lasting works of literature. Over time, hiragana took its place alongside katakana as part of Japan's written language.

Heian writers took care to present their work in a beautiful manner, since calligraphy skills were viewed as important as the ability to create poetry. People believed that handwriting revealed their character and goodness better than the words they used. Calligraphy was often displayed on colorful, handmade paper, and sometimes the paper was even perfumed.

Women Become Japan's Leading Writers The female companions to the courtiers of Heian-kyo were usually selected for their intelligence. They often took a great interest in literature and, as a result, women led in the flowering of Japanese literature in the golden age of the 10th and 11th centuries.

The best-known Heian writer was Murasaki Shikibu, often referred to as Lady Murasaki. Born into the Fujiwara family, she served as a lady-in-waiting to one of the daughters of Fujiwara Michinaga. Her novel, the *Tale of Genji* (GEN-jee), is a Heian masterpiece and is today considered one of the great works of world literature.

The *Tale of Genji* is often called the world's first novel. The book follows the life of Genji, a fictional prince, and paints a vivid picture of life in the Heian court. Much of the book focuses on the thoughts and feelings of the characters, particularly the women. For this reason, the *Tale of Genji* has served as a model for the modern romance novel.

Murasaki also kept a diary about her life in the court. Like her novel, her diary offers a close look at court life in the period.

The other leading writer of the time was Sei Shonagon. Like the *Tale of Genji*, Shonagon's *Pillow Book* presents a detailed picture of life in Heian-kyo. *Pillow Book* is a collection of clever stories, character sketches, conversations, descriptions of art and nature, and various lists. Here is Shonagon's list of "Things That Should Be Short":

> *a piece of thread when one wants to sew something in a hurry*
> *a lamp stand*
> *the hair of a woman of the lower classes*
> *the speech of a young girl*

Like Sei Shonagon, many Heian women wrote their thoughts and experiences in diaries. A book called *The Gossamer Years* is the earliest existing example. This diary by an unknown noblewoman describes her unhappy life as companion to a Fujiwara leader. Writers often included artwork, poems, and letters in their diary entries.

The *Tale of Genji* describes the life of Japanese nobles during the Heian period. This is an illustration of a scene from a 19th-century version of the novel.

Tale of Genji a Japanese novel and Heian masterpiece written by Murasaki Shikibu; considered one of the great works of world literature

Minamoto Yoritomo's rise to power in 1185 marked the end of the Heian period and the beginning of military control of Japan.

8. The End of the Heian Period

The Heian period is known as Japan's golden age of peace. However, despite the glittering imperial court, problems were brewing that would bring an end to this flourishing cultural era.

Aristocrats in Heian-kyo lived very well, but in Japan's rural areas most people were quite poor. The peasants' farming and other work supported Heian-kyo's rich. Even so, the wealthy looked down on the poor and ignored their problems.

While the rich focused on culture in Heian-kyo, events in the countryside began to weaken the Heian court. The practice of giving large estates to top nobles slowly **eroded** the emperors' power. Those who owned these estates paid no taxes. Eventually, tax-free land was so common that the government could no longer collect enough taxes to support the emperor.

Japan's rulers began to lose control. Bandits roamed the countryside, and people of different religions began to band together to attack and rob one another. The government was now too weak to provide law enforcement, so estate owners created their own police forces and armies to protect their lands. The profits from landowners' estates went to paying the warriors instead of supporting the emperor.

By the 12th century, the power of some local lords rivaled that of the weakened imperial government. Fighting broke out over control of the land, while various clans struggled for power in the capital. By 1180, there was civil war in Japan.

In 1185, Minamoto Yoritomo (meen-ah-MOE-toe yor-ee-TOE-moe), the head of a military family, seized power. A new era began in which military leaders controlled Japan.

9. The Effect of the Heian Period on Japan Today

As you have learned, the Heian period witnessed the birth of a unique Japanese culture, and the effects of this cultural flowering are still felt today. In fact, much of Japan's culture has remained quite constant since the Heian period, which can be seen most clearly in Japan's literature and drama.

Heian authors influenced many later Japanese writers. The *Tale of Genji* by Murasaki Shikibu and *Pillow Book* by Sei Shonagon are classics that are as basic to Japanese culture as Shakespeare's works are to the English-speaking world.

The success of these writers had a major effect on Japan's written language. Today, Japanese people write with the same characters used in the *Tale of Genji*.

Heian influence is also seen in modern poetry. The short poems called tanka were very popular in Heian times, and this type of poetry remains a vibrant part of Japanese literature.

Modern Japanese drama also shows Heian influences. As you may recall, the bugaku performances of Heian times blended dance and drama. Bugaku led to Japan's unique Noh theater. In Noh dramas, a chorus sings a heroic story as performers dance and act it out. Noh theater is centuries old, but it is still a popular form of entertainment in Japan.

Lesson Summary

In this lesson, you learned about the golden age of Japanese culture, called the Heian period.

A New Capital and the Fujiwara Family In 794, the emperor Kammu built a new Japanese capital, Heian-kyo, marking the beginning of the Heian period. Aristocrats—especially the Fujiwara family—dominated the new imperial court and helped to create a uniquely Japanese culture.

Social Position, Beauty and Fashion, and Entertainment Born into a particular social rank, the aristocrats of Heian-kyo lived in great luxury. They prized beauty, elegance, and correct manners.

Sculpture, Painting, Writing, and Literature Heian artists created new Japanese forms of sculpture and painting. Court women, such as Lady Murasaki, wrote classic works of Japanese literature.

The End of the Heian Period and Its Effects The Heian period ended in civil war and the rise of new military leaders. However, the effects of this golden age are still felt in Japan today. Japan's culture has remained fairly constant since the Heian period, especially in literature and drama.

Why Was Lady Murasaki an Important Figure in Japan's History?

Many great works of art and literature came out of Japan's Heian period, from the late 8th to the late 12th centuries. One woman writer, Murasaki Shikibu, became so famous that one of her books is today known as a great masterpiece of world literature. You will examine four primary sources about "Lady Murasaki" and write a claim about why she was an important figure in Japan's history.

Murasaki Shikibu was born in Japan around 978 into a lower branch of the noble Fujiwara family. Historians do not know her real name since women in Heian Japan used nicknames. While growing up, she was taught to read and write in Chinese, skills that usually were taught only to boys. In the year 1005, she became a lady-in-waiting to a queen who was also one of the daughters of the powerful leader, Fujiwara Michinaga. Before and during her life in the royal court, Murasaki spent many hours writing poetry and keeping a very detailed diary of the daily life around her. These finely detailed writings became famous throughout the world.

This is a page from a Japanese book printed in 1670. The artist made the picture of Lady Murasaki with a hand-colored woodblock print. One of her poems is printed around her picture.

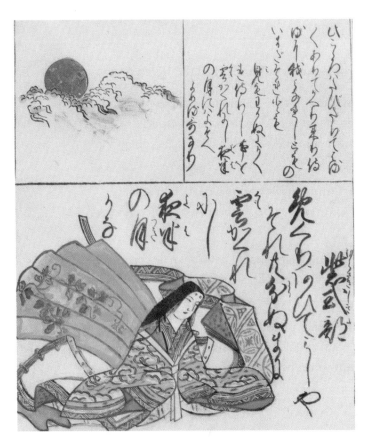

This artifact shows an image of Lady Murasaki with one of her poems. It is a hand-colored woodblock print from a page of a Japanese book whose title translates to "One Hundred Poems by One Hundred Poets." The print was created by Hishikawa Moronobu in Japan around 1670. Lady Murasaki's poem is translated as:

"I WANDERED forth this moonlight night,
*   And some one hurried by;*
But who it was I could not see,—
*   Clouds driving o'er the sky*
*   Obscured the moon on high."*

As you examine the woodblock, what details from the poem do you see in the art? What do you notice about the clothing that Murasaki is wearing, and what does it indicate about her status in society? What does the fact that Murasaki is represented on a page in this book tell you about her importance in Japan's history?

The Diary of Murasaki

The under garments were in deep and pale jasmine yellow or in green and white. Some wore scarlet and green, and others dresses trimmed with three folds. Among those who were not permitted to wear figured silk the elderly persons wore blue, or dull red . . . The colour of the sea painted on their trains was tasteful and quiet. On their belts was a repeated design.

The younger ladies wore . . . chrysanthemum colours according to their taste . . . I saw some fans exquisitely strange and original . . . Their faces and heads were hidden by fans . . .

To serve dinner Ladies-in-Waiting . . . came out near the square pillar where the court ladies sat. They were like beautiful angels . . .

When night came we had beautiful dances. The court nobles presented themselves before the King [to dance] . . .

When they danced the "Long-Pleasing Son," the closing one, they went out singing and danced along the road beyond the garden hills. As they went farther away the sound of flute and drum mingled with the sound of wind in the pine-wood towards which they were going . . .

The dancing before the King had begun and it was very delightful, when the voice of the young Prince was heard crying beautifully. The Minister of the Right said flatteringly that the August Child's voice was in accord with the music.

—Lady Murasaki, 1007

Lady Murasaki was a keen observer of life around her. She kept a detailed diary of her observations and reactions, especially after she became a member of the Fujiwara court.

Murasaki was influential in spreading the use of the Japanese language, which was just developing during this period. Most men wrote in Chinese, the official language of the government. But, according to Murasaki's diary, women were discouraged from knowing the language. Women, including Murasaki, developed their own written Japanese language to express their thoughts and stories.

Here is an excerpt from Lady Murasaki's diary, in which she writes of living at the home of Prime Minister Fujiwara, the father of the Queen. The diary describes a celebration of the birth of the Queen's new son. How does Murasaki describe the women who are attending the celebration? What does this excerpt reveal about members of high society during the Heian period?

The Diary of Sarashina

I looked at these poems which were written in such a beautiful handwriting, and I shed more tears. I sat brooding until mother troubled herself to console me. She searched for romances and gave them to me, and I became consoled unconsciously. I read a few volumes of Gengi-monogatari and longed for the rest, but as I was still a stranger here I had no way of finding them. I was all impatience and yearning, and in my mind was always praying that I might read all the books of Gengi-monogatari from the very first one.

. . . One day I visited my aunt . . . she said: "What shall I give you? You will not be interested in serious things: I will give you what you like best." And she gave me more than fifty volumes of Genji-monogatari put in a case . . .

Now I could be absorbed in these stories, taking them out one by one, shutting myself in behind the kichō. To be a Queen were nothing compared to this!

All day and all night, as late as I could keep my eyes open, I did nothing but look at the books.

. . . Although I was still ugly and undeveloped [I thought to myself] the time would come when I should be beautiful beyond compare, with long, long hair. I should be like the Lady Yugao [in the romance] loved by the Shining Prince Genji . . . I indulged in such fancies—shallow-minded I was, indeed!

—Lady Sarashina, 1059

Many Japanese people grew up reading Lady Murasaki's writing, especially her most famous book the *Tale of Genji*, also known as *Genji-monogatari*. This book about a handsome fictional prince, Genji, and the beautiful women he falls in love with captivated readers during the Heian period, and continues to be a well-loved novel today.

Lady Sarashina, another successful female writer during the Heian period, read much of Murasaki's works as a young girl. Sarashina recorded her thoughts and feelings in diaries the way Lady Murasaki did. Only a few copies of Sarashina's diaries have been preserved.

Here is an excerpt from one of Sarashina's diaries about her life as a twelve-year-old girl. According to this passage, how did Lady Murasaki's work influence young Sarashina? Compare this diary text with the one by Murasaki. Why might each diary be considered a valuable primary source for evaluating the importance of Lady Murasaki? What are the limitations of each one?

The Diary of Murasaki

Lady Izumi Shikibu corresponds charmingly...She writes with grace and ease and with a flashing wit. There is fragrance even in her smallest words. Her poems are attractive, but they are only improvisations which drop from her mouth spontaneously. Every one of them has some interesting point, and she is acquainted with ancient literature also, but she is not like a true artist who is filled with the genuine spirit of poetry. Yet I think even she cannot presume to pass judgment on the poems of others . . .

Lady Seishonagon. A very proud person. She values herself highly, and scatters her Chinese writings all about. Yet should we study her closely, we should find that she is still imperfect. She tries to be exceptional, but naturally persons of that sort give offence. She is piling up trouble for her future. One who is too richly gifted, who indulges too much in emotion, even when she ought to be reserved, and cannot turn aside from anything she is interested in, in spite of herself will lose self-control. How can such a vain and reckless person end her days happily!

—Lady Murasaki, 1008

As you observed in an earlier diary excerpt, Lady Murasaki often described in vivid detail the aristocratic people and events in the world she lived in. There are other passages from her diary in which she expressed her strong opinions, particularly about other female writers of the Heian period.

Here are excerpts from Lady Murasaki's diary in which she comments on two famous writers. Lady Izumi Shikibu was considered by many to be one of the great Japanese poets of all time. She served in the same queen's court as Murasaki. Lady Seishonagon served a different queen and was famous for her knowledge and wit.

Do you think a diary is a reliable source of information? Based on this excerpt, why does Lady Murasaki disapprove of the work of each of these successful female writers?

You have seen how one artist and one writer portrayed Lady Murasaki, and you have read two parts of Murasaki's own diary. Do you think you have a nearly complete picture of Murasaki's importance? What other sources might be helpful? Write a claim about her importance in Japan's history, citing evidence from these primary sources. Exchange claims with other students and give critiques about how well they supported their claims.

The Rise of the Warrior Class in Japan

What was the role of the samurai in the military society of medieval Japan?

Introduction

During the Heian period, Japan experienced a golden age. That period was followed by civil war. During this time of strife, a powerful warrior class arose—the *samurai*.

Minamoto Yoritomo came to power in Japan in 1185 and, by 1192, had taken the title of *shogun*, or commander-in-chief. Yoritomo did not replace the emperor, but he did set up a military government with its own capital in the city of Kamakura. While the imperial court remained in Heian-kyo, emperors played an increasingly less important role in the government of Japan.

The start of the Kamakura government marked the beginning of a new era in Japanese history. Eventually, professional warriors—the samurai—became Japan's ruling class. The era of the samurai lasted for 700 years, until the emperor was restored to power in 1868.

Over time, an elaborate culture and code of conduct grew up around the samurai. A samurai was expected to be honest, brave, and intensely loyal to his lord. In fact, the word *samurai* means "those who serve." The samurai code was very strict. Samurai sometimes killed themselves with their own swords rather than "lose face," or personal honor.

The samurai were more than fearless fighters. They were educated in art, writing, and literature, and many were devout Buddhists. Their religious faith helped them prepare for their duties and face death bravely.

In this lesson, you will meet Japan's samurai. You will learn about their armor, weapons, and the physical training needed for their strenuous battles. You also will find out about their mental training in self-control, their code of conduct, and the role they played in the military society of medieval Japan.

Social Studies Vocabulary

Amida Buddhism

Bushido

daimyo

martial arts

restoration

samurai

shogun

Zen Buddhism

◀ Fierce samurai fought individual battles with samurai of equal rank.

Tokugawa Ieyasu became shogun in 1603 and established Edo, present-day Tokyo, as the capital. This statue of Ieyasu is at Nikko Tosho-gu, a Shinto shrine dedicated to him.

1. The Rise of the Samurai

The military government established by Minamoto Yoritomo was led by a **shogun,** or commander-in-chief. Although emperors continued to rule in name, the real power shifted to the shoguns.

Samurai Under the Shoguns Shoguns, such as Yoritomo and his successors, rewarded warriors, or **samurai,** with appointments to office and land grants. In return, the samurai pledged to serve and protect the shogun.

The rise of the samurai brought a new emphasis on military values in Japanese culture. All samurai trained in the arts of war, especially archery. During this period, women, as well as men, could be samurai, so girls and boys alike were trained to harden their feelings and to use weapons. One samurai wrote,

> *Of what use is it to allow the mind to concentrate on the moon and flowers, compose poems, and learn how to play musical instruments? . . . Members of my household, including women, must learn to ride wild horses, and shoot powerful bows and arrows.*

Shifting Loyalties By the 14th century, Japan's warrior society resembled the lord-vassal system of medieval Europe. The shogun now ruled with the help of warrior-lords called **daimyos** (DIE-mee-os), who, in turn, were supported by large numbers of samurai. The daimyos expected to be rewarded for their obedience and loyalty with land, money, or administrative office, and the samurai expected the same from the daimyos they served.

Over time, the position of the shogun weakened as daimyos became increasingly powerful and began to view their lands as independent kingdoms. Samurai now allied themselves with their daimyo lords.

In the late 15th century, Japan fell into chaos as daimyos warred with one another for land and power. Samurai fought fierce battles on behalf of their lords.

After a century of bloody warfare, a series of skilled generals defeated rival daimyos and reestablished a strong military government. In 1603, the last of these leaders, Tokugawa Ieyasu (TAW-koo-GAH-wah EE-yeh-YAH-soo), became shogun and established a new capital in Edo, present-day Tokyo.

For the next 250 years, Japan was at peace. Samurai served under shoguns and **administered** the government. It was during this time that the samurai ideal came to full flower. Let's look now at the samurai way of life.

shogun the head of the military government of Japan in the era of the samurai

samurai a member of a powerful warrior class in Japan

daimyo a local lord in Japan in the era of the samurai

2. The Samurai's Armor and Weapons

A samurai was first and foremost a warrior. Let's look at what the samurai wore in battle and the weapons they used.

Armor Samurai went into battle dressed in heavy armor, under which was a colorful robe called a *kimono* and baggy trousers. Leather or cloth shin guards protected their legs.

Samurai armor was unique. It was made of rows of small, lacquer-coated metal plates that were laced together with colorful silk cords. This type of armor was strong yet flexible enough for the samurai to move freely.

Boxlike panels of armor covered samurai's chest and back, and metal sleeves covered their arms. Broad shoulder guards and panels that hung over their hips provided additional protection. Some samurai wore thigh guards as well.

After dressing in body armor, samurai put on a ferocious-looking iron mask that was designed to frighten opponents as well as to protect their face. Last came the helmet. Before putting on the helmet, samurai burned incense in it so that their head would smell sweet if cut off in battle.

The clothing and armor of a samurai was extremely complex and took several stages to complete.

Samurai wore elaborate armor with many layers. The layers protected the samurai while allowing free movement.

Weapons Samurai fought with bows and arrows, spears, and swords. Their wooden bow could be up to eight feet long and, as such, required great strength to use. In battle, samurai on horseback rode toward each other, pulling arrows from the quivers on their backs and firing them at the enemy.

In hand-to-hand combat, some foot soldiers used spears to knock riders off their horses and to kill an enemy on foot with a powerful thrust.

Samurai's most prized weapons, however, were their swords. Japanese sword makers were excellent craftsmen, and samurai swords were considered the finest in the world. They were flexible enough not to break but hard enough to be razor sharp. Samurai carried one long sword and one short sword, both of which had curved blades.

Wearing a sword was the privilege and right of the samurai, and swords were passed down through generations of warrior families and given as prizes to loyal warriors. Even after peace was established in the 17th century, samurai proudly wore their swords as a sign of their rank.

3. Military Training and Fighting

The way the first samurai warriors trained and fought was called "The Way of the Horse and the Bow." Later, the art of swordsmanship became more important than archery.

Military Training Learning the skills of a samurai required extensive training. Young samurai were apprenticed to archery masters who taught them mental and physical techniques. Samurai practiced until they could shoot accurately without thinking. They also learned to breathe properly and to shoot at their enemies while riding on the back of a galloping horse.

The art of fencing, or swordsmanship, was just as demanding. Samurai had to learn how to force an enemy to make the first move, how to stay out of range of an enemy sword, and how to fight in tight spaces or against multiple opponents. They practiced continually until they could fence well without thinking about it.

Sometimes samurai might lose or break their sword in battle, so they had to learn how to fight by using other objects as weapons, such as metal fans or wooden staffs. They also learned how to fight without weapons by using **martial arts**. This type of fighting often involves using an opponent's strength against him.

martial arts styles of fighting or self-defense, such as modern-day judo and karate, that began mostly in Asia

Battle According to early texts, the samurai had a unique style of battle. First, messengers from opposing sides met to determine the time and place of combat. Then the two armies faced each other a few hundred yards apart. Samurai on both sides shouted out their names, ancestors, heroic deeds, and reason for fighting. Finally, the armies charged at each other, with mounted samurai firing arrows as they urged their horses forward.

As the two armies clashed, samurai fought each other in hand-to-hand combat. Enemies fought a series of one-on-one duels. Samurai found opponents who were matched in rank. They would then try to knock them off their horses, wrestle them to the ground, and kill them.

Samurai classes in swordsmanship, or fencing, taught samurai essential skills for battle.

4. Mental Training

A samurai's education in the art of war included mental training. Samurai had to develop self-control so that they could overcome emotions that might interfere with fighting, especially the fear of death. They also learned to be always alert and prepared to fight.

Training in Self-Control To learn how to endure pain and suffering, young samurai went for days without eating, marched barefoot in snow on long journeys, and held stiff postures for hours without complaining. To overcome the fear of death, they were told to think of themselves as already dead.

Training in Preparedness A samurai could never relax because an attack could come when least expected, even while playing music or dancing. For this reason, samurai had to develop a "sixth sense" about danger and did so through long and grueling training.

The experience of one young samurai illustrates this kind of training. The young man's fencing master used to whack him with a wooden sword throughout the day whenever he least expected it. These painful blows eventually taught the young student to always stay alert.

Teachers also told stories about being prepared. One story was about a samurai who was peacefully writing when a swordsman tried to attack him. Using his sixth sense, the samurai felt the attack coming. He flicked ink into his attacker's eyes and escaped. In another story, a samurai woman who was suddenly attacked thrust a piece of rolled-up paper into her attacker's eyes and gave a war shout, prompting her attacker to run away.

Samurai learned to control their emotions and to always be prepared. They developed a "sixth sense" so that they would be ready to defend themselves in case of a surprise attack.

5. Training in Writing and Literature

By the more peaceful 17th century, samurai had to be students of culture, as well as fierce warriors. They were expected to be educated in both writing and literature.

Samurai practiced calligraphy, the art of beautiful writing. A calligrapher's main tools were a brush, a block of ink, and paper or silk. The calligrapher moistened the ink block, rubbed it on an ink stone until the ink reached the right consistency, and then carefully drew each character with the brush.

Samurai also wrote poetry. One famous samurai poet was Matsuo Basho, who invented a new form of short poetry that was later called *haiku* (high-KOO). A haiku has three lines of 5, 7, and 5 syllables, making 17 syllables in all. A haiku poet uses imagery to suggest an idea or create a mood. Basho added to the beauty of haiku by choosing simple words. Here is his most famous haiku:

Furu ike ya	*An ancient pond*
Kawazu tobikumu	*A frog jumps in*
Mizu no oto	*The splash of water*

Samurai were students of culture. They were trained in the art of writing, or calligraphy, and studied literature.

Amida Buddhism a form of Buddhism founded on the belief that all people can reach paradise by relying on the mercy of Amida Buddha

Many samurai worshipped the Amida Buddha, shown in this statue.

6. Training for the Tea Ceremony

Another aspect of culture that samurai studied was the tea ceremony. The tea ceremony fostered a spirit of harmony, reverence, and calm among these warriors, and it also served as an important way to form political alliances.

Each step of the ceremony had to be performed in a certain way. A tea master invited guests into a small room, which they entered through a doorway so low that they had to crawl.

The tearoom was very simple, with only a scroll painting or an artistic flower arrangement for decoration. The guests sat silently, watching the master make and serve the tea. They then engaged in **sophisticated** discussions as they admired the utensils and the beautiful way the tea master had combined them.

To make the tea, the master heated water in an iron urn over a charcoal fire. Then he scooped powdered green tea from a container called a tea caddy into a small bowl. He ladled hot water into the bowl with a wooden dipper and then whipped the water and tea with a bamboo whisk. Each guest in turn took the bowl, bowed to the others, took three sips, cleaned the rim with a tissue, and then passed the bowl back to the master to prepare tea for the next guest.

7. Training in Spiritual Strength

Most samurai were Buddhists. Two forms of Buddhism that became popular in Japan were Amida and Zen. Samurai were drawn to both kinds of Buddhism, but especially to Zen.

Amida Buddhism In the 12th century, a monk named Honen founded a popular form of Buddhism, **Amida Buddhism**. These Buddhists believed that all people could reach paradise. Honen taught that believers could do this by relying on the mercy of the Amida Buddha.

Amida had been an Indian prince. When he became a Buddha, it was said, he set up a western paradise called the Pure Land. Honen said that believers could enter the Pure Land by prayerfully repeating Amida's name over and over—up to 70,000 times a day. Then, when a believer died, Amida Buddha and a group of bodhisattvas would be waiting to escort the believer into the Pure Land.

Honen's disciple Shinran made this "Pure Land Buddhism" even more popular. He taught that believers could reach the western paradise by sincerely saying Amida's name only once.

Zen Buddhism The form of Buddhism called Zen appealed to many samurai because of its emphasis on effort and discipline. Zen stresses self-reliance and achieving enlightenment through meditation.

To reach enlightenment, Zen Buddhists meditate for hours, during which they must sit erect and cross-legged without moving. According to the beliefs of **Zen Buddhism,** becoming enlightened requires giving up everyday, logical thinking. To jolt the mind into enlightenment, masters pose puzzling questions called *koans* (KOH-ahnz). Probably the most well-known koan is, "What is the sound of one hand clapping?"

Zen masters created artfully arranged gardens to aid in meditation. These often simple and stark gardens symbolized nature instead of imitating it. Rocks in sand, for example, might represent islands in the sea.

Zen Buddhism was a good match for the samurai way of life. Zen helped samurai learn discipline, focus their minds, and overcome their fear of death.

8. The Code of Bushido and Samurai Values

The samurai code developed over several centuries. By the 17th century, it took final form in **Bushido,** "The Way of the Warrior."

The code of Bushido, like the code of chivalry in medieval Europe, governed a samurai's life. It called on samurai to be honest, fair, and fearless in the face of death, and samurai were expected to value loyalty and personal honor even more than their lives.

Samurai who believed in Zen Buddhism might have sat in simple gardens like this one when they meditated.

Zen Buddhism a form of Buddhism that stresses self-reliance and enlightenment through meditation

Bushido a samurai code that called on warriors to be honest, fair, and fearless

Samurai were fair, honest, and loyal to their lords, above all else. They would fight deadly duals to avenge an insult or their lord's death.

Loyalty and Personal Honor The **supreme** duty of samurai was to be so loyal to their lord that they would gladly die for him. If their lord were murdered, samurai might avenge his death. A samurai poem says,

> *Though a time come*
> *when mountains crack*
> *and seas go dry,*
> *never to my lord*
> *will I be found double-hearted!*

Samurai were also expected to guard their personal honor. The smallest insult on the street could lead to a duel. One samurai, for example, accidentally knocked his umbrella against another samurai's umbrella. This quickly turned into a quarrel and then a sword fight, resulting in the first samurai's death.

Ritual Suicide The price for failing to live up to the code of Bushido was *seppuku*, or ritual suicide. There were many reasons for seppuku, including preserving personal honor and avoiding capture in battle. Samurai might also perform seppuku to pay for a crime, a shameful deed, or an insult to a person of higher rank. Some samurai even killed themselves when their lord died or as a form of protest against an injustice.

9. Women in Samurai Society

The position of women in samurai society declined over time. In the 12th century, the women of the warrior class enjoyed honor and respect, but by the 17th century, samurai women were treated as inferior to their husbands.

Samurai Women in the 12th Century In the 12th century, samurai women enjoyed considerable status. A samurai's wife helped manage the household and promote the family's interests. When her husband died, she could inherit his property and perform the duties of a vassal. Although women rarely fought, they were expected to be as loyal and brave as men.

Some women, like Tomoe Gozen (TOH-moh-eh GO-zen), did take part in battles alongside men. Fighting one-on-one, she killed several enemies in a battle. Then she fenced with the enemy leader, who tried to drag her from her horse. When he tore off her sleeve, she spun her horse around and killed him.

A woman named Koman is another famous warrior. During a battle on a lake, she saved her clan's banner by swimming to shore under a shower of arrows with the banner clenched in her teeth.

In the 12th century, women, as well as men, were taught the military skills needed to become samurai.

Samurai Women in the 17th Century As the warrior culture developed, women's position weakened, and by the 17th century, samurai men were the unquestioned lords of their households. According to one saying, when young, women should obey their fathers; when grown, their husbands; and when old, their sons.

Girls did not choose their own husbands. Instead, families arranged marriages for their daughters to increase their position and wealth. Wives were expected to bear sons, manage the home, and look after their husbands.

A popular book of the time told women how to behave. They were to get up early and go to bed late. During the day they must weave, sew, spin, and take care of their households. They must stick to simple food and clothes and stay away from plays, singing, and other entertainment.

Not all Japanese women were treated the same way. Peasant women had some respect and independence because they worked alongside their husbands. However, in samurai families, women were completely under men's control.

10. Comparing Japan and Europe in the Middle Ages

The Japan of the samurai period was both like and unlike Europe during the Middle Ages. In both societies, ties of loyalty and obligation bound lords and vassals. Both had rulers who rose to power as military chiefs. However, in Europe, a military leader like William the Conqueror ruled as king; whereas in Japan, the shogun ruled in the name of the emperor.

The daimyos of Japan were like the landholding lords of medieval Europe. Both types of lords built castles and held estates that were worked by peasants.

Both the samurai of Japan and the knights of Europe were warriors who wore armor, rode horses, and owned land. Just as European knights had a code of chivalry, the samurai had the code of Bushido. The samurai code, however, was much stricter, because it demanded that a samurai kill himself to maintain his honor.

11. The Influence of Samurai Values and Traditions in Modern Times

Japan's warrior society lasted until 1868, when political upheavals led to the **restoration** of the emperor to ruling power. Modern Japan still feels the influence of the long era of the samurai.

In the 1940s, the Japanese who fought in World War II stayed true to the samurai warrior code. Many soldiers killed themselves rather than surrender, and suicide pilots crashed planes loaded with explosives into enemy battleships. These pilots were called *kamikazes* ("divine winds") after the storms that helped destroy an invading Chinese fleet in the 13th century.

restoration the return of a past state, situation, or ruler

Samurai fought individual battles with other samurai of equal rank. Like the medieval European knights, the samurai also fought on horseback.

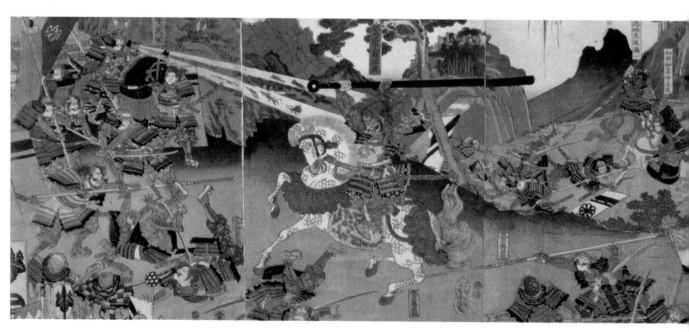

Today, instructors teach samurai fighting techniques to students wearing traditional padded armor. These students are practicing the ancient martial art of kendo.

Japanese and other peoples around the world study martial arts. Sports such as judo and fighting with bamboo swords reflect samurai discipline and skill.

Other elements of samurai culture persist today. People in Japan continue to write haiku and practice calligraphy. Zen gardens and the tea ceremony remain popular. And the samurai ideals of loyalty to family and respect for rank are still alive in modern Japan.

Lesson Summary

In this lesson, you learned how a class of warriors, called samurai, rose to prominence in medieval Japan. They dominated Japan for nearly 700 years, serving shoguns and daimyos, and over time, an elaborate samurai culture developed.

Armor, Weapons, and Military, Mental, and Spiritual Training Samurai wore flexible armor, rode horses, and fought with bows, spears, and swords. They were trained as fearless fighters. The discipline of Zen Buddhism especially appealed to them.

Training in Writing, Literature, and the Tea Ceremony Samurai also studied literature, the arts, and the complex tea ceremony. They were expected to be skilled at poetry and calligraphy.

Bushido and Samurai Values Samurai were expected to live by a strict code called Bushido. This code prized honor, loyalty, and fearlessness.

Women Samurai Women enjoyed high status in early samurai society, and some women fought as warriors. Over time, however, the status of samurai women declined.

Japan and Europe in the Middle Ages Japan's samurai society, with its lord-vassal system, resembled feudalism in medieval Europe. Samurai and European knights both had a code of behavior, fought on horseback, and pledged loyalty to their lords.

The Samurai Influence Today Samurai values and traditions continue to influence Japan. For example, people practice samurai martial arts, write haiku, and create Zen gardens.

Female samurai Tomoe Gozen is a legendary hero to the Japanese. She was first mentioned in *The Tale of the Heike*, medieval Japan's most famous epic.

Tomoe Gozen: History or Legend?

Japanese history tells stories about women warriors of the samurai period. Strong and skillful fighters, they were willing to die with honor rather than face defeat and disgrace. Tomoe Gozen is one of the best known of these fierce Japanese women samurai. The tales say that she was an important figure in the wars of the late Heian period, but was she a real woman or a fictional character?

Tomoe Gozen is first mentioned in *The Tale of the Heike* (HAY-keh), the most famous epic from medieval Japan. The tale is actually a series of stories about the Genpei War, which took place in the 1180s, during the late Heian period. The war was a struggle between two powerful rival clans for control of Japan.

The Tale of the Heike had numerous authors because storytellers repeated the narrative over several generations before it was written down. Experts say the most definitive version of the Heike tale probably was first recorded in the 1300s, but many other versions and translations have appeared since then.

A Woman Warrior

Although Tomoe appears only briefly in *The Tale of the Heike*, fighting for a general named Yoshinaka, she makes a strong impression:

> *Tomoe was especially beautiful . . . She was also a remarkably strong archer, and as a swordswoman, she was a warrior worth a thousand, ready to confront a demon or a god, mounted or on foot. She handled unbroken horses with superb skill; she rode unscathed [unhurt] down perilous descents. Whenever a battle was imminent [about to begin], Yoshinaka sent her out as his first captain, equipped with strong armor, an oversized sword, and a mighty bow; and she performed more deeds of valor than any of his other warriors.*

Some versions of the story say that Tomoe was General Yoshinaka's wife, while others indicate that she was not. Regardless, she was a strong woman warrior. In the final battle of the Genpei War, as described in the Heike tale, Tomoe fights bravely, but General Yoshinaka is mortally wounded. Although she wants to remain and die with him, he orders her to leave the battlefield, and Tomoe obeys. Frustrated, she thinks, "Ah! If only I could find a worthy foe! I would fight a last battle for His Lordship to watch."

Suddenly, a powerful and strong enemy leader appears nearby. Tomoe rides toward him, drags him from his horse, pulls him down against her saddle, cuts off his head, and throws it aside. When she is finished, she removes her armor and helmet and rides off toward the eastern provinces.

Was Tomoe a Real Person?

This brief but powerful appearance of Tomoe in *The Tale of the Heike* is all we know about her. Was she a real person? To decide, historians looked at the evidence. Because *The Tale of the Heike* is one of the main sources for historical knowledge of the Genpei War, historians had to read every version of it written over the centuries.

Historians have good evidence that Tomoe did, in fact, really exist. First, much samurai history indicates that there actually were female warriors, like Tomoe, who fought just as skillfully and fiercely as men. Second, *The Tale of the Heike* says that General Yoshinaka "had brought . . . two female attendants, Tomoe and Yamabuki" with him to the wars. Because other figures and events in the book are real, historians have concluded that Tomoe was most likely real, too.

Not only was Tomoe Gozen a brave and talented warrior, she was also an excellent horsewoman. Here, she rides ahead into battle.

Actors, such as the one in the center of this image, took on the role of Tomoe Gozen. Stories and plays about her allowed her legend to grow.

The Legend Begins

How does a legend start? Generally, it starts with a historical figure, and over time, people retell the person's story and add new details with each passing generation. These details often make the story more exciting but less realistic, with the historical figure becoming superhuman, extremely wise, strong, or magical. Moreover, that individual may become a symbol, standing for positive or negative characteristics that capture people's imagination.

Robin Hood is a good example of a legendary figure in Western culture. Some historians believe he might have been real, but as his story was retold, he turned from a historical figure into a legend, fighting for the poor against the rich. Countless ballads, plays, poems, movies, and TV series have been written about his adventures.

Similarly, over the centuries, Tomoe became a legend in Asian culture. Her story was retold over centuries in Japan, and details were added to explain what happened to her after she went off to the eastern provinces. Various versions have her running away, dying with Yoshinaka, getting married, or becoming a Buddhist nun.

One thing is certain: over time, Tomoe came to symbolize loyalty, strength, and bravery, and she became a role model of a strong and powerful woman. Her unknown fate would be the seed of her growing legend, and eventually, Tomoe the Heian warrior became Tomoe Gozen. *Gozen* is a title of respect, similar to the English title "Lady."

The Legend Grows

Between the 14th and the 17th centuries, Tomoe and her story were a favorite theme for dramatists. *Tomoe* is the title of a haunting Japanese drama written in the 14th century. The story takes place at a shrine built where General Yoshinaka died. There, a figure appears— the spirit of Tomoe. She cries as she recounts the story of Yoshinaka and Tomoe and says that Yoshinaka ordered her to leave him dying on the battlefield so that someone would live to tell his story. A monk comforts her ghost. The audience is left with the idea that Tomoe will someday reappear. "For where I suffered . . . I shall rise," the ghost says.

Traveling entertainers also helped keep her story alive. Many became the character of Tomoe, and these "Tomoes" earned a living by traveling to famous battle sites. Audiences watched in awe as the actor "Tomoe" related the sad story of Yoshinaka's death as if he or she had been an eyewitness. In this way, her story spread.

New and largely made-up details were added to Tomoe's story by these wandering entertainers. One expert believes that it was these entertainers who created most of the later explanations of Tomoe's fate. Their storytelling helped to make her one of the most important cultural icons in the history of Japan.

Between the 17th and 19th centuries, Tomoe Gozen's image and story became even more popular. She appeared as a character in Kabuki theater, a type of Japanese drama with song and dance and very elaborate costumes. Artists also created both painted scrolls and woodblock prints showing some of the best-known incidents in her life. In fact, there are many more print portraits of Tomoe Gozen than of her more famous commander, Yoshinaka.

Tomoe Gozen Today

Today, Tomoe Gozen continues to inspire many types of artistic expression. Artists and writers have given Tomoe Gozen new life in novels, comic books, graphic novels, TV series, anime films, and video games. Some, like the wandering entertainers of the past, add details to her story to explain her life after Yoshinaka's death, while others reinvent her into a modern woman warrior.

In the Japanese comic book *Samurai Deeper Kyo*, Tomoe comes back to life as the character Saisei (SIGH-say). In the Japanese samurai comic *Usagi Yojimbo*, Tomoe Ame (AH-meh) is a woman warrior partly based on the historic Tomoe. In the 21st century, Tomoe Gozen has become almost a superhero, like Superman or Batman.

Tomoe Gozen's name and image have survived for more than 800 years. Whether she lived or not, may not be important; her loyalty, bravery, and strength make her an important role model.

A participant in Kyoto's famous Jidai Matsuri, or Festival of the Ages, dresses as Tomoe Gozen for a historical reenactment parade.

Japan During Medieval Times

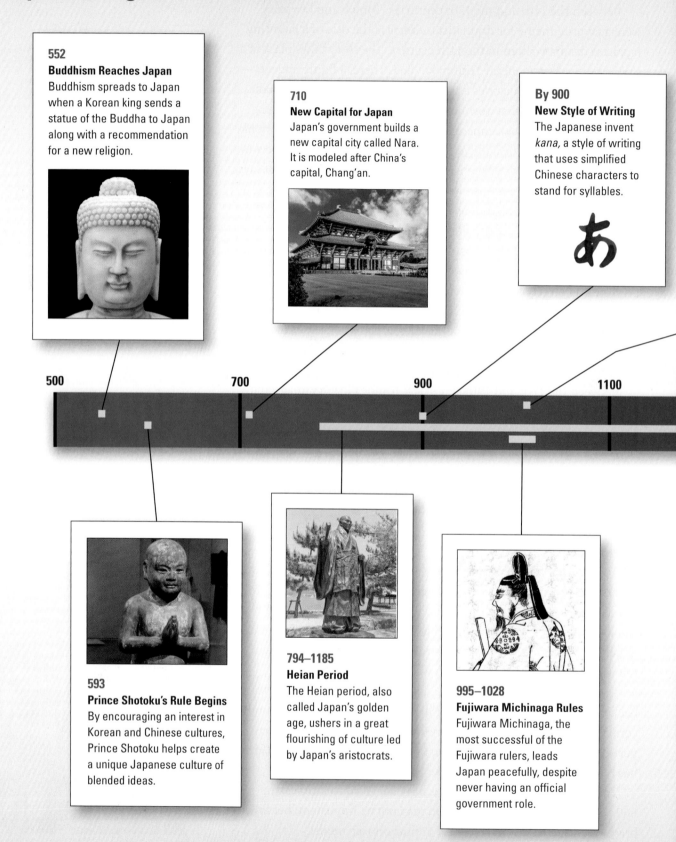

552
Buddhism Reaches Japan
Buddhism spreads to Japan when a Korean king sends a statue of the Buddha to Japan along with a recommendation for a new religion.

710
New Capital for Japan
Japan's government builds a new capital city called Nara. It is modeled after China's capital, Chang'an.

By 900
New Style of Writing
The Japanese invent *kana,* a style of writing that uses simplified Chinese characters to stand for syllables.

500   700   900   1100

593
Prince Shotoku's Rule Begins
By encouraging an interest in Korean and Chinese cultures, Prince Shotoku helps create a unique Japanese culture of blended ideas.

794–1185
Heian Period
The Heian period, also called Japan's golden age, ushers in a great flourishing of culture led by Japan's aristocrats.

995–1028
Fujiwara Michinaga Rules
Fujiwara Michinaga, the most successful of the Fujiwara rulers, leads Japan peacefully, despite never having an official government role.

About 1010
Tale of Genji Completed
Murasaki Shikibu finishes writing the *Tale of Genji,* considered to be the world's first novel.

1185
Minamoto Yoritomo Comes to Power
Minamoto Yoritomo, head of a military family, seizes control and sets up a military government in Japan.

1300   1500   1700   1900

1180
Civil War in Japan
As the power of local feudal lords grows and the imperial government weakens, civil war erupts, clans struggle for power, and local rulers fight to control land.

1192–1867
Feudalism in Japan
A lord-vassal system of shoguns, daimyos, and samurai dominates Japan. A warrior code known as *Bushido* develops.

1603–1867
Samurai Culture
Samurai culture flourishes under the Tokugawa shogunate, which begins with the reign of Tokugawa Ieyasu.

Civilizations of the Americas

The Maya constructed immense stone pyramids in what is now present-day Mexico. Shown here is a step pyramid on the Yucatán Peninsula at Chichén Itza with stairways on four sides leading to the top.

Physical Features of Mexico, Central America, and South America

NORTH AMERICA

BAJA CALIFORNIA

Gulf of California

SIERRA MADRE OCCIDENTAL

MEXICAN PLATEAU

SIERRA MADRE ORIENTAL

Cabo San Lucas

Tropic of Cancer

Pico de Orizaba (18,855 ft. 5,747 m) ▲

YUCATÁN PENINSULA

Gulf of Mexico

Cuba

BAHAMAS

WEST INDIES

ATLANTIC OCEAN

Tropic of Cancer

40°N

20°N

Jamaica

Hispaniola

Caribbean Sea

Lake Managua

Lake Nicaragua

ISTHMUS OF PANAMA

Gulf of Panama

Lake Maracaibo

LLANOS

Orinoco River

GUIANA HIGHLANDS

Angel Falls

Marajó Island

Equator

GALÁPAGOS ISLANDS

Gulf of Guayaquil

Negro River

AMAZON BASIN

SELVAS

Amazon River

Equator

0°

ANDES MOUNTAINS

Madeira River

Xingu River

Tocantins River

São Francisco River

PACIFIC OCEAN

Lake Titicaca

MATO GROSSO PLATEAU

BRAZILIAN HIGHLANDS

Tropic of Capricorn

ATACAMA DESERT

GRAN CHACO

Paraná River

Iguazú Falls

Uruguay River

Tropic of Capricorn

20°S

Mt. Aconcagua (22,831 ft. 6,959 m) ▲

ANDES

PAMPAS

Río de la Plata

ATLANTIC OCEAN

N
W   E
S

120°W

CHONOS ARCHIPELAGO

PATAGONIA

Gulf of San Jorge

0   500   1,000 miles
0   500   1,000 kilometers
Lambert Azimuthal Equal-Area Projection

40°S

Laguna del Carbón (-344 ft. -105 m)

FALKLAND ISLANDS

Strait of Magellan

Tierra del Fuego

Cape Horn

100°W   80°W   60°W   40°W   20°W

Elevation

Feet	Meters	
Over 10,000	Over 3,050	
5,001–10,000	1,526–3,050	
2,001–5,000	611–1,525	
1,001–2,000	306–610	
0–1,000	0–305	
Below sea level	Below sea level	

▲ Mountain peak

Present-day boundary

Civilizations of the Americas

In this unit, you will learn about the civilizations that developed in Mexico, Central America, and South America. This region is also known as Latin America.

If you could fly over this entire region in just a few hours, what would you see? Beginning in Mexico and Central America, and flying south, you would see mostly rugged mountains. In the middle of the country, these highlands include volcanoes and vast farmlands that span for miles. In the southernmost part of this region, the land becomes very narrow, only 30 miles wide.

This thin land bridge leads into South America. From your plane, you would see a dramatic mountain range called the Andes, which extends along nearly the entire western coast of South America. East of the Andes, in the central part of the continent, are rainforests, deserts, and grasslands. You would glimpse rivers like the Amazon, the longest river in South America, flowing through the rainforests. As you complete your flight, you would cross over the pointy tip of South America, a flat area that rises from the Atlantic to the Andes.

Mexico, Central America, and South America were home to several advanced early civilizations. In the Andes, a group known as the Incas developed the largest empire in the Americas. To connect their huge mountain empire, they constructed roads and bridges across deep ravines and raging rivers.

Two groups of people lived in Mexico and Central America: the Maya and the Aztecs. The Maya survived by learning to grow food in the hills, swamps, and forests they inhabited. The Aztecs also used their natural resources and developed an elaborate system of canals by which they traded with distant lands. You will begin your exploration of these early civilizations with the Maya.

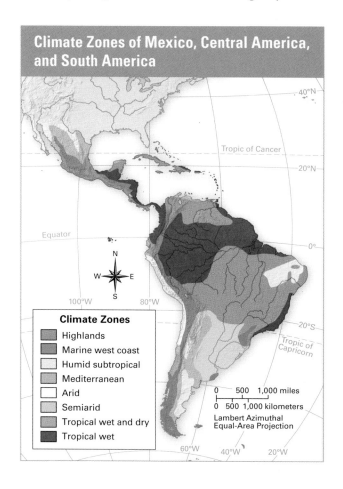

Climate Zones of Mexico, Central America, and South America

Climate Zones
- Highlands
- Marine west coast
- Humid subtropical
- Mediterranean
- Arid
- Semiarid
- Tropical wet and dry
- Tropical wet

0   500   1,000 miles
0 500 1,000 kilometers
Lambert Azimuthal
Equal-Area Projection

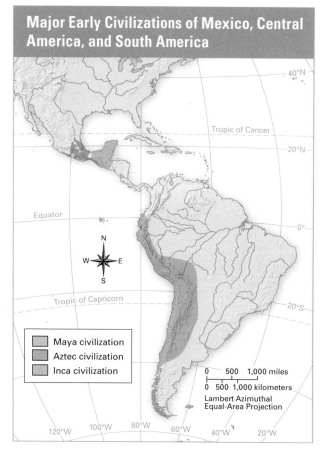

Major Early Civilizations of Mexico, Central America, and South America

- Maya civilization
- Aztec civilization
- Inca civilization

0   500   1,000 miles
0 500 1,000 kilometers
Lambert Azimuthal
Equal-Area Projection

Lesson 26

The Maya

What led to the rise, flourishing, and fall of the Maya civilization?

Introduction

The Maya civilization, which lasted 3,500 years, from about 2000 B.C.E. to 1500 C.E., included lands located in present-day southern Mexico and large portions of Central America. Visitors can still see the ruins of some amazing stone cities built by the Maya (MY-uh). The ruins of the ancient city of Tikal (tee-KAHL), shown here, lie deep in the jungles of present-day Guatemala.

Picture yourself standing at the heart of this city in the year 750 C.E. You are in a large, open plaza surrounded by eight soaring temple-pyramids. On the ground, as far as you can see, are brightly colored structures on raised platforms. Nearby, in the center of the city, you see large palaces made of limestone blocks that serve as the homes of the ruler, priests, and nobles. Farther out are the stone houses of the merchants and artisans, whom you might see making colorful murals or statues of different Maya gods.

At the very edge of the city are thousands of small, thatched-roof house-mounds where the peasants live. The peasants might be farming or weaving, or may even be building elaborate temples. You might notice that people from different classes performed specific duties, but all contributed to ancient Maya society.

Tikal was only one of more than 40 Maya cities. How did the Maya create such great cities and such an advanced civilization? In this lesson, you will trace the development of Maya civilization and some of its most important achievements. You will also take a closer look at several aspects of Maya culture, including class structure, family life, religious beliefs and practices, and agricultural techniques.

Social Studies Vocabulary

ceremonial center

hieroglyphic

Maya

Mesoamerica

ritual

sacrifice

slash-and-burn agriculture

social pyramid

◀ The Maya built great stone pyramids such as this one at Tikal.

The Maya **371**

Maya the people of an important Mesoamerican civilization that lasted from about 2000 B.C.E. to 1500 C.E.

Mesoamerica the region extending from modern Mexico through Central America

ceremonial center a large plaza in a city center, surrounded by temples and palaces, where religious rituals and other public ceremonies took place

One of the great achievements of the Olmecs was the creation of monumental stone heads, believed to be portraits of their leaders. More than 30 of them have been found. They stand over eight feet high and weigh about ten tons. The massive heads were sculpted without metal tools.

1. The Development of Maya Civilization

The **Maya** were creating an advanced civilization in the Americas around the same time the Roman Empire was declining in western Europe. Maya civilization reached its height between 200 and 900 C.E. During this time, Maya culture spread over a great deal of **Mesoamerica,** including part of present-day southern Mexico, Belize, most of Guatemala, and parts of Honduras and El Salvador.

The landscape in which the Maya lived varied greatly. In the south, pine forests covered the mountain highlands, while the northern and central regions were covered in rainforests, grasslands, and swamps. These northern and central regions are known as the lowlands, parts of which were covered in thick jungle. This area, today called the Petén (pay-TAYN) region of Guatemala, is where Maya civilization reached its highest development.

The Origins of Maya Civilization The Maya built their civilization, in part, on ideas they inherited from a people called the Olmecs, who lived in the jungle areas on the east coast of Mexico. Their civilization reached its peak between 1200 and 500 B.C.E.

Like early civilizations in other parts of the world, the Olmec civilization was based on agriculture. By 2000 B.C.E., people in parts of Mexico had turned from hunting and gathering to farming as their main source of food. A particularly important crop at the time was maize, or corn.

Farming allowed the Olmecs to create permanent settlements. The Olmecs established farming villages throughout the region and created trade routes that stretched for hundreds of miles.

By 1400 B.C.E., the Olmecs had a capital city that boasted palaces, temples, and monuments. They were the first Mesoamericans to develop large religious and **ceremonial centers,** as well as the first to use a solar calendar, or a calendar based on the cycles of the sun. The Maya , and other contemporary Mesoamerican cultures, would build on all these achievements.

Three Periods of Maya Civilization Maya civilization began to develop in eastern and southern Mexico around 2000 B.C.E. Historians divide the history of Maya civilization into three main periods: Pre-Classic, Classic, and Post-Classic.

The long Pre-Classic period lasted from about 2000 B.C.E. to 200 C.E. During this time, the Maya farmed the land and lived in simple houses and compounds, or groups of buildings.

Gradually, Maya culture became more complex. As the Maya population grew, settlements became larger. Other changes occurred with this growth. For instance, the Maya began constructing public buildings for governmental and religious purposes.

Possibly as early as 300 B.C.E., they began to adapt the writing system of the Olmecs and to develop their own system of **hieroglyphic** writing. Maya civilization reached its peak during the Classic period, from around 200 to 900 C.E. The achievements you will study in this lesson date from this time.

During the Classic period, the Maya adapted and developed other ideas they had learned from the Olmecs. For example, they improved on Olmec building techniques. Even though the Maya lacked metal tools and had not discovered the wheel, they built enormous stone cities with elaborate and highly decorated temple-pyramids and palaces. The Maya also built observatories where they charted the movements of the moon, stars, and planets. They used their knowledge of astronomy and mathematics to create complex and highly accurate calendars.

Maya society during the Classic period consisted of many independent states. Each included farming communities and one or more cities. At its height, the Maya Empire included more than 50 cities, including Tikal, Copan (kaw-PAHN), Chichén Itzá, and Palenque (pah-LENG-kay).

Around 900 C.E., the Classic civilization collapsed. The Maya **abandoned** their cities in the southern lowland area, and the once thriving communities fell into ruin in the jungle. To this day, no one knows for certain why this happened. At the end of this lesson, you will look at some theories that may explain this mystery.

To the north, on the Yucatán (you-kuh-TAN) Peninsula, Maya cities continued to prosper during the Post-Classic period. This period lasted from about 900 C.E. to 1500 C.E. During this time, the Maya continued their warfare and empire building, but they had fewer great artistic and cultural achievements.

Even at the height of their empire, the Maya were not one unified nation, but rather a collection of city-states with their own governments. What united them as Maya was their common culture: their social system, languages, calendar, religion, and way of life.

hieroglyphic writing that uses pictures as symbols

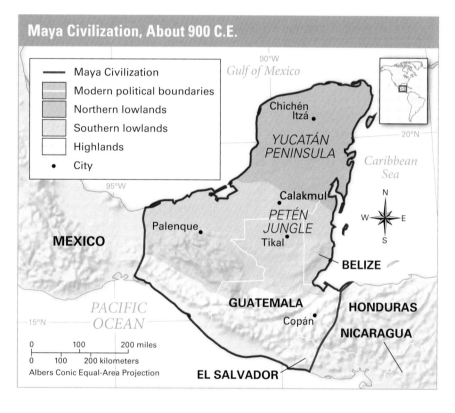

At the height of their civilization, the Maya occupied large parts of modern Central America. Even though their cities in the southern lowland area were abandoned by 900 C.E., their cities to the north continued to thrive. Among the largest cities in this area were Tikal and Calakmul.

2. Class Structure

Within each Maya city-state, society was structured like a pyramid. The ruler of each city-state was at the top of this **social pyramid**, while the rest of the members of Maya society were organized into a series of ranks below the ruler.

social pyramid a social structure in the shape of a pyramid, with layers representing social classes of different rank

The Ruler The highest authority in the state was the *halach uinic* (hah-lach WEE-nik), a Maya phrase that means "true man." He ruled the state with the help of his advisers and decided when and with whom to go to war.

The Maya ruler was considered a god-king. During religious ceremonies, he wore a headdress that was as tall as a person. When he died, a son or another close male relative succeeded him. Maya rulers were almost always men, but scholars believe that some women had **considerable** influence, probably through family relationships.

Nobles and Priests The next layer in the social pyramid was made up of nobles and priests. They, along with the ruler, were the only members of Maya society who knew how to read and write.

The nobles served as scribes and officials, and oversaw the administration of the states. They gathered taxes, supplies, and labor for projects, such as the construction of temples. Nobles led peasant armies in times of war. During battles, they wore elaborate costumes, including gold jewelry and animal robes made from the skins of jaguars.

The social pyramid of the Maya civilization shows the ruler of each city-state at the top, with the rest of Maya society below him. Each layer of the pyramid represents the people at different levels of importance. Notice that there are many more people at the bottom of the pyramid than at the top.

Priests were important because it was their job to maintain favor with the gods. Like nobles, priests inherited their position from their fathers. Priests led **rituals,** offered **sacrifices,** and foretold the future. They were consulted to determine the best days for going to battle. In addition to their religious duties, priests were often mathematicians, astronomers, and healers.

Merchants and Artisans Although the Maya economy was based mostly on farming, trade and crafts were also important. These functions were carried out by merchants and artisans.

The Maya were accomplished traders, traveling by sea, river, and well-constructed roads to trade with other city-states. Merchants in the lowlands imported valuable products from the highlands. These products included stones such as obsidian and jade; copal, a tree sap that the Maya used as incense during religious ceremonies; and quetzals, birds whose shiny green feathers were used in headdresses.

Maya artisans made a wide variety of objects, many of them designed to pay tribute to the gods. They painted books on paper made from the bark of fig trees. Artists painted murals of Maya life, important battles, and other major events. They created sculptures for temples and decorative designs on palace walls. The Maya were also skilled weavers and potters.

Peasants The peasants were the backbone of Maya society. They worked hard on the land, growing maize, squash, beans, and other crops to feed the population. During the growing season, men spent most of the day in the fields, farming with wooden hoes. Women usually stayed closer to home, preparing food, weaving, and sewing.

When they were not farming, peasants had to spend time building pyramids and temples. In exchange for their work, they sometimes attended royal weddings and religious events. Peasants also served as soldiers during wars and paid taxes to the nobles.

Slaves At the bottom of the social pyramid were the slaves, who performed manual labor for their owners. While some were born into slavery, free people sometimes became slaves. For instance, a parent might sell their child to feed the rest of the family, or a person who committed a serious crime might be enslaved as punishment. Once captured, war prisoners of humble origin were also enslaved. (Those of higher rank were sacrificed to the gods.)

In general, the Maya did not mistreat slaves. Sometimes, slaves actually had easier lives than peasants, depending on their jobs and owners' social rank. However, slaves were not free to come and go as they pleased and were often sacrificed when their owners died.

ritual a set of actions that is always performed the same way as part of a religious ceremony

sacrifice a gift of an animal for slaughter to honor the gods

Maya artists created many objects, such as this terra-cotta figure, to honor their gods. They, as well as farmers and hunters, paid taxes to Maya nobles.

Maya peasants lived in one-room huts made out of mud and interwoven poles, like the one shown here. Families would build their huts in groups around a single shared courtyard.

3. Family Life

In city-states like Copan, located in present-day Honduras, Maya peasants lived in one-room huts built of interwoven poles and covered with dried mud. Several family houses were often grouped around a shared courtyard. A separate kitchen building might be directly behind the main house. Peasant families worked hard, but ceremonies and rituals provided a break from work and a chance to celebrate important events.

Duties of Family Members Life for Maya peasant families was not easy. Maya women rose before dawn to get the fire burning in the fireplace. With the help of her daughters, a Maya woman cleaned the corn that had been boiled and left to soak and soften overnight. Then she set to work at the grinding stone, pounding corn into meal. She patted the meal into *tortillas* (tawr-tee-uhs), a Spanish word meaning "little breads," or *tamales* (tuh-MAH-leez) and cooked them over the fire. These might serve as the morning meal or they might be saved for dinner. On special days, the family might also have hot chocolate, a drink the Maya made from cacao (kuh-KAY-oh) beans.

During the day, women and older girls cared for small children and for the family's few animals, like ducks and turkeys. They swept their homes, and they gathered, spun, and wove cotton into cloth.

Maya fathers and sons ate their morning meal quickly before leaving to work in the fields. When they were not busy with the crops, men and boys hunted and trapped animals.

Special Occasions Maya families took time to celebrate the important events in their lives. The birth of a child was a time for rejoicing. As soon as possible after the birth, the family called in a priest to perform a ceremony much like baptism. The priest would forecast the baby's future and give advice to help guide the parents in raising the child.

At three months of age, girls went through another ceremony. The number three was special to Maya women because it represented the three stones of the home hearth, or fireplace. In the three-month ceremony, the baby girl was introduced to the tools she would use throughout her life. Small items were placed in the baby's hands, such as tools for spinning and weaving, carrying water and cooking, and soaking and grinding maize.

A similar ceremony was held for boys at four months of age. The number four was special to Maya men because it represented the four sides of the plot of land where a boy would spend his life. The baby boy was given farmer's tools, such as axes and planting sticks, and the spears, knives, and traps of a hunter.

Another important event in every Maya child's life was the coming-of-age ceremony. Girls went through this ceremony at age 12, boys at 14. The long ceremony involved confessing, cleansing with water, and reciting the rules of behavior. Finally, the priest cut a white bead from the boys' hair and removed a string of red shells from around the girls' waists. Boys and girls had worn these symbols of innocence since they were quite young.

Marriage Customs The next big moment in the life of a Maya youth was marriage. Men usually married around age 20, while women married when they were as young as 14.

The bride and groom did not choose each other. Instead, marriages were negotiated by the village *atanzahab*, or matchmaker. Families had to agree on how much food and clothing would be given to the bride's family. They also had to agree on the number of years a young man would work for his new wife's family.

Once the details of a marriage were arranged, the villagers built a hut for the couple behind the home of the bride's parents. When the home was ready, the bride and groom put on clothing woven for the occasion. After a priest blessed the marriage, the villagers celebrated.

The Maya held special ceremonies for boys and girls at a young age. Pictured here is a mortar and pestle, a tool given to young girls to grind maize.

4. Religious Beliefs and Practices

Religion was very important to the Maya, who built their cities around religious and ceremonial centers. Their magnificent temple-pyramids rose high above the jungle canopy, like mountains reaching into the sky. Temple plazas provided gathering places for people to attend rituals and ceremonies.

Scholars have learned about the Maya religion from studying present-day Maya practices, ancient artifacts, and documents written during the Post-Classic period. Here are some things they discovered.

Beliefs and Rituals The Maya religion was polytheistic, which means it included many gods. The Maya believed in more than 160 gods, but the primary Maya gods were forces or objects in nature that affected people's daily lives, such as rain, corn, and death. Many gods had animal characteristics. The jaguar was especially important to the Maya.

The Maya believed that the gods had created the world and could influence or even destroy it. The same god that sent life-giving rain could also ruin the crops with hailstones. So, it was extremely important to honor the gods.

According to Maya beliefs, only priests could explain **divine** signs and lead people through rituals aimed at pleasing the gods. Priests performed sacrifices and conducted ceremonies. They consulted sacred books, read omens, interpreted signs, and predicted the future. No decision was made without seeking the gods' advice, and no action was taken without first honoring the gods.

The Maya honored their gods with offerings such as plants, food, flowers, feathers, jade, and shells. The Maya believed that blood gave the gods strength, so they also made blood offerings by sacrificing animals and, sometimes, humans. The people who were sacrificed were usually orphans, slaves, or nobles captured during war.

The Maya believed there were many gods and did their best to honor them. In this stone carving, a summoned spirit appears out of the mouth of a two-headed snake.

Human sacrifice also played a role in an ancient Maya game called *pok-a-tok*. Every Maya city had at least one ball court where the game took place. Scholars believe that the game was played between two teams of nobles who tried to hit a solid rubber ball through a stone ring by using their leather-padded elbows, wrists, and hips. People from all levels of Maya society attended the popular games. Unfortunately, the outcome often had serious results. Surviving art from the ball courts shows members of the losing team being sacrificed and the captain of the defeated team being beheaded.

The Sacred Calendar The Maya used their knowledge of mathematics and astronomy to develop a complex calendar system composed of two main calendars for religious and other purposes. The first was a daily calendar, based on the solar (sun) year that divided the year into 18 months of 20 days each, plus 5 "unlucky" days. This totaled 365 days, as our calendar does.

The second calendar was the sacred, or ritual, calendar called the *tzolkin* (TSAWL-keen), or Sacred Round. The Sacred Round was based on 13 months of 20 days each, making 260 days in all. It had two cycles that worked together to identify a particular day. One cycle was made up of the numbers 1 to 13, while the other cycle was a set of 20 day names. Each of the day names represented a particular god. Every 260 days, a given combination of numbers and day names, such as *1 Ik*, would occur.

Only priests could "read" the hidden meaning of the Sacred Round. Priests used the sacred calendar to determine the best days to plant, hunt, cure, do battle, and perform religious ceremonies. To this day, there are calendar priests in southern Mexico who still use the 260-day calendar in this way.

Like Maya art and architecture, the calendar system reflects a highly advanced civilization. This high level of civilization was possible due to the ability of the Maya to create a stable food supply.

This is the ball court at the ancient Maya city of Chichén Itzá. Notice the height of the stone rings embedded in the walls and how small the holes are.

Cutting and burning plants and trees is an easy way to clear land for farming, and the ashes help to fertilize crops. However, this slash-and-burn technique uses up the soil quickly and can be dangerous, as fires sometimes get out of control.

slash-and-burn agriculture
a farming technique in which vegetation is cut away and burned to clear land for growing crops

5. Agricultural Techniques

The Maya were creative, skillful farmers and used their knowledge of calendars and seasonal change to help them become even better at growing food. But Maya farmers faced many challenges, such as crop failure, which may have played a key role in the collapse of the Classic Maya civilization.

Challenges Facing Maya Farmers The primary Maya food was maize, or corn. Other typical crops were beans, squash, and chili peppers. Fortunately, beans and squash, when eaten with corn, supply people with a naturally healthful and balanced diet.

One of the most difficult challenges the Maya faced was how to grow enough food to feed their growing population. Farming was difficult in the regions where they lived due to dense forests, little surface water (such as lakes or streams), and poor soil.

The Maya responded to this challenge by developing different agricultural techniques for the various environments in which they lived. In the mountainous highlands, they built terraces, or flat earthen steps, into the hills to make more land available for planting. In the swampy lowlands, the Maya constructed raised-earth platforms surrounded by canals that drained off extra rainwater. This technique helped them to grow more food without having to conquer or clear more land.

A different technique was used in the densely forested lowland areas. In city-states like Palenque (in present-day Mexico), the Maya used **slash-and-burn agriculture**. First, they cleared the land by cutting and burning plants and trees, and then they planted their crops. Unfortunately, this type of farming wears out the soil. Lowland soil was not very rich to begin with, so land that was planted for two to four years had to be left to rest for two to ten years. Slash-and-burn farmers had to have a lot of land since each year some areas were planted while others were recovering.

The Maya agricultural system worked as long as settlements were spread out and not too large. As populations increased, the Maya had trouble raising enough food to feed everyone. In the constant quest for land, they drained swamps and cleared hillsides. They also used household gardens in the cities to help supplement the food supply.

The End of the Classical Period Creative agricultural techniques were not enough to save Classic Maya civilization. For about 600 years, the great cities of the southern lowlands thrived. Then, around 750 C.E., the civilization that supported these centers fell apart. By 900 C.E., the Maya had abandoned their large cities to the jungle.

The collapse of Classic Maya civilization is one of the great mysteries of Mesoamerican history, and many theories have been offered to explain what happened. Some historians believe that the populations of the cities grew faster than the Maya farming systems could **sustain** them. Scholars have also proposed that long periods of drought caused massive crop failure.

Another possible cause of the Maya's downfall was uncontrolled warfare. In the centuries after 300 C.E., the skirmishes that were common among city-states grew into full-fledged wars. A final possibility is that invaders from central Mexico helped to destroy the Maya city-states.

Perhaps a combination of factors ended the Classic period. What we do know is that the great cities disappeared. The Maya migrated away from the old Maya heartland and returned to village life. Stone by stone, the jungle reclaimed the great pyramids and plazas.

Although the great Maya cities are ruins today, Maya culture lives on. About two million Maya still live in the southern Mexican state of Chiapas, with millions more spread throughout the Yucatán Peninsula and the cities and the rural farm communities of Belize, Guatemala, Honduras, and El Salvador.

The walls of Maya tombs were painted with scenes of important events and daily life. This tomb painting shows warriors in battle.

Lesson Summary

In this lesson, you read about the Maya civilization, which existed in what is now Mexico and Central America between about 2000 B.C.E. and 1500 C.E.

The Development of Maya Civilization The Maya's greatest achievements came in the Classic period, between 200 and 900 C.E. With a writing system and building techniques adapted from the earlier Olmecs, the Maya built complex, stone cities. At its height, their empire consisted of more than 40 city-states and covered much of Central America.

Class Structure and Family Life Maya society was a social pyramid, with the ruler at the top. Most Maya were peasants. Women and girls cared for small children, kept house, and cooked the meals. Men and boys worked in the fields or hunted. Maya girls celebrated reaching adulthood at 12; boys did so at 14. Marriages were arranged by a matchmaker.

Religious Beliefs and Practices Maya religion was polytheistic. The gods were forces of nature who could influence or destroy the world. Only priests could understand divine signs and read the sacred calendar, and no decisions were made without first consulting the gods.

Agricultural Techniques Farming techniques, such as terraces, slash-and-burn agriculture, and raised-earth platforms, allowed the Maya to create a stable food supply.

Lesson 27

The Aztecs

How did the Aztecs rise to power?

Introduction

The Aztecs were a Mesoamerican people who built a vast empire for nearly 100 years in what is today central Mexico. Their empire flourished from 1428 C.E. until 1519 C.E., when it was destroyed by invaders from Spain.

The Aztecs told a legend about the beginnings of their empire. Originally a wandering group of hunter-gatherers, the Aztecs believed that one day they would receive a sign from the gods in the form of an eagle perched on a great cactus with "his wings stretched out toward the rays of the sun." In its beak, the eagle would hold a long snake. When they saw this eagle, the Aztecs would know they had found the place where they would settle and build a great city.

In the mid-1200s C.E., the Aztecs entered the Valley of Mexico, a fertile basin in present-day central Mexico. Several times, other groups pushed the Aztecs away from their lands in the valley.

In 1325, the Aztecs took refuge on an island in Lake Texcoco, where Aztec priests saw the eagle on the cactus, just as the gods had promised. The Aztecs set about building a city on the site, which they called Tenochtitlán (tay-nawh-tee-TLAHN), and made use of the land's abundant resources. Its name means "the place of the fruit of the prickly pear cactus." In time, the island city became the center of the Aztec Empire.

How did the Aztecs create one of the great empires of the medieval world? In this lesson, you will learn where the Aztecs came from and how they built their magnificent capital city. You will also discover how the Aztecs formed influential relationships with other groups and rose to power.

Social Studies Vocabulary

Aztecs

causeway

conformity

mercenary

plaza

Tenochtitlán

◀ These drawings were created in Mexico around 1540 and show details of Aztec life.

Teotihuacán, the "City of the Gods," was a large city of plazas, pyramids, and avenues. The Pyramid of the Moon, shown here, was constructed of volcanic rock and limestone.

Aztecs a Mesoamerican people who built an empire in central Mexico that flourished from 1428 to 1519 C.E.

1. The Aztecs in the Valley of Mexico

The Aztec Empire arose in the Valley of Mexico, a fertile area nearly 8,000 feet above sea level. By the time the **Aztecs** arrived, in the mid-1200s C.E., the valley had been a center of civilization for more than 1,000 years. Two earlier groups, in particular, had built civilizations there that strongly influenced the Aztecs.

Civilizations in the Valley of Mexico From about 100 to 650 C.E., the Valley of Mexico was dominated by the Teotihuacáns (TEH-aw-tee-wah-KAHNZ). These people built an **enormous** capital city, Teotihuacán. One of the city's buildings, the Pyramid of the Sun, was more than 200 feet high.

After Teotihuacán's collapse around the 700s, a group from the north, the Toltecs (TOHL-teks), migrated into the valley. Toltec civilization reached its height in the 10th and 11th centuries. The Toltecs built a number of cities, including their capital Tollán (toh-LAHN), which boasted large pyramids topped with temples.

During the 1100s, new groups invaded the valley, took over Toltec cities, and then established new city-states. But the influence of the Teotihuacáns and the Toltecs continued to be felt in the new culture that was developing in the valley.

The Arrival of the Aztecs Sometime around 1250 C.E., a new group of people arrived in the Valley of Mexico. This nomadic band of hunter-gatherers called themselves the *Mexica* (meh-HEE-kah). We know them today as the Aztecs.

The name *Aztec* comes from Aztlán (az-TLAN), the Mexicans' legendary homeland. According to Aztec tradition, Aztlán was an island in a lake northwest of the Valley of Mexico. After the Aztecs left the island around 1100 C.E., they wandered through the deserts of northern Mexico for many years before coming to the Valley of Mexico.

When the Aztecs came to the heart of the valley, they found lakes dotted with marshy islands. Thriving city-states controlled the land around the lakes.

The Aztecs had a difficult time establishing themselves in the valley. The people living in the city-states thought the Aztecs were crude barbarians. But the Aztecs were fierce warriors, and the city-states were willing to employ them as mercenaries.

After they settled in the valley, the legacy of the Teotihuacáns and the Toltecs began to influence the Aztecs. They made pilgrimages to the ancient ruins of Teotihuacán and adopted Quetzalcoatl (ket-sahl-koh-AHT-l), the Teotihuacáns' feathered serpent god, as one of their own gods.

The Aztecs considered the Toltecs to be the rulers of a golden age. Aztec rulers married into the surviving Toltec royal line and even began to claim the Toltecs as their own ancestors.

In 1319, stronger groups forced the Aztecs to move away from Chapultepec (chuh-PUHL-teh-pek), a rocky hill where they had made their home. The Aztecs fled to the south and became mercenaries for the city-state of Culhuacán. But trouble came again when the Aztecs sacrificed the daughter of the Culhua chief. This led to a war with the Culhuas, who drove the Aztecs onto an island in the shallow waters of Lake Texcoco.

It was here, the Aztecs said, that they spotted an eagle perched atop a cactus with a long snake in its beak. The Aztecs took this as a sign that they should stay in this place, and they set to work building the city they called Tenochtitlán.

The island turned out to be a good site for the Aztecs' city. The lake provided fish and water birds for food, and the island was easy to defend. Over time, the Aztecs' new home would grow into one of the great cities of the world.

From Mercenaries to Empire Builders The Aztecs started building Tenochtitlán in 1325 C.E. For the next 100 years, they again served as mercenaries for a powerful group called the Tepanecs. Through this alliance, the Aztecs gained land, trading connections, and wealth.

Eventually, however, the Aztecs rebelled against the heavy-handed rule of the Tepanecs. Under the Aztec leader Itzcoatl (itz-koh-AHT-l), Tenochtitlán joined with two other city-states in what was called the Triple Alliance. In 1428, the alliance fought and defeated the Tepanecs. Together, the allies began a series of conquests that laid the foundation for the Aztec Empire.

As Tenochtitlán became a great power, Itzcoatl set out to reshape Aztec history. He burned records that referred to his people's humble origins and connected the Aztecs to the distinguished Toltecs.

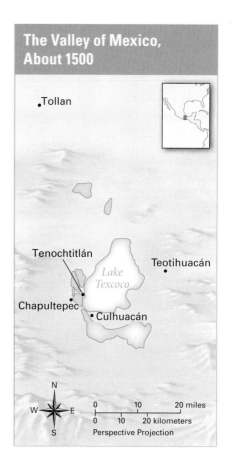

The Valley of Mexico, About 1500

The Aztecs settled in the Valley of Mexico around 1250. By 1500, they controlled most of the region.

mercenary a professional soldier who is paid to fight for another country or group

Tenochtitlán the capital city of the Aztec Empire

2. Tenochtitlán: A City of Wonders

As the Aztecs' power grew, their capital city of Tenochtitlán developed into one of the largest cities in the world. When Spanish explorers first arrived at Tenochtitlán in 1519, they were amazed to see a majestic city crisscrossed by canals and boasting **impressive** temples and palaces. With a huge population for the time of between 200,000 and 300,000 people, Tenochtitlán was larger than London, Paris, or Venice.

How did the Aztecs turn an island into such a great city? First, they reclaimed land from the lake by sinking timbers into the water to serve as walls. Then, they filled in the area between the timbers with mud, boulders, and reeds. In this way, they created small islands called *chinampas*, or "floating gardens." Eventually, the Aztecs expanded the city's land surface until it covered over five square miles. They even merged Tlatelolco (tlah-TEH-lohl-koh), originally a separate island, with Tenochtitlán.

Gradually, Tenochtitlán grew into the magnificent city that later amazed the Spanish. At the center of the city lay a large ceremonial **plaza** where the Aztecs gathered for religious rituals, feasts, and festivals. An eight-foot wall that was studded with sculptures of serpents enclosed this area. The palaces and homes of nobles lined the outside of the wall.

Inside the plaza, a stone pyramid called the Great Temple loomed 150 feet into the sky. People could see the pyramid, which was decorated with bright sculptures and murals, from several miles away.

plaza a public square or open area in a city where people gather

The Aztecs of Tenochtitlán built the city and farmed on chinampas, small artificial islands they constructed from timbers, mud, and plants. In this artist rendering, you can see the chinampas as rectangular islands in the middle of the water.

The Great Temple had two steep stairways leading to double shrines, one of which was dedicated to the chief god, Huitzilopochtli (wee-tsee-loh-POHCH-tlee). The other was dedicated to Tlaloc (tlah- LOHK), the rain god. In front of the shrines stood the stone where priests performed human sacrifices. An altar, called the *tzompantli* ("skull rack"), displayed the skulls of thousands of sacrificial victims. Other structures in the plaza included more shrines and temples, the ritual ball court, military storehouses, and guest rooms for important visitors.

Temples dedicated to various gods rose along the streets and canals of the city of Tenochtitlán. These are the ruins of the Great Temple, located in present-day Mexico City.

Just outside the plaza stood the royal palace, which was two stories and functioned like a small town. The palace was the home of the Aztec ruler, but it also had government offices, shrines, courts, storerooms, gardens, and courtyards. At the royal aviary, trained staff plucked the valuable feathers from parrots and quetzals. Wild animals captured throughout the empire, such as pumas and jaguars, prowled cages in the royal zoo.

The city's main marketplace was located in the northern section, in Tlatelolco. Each day, as many as sixty thousand people came from all corners of the Aztec Empire to sell their wares. Goods ranged from luxury items, such as jade and feathers, to necessities, such as food and rope sandals. Merchants also sold gold, silver, turquoise, animal skins, clothing, pottery, chocolate, vanilla, tools, and even slaves.

Although Tenochtitlán spread over five square miles, people had an easy time getting around. Four wide avenues met at the foot of the Great Temple. A thousand workers swept and washed down the streets each day, keeping them cleaner than streets in European cities. At night, pine torches lit the way. People also traveled on foot on smaller walkways or by canoe on the canals that crossed the city. Many of the canals were lined with stone and had bridges.

The island connects to the mainland by three **causeways,** the longest of which stretched five miles. The causeways were 25 to 30 feet wide, and all had wooden bridges that could be raised to let boats through or to protect the city in an enemy attack.

causeway a solid earthen roadway built across water or low ground

The city boasted other technological marvels, like the aqueducts that carried fresh water for irrigation. Twin pipes ran from the Chapultepec springs, three miles away. While one pipe was being cleaned or repaired, the other could transport water. A dam ten miles long ran along the east side of the city to hold back floodwaters.

3. The Aztec Empire

Tenochtitlán began simply as the Aztecs' home city, but after the Aztecs and their allies defeated the Tepanecs in 1428 C.E., it became the capital of a growing empire. Under Moctezuma I, in the mid-1400s, the Aztecs extended the area under their control.

By the early 1500s, the Aztec Empire stretched from the Gulf of Mexico to the Pacific Ocean, as you can see on the map shown here. It covered much of Central Mexico, and reached as far south as Mexico's current border with Guatemala. At its height, the empire ruled more than five million people.

An Empire Based on Tribute Unlike other empire builders, the Aztecs neither established colonies, nor forced **conformity** on their subjects. Instead, the Aztec Empire was a loose union of hundreds of city-states that had to pay tribute to the Aztecs.

Collecting tribute was the empire's most **vital** business because they relied on tribute to support Tenochtitlán's huge population. Tribute took the form of whatever valuable items a city could provide. Cities might pay in food, cacao, gems, cotton, cloth, animals, animal skins, shells, building materials, or even soldiers. Tax collectors stationed around the empire made sure that cities paid regularly.

Each year, huge amounts of goods flowed into Tenochtitlán. An average year brought 7,000 tons of maize; 4,000 tons each of beans, seed, and grain; and at least 2 million cotton cloaks. Warriors, priests, officials, servants, and other workers and craftspeople all received payment in tribute goods.

conformity uniform behavior according to a set of social or cultural rules or beliefs

By the 1500s, the Aztecs had established a huge and powerful empire in the Valley of Mexico.

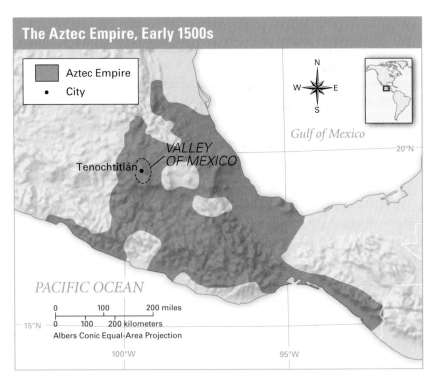

The Aztec Empire, Early 1500s

- Aztec Empire
- • City

N W E S

Gulf of Mexico

20°N

Tenochtitlán

VALLEY OF MEXICO

PACIFIC OCEAN

| 0 | 100 | 200 miles |
| 0 | 100 | 200 kilometers |

Albers Conic Equal-Area Projection

15°N

100°W   95°W

Warfare Warfare was the center of Aztec life. Successful battles allowed the Aztecs to increase their sources of tribute and gain additional territory, laborers, and sacrificial victims.

Every male Aztec was trained to be a soldier. In battle, the Aztecs used bows and arrows, spears, clubs, and swords with sharp stone blades. Warrior knights carried shields decorated with figures of animals, such as the jaguar and eagle, to represent different strengths that the Aztecs believed they received from these animals.

An Aztec declaration of war followed a ritual pattern. First, the Aztecs asked a city to join the empire as an ally. The city had 60 days to agree. If the city's ruler refused, the Aztecs declared war.

Most wars ended after one battle, usually with an Aztec victory. Afterward, the Aztecs brought the soldiers they had **captured** to Tenochtitlán. Some became slaves, but most ended up as sacrifices.

The Aztecs made only a few demands on the defeated city. The people had to pay tribute, honor the god Huitzilopochtli, and promise obedience to the Aztec ruler. In most other ways, conquered cities remained independent. They kept their religion, customs, and language. They usually even kept their leaders.

While these conditions made it easy for the Aztecs to rule, most of the conquered people never thought of themselves as true Aztecs. They wanted their freedom and resented paying tribute. These feelings led to a lack of unity in the Aztec Empire. Eventually, the Spanish would take advantage of that weakness by making allies of the Aztecs' enemies when they invaded Mexico in 1519.

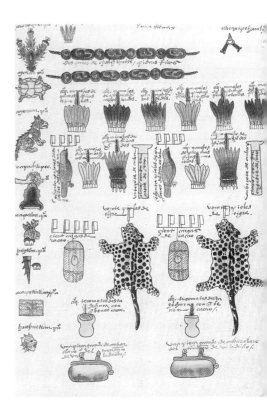

These drawings show some of the many forms of tribute paid to the Aztecs, such as feathers, jade, and jaguar skins.

Lesson Summary

In this lesson, you learned about the rise of the Aztecs from a band of nomads to the masters of a great empire.

The Aztecs in the Valley of Mexico The Aztecs arrived in the Valley of Mexico in the mid-1200s C.E. For a long time, they served as mercenaries for, and adapted the gods and culture of, more powerful groups, such as the Teotihuacáns, Toltecs, and Tepanecs.

Tenochtitlán In 1325, the Aztecs began building their great capital, Tenochtitlán, in Lake Texcoco. They chose the location based on a sign from the gods—an eagle perched on a cactus, with a snake in its beak. At its height, the impressive city boasted huge stone temples, canals, and a population greater than any European city of the time.

The Aztec Empire The Aztec Empire began in 1428, when the Aztecs and their allies won a victory against the Tepanecs. The Aztecs went on to conquer most of the Valley of Mexico. Over the next nearly 100 years, the Aztecs expanded their empire through warfare and alliances. Eventually the empire included hundreds of cities and millions of people, who supported the Aztecs through vast amounts of tribute goods.

Lesson 28

Daily Life in Tenochtitlán

What was daily life like for Aztecs in Tenochtitlán?

Introduction

The Aztecs built their large empire in central Mexico and governed it from Tenochtitlán, their capital city. Built on an island in the middle of Lake Texcoco, Tenochtitlán was an impressive city that was home to almost 200,000 people.

Suppose you are an Aztec child living outside Tenochtitlán in the 1400s C.E. One morning your father, a chili pepper farmer, takes you to the Great Market at Tenochtitlán. You pass by a stand with glimmering gold and silver for trade and another with fresh produce. Your father finds the vegetable section, spreads out a mat to display peppers for trade, and then begins to shout out prices. He gladly trades with a noblewoman, exchanging peppers for precious cacao beans. Later he trades his remaining peppers for a handmade clay cooking pot for your mother.

After all the peppers are gone, your father takes you on a walk around the city. You see the Great Temple where priests perform sacrifices, and the ball court where nobles play a game called *tlachtli*. You gaze in wonder at the beautiful houses of the noble families and the splendid palace of the Aztec ruler. You might see carvings and statues of Aztec gods that you recognize. When you return home, you eat a simple mush made of maize before going to sleep.

This imaginary trip to Tenochtitlán shows aspects of daily life experienced by many Aztecs in the 1400s. In this lesson, you will learn more about how the people of Tenochtitlán lived. You will explore Aztec class structure, marriage, family life, food, markets, religious practices, and recreation.

Social Studies Vocabulary

hereditary

polygamy

semidivine

ward

◀ The Great Market in the city of Tenochtitlán was a center of daily life for the Aztecs.

1. Class Structure

Aztec society was divided into five main social classes. At the top of the class structure were the ruler and his family, followed by a noble class of government officials, priests, and high-ranking warriors. The third and largest class was made up of commoners, citizens who were not of noble rank. Below the commoners were the peasants, who were neither slaves nor citizens. At the bottom of the class structure were the slaves.

Each class had its own privileges and responsibilities. However, an Aztec's status was not fixed. Commoners could move up in social class by performing brave deeds in war or by studying to be priests, and nobles could fall in rank if they failed to live up to their responsibilities.

The Ruler The Aztec ruler, or emperor, was considered **semidivine**. Called *tlatoani*, or "he who speaks," the emperor maintained the empire and decided when to wage war.

The position of ruler was not **hereditary,** as it was in many other societies. When an emperor died, his son did not automatically become ruler. Instead, a group of advisers chose the new ruler from the emperor's family. Each new ruler was expected to acquire new wealth of his own, which was an important motive for constant warfare.

Government Officials, Priests, and Military Leaders The emperor was supported by a noble class of government officials, priests, and military leaders. Officials in Tenochtitlán counseled the emperor, worked as judges, and governed the city's four districts.

Other nobles throughout the large empire ruled cities, collected tribute, or managed the construction of public buildings and roads.

The emperor appointed government officials for life. Although noble status was not hereditary, most sons of nobles earned high offices themselves.

Priests conducted all religious rites and served individual gods. Some priests ran the schools that trained boys for government jobs and the priesthood, while others studied the skies and made predictions about the future. Generally, only nobles became priests, but sometimes an Aztec from lower classes was **elevated** to this position. Girls also had the ability to become priestesses.

semidivine half-human and half-god

hereditary passed on from parent to child; inherited

This artwork shows people from various classes of Aztec society. Use the information from the text and visual clues in the image to identify which group in the Aztec class structure each figure represents.

Since all Aztec men were trained to be soldiers, commoners could also rise to become military leaders. A common soldier could become a leader by capturing enemies in battle. Military leaders commanded groups of soldiers and took part in war councils.

Commoners The broad class of commoners included several smaller classes. The highest-ranking commoners were professional traders called *pochteca*. The pochteca led caravans to distant lands to acquire exotic goods. Some also served as spies for the emperor, reporting what type of tribute a city could provide.

The pochteca worshipped their own god and lived in a separate section of Tenochtitlán. They paid taxes with rare goods and enjoyed many privileges. For example, they could own land and send their children to the nobles' schools. Unlike the nobles, membership in this class was hereditary.

Below the pochteca came craftspeople and artisans, such as potters, jewelers, and painters. Some worked in their homes and traded their goods at the market, while others worked in the royal palace and made items especially for the emperor.

Aztec artisans created beautiful works of art for emperors and other high ranking officials. Pictured here is a terra-cotta vessel depicting Tlaloc, the god of rain.

Most commoners worked as farmers, fishers, laborers, and servants. Instead of owning land, they were loaned plots of land for homes and farms by their *calpulli*, or **ward**. All commoners paid tribute to the nobility in the form of crops, labor, or manufactured goods.

Peasants About 30 percent of the Aztec people were peasants. Unlike slaves, people in this class were free, but were considered inferior to commoners. Peasants did not belong to a calpulli and were not loaned land to farm. Instead, they hired out their services to nobles.

> **ward** a political unit within a city, often a neighborhood

Slaves At the bottom of Aztec society were the slaves. Prisoners of war, lawbreakers, or debtors might be forced into slavery. Unlike slaves in many societies, Aztec slaves had a number of rights, which included owning property, goods, and even other slaves. In addition, slaves did not pass their status on to their children, who were born free. In fact, the mother of the emperor Itzcoatl was a slave. Many slaves could be **emancipated** after working off a debt, upon completing their term of punishment for a crime, or when their masters died.

2. Marriage

Marriage and family life were important to Aztecs of all social classes. Marriage marked an Aztec child's entry into adulthood. Most men married around age 20, while young women tended to marry around 16.

Marriages were arranged by the families of the bride and groom. The young man's family chose the bride. They then engaged the services of a matchmaker, an older woman who approached the bride's family. It was customary for the bride's family to refuse at first, prompting the matchmaker to then return a few days later. This time the bride's family usually accepted the union and set the dowry, or the money or goods a woman brought to her husband upon marriage.

Even among commoners, an Aztec wedding was as elaborate as the families could afford. The festivities began at the bride's house where relatives, friends, the groom's teachers, and the important people of the calpulli enjoyed a banquet with the bride and gave her presents.

That evening, the guests marched to the groom's home for the wedding ceremony. An old woman, usually the matchmaker, carried the bride on her back. To symbolize the bond of marriage, during the ceremony the matchmaker tied the groom's cloak to the bride's blouse.

After the ceremony, the young couple went to the bridal chamber to pray for four days, while their guests celebrated. On the fifth day, the couple emerged and attended another grand banquet before settling down on a piece of land in the groom's calpulli.

This page from the *Codex Mendoza* shows a young couple's marriage festivities. (A codex is a kind of early book.) Can you identify the bride, the groom, and the matchmaker?

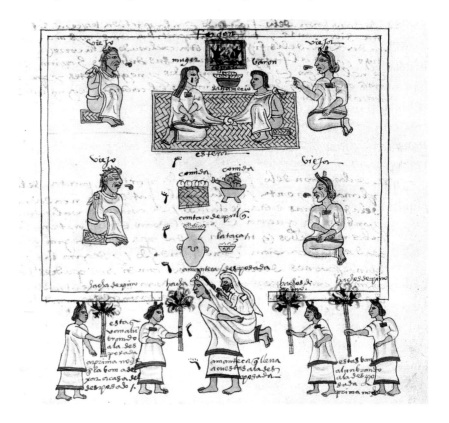

The Aztecs permitted men to practice **polygamy,** or to have multiple wives. An Aztec man could take as many wives as he could afford. However, only one of the wives was considered the primary wife, and only marriage to the primary wife was celebrated with special rites and ceremonies.

When a marriage was unhappy, either spouse could ask for a divorce. A man could divorce his wife if she neglected her duties at home, had a bad temper, or did not bear any children. A woman could divorce her husband if he beat her, deserted her, or failed to support her and her children. However, Aztec society encouraged divorced women to remarry.

polygamy having more than one spouse at one time

3. Family Life

Men had higher status than women in Aztec society. Within the family, the father was the master of the house. Aztec women, however, had their own rights and responsibilities. Married women could own property and sell goods. Some older women also practiced a profession, such as matchmaking or midwifery.

Among commoners, the skills of both men and women were necessary to care for the household and the family. Men built the house and worked as farmers or at a craft, while women fixed meals, tended the garden, and looked after livestock. Many Aztec women wove beautiful cloth of many colors, and some made cloaks in patterns of sun designs or with images of shells, fish, cacti, snakes, or butterflies. Women traded these cloaks for other goods at the market.

In this artist's depiction of an Aztec home, Aztec family members perform daily tasks such as fishing, collecting firewood, cooking, childcare, and weaving.

One of a woman's most important jobs was to have and care for children. The Aztecs believed that the purpose of marriage was to bring children into the world, so they honored a woman's role in giving birth as much as they did a man's role in fighting wars.

Aztec parents began training their children at a young age. All children of commoners helped out around the house. Young boys fetched water and wood, while older boys learned how to fish and handle a canoe. Eventually, boys accompanied their fathers to work or to the market. Girls' tasks centered on running a home, and included cleaning house and grinding maize. When they were about 7 years old, girls began learning to weave from their mothers.

In addition to working, all boys attended school. Commoners probably started school around the age of 6, but they only attended part-time. At the *telpochcalli*, or "house of youth," boys mostly trained to be soldiers, but the sons of nobles went to the *calmecac* instead. There, they learned the skills to become priests, government officials, or military commanders.

4. Food

The Aztecs of Tenochtitlán ate both homegrown foods and foods imported from distant places. The mainstay of the Aztec diet, however, was maize, which the Aztecs found useful because it could be dried and then stored for a long time. Women boiled and skinned maize kernels and ground them into flour, and then they baked fresh tortillas for each meal on clay griddles. They also made tamales by wrapping maize in its husks and steaming it.

The daily routine of Aztec commoners shows the importance of maize. After working for several hours, commoners ate a simple meal in the late morning that usually consisted of a maize porridge called *atole*. The porridge was often seasoned with peppers

The preparation of tortillas and other foods was a daily task for Aztec women. In this photo, a woman prepares tortillas using methods similar to that of the Aztecs.

or sweetened with honey. At midday, commoners ate their main meal of tortillas, maize cakes, boiled beans, or tamales. Pepper or tomato sauce sometimes spiced up these dishes. Most families had only two meals, but some people ate a thin porridge, usually made of maize, just before going to bed.

Aztec commoners had occasional variety in their meals. To provide meat for special occasions, families might raise a few turkeys or hunt wild game, such as rabbits and pigeons.

Aztec farmers also grew such crops as red peppers, tomatoes, sage, squash, green beans, sweet potatoes, and avocados. In periods when crops were bad, the Aztecs turned to other sources of food. They caught frogs and shrimp, collected insect eggs, and even skimmed algae, a type of plant, off the surface of the lake and formed it into small cakes.

The wealthy ate quite a different diet, both on a daily basis and at the feasts they attended. They prized delicacies, such as winged ants and a lizard-like creature called an *axolotl*. They enjoyed cocoa with their morning meals and pineapples, oysters, and crabs at their banquets.

5. Markets

Markets were an important part of the Aztec economy. Each city in the empire had its own market, usually located in the plaza in front of the town's temple. Large towns held markets every day, while small villages held them about every five days. Since some towns had their own specialties, the people of Tenochtitlán might travel to places like nearby Texcoco for fine cloth or to faraway Acolman to buy meat.

At Tlatelolco, the bustling market in Tenochtitlán, people bought and sold everything from food and utensils to warrior costumes, quetzal feathers, and slaves. Instead of using money, Aztecs used a barter system, trading one kind of good for another. Some expensive goods had an agreed-upon value, like a warrior's costume and shield for instance, which were worth about 60 cotton cloaks.

Many individuals brought their wares to market. Farmers brought their surplus crops, while craftspeople brought goods they had made. The pochteca had a special place in the markets because they imported goods from faraway places and provided raw materials that were unavailable around Tenochtitlán. For example, they sold metals, such as gold and silver, as well as tortoiseshells for making spoons.

Guards watched over the market to make sure sellers acted honestly. When a **dispute** arose—for example, if a buyer accused a seller of cheating—the guards took the parties to a court located at one end of the market. Three judges sat there, waiting to hear each case and to give their verdict.

The market also had a social purpose for people who went there to meet friends, gossip, and hear the news of the day. Some people simply enjoyed strolling up and down the aisles, buying snacks and browsing among all the items the sellers had to offer.

At Tlateloco, Tenochtitlán's market, people bartered, or traded, in the marketplace for the things they needed. This illustration demonstrates how the market was an opportunity for townspeople to socially gather and for merchants and farmers to sell their wares.

Aztec priests used decorative ceremonial knives made out of obsidian to make their sacrifices. Historians believe the Aztecs may have used human sacrifice as a way to scare other tribes into accepting Aztec rule.

6. Religious Practices

Religion was central to Aztec life and society because the Aztecs believed that humans needed the gods for survival. It was the gods who granted a good harvest or sent earthquakes and floods if they were displeased, so it was important to please them through elaborate rituals and ceremonies. Priests presented the gods with flowers, ears of maize, clothing, or images made of wood.

The Aztecs adopted some of their gods from other Mesoamerican groups. For example, Tlaloc, the rain god, was an ancient Mesoamerican god. Quetzalcóatl ("feathered serpent") had been worshipped by the Teotihuacans. But the Aztecs' own chief god was Huitzilopochtli, the god of the sun and of war. In fact, the Aztecs called themselves the "people of the sun."

The Aztecs saw the sun as a warrior who fought each night against the forces of darkness. In Aztec belief, the survival of the universe depended upon the sun winning these battles. The way to keep the sun strong was to offer him nourishment in the form of blood.

For this reason, most Aztec rituals included some form of blood sacrifice. Every morning, Aztec priests sacrificed hundreds of birds to Huitzilopochtli. Priests also pierced their skin with cactus spikes to offer their own blood.

The highest form of sacrifice, however, was that of humans. The Aztecs particularly valued the sacrifice of warriors captured in battle because they believed that the blood of strong warriors was especially nourishing to Huitzilopochtli. Scholars think the Aztecs also used human sacrifice to frighten other groups into accepting their rule.

In Tenochtitlán, up to several thousand people may have gone to sacrificial deaths each year. Four priests pinned the victim to the stone in front of Huitzilopochtli's temple, while another cut out his heart. Some victims may have died willingly in the belief that they would accompany the sun god in his daily battle across the sky.

The Aztecs also made sacrifices to other gods. For example, honoring the fire god would include throwing sacrificial victims into a great blaze, while honoring the corn goddess would mean cutting off women's heads. Overall, the Aztecs practiced human sacrifice on a much larger scale than other Mesoamerican groups.

7. Recreation

While work, warfare, and ritual were all important to the Aztecs, they also had some time for recreation. They enjoyed music and dancing, and nobles liked to go on hunts.

One entertainment was *patolli*, a game played on a cross-shaped board divided into 52 squares. The board symbolized the 260-day calendar, which the Aztecs shared with the Maya and other Mesoamerican peoples. Five times around the board equaled 260 days.

To move around the board, players threw beans marked with holes, similar to dice. The holes told them how many spaces to move the colored stone game pieces. The first person around the board five times won.

All social classes played patolli, but it's likely that only members of the nobility played the ball game *ōllamalitzli*. Ōllamalitzli was played on a *tlachtli*, which is a long, narrow court shaped like the letter *I* and with high walls. Two teams faced each other across a line that ran between two small rings that projected over the court from each side wall. The object was to get a rubber ball through the ring on the other team's side. Players could not touch the ball, so they threw themselves on the ground to hit the ball with their elbows, knees, and hips.

Along with its entertainment value, Ōllamalitzli had a religious meaning. The Aztecs believed that the tlachtli court represented the world and that the ball represented a heavenly body. Because of this, the Aztecs built the tlachtli courts near the most important temples, like the Great Temple in Tenochtitlán.

Ōllamalitzli, similar to the Mayan ball game pok-a-tok, held a deep religious meaning for the Aztecs. In this photo, players recreate what the game may have looked like by wearing traditional dress.

Lesson Summary

In this lesson, you learned about daily life in the Aztecs' capital city of Tenochtitlán.

Class Structure Aztec society had five classes. At the top was the ruler and his family, followed by the nobles, priests, and high-ranking warriors. Next came the commoners. Below them were the peasants. Slaves were the lowest class, but their children were born free.

Marriage and Family Life Aztec marriages were arranged; men married at about 20 and women at about 16. Men had higher status, but both spouses worked to run the home, and women were honored for their ability to give birth. Men farmed and hunted, while women raised the children and wove cloth. Children did chores around the house.

Food and Markets Maize was the main food, but the Aztecs enjoyed other local and imported foods, as well as fish and game. Markets were an important part of the Aztec economy. In daily or weekly markets, using a barter system, the Aztecs bought and sold everything from food and armor to clothing and slaves.

Religious Practices Religion was central to Aztec society. They believed that their chief god, Huitzilopochtli, god of the sun and of war, needed blood for nourishment. Because of this, the Aztecs practiced human sacrifice more than other Mesoamerican groups.

Recreation The Aztecs enjoyed games, including a board game called patolli and a ball game called Ōllamalitzli.

How Did Religion Influence Aztec Culture?

Gods of sun, rain, war, and more were all-important to the ancient Aztecs. Archaeologists have discovered artifacts that give valuable clues to the Aztecs' religious practices. You will investigate four of these to make and support a claim about the role that religion played in Aztec culture.

The Aztecs honored many gods and goddesses, several of which they adopted from other Mesoamerican civilizations. Among them there were deities for war and farming, as well as all-powerful deities who created the world. By studying artifacts, historians have learned that the Aztecs honored these gods by building temples, carving statues, and making offerings to them.

This vessel is in the image of Tlaloc, who was a rain god for the Aztec people. It is about 14 inches high and was discovered in Tomb Number 21 at *Templo Mayor* in Tenochtitlán, Mexico. This vessel may have been used in a religious ceremony.

Tlaloc, the Rain God

This Aztec vessel from the 1400s portrays Tlaloc, a rain god who was both cherished and feared for his powers. He was important to agriculture, as he brought rain to help grow the crops. However, he also was believed to bring more destructive forms of water, like frightening floods and storms.

Images of Tlaloc appeared on many Aztec objects, such as this vessel. Sometimes a vessel of Tlaloc would be filled with water and broken in a religious ceremony. What do you think this ritual represented?

Closely examine this vessel, and come up with words to describe this image of Tlaloc. What colors and shapes do you see? What do you think these colors and shapes represent? Why do you think Tlaloc was considered such an important god to the Aztecs? How is this vessel an example of the influence of religion on Aztec culture? What other sources might help you support this claim?

Quetzalcóatl, the Feathered Serpent

The Aztecs used art to represent the gods and goddesses they worshipped, as with this sculpture carved from stone during the 1400s. It is a model of Quetzalcóatl or "Feathered Serpent," who was one of the most important deities in Aztec religion.

Through Mesoamerican history, Quetzalcóatl represented many different powers. For example, people believed he was a serpent who crawled on the ground and rose to the sky, a concept that represented rebirth after death. Examine this picture of the artifact, and explain how earth and sky are represented in this statue.

People also believed that Quetzalcóatl was the protector of craftspeople, the inventor of the calendar, and the god of learning. For this reason, he was honored in religious colleges where students of the priesthood were educated.

Archaeological findings tell us that the Aztecs carved their statues from a variety of substances. They carved some from ordinary volcanic rock and others from precious gems.

This stone carving of Quetzalcóatl dates back to the 15th century. According to stories passed down through the generations, the Aztecs believed that Quetzalcóatl was the inventor of the calendar and god of learning.

Most statues created by the Aztecs represented the gods and goddesses that they worshipped. While the location of this particular sculpture is unknown, often such sculptures were placed in temples or shrines in Tenochtitlán. The collection of sculptures left by the Aztec people helps historians understand their religion.

Examine this sculpture, and observe its colors, textures, and carvings. What words would you use to describe this Aztec statue? Use what you know about the Aztecs to try to figure out how they may have used this statue.

Codex Mendoza

You have learned that the Aztecs demonstrated their religion by worshipping gods, building shrines to them, and performing rituals, but these were not the only ways that religion shaped Aztec culture. Here are two other primary sources that demonstrate how religion was prominent in other parts of Aztec daily routines.

This Aztec illustration from 1541 shows different members of the society interacting with one another. It is from an Aztec book called the *Codex Mendoza*. A codex is a book created by Aztec people that used pictures and writing to show situations in daily life, such as sharing mythological stories and performing rituals.

The *Codex Mendoza* was written after Spanish soldiers invaded and conquered the Aztecs. Many historians claim that the Spanish leader Antonio Mendoza likely required Aztec people to record pictures of their daily life so that Mendoza could send the book to the King of Spain. Unfortunately for Mendoza, pirates captured it and took it to France instead.

As you can see at the top of this picture, a man is making music and singing. Often times, the Aztecs played flutes, drums, and bells during ceremonies and festivals. They hoped the music pleased the gods enough to bring good fortune, such as a healthy agricultural season. There are many objects in this scene, including a drum made from the skin of an ocelot, a member of the wild cat species.

What does this illustration suggest about Aztec recreation? What do you think the objects in the picture represent? How might this picture help you explain the influence of religion on daily life? What other sources might help you support this claim?

The Aztecs illustrated their daily life in books like this *Codex Mendoza*. The musician in the top picture is singing, possibly a song to the gods. Primary source illustrations such as these can help you explain how religion influenced Aztec culture.

This drawing from the *Codex Magliabechiano* depicts an ancient ball game called *ōllamalitzli*. Sometimes the Aztecs played games to please the gods. By studying ancient artwork like this, you can learn how religion influenced the culture of the Aztecs.

Codex Magliabechiano

Primary sources have also provided information about the games and sports in Aztec daily life. According to historians, there were many connections between Aztec games and their religious beliefs and rituals.

This picture from the mid-1500s shows two men playing a game. It is a drawing from the *Codex Magliabechiano*, which described and illustrated the Aztecs' customs, gods and goddesses, and other information about their lives. This game of *ōllamalitzli* has been compared to the modern game of basketball. In this Aztec ball game, two teams competed to get a ball through circular rings on the walls of the court without using their hands.

As you have learned, the game had religious value in addition to being a form of entertainment. For example, the courts were often constructed near the most important temples. The *tlachtli*, or court, represented the world while the *ōllamaloni*, or ball, represented the sun or moon, and the rings represented sunrise and sunset. According to some stories passed down by the people of these early cultures, the game was a competition between the gods of day and night. Sometimes the captain of a team was killed as a sacrifice to the gods. Describe what might be happening in this picture. What might be the significance of the skulls on the court? What might it have been like to be a spectator?

Think about the four primary sources you just learned about. Based on these sources, what claim can you make about how religion influenced the culture of the Aztecs? Use what you already learned as well as research from reliable sources to help form your claim and support it.

Tenochtitlán (1428–1600)

Tenochtitlán was a site of encounter from 1428, when the development of the city took off after the defeat of the Atzcapotzalco. The Aztec Empire was not ruled by people from a single culture, with a single language, and a shared set of social norms, as was often the case in the Old World.

Early Steps Toward Creating a Site of Encounter

Marriage Even before they began their empire, the Aztecs created a multi-ethnic community as a matter of policy. They used marriage to bind them to the Colhua community for whom they provided mercenary services before founding their own empire. After founding the empire, Aztec nobility formed marriage alliances with conquered city-states, continuing to incorporate people from other ethnic backgrounds into their highest ranks.

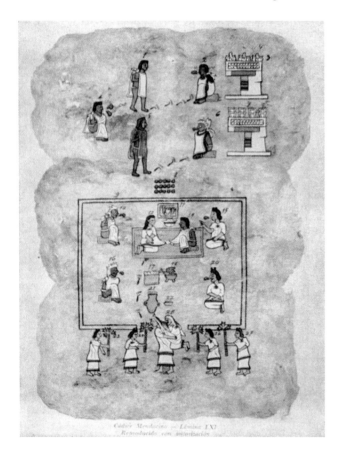

This image, created in the 16th century, shows a marriage ceremony. Marriage was important for forming alliances and binding people to the Colhua community.

The "Triple Alliance" The earliest Aztec rulers came to power when the Aztec had founded Tenochtitlán, but they were still paying tribute to Atzcapotzalco. The Aztec leader Itzcoatl allied his city with Texcoco and Tlacopan. This Alliance became known as the "Triple Alliance." It is now believed that Tenochtitlán was the dominant state from the beginning. After Atzcapotzalco was conquered, the city grew enormously. Immigration of people to Tenochtitlán increased the city's population, as well as its diversity.

Cultural Encounter Through War

Some scholars believe that the main purpose of Aztec wars to expand the empire was economic. Conquered states paid tribute, and tribute was a central element of the empire. Tribute took many forms, including food, everyday goods, luxury items, and raw materials for craftsmen in Tenochtitlán to use. Some scholars divide tribute into five categories: food, textiles, warriors' costumes, luxury goods, and other specialty items. In recent studies, scholars distinguish tribute provinces from strategic provinces. While tribute provinces provided goods, strategic provinces provided a buffer between the Aztec Empire and enemies.

Adaptation and Adoption

Adaptation is the action of making a change to something, while keeping other parts the same. Adoption is incorporating something that wasn't included before. One key adaptation that helped the multi-ethnic society function was a common language. The Aztec language Nahuatl was used as a lingua franca, or common language among people whose native languages are different. A common language was also useful for what archaeologists refer to as trade across the Mesoamerican world system.

The Aztecs adopted "foreign" products into their rituals. Some of these products they may have obtained through trade. Others they obtained through tribute. In some cases, tribute was generic items, but in other cases, the Aztecs demanded tribute to be paid in items that were local specialities.

The Templo Mayor Project, which excavated the sacred precinct of Tenochtitlán from 1978 to 2011, helped reveal the Aztecs' use of

The Aztec capital in Tenochtitlán imported local products from across the empire and incorporated them into their imperial strategies. Items such as liquidambar (sweet gum) in a pot in the middle of the second row from the bottom on the left-hand page and jaguar skins on the right-hand page, were not available in the capital city.

Record of Tribute from the Provinces of Tochtepec (left) and Xoconochco (right) in the Codex Mendoza

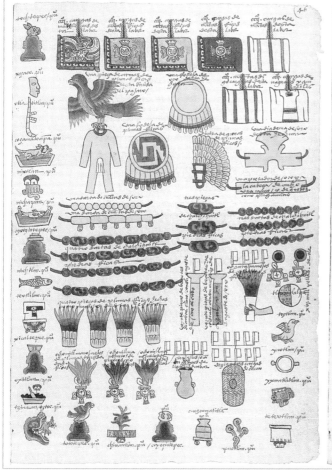
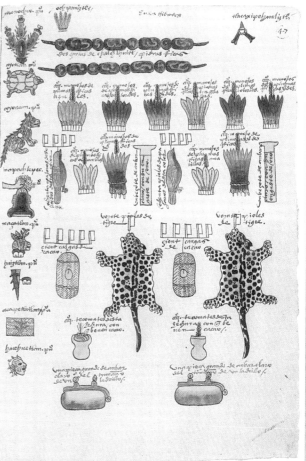

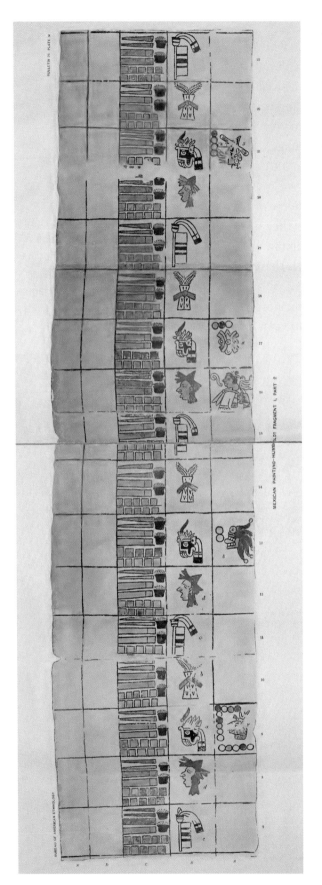

goods from distant regions. This is an example of how archaeology during the past 30 years has changed understandings of Aztec culture, which were previously based entirely on documents. The burial sites they excavated contained animal remains from a wide range of species from regions far from the Basin of Mexico, where Tenochtitlán was situated. These included animals from a wide variety of ecosystems, including the sea and the rainforest. These animals were either imported or provided as tribute.

Diffusion

The empire did not have beasts of burden or many waterways that could be used for travel. Despite the high cost of transporting goods, trade increased, and with it, the diffusion of goods from Tenochtitlán. (Diffusion is the spread of goods and ideas through contact between people of different regions and cultures.) The empire took advantage of the pre-existing networks of the Mesoamerican world system and built on them to bring goods into Tenochtitlán from across the region. At the same time, goods from Tenochtitlán were diffused across the empire.

Products were not the only elements from Tenochtitlán that spread. One aspect of culture that was diffused was the manuscript painting style developed in the capital. When provincial painters adopted imperial style, they demonstrated commitment to and integration with the rulers.

Here's a particular example. Artists in Tenochtitlán invented year-count annals to record historic events. This form of document and its particular style spread throughout the empire. But when artists from other parts of the empire made year-count annals, they always included Tenochtitlán events along with their own. As a result, events in Tenochtitlán were included in all records across the empire.

◀ This tribute list from Humboldt Fragment 1 was created in an Aztec province in Guerrero, on the Pacific coast. Scholars say the diffusion of the Aztec manuscript painting style to this province can be seen in the images in the third column. These images show the four quarterly periods for tribute payment and are created in the Aztec style.

Tenochtitlán Transforms

Although the Aztec Empire was conquered and Tenochtitlán was transformed into Mexico City, Mexico City retained many of the people and the material elements of the former empire. Scholars identify five types of cultural interaction between the Spaniards and the previous society. These are destruction, appropriation, continuity, reconstruction, and change in use.

In the war between the Spaniards and indigenous people against the Aztec Empire, buildings, monuments, and smaller cultural artifacts were destroyed. For example, the Templo Mayor, the main temple, was almost completely in ruins. In an example of appropriation, the Spanish built the Metropolitan Cathedral in a space previously used for Aztec rituals. Continuity can be found in Spanish streets being laid out on the pattern the Aztecs had created. Reconstruction took place when foundations from pre-hispanic buildings were used for new structures. And change of use was found both in Aztec and Spanish structures built on previous structures that had a different purpose.

Mexico City continued as a multi-cultural city through colonial times. Residents ate a diet that combined European and Mesoamerican products. And the Spanish and their African slaves added to the already existing ethnic diversity.

The Metropolitan Cathedral still stands in downtown Mexico City today.

The Incas

How did the Incas manage their large and remote empire?

Introduction

The Inca Empire was a complex society that developed in the Andes Mountains of South America. It flourished in what is now present-day Peru between the 1400s C.E. and 1532, when the Incas were conquered by Spanish explorers.

From north to south along the South American continent, the Inca Empire stretched for over 2,500 miles and included millions of people. To communicate across this vast distance, the Incas used runners called *chasquis* (CHAHS-kees) to relay messages from one part of their territory to another.

Picture yourself as a young chasqui. From your messenger station along the Royal Road, you see another chasqui racing toward you carrying an important message from the emperor.

You dart out of the messenger station and run alongside the other runner while he hands you a set of strings called a *quipu* (KEE-pooh). You quickly study the knots tied at different places in the strings, which stand for numbers that will help you remember the message. The other chasqui also gives you a verbal message. Once he is certain that you have both parts of the message, he stops running. Now that his work is over, it is up to you to get the message to the next station as quickly as possible.

This remarkable relay system helped the Incas manage their far-flung empire. In this lesson, you will explore how the Incas built and maintained their empire. You will discover the role of the Sapa Inca, the emperor, and how he helped expand the territory. You will also learn about the Incas' class structure, family life, religion, and relations with other peoples.

Social Studies Vocabulary

ayllu

communal

Incas

oracle

◀ The city of Machu Picchu may have been a religious center during the Inca Empire.

Incas people of a culture in the Andes Mountains of South America that arose in the 1400s C.E. and lasted until 1532

The Inca Empire consisted of a huge territory that stretched along most of the west coast of South America. After settling the area around their capital, Cuzco, in the 1200s C.E., the Inca Empire expanded over the next 300 years until they were conquered by the Spanish in 1532.

1. The Rise of the Inca Empire

At the height of their power in the early 1500s C.E., the **Incas** ruled over a vast, well-organized empire of perhaps 10 million people. From north to south, the Inca Empire stretched almost the length of the Andes mountain range, a distance of about 2,500 miles. It reached from the Pacific Coast in the west to the Amazon River Basin in the east. Today, this territory includes most of Peru and Ecuador, as well as parts of Bolivia, Chile, and Argentina.

How did the Incas build and manage such a huge empire? In part, they adopted ideas and institutions that had been pioneered by earlier cultures. Two peoples who had an especially strong influence on the Incas were the Moches (MOH-chayz) and the Chimus (chee-MOOZ).

The Moches lived along the northern coast of Peru from about 100 B.C.E. to 700 C.E. They built cities, dug irrigation canals, and developed special classes of workers.

The Chimu kingdom in northern Peru flourished during the 1300s and 1400s. Like the Moches, the Chimus built well-planned cities and used elaborate irrigation methods. They preserved the artistic traditions of the Moches and passed them on to the Incas. They also built good roads and created a message system using runners. The Incas **adapted** and improved upon all these advances.

Beginnings of the Empire The center of the Inca Empire was the capital of Cuzco (KOOZ-koh), which was located high in the mountains of southern Peru. The Incas first settled in this area around 1200 C.E. Apart from this fact, their early history is cloaked in legend.

According to one Incan legend, the people were descended from Inti, the sun god. Inti commanded his son, Manco Capac, to rise from the waters of Lake Titicaca. Manco Capac then founded the Inca tribe.

In another legend, Inti appeared before a later Incan ruler and declared the Incas must become a great power and educate the people they meet. But for more than 200 years, the Incas increased their territory by only about a dozen miles around Cuzco.

The Incas began expanding their empire in 1438, after they were attacked by the neighboring Chancas. Even though the Incan emperor and many citizens fled Cuzco, one of his sons, Yupanqui, stayed behind and led his army against the Chancas. Incan legend says that the stones on the battlefield turned into powerful warriors. Yupanqui's victory made his people the strongest group in the area.

After driving off the Chancas, Yupanqui seized the throne and took the name Pachacuti, which means "earthshaker." Pachacuti and his son, Topa Inca, then launched a series of conquests against other nearby tribes. With each victory, the Incan army became larger and more skilled.

Chasquis counted the knots and strings on quipus, like the one pictured here, to relay messages about various matters, such as the number of people in a military troop or the amount of goods given in tribute to an Incan leader.

Soon the Incas controlled almost every major group in the central Andes region. In 1470, they conquered the Chimus. By the 1500s, their empire covered about 350,000 square miles.

Roads and Messengers To manage the empire, Incan leaders came to rely on a system of two main roads connected by several smaller ones. The main routes were the coastal road and the inland road, which was called the Royal Road.

Some historians have said that the Incas' system of roads was as impressive as that of ancient Rome. About 25,000 miles of road linked all corners of the empire and crossed tropical jungles, high mountains, and raging rivers. Incan officials used the roads to travel throughout the empire. There was a shelter along the roads every 15 to 30 miles to give travelers a place to rest.

The roads allowed the emperor at Cuzco to communicate with officials in distant places. The Incas sent messages by an elaborate relay system that included messenger stations every couple of miles along the main roads. Chasquis, or messengers, carried the messages from one station to the next. Using this system, messages could travel more than 150 miles a day.

A message consisted of memorized words and sets of strings called quipus, which served as memory aids. Knots tied at various places and on strings of different colors represented numbers.

In contrast to the Maya, the Incas had no system of writing, but the quipus proved to be an effective substitute for written language. The Incas used them to keep track of civil and military populations, as well as to record their legends and achievements.

Incan legend says that the emperor was descended from Inti, the sun god, making him the "son of the sun." Shown here is Atahualpa, the last emperor to rule before the Spanish conquered the Inca Empire.

2. Class Structure

Incan society was based on a strictly organized class structure made up of three broad classes: the emperor and his immediate family, nobles, and commoners. Throughout Incan society, people who were "Incan by blood"—those whose families were originally from the capital city of Cuzco—had higher status than non-Incas. As the empire grew, its class structure became more complex.

The Emperor At the top of Incan society was the emperor, called the Sapa Inca. The Incas believed that the Sapa Inca was descended from Inti, the sun god, and for this reason he ruled with complete authority.

Everything in the empire belonged to the Sapa Inca, who lived in great splendor. When the Spanish came to Cuzco in the 1500s, they were dazzled to see fine gardens, golden statues, and jars made of gold and silver studded with emeralds. Servants carried the Sapa Inca everywhere on a golden litter, an elaborate covered chair. His subjects dared not look him directly in the eye.

The Sapa Inca could have many wives and hundreds of children. But he had one primary wife, who was called the Coya.

Nobles Below the Sapa Inca were the nobles. The Incan nobility was made up of leaders who helped to rule and administer the vast empire.

All nobles enjoyed certain privileges, such as gifts of land, servants, llamas, and fine clothing. They did not pay taxes, and the men had the right to marry more than one wife. However, nobles were not all of equal rank. There were three main classes of nobles: Capac Incas, who were considered relatives of the emperor; Hahua Incas, who did not share the royal blood; and *curacas*, who were leaders of people conquered by the Incas.

The highest-ranking nobles were the Capac Incas. Like the emperor himself, they were believed to be descended from Manco Capac, the legendary founder of the Incan dynasty.

Capac Incas controlled the empire's land as well as its valuable resources, such as llamas, coca leaves, and gold. They held the most important posts in the government, the army, and the priesthood. The *apus*, or governors, of the four quarters of the empire belonged to the group of Capac Incas.

As the empire grew, the Incas needed more nobles to staff the government's complex bureaucracy. As a result, some people who were not true Incas also gained entry into the noble class. Called Hahua Incas, they were considered "Incas by privilege." Non-royal leaders from around Cuzco often became Hahua Incas, and people of common birth sometimes gained this status as well.

Additional conquests created a need for the third class of nobles, called curacas, who were local leaders of conquered peoples. Curacas carried out various jobs. While many collected taxes, others worked as inspectors by making sure everyone followed Incan laws and customs, including wearing proper clothing and keeping clean homes. Curacas were required to spend time in Cuzco learning these laws and customs. They were allowed to rule their people only if they followed Incan ways.

Commoners Most people in the Inca Empire were commoners who worked as farmers and herders. The Incas did not practice slavery in the usual sense of the word. However, they did require commoners to support the government, both through the products of their labor and by working on government-sponsored projects. Men did jobs like building roads, while women might weave cloth.

Incan farmers grew a variety of crops, including squash, peppers, beans, peanuts, more than 20 types of corn, and more than 200 types of potato. The most important crop was the potato, which could survive heavy frosts at altitudes as high as 15,000 feet above sea level. Corn could be grown nearly as high up, and the Incas enjoyed it fresh, fried, and popped.

Incan farmers were required to give most of their crops to the government, which placed the crops it collected in storehouses throughout the empire. The food was then distributed to warriors, temple priests, and people in need. For example, the government gave food to people who could no longer work, particularly the aged, the sick, and the disabled.

The Capac Incas held some of the most important posts in the Incan Empire. This drawing, dating from about 1565, depicts a Capac Inca as an army captain.

3. Family Life

ayllu an Incan clan (group of related families), the basic unit of Incan society

communal shared by a community or group

Families in the Inca Empire belonged to larger groups, or clans, called **ayllus**. The ayllu (EYE-yoo) was the foundation of Incan society. Everyone was born into an ayllu, and most people lived their entire lives within the borders of its land. So, to understand family life in the Inca Empire, we need to begin with the ayllu.

Life in the Ayllu Groups of families made up the ayllus, which ranged in size from small villages to large towns. Each ayllu had its own farmland and homes, but the ayllu did not own the land. As you have read, everything in the empire belonged to the emperor. The government loaned land to the ayllus for living and for farming, and the people of an ayllu then worked this communal land cooperatively to grow crops and produce goods.

Everyone had responsibilities to the ayllu and to the government, and all members of the ayllu had to work, except for the very young and the very old. The leaders of the ayllu made sure all the work got done. For instance, a leader might assign some men to clear the fields and others to dig irrigation ditches.

The households of the ayllu came under the authority of a series of curacas. One head of household ruled every ten households. Fifty of these heads of household came under the supervision of a higher-level curaca. At still higher levels, curacas managed groupings of 100, 500, 1,000, 5,000, and 10,000 households.

Incan men were required to pay the mit'a, or public tax, by participating in government projects, such as working in salt mines like the ones shown here. The work was assigned to members of the ayllu by their head of household.

One of the functions of the curacas was to make sure ayllus paid their taxes. The Incas had no currency, so taxes were paid in the forms of goods and labor. The Sapa Inca claimed one-third of everything an ayllu produced. Another third supported the Incan temples. Commoners kept the remaining third for themselves.

In addition, men had to pay the *mit'a*, or public duty tax, by contributing labor to government projects each year. In response to the government's needs, the leaders of an ayllu assigned work to members. For example, men might repair roads, build storehouses, or work in the mines.

Childhood Most Incan children were born into ayllus of hardworking commoners where they learned about their responsibilities early in life. Young children performed simple tasks around the home. As they grew older, girls took care of the babies, fetched water, cooked, made clothing, and learned to weave. Boys looked after the animals and helped in the fields.

The sons of Incan nobles had to pass month-long tests of courage and discipline before they could receive the weapons of an Incan warrior. Incan weapons, such as the ones shown here, were often made of stone or metal and attached to a long wooden handle.

The children of most commoners did not receive any formal education. Instead, they learned the skills they needed, as well as Incan customs, from their elders. Some especially talented boys were trained in crafts or record keeping so they could serve the emperor.

Unlike boys from commoner families, the sons of nobles had special *amautas*, or tutors. Amautas taught religion, geometry, history, military strategy, public speaking, and physical training.

At about age 15, all boys received a loincloth, a strip of cloth worn around the waist. However, the sons of nobles underwent a much more elaborate ritual in which they had to pass month-long tests of courage, strength, and discipline. After passing these tests, the boys swore loyalty to the Sapa Inca and received the weapons of an Incan warrior.

Marriage Young men and women remained at home until they married. Unlike the emperor and the nobility, male commoners married only one wife. Young men married in their early 20s, while girls could marry at 16.

People usually married within their ayllu. Some marriages were arranged by families or by the young people themselves, but in other cases, the local curaca chose a wife for a young man who was not yet married. When a couple agreed they would marry, they held hands and exchanged sandals.

Once married, a couple established their own home. Commoners typically lived in one-room houses made of adobe bricks or stone, whereas noble families had fancier houses with several rooms. While nobles enjoyed the help of servants, commoners worked hard to produce their own food and clothing and to fulfill their responsibilities to the ayllu.

4. Religion

Religion was an important part of Incan life. Like other early groups in the Americas, the Incas believed that the gods influenced their daily lives. As a result, they showed their devotion to the gods through a number of practices.

The Inca believed that a supreme god named Viracocha created the world and gave power to all other gods. This statue depicting Viracocha is located in the Andes Mountains in Peru.

Religious Beliefs The Incas believed in many gods who controlled various aspects of nature. For example, Illapu was the weather god and rain giver, Paca Mama was the Earth Mother, and Mama Cocha was the goddess of the sea. The Incas believed that all these gods had received their power from a supreme god called Viracocha, the creator of the world.

But to the Incas, the most important god was Inti, the sun god. Inti was important for two reasons. First, Incas believed that the emperor's family was descended from Inti. Second, Inti was also the god of agriculture, which was the basis of Incan life.

The Incas also believed that spirits dwelled in certain sacred objects and places, called *huacas*. Huacas (WHAH-kuz) included temples, charms, and places in nature such as springs and rocks. Because the Incas believed in an afterlife, the tombs and bodies of the dead were also considered huacas. People often prayed and made offerings to all these huacas.

Religious Practices The Incan religion was highly formal and required a large number of priests to conduct rituals and ceremonies. Priests worked at temples and shrines devoted to the gods.

The most important temples were those **dedicated** to Inti. The high priest, a close relative of the Sapa Inca, presided over the Sun Temple in Cuzco. Priests who worked in the sun temples in the countryside came from the families of curacas.

Like the Maya and the Aztecs, the Incas offered sacrifices to the gods. Some sacrifices took place regularly. For example, each day priests threw corn on a fire to encourage the sun to appear. "Eat this, Lord Sun," the priests said, "so that you will know we are your children." In many rituals, the Incas sacrificed live animals, usually llamas or guinea pigs. The Incas also practiced human sacrifice, but only on the most sacred occasions or in times of a natural disaster.

In addition to performing rituals and sacrifices, priests practiced divination, or the art of predicting the future. Divination helped the Incas decide upon a course of action. For example, a priest might ask an **oracle** when the army should attack another tribe.

This gold figurine depicts one of the Chosen Women, who were honored as servants of Inti. Girls as young as 8 were selected for this role and served as a Chosen Woman for the rest of their lives.

Chosen Women A unique aspect of Incan religion was the role played by women. Each year, government officials visited all the towns in the empire to search for the most beautiful, graceful, and talented girls between the ages of 8 and 10. Selected girls were honored as Chosen Women and taken to live in convents where they studied Incan religion. They learned how to prepare special food and drink for religious ceremonies and wove garments for the Sapa Inca and the Coya.

Around age 15, many Chosen Women left their convents. Some went to work in temples or shrines, while others became convent teachers, called *mamaconas*. Still, others went to Cuzco and became wives of nobles or secondary wives of the Sapa Inca himself.

A few Chosen Women were sacrificed at important religious ceremonies, but the majority spent almost their entire lives either serving Inti or fulfilling their roles as wives of nobles or the emperor. Only in old age were they sometimes allowed to return to the homes and families they had left so many years earlier.

oracle a person through whom a god or spirit is believed to speak about the future

5. Relations with Other Peoples

The Incas had several methods of bringing other groups of people into the empire. Instead of immediately declaring war, the Sapa Inca generally sent a delegate to meet with a tribe. The delegate explained that the tribe could join the Inca Empire and enjoy peace and prosperity, but everyone understood that the **alternative** was war with the strong Incan army.

When faced with these options, many tribes chose to join the empire. Their leaders were then allowed to retain some local power. In this way, the Incas expanded their empire without always having to fight.

If a tribe resisted, however, the two sides met in battle. The Incas used a variety of weapons, including spears, axes, and clubs. They were especially skilled at hurling stones with a sling. The fighting often cost the enemy tribe many of its men, and the Incas usually won. Sometimes, the Incas moved a defeated tribe to other parts of the empire so that its people lost their native lands as well.

Becoming part of the empire meant adopting Incan ways. The leaders of a conquered tribe had to build a sun temple. While the tribe could go on worshipping its own gods, it had to accept the Incan gods as the most powerful. Local leaders and their sons were brought to Cuzco to study Incan laws, as well as the official language, Quechua (KECH-wah), before they returned to their people as curacas.

As the new territory accepted Incan ways, teachers arrived to create Incan-style villages. When necessary, they organized ayllus and taught the people how to build storehouses, irrigation systems, and terraced fields for farming.

As the Incas expanded their empire, foreign tribes could choose to join the empire or face Incan warriors in battle. The consequences of losing to the Incas in battle could be severe.

Meanwhile, the Incas took an important religious object belonging to the tribe and kept it in Cuzco. The Incas claimed they acted out of respect for the local religion, but in reality, the object was held "hostage." If the tribe rebelled, the government could destroy the sacred object.

Despite these efforts, sometimes the Incas failed to bring a tribe fully into their empire. In such cases they might remove—and usually kill—the local leader. The government forced some **rebellious** tribes to move far away and then settled loyal members of the empire in their place. In this way, the Incas reduced the chance of resistance to their rule.

The Incas believed that even after death the Sapa Inca kept his wealth and lands. In order to honor their dead ruler, the Incas created beautiful funeral masks made out of gold.

Many historians have wondered what motivated the Incas to conquer such a huge empire. Part of the answer may lie in the Incan belief that even after death the Sapa Inca continued to rule the lands he had conquered. In order for the new emperor to establish his own source of power and wealth, he had to take new lands. Only then would he have land that belonged to him alone.

Lesson Summary

In this lesson, you learned about life in the Inca Empire, which arose in the west of South America in the 1400s C.E.

The Rise of the Inca Empire In the 1400s, the Incas began rapidly expanding their power from their capital city, Cuzco. Eventually, they created a huge empire that extended almost the length of the Andes. An impressive system of roads and messengers helped the emperor manage his vast territory.

Class Structure, Family Life, and Religion Incan class structure had three main levels: the emperor and his family, the nobility, and the commoners. All Incas belonged to ayllus, which provided the empire with crops, goods, and labor. Like other early peoples in the Americas, the Incas engaged in many religious practices to maintain proper relationships with their gods, especially their chief god, Inti, god of the sun.

Relations with Other Peoples The Incas used a variety of means to bring others under their control. Conquered peoples had to build a sun temple, study Incan laws, and learn Quechua. The Incas also took a sacred object as a hostage. Rebellious tribes were forced to relocate.

Achievements of the Maya, Aztecs, and Incas

What were the significant achievements of the Maya, Aztecs, and Incas?

Introduction

The three great peoples of the early Americas—the Maya, the Aztecs, and the Incas—each had unique cultures and achievements. The history of these civilizations stretches from very ancient times to just a few centuries ago. Maya civilization dates back to 2000 B.C.E. and reached its height in what is called the Classic period, which lasted about 200 to 900 C.E. The Aztecs and the Incas, on the other hand, built their empires in the two centuries before the Spanish arrived in the 1500s.

Scholars have learned about these cultures in various ways. They have studied artifacts found at the sites of old settlements and have also read accounts left by Spanish soldiers and priests. In addition, scholars have observed several traditions that have been passed down for generations. These traditions can still be found among the descendants of the Maya, Aztecs, and Incas.

The more we learn about these cultures, the more we can appreciate what was special about each of them. For example, the Maya made striking advances in writing, astronomy, and architecture. Both the Maya and the Aztecs created highly accurate calendars. The Aztecs adapted earlier pyramid designs to build massive stone temples. In addition to managing their huge empire, the Inca showed great skill in engineering.

In this lesson, you will study these and other achievements of the Maya, the Aztecs, and the Incas. You will focus on three main areas of culture: science and technology, arts and architecture, and language and writing.

Social Studies Vocabulary

dialect

glyph

pictograph

solar year

stele

suspension bridge

trephination

◀ The cultures of Mexico, Central, and South America produced great art work, such as this gold ornament made by the Incas.

1. Achievements of the Maya

Many of the greatest achievements of the Maya date from the Classic period (about 200 to 900 C.E.). Hundreds of years later, their ideas and practices continued to influence other Mesoamerican groups, including the Aztecs.

Science and Technology The Maya made important breakthroughs in astronomy and mathematics. Throughout Maya lands, priests studied the sky from observatories, where they tracked the movements of stars and planets with great accuracy. The Maya used their observations to calculate the **solar year**. The Maya figure for their year of 365.2420 days is amazingly precise.

These calculations allowed the Maya to create their solar calendar of 365 days. They also had a sacred 260-day calendar. Every 52 years, the first date in both calendars fell on the same day, giving the Maya a longer unit of time that they called a Calendar Round. For the ancient Maya, this 52-year period was something like what a century is to us.

Maya astronomy and calendar-making depended on a deep understanding of mathematics, and in some ways, the Maya number system was similar to ours. The Maya used place values for numbers, just as we do. However, instead of being based on the number 10, their system was based on 20. So, instead of place values for 1s, 10s, and 100s, the Mayas had place values for 1s, 20s, 400s (20 times 20), and so on.

solar year the time it takes Earth to travel once around the sun

Maya priests are still active today. This priest takes part in a Maya ceremony in Guatemala.

The Maya also recognized the need for zero—a discovery made by few other early civilizations. In the Maya system for writing numbers, a dot stood for one, a bar for five, and a shell symbol for zero. To add and subtract, people lined up two numbers and then combined or took away dots and bars.

Arts and Architecture The Maya were equally gifted in the arts. We can see the artistry of Maya painters in the Bonampak murals, which were found in Chiapas, Mexico. The murals, made with colors mixed from minerals and plants, show nobles and priests, as well as battle scenes, ceremonies, and sacrifice rituals.

The Maya also constructed upright stone slabs called **steles** (STEE-leez), which they often placed in front of temples. Most steles stood between 5 and 12 feet tall, although some rose as high as 30 feet. Steles usually had three-dimensional carvings of gods and rulers. Sometimes, the Maya inscribed them with dates and hieroglyphics in honor of significant events.

Another important art was weaving. We know from steles and paintings that the Maya wove colorful fabric in complex patterns. Women made embroidered tunics called *huipiles* and fashioned lengths of cloth for trade. Maya women still make their huipiles in traditional designs using similar techniques today. People from different towns can be distinguished by the colors and patterns of their garments.

In architecture, the Maya built temple-pyramids from hand-cut limestone bricks. An unusual feature of Maya buildings was a type of arch called a corbel vault, which was made when builders stacked stones so that they gradually angled in toward each other to form a triangular archway. At the top of the arch, where the stones almost touched, one stone joined the two sides. The archway always had nine stone layers, representing the nine layers of the underworld (the place where souls were thought to go after death).

Language and Writing The Maya developed the most complex system of writing in the ancient Americas, using hieroglyphics, or picture symbols, to represent sounds, words, and ideas. Hieroglyphic inscriptions have been found on stoneware and other artifacts dating from possibly as early as 300 B.C.E.

Over time, the Maya created hundreds of **glyphs,** eventually allowing scribes to write down anything in the spoken language. They often wrote about rulers, history, myths and gods, and astronomy.

However, not all Maya groups shared the same language. Instead, they spoke related **dialects**. Today, about four million Mesoamericans still speak one of thirty or so Maya dialects.

Huipiles, colorful blouses woven with complex patterns, are still worn by Maya women today. These huipiles on sale in a Guatemalan market show the artistry with which these clothes are made.

stele a vertical stone slab or pillar with carvings or inscriptions

glyph a symbol for a word, idea, or sound in a hieroglyphic system of writing

dialect a regional variety of a language

2. Achievements of the Aztecs

The Aztecs adapted many ideas from earlier groups, including their calendars and temple-pyramids. But the Aztecs improved on these ideas and made them their own.

Science and Technology One of the Aztecs' most remarkable technological achievements was the construction of their island city, Tenochtitlán. The Aztecs enlarged the area of the city by creating artificial islands called *chinampas*. Today, flower farmers in Xochimilco, near Mexico City, still use chinampas. Tourists enjoy taking boat trips to see these "floating gardens."

Just as impressive as the chinampas were the three causeways that connected Tenochtitlán to the mainland. The causeways were often crowded with people traveling in and out of the capital. During the rainy season, when the waters of the lake rose, the causeways also served as dikes.

To manage time, the Aztecs adapted the Maya solar and sacred calendars. The 365-day solar calendar was especially useful for farming, since it tracked the seasons. Priests used the sacred 260-day calendar to predict events and to determine "lucky" days for such things as planting crops and going to war.

Adapted from the Maya calendar, the Sun Stone calendar shows the face of the Aztec sun god. It includes a 365-day agricultural calendar and a 260-day sacred calendar.

One of the most famous Aztec artifacts is a calendar called the Sun Stone, which depicts the face of the sun god at its center. This beautifully carved stone is nearly twelve feet wide and weighs almost twenty-five tons. Today, the Sun Stone is a well-known symbol of Mexico.

Arts and Architecture The Aztecs practiced a number of arts, including poetry, music, dance, and sculpture. Poets wrote verses to sing the praises of the gods, to tell stories, and to celebrate the natural world. Poetry was highly valued, and Aztec poets sung their poems or recited them to music. Sometimes, actors performed them, creating a dramatic show with dialogue and costumes.

Music and dance were important features of Aztec ceremonies and holidays, and people dressed up for these special occasions. Women wore beautiful blouses over their skirts while men painted their faces, greased their hair, and wore feathered headdresses. The dancers formed large circles and moved to the beat of drums and the sound of rattle bells. The dances had religious meaning, and the dancers had to perform every step correctly. Sometimes, thousands of people danced at one time. Even the emperor occasionally joined in.

The Aztecs were also gifted painters and sculptors. Painters used brilliant colors to create scenes showing gods and religious ceremonies. Sculptors fashioned stone statues and relief sculptures on temple walls. They also carved small, lifelike figures of people and animals from rock and semiprecious stones, such as jade. In technical craft and beauty, their work surpassed that of earlier Mesoamerican cultures.

In architecture, the Aztecs are best remembered today for their massive stone temples. The Aztecs were unique in building double stairways, like those of the Great Temple in Tenochtitlán. The staircases led to two temples, one for the sun god and one for the god of rain. Smaller pyramids nearby had their own temples, where sacrificial fires burned before huge statues of the gods.

Language and Writing Spoken language was raised to an art in Aztec society. Almost any occasion called for dramatic and often flowery speeches. The rich **vocabulary** of the Aztec language, Nahuatl, allowed speakers to create new words and describe **abstract** concepts.

The Aztec system of writing used both glyphs and pictographs. A pictograph is a drawing that depicts a word, phrase, or name, rather than symbolizes it. For example, the Aztec pictograph for war was a symbol of a shield and a club. However, the Aztecs did not have enough pictographs and glyphs to express everything that could be spoken in their language, so scribes instead used writing to list data or to outline events. Priests used these writings to spark their memories when relating stories from the past.

This woman performs a traditional dance in Mexico City, where Aztec dancers celebrated over 600 years ago.

pictograph a drawing that stands for a word, phrase, or name

suspension bridge a bridge held up by cables anchored at each end

trephination a type of surgery in which a hole is made in the skull

Terraces anchored with stones can still be seen in the ruins of the Incan city of Machu Picchu.

3. Achievements of the Incas

Like the Aztecs, the Incas often borrowed and improved upon ideas from other cultures. However, the Incas faced a unique challenge in managing the largest empire in the Americas, and maintaining tight control over such an enormous area was one of their most impressive accomplishments.

Science and Technology The Incas' greatest technological skill was engineering. The best example is their amazing system of roads.

The Incas built roads across the length and width of their empire. To create routes through steep mountain ranges, they carved staircases and gouged tunnels out of rock. They also built **suspension bridges** over rivers made from thick rope cables anchored at stone towers on either side of the river. Two cables served as rails, while three others held a walkway.

In agriculture, the Incas showed their technological skill by vastly enlarging the system of terraces already in use by earlier Andean farmers. The Incas anchored their step-like terraces with stones and improved the drainage systems in the fields. On some terraces, they planted different crops at elevations where the plants would grow best.

To irrigate the crops, the Incas built canals that brought water to the top of a hillside of terraces. From there, the water ran down, level by level. People in South America still grow crops on Incan terraces.

The Incas also made remarkable advances in medicine. Incan priests, who were in charge of healing, practiced a type of surgery called **trephination**. Priests operated on the patient—usually an injured warrior—by cutting into the skull to remove bone fragments that were pressing against the brain. As **drastic** as this sounds, many people survived the operation and recovered full health.

Arts and Architecture Making textiles for clothing was one of the most important Incan arts. The quality and design of a person's clothes were a sign of status. The delicate cloth worn by Incan nobles often featured bright colors and bold geometric patterns. Incan women also made feather tunics, or long shirts, weaving feathers from jungle birds right into the cloth.

The Incas fashioned valuable objects out of prized gold, which they called the "sweat of the sun." Gold covered almost every inch inside the Temple of the Sun in the Incan capital city of Cuzco. Incan goldsmiths also fashioned masks, sculptures, knives, and jewelry.

Music was a major part of Incan life, and the Incas played many instruments, including flutes, seashell horns, rattles, drums, and panpipes. Scholars believe that the modern music of the Andes region preserves elements of Incan music.

In architecture, the Incas are known for their huge, durable stone buildings. The massive stones of Incan structures fit together so tightly that a knife blade could not be slipped between them. Incan buildings were sturdy, too—many remain standing today.

Language and Writing The Incas made their language, Quechua, the official language of the empire, and as a result, Quechua spread far and wide. About ten million people in South America still speak it.

Because the Incas did not have a written language, they developed an **ingenious** substitute: the knotted sets of strings called *quipus*. The Incas used quipus as memory aids when sending messages and recording information.

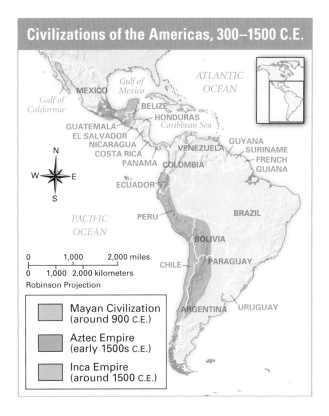

Civilizations of the Americas, 300–1500 C.E.

Mayan Civilization (around 900 C.E.)

Aztec Empire (early 1500s C.E.)

Inca Empire (around 1500 C.E.)

Between 300 and 1500 C.E., three major powers arose: the Maya and Aztecs in Mexico and Central America and the Incas in South America.

In this lesson, you explored the cultural achievements of the Maya, Aztecs, and Incas. All three peoples accomplished advances in science and technology, arts and architecture, and language and writing.

Achievements of the Maya The Maya are admired for their writing system, calendar, knowledge of astronomy, and architecture. They were able to calculate the length of a solar year and also developed the concept of zero. Maya steles and other structures stand today.

Achievements of the Aztecs The Aztecs are noted for their calendar and their massive temples, as well as their great capital city. People still travel to Mexico to visit the remains of Tenochtitlán and view the chinampas, the floating islands invented by the Aztecs.

Achievements of the Incas The Incas showed great skill in managing their huge empire and in engineering. They built an extensive road system of about 15,000 miles. Quipus allowed them to record and transport important information. They also made remarkable advances in medicine, such as a type of surgery called trephination.

Walking Across Space: Incan Rope Bridges

Talented engineers, the Incas developed a way to create safe bridges out of grass rope. The technology is still used today.

You're standing at the edge of a canyon high in the Andes Mountains looking down at a raging river far below. You look across to the other side and see that the only way to get there is to walk across a narrow rope bridge. You grit your teeth, step out into space, and feel the bridge sink beneath your weight. Will the bridge hold, or will it flip you over into the gorge below? Don't worry—this bridge was built by people who really know what they're doing!

The Incas lived in a land of high mountains separated by rivers and deep valleys. In order to help them travel and communicate, they built a vast system of roads, including amazing bridges that crossed the vast chasms between cliffs and canyons. These bridges were made of thick rope cables woven from grass. That's right—grass.

For centuries, these rope bridges played a critical role in transportation throughout the Andes Mountains. Massachusetts Institute of Technology (MIT) professor John Ochsendorf, a structural engineer who has spent years studying Incan rope bridges, thinks that the bridges were just as important as the Incan road system. They allowed the Incas to cross natural barriers, such as canyons and rivers. Without the amazing engineering that created these rope bridges, the Incas could not have connected the roads into the effective communication system that helped them create and control their large empire.

Bridges Made from Grass

A grass rope bridge is called a *Keshwachaka* in the Quechua language. According to Ochsendorf, there were two types of rope bridges: large and small. Each type was carefully planned and maintained. There is evidence that the Incan emperor himself drew plans for large bridges and made sure that they were repaired and protected.

Large bridges had a *Chaka Camayoc*, which means "bridgekeeper" in the Quechua language. Living at the bridge, the Chaka Camayoc was responsible for guarding and repairing it. Large bridges were usually located on the Royal Road, built between the present-day cities of Cuzco, Peru, and Quito, Ecuador.

Smaller bridges connected rural communities to one another and to the Royal Road. As part of their annual service to the empire, the local people worked together to repair or rebuild these bridges every year.

Building a Rope Bridge

The last remaining Incan rope bridge is believed to be located in the remote village of Huinchiri, Peru. It hangs about two hundred feet over the Apurimac River and spans a distance of over one hundred feet. People in the area use a modern metal bridge for everyday transportation across the river. But each year, Quechua villagers hold a three-day festival during which they cut down the old rope bridge and build a new one. Using weaving and construction techniques that have passed from generation to generation, they honor their culture and ancestors. Tourists come from around the world to watch the villagers rebuild the bridge.

During the festival, villagers organize the work in the same way it has been done for centuries. Each household is responsible for helping with one of four key tasks in constructing a bridge: making rope; braiding it into cables; repairing or rebuilding the stone anchors on either side of the river; and making the ties, the handrails, and a floor system.

The basic material that makes up the huge cables needed to hold up the bridge is a thin, two-ply rope that hundreds of families craft before the festival begins. They start by gathering dry stalks of grass and twisting them together. As they add grass, the rope becomes longer and longer. The villagers make the rope in lengths of about fifty yards until they have enough to create approximately ten miles of rope needed to build the bridge.

During a three-day festival, Quechua villagers rebuild a rope bridge over the Apurimac River in Peru, using the methods of their Incan ancestors. This photo demonstrates how heavy the rope is once the villagers finish making it.

To form the bridge, thick rope cables are first strung across the river using guide ropes and then anchored to each bank. Villagers will use timber or large stones to anchor the cables before constructing the rest of the bridge.

On the first day of the festival, construction begins. Families bring their handmade thin ropes to the bridge site. The chief bridge builder and the priest make offerings to *Paca Mama,* or Mother Earth. They ask that she bless their work, and they also request that the bridge stay safe and strong until they rebuild it next year.

Next, the men make large cables by braiding the thin ropes together, three at a time, to make thicker cables. Then they braid these cables together to make an even thicker one that will measure 6 inches in diameter, weigh about 150 pounds, and is 150 feet long. Six of these big cables are needed to make the bridge. Four cables form the bridge floor to carry the weight of people and animals, and the remaining two cables serve as handrails.

On the second day, the villagers cut down the old bridge and let it fall into the river. Then the men put up new cables. Using guide ropes attached to each cable, the men pull the cables across the river. They lift each one to the top of the cliff on the other side of the canyon and pull on the cables to make sure they are very tight. Finally, they connect the cables to strong timbers and stone anchor blocks located on each side of the river.

On the festival's final day, people gather at the bridge in colorful party clothes to watch the current bridgekeeper connect rope ties from the floor cables to the handrail cables. Other men lay down crossties, or sticks that will help keep the floor cables in place. Finally, they lay reed floor mats over the crossties and floor cables to complete the rope bridge.

Walking Across the Rope Bridge

Once the bridge is finished, a celebration begins. The villagers may offer guests or tourists a traditional Quechua meal before inviting visitors to walk across the bridge. Would you walk across it?

When Spanish soldiers first saw these bridges, they were so terrified that some soldiers crawled across them on their hands and knees. The bridges were strong and safe, however, and the Spanish even crossed them with their horses and cannons.

Ephraim George Squier, an American visitor to Peru in the 1870s, gave good advice about crossing the rope bridge over the Apurimac. He wrote, "It is usual for the traveler to time his day's journey so as to reach the bridge in the morning, before the strong wind sets in; for, during the greater part of the day, it sweeps up the canyon of the Apurimac with great force, and then the bridge sways like a gigantic hammock, and crossing is next to impossible."

An American scientist who crossed the newly rebuilt bridge described her walk with words that echoed those of Ephraim Squier from the 1870s. As she crossed slowly to keep the bridge from swaying too much or flipping over, she said, "I want to look down, but I'm afraid to look down, so I'm looking at everybody across. I know I can do this. I think I'm going to be sick. No, I'm not."

Many tourists accept the invitation to walk across the newly finished bridge. After watching its construction, they feel sure that it is sturdy and safe. Laboratory tests done by Professor John Ochsendorf show that the bridge is strong enough to hold 56 people spread out in a row across the bridge at one time, or 4,200 pounds of weight.

What the Incas accomplished centuries ago makes their Quechua descendants very proud. They know that their ancestors were gifted engineers. The Incas solved the problem of connecting roads by using the resources at hand. They also know that these bridges function well, since they were rebuilt again and again for more than 400 years, until metal bridges started to replace them in the 19th century. Anyone watching the Incas' Quechua descendants build a bridge in just three days will see that they are living examples of a way of life that has endured for centuries.

The Incan method of bridge building has been in use for over 400 years. This illustration, made in 1752, displays rope bridges similar to the one made by the villagers in Huinchiri.

The Incan bridge is extremely strong. It can hold more than two tons of weight at a time.

Civilizations of the Americas

About 2000 B.C.E.–1500 C.E.
Maya Civilization
The Maya civilization consists of independent states that contain elaborate stone cities and extensive farming communities.

About 200 C.E.–900 C.E.
Classic Period of Maya Civilization
Great cultural achievements, including the construction of observatories and the development of an accurate 365-day solar calendar, occur during the Classic period of Maya civilization.

2000 B.C.E.	1500 B.C.E.	1000 B.C.E.	500 B.C.E.	1 C.E.

About 300 B.C.E.
Maya Hieroglyphics Developed
The Maya develop hieroglyphics, which can be found on stoneware and other artifacts from the Pre-Classic period.

About 1200 C.E.
Incas Settle in Cuzco
The Incas settle in Cuzco, high in the Andes Mountains of southern Peru, where they live for more than 200 years before beginning to expand their empire.

About 1325 C.E.
Aztecs Build Tenochtitlán
The Aztecs build their capital of Tenochtitlán in Lake Texcoco by creating artificial islands called *chinampas*.

1438 C.E.–1532 C.E.
Inca Empire
The Inca Empire expands rapidly by forcing defeated tribes to adopt the ways of the Incas, including Incan-style villages with communal land.

1300s–1400s C.E.
Aztec Religious Practices
Aztec religious practices include human sacrifice.

1519–1532 C.E.
Aztec and Incan Civilizations Conquered
The Spanish defeat the Aztec Empire in 1519 and the Inca Empire in 1532.

1 C.E.   500 C.E.   1000 C.E.   1500 C.E.   2000 C.E.

1428 C.E.–1519 C.E.
Aztec Empire
The Aztec Empire expands to include most of central Mexico. The Aztecs make many enemies through warfare and an empire system based on tribute.

1479 C.E.
Aztec Calendar
The Aztecs adapt the Maya 365-day solar calendar, which is especially useful for farming since it tracks the seasons. This Aztec calendar dates to 1479.

1400s–1500s C.E.
Incan Roads and Bridges
The Incas build an extensive system of roads and bridges to help them manage their empire.

The Sultan Han in Turkey was built in 1229.
Here, traders would stop and rest as they
made their way along the Silk Road.

Physical Features of Afroeurasia

Arctic Circle

°N

SCANDINAVIA

Ob R.

Yenisey R.

Lena R.

Volga R.

URAL MTS.

ALPS

Mt. Elbrus
(5,642 m,
▲18,510 ft.)

GOBI
DESERT

Huang He

ATLAS MTS.

°N

Nile R.

ARABIAN
PENINSULA

Mt. Everest
(8,850 m,
29,035 ft.)
▲

HIMALAYA

Chang Jiang

Tropic of Cancer

S A H A R A

DECCAN
PLATEAU

ETHIOPIAN
HIGHLANDS

Congo R.

CONGO
BASIN

Kilimanjaro
(5,895 m,
▲19,341 ft.)

Equator

KALAHARI
DESERT

Tropic of Capricorn

ATLANTIC
°S
OCEAN

INDIAN OCEAN

°S

60°E

90°E

120°E

150°E

Antarctic Cir

Elevation

Feet	Meters
Over 10,000	Over 3,050
5,001–10,000	1,526–3,050
2,001–5,000	611–1,525
1,001–2,000	306–610
0–1,000	0–305
Below sea level	Below sea level

▲ Mountain peak

Present-day
boundary

N
W E
S

0   1,000   2,000 miles
0   1,000   2,000 kilometers
Miller Projection

180°

The Medieval World, 1200–1490

The continents of Africa, Europe, and Asia are sometimes referred to as Afroeurasia. The continents that form Afroeurasia are connected by both land masses and a shared history.

As you can see on the map, Africa and Europe have lower elevations, whereas large portions of Asia have higher elevation. The Himalayan Mountain Range forms a boundary between India and the rest of Asia and thus hindered trade in that region. However, the construction of the Silk Road helped to facilitate trade throughout Afroeurasia. Afroeurasia also has access to oceans and waterways, which made trade by sea possible.

The Mongol Empire also thrived in Afroeurasia. Once one of the largest land empires, the nomadic Mongols, led by Genghis Khan, conquered parts of Europe and Asia. After Genghis Khan's death, the Mongol Empire was divided into four khanates ruled by his sons and grandsons.

Due to the expanse of the empire, the Mongols controlled the entire Silk Road. The Mongols encouraged trade of goods and culture and worked to protect travelers along this route.

You will also study the development of networks of trade. Spices, rare in Europe yet plentiful in Asia and the Middle East, were a valuable trade commodity. The Silk Road promoted trade between the Middle East and Asia, and the access to waterways allowed sea trade with the Europeans. Not only goods were exchanged by these means, but also religion and naval technologies. These commercial, technological, and cultural exchanges ultimately helped create greater interconnectedness among the people of Afroeurasia.

Both the expansion of trade and the conquest by the Mongol Empire led to major changes throughout Afroeurasia. In this unit, you will explore how the world became more interconnected during the Medieval period.

Trade and Interconnectedness c. 1300

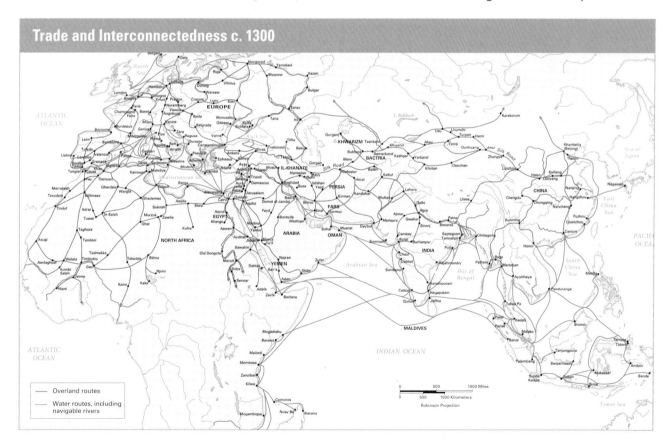

Legend:
— Overland routes
— Water routes, including navigable rivers

The Mongol Empire

How did the Mongol Empire destroy states and increase the interconnection of Afroeurasia?

Introduction

After 1000, agricultural innovations enabled increased productivity and population growth, which in turn fueled expansion of manufacturing and trade. States across Afroeurasia prospered as they produced and traded an increasing range of goods. Commercial, technological, and cultural exchange networks grew. Products, technologies, and ideas traveled across the continents. This helped create stronger links between states, particularly in the period from 1200 to 1490. These networks flourished thanks in part to the support of the Mongol Empire.

The Mongols emerged as an empire under the leadership of Genghis Khan, who united the Mongol and Central Asian tribes. He transformed these separate groups into a military power that used terror and destruction to expand its territory. Eventually, it reached across Asia and into Europe. After Genghis Khan's death, the empire continued under the leadership of his sons and grandsons, including his grandson Kublai Khan, who became emperor and united China under Mongol rule.

Although the Mongols used brutality to gain power and territory, they embraced the cultures and ideas of those they conquered. Moreover, their unified rule brought safety and stability to many parts of Asia. Greater trade and, thus, greater cultural exchange occurred as a result. Trade boomed, and ideas, innovations, and technologies moved within the Mongol Empire and beyond. However, the success of the Mongol Empire did not last long.

Here, you will study how Genghis Khan transformed nomadic tribes into an empire. You will learn how the Mongols ruled their empire across Asia and what life was like under their rule. Finally, you will examine the factors that led to the decline of the empire.

Social Studies Vocabulary

khagan

khan

khanate

shamanism

◀ Genghis Khan became the first Mongol emperor after he unified the Mongol and Central Asian tribes.

Mongol warriors were known for their horse riding skills, which gave them mobility. This Persian image shows Mongol warriors heading into battle in the 13th century.

Khan the title used by the rulers of Mongol tribes

khagan title in the Mongolian language equal to the status of emperor and used to refer to someone who rules a khanate or empire

khanates a territory led by a khan. The khanates were the four divisions of the empire

1. The Rise of the Mongol Empire

At its height, the Mongol Empire was one of the largest land empires that the world has ever seen. The Mongol Empire grew as a result of conquest across Eurasia. The Mongols were mobile warriors from the steppes north of China. Although their population was not large, they were viewed as fierce fighters. People feared the terror and destruction they brought.

The Mongols were not a single group, but rather they were groups of nomadic tribes. They were united by Genghis **Khan**, who brought together both the Mongol tribes and the Central Asian tribes. Genghis Khan was not the first nomadic conqueror to emerge, but he was the most successful. Enemies, rivals, and anyone who tried—or might try—to resist were eliminated. By destroying tribal loyalties, he reorganized the social structure and developed obedience to his rule. He was made **khagan** in 1206.

After uniting the Mongol and Central Asian tribes, Genghis Khan began to look beyond Mongolia to expand his territory. Initially, the Mongol military campaigns began as raids. However, as they became increasingly successful and met decreasing resistance, Genghis Khan decided to keep the conquered territories. As the Mongols gained new territories, advisers to the former rulers of these lands became advisers to Genghis Khan and his successors. They helped them recognize the importance of keeping (and not destroying) towns and the value of ruling over people who could produce taxable goods.

By 1225, the Mongols had taken provinces in China and regions of Central Asia. Some territories even asked the Mongols for protection. When Genghis Khan died in 1227, Mongol territory stretched across Asia.

2. The Empire after Genghis Khan's Death

After Genghis Khan's death, leadership passed to his sons and grandsons. His third son, Ögödei, became the overall ruler. Over time, the empire was divided into four **khanates**.

The Chagatai Khanate was led by the Genghis Khan's son Chagatai. It included the southern part of modern-day Xinjiang Uyghur Autonomous Region in China and parts of modern-day Uzbekistan, Kazakhstan, and Turkmenistan.

The Khanate of the Golden Horde was established by Batu, Genghis Khan's grandson. Batu's father, Jochi, was supposed to inherit the western portion of the Mongol Empire. However, he died before his father, so Batu became the leader of this region. Batu expanded the region. At its peak, the Golden Horde extended from Siberia to Poland and Hungary in the west and to the Black Sea and Caspian Sea in the south.

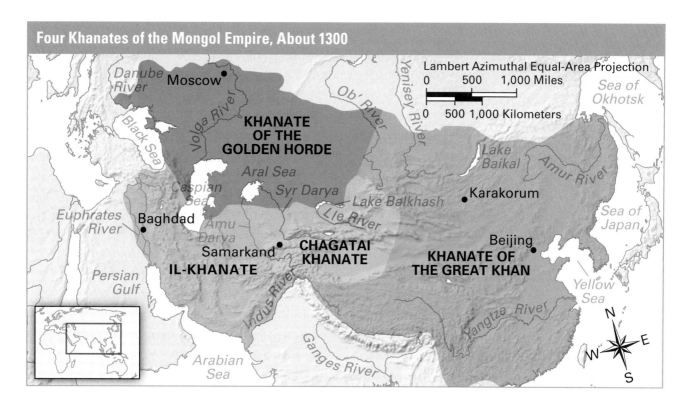

The Il-Khanate was created by another of Genghis Khan's grandsons, Hulagu, in 1256. Hulagu was given the task of extending Mongol power into Islamic regions in the Middle East. Before the rise of Hulagu, much of the region had been divided in minor kingdoms. In extending the Mongol Empire, Hulagu unified the region, including Persia, Syria, and part of Anatolia (modern-day Turkey). His army also defeated the Abbasid Caliphate, executed the last Abbasid caliph, and seized and destroyed Baghdad, the religious and cultural capital of Islam. Some feared that the Mongol Empire would destroy the Muslim world. However, Hulagu was defeated by Mamluk Egypt in 1260, after which he settled in Persia to rule.

The final khanate was the Khanate of the Great Khan, led by Kublai Khan, the grandson of Genghis Khan. Kublai Khan became the fifth emperor of the Mongol dynasty in 1260 and was the overlord of all four khanates. In 1279, Kublai Khan defeated the Song dynasty to complete the Mongol's conquest of China and became the first Yuan ruler of the nation. Like his grandfather, Kublai Khan depended on foreign advisers to help govern his empire. Although he embraced the Chinese way of governing, he got rid of civil service exams and replaced Confucian scholar-officials.

The conquest of China extended Mongol rule to the Pacific Ocean. Kublai Khan tried to push further south and east, but these attempts ultimately failed. His campaigns in Myanmar and Southeast Asia met with initial success, but then the Mongols were forced to withdraw. Attempts to invade Japan in 1274 and 1281 were disastrous failures.

By 1300, the Mongol Empire had been divided into four khanates. Each was led by one of Genghis Khan's family members.

shamanism Mongol religion characterized by a belief that gods, demons, and ancestral spirits respond to a shaman, a priest

3. Life Under the Mongols

The Mongol Empire has been noted for its brutal and destructive conquests. However, the Mongols were also known for their tolerant attitude toward different religions. The Mongols practiced **shamanism** and believed that forcing their religion on their conquered subjects would undermine their leadership. Rather, they allied themselves with members of the clergy to gain the support of members of each religion.

The Mongols were not merely tolerant of other religions; they also welcomed foreigners and foreign influences. Government advisers and administrators came from throughout the empire. Administrators of different ethnicities helped in the process of conquest by aiding communication between the Mongols and different groups. However, in China, the Mongols employed foreign administrators, including Persians and Turks, because they did not trust the Chinese.

Foreign influence also came from those who traveled from different parts of the world. Since the end of the Tang dynasty (907), most had traveled to China by sea because improved technology had made sea travel easier. Fewer traders used the Silk Road, the land route that linked the Mediterranean and China. This changed under the Mongol Empire, and trade boomed.

The Silk Road stretched from one side of Asia to the other, connecting China to the Middle East. The part of the road shown here links Sikkim, India, to China.

This Chinese coin from the 1300s is one example of cultural exchange on the Silk Road. The markings on it show a Tibetan-Mongolian inscription.

With much of Asia in Mongol hands, the entire Silk Road sat within the empire. Under the control of one government, the Silk Road became a safe route of travel. Additionally, the Mongols set up stations along the Silk Road so that travelers would have a place to eat and sleep. By welcoming traders and other foreigners, such as Marco Polo, who traveled by land and by sea, the Mongols encouraged trade and cultural exchange.

With increased travel within, and to and from, the Mongol Empire, new goods, ideas, and technologies spread throughout Afroeurasia. Technologies such as gunpowder, mechanical printing, and the blast furnace were brought west by those who had traveled from China. Knowledge about history, geography, science, medicine, and the arts reached different parts of the world as travelers learned new information and carried it with them. For example, cobalt blue dyes used in ceramics in the Il-Khanate made their way to artisans in China. Also, Mongol rulers embraced medical treatments from different ethnic and religious groups. Traders bought and sold textiles, glass, gemstones, porcelain, and spices. The opening of the Silk Road reduced the price of many goods, such as silk, because travel and security costs had decreased.

Despite the benefits brought by cultural exchange, Yuan policies about foreigners in China ultimately created division. This contributed to the decline of the empire.

4. The Decline of the Mongol Empire

After the death of Kublai Khan in 1294, Mongol rule became unstable as questions arose about succession. Between 1308 and 1333, there were eight emperors. Additionally, the Mongols depended on subjects and foreigners to run their empire. This weakened their power and caused feuds within governments.

At the same time, the Chinese were becoming increasingly angered by policies that favored Mongols and foreigners. Unlike the local population, they paid no taxes and received special privileges. In contrast, the Chinese were excluded from government positions and could not benefit from the empire's trade. Most Chinese people became poorer during the Yuan dynasty. Over the years, the Chinese increasingly resented these Mongol policies.

In the 14th century, anger and resentment resulted in peasant unrest. An uprising in 1368 ultimately brought down the empire and led to the creation of the Ming dynasty.

Elsewhere, new states and empires arose as the Mongol khanates fell. For example, Turkic groups such as the Uzbeks and Kazakhs emerged from the Golden Horde, and the Uzbeks briefly established their own empire. Further west, Turkic groups were instrumental in ending the Il-Khanate. Some Turkic groups had migrated west from Central Asia as part of Mongol policies or to avoid the Mongols. One such group was the Oghuz Turks, who moved to Anatolia. One of their leaders, Osman, established the Ottoman Empire in 1326. The Ottomans extended their power in the region over the next century, conquering all of Anatolia, Greece, and parts of the Balkans.

The Sher-Dor Madrasah in Samarkand was built in the 17th century, during the rule of the Shaybanid dynasty. This Uzbek dynasty was founded by descendants of Genghis Khan.

The Il-Khanate rulers led parts of the empire until 1353. Around 1300, this branch of the Mongol Empire lost contact with leaders in China. However, as in China, these rulers experienced disturbances and unrest. As the Il-Khanate declined, other empires also emerged, including the Safavid Empire in Persia in 1501 and the Mughul Empire in India in 1526. Babur, the first Mughul emperor—mughal is the Persian word for Mongol—even traced his lineage to Genghis Khan.

Although the khanates lost most of their power within 100 years of the uniting of the territory, the Mongol Empire achieved one of the largest land empires in the history of the world. The empire's approach to warfare, trade, and religion affected and influenced territories throughout Europe and Asia.

This statue of Kublai Khan sits at Shangdu, also known as Xanadu, the first capital of the Yuan dynasty. After his death, Mongol rule became unstable.

Lesson Summary

You have learned about the Mongol Empire, from rise to fall.

The Rise of the Mongol Empire Genghis Khan unified nomadic Mongol and Central Asian tribes. Under his leadership, these fierce warriors went from raiding groups to conquering their lands. By the time Genghis Khan died, the Mongol Empire controlled parts of China and Central Asia.

The Empire After Genghis Khan's Death After Genghis Khan's death, his sons and grandsons took over his empire. The empire was later divided into four khanates. Kublai Khan, Genghis Khan's grandson, eventually became the emperor. He unified China and established the Yuan dynasty.

Life Under the Mongols Although the Mongols were brutal in their conquest of foreign territory, they embraced foreigners and foreign ideas. They welcomed commercial, technological, and cultural exchange, which flourished across Afroeurasia.

Decline of the Mongol Empire After Kublai Khan's death, Mongol rule became unstable. The Mongols' power was further weakened by their dependence on subjects and foreigners to run their empire. As the empire fell apart, new states and empires arose, including the Ottoman Empire in Turkey, the Safavid Empire in Persia, and the Mughal Empire in India.

Lesson 32

Increasing Trade and Competition

How did increasing trade lead to the exchange of ideas and new conflicts?

Introduction

Between 500 and 1500 C.E., the need for long-distance trade became increasingly important. Between the different regions of the world, there was an imbalance of goods and resources both natural and human-made. This meant that people were unable to get certain goods or products from local sources. It motivated the need for exchange between different societies.

This imbalance of goods existed because different countries had their own unique features and climates. These different regions allowed people to produce different types of goods. China, Persia, Syria, and Egypt were able to produce goods such as silk, while India and Egypt produced cotton. The societies of West Africa had gold, and Southeast and South Asia were rich with spices.

Because most states and empires wanted access to goods that they couldn't produce themselves, these civilizations began to trade with one another. As they did, they began to build a network of trade routes that extended all across Africa, Europe, and Asia. Merchants trading along these routes brought not only goods, but also new religious and cultural ideas to the places they visited.

Many of these early trade networks were over land. However, as navigational technology developed—and European ambition to discover new and cheaper trade routes in the spice trade grew—explorers set out to discover new trade routes over water.

As these cultures interacted with one another, many different cultures chose to work together peacefully in order to trade and coexist. However, conflicts also emerged between different religions over land and resources.

◀ Pictured here is a map explorers would have used to find new trade routes at sea.

Social Studies Vocabulary

portolan charts

Moor

Pictured here are green black pepper pods, black peppercorns, and ground black pepper.

1. The Spice Trade

Today, your kitchen at home may be stocked with seasonings like cinnamon, ginger, and turmeric. Most of the spices you can find inexpensively at your local grocery store. But during the medieval period, these spices were remarkably valuable and rare. Many other goods were traded, but spices remain the oldest and arguably the most important commodity in the evolution of trade.

Most of these spices were grown in South Asia and Southeast Asia. For example, black pepper was found in India in the form of peppercorns. Cardamom, turmeric, ginger, and cloves also grew in these areas. Cinnamon was from Sri Lanka. Parts of Indonesia were known as the Spice Islands because of the rich supply of mace, nutmeg, and black pepper. Others like frankincense and myrrh were grown in the Middle East. Many of these spices can still be found in their countries of origin.

As early as 5,000 B.C.E. in the Middle East and Egypt, spices were used as medicines and in religious rituals. Cinnamon and nutmeg were used to preserve the dead during the embalming process. Rome began a spice trade with India for three centuries. Romans used spices in wine, lamp oils, perfumes, and incense. Different spices became important ingredients for cooking as well. For the bland dishes of the time, the extra bit of seasoning provided delicious flavors.

Europe, the center of medieval Christendom, had one of the least developed but fastest growing economies in Afroeurasia. The demand for goods, like spices, increased. However, although spices were found in various parts of the world, none were native to Europe. This made spice highly desirable. There was little Europe had in return for the foreign goods except for gold and silver. For a time, these items were the continent's only way to pay for the exotic items.

Before the Crusades, spices in Europe were costly and mainly used by the wealthy. A pound of saffron cost the same as a horse; a pound of ginger was as much as a sheep; two pounds of mace was worth as much as a cow. A German price table from 1393 lists a pound of nutmeg equaling seven fat oxen. Black pepper became the most sought after spice by Europeans.

As trade networks grew, trading cities surfaced and controlled the flow of goods between Europe, Asia, and the Middle East. Other goods, like Chinese rice, silk, tea, porcelain, and jade, also became popular trade items. In fact, much of the silver exported from Europe ended up in China. Many rulers saw the benefits of acting as intermediaries. Serving as trading posts, these cities could profit off taxes placed on trade.

Arabia, Syria, and Egypt provided well-organized markets along the major recognized spice routes. Trade was established on land and

Spices like these are still used today to help provide delicious flavors to food.

sea routes to Seville in Spain, Lisbon in Portugal, and the major port cities of England, Belgium, and the Netherlands. Italian ports, such as Venice and Genoa, grew quickly and prospered.

2. Cooperation and the Exchange of Ideas

Trade led to extensive economic growth in places around Afroeurasia. It also led to the diffusion of new ideas and religions.

This spread of beliefs allowed religions like Islam, Buddhism, and Hinduism to continue expanding in Asia. Monks, scholars, and merchants all traveled on various trade routes like the Silk Road. They would bring religious books, songs, and stories back to their own countries to teach people.

Christianity and Roman Catholic missionaries later followed as the Europeans began discovering and using more trade passages. Missionaries converted native peoples in South America, Africa, and Asia. The new religions were not always accepted and sometimes led to violent encounters. However, missionaries also protected indigenous people from the cruelty of Europeans.

Spread of Naval Ideas Naval technologies were exchanged throughout the centuries and improved upon as sea trade grew. From the 15th to the 17th centuries, the Spanish and Portuguese used ships called caravels. They were light and perfect for exploring. Over time, the sails on the caravels were improved to move across the water quicker than previous ships could. The lateen sail was shaped like a triangle and could move in almost any direction. This was the only method used for a long time. Later on the Europeans started using the square sail with the lateen. The square sail helped move ships forward if the wind was blowing from behind.

Another useful sailing device was the compass. The Chinese invented the compass in the 12th century. By the next century, the Islamic world and Europeans were using compasses too—though historians are unclear how the technology transferred. Compasses first helped sailors figure out wind direction. They were improved through magnetizing the pointer to point north.

Portolan charts, or sea maps, appeared around the same time Europeans began using magnetized compasses. They were first made in Italy and Spain in the 13th century. The charts were carefully made with rhumb lines (lines showing the direction of the winds or compass points), a compass, coastlines, and port names.

Astrolabes were used to determine latitude by measuring the angle between the horizon and the sun, moon, or stars. Astrolabes are also old instruments that were used since the Roman period. They weren't used on the sea until after the 1300s.

portolan charts navigational maps based on compass directions and observations of pilots at sea

This diagram of a compass was drawn in a 14th century manuscript called *Epistola de magnete*.

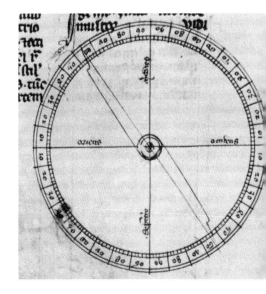

3. Conflicts Emerge

As trade increased, many new conflicts emerged. States of Western Christendom, such as England, France, Castile, and Aragon, grew powerful and centralized because of increasing access to trade. As these states came into contact with other countries throughout Afroeurasia, competition for land and resources, and between the followers of different religions, made many of these encounters violent.

Moor a name given to Muslims who lived in the Iberian peninsula

Religion in Iberia Spain was once called Iberia and was comprised of several different territories. In 711, Umayyad Muslim armies conquered most of Iberia. The Umayyad dynasty was the first great Muslim empire. They called their Iberian territory al-Andalus. Iberian Christians used the name "**Moors**" for Muslims in Iberia.

Under Umayyad rule, Córdoba was made the capital. The Muslim rulers remained tolerant of the other religions and allowed cultural diversity. Along with Jewish people, there were still small Latin Christian kingdoms in the north who were followers of the pope.

Through religious tolerance and the exchange of ideas, Iberia thrived culturally and economically. Lavish palaces, mosques, and libraries were built all over the city. Silks, leatherwork, and jewelry were prized throughout Europe and the East. Trade with Africa was prosperous and accessible through its many Mediterranean ports.

However, the peace did not last. Religion eventually became a problem as non-Muslim groups were taxed higher. As rulers changed over the years, the edicts for non-Muslim religions became stricter, and the small disputes grew larger. Christian territories banded together to overthrow the Iberian Muslim empire.

The Mosque-Cathedral of Córdoba, or Great Mosque of Córdoba, was built in the late 900s C.E.

Called the Reconquista, or Reconquest, the Christian kingdoms of Castile, Aragon, Asturias, Catalan, and others overthrew the Muslim rulers in al-Andalus. By mid-13th century, only the small kingdom of Granada belonged to the Muslims, but it was ultimately conquered as well.

Majorca and Trade With the help of the neighboring regions, and especially the Catalan navy, King James I of Aragon was able to conquer the island of Majorca in 1229. Situated off the eastern coast of the Iberian Peninsula, Majorca was first ruled by Muslim Almohad rulers. The Almohad was the group that governed after the Umayyad and Almoravid kingdoms fell.

Religious differences were only partially responsible for James actions. Majorca's position as a trading and shipping center for the western Mediterranean and the Maghrebi ports was also a major factor. These ports controlled the gold trade with Mali. During his rule of Aragon, James wrote an autobiography called The Book of Deeds. Its pages detail how Catalan merchants urged him to take over Majorca because they wanted to gain access to those markets.

> *Pere Martel, a citizen of Barcelona, who had great knowledge of the sea, invited me to dinner one day, and all the barons who were with me. Towards the end of dinner a conversation began among them. And I asked: "What kind of country is Majorca, and what is the extent of that kingdom?" They asked Pere Martel, because he was a shipmaster; and Pere Martel said that he would give an account of it, as he had been there once or twice. When dinner was over, they came before me, and said:*

> *My lord, we have asked Pere Martel about Majorca, and he has told us something we think will please you. It is a good-sized island, in the midst of other smaller islands, called Minorca, Ibiza, and Formentera, all of which are subject to the King of Majorca . . .*

As James gained control of Majorca, he created similar rules to the ones imposed by Muslims. Under his rule, non-Christian religions were tolerated and taxed. Jews traded and engaged in moneylending. They were also often contracted by the monarchy to collect royal taxes. James himself wrote that he would allow Muslims to stay in Majorca but if there was resistance, they would be exiled.

In the 1500s, when Ferdinand II of Aragon and Isabella I of Castille unified the two kingdoms of Iberia, Catholicism reigned supreme. In 1492, the Alhambra Decree was issued. Even though a large portion of the Spanish population was Jewish, the decree ordered them to leave Iberia. If Jews wanted to stay, they had to convert to Catholicism or be executed. Shortly after, Muslims were persecuted as well. In 1501, Muslims were ordered to convert or flee. Many people converted and stayed. By 1609, Muslim converts were expelled anyway.

Other European countries, such as England and France, also persecuted Jews. Over time, many of these European Jews fled to countries like Poland, where they were given security and rights. Other Jews fled to Russia and countries throughout eastern Europe.

A statue of King James I of Aragon can be found near the Royal Palace of Madrid in Spain.

4. Trade Leads to the Age of Exploration

As Europeans fought each other over religion and continued to war with Muslim empires, trade routes became more valuable. Several countries turned to military might to control the main trade ports and routes. Chiefly important were Venice and Genoa. In the 10th century, these Italian cities became rich and powerful through their domination of the spice trade routes.

Situated nearest the Mediterranean, Italy was able to secure a trade agreement with Byzantium. This paved the way for massive expansion in the Black Sea. Venice had a strong army and navy. With its military, the city was able to help secure various islands and create ports for trading. Many colonies were founded around the Black Sea. Genoa, while smaller, also had several naval victories. This allowed the growing city-state to establish its own trade ports and colonies.

Until the mid-15th century, Venice and Genoa monopolized all trade in Europe. Then war, growing trade demands within Europe, and a strong Venetian government toppled the competition. All goods, including the highly desired spice from the far East, Middle East, and parts of the western Mediterranean had to go through Venetian ports. Venice became the world's biggest trade center for Europe.

Genoa was one of the main trade ports in Europe up until the mid-15th century. It is still one of the major ports in Mediterranean today.

As Venice continued to control the major sea trade routes, the rest of Europe was looking for its own cheaper and quicker routes. Beginning in 1418, explorers were encouraged by Portugal's Prince Henry to chart new, more direct trade passages. Like many other countries, Portugal wanted to find a way to trade with India and Southeast Asia without using the Venetian ports.

Several other Portuguese explorers were able to discover new passages around the world. Vasco de Gama charted a route to India where he landed in Calicut and was able to trade his goods for cinnamon and pepper. Spain followed shortly afterwards in 1492 and funded the voyages of Christopher Columbus who claimed an island in the Caribbean Sea. Portuguese explorer Ferdinand Magellan also sailed under Spain's flag. He undertook a massive expedition along South America and across the Pacific Ocean.

The Discoveries Monument in Portugal was built to commemorate Prince Henry the Navigator.

Lesson Summary

In this lesson, you learned how trade, competition, and the exchange of new ideas like religion and technology led to the Age of Exploration.

Spice Trade Spices were used for centuries but during the Middle Ages, they became even more valuable. Spices were found in parts of the Middle East and Africa, but the most desired spices were in Southeast Asia.

Sharing Technology Technology was shared between nations through trade. Naval technologies continued to grow and develop as people borrowed ideas from the places that they visited. Ships like caravels were improved with better sails to travel across the sea faster. To aid in more accurate navigation, compasses, astrolabes, and sea charts were improved as well.

Religious Expansion Different religions tolerated one another for a time, but disputes turned violent and wars erupted. Forms of Christianity and Catholicism took over pushing out Islam and Judaism. Missionaries wanting to spread religion joined ships bound for new trade territories.

Trade Monopoly As trade grew and spice costs skyrocketed, Venice and Genoa took advantage of their position in the Black Sea. This gave the cities control over the most important trade route to Southeast Asia.

Age of Exploration Begins In response to Italy's trade monopoly, Europe began searching for cheaper, quicker journeys to trade with Southeast Asia. Starting with Portugal and Spain, explorers set sail to find new trade routes.

The Medieval World, 1200–1490

About 1111
Invention of the Compass
The Chinese begin using compasses for maritime navigation.

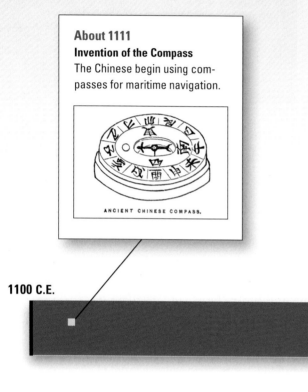

ANCIENT CHINESE COMPASS.

1229
Majorca Conquered
King James I gains control of Majorca.

1100 C.E.

1200 C.E.

1300 C.E.

1216–1227
Rise of Genghis Khan
After bringing together Mongol and Central Asian tribes, Genghis Khan rules and expands the Mongol Empire.

1368
Fall of the Mongol Empire
A peasant uprising brings down the empire and leads to the rise of the Ming Dynasty.

1300 C.E.

1400 C.E.

1500 C.E.

1279
Mongol Conquest of China
Kublai Khan defeats the Song dynasty to conquer China and become the first Yuan ruler of the nation.

1418
Exploration from Portugal
Portugal's Prince Henry starts sending explorers to chart new trade routes.

Unit 9

Europe's Renaissance and Reformation

The cathedral of Santa Maria del Fiore, also called the Duomo, is one of the most important buildings in Florence, Italy. Its construction ended in 1496 during the Renaissance. In this unit, you will find out what feature makes the cathedral so famous.

ICELAND

ATLANTIC
OCEAN

Norwegian
Sea

FAROE ISLANDS
(Den.)

SHETLAND ISLANDS
(U.K.)

Ben Nevis
(4,406 ft., 1,343 m)

BRITISH
ISLES

North
Sea

SCANDINAVIA

NORTHERN EUROPEAN PLAIN

Baltic Sea

Celtic
Sea

English Channel

Thames
River

Rhine River

Elbe River

Seine River

Loire River

CARPATHIAN MOUNTAINS

Danube River

Bay of
Biscay

Mont Blanc
(15,781 ft., 4,810 m)

A L P S

Po River

PYRENEES

IBERIAN
PENINSULA

Corsica

Adriatic Sea

APENNINES

BALKAN MTS

BALKAN
PENINSULA

Black Sea

Bosporus

Sardinia

Tiber
River

ITALIAN
PENINSULA

Tyrrhenian Sea

Balearic
ISLANDS

Strait of Gibraltar

Ionian
Sea

PELOPONNESUS

Aegean Sea

ASIA

Sicily

Mediterranean Sea

Crete

AFRICA

Elevation

Feet	Meters
Over 10,000	Over 3,050
5,001–10,000	1,526–3,050
2,001–5,000	611–1,525
1,001–2,000	306–610
0–1,000	0–305
Below sea level	Below sea level

▲ Mountain peak

Present-day
boundary

Arctic Circle

80°N
70°N
60°N
50°N
40°N

40°W
30°W
20°W
10°W
0°
10°E
20°E
30°E
40°E
50°E
60°E
70°E
80°E

0   250   500 miles
0   250   500 kilometers
Lambert Azimuthal Equal-Area

N
W   E
S

Europe's Renaissance and Reformation

Understanding the political geography of Europe during the 1300s to the 1600s will give you a foundation on which to build your upcoming study of two crucial periods: the Renaissance and the Reformation.

Much of the power in Europe from the 1300s to the 1600s lay in three major areas: the city-states of Italy, the Papal States, and the Holy Roman Empire.

During these years, Italy was not the unified country it is today. Instead, it was a collection of city-states, or large, self-governing cities and their surrounding communities and farms. From the 1300s to the 1600s, several of these independent city-states prospered. Places such as Florence, Venice, and Milan grew in power and influence, due mostly to an increase in trade and banking.

Additionally, the city of Rome was a prosperous and important city that belonged to an area known as the Papal States. These were territories in central Italy controlled by the pope, the spiritual leader of the Roman Catholic Church. Life was changing in Europe in the 1500s, however, and the power of the Church and the Papal States was just beginning to weaken.

To the north of the Papal States and the Italian city-states lay the Holy Roman Empire. Established by King Charlemagne in the 700s, the empire during the period of the Renaissance encompassed a large piece of land that stretched to the North Sea. Its borders changed often, as territories were won and lost. Within the Holy Roman Empire, powerful princes ruled over smaller territories. The influence of the empire as a whole, however, was beginning to weaken, despite repeated attempts by successive emperors to gain an advantage over the pope and the Catholic Church.

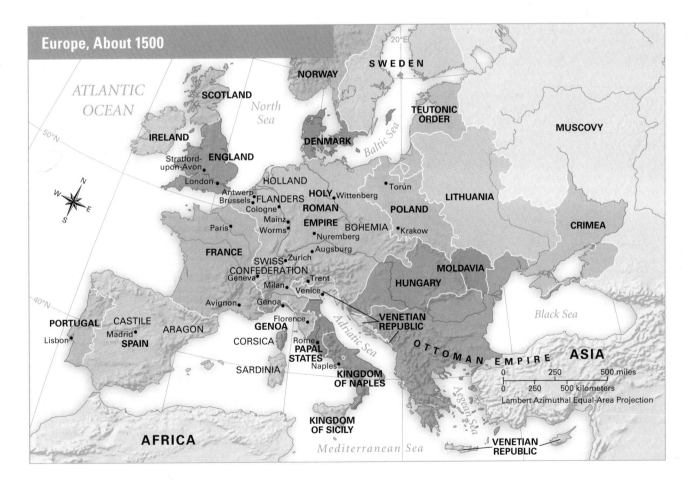

Europe, About 1500

Lesson 33

The Renaissance Begins

What changes in Europe led to the Renaissance?

Introduction

Toward the end of the Middle Ages, a great flowering of culture called the Renaissance began in Italy. The Renaissance inspired interest in art and education throughout Europe.

Renaissance is a French word that means "rebirth." Historians use the word to describe the rebirth of widespread interest in classical art and learning that occurred in Europe from about 1300 to about 1600 C.E. "Classical" refers to the cultures of ancient Greece and Rome. Although there was no sudden end to the Middle Ages, the Renaissance changed many aspects of people's lives over time.

Medieval European society was based on feudalism. Most people lived on feudal manors. The Roman Catholic Church encouraged people to think more about life after death than about daily life on Earth. Few people, except for the clergy, were educated.

By the Late Middle Ages, changes were occurring that paved the way for the Renaissance. Trade and commerce increased, cities grew larger and wealthier, and newly wealthy merchants and bankers supported the growth of arts and learning. In addition, a renewed interest in ancient cultures started a flood of new ideas. Greek and Roman examples inspired new styles of architecture, approaches to the arts, and ways of thinking.

Beginning in Italy, a philosophy called *humanism* developed. Humanists believed in the worth and potential of all individuals and balanced religious faith with belief in the power of the mind. This thinking contributed to the burst of creativity during the Renaissance.

In this lesson, you will explore how the Renaissance differed from the Middle Ages and classical times. Then you will examine some changes in European life that led to the Renaissance.

Social Studies Vocabulary

city-state

classical art

humanism

humanities

individualism

Renaissance

republic

◀ Built in 1502, the Tempietto chapel in Rome reinterprets the classical architecture of Greece and Rome.

Renaissance a great flowering of culture, based on classical Greek and Roman ideas and art, that began in Italy in the Late Middle Ages and spread throughout Europe

classical art art influenced by the styles and techniques of ancient Greece and Rome

This Roman copy of a Greek statue was created in 450 B.C.E. It shows a discus thrower and celebrates the classical ideals of athleticism, balance, and power.

1. What Was the Renaissance?

The **Renaissance** began in Italy in the 1300s and spread to other parts of Europe in the 1400s and 1500s. Let's look more closely at this "great rebirth" of interest in **classical art** and learning. Then we will explore the link between the Renaissance and the classical world.

Renewed Interest in the Classical World The Renaissance began with the rediscovery of the classical world of ancient Greece and Rome. After the fall of Rome in the 5th century C.E., classical culture was never entirely forgotten. Clergy of the Roman Catholic Church helped keep knowledge of ancient times alive by copying documents that survived from the classical period. However, this knowledge reached relatively few people during most of the Middle Ages.

In the Late Middle Ages, merchants and Crusaders returned with goods and ideas from the East, including classical learning that had been preserved in the Byzantine Empire. Europeans also read classical works that came to them from Muslim scholars.

This flow of ideas led to a rediscovery of Greek and Roman culture. Scholars started collecting and reading ancient manuscripts from monasteries, and artists and architects studied classical statues and buildings. The renewed interest in classical culture led to the great flowering of art and learning that we call the Renaissance.

Exploring the Rebirth of Classical Ideals Through Art We can trace the link between the classical world and the Renaissance by looking at art. Let's explore some of the characteristics of art from classical, medieval, and Renaissance times.

Classical Art The classical period lasted from about 500 B.C.E. to 500 C.E. The classical artists of Greece and Rome created sculptures, pottery, murals, and mosaics to show the importance of ordinary people and civic leaders, as well as gods and goddesses. Here are additional characteristics of classical art:

- Artists valued balance and harmony.
- Figures were lifelike but often idealized, or more perfect than in real life.
- Figures were nude or draped in togas, or robes.
- Bodies looked active, and motion was believable.
- Faces were calm and without emotion.
- Scenes showed either heroic figures or real people doing tasks from daily life.
- In paintings, there was little background or sense of perspective. *Perspective* is a visual technique used to make people and objects look closer or farther away and to give realistic depth to a scene.

Medieval Art The medieval period lasted from about 500 to about 1300 C.E. Medieval artists created stained glass windows, sculptures, illuminated manuscripts, paintings, and tapestries, all of which were primarily used to teach religion to people who could not read or write. Here are additional characteristics of medieval art:

- Most art was religious, showing Jesus, saints, and people from the Bible.
- Important figures in paintings were shown larger than others around them.
- Figures looked stiff, with little sense of movement.
- Figures were fully dressed in stiff-looking clothing.
- Faces were serious and showed little expression.
- Painted figures looked two-dimensional, or flat.
- Paint colors were bright.
- Backgrounds were mostly one color, often blue or gold.

This example of medieval art was created for a church in France in 1120 C.E. Jesus, the central figure, is shown as much larger than the people around him.

This example of Renaissance art is titled *The School of Athens*. It was painted by the artist Raphael around 1510. Ancient Greek philosophers, such as Plato and Aristotle, are shown here, surrounded by some of the Renaissance artists they later inspired.

Renaissance Art The Renaissance lasted from the 1300s to the early 1600s. Artists used new techniques to create sculptures, murals, drawings, and paintings. The aim of much Renaissance art was to show the importance of people and nature, not just religious ideas. Here are additional characteristics of Renaissance art:

- Artists showed religious and nonreligious scenes.
- Art reflected a great interest in nature.
- Figures looked lifelike and three-dimensional, reflecting an increasing knowledge of anatomy.
- Figures were shown in action.
- Figures were either nude or clothed.
- Scenes showed real people doing everyday tasks.
- Faces expressed what people were feeling.
- Colors were shown responding to light.
- Paintings were often symmetrical, or balanced, with the right and left sides having identical elements.
- Full backgrounds showed perspective, adding depth.

If you compare classical, medieval, and Renaissance styles, you can see that Renaissance artists were inspired more by classical art than by medieval art. Like classical artists, Renaissance painters and sculptors depicted subjects that were not always religious. They tried to capture the way things look in the real world by making people appear more lifelike and engaged in everyday activities.

Renaissance art reflects a rebirth of interest in the classical world. What changes brought about this revival of classical culture?

2. The Growth of Trade and Commerce

One reason for the flowering of culture during the Renaissance was the growth of trade and commerce. Trade brought new ideas as well as goods into Europe. A bustling economy created prosperous cities and new classes of people with the wealth to support art and learning.

Increased Contact Between East and West Starting in the 11th century, the Crusades strengthened contacts between western Europe and Byzantine and Muslim cultures. Merchants brought goods and ideas from the East that helped to reawaken interest in classical culture. In the 13th century, the Mongol conquests in Asia made it safer for traders to travel along the Silk Road to China. The tales of the Italian traveler Marco Polo sparked even greater interest in the East. Food, art, and luxury goods, such as silk and spices, moved along the trade routes linking Europe to Africa and Asia.

Cities, such as Venice and Genoa in Italy, were centrally located on the trade routes that linked western Europe with the East. They became bustling, prosperous trading centers that attracted merchants and customers, as did cities in northern Europe, such as Bruges and Brussels. Trade ships carried goods to England, Scandinavia, and present-day Russia by way of the English Channel and the Baltic and North seas. Towns along the routes connecting southern and northern Europe, such as Cologne and Mainz in Germany, provided inns and other services for traveling merchants.

This 15th-century French illustration shows people exchanging goods for money in a shop in a Renaissance town.

city-state an independent state consisting of a city and its surrounding territory

A New Economy The increase in trade led to a new kind of economy. During the Middle Ages, people bartered, or traded, goods. By the Renaissance, people were using coins to buy merchandise, which created a money economy. Coins came from many places, so money changers were needed to convert one type of currency into another.

As a result of all this activity, craftspeople, merchants, and bankers became more important in society. Craftspeople produced goods that merchants traded across Europe, while bankers exchanged currency, loaned money to merchants and rulers, and financed their own businesses.

Some merchants and bankers grew very rich, and their abundant wealth enabled them to make their cities more beautiful. In addition to helping found universities, wealthy patrons commissioned (ordered and paid for) new buildings and art. Prosperous Renaissance cities grew into flourishing educational and cultural centers.

3. The Influence of Italian City-States

The Renaissance began in northern and central Italy. One reason why it began there was the prosperity of Italian **city-states**.

In the Late Middle Ages, most of western Europe was made up of fiefs ruled by nobles, who in turn were ruled by monarchs. In Italy, however, growing towns developed into independent city-states. Each city-state consisted of a powerful city and the surrounding **territory**, which might include other towns.

This is a late-15th-century map of Florence, one of Italy's most powerful city-states. Outside the walls of Florence, you can see smaller communities.

FIORENZA

Major Italian City-States During the Renaissance

Venice
Milan
Mantua
Padua
Turin
Parma
Genoa
Ferrara
Bologna
Florence
Ravenna
Siena
Urbino
Rome
Naples

Adriatic Sea

Tyrrhenian Sea

Mediterranean Sea

Naples
Papal States
Siena
Florence
Milan
Genoa
Venice
Sicily
Minor city-states

0 100 200 miles
0 100 200 kilometers
Lambert Azimuthal Equal-Area Projection

N
W E
S

At the time of the Renaissance, Italy was not a unified nation. It was divided into many different city-states, some of which were extremely powerful.

The Italian city-states conducted their own trade, collected their own taxes, and made their own laws. Some, such as Florence, were **republics** that were governed by elected councils.

In theory, the power in republics belonged to the people, but in reality, it often lay in the hands of rich merchants. During the Middle Ages, guilds of craftspeople and merchants became very powerful. During the Renaissance, groups of guild members, called boards, often ruled Italian city-states. Although boards were supposed to change members frequently, wealthy families often gained long-term control. As a result, some city-states were ruled by a single rich family, such as the Medici (MED-uh-chee) family in Florence.

Trade made the Italian city-states dazzlingly wealthy. Italy's central Mediterranean location in the middle of the trade routes connected distant places with the rest of western Europe. People from all over Europe came to northern Italy to buy, sell, and do their banking.

Some Italian city-states developed specializations. Florence became a center for cloth making and banking. Milan produced metal goods and armor. The port city of Genoa was a trade center for ivory and gold from northern Africa. Venice, the most powerful city-state, had hundreds of ships that controlled the trade routes in the Mediterranean Sea. Silk, spices, and perfume from Asia flowed into Venice.

republic a form of government in which citizens elect representatives to rule for them

The city-states' wealth encouraged a boom in art, literature, and learning. Rich families paid for the creation of statues, paintings, beautiful buildings, and elegant avenues. They built new centers of learning, such as universities and hospitals. From the city-states of Italy, Renaissance ideas spread to the rest of Europe.

4. The Growth of Humanism

The interest in learning during the Renaissance was spurred on by **humanism**. This way of thinking sought to balance religious faith with an **emphasis** on individual dignity and an interest in nature and human society.

Humanism first arose in Italy as a result of the renewed interest in classical culture. Many early humanists eagerly hunted for ancient Greek and Roman books, coins, and other artifacts that could help them learn about the classical world.

One of the first humanists was an Italian poet named Francesco Petrarch, who was particularly interested in old books. He searched for them all over Europe and encouraged his friends to bring him any they found. Eventually, he created a large collection of ancient Latin and Greek texts, which he made available to other scholars.

Scholars from all over Europe traveled to Italy to learn about the new humanist ideas inspired by classical culture. In addition to reading classical history and poetry, they studied such subjects as art, architecture, government, and language. They began to ask probing questions. What did classical artists find most beautiful about the human body? How did the Romans construct their buildings?

In their studies of classical culture, humanists discovered a new way of looking at life. They began to create a philosophy based on the importance and dignity of each individual. Humanists believed that all people have the ability to control their own lives and achieve greatness. In education, they stressed study of the **humanities**—a group of subjects that focus on human life and culture, which includes grammar, rhetoric (the study of persuasive language), history, poetry, and ethics (the study of moral values and behavior).

Humanists tried to put ancient ideas into practice. Architects, for example, studied Greek and Roman ruins and designed buildings with pillars, arches, and courtyards like those of classical buildings.

The humanists did not simply imitate classical achievements, but rather they tried to improve on the work of the ancient Greeks and Romans. In universities, scholars began to teach methods of observation and experimentation. Renaissance scientists proposed new ideas about the stars and planets. Artists and students of medicine closely studied human anatomy. Poets wrote about both religious subjects and everyday experiences. Writers produced works of history and studies of politics.

Francesco Petrarch is considered to be the founder of Italian Renaissance humanism. A well-known poet, he wears a laurel wreath in this portrait to symbolize his crowning as poet laureate in Rome in 1341.

humanism a philosophy that tries to balance religious faith with an emphasis on individual dignity and an interest in nature and human society

humanities collectively, areas of study that focus on human life and culture, such as history, literature, and ethics

The influence of classical ideals changed ideas about government. Humanists separated the state and its right to rule from the Church and, in doing so, helped lay the foundation for modern thinking about politics and government.

Humanist ideals also changed people's thinking about social standing. In feudal times, people were born into a certain status in society. If someone was born a peasant, he or she would always have less status than a noble. In general, Renaissance thinkers prized individual achievement more than a person's class or family. This emphasis on **individualism** was an enormous shift from medieval thinking.

The humanists' new ideas sometimes brought them into conflict with the Catholic Church. The Church taught that laws were made by God and that those who broke them were sinful. It encouraged people to follow its teachings without question to save their souls. For the Church, life after death was more important than life on Earth. In **contrast,** humanists believed that people should use their minds to question everything. Most tried to balance religious faith and its emphasis on the afterlife with an active interest in daily life, but some directly challenged teachings that were important to the Church. An Italian humanist, Giordano Bruno, paid for his ideas by being burned at the stake.

individualism the belief in the importance of an individual's achievements and dignity

Giordano Bruno, a humanist scholar, was noted for being a philosopher, astronomer, and mathematician.

Lesson Summary

In this lesson, you explored the beginnings of the period in Europe that followed the Middle Ages, called the Renaissance.

What Was the Renaissance? The Renaissance was a flowering of art and learning that was inspired by a rediscovery of the classical cultures of Greece and Rome. It began in Italy around 1300 and spread throughout Europe, lasting to the early 1600s.

The Growth of Trade and Commerce Italy's location made it a perfect crossroads for trade between Europe and Asia, which began to increase at this time. This growth of trade and commerce created prosperous cities and classes of people with enough wealth to support education and the arts.

The Influence of Italian City-States The developing wealth and power of the individual Italian city-states helped to promote and spread Renaissance ideas. Civic leaders and wealthy private individuals paid for new works of art and built new centers of learning.

The Growth of Humanism The new philosophy of humanism spurred interest in learning and fresh ways of thinking. Humanists, such as Francesco Petrarch, sought to balance religious faith with an emphasis on individualism, the workings of the natural world, and human society. They sought to separate the workings of government from the Church.

How Does Renaissance Art and Literature Reflect Humanist Ideals?

If you compare art and literature from the Renaissance to earlier examples from medieval times, you will notice that the Renaissance placed less emphasis on religion and more on individuals in everyday life. Much of the Renaissance culture grew out of a philosophy of humanism. You will analyze primary sources by a humanist artist and three humanist writers and explore what their work reveals about this philosophy. Then you will construct a claim about how Renaissance art and literature reflect humanist ideals.

St. Peter Healing the Sick with His Shadow, an example of Renaissance art, can be seen in Brancacci Chapel in Florence, Italy. The artist Masaccio painted this in the 1420s as one of many scenes of St. Peter's life.

The work of Renaissance scholars, artists, and writers reflected ideas of humanism, a way of thinking that focuses on human potential and individual accomplishments. Humanism began in Italy in the 13th century, and by the 15th century it had become popular throughout Europe. Humanism affected art, literature, education, and science that was developed at the time. It encouraged attention on what individuals could accomplish, regardless of the status of their families. Art and literature portrayed a balance of religious faith with an interest in nature and human society. In education and in fields of science, humanism encouraged questioning, observations, and experimentation.

Examine this painting entitled *St. Peter Healing the Sick with His Shadow*. It is a fresco painting created by the artist Masaccio in the 1420s and can be seen today in the Brancacci Chapel located in Florence, Italy. A fresco is a painting on a wall or ceiling. The artist used light and shade to highlight the facial expressions of the people in the scene. As you look closely at the painting's details, what do you notice about the background? How would you describe the facial expression of each person portrayed by the artist? What elements of humanism can you identify in this piece of Renaissance art?

Historians examine the works of Petrarch to learn about the development of the philosophy of humanism during the Renaissance. Petrarch was an Italian scholar, writer, and poet who was born in Tuscany in 1304. He became a priest, but unlike many priests before him, he emphasized the importance of balancing Christian beliefs with classical learning of literature and art. Petrarch believed that a powerful deity guides the world, and humans are at the center of that world.

In addition to his involvement in religion, Petrarch had an inquiring mind and a love of poetry. During his lifetime, he wrote more than 300 love sonnets to a woman named Laura. A sonnet is a type of poem that often has a specific line count and number of syllables in each line. In these sonnets, Petrarch describes his intense feelings for Laura. His poems inspired other writers to use a similar style of emotional poetry, and this new style of writing on secular (nonreligious) subjects in a language other than Latin became hallmarks of Renaissance writing.

Read this sonnet from Petrarch's collection. What is the main message of this poem? What secular language is used, and what religious language is used? Which humanist ideas can you identify in the poem?

The Italian writer and poet Francesco Petrarco, known as Petrarch, is considered to be the founder of Italian Renaissance humanism. This painting of him was a fresco transferred to canvas around 1450.

Sonnet CXXVI

HE EXTOLS THE BEAUTY AND VIRTUE OF LAURA.

In what ideal world or part of heaven
Did Nature find the model of that face
And form, so fraught with loveliness and grace,
In which, to our creation, she has given
Her prime proof of creative power above?
What fountain nymph or goddess ever let
Such lovely tresses float of gold refined
Upon the breeze, or in a single mind,
Where have so many virtues ever met,
E'en though those charms have slain my bosom's weal?
He knows not love who has not seen her eyes
Turn when she sweetly speaks, or smiles, or sighs,
Or how the power of love can hurt or heal.

—*Petrarch, 14th century*

In addition to being a poet, Petrarch was a scholar who traveled to libraries throughout Europe to study classical writing. He wrote an epic poem about war and a series of biographies about heroes. An epic poem is a long, serious poem that tells a story about an event.

Petrarch also wrote hundreds of letters to express his thoughts and ideas. He wrote to friends, family, and even historical figures whom he did not personally know. These letters shed more light on Petrarch's philosophy and on humanism. Around 1340, Petrarch's writing showed that he struggled to explain the relationship between his intense faith in God and his interest in worldly and individualistic endeavors.

This passage is from a letter that Petrarch wrote to his brother Gherardo, who had entered a monastery and devoted his life to religion. Written in the mid-1300s, Petrarch talks about whether theology (the study of religion) can coexist with poetry. He points to examples of poetry in Scriptures (the Bible). According to this passage, what does Petrarch say is the relationship between poetry and religious texts? What argument does Petrarch make in this letter, and how does it relate to humanism?

On the Nature of Poetry

I judge, from what I know of your religious fervour, that you will feel a sort of repugnance toward the poem which I enclose in this letter, deeming it quite out of harmony with all your professions, and in direct opposition to your whole mode of thinking and living. But you must not be too hasty in your conclusions. What can be more foolish than to pronounce an opinion upon a subject that you have not investigated? The fact is, poetry is very far from being opposed to theology. Does that surprise you? One may almost say that theology actually is poetry, poetry concerning God. To call Christ now a lion, now a lamb, now a worm, what pray is that if not poetical? And you will find thousands of such things in the Scriptures, so very many that I cannot attempt to enumerate them . . .

But you will object, and say, "I certainly can believe the saint, if not the other learned men; and yet the fact remains that the sweetness of your poetry is inconsistent with the severity of my life." Ah! but you are mistaken, my brother. Why, even the Old Testament fathers made use of poetry, both heroic song and other kinds. Moses, for example, and Job, and David, and Solomon, and Jeremiah. Even the psalms, which you are always singing, day and night, are in metre, in the Hebrew . . .

—Petrarch, mid-1300s

Another influential writer of the Renaissance was Giovanni Boccaccio. He often wrote on medieval themes, such as chivalry, but his work also reflected humanist themes, such as love, with real-life details. Boccaccio met Petrarch in Florence in 1350, a moment that became a turning point in his life. Boccaccio respected the older Petrarch who offered him advice and counselling, and the two exchanged ideas that shaped their humanist writing.

At the time of their meeting, Boccaccio was working on *The Decameron*, which he wrote between 1348 and 1353. The book is comprised of 100 fictional stories told by 10 fictional characters who have fled from Florence during the Black Death. Each of the 10 people takes turns telling stories on themes such as virtue, tragic love, and trickery. The stories reflect Boccaccio's ideas of human nature.

This passage is from the Introduction to *The Decameron* and describes how people are coping with the tragic conditions of the Black Death in Europe. What mood does Boccaccio set with this introduction? How do people respond to the fear of the deadly plague?

Consider the examples of art and literature that you've just examined. How does each reflect the influence of humanism that was evolving at the time? Use these sources to write an argument about how Renaissance art and literature reflect humanist ideals.

Giovanni Boccaccio was an Italian poet and scholar whose writing represented humanism during the Renaissance. He wrote stories and poems that reflect realistic aspects of human nature, including his famous *Decameron* about 10 characters that have fled from the Black Death.

The Decameron

From these things and many others like unto them or yet stranger divers fears and conceits were begotten in those who abode alive, which well nigh all tended to a very barbarous conclusion, namely, to shun and flee from the sick and all that pertained to them, and thus doing, each thought to secure immunity for himself. Some there were who conceived that to live moderately and keep oneself from all excess was the best defence against such a danger; wherefore, making up their company, they lived removed from every other and shut themselves up in those houses where none had been sick and where living was best; and there, using very temperately of the most delicate viands and the finest wines and eschewing all incontinence, they abode with music and such other diversions as they might have, never suffering themselves to speak with any nor choosing to hear any news from without of death or sick folk. Others, inclining to the contrary opinion, maintained that to carouse and make merry and go about singing and frolicking and satisfy the appetite in everything possible and laugh and scoff at whatsoever befell was a very certain remedy for such an ill.

—Giovanni Boccaccio, mid-14th century

Lesson 34

Florence: The Cradle of the Renaissance

What advances were made during the Renaissance?

Introduction

The Renaissance began in 14th-century Italy. During this time, the Italian city-state of Florence was home to many advances, leading it to be called the "cradle of the Renaissance."

Florence is located on the Arno River, just north of central Italy. Between 1300 and 1600, it was home to some of the greatest artists and thinkers of the Renaissance.

During the Renaissance, Florence was—as it still is—a beautiful city. One of its most notable buildings is the cathedral of Santa Maria del Fiore with its towering *duomo* (DWOH-moh), or dome. The cathedral was the center of the city's religious life. Nearby is the Palazzo Vecchio (VEK-ee-oh), or Old Palace, which was the headquarters of the city government. The grand Palazzo Medici was the home of Florence's ruling family, the Medici. A more humble house was the Casa di Dante (kah-sah dee DAHN-tay), or Dante's House. Dante is one of Italy's most celebrated poets.

Florence was the banking center of Europe during the Renaissance. People came to the Mercato Nuovo to trade their coins for florins, the gold coins of Florence. Another popular spot in the city was the Ponte Vecchio, a beautiful stone bridge that spanned the Arno River and, even today, is lined with the shops of fine jewelers and goldsmiths.

Florence's wealth helped to make it a leading cultural center of the Renaissance. In this lesson, you will explore Renaissance Florence's architecture and engineering, painting, sculpture, literature, science, and mathematics. You will also find out about Florentine politics, commerce, and trade.

Social Studies Vocabulary

Dante Alighieri

Donatello

Florence

Leonardo da Vinci

Michaelangelo

Niccolò Machiavelli

secular

◀ The city of Florence, Italy, was the center of Europe's Renaissance.

During the Renaissance, the Palazzo Vecchio housed the government of Florence. Today, city officers are still in the building, but parts are also a museum.

1. The City of Florence

Florence was Italy's leading cultural center during the Renaissance. The city was the birthplace of the great poet Dante Alighieri (ahl-ee-GAIR-ee). The famed painter and sculptor Michelangelo grew up there, as did the brilliant thinker and artist Leonardo da Vinci. Other Florentines, such as the sculptor Donatello and the painter Botticelli, also achieved great works of art, wealth, and fame during the Renaissance.

What factors helped Florence to become such a wealthy city? One answer is its location. Renaissance Italy was divided into city-states, one of which was Florence. The city's location on the Arno River made it an important center for trade and commerce. Florence became the hub of woolen-cloth trading for all of Europe. In the early 14th century, Florence also became Europe's banking center. About 100,000 people lived inside the city walls.

Renaissance Florence was dominated by a single family known as the Medici, who had acquired their wealth through banking. With their help, Florence became the banking center of Europe.

Banking, along with the wool trade, created wealth that supported **intense** cultural activity in Florence. The city and its rich residents could afford to be patrons of talented artists and thinkers. The Medici family, for example, spent lavish sums on art. Their home was a gathering place for artists, such as Michelangelo, philosophers, and poets.

Over time, Florentines inspired still more creative activity. People learned from one another, and they sometimes competed to produce even greater works of art. Florentines were also influenced by ideas from other places since the city drew travelers from many parts of the world. Some came to do business. Some came to study art with Florence's master artists. Others came to learn at the city's schools and libraries. These visitors brought new ideas, goods, and technologies to the city.

Florentines were also inspired by the freedom of ideas that was at the core of humanism. Humanists prized the individual and tried to look with fresh eyes at nature and human society. You will see the influence of humanism throughout this lesson as you study examples of Renaissance advances.

2. Advances in Architecture and Engineering

Like humanist scholars of the Renaissance, architects and engineers were also influenced by classical ideas. Renaissance architects studied Greek and Roman ruins, modeling their own buildings on what they learned. They were particularly attracted to rounded arches, straight columns, and domed roofs.

Renaissance Architecture and Engineering Renaissance architects also added their own ideas to classical building styles. During the Renaissance, wealthy families built private townhouses known as *palazzi* (pahl-AH-tzee), which is Italian for "palaces." Many had shops on the ground floor and homes above. Most *palazzi* were built around a private courtyard, which might contain statues or other works of art.

Public spaces were often influenced by humanist ideals. For example, humanists valued good citizenship. Architects designed public buildings with outdoor plazas where citizens could gather in settings that were grand, yet welcoming.

Innovations in engineering made new kinds of architecture possible. One of the most impressive architectural feats of the Renaissance is Santa Maria del Fiore, the great cathedral in Florence. Florentines started building this eight-sided cathedral in 1296, but they had to leave an opening for the dome because, at the time, they did not know how to build a sufficiently large dome that would not collapse. It took a Renaissance architect, Filippo Brunelleschi (feel-EE-poh broon-el-ES-key), to solve the problem.

The dome of Santa Maria del Fiore in Florence rises from the octagonal (eight-sided) cathedral. The dome's design is one of the great engineering achievements of the Renaissance.

Building Florence's Dome Brunelleschi had studied ancient ruins in Rome and had also learned about the mathematics involved in constructing buildings. The dome he designed for the cathedral required true engineering genius. It used no internal support beams or columns. Instead, eight huge stone arches met at the top of the dome and leaned against each other. Hoops of iron, wood, and brick wrapped around the arches, keeping them in place.

The magnificent dome, which was completed in 1436, rose more than 300 feet above the city. Santa Maria del Fiore, also known as the Duomo, still stands today, more than five hundred years later. From its top you can see most of the city of Florence.

3. Advances in Painting

Wealthy patrons made Renaissance Florence a thriving center of art. The Medici family spent huge amounts of money on fine palaces, paintings, and statues. The Palazzo Medici was filled with works of art commissioned, or ordered, by the family. Patrons such as the Medici family created opportunities for talented painters, who made a number of advances in style and technique.

Renaissance painters were influenced by the renewed interest in classical culture and the spread of humanism. They wanted to depict real people who were posed in lifelike ways and whose faces expressed emotions. Additionally, they wanted to include realistic settings. The result was a new style of painting.

Renaissance painters were the first to use techniques of perspective. This is Botticelli's *Adoration of the Magi*. Notice the sense of distance, or depth, in the painting.

The Use of Perspective One key advance made by Renaissance painters was the use of perspective, which created the appearance of depth on a flat surface. Renaissance artists used several techniques to achieve depth. One was the size of objects. The smaller a painted object, the farther away it appears to be. The larger an object, the closer it appears to be. Painters also learned that a feeling of depth could be created by lines that came closer together as they receded into the distance. They discovered that careful shading could give figures and objects depth to make them look three-dimensional. *Adoration of the Magi*, a famous painting by Sandro Botticelli, demonstrates some of these techniques.

This is a small detail from a painting by Florentine artist Mosaccio. This artwork was influenced by Mosaccio's interest in geometry and still stands today in a chapel in Florence.

The Influence of Science and Mathematics Science and mathematics also helped artists make other advances. The Florentine artist Masaccio used geometry to figure out how to divide the space in a painting to make scenes appear more lifelike. Some artists studied anatomy by observing bodies and how they moved. Their studies helped them to portray the human body more realistically.

Renaissance science gave painters new materials, such as oil-based paints, which were made by mixing powdered pigments with linseed oil. This type of paint was thicker and dried more slowly than the older, egg-based paint, so artists did not have to work so quickly. Oil paint also allowed artists to paint over previous work and to show details and **texture** in new ways.

4. Advances in Sculpture

Like painters, Renaissance sculptors were influenced by the humanist interest in realism. Also inspired by ancient Roman statues dug up from ruins, sculptors began carving figures that looked like real people.

For the first time since the days of ancient Greece and Rome, sculptors made freestanding statues that could be viewed on all sides. This was very different from the sculptures of medieval times, so the new statues caused a sensation. They seemed to symbolize the humanist ideals of nature, realism, and the importance of the individual.

The Work of Donatello A Florentine artist named **Donatello** was one of the first sculptors to use the new, more lifelike style in his work, which expressed personality and mood. A good example is his life-sized statue of David, the young warrior in the Bible story of David and Goliath. In the 1500s, Giorgio Vasari, an architect and painter, wrote that Donatello's *David* is "so natural . . . it is almost impossible . . . to believe it was not molded on the living form." This statue is thought to be the first freestanding statue since ancient times.

Donatello a Florentine sculptor who was one of the first to use a realistic, lifelike style

Michelangelo's *David* (left) and *La Pietà* (right), are two of the world's most-admired sculptures. The term *pietà* refers to any image of Mary holding the body of her son Jesus after his crucifixion.

Michelangelo a Renaissance artist, renowned for his painting and sculpture

The Work of Michelangelo Donatello's *David* influenced **Michelangelo,** another great artist of the Renaissance who is known for both for his painting and his sculpture. He was also a talented poet and architect. Of all these arts, he preferred sculpture because it seemed to bring his subjects to life.

Michelangelo created his own majestic statue of David, which may be the world's most widely admired sculpture. Carved in white marble, Michelangelo's *David* stands about seventeen feet tall. The statue's expression shows the concentration and tension of a real youth on the verge of battle.

Michelangelo's *David* was installed in the Piazza della Signoria, the plaza in front of the Palazzo Vecchio. It became the prized expression of Renaissance genius in Florence, and Michelangelo had an enormous influence on other artists.

5. Advances in Literature

During the Renaissance, literature also changed with the rebirth of interest in classical ideas and the rise of humanism. The topics that people wrote about changed, as did their style of writing and the language in which they wrote.

New Topics and Styles of Writing In medieval times, literature usually dealt with religious topics. Most writers used a formal, impersonal style and wrote in Latin. Their work could be read only by a few highly educated people.

In contrast, Renaissance writers were interested in individual experience in the real world. Writing about **secular,** or nonreligious, topics became more common. Writers used a more individual style and expressed thoughts and feelings about life. Most importantly, by the end of the Renaissance, most writers were writing in their own languages, instead of in Latin. As a result, far more people could read their work.

Dante and *The Divine Comedy* The first well-known writer to create in a native language was Dante Alighieri (DAHN-tay ahl-ee-GAIR-ee) of Florence. He wrote his best-known work, *The Divine Comedy*, in Italian in the early 1300s. This long poem describes Dante's imaginary journey through the afterlife. With the spirit of the ancient Roman poet Virgil as his guide, Dante witnesses the torments of souls condemned to the *Inferno*, which according to Christian belief is the place of punishment after death for one's sins. Virgil also takes Dante to *Purgatorio*, which according to Catholic tradition is a place where souls await entry into heaven. Then a beautiful woman named Beatrice shows Dante *Paradiso*, or heaven, which according to Christianity is a place of eternal life.

The Divine Comedy is a social commentary containing characters who were real people. The inhabitants of the *Inferno* include people of whom Dante disapproved, whereas people he admired appear in *Paradiso*.

Dante's work became a model for other Renaissance writers, such as Petrarch and Boccaccio. They described people's lives with a new intensity of feeling. Like Dante, they wrote using the **vernacular,** or common language, so their words reached many more people.

secular relating to earthly life rather than to religious or spiritual matters

Dante Alighieri a great Italian author of the Renaissance who wrote *The Divine Comedy*

Dante Alighieri, a Renaissance author in Florence, wrote a long narrative poem called *The Divine Comedy*. This plaque in Florence shows Dante with scenes described in his poem. The city of Florence is shown on the right.

6. Advances in Science and Mathematics

The Renaissance was not just a time of progress in the arts. Scholars and others also made great advances in science and mathematics.

Before the Renaissance, most of what people believed about the natural world was based on ideas in ancient Greek and Roman texts. As the humanist spirit took hold, people started questioning old ideas and began carefully observing the world around them. Instead of relying on old books and theories, scientists began to perform experiments and analyze the results using mathematics and logic. This approach to research changed the study of science.

Leonardo da Vinci

One of the most creative Renaissance thinkers was **Leonardo da Vinci**. Leonardo was an artist, a scientist, an engineer, and an inventor who studied under artists in Florence and did his early work there.

Leonardo da Vinci studied many topics, including human anatomy. These sketches of the muscles of the arm are from his notebooks.

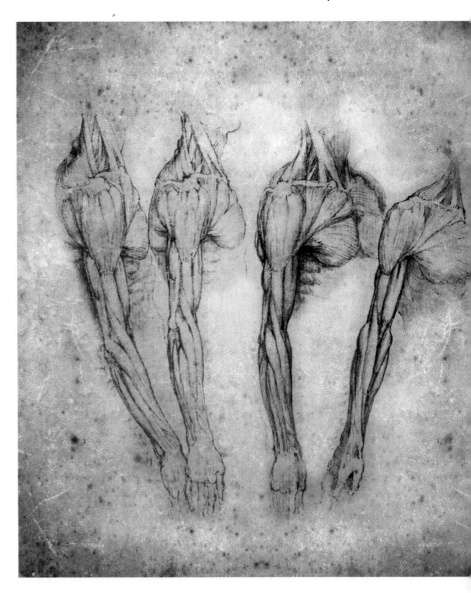

Leonardo was endlessly curious about all aspects of the world around him, refusing to accept anything as true until he had proved it himself. In his notebooks, he made sketches and wrote about an amazing variety of topics such as geometry, engineering, sound, motion, and architecture. He studied anatomy, including the circulation of blood and the workings of the eye. He learned about the effects of the moon on Earth's tides. He was the first person to draw maps from an aerial, or above-ground, view. He designed bridges, weapons, and many other machines. Among his many farsighted ideas were an underwater diving suit and a helicopter.

Paving the Way of Modern Science and Mathematics

Other Italian scientists and mathematicians made breakthroughs as well. Girolamo Cardano solved complex equations in algebra and did pioneering work in probability, the science of chance. Galileo Galilei conducted important experiments about gravity, proving that a heavier object and a lighter object fall at the same rate. If the two objects are dropped from the same height, they reach the ground at the same time. Galileo also built the first telescope used to look into space. With his telescope, he was able to discover sunspots and the moons of the planet Jupiter. By emphasizing observation and experimentation, Galileo and other Renaissance scholars paved the way for modern science and mathematics.

7. Florentine Politics

The local government of Florence was housed in the Palazzo Vecchio, or Old Palace. Like other Italian city-states, Florence was ruled under a series of governing boards that were often controlled by rich families. The powerful Medici family controlled Florence for nearly three centuries.

Galileo Galilei made fundamental contributions to science. His success inspired others to conduct their own experiments using the scientific method he developed.

The Medici Family The Medici maintained their power in a number of ways. With their vast wealth, they built palaces and were able to maintain a strong army. They were involved in or controlled all aspects of life in the city. They were great sponsors of artists, writers, and musicians, whose works beautified Florence and made the city famous. The Medici also were constantly watchful for enemies who plotted against the family.

One of the most powerful members of the Medici family was Lorenzo the Magnificent. A leading patron of art and scholarship, Lorenzo ruled Florence for more than twenty years, from 1469 until his death in 1492. Two years later, a revolution forced the Medici into temporary exile until the family regained power in 1512.

The Procession of the Magi is a fresco in one of the Medici palaces. It includes images of three generations of the powerful Renaissance family.

Niccolò Machiavelli a Renaissance statesman and historian who wrote *The Prince*

A Book About Politics A Florentine statesman and historian, **Niccolò Machiavelli** (mahk-ee-uh-VEL-ee), watched these struggles for power. During the Medici's exile, he reorganized the city's defenses. He also served as a diplomat and spent time observing the actions of other Italian rulers.

Machiavelli used his experiences to write a book called *The Prince*, which is his account of how politics and government really work. Machiavelli advises rulers to make their states strong by doing what works best, rather than by doing what is good or moral. He said that they should even lie if it helps them to rule. In his view, the end, or purpose, justifies the means—the actions taken to achieve that purpose. Rulers, he wrote, should be feared rather than loved.

The Prince seems to contradict humanist ideals about people's goodness. Its cold realism shocked many readers of the time. Yet in other ways, the book shows the influence of humanist ideas since it is the product of one individual's careful observation and thinking and is concerned with how things really work in the world. It also separates ideas about government from ideas about religion, making *The Prince* a very modern work.

8. Florentine Commerce and Trade

One reason why Florence became a cultural center was the wealth that trade and commerce brought to the city. A thriving banking industry developed. Over time, Florence became Europe's banking hub and grew richer than the largest kingdoms in Europe. Popes and kings alike borrowed money from its 80 banks.

There were two market centers in Renaissance Florence. At the Mercato Vecchio, or Old Market, people bought everyday items, such as food. The Mercato Vecchio was crowded and noisy since people from all over Europe came there to buy and sell goods.

The Mercato Nuovo, or New Market, was built in the mid-1500s as a center for the city's cloth and banking industries. City officials banned food and weapons there because they wanted it to be clean and orderly to show that commerce was highly valued in Florence.

The Mercato Nuovo became one of the largest financial market-places in Europe. People traveled from far and wide to get loans or to convert their money into florins, which could be exchanged for goods anywhere in Europe.

During the Renaissance, florins, the coins of Florence, were the most valuable coins in all of Europe.

Lesson Summary

In this lesson, you visited Renaissance Florence to learn about advances that were made there in a number of fields.

The City of Florence Florence was the leading culture center of the Renaissance. Many Renaissance figures were born or grew up there. Located on the Arno River, the city also became a business center. Florentines used their wealth to support the arts and education.

Advances in Architecture and Engineering Renaissance architects and engineers studied Greek and Roman structures. They created new works based on classical styles, but were influenced by humanism and their own ideas. Brunelleschi's cathedral dome is a lasting symbol of Renaissance achievements in architecture and engineering.

Advances in Painting, Sculpture, and Literature Renaissance humanism also influenced artists, such as Donatello and Michelangelo, and writers, such as Dante. They created works based on experience in the real world. Dante was the first major writer to use the vernacular.

Advances in Science and Mathematics Renaissance thinkers began to experiment and use mathematics and logic to analyze the world. Figures such as Leonardo da Vinci and Galileo emphasized direct observation, paving the way for modern scientific methods.

Florentine Politics, Commerce, and Trade The powerful Medici family controlled Florence for nearly three centuries and were involved in all aspects of the city's life. Niccolò Machiavelli used his experience and observations of Florentine politics to write *The Prince*. Under the Medici, the city became Europe's banking hub. The Mercato Vecchio and the Mercato Nuovo became two major centers of European trade and commerce.

Lesson 35

Leading Figures of the Renaissance

In what ways have various leading figures of the Renaissance affected modern society?

Introduction

The period in Europe known as the Renaissance began in Italy around 1300. From the 14th through the 16th centuries, Europe crackled with energy. Cities expanded while trade and commerce boomed. As artists and writers were experimenting with their crafts and creating wonderful works of art and literature, new ways of thinking led to many important inventions and scientific discoveries. Rulers and wealthy patrons supported the work of artists, scientists, and explorers.

Why was there so much creative energy during the Renaissance? One reason was that many people from all over Europe were traveling to Italy for trade and would spread Renaissance ideas after returning home. Another reason was the Renaissance idea that people should be educated in many areas. People who studied art or music, for example, were also interested in science. To this day we still use the term "Renaissance person" to describe someone who is skilled and knowledgeable in many fields.

Leonardo da Vinci is often considered to be the ideal Renaissance person. Leonardo trained mainly as a painter, but he was also a scientist, engineer, musician, and architect. In addition to designing fortifications, waterways, and machines, he studied and drew plants, animals, and people. He also sketched ideas for inventions that were far ahead of his time.

Leonardo is just one of the ten influential Renaissance figures you will study in this lesson. You will learn how contributions made by these leading figures affect society today. Additionally, you will learn how the Renaissance spread from its birthplace in Italy throughout Europe.

Social Studies Vocabulary

Johannes Gutenberg

Miguel Cervantes

New World

William Shakespeare

◀ Renaissance artist Albrecht Dürer painted this self-portrait at age 26.

1. The Renaissance Spreads Through Europe

As you have read, the Renaissance began in Italy. From there, it spread to France, Germany, Flanders (modern-day Belgium), Holland, England, and Spain.

The diffusion of Renaissance ideas occurred through trade, travel, and education. Italy was the gateway to Europe for much of the trade from Asia, Africa, and the Greek-speaking cities of the east. Traders moved through Italy to the rest of Europe, bringing a rich flow of new ideas along with their goods.

Visitors to Italy also helped spread Renaissance ideas. People from all over Europe traveled to Italy to learn, as well as to trade. Scholars went to study humanism and medicine, while artists studied Italian painting and sculpture to learn new styles and techniques.

When these travelers returned home, many of them founded art schools and universities. Artists taught others what they had learned in Italy, and scholars began to teach the new ideas of experimentation, observation, and logic.

The spread of ideas was made even easier by the invention of the printing press, a machine that pressed inked type or plates onto paper to create many copies of a work. You may recall that the Chinese had learned to make paper and to print using wooden blocks, and the Koreans had invented a kind of movable type. Gradually, knowledge of papermaking and examples of Asian printing reached Europe.

After Gutenberg invented movable type, print shops, such as this one, created books and pamphlets more quickly and easily.

In about 1450, a German named **Johannes Gutenberg** dramatically improved on existing printing methods when he invented a printing press that used movable type—characters that could be rearranged and used over again. Unlike the Chinese, who used wooden blocks, Gutenberg cast his type in metal, which was much more durable.

Before Gutenberg's invention, most books were written and copied by hand. It could take four or five months to copy a 200-page book. The new press could produce 300 pages in a single day. As a result, books and short works, called pamphlets, could be made much more quickly and cheaply.

The number of printers in Europe increased rapidly. People used printed matter to communicate new ideas, discoveries, and inventions. And, since printed material was more widely **available,** more people learned to read.

2. Michelangelo, Italian Sculptor and Painter

Michelangelo (1475–1564) was one of the leading artists of the Renaissance. He was born in a small village near Florence and grew up to be one of the greatest painters and sculptors in history.

Personality and Training Historians say that Michelangelo had a difficult childhood. His mother died when he was six years old, and his father was stern and demanding. Perhaps this troubled early life contributed to Michelangelo's famously bad temper. Although he was very religious, he was known to use fierce words when he was angry. He was also intensely ambitious.

When Michelangelo was 13, he became an apprentice to a painter in Florence. At 15, he began studying with a sculptor who worked for the powerful Medici family. Michelangelo lived for a time in the Medici household, where he met many leading thinkers, artists, and writers.

Talents and Achievements Michelangelo was gifted in both sculpture and painting. His art combines Renaissance ideals of beauty with **emotional** expressiveness.

Michelangelo's sculptures show his amazing talent for carving lifelike figures from blocks of marble. When he was just 24, he carved his famous *La Pietà*, which shows Mary tenderly holding the body of Jesus across her lap. (A *pietà* is a depiction of Mary, the mother of Jesus, mourning over her dead son.)

In this famous scene from the Sistine Chapel ceiling by Michelangelo, God reaches out to give life to Adam. According to the Bible story of creation, Adam was the first human on Earth.

Two other magnificent sculptures by Michelangelo are his *David* and *Moses*. Michelangelo's *David*—standing 17 feet tall—combines great beauty with the intense look of a youth who is about to go into battle. Michelangelo's *Moses* shows the strong, powerful figure of Moses holding the Ten Commandments, which, according to the Bible, he received from God.

Michelangelo is perhaps best known for painting the ceiling of the Sistine Chapel, the pope's chapel in Rome. He labored for almost four years on a high platform to complete this work. The curved ceiling, covered with brilliantly colored scenes from the Bible that contain over three hundred figures, continues to awe visitors to Rome today.

3. Titian, Italian Painter

Titian (TISH-uhn), who lived from about 1488 to 1576, was born in the Italian Alps. Early in life, his talent took him to the wealthy city-state of Venice where he became the city's greatest painter.

Personality and Training As a boy, Titian was sent to Venice to train with famous painters. He worked with an artist named Giorgione, who was a master of fresco painting. A *fresco* is a painting made on the wet plaster of a wall or ceiling. Titian also studied examples of art from Rome and Florence, but in time, he outgrew the influence of his teachers and created his own style.

Titian was a persuasive man. Long after he became famous, he persuaded patrons to support his art by claiming to be poor. However, despite his financial troubles, he was also quite generous with his friends and sometimes gifted them portraits at no cost.

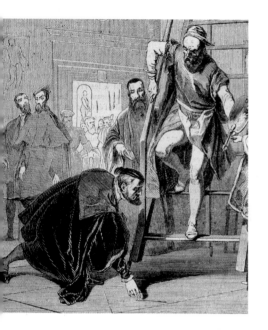

This drawing illustrates the story of Charles V picking up a paint brush dropped by Titian. Titian was so beloved that Charles made him a knight, the first time the honor had ever been bestowed on a painter.

Talents and Achievements Titian's early work was precise and detailed, but he later developed a freer style that involved using blobs of paint to create vivid forms, colors, and textures. He was known for his inspired use of color and for loose, lively brushwork that made his pictures appear lifelike. His art also had a flair for expressing human personality.

In addition to painting many scenes of classical myths and Bible stories, Titian created portraits of the rich and powerful. In 1516, he was named the official painter of Venice and was later named court painter of Italy by Holy Roman emperor Charles V. Titian made many portraits of Charles V and other royalty.

Charles V greatly admired Titian's work. There is a story that the emperor once picked up a paintbrush that had fallen to the floor. Titian protested, "I am not worthy of such a servant." The emperor replied, "Titian is worthy to be served by Caesar," referring to the emperor of ancient Rome. Charles even made Titian a knight—a first-time honor for a painter.

4. Albrecht Dürer, German Artist

Albrecht Dürer (AHL-brekht DOOR-er), who lived from 1471 to 1528, was from the German city of Nuremberg. He earned fame for his paintings, drawings, prints, and essays about art.

Personality and Training As a boy, Dürer received a diverse education. The son of a goldsmith, he learned his father's trade. At 15, he began training with a well-known painter and printmaker, a person who uses printing to make copies of works of art. Dürer also studied math, Latin, and classical literature.

As a young man, Dürer traveled through Germany, Italy, and the Netherlands and became friends with many humanist artists, writers, and thinkers. He studied classical sculpture for years to learn ideal human **proportions** because he wanted to be able to show the parts of the human body correctly sized in relation to each other.

Dürer's self-portraits show him to be a fashionable, confident man. He had an intellectual approach to life and art. His art was an attempt to answer the question "What is beauty?"

Dürer's woodcut *The Four Horsemen of the Apocalypse* illustrates a vision of the end of the world described in the Christian Bible. Dürer's woodcuts set a new standard for quality of expressiveness and clarity of detail.

Talents and Achievements In his painting, Dürer blended the detailed style of Germany with the perspective and idealized beauty he learned from Italian painting. He encouraged all artists to study mathematics as the key to understanding Renaissance and classical art.

Dürer was especially skilled at making engravings and woodcuts, prints made from an original that is specially prepared for printing. The original may be etched, or engraved, in metal or it may be cut into a block of wood before it is inked and re-inked to make copies. In Renaissance times, printers used engravings and woodcuts to illustrate books.

Much of Dürer's art shows religious figures or subjects from myths. Like other artists of his time, he made many portraits of royalty and wealthy patrons. He worked for years as a court artist for the Holy Roman emperor Maximilian I.

Dürer's work is widely admired, particularly his beautiful engravings and woodcuts. They set a new standard in printmaking because of their clarity, expressiveness, and fine detail.

5. Nicolaus Copernicus, Polish Scientist

Nicolaus Copernicus (1473–1543) was born in Torun, Poland. He is often called the "father of modern astronomy."

Personality and Training When Copernicus was ten years old, his father died, so his uncle, a Catholic bishop, became his guardian. He made sure that Copernicus received a good education.

As a young man, Copernicus attended the University of Krakow in Poland before heading to Italy to study medicine and Church law. In Italy, he rented rooms from an astronomy teacher and soon became fascinated by astronomy.

Copernicus's scientific work would show that he was highly creative. He was also a free thinker, unafraid to question accepted beliefs.

Talents and Achievements Copernicus was skilled in mathematics and observation. He based his thinking on what he truly saw, rather than on what he thought he should see.

Like other people of his time, Copernicus had been taught that Earth was at the center of the universe. According to this idea, the sun, stars, and planets travel around Earth.

As Copernicus studied the motion of the planets, he became dissatisfied with this explanation and proposed the revolutionary idea that Earth and the other planets **orbit** the sun. When Earth rotates, or turns, on its axis, it makes the sun and other objects in the heavens seem to move across the sky around Earth.

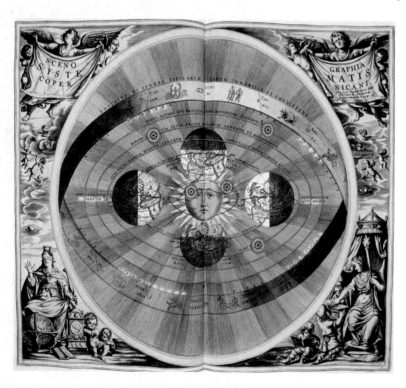

Since ancient times, most people believed that Earth was at the center of the universe. This engraving illustrates Copernicus's theory that Earth and the other planets travel around the sun.

In 1514, Copernicus printed a booklet that outlined his theory. Then he began years of work on a full-length book titled *On the Revolutions of the Celestial Spheres*. (*Celestial* means "heavenly.")

Copernicus dedicated his book to the pope. However, the idea of Earth traveling around the sun went against the Roman Catholic Church's belief that God had placed humans at the center of the universe. In 1616, the Church forbade people to read Copernicus's book.

Despite the Church's disapproval, Copernicus's theory had a major influence on a few key scientists, and it was eventually proved to be correct. Today, the Copernican theory is part of the basis of modern astronomy.

6. Andreas Vesalius, Belgian Scientist

Andreas Vesalius (1514–1564) was born in Brussels, in what is now Belgium. He became an outstanding scientist whose work changed medicine and the study of anatomy.

Personality and Training Vesalius came from a family of doctors and pharmacists, or people who prepare medicines. He was always interested in living things and especially in anatomy.

Vesalius attended universities in Flanders, France, and Italy. In 1537, he earned his medical degree, specializing in anatomy, and later became a personal doctor to Italian and Spanish royalty.

Vesalius was hardworking, curious, and confident. He was also said to be gloomy and distant at times.

Talents and Achievements Vesalius was a talented observer and an independent thinker. He also had the artistic skill necessary to make detailed drawings of his scientific observations.

In Vesalius's time, physicians' understanding of human anatomy was based on the works of the ancient Greek physician Galen. Vesalius studied Galen, but he soon broke with this tradition because, like Copernicus, he was determined to observe things for himself.

Vesalius began dissecting, or cutting apart to study, dead human bodies. His research showed that Galen's work had relied on studies of animals, and as a result, it had many errors when applied to human anatomy and medicine.

Vesalius made many discoveries about the human body. For example, he showed that the human heart has four hollow areas, called chambers.

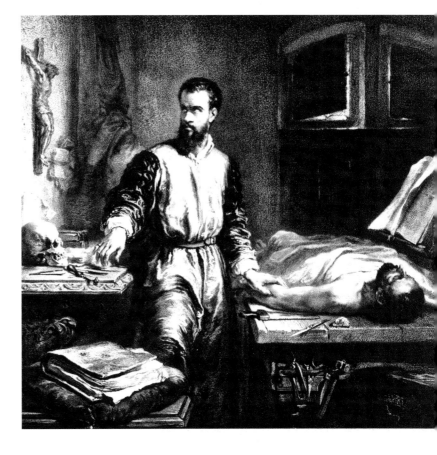

Vesalius dissected dead bodies to study human anatomy. He insisted on performing dissections himself, rather than relying on untrained assistants.

His discoveries led him to write his own seven-volume textbook of anatomy called *On the Structure of the Human Body*. It explains how the body functions and contains prints by artists that were based on Vesalius's drawings of the body.

Vesalius's book was a major breakthrough. In addition to changing what people knew about human anatomy and how they studied it, it also changed physicians' understanding of medicine. His book is considered to be the world's first modern medical textbook.

Queen Isabella I helped sponsor Christopher Columbus's attempt to find a route across the Atlantic Ocean to Asia. Instead of Asia, Columbus found the Americas.

7. Isabella I, Queen of Spain

Queen Isabella I (1451–1504) was born in the Spanish kingdom of Castile. She is best known for creating a unified Spain and for sponsoring the voyages of Christopher Columbus.

Personality and Training Isabella was the daughter of the king of Castile. She was highly intelligent, strong-willed, and a devoted Catholic. Girls at that time received little education, so Isabella's schooling was limited. In adulthood, she educated herself by learning Latin. As queen, she supported scholarship and art, collected fine paintings, and built schools.

Talents and Achievements Isabella was a forceful and brave ruler. In 1469, she married Prince Ferdinand of Aragon, the other major kingdom in Spain at that time. In 1474, Isabella became queen of Castile. When Ferdinand inherited the throne of Aragon in 1479, the two monarchs ruled jointly over much of Spain. They fought several battles to unify the rest of the nation.

Isabella and Ferdinand actively encouraged exploration. Isabella gave her support to Christopher Columbus, an Italian who proposed finding a new sea route to Asia. In 1492, Columbus sailed across the Atlantic and stumbled upon the Americas. His discovery of this so-called **New World** would lead to a Spanish empire and create great wealth for Spain.

New World the name given by Europeans to the Americas, which were unknown to most Europeans before the voyages of Christopher Columbus

Isabella and Ferdinand also sought to strengthen Spain as a unified Catholic country, but this meant that Jews who refused to convert to Catholicism were forced to leave. This harsh action was not only a tragedy for Spanish Jews, but it also cost Spain many of its most talented and productive citizens.

8. Elizabeth I, Queen of England

Queen Elizabeth I (1533–1603) was one of England's most popular and successful monarchs. Born in London, she was the daughter of King Henry VIII and his queen at the time, Anne Boleyn.

Personality and Training When Elizabeth was two years old, King Henry lost interest in Queen Anne. Claiming that Anne had been unfaithful to him, he ordered her beheading.

Elizabeth was raised in a separate household, largely away from the royal court. An English scholar became her teacher and educated her as a possible future monarch. Elizabeth was a gifted student and became highly educated, learning to speak Greek, Latin, French, and Italian.

Elizabeth was a strong-minded ruler, but she was not stubborn. As monarch, she was willing to listen to good advice and always considered what was best for the people of England.

Talents and Achievements Elizabeth became queen at age 25 and reigned for 45 years until her death in 1603. She never married because she feared that a husband would take her power. She said she was married to the people of England.

One of the great monarchs of England, Elizabeth I created peace and stability during her long rule. During Queen Elizabeth I's rule, culture thrived, England expanded its territories, and the English navy defeated the Spanish Armada.

William Shakespeare an English Renaissance poet and playwright whose plays show a deep understanding of human behavior

Shakespeare wrote about life with both humor and drama. This is a scene from *Macbeth,* one of Shakespeare's most popular tragedies.

Elizabeth was a hard-working and able ruler. Although she was independent, she was also flexible and willing to change unpopular policies. She showed political skill in balancing the interests of different people in her court and inspired great love and loyalty from her subjects, who called her "Good Queen Bess."

Elizabeth's long reign is often called England's Golden Age. Culture thrived under her rule in part because she supported theater, fashion, literature, dance, and education. Poets and playwrights during her rule composed some of the greatest works in the English language.

Elizabeth worked to strengthen England's economy, and she encouraged trade and commerce. She **authorized** English trading companies in Africa, Asia, and the Americas. Her funding of sea exploration helped England gain territory in North America. In 1588, the English navy defeated the Spanish Armada, a mighty fleet that tried to attack England. This victory sparked a national celebration and further strengthened England's sea power. By the time Elizabeth died, England was one of the strongest and richest countries in the world.

9. William Shakespeare, English Poet and Playwright

William Shakespeare (1564–1616) was born in the English town of Stratford-upon-Avon. He was a major figure of the English Renaissance and is widely considered to be the world's greatest playwright and one of its finest poets.

Personality and Training As a boy, Shakespeare studied Latin and classical literature in grammar school. Although he never went to a university, his plays show a broad knowledge of many subjects, from history and politics to music and art.

In his early twenties, Shakespeare became an actor with a theater company in London and learned about drama by performing and writing plays. Many of his plays were first presented at London's Globe Theatre where Queen Elizabeth, among many others, enjoyed his work.

Shakespeare had a reputation for being quiet and a bit mysterious, but his writings show that he was curious and keenly observant. He thought deeply about life and its sufferings, yet he also had a sense of humor and found much to laugh at in life.

Talents and Achievements Shakespeare was a skilled actor, but he was an even greater poet and playwright. He had an enormous talent for expressing thoughts and feelings in memorable words. His plays show that he had a deep understanding of human behavior and emotions. Above all, he had the skill to present his understanding through vivid characters and exciting drama.

Shakespeare's poetry is widely admired, especially the 14-line poems called sonnets. However, he is best known for his 38 plays, which include comedies, tragedies, and histories. Many of his plays are still performed around the world, and several have been made into television series or movies. Among the most popular are *Romeo and Juliet, Hamlet, Macbeth, Julius Caesar, All's Well That Ends Well,* and *The Merchant of Venice.*

Shakespeare's plays cover a broad range of subjects, including romance, politics, prejudice, murder, and war. His plays remain popular in part because he wrote about timeless, universal themes such as love, jealousy, power, ambition, hatred, and fear.

Shakespeare has had a deep influence on later writers and has also left a lasting mark on the English language. Many common sayings come from Shakespeare, such as "Much ado about nothing." People often quote his witty, wise lines, sometimes without knowing that they owe their clever or graceful words to Shakespeare.

Miguel Cervantes the Spanish Renaissance author of the masterpiece *Don Quixote*

10. Miguel Cervantes, Spanish Writer

Miguel Cervantes (mi-GEL ser-VAN-tayz) was born near Madrid, Spain. He lived from 1547 to 1616. He is best known for his comic novel *Don Quixote* (DON kee-HOH-tay).

Personality and Training Little is known about Cervantes's education. He may have studied with priests influenced by humanism. It is certain that he loved to read.

Much of Cervantes's education came through experience. At 23, he became a soldier. He was shot twice in the chest in a battle at sea, and at one time he injured his left hand so badly that the hand became useless. Several years later, he was taken prisoner at sea by pirates and spent five years as a slave in North Africa until his family bought his freedom.

Cervantes's early life shows that he was adventurous and courageous. His sense of humor could be biting, but he also turned it on himself. He once bragged that the public liked his plays enough not to boo them off the stage or throw vegetables at the actors.

Talents and Achievements A gifted writer with a particular talent for satire, Cervantes wrote many plays, poems, and novels. His masterpiece, *Don Quixote*, pokes fun at romantic stories of heroic knights, as well as at Spanish society. The novel's title character, Don Quixote, is an elderly man who has read too many tales of glorious knights. Although the age of knights is past, he dresses up in rusty armor and sets out to do noble deeds. He is accompanied by short, stout Sancho Panza, who is an ordinary farmer that rides a mule but is seen by Don Quixote as a faithful squire, or armor bearer.

Don Quixote is the hero of Cervantes's comic novel of the same name. This sculpture in Spain shows Don Quixote dressed as a knight and Sancho, a farmer whom Don Quixote named as his squire.

Together the two men have a series of comic adventures. In Don Quixote's imagination, country inns turn into castles and windmills become fearsome giants. While his adventures are very funny, there is something noble about the way he bravely fights evil, even if his deeds are only in his mind.

Don Quixote was very popular in Spain. King Philip III supposedly saw a man reading and laughing so hard that he was crying. The king said, "That man is either crazy or he is reading *Don Quixote*." Today, *Don Quixote* is considered one of the masterpieces of world literature.

11. Leonardo da Vinci, Renaissance Person

Leonardo da Vinci (1452–1519) was born in a village near Florence in Italy. His wide range of interests and accomplishments made him a true Renaissance person.

The *Mona Lisa* is one of Leonardo da Vinci's best-known paintings. This surprisingly small painting—only about 20 by 30 inches—has had a huge and lasting influence on other artists.

Personality and Training Leonardo trained in Florence under a master sculptor and painter. All his life he studied many subjects, including painting, sculpture, music, math, anatomy, botany, architecture, and engineering.

Leonardo spent much of his life in Florence and Milan where he worked as an artist, engineer, and architect for kings, popes, and wealthy commoners. He had a special love for animals and sometimes bought caged animals at the market and set them free. He also was a vegetarian, which was quite unusual at the time.

Talents and Achievements Leonardo was gifted in many fields. He was an accomplished painter, sculptor, architect, and engineer.

Leonardo's notebooks show him to be one of the greatest creative minds of all time. Like Albrecht Dürer, he closely studied proportions and made precise drawings of people, animals, and plants. He also sketched out ideas about geometry and mechanics, the science of motion and force. He designed weapons, buildings, and a variety of machines. Many of the inventions he imagined, such as a helicopter and a submarine, were centuries ahead of their time.

Leonardo's paintings are among the world's greatest works of art. One of his masterpieces, the *Mona Lisa*, is a painting of a woman with a mysterious smile and is among the most famous paintings in the world. Like his other works, it displays a remarkable use of perspective, balance, and detail. The rich effects of shade and color reveal his close study of light. Students of his art also detect how principles of geometry helped him organize the space in his paintings.

Leonardo's work inspired other great artists, such as Michelangelo. With his many interests and talents, Leonardo is a perfect example of the spirit of the Renaissance.

In this lesson, you learned how the Renaissance spread from Italy across Europe. Then you studied the lives and accomplishments of ten major Renaissance figures.

The Renaissance Spreads Through Europe Renaissance ideas spread through trade, travel, and education. People from across Europe went to Italy to learn and to trade. When they returned home, many passed on new ideas by founding schools and universities. The spread of the Renaissance was made even easier by Gutenberg's new printing press.

Michelangelo, Titian, and Dürer Renaissance artists like Michelangelo, Titian, and Dürer created many kinds of art. They studied human anatomy and mathematics that helped them to create works of art based on humanist ideals of realism and beauty.

Copernicus and Vesalius Through observation and fresh thinking, scientists Copernicus and Vesalius dramatically increased human knowledge. Copernicus discovered that Earth and other planets in our solar system revolve around the sun, not Earth. Vesalius's studies of anatomy and his detailed drawings changed how people understood the human body.

Isabella I and Elizabeth I Queen Isabella and Queen Elizabeth were strong leaders who supported the arts and encouraged exploration. Both monarchs improved their nations and financed important explorations that increased Europeans' knowledge of the world.

Shakespeare and Cervantes Shakespeare and Cervantes created masterpieces of world literature. Both writers created lyrical and expressive works that explored humanist ideas and enriched their native languages.

Leonardo da Vinci Leonardo da Vinci was a creative genius who embodied the spirit of the Renaissance. His studies in topics such as art, architecture, and engineering led him to invent many devices that were far ahead of his time, as well as timeless works of art.

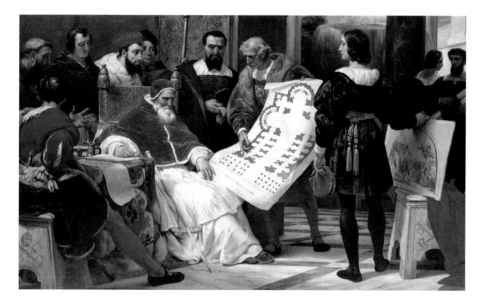

The Renaissance popes were important art patrons. Here, Pope Julius II (seated) reviews plans for St. Peter's Basilica with architect Donato Bramante (center), Michelangelo (left of Bramante), and the artist Raphael (right of Bramante).

Johannes Gutenberg's invention of movable metal type revolutionized the transfer of information in Europe. His printing press gave people unprecedented access to inexpensive books.

From Gutenberg to the Internet

Around 1450, Johannes Gutenberg invented a printing press that used movable metal type. Before Gutenberg's press, books and other printed materials were made by hand. Printed material was costly to produce and to buy. Gutenberg's invention changed Europe by making books more affordable and by distributing information faster and to more people. Today, Gutenberg is known as the inventor of printing in Europe. Although his achievements were well deserved, his invention was almost taken away from him.

The year is 1455, and Johannes Gutenberg sits in a courtroom across from his bitter enemy Johann Fust, who has sued Gutenberg. Gutenberg shifts nervously, waiting for the judges' decision. If the judges rule against him, he will lose everything—including the printing press that he has worked for 20 years to perfect.

Gutenberg was born in Mainz, Germany, sometime between 1394 and 1400. He found, at a young age, that he loved to work with metal. He worked with craftsmen in the city and slowly learned their secrets. He demonstrated an extraordinary talent, mastering the technology of turning metal into beautiful objects. He was also fueled with the ambition to do something special and memorable.

In 1428, Gutenberg moved from Mainz to Strasbourg and started a business cutting gemstones to create jewelry. The company thrived, and he formed a business partnership with three other men. Soon they were making mirrors and other quality products.

Early Printing and Movable Type

During the 1430s, Gutenberg saw the opportunity to do something even greater—to develop a printing press that lowered the cost of books. Printing was first developed in China and Japan in the 8th century. Craftspeople in those countries spent hours carving an image into a block of wood, rolling ink onto the raised parts, and pressing the image against paper.

Korean craftspeople were the first to develop metal movable type, in which the characters could be rearranged to form different words. During the 13th century, they formed type by heating bronze to a temperature high enough to make it liquid. They poured the bronze into molds formed in sand, and the bronze hardened and formed type. They then used the type to form all the words on a page, applied ink to the type, and rubbed paper against it, producing a printed page.

In 1377, the Koreans printed a text for Buddhists. It is the oldest known book in the world printed with movable metal type.

Europeans did not develop movable type for another 200 years. Until then, monks and nuns in monasteries painstakingly copied books by hand. Many of the books were unique works of art because they had huge, colorful capital letters, complex illustrations, and the edge of each page was lined with gold. However, these books were incredibly expensive, because one individual had to work an average of 300 days to create just one book. Historians estimate that the typical book might cost between $200 and $250 in today's dollars. Only the very wealthy could afford such items.

Inventing Type, a Press, and Ink

When Gutenberg turned his creative genius to developing an inexpensive way to print books, he faced three challenges—developing type, creating a printing press, and mixing the right ink. To create type, he had to decide what metal to use. It couldn't be too hard because then it wouldn't melt, but it couldn't be too soft because then the type wouldn't last. Finally, he landed on a brilliant idea. Instead of one metal, he would blend different metals. He created an alloy—or combination of metals—which included 80 percent lead, 5 percent tin, and 15 percent of a metal called antimony.

To make the letter *a*, for example, he heated the metal until it melted, poured it into a mold, let it cool, and then removed the metal from the mold. Now he had the type for the letter *a*, which he could use over and over again. He repeated the process for all the other letters and for punctuation.

With movable type, the printer selects individual letters to form words. The letters can be used repeatedly in different combinations. Although movable type has been mostly replaced by new technology, huge printing presses produce vast amounts of printed information every day.

Although much of the work of type setting and printing books was still completed by hand on Gutenberg presses like this one, it was vastly quicker than writing out each copy. This press still stands in the Gutenberg Museum in Mainz, Germany.

Next, Gutenberg needed to find the right ink. It couldn't be too thin because then it would leave smudges on the paper, but it couldn't be too thick, or it would clog the type. Gutenberg experimented for a long time and finally used linseed oil. To make it black, he added soot, which he got from lamps.

Finally, Gutenberg had to construct a press. Historians believe that he probably adapted a press that papermakers used to dry stacks of paper. In his press, Gutenberg set the type and rolled ink onto the type. Then he turned a giant screw that lowered the type onto paper. In a few seconds, he could print a page that would have taken a monk hours to copy. More importantly, he could make many copies of the same page very quickly.

Printing Success and Business Setbacks

Gutenberg made great progress on the printing press, but he faced some serious business problems. First, one of his partners died. Then the man's relatives sued Gutenberg to get control of the business. Gutenberg was relieved when the court ruled in his favor. But regardless of his victory, the lawsuit prevented him from finishing his printing press.

Gutenberg's problems worsened. He ignored the jewelry business, and his income sank. Yet he was spending money to buy metals, a press, and inks. He went into debt, but he continued working on the printing press. Finally, in 1446, he had his first major triumph, when he printed a short poem. Soon after, he printed a grammar book, which became a bestseller throughout Europe.

These early books were plain, and Gutenberg wanted to produce something wonderfully beautiful. Since money was still a big problem, Gutenberg formed a partnership with Johann Fust, a wealthy businessman in Mainz who loaned him 1,600 guldens, which at that time was a fortune. Historians have estimated that just 100 guldens could purchase a small farm. The two men planned to print a book that would sell extremely well and give them a good return on their investment. But what kind of a book should it be?

Printing a Bible

Finally they came up with a brilliant idea—they would print a Bible that was extraordinary in every way. Around 1455, Gutenberg started preparations. The Bible would have two volumes: the Old Testament and the New Testament. It would have 42 lines per page, and the two volumes together would contain 1,282 pages. Every page would have 2,000 letters. For this monumental task, Gutenberg had to create 290 pieces of type, including capital letters, lower case letters, and punctuation. He planned to print 210 copies.

While Gutenberg was aiming for perfection, Fust was growing impatient. He had invested 1,600 guldens in the printing press, but in five years, the investment had not earned him one penny. He filed a lawsuit against Gutenberg, demanding that his money be returned. Gutenberg simply did not have the money, so he desperately needed the judges to find in his favor.

But the judges ruled against Gutenberg, arguing that Fust had waited long enough to earn a profit on the money that he had invested. Gutenberg had to repay Fust. Since Gutenberg did not have the funds, the court allowed Fust to take over the business, including the type-faces and the printing press. Fust even hired away Gutenberg's most skilled assistant. Together, they finished work on the Bible that Gutenberg had started and began to sell it. This remarkable book became an instant bestseller, so Fust made a good deal of money from the sweat, tears, and genius that Gutenberg had poured into the project.

Yet Gutenberg was an amazingly stubborn man. Fust had taken away his business, but he could not take away Gutenberg's knowledge and skills. He found another financial backer, Dr. Konrad Humery, who helped him establish a printing shop in Mainz. Gutenberg printed philosophical writings, a dictionary, and other works, all with the extraordinary quality that was his trademark. He also trained printers, who spread his printing technology throughout Europe.

Books: The Internet of the Time

Gutenberg's amazing invention made books the Internet of the time. The printing press made it possible to produce books much more quickly and cheaply than ever before. By 1463, printed Bibles cost one-tenth of hand-copied Bibles. The demand for books exploded and, by 1500, Europe had more than 1,000 printers and 7,000 books in print.

Like the Internet, books spread new ideas quickly and sped up the process of change. For example, as a young sailor in Genoa, Christopher Columbus was thrilled when he read Marco Polo's famous *Travels*, in which he described his journeys to China. Books also planted the seeds of democracy and human rights in the next generation of thinkers, while newspapers and pamphlets generated information and ideas even faster.

In 1465, the Archbishop of Mainz gave Gutenberg a pension for the "agreeable and willing service" that he had provided to the city and to Germany. Gutenberg died in 1468, and Dr. Humery inherited everything. However, the Archbishop refused to let the doctor move Gutenberg's printing press. The city was honored to be the birthplace of printing in Europe, and Gutenberg would always be known as the father of an invention that truly changed the world.

One advantage of the new, printed books, like the Gutenberg Bible (bottom), over the earlier, hand-copied versions (top) was that each printed copy was neat and exactly the same.

Lesson 36

The Reformation Begins

What factors led to the weakening of the Catholic Church and the beginning of the Reformation?

Introduction

At the height of the Renaissance, western Europe was still Roman Catholic, but this changed with the beginning of the Reformation. This movement led to the start of many new Christian churches that broke away from the Catholic Church.

The Reformation began in the early 1500s and lasted into the 1600s. Until then, all Christians in western Europe were Catholics. However, even before the Reformation, the Church's religious and moral authority was starting to weaken. One reason for the weakening of the Church was the humanism of the Renaissance. Humanists often were secular, or nonreligious, in their thinking, and they believed in free thought and questioned many accepted beliefs.

Problems within the Church added to this spirit of questioning. Many Catholics were dismayed by worldliness and corruption (immoral and dishonest behavior) in the Church. Sometimes, bishops and clergy used questionable practices to raise money. Some popes seemed more concerned with power and wealth than with spiritual matters.

These problems led a number of Catholics to call for reform. They questioned the authority of Church leaders and some of the Church's teachings. Those who broke away from the Church entirely became known as "Protestants" because of their protests against the Catholic Church. The establishment of Protestant churches divided Christians into many separate groups.

In this lesson, you will learn about the factors that weakened the Roman Catholic Church and how a German priest, Martin Luther, ignited a movement that ended the religious unity of Europe. You will also learn about other early reformers and leaders of the Reformation.

Social Studies Vocabulary

denomination

indulgence

Martin Luther

Protestant

Reformation

simony

◀ Corruption in the Church, particularly moneymaking schemes, led to questions about the morals of Church officials.

indulgence a grant by the Catholic Church that released a person from punishment for sins

simony the selling and buying of positions in the Catholic Church

1. The Weakening of the Catholic Church

By the Late Middle Ages, two major problems were weakening the Roman Catholic Church. The first was worldliness and corruption within the Church, and the second was political conflict between the pope and European monarchs.

Worldliness and Corruption Within the Church During the Middle Ages, the Catholic Church united the Christians of western Europe in a single faith. However, the Church was a political and economic institution as well as a religious one. By the 1300s, many Catholics felt that the Church had become too worldly and corrupt.

Too frequently, Church officials failed to live up to their role as spiritual leaders. For example, priests, monks, and nuns made vows, or solemn promises, not to marry or have children, but many broke these vows. Others seemed to ignore Christian values, and Church leaders often behaved like royalty instead of God's servants. For example, the popes, and many cardinals and bishops, were extremely wealthy and powerful.

People were also troubled by the way numerous Church officials raised money to support the church. One method was the practice of selling **indulgences**. An indulgence is a release from punishment for sins.

The practice of selling indulgences suggested that people could buy forgiveness for their sins. This and other moneymaking practices led people to distrust the Church.

During the Middle Ages, the Church granted indulgences in exchange for gifts to the Church and good works. People who received indulgences were not required to perform good deeds to make up for their sins. Over time, popes and bishops started selling indulgences as a way of raising money. This practice made it seem that people could buy forgiveness for their sins, an abuse that deeply disturbed many Catholics.

The Church also sold offices, or leadership positions, a practice called **simony**. Instead of being chosen based on their merit and accomplishments, buyers simply paid for their jobs. Buying an office was worthwhile because it could be a source of income. Often, people acquired multiple offices in different locations without actually going there to perform their duties.

People questioned other practices as well. Some clergy charged pilgrims to see holy objects, such as the relics of **saints**.

In addition, all Catholics paid taxes to the Church. Many people resented having to pay taxes to Rome in addition to their own governments.

Political Conflicts with European Rulers In the Middle Ages, the pope became a powerful political figure, as well as a religious leader, and the Church accumulated vast amounts of wealth. Its political and economic power presented a problem for monarchs because the Church claimed that its clergy were independent of political rulers' control.

The Popes' Palace became the seat of the pope when the papacy moved to Avignon, France in 1309.

As monarchs attempted to increase their own power, they frequently came into conflict with the pope. They quarreled with the pope over Church property and the right to make appointments to Church offices. In addition, popes became involved in other political conflicts, which prompted many to question the pope's authority and also damaged the Church's reputation.

One dramatic crisis unfolded in France in 1301. When King Philip IV tried to tax the French clergy, the pope threatened to force him out of the Church. In response, soldiers hired by the king kidnapped the pope. The pope was soon released, but he died a few weeks later.

The quarrel with the king ended under Pope Clement V. In 1309, Clement moved his headquarters from Rome to the French city of Avignon. During his reign, he appointed 24 new cardinals, 22 of whom were French. The next six popes also lived in Avignon and named more French cardinals. Many Europeans believed that France's kings now controlled the papacy, or the office of the pope, causing them to lose respect for the pope as the Church's supreme leader.

An even worse crisis developed after Pope Gregory XI returned the papacy to Rome in 1377. When Gregory died in 1378, an Italian was elected pope and refused to move back to Avignon. A group of cardinals, most of them French, left Rome and elected a rival pope, leading the Church to have one pope in Rome and one in Avignon. Later, a Church council elected a third pope. Each pope claimed to be the real head of the Church.

This division in the Church is called the Great Schism. For nearly 40 years, the various lines of popes denounced each other as impostors, which divided and confused Catholics. The Great Schism lessened people's respect for the papacy and sparked calls for reform.

Priest Jan Hus was an early reformer who agreed with Wycliffe's ideas and spoke against the pope. For this, he was burned at the stake as a heretic.

Reformation a religious reform movement from the early 1500s to the 1600s that led to the formation of new Christian groups

2. Early Calls for Reform

By the 1300s, the Church was beginning to lose some of its moral and religious standing. Many Catholics, including clergy, criticized the corruption and abuses in the Church. They challenged the authority of the pope, questioned Church teachings, and started to develop new forms of Christian faith.

Reformers wanted to purify the Church, not destroy it. By challenging the Church's practices and teachings, however, they helped pave the way for the dramatic changes of the **Reformation**.

John Wycliffe (About 1330–1384) John Wycliffe (WIH-cliff) was an English scholar who challenged the Church's right to money that it demanded from England. When the Great Schism began, he publicly questioned the pope's authority and criticized indulgences and immoral behavior on the part of the clergy.

During the Middle Ages, Church officials attempted to control how the Bible was interpreted. Wycliffe believed that the Bible, not the Church, was the supreme source of religious authority. Against Church tradition, he had the Bible translated from Latin into English so that common people could read it.

The pope accused Wycliffe of heresy, or opinions that contradict official **doctrine**. Wycliffe's followers were persecuted, and some of them were burned to death as heretics, or people who behave against official teachings. After his death, the Church had Wycliffe's writings burned, too. Despite the Church's opposition, however, Wycliffe's ideas had wide influence.

Jan Hus (About 1370–1415) Jan Hus (huhs) was a priest in Bohemia, which today is in the Czech Republic. He read Wycliffe's writings and agreed with many of his ideas. Hus criticized the Church's vast wealth and spoke out against the pope's authority. The true head of the Church, he said, was Jesus Christ.

Hus sought to purify the Church, return it to the people, and end corruption among the clergy. He wanted both the Bible and mass to be offered in the common language of the people instead of in Latin. Hus was arrested and charged with heresy in 1414 and was burned at the stake in July 1415.

Like Wycliffe, Hus had a major influence on future reformers. Martin Luther would later say that he and his supporters were "all Hussites without knowing it."

Catherine of Siena (1347–1380) Catherine of Siena was a mystic—a person deeply devoted to religion and who has spiritual experiences. Born in the Italian city of Siena, she began having visions of Jesus when she was a child.

Catherine spent many long hours in prayer and wrote numerous letters about spiritual life. In addition, she involved herself in Church affairs. Her pleas helped to convince Pope Gregory XI to return the papacy to Rome from Avignon. Later, she traveled to Rome to attempt to end the Great Schism.

In 1461, the Church declared Catherine a saint. Her example showed that people could lead spiritual lives that went beyond the usual customs of the Church. She and other mystics emphasized personal experience of God more than formal observance of Church practices. This approach to faith helped prepare people for the ideas of the Reformation.

Desiderius Erasmus (1466–1536) Desiderius Erasmus was a humanist from Holland. A priest and devoted Catholic, he was one of the most outspoken figures in the call for reform.

In 1509, Erasmus published a book called *The Praise of Folly*. (*Folly* means "foolishness.") The book was a sharply worded satire of society, including abuses by clergy and Church leaders, that argued for a return to simple Christian goodness.

Erasmus wanted to reform the Church from within and angrily denied that he was a **Protestant** who wanted to break away from the Catholic Church. However, perhaps more than any other individual, he helped to prepare Europe for the Reformation. His attacks on corruption in the Church contributed to many people's desire to leave Catholicism. For this reason, it has frequently been said that "Erasmus laid the egg, and Luther hatched it."

Protestant a Christian who separated from the Roman Catholic Church during the reformation; today, any member of a Christian church founded on the principles of the Reformation

Catholic priest Erasmus of Holland was perhaps the most influential person in spreading the ideas of reform before the Reformation.

3. Martin Luther Breaks Away from the Church

In the early 1500s in Germany, then part of the Holy Roman Empire, a priest named **Martin Luther** became involved in a serious dispute with Church authorities. Condemned by the Catholic Church, Luther established the first Protestant church, which started the Reformation.

Luther's Early Life Luther was born in Germany in 1483 and was raised as a devout Catholic. Luther's father wanted him to become a lawyer. As a young man, however, Luther was badly frightened when he was caught in a violent thunderstorm. As lightning flashed around him, he vowed that if he survived he would become a monk.

Luther kept his promise, joined an order of monks, and later became a priest. He studied the Bible thoroughly and developed a reputation as a scholar and teacher.

Luther Pushes for Change in the Catholic Church The Church stressed that keeping the sacraments and living a good life were the keys to salvation. Luther's studies of the Bible led him to a different answer. He believed that it was impossible to earn salvation because it was a gift from God that people received in faith. People, he said, were saved by their faith, not by performing good works.

Luther's views brought him into conflict with the Church over indulgences. In 1517, Pope Leo X needed money to finish building St. Peter's Basilica, the grand cathedral in Rome. He sent preachers around Europe to sell indulgences. Buyers were promised pardons of all of their sins and those of friends and family. Luther was outraged because he felt that the Church was selling false salvation to uneducated people.

Luther posted a list of arguments, called **theses,** against indulgences and Church abuses on a church door in the town of Wittenberg. He also sent the list, called the Ninety-Five Theses, to Church leaders.

Martin Luther a German priest who broke away from the Catholic Church to start his own religion, Lutheranism. His posting of the Ninety-Five Theses started the Reformation.

Luther nailed his list of 95 arguments, called the Ninety-Five Theses, to a church door in Wittenberg, Germany. Church leaders condemned the ideas in this document.

Luther's theses caused considerable controversy. Many people were excited by his ideas, despite being condemned by the Church. Gradually, he was drawn into more serious disagreements with Church authorities.

In response to critics, Luther published pamphlets that explained his thinking. He argued that the Bible—not the pope or Church leaders—was the ultimate source of religious authority. The only true sacraments, he said, were baptism and the Eucharist. The Church's other five sacraments had no basis in the Bible. Moreover, Luther said that all Christians were priests and, therefore, all should study the Bible for themselves.

In the eyes of Church leaders, Luther was attacking fundamental truths of the Catholic religion. In January 1521, Pope Leo X excommunicated him, which meant he was no longer allowed membership in the Church.

In April 1521, Luther was brought before the Diet, an assembly of state leaders, in the German city of Worms. At the risk of his life, he refused to take back his teachings, prompting the Holy Roman emperor, Charles V, to declare Luther a heretic and forbid the printing or selling of his writings. For a time Luther went into hiding, but the movement he had started continued to spread.

denomination a particular religious group within a larger faith. For example, Lutheranism is one denomination within Christianity.

Luther Starts His Own Church Many Germans viewed Luther as a hero. As his popularity grew, he continued to develop his ideas. Soon he was openly organizing a new Christian **denomination** known as Lutheranism, which emphasized studying the Bible. Luther not only translated the Bible into German, but he also wrote a baptism service, a mass, and new hymns (sacred songs) in the language.

Having rejected the Church's hierarchy, Luther looked to German princes to support his church. When a peasants' revolt broke out in 1524, the rebels expected Luther to support their demands for social and economic change. Instead, Luther denounced the peasants and sided with the rulers because he needed their help to continue his new church's growth. By the time the uprising was crushed, tens of thousands of peasants had been brutally killed, so many rejected Lutheranism.

Several princes, however, supported Luther, and Lutheranism continued to grow. Over the next 30 years, Lutherans and Catholics were often at war in Germany. These religious wars ended in 1555 with the Peace of Augsburg, a **treaty** that permitted each prince within the Holy Roman Empire to determine the religion of his subjects.

The Peace of Augsburg was a major victory for Protestantism. Christian unity was at an end, and not only in Germany. As you will learn next, by this time a number of other Protestant churches had sprung up in northern Europe.

Martin Luther burned the papal bull, or letter, informing him that he was being excommunicated from the Catholic Church.

The printing press and booksellers, such as this man, helped to spread the ideas of the Reformation.

4. Other Leaders of the Reformation

The movement started by Martin Luther swept across much of Europe. Many people who were dismayed by abuses in the Church remained loyal Catholics, whereas others were attracted to new forms of the Christian faith. The printing press helped spread new ideas, as well as translations of the Bible, faster than ever before. In addition, government leaders had learned from Luther's experience that they could win religious independence from the Church. The Reformation succeeded most where rulers embraced Protestant faiths.

Many reformers contributed to the spread of Protestantism. Let's take a look at four leaders of the Reformation.

Huldrych Zwingli (1484–1530) Huldrych Zwingli (HUL-drick ZVING-lee) was a Catholic priest in Zurich, Switzerland who was influenced by both Erasmus and Luther. After reading Luther's work, he persuaded the local government to ban any form of worship that was not based on the Bible. In 1523, Zurich declared its independence from the authority of the local Catholic bishop.

Zwingli wanted Christians to focus solely on the Bible, and he attacked the worship of relics, saints, and images. In the Protestant churches he founded, there were no religious statues or paintings, and services were very simple, without music or singing.

Zwingli carried his ideas to other Swiss cities. In 1530, war broke out between his followers and Swiss Catholics, and Zwingli died during the fighting.

John Calvin (1509–1564) In the late 1530s, John Calvin, a French humanist, established another Protestant group in Geneva, Switzerland. His book, *Institutes of the Christian Religion,* became one of the most influential works of the Reformation.

Calvin emphasized that salvation came only from God's grace. He said that the "saved" whom God elected, or chose, lived according to strict standards. He believed firmly in hard work and thrift, or the careful use of money. Success in business, he taught, was a sign of God's grace. Calvin tried to establish a Christian state in Geneva that would be ruled by God through the Calvinist Church.

Calvin influenced many other reformers, including John Knox, a Scotsman who lived in Geneva for a time. Knox led the Protestant reform that established the Presbyterian Church in Scotland.

King Henry VIII (1491–1547) England's Protestant Reformation was led by King Henry VIII. In 1534, Henry formed the Church of England, also called the Anglican Church, and named himself as its supreme head.

Unlike Luther and Calvin, King Henry did not have major disagreements with Catholic teachings. His reasons for breaking with the Church were personal and political. On a personal level, he wanted to end his first marriage, but the pope had denied him a divorce. On a political level, he no longer wanted to share power and wealth with the Church. In 1536, Henry closed down Catholic monasteries in England and took their riches.

William Tyndale was an English priest, scholar, and writer who traveled to Germany and met Martin Luther. As his views became increasingly Protestant, he attacked corruption in the Catholic Church and defended the English Reformation. After being arrested by Catholic authorities in the city of Antwerp, in present-day Belgium, he spent over a year in prison and was burned at the stake in 1536.

Tyndale is especially important to the Reformation because of his translations of the Bible. To spread knowledge of the Bible, he translated the New Testament and parts of the Old Testament into English. In the early 1600s, his work was used in the preparation of the King James, or Authorized, Version of the Bible. Famed for its beautiful language, the King James Bible had an enormous influence on English worship, language, and literature.

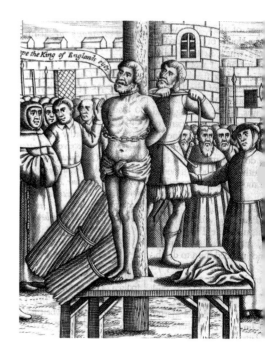

Writer and scholar William Tyndale was burned at the stake for his Protestant beliefs.

Lesson Summary

In this lesson, you learned about the Reformation, which began in the early 1500s. This movement led to the founding of many new Christian denominations in Europe.

The Weakening of the Catholic Church By the Late Middle Ages, the Catholic Church was weakened by corruption, political struggles, and humanist ideas. Many Catholics were dismayed by worldliness and immorality in the Church, including the sale of indulgences and the practice of simony.

Early Calls for Reform A number of Catholics began to call for reform, including John Wycliffe, Jan Hus, Catherine of Siena, and Erasmus. They questioned the practices of Church leaders and some of the Church's teachings.

Martin Luther Breaks Away From the Church In the early 1500s, German priest Martin Luther became involved in a major dispute with the Church over indulgences and other practices. Excommunicated, Luther established the first Protestant church, which started the Reformation.

Other Leaders of the Reformation Other Protestant reformers began to separate from the Catholic Church. The printing press helped to spread their ideas. Zwingli and Calvin began churches in Switzerland. William Tyndale translated the Bible into English. Henry VIII became the supreme head of the new Church of England.

Lesson 37

The Spread and Impact of the Reformation

What were the effects of the Reformation?

Introduction

In this lesson, you will learn more about the movement called the Reformation and the Protestant churches that emerged in the 1500s. You will also explore the impact of the Reformation on the Catholic Church and on the history of Europe.

As Protestantism spread, it branched out in several directions. By the start of the 1600s, there were already many different Christian churches in Europe.

Each Protestant denomination had its own beliefs and practices. However, all Protestants had much in common, including a shared belief in the authority of the Bible, individual conscience, and the importance of faith. In addition, they were united in their desire to **reform** Christianity.

The growth of Protestantism also helped to encourage a reform movement within the Catholic Church called the Counter-Reformation. As part of this movement, Church leaders worked to correct abuses, clarify and defend Catholic teachings, and condemn what they saw as Protestant **errors**. Additionally, they tried to win back areas of Europe that had been lost to the Catholic Church.

The many divisions among Christians led to a series of wars and persecutions. People suffered because of their beliefs. Catholics fought Protestants, and Protestants fought one another. These struggles involved political, economic, and cultural differences, as well as deep religious beliefs.

The Reformation brought much conflict to Europe, but it also created many new forms of the Christian faith. Three new branches of Christianity that developed early in the period were Lutheranism, Calvinism, and Anglicanism.

Social Studies Vocabulary

absolute monarchy

Anglicanism

Calvinism

Counter-Reformation

Lutheranism

nationalism

Puritans

theocracy

◀ Catholic leaders worked to strengthen the Church in response to the Reformation.

Lutheranism a Protestant denomination of Christian faith founded by Martin Luther

1. Lutheranism

The first major Protestant sect was **Lutheranism**. Lutheranism began in Germany after Martin Luther was excommunicated by the Catholic Church in 1521.

Luther was a Catholic priest and scholar who taught scripture and theology (the study of religion) at the University of Wittenberg. As he studied the Bible, Luther became troubled because he could not find a basis for many Church teachings and practices. He was also upset about corruption in the Church, especially the sale of indulgences.

Luther tried to work out his differences with the Church. However, after his views were condemned, he started the separate movement that became Lutheranism.

Beliefs About Sin and Salvation Luther and his followers disagreed with the Catholic Church about sin and salvation. Catholics believed that people earned salvation by following the teachings and practices of the Church. Taking part in the sacraments was essential. For example, the sacrament of baptism wiped away original sin. In Christian belief, this was the sinful condition passed on to all people by Adam, the first man created by God. Once they were baptized, people needed to pray, take the sacraments, follow rules laid down by the Church, and perform good works.

Lutherans did not believe that people could do anything to earn their salvation, rather it was God's gift, which people received in faith. People would be "justified," or saved, if they sincerely believed in Jesus Christ, were sorry for their sins, and accepted the words of the Bible as truth. Luther called this "justification by faith." According to Luther, those who have faith perform good works and avoid sin because God commands them to, not in order to earn salvation.

The Augsburg Confession, or statement of faith, was prepared by German reformer Melanchthon in 1530, with Luther's approval. In its modern form, it is the basis of Lutheranism for millions of people around the world.

Ultimate Source of Authority Lutherans rejected traditional sources of religious authority, such as Church councils and the pope, and instead believed that the Bible was the only true source of religious guidance. Reading the Bible was the only way to learn how to lead a good life and gain faith in God. Lutherans published the Bible in several languages so that people could read it for themselves.

Rituals and Worship Lutheran services combined Catholic practices with new Lutheran ones. Lutherans met in church buildings that had originally been Catholic. Like Catholics, they used an altar, candles, and a crucifix, which represented the crucifixion of Jesus.

Lutheran services resembled the Catholic mass in several ways. The services included Holy Communion, the Christian ritual of sharing bread and wine to commemorate the last meal Jesus shared with his disciples before his death. Lutheran services also included Bible readings and a sermon, in which clergy explained the day's lesson from the Bible. Like Catholics, Lutherans sang hymns. Luther wrote these hymns in German for his followers and often set them to popular tunes so everyone could learn them more easily.

Other parts of Lutheran worship were different from Catholic practice. Prayers were written and spoken in German, not in Latin, so that everyone could participate. Instead of having seven sacraments, Lutherans had just two, baptism and Communion, which Luther believed were the only sacraments clearly named in the Bible.

This painting of a Reformation church shows Lutheran clergy ministering the sacraments of baptism (far left) and Communion (center and right). Luther preaches from the altar at the far right.

Calvinism a Protestant denomination of Christian faith founded by John Calvin

Community Life Luther gave his followers certain rules for how to live. Over time, he preached less about the Bible and instead started to place greater importance on discipline and strong families. He believed that fathers should teach their children religion by having them pray before meals and before bed. "Unless they [pray]," he said, "they should be given neither food nor drink." He also thought that women should get married and give birth to as many children as possible. He felt that these rules would help to strengthen Lutheran communities.

Unlike Catholic priests, Lutheran ministers, or members of the clergy, were allowed to marry. Luther himself married a former nun.

2. Calvinism

Calvinism was founded by John Calvin, a French humanist who did his most influential work in Geneva, Switzerland. In 1541, Calvin took over the leadership of the reform movement in Geneva.

Beliefs About Sin and Salvation Calvinists agreed with Lutherans that people depended entirely on God to be saved. No one deserved salvation, and no one could "force" God to grant it by doing good works. Instead, God chose certain people, the "elect," to be saved and to enjoy eternal life. Religious faith and salvation were God's gifts to the elect, and everyone else was doomed to spend eternity in hell.

Calvin maintained that God knew from the beginning of time who would be saved and who would be condemned, an idea called *predestination*. There was nothing people could do to change their destiny because, as Calvin said, everything is under God's control.

Calvinists believed that the elect could be known by their actions. They believed that the world was full of opportunities to sin, but only people who were destined not to be saved would sin. Good behavior indicated that a person was an elect destined for heaven. The reason for good behavior was to honor God, not to "buy" one's salvation.

Calvinists had many strict rules defining good behavior. For example, singing, dancing, playing cards, and wearing fancy clothing were all forbidden. Many people followed these rules to show that they were saved.

John Calvin led a Reformation church in Geneva, Switzerland. Calvinists lived by strict rules that they felt showed them to be good Christians.

Ultimate Source of Authority Like Lutherans, Calvinists thought that the Bible was the only true source of religious guidance. Part of the task of church leaders was to interpret the Bible and make laws from it. Calvinists believed that all of life should be lived according to God's law. **Consequently,** in a Calvinist state, religious rules also became government laws, meaning that anyone who sinned was also committing a crime. A lawbreaker was punished first by Calvinist clergy and then by the local court system. Sins such as blasphemy (showing disrespect to God) were treated as serious crimes.

Rituals and Worship Calvinist churchgoers attended services up to five times a week. Services included sermons that lasted for hours and that explained how to live according to the Bible.

Calvinist church buildings reflected Calvin's belief in simplicity. Churches were paneled in plain wood and had no paintings, statues, or stained glass windows. People sat on long wooden benches, while the minister preached from a pulpit in the middle of the room. Men sat on one side of the church, and women and children sat on the other side. Children had to be prepared to answer questions from the minister at a moment's notice. Failure to answer correctly would bring them shame or even punishment.

Like Lutherans, Calvinists used only the two sacraments they found in the Bible: baptism and Communion. Calvinists were not allowed to sing any words except those in the Bible. At services, they sang verses from the Bible set to popular tunes or to melodies that had been specially written for them.

Community Life Calvinists believed that each community should be a **theocracy,** or a state governed by God through religious leaders. Calvinists had a duty to try to establish communities in which church and state were united.

Calvinist communities had strict laws based on the Bible. Parents could name babies only certain names from the Bible. Guests at local inns were prohibited from swearing, dancing, playing cards, or insulting anyone at the inn. Innkeepers were required to report anyone who broke these rules. The same rules applied to people in their homes, which church leaders could inspect yearly to see whether families were living by the strict Calvinist laws. Offenders were punished severely, and some were even banished.

theocracy a government or state in which God is the supreme ruler, and religious officials govern in God's name

Calvinist churches reflected Calvin's belief in simplicity. They were practical with few decorations such as paintings or stained glass.

3. Anglicanism

Anglicanism was founded in 1534 by King Henry VIII in
England. Henry was not a religious reformer like Martin Luther or
John Calvin. Instead, he broke away from the Catholic Church for
political and personal reasons.

Politically, Henry did not want to share either his power or his
kingdom's wealth with the Church. Personally, he wanted to get a
divorce so that he could marry another woman, Anne Boleyn. He
wanted a male heir, and he and his first wife, Catherine of Aragon,
failed to have a male child.

When the pope refused to grant permission for a divorce, Henry
took matters into his own hands and compelled Parliament, England's
lawmaking body, to declare him the head of the English church. So
began the Church of England, or Anglican Church, with the monarch
as its leader.

Under Henry, the Church of England continued to greatly
resemble the Catholic Church. Over time, however, it blended elements of Catholicism and Protestantism.

Beliefs About Sin and Salvation Anglican beliefs had much
in common with the beliefs of the Catholic Church. Like Catholics,
Anglicans believed that baptism washed away original sin. Anglicans,
however, were also influenced by Protestant ideas and accepted
Luther's idea of justification by faith. To go to heaven, people needed
only to believe in God, regret their sins, and receive God's mercy.

Later, Anglicans believed that people should have privacy in how
they practiced religion. It was up to individuals to determine how to
live by their religious beliefs.

Despite the pope's refusal to grant
Henry VIII a divorce from his first wife,
Henry (left) secretly married his second
wife, Anne Boleyn (right), in early 1533.
Their marriage signaled Henry's break
with the Catholic Church.

Ultimate Source of Authority Anglicans based their beliefs on the Bible, but the English monarch, as head of the Church, was the main interpreter of the Bible's meaning. The highest-ranking bishop in England, the Archbishop of Canterbury, assisted the monarch with this task. Local clergy and churchgoers could interpret Church teachings in their own ways, as long as they were loyal to the monarch.

Rituals and Worship Anglican services were similar to both Roman Catholic and Lutheran services. Two versions of the Anglican Church service developed. The High Church service was much like the Catholic mass and very formal, whereas the Low Church service was similar to the Lutheran service.

Anglican services were held in former Catholic Church buildings that had been stripped of their paintings, statues, and other decorations. The inside of each church was painted white, and the Ten Commandments were painted on a plain white wall. Churchgoers sang simple hymns with English words and easy melodies.

Like other Protestant groups, Anglicans used only two sacraments: baptism and Communion. English slowly replaced Latin in Anglican services. Under Henry's son, King Edward VI, an official prayer book, the *Book of Common Prayer*, was published, and it provided English-language prayers for services and morning and evening prayers. It also expressed the basic ideas of Anglican doctrine. In the early 1600s, King James I had a committee of scholars prepare a new English translation of the Bible, known as the Authorized Version, or the King James Version.

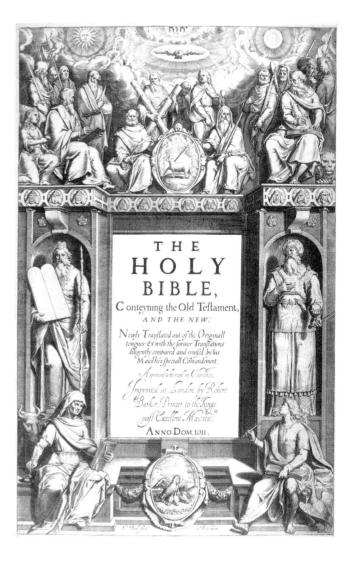

During the Reformation, Protestants published many vernacular versions of the Bible in English, including the King James Version.

Community Life Anglican communities were not all alike. High Church communities were made up mostly of wealthy people, whereas Low Church communities were usually made up of middle-class and working-class people.

Henry VIII's daughter, Queen Elizabeth I, said that no one should be forced to believe or practice a particular kind of Anglicanism. People could choose how to worship as long as they obeyed the laws of England and were loyal to the monarch. Heresy ceased to be a crime, but citizens had to take care not to attack the monarch or the Anglican Church's place as the official Church of England.

4. The Counter-Reformation

As Protestantism spread, the Catholic Church responded with a program of serious reform. It **clarified** its teachings, corrected abuses, and tried to win people back to Catholicism. This movement is known as the **Counter-Reformation**.

The Council of Trent A major feature of the Counter-Reformation was the Council of Trent, a meeting of Catholic leaders that began in Trent, Italy, in 1545. Pope Paul III summoned the council to combat corruption in the Church and to fight Protestantism. The council continued its work in more than 20 sessions over the next 18 years.

In response to Protestant ideas, the council gave a more precise statement of Catholic teachings. It rejected predestination, declaring that individuals do have a role to play in deciding the fate of their souls. The council agreed with Protestants that faith was important and that salvation was God's gift, but it rejected justification by faith alone. The council insisted that faith, good works, and the sacraments were all necessary for salvation. It reaffirmed the Catholic belief in seven sacraments.

Counter-Reformation a movement of the Catholic Church, in reaction to the Reformation, in which Catholic leaders worked to correct abuses, to clarify and defend Catholic teachings, to condemn what they saw as Protestant errors, and to win back members

This scene from the Council of Trent shows Roman Catholic leaders as they meet to reform their own church and consider ways to fight against the spread of Protestantism.

The council acknowledged the importance of the Bible. It insisted, however, on the Church's authority to interpret the Bible and stated that the Latin Bible was the only official scripture.

The council also took action to make needed changes in the Church. It required better education and training of its clergy and called for priests and bishops to spend more time preaching. It corrected many of the abuses involving money and Church offices. Additionally, it established rules for services so that they would be more consistent from church to church.

The Council of Trent went a long way toward achieving the goals of Pope Paul III. The council's work brought a higher standard of morality to the Church's clergy and leadership, while its statements of Catholic belief and practices helped to unify the Church. The reformed Church was now better able to compete with Protestantism for the loyalties of Christians.

Teresa of Avila, a nun, established a new religious order in Spain and helped reform the lives of the clergy. Her writings inspired many Catholics to return to the religion.

Catholic Reformers and Missionaries The spirit of reform brought new life to the Catholic Church and its followers. Many individuals and groups helped to reform the Church and spread its message. For example, Teresa of Avila, a nun, started a new religious order in Spain and helped reform the lives of priests and nuns. Her example and writings inspired many Catholics to return to the values taught by Jesus.

Other new orders were formed to preach, to educate people, and to perform such services as feeding the poor. The most important of these orders was the Society of Jesus, also known as the Jesuits.

The Jesuits were founded by Ignatius of Loyola, a Spanish nobleman. As a young soldier, Ignatius had his leg shattered by a cannonball. While he was recovering, he read about the lives of saints. He then vowed to become a "soldier for Jesus."

After years of study, Ignatius started the order that became the Society of Jesus, or the Jesuits. The Jesuits were dedicated teachers and missionaries who founded schools and colleges. They brought many Europeans back to the Church and also worked to spread Catholicism in Africa, Asia, and the Americas. They became the largest order in the Church and actively supported the pope.

Fighting the Spread of Protestantism The Catholic Church also fought the spread of Protestantism by condemning beliefs that it considered to be errors and by dealing harshly with those it labeled as heretics. It looked to Catholic rulers to support its efforts and to win back lands lost to Protestantism.

Those considered heretics during the Spanish Inquisition participated in a ritual of public penance during which their sentence was announced. After the ceremony, the civil authorities would carry out the punishment.

To deal with heresies during the Middle Ages, the Church had established the Inquisition. This body was made up of clergy called inquisitors who sought out and tried heretics. Inquisitors could order various punishments, including fines and imprisonment, and they sometimes turned to civil rulers to put heretics to death.

King Ferdinand and Queen Isabella used the Spanish Inquisition to persecute Jews and Muslims. With the start of the Reformation, the Spanish Inquisition also fought the spread of Protestantism. In Rome, the pope established a new Inquisition. The Roman Inquisition similarly sought out and condemned people whose views were considered dangerous.

5. Effects of the Reformation

The Reformation brought lasting change to Europe. Through the influence of Europeans, it also affected other parts of the world.

Religious Wars and Persecution The religious divisions of the Reformation led to a series of wars and persecutions during the 16th and 17th centuries. Catholics and Protestants alike persecuted members of other denominations, as well as each other.

Many people died for their beliefs. Others, like the French Protestants who moved to Switzerland, fled to Protestant countries.

Bloody civil wars erupted in many countries. In France, for example, wars between Catholics and Protestants between 1562 and 1598 left over a million dead.

The wars in France were not only about religion, but they were also about the power of the Catholic monarchy. Similarly, the last major war of the Reformation, which was fought in Germany, was both political and religious. The war, later called the Thirty Years' War (1618–1648), pitted Catholics against Protestants, and Protestants against each other. However, it was also a struggle for power that involved most of the nations of Europe, which fought for their own interests, as well as for religious reasons. Catholic France, for example, sided with Protestants to combat the power of the Holy Roman Empire.

The Thirty Years' War ended in 1648 with the signing of the Peace of Westphalia, a treaty that called for peace between Protestants and Catholics. By deciding the control of territory, it set boundaries between Catholic and Protestant lands. Most of northern Europe, including much of Germany, was Protestant. Spain, Portugal, Italy, and France remained Catholic. So did Bohemia, Austria, and Hungary. This religious division survived for many centuries.

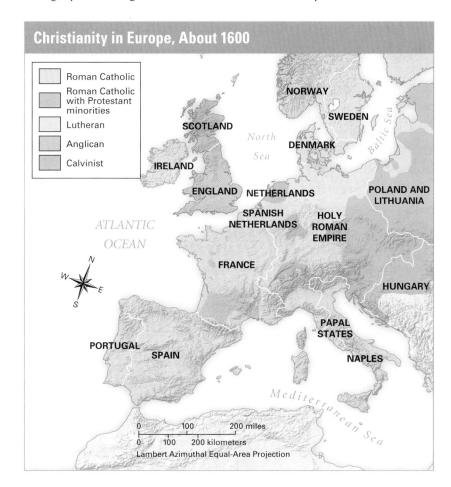

By 1600, Protestantism had spread across much of northern Europe, especially in the Holy Roman Empire, Scandinavia, and the British Isles. Small groups were also in the largely Catholic nations of France, Poland, and Hungary.

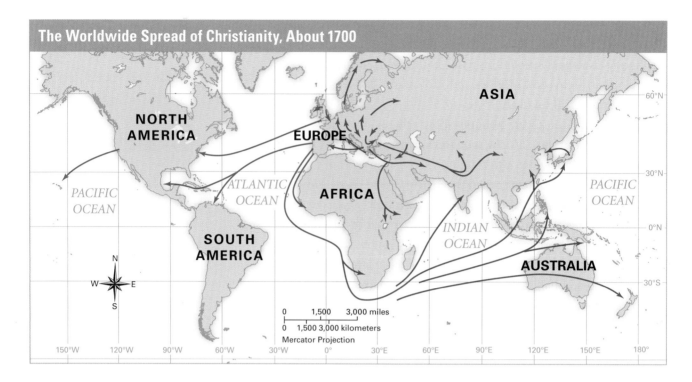

The Worldwide Spread of Christianity, About 1700

As Europeans began to explore beyond their continent, they brought their religious beliefs with them. By the 18th century, Christianity had been carried around the world.

The Rise of Nationalism and Democratic Practices The spread of Protestantism went hand in hand with a growing feeling called **nationalism**. Increasingly, people identified with their nation rather than with their local area or lord. Throughout Europe, official state religions strengthened national unity.

Along with nationalism, monarchies were also growing stronger. Protestant rulers claimed authority over religious, as well as secular, matters. Even Roman Catholic rulers became increasingly independent of the pope.

These changes led to what is often called "The Age of Monarchs." Monarchs revived the old idea of the divine right of kings. According to this idea, rulers received their authority directly from God. This way of thinking reached its height in the late 17th and early 18th centuries when some rulers established **absolute monarchies**.

Yet the Reformation also planted the seeds of democratic ideas and practices. Beginning with Martin Luther, Protestants emphasized being true to the Bible and to their own consciences. This belief made people more willing to resist authority and to fight for their own ideas and rights.

Some persecuted groups sought freedom to worship in their own ways. For example, the Calvinist **Puritans** fled England for North America in search of religious liberty. Many Protestant local groups, or congregations, insisted on their right to control their own affairs. In addition, the leaders of Protestant churches were elected by congregation members, not just by the powerful. Such beliefs about religious freedom and church government helped pave the way for democracy.

The Spread of Christianity By the time of the Reformation, Europeans had embarked upon a great age of exploration. As they voyaged around the world, both Catholics and Protestants worked to spread their faith. By the 1700s, there were missionary societies in several European countries. Jesuit missionaries were particularly active in spreading Roman Catholicism in places such as India, China, Japan, and Southeast Asia. Protestant missionaries worked in Ceylon (now Sri Lanka), India, and Indonesia.

The religious divisions in Europe were repeated in areas controlled by Europeans around the world. This was especially true in the Americas. Most people in English colonies in North America were Protestant. Missionaries and settlers from France brought Catholicism to parts of Canada and the Mississippi Valley. The Spanish and Portuguese brought Catholicism to the American southwest, Mexico, and South America. These patterns of religious faith are evident today.

Lesson Summary

In this lesson, you read about three branches of Protestantism—Lutheranism, Calvinism, and Anglicanism. You also learned about the Catholic response to the Reformation and some of the Reformation's lasting effects.

Lutheranism, Calvinism, and Anglicanism Started by Martin Luther in 1521, Lutheranism was the first Protestant sect. Calvinism was started by John Calvin in Switzerland in 1541. The Anglican Church was founded when English king Henry VIII separated from the Catholic Church in 1534. All three sects believed that the Bible was the only religious authority and rejected all sacraments except for baptism and Communion. Services were held in the vernacular, not Latin. Clergy could marry. Unlike Lutherans and Anglicans, Calvinists believed in predestination—that salvation of "the elect" was predetermined by God. They also believed that the Bible should form the basis for secular, as well as religious, law.

The Counter-Reformation The Catholic Church responded to Protestantism with the Counter-Reformation, a period of serious reform. At the Council of Trent, Catholic leaders created a more precise statement of Catholic belief and worked to end corruption. Reformers, such as the Jesuits, actively fought the spread of Protestantism through missionary work and the Inquisition.

Effects of the Reformation By the end of the wars that followed the Reformation, medieval Europe was largely a thing of the past. The Peace of Westphalia in 1648 set boundaries between Catholic and Protestant lands. This religious division survived into modern times and spread to wherever Europeans controlled territory around the world. In the period following the Reformation, Europe experienced a rise in nationalism and a strengthening of the monarchies. Yet, Protestantism also led to the beginnings of modern democracy.

Europe's Renaissance and Reformation

1296
Work Begins on Florence's Cathedral
The cathedral is completed in 1436 with a dome designed by architect Filippo Brunelleschi.

About 1300–1600
Renaissance in Europe
The Renaissance is a rebirth in classical art, learning, and culture, including the development of a new philosophy known as humanism.

1501–1504
Michelangelo Creates *David*
Michelangelo sculpts *David,* now one of the most admired statues in the world.

1200   **1300**   **1400**

1309–1377
Pope's Headquarters in France
The office of the pope is located in Avignon, France, causing many Europeans to believe that the French monarchy controls the papacy.

1450
Invention of the Printing Press
Johannes Gutenberg invents a printing press that uses movable type.

1509
The Praise of Folly
Desiderius Erasmus publishes a book that criticizes abuses by church leaders and calls for a reformation of the Catholic Church.

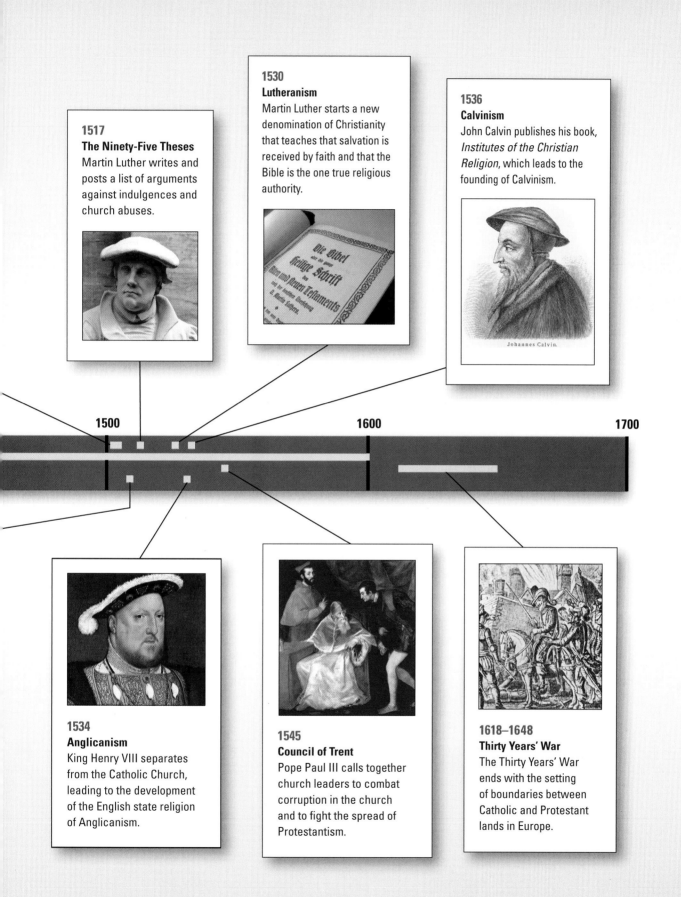

1517
The Ninety-Five Theses
Martin Luther writes and posts a list of arguments against indulgences and church abuses.

1530
Lutheranism
Martin Luther starts a new denomination of Christianity that teaches that salvation is received by faith and that the Bible is the one true religious authority.

1536
Calvinism
John Calvin publishes his book, *Institutes of the Christian Religion*, which leads to the founding of Calvinism.

Johannes Calvin.

1534
Anglicanism
King Henry VIII separates from the Catholic Church, leading to the development of the English state religion of Anglicanism.

1545
Council of Trent
Pope Paul III calls together church leaders to combat corruption in the church and to fight the spread of Protestantism.

1618–1648
Thirty Years' War
The Thirty Years' War ends with the setting of boundaries between Catholic and Protestant lands in Europe.

1500   1600   1700

Europe Enters the Modern Age

Full-sized replicas of the Niña, the Pinta, and the Santa Maria sailed from Spain to the United States to mark the 500th anniversary of Columbus's first voyage to the Americas. The largest ship was the Santa Maria, and the smallest was the Niña.

Europe Enters the Modern Age

In this unit, you will learn about Europe during the early modern age, which lasted from the 1400s to the 1700s. While Europe was immersed in the Renaissance and the Reformation, other major changes were taking place in the world. These changes originated in Europe, but soon involved other continents. The changes began with a series of voyages during the 1400s, 1500s, and early 1600s when European explorers ventured into the Atlantic and Pacific oceans. Historians call this period the Age of Exploration.

With today's global positioning satellites, Internet maps, cell phones, and rapid travel, it is difficult to imagine exactly how it might have

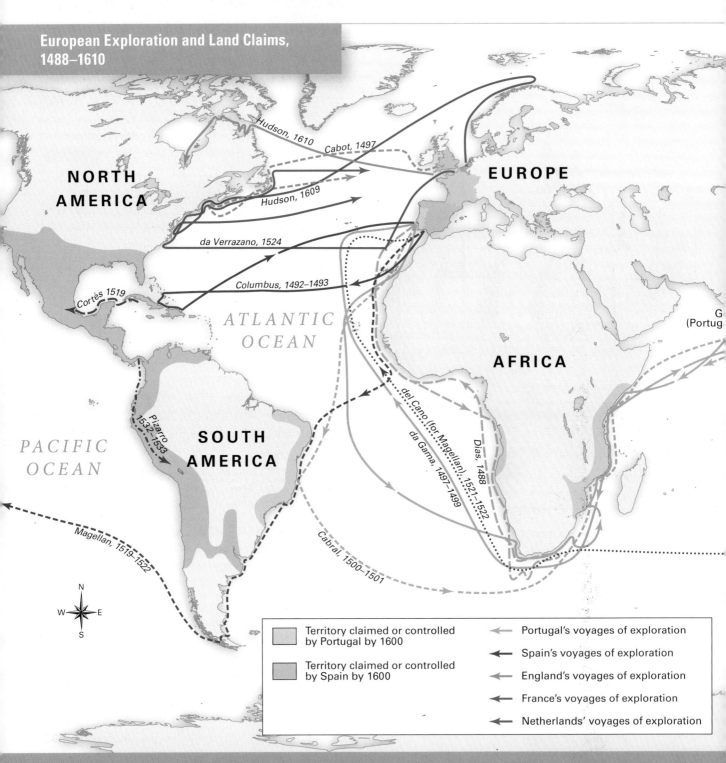

European Exploration and Land Claims, 1488–1610

Hudson, 1610

Cabot, 1497

Hudson, 1609

da Verrazano, 1524

Columbus, 1492–1493

Cortés 1519

Pizarro 1532–1533

Magellan, 1519–1522

del Cano (for Magellan), 1521–1522

da Gama, 1497–1499

Dias, 1488

Cabral, 1500–1501

G (Portug

NORTH AMERICA

EUROPE

AFRICA

SOUTH AMERICA

ATLANTIC OCEAN

PACIFIC OCEAN

	Territory claimed or controlled by Portugal by 1600	← Portugal's voyages of exploration
	Territory claimed or controlled by Spain by 1600	← Spain's voyages of exploration
		← England's voyages of exploration
		← France's voyages of exploration
		← Netherlands' voyages of exploration

felt to embark on a voyage across an unknown ocean. In the early 1400s in Europe, few people knew what lay across the ocean. How long it took to reach a destination depended on the wind, the weather, and the distance. Days would have run together, with no sounds other than the voices of the captain and the crew, the creaking of the sails, the blowing wind, and the splash of waves against the ship's hull.

ASIA

PACIFIC OCEAN

Magellan died, 1521.

Magellan, 1519–1522

Malacca (Portugal)

INDIAN OCEAN

del Cano (for Magellan), 1521–1522

AUSTRALIA

Would you be courageous enough to undertake such a voyage? Only those most adventurous, brave, and confident in their abilities to sail in any weather, manage any crew, and meet any circumstance dared do so. They sailed west from England, Spain, and Portugal to North America. They sailed south from Portugal and Spain to South America, to lands where the Incas lived. They traveled to Africa, past the kingdoms of Ghana, Mali, and Songhai. The crew of one Portuguese expedition even sailed completely around the world.

European explorers changed the world in many dramatic ways. Because of them, cultures divided by 3,000 miles or more of water began interacting and developing relationships. European countries claimed large parts of the world. As nations competed for territory, Europe had an enormous impact on people living in distant lands.

The Americas, in turn, made significant contributions to Europe and the rest of the world. For example, from the Americas came crops such as corn and potatoes, which flourished in Europe. By increasing Europe's food supply, these crops helped create population growth.

Another drastic change during the early modern age was the Scientific Revolution. Between 1500 and 1700, scientists used observation and experiments to make dramatic discoveries. For example, Isaac Newton formulated the laws of gravity. Additionally, the Scientific Revolution led to the invention of new tools, such as the microscope and the thermometer.

Advances in science helped pave the way for a period called the Enlightenment, which began in the late 1600s. Enlightenment thinkers used observation and reason to attempt to solve problems in society. Their work led to new ideas about government, human nature, and human rights.

The Age of Exploration, the Scientific Revolution, and the Enlightenment helped to shape the modern world. In this unit, you will begin exploring the early modern age with the Age of Exploration.

C. frio
Rio bravo
C. Hermoso
Cabo blanco
Cabo del Engaño
Tierra de las palmas
R. grande
Baia hermosa
R. hermoso
Braco
Mar Ver=
mejo.
Cali=
fornia.
Ponto de bue.
na Jheranja
Ancon de S. Andres
S. Augustin
Laguna del rasto
R. de S. Francesco.
Islas hermosas
Islas de los
Cedros
Islas de
los diamantes
Laguna de
caldera
P. de Pedro y S. Paulo.

Noua Hispania.
Messico.

Florida.

MARI

SIVE M

Cuba

Y. de S.
Thomas.
La anublada
C. de
California
Las Marias
Isleos colima
Colima
P. di na
vidad
Quebibo
Guatulco
Coconiseo
Staya
Pasado
P. de Picu
gualco.
YVCATAN.
co.

Iamaica

Rocca partida.
Simarron
Cagnados
C. de los
Farillones.
Repegu
Rimalle
Lempa
Badia de Gi.
S. Pe
Nicaragua
Blanco
R. de per=
dicion.
Medico
Nombre de Dios

Cartagena

VOD VVLGO

Y. de Cocos
Malpelle
P. de Gue:
vara.
Montaffe
Colin
Pana
ma
C. de forta.
Rio de S. Ioan.
Mangrales.
Rio de S. Iago

Y. de Galopagos.
P. de S. Matheo
30º
Quito.

24º   25º   26º   27º   28º   29º

Circulus Aequinoctialis.
Isola de la
plata
S. Clara.
Isola de
lobos
Badia de caraque.
Charapanton
de puna.
R. de S. Iago.
R. de tambes
R. de S. Miguel.
Paira
C. de laguia
Y. de Salinas.

Peru.

NOMI=NANT,
Isolas de lobos
Limocin
Civdad de los reiz.
Pachacania
Garico.
Laguna

Isolas de
cuervos.
Laanasca
Machate
R. de Montagr
Isleo de
arecife
R. Decumana
R. de arecipo,
Tambopele

S. Petri
C. de Fortuna
R. de buena madre

MAR
DEL
Cunhamu
co
C. Blanco
Arb
Las
Baa
Be

C. dela isla
C.
los

Prima ego velivolis ambivi cursibus Orbem,
Magellane novo te duce ducta freto.
Ambivi, meritoq3 vocor VICTORIA: sunt mî
Vela, alæ; precium, gloria; pugna, mare.

ZVR.

TRALIS,
ANICA, NON=

The Age of Exploration

How did the Age of Exploration change the way Europeans viewed the world?

Introduction

The Age of Exploration was a period of discovery that lasted from about 1418 to 1620. During this time, European explorers made numerous daring voyages that changed the world.

A major reason for these voyages was the desire to discover ocean routes to East Asia, which Europeans called the Indies. When Christopher Columbus sailed west across the Atlantic Ocean, he was looking for such a route. Although he thought he had reached the Indies, Columbus had actually reached the Americas. Eventually, Europeans would realize that Columbus had found what they called the "New World," and the Indies in the Atlantic became the West Indies. European nations soon rushed to claim lands in the Americas and elsewhere.

Early explorers often suffered terrible hardships. In 1520, Ferdinand Magellan departed South America with three ships to cross the Pacific Ocean. He had guessed, correctly, that Asia was located west of South America. However, Magellan was unaware of how vast the Pacific Ocean was. He thought his crew would sail for several weeks at most, but the crossing lasted three months. While the ships were still at sea, the crew ran out of food, nearly **starving** to death. One sailor wrote about the terrible time. "We ate biscuit . . . swarming with worms . . . We drank yellow water that had been putrid [rotten] for days . . . and often we ate sawdust from boards."

Why did explorers brave such dangers? In this lesson, you will discover some of the reasons for the Age of Exploration. You will learn about the voyages of explorers from Portugal, Spain, and other European countries. You will also learn how the Age of Exploration changed the way people viewed the world.

Social Studies Vocabulary

Age of Exploration

capitalism

cartography

colony

cottage industry

epidemic

market economy

mercantilism

◀ In the Age of Exploration, European nations competed to claim new lands.

1. The Causes of European Exploration

Why did European exploration begin to flourish in the 1400s? Two main reasons stand out. First, Europeans of this time had several **motives** for exploring the world. Second, advances in knowledge and technology helped to make the **Age of Exploration** possible.

Motives for Exploration For early explorers, one of the primary motives for exploration was the desire to establish new trade routes to Asia. By the 1400s, merchants and Crusaders had brought numerous goods to Europe from Africa, the Middle East, and Asia. Demand for these goods increased the desire for trade.

Europeans were especially interested in spices from Asia. They had learned to use spices to help preserve food during winter and to conceal the taste of food that was no longer fresh.

Trade with the East, however, was difficult and very expensive, in part because Muslims and Italians controlled the flow of goods. Muslim traders carried goods to the east coast of the Mediterranean Sea, and Italian merchants then brought the goods into Europe. Problems arose when Muslim rulers sometimes closed the trade routes from Asia to Europe. Also, the goods passed through many hands, and each trading party increased the price.

European monarchs and merchants wanted to break the hold that Muslims and Italians had on trade. One way to do so was to find a sea route to Asia. Portuguese sailors looked for a route that went around Africa, and Christopher Columbus tried to reach Asia by sailing west across the Atlantic.

Age of Exploration a period of European exploration and discovery that lasted from about 1418 to 1620

Mapmakers created better, more accurate maps by using navigational tools and information brought back by explorers.

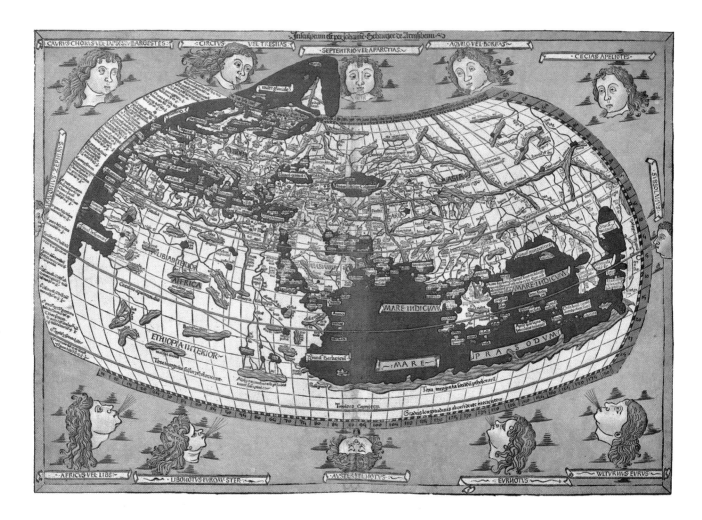

Europe's Age of Exploration produced key advances in cartography. This map dates from the 1400s. How accurate is it compared to a modern map?

Other motives also came into play. Many people were excited by the opportunity for new knowledge, while explorers sought the chance to earn fame and glory, as well as wealth. As new lands were discovered, nations wanted to claim the lands' riches for themselves.

A final motive for exploration was the desire to spread Christianity beyond Europe. Both Protestant and Catholic nations were eager to make new converts, with missionaries of both faiths following the paths blazed by explorers.

Advances in Knowledge and Technology The Age of Exploration began during the Renaissance. The Renaissance was a time of new learning when a number of advances occurred that made it easier for explorers to venture into the unknown.

One key advance was in **cartography,** the art and science of map-making. In the early 1400s, an Italian scholar translated an ancient book called *Guide to Geography* from Greek into Latin. The book was written by the thinker Ptolemy (TOL-eh-mee) in the 2nd century C.E. Printed copies of the book inspired new interest in cartography, and European mapmakers used Ptolemy's work as a basis for drawing more accurate maps.

cartography the science and art of making maps

Discoveries by explorers provided mapmakers with new information to use. The result was a dramatic change in Europeans' view of the world. By the 1500s, Europeans made globes showing Earth as a sphere. In 1507, a German cartographer made the first map that clearly showed North and South America as separate from Asia.

In turn, better maps made navigation easier. The most important Renaissance geographer, Gerardus Mercator (mer-KAY-tur), created maps using improved lines of longitude and latitude, which were a great help to navigators.

An improved ship design also helped explorers. By the 1400s, Portuguese and Spanish shipbuilders were making a new type of ship called a caravel. These ships were small, fast, and simple to maneuver and had special bottoms that made it easier for explorers to travel along coastlines where the water was shallow. Caravels also used lateen sails, a triangular style adapted from Muslim ships that could be positioned to take advantage of the wind regardless of its direction.

Along with better ships, new navigational tools helped sailors travel more safely on the open seas. By the end of the 1400s, the compass, which sailors used to find their bearing, or direction of travel, was much improved. The astrolabe helped sailors determine their distance north or south from the equator.

Finally, improved weapons gave Europeans a huge advantage over the people they met in their explorations. Sailors could fire their cannons at targets near the shore without leaving their ships. On land, the weapons of native peoples often were no match for European guns, armor, and horses.

2. Portugal Begins the Age of Exploration

The Age of Exploration began in Portugal, a small country located on the Iberian Peninsula. Its rulers sent explorers first to nearby Africa and then around the world.

Key Portuguese Explorers The major figure in early Portuguese exploration was Prince Henry, the son of King John I of Portugal. Nicknamed "the Navigator," Prince Henry was not an explorer himself, but he encouraged exploration and planned and directed many important expeditions.

Beginning in about 1418, Henry sent explorers to sea almost every year. He also started a school of navigation where sailors and mapmakers could learn their trades. His cartographers made new maps based on the information ship captains brought back.

Henry's early expeditions focused on the west coast of Africa. He wanted to continue the Crusades against the Muslims, find gold, and participate in Asian trade.

Prince Henry the Navigator promoted Portugal's exploration and began a school of navigation.

Gradually, Portuguese explorers made their way farther and farther south. In 1488, Bartolomeu Dias became the first European to sail around the southern tip of Africa.

In July 1497, Vasco da Gama set sail with four ships to chart a sea route to India. Da Gama's ships rounded Africa's southern tip and then sailed up the east coast of the continent. With the help of a sailor who knew the route to India from there, they were able to cross the Indian Ocean.

In May 1498, Da Gama arrived in the port of Calicut, India, where he obtained a load of cinnamon and pepper. On the return trip to Portugal, da Gama lost half of his ships. However, his valuable cargo paid for the voyage many times over. His trip increased the Portuguese's eagerness to trade directly with Indian merchants.

In 1500, Pedro Cabral (kah-BRAHL) set sail for India with a fleet of 13 ships. Cabral first sailed southwest to avoid areas without winds to fill sails, but he sailed so far west that he reached the east coast of present-day Brazil. After claiming this land for Portugal, he sailed back to the east, rounded Africa, and headed toward Calicut, where he established a trading post and signed trade treaties. He returned to Portugal in June 1501.

Portugal's explorers changed Europeans' understanding of the world in several ways. They explored the coasts of Africa and brought back gold and enslaved Africans. They also found a sea route to India. From India, explorers brought back spices, such as cinnamon and pepper, and other goods, such as porcelain, incense, jewels, and silk.

Vasco da Gama reached India by sailing around Africa and across the Indian Ocean.

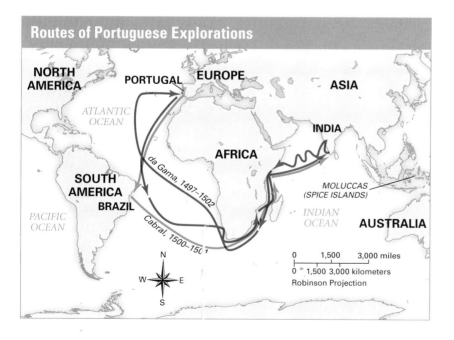

Routes of Portuguese Explorations

NORTH AMERICA
PORTUGAL
EUROPE
ASIA
ATLANTIC OCEAN
INDIA
AFRICA
da Gama, 1497–1502
MOLUCCAS (SPICE ISLANDS)
SOUTH AMERICA
BRAZIL
Cabral, 1500–1501
PACIFIC OCEAN
INDIAN OCEAN
AUSTRALIA
N
W E
S
0   1,500   3,000 miles
0   1,500   3,000 kilometers
Robinson Projection

Explorers from Portugal were among the earliest Europeans to make long sea voyages of explorations.

Although he initially set sail for India, Pedro Cabral reached present-day Brazil and claimed it for Portugal.

colony a territory, often very large, under the political and economic control of another country

After Cabral's voyage, the Portuguese took control of the eastern sea routes to Asia. They seized the seaport of Goa (GOH-uh) in India and built forts there. They attacked towns on the east coast of Africa. They also set their sights on the Moluccas, or Spice Islands, in what is now Indonesia, where, in 1511, they attacked the main port and killed the Muslim defenders. The captain of this expedition explained what was at stake. If Portugal could take the spice trade away from Muslim traders, he wrote, then Cairo and Mecca "will be ruined." As for Italian merchants, "Venice will receive no spices unless her merchants go to buy them in Portugal."

Portugal's control of the Indian Ocean ended Muslim and Italian control over Asian trade. With the increased competition, prices of Asian goods—such as spices and fabrics—dropped, enabling more Europeans to afford them.

During the 1500s, Portugal also began to establish colonies in Brazil. The native people of Brazil suffered greatly as a result, in part, because the Portuguese forced them to work on sugar plantations, or large farms. They also tried to get them to give up their religion and convert to Christianity. Missionaries sometimes tried to protect the native people from abuse, but countless natives died from overwork and from European diseases. Others fled into the interior of Brazil.

The colonization of Brazil also negatively affected Africa as well. As the native population of Brazil decreased, the Portuguese needed more laborers, so they turned to Africa beginning in the mid-1500s. Over the next 300 years, ships brought millions of enslaved West Africans to Brazil.

3. Spain's Early Explorations

In the late 1400s, King Ferdinand and Queen Isabella of Spain were determined to make their country a powerful force in Europe. One way they thought to do this was to sponsor explorations to claim new lands for Spain.

Key Explorers for Spain It was Ferdinand and Isabella who sponsored the voyages of Christopher Columbus. The Italian-born Columbus thought that the Indies, or eastern Asia, lay on the other side of the Atlantic Ocean and believed sailing west would be the easiest route to reach it.

When Columbus failed to win Portuguese support for his idea, Ferdinand and Isabella agreed to pay for the risky voyage. They wanted to beat Portugal in the race to control the trade wealth of Asia. They also wanted to spread Christianity.

In August 1492, three ships left Spain under Columbus's command. For the crew, venturing into the open ocean was frightening.

Christopher Columbus landed on an island in the Caribbean Sea when he tried to reach the Indies by sailing west across the Atlantic Ocean.

As the weeks passed, some of the men started to fear they would never see Spain again. Then, on October 12, a lookout sighted land. Columbus went ashore on an island in the Caribbean Sea and claimed it for Spain.

For three months, Columbus and his men explored nearby islands with assistance from native islanders, whom the Spanish called Taino (TY-noh). Thinking they were in the Indies, the Spanish soon called all the local people "Indians."

In March 1493, Columbus arrived back in Spain and proudly reported that he had reached Asia. Over the next ten years, he made three more voyages to what he called the Indies. He died in Spain in 1506, still insisting that he had sailed to Asia.

Many Europeans, however, believed that Columbus had actually found a land mass between Europe and Asia. One of these was Ferdinand Magellan (muh-JEL-uhn), a Portuguese explorer.

Magellan believed he could sail west to the Indies if he found a strait, or channel, through South America. The strait would connect the Atlantic and Pacific oceans, allowing ships to continue on to Asia. Magellan won Spain's support for a voyage to find the strait and, in August 1519, set sail with five ships and about 250 men.

Magellan looked for the strait all along South America's east coast and finally found it at the southern tip of the continent. Today, it is called the Strait of Magellan.

Explorer Christopher Columbus convinced King Ferdinand and Queen Isabella of Spain to support his westward voyages.

Ferdinand Magellan sailed around South America in search of a strait that linked the Atlantic and Pacific oceans.

To increase their nation's power, Ferdinand and Isabella of Spain sponsored several expeditions in search of better trade routes and new lands to control.

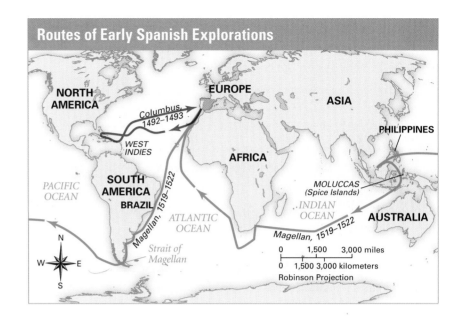

Routes of Early Spanish Explorations

After passing through the strait, Magellan reached the Pacific Ocean in November 1520, but it took another three months to cross the Pacific. Continuing west, Magellan visited the Philippines, where he became involved in a conflict between two local chiefs. In April 1521, Magellan was killed in the fighting.

Magellan's crew sailed on to the Spice Islands. Three years after the expedition began, the only ship to survive the expedition returned to Spain. The 18 sailors on board were the first people to travel completely around Earth.

The Impact of Early Spanish Exploration The early Spanish explorations greatly changed Europeans' view of the world. The voyages of Christopher Columbus revealed the existence of the Americas, and Magellan's expedition opened up a westward route to the Indies. It showed that it was possible to sail completely around the world. It also proved that Columbus had indeed found a "New World"—one that Europeans had not realized was there.

Columbus's voyages marked the beginning of Spanish settlement in the West Indies, which earned Spain great wealth. Settlers mined for precious minerals, such as gold and silver, and started sugar plantations. The Spanish also brought new crops, such as sweet potatoes and pineapples, to Europe.

For the native people of the West Indies, however, Spanish settlement was extremely **detrimental**. The Spanish forced native people to work as slaves in the mines and on the plantations, and priests forced many of them to become Christians. When the Spanish arrived, perhaps one or two million Taino lived on the islands. Within 50 years, fewer than 500 Taino were left, with most having died of starvation, overwork, or European diseases.

Like Portugal, Spain looked to West Africa for new laborers. From 1518 through the mid-1800s, the Spanish brought millions of enslaved Africans to work in their American colonies.

4. Later Spanish Exploration and Conquest

After Columbus's voyages, Spain was eager to claim even more lands in the New World. To explore and conquer "New Spain," the Spanish turned to adventurers called *conquistadors*, or conquerors. The conquistadors were allowed to establish settlements and seize the wealth of natives. In return, the Spanish government claimed some of the treasures they found.

Key Explorers In 1519, Spanish explorer Hernán Cortés (er-NAHN koor-TEZ) and a band of fellow conquistadors set out to explore present-day Mexico. Native people in Mexico told Cortés about the Aztecs, who had built a large and wealthy empire in Mexico.

With the help of a native woman named Malinche (mah-LIN-chay), Cortés and his men reached the Aztec capital, Tenochtitlán (tay-nawh-tee-TLAHN). The Aztec ruler, Montezuma II, welcomed the Spanish with great honors. Determined to break the power of the Aztecs, Cortés took Montezuma hostage.

When Spanish explorer Cortés (right) first entered Mexico, he was welcomed by the Aztec ruler, Montezuma II (left).

With the assistance of native allies who resented Aztec rule, Hernán Cortés captured the Aztec leader and brought down the Aztec Empire.

epidemic an outbreak of a contagious disease that spreads quickly and over a wide geographic area

Cortés now controlled the Aztec capital. In 1520, he left the city of Tenochtitlán to battle a rival Spanish force. While he was away, a group of conquistadors attacked the Aztecs in the middle of a religious celebration. In response, the Aztecs rose up against the Spanish. The soldiers had to fight their way out of the city, and many were killed during the escape.

The following year, Cortés mounted a siege of the city, aided by thousands of native allies who resented Aztec rule. The Aztecs ran out of food and water, yet they continued to fight desperately. After several months, the Spanish captured the Aztec leader, and Aztec resistance collapsed. The city was in ruins, and the mighty Aztec Empire was no more.

Four factors contributed to the defeat of the Aztec Empire. First, Aztec legend had predicted the arrival of a white-skinned god. When Cortés appeared, the Aztecs welcomed him because they thought he might be this god, Quetzalcoatl. Second, Cortés was able to make allies of the Aztecs' enemies. Third, their horses, armor, and superior weapons gave the Spanish an advantage in battle. Fourth, the Spanish carried diseases that caused deadly **epidemics** among the Aztecs.

Aztec riches inspired Spanish conquistadors to continue their search for gold. In the 1520s, Francisco Pizarro received permission from Spain to conquer the Inca Empire in South America. The Incas ruled an empire that extended throughout most of the Andes Mountains. By the time Pizarro arrived, however, a civil war had weakened that empire.

Routes of Later Spanish Explorations

Spanish explorations in the Americas, especially in Mexico and Peru, gained much territory and great wealth for Spain.

In April 1532, the Incan emperor, Atahualpa (ah-tuh-WAHL-puh), greeted the Spanish as guests. Following Cortés's example, Pizarro launched a surprise attack and kidnapped the emperor. Although the Incas paid a roomful of gold and silver in ransom, the Spanish killed Atahualpa. Without their leader, the Inca Empire quickly fell apart.

The Impact of Later Spanish Exploration and Conquest The explorations and conquests of the conquistadors transformed Spain. The Spanish rapidly expanded foreign trade and overseas colonization. For a time, wealth from the Americas made Spain one of the world's richest and most powerful countries.

Besides gold and silver, ships from the Americas brought corn and potatoes to Spain. These crops grew well in Europe, and the increased food supply helped spur a population boom. Conquistadors also introduced Europeans to new luxury items, such as chocolate.

In the long run, however, gold and silver from the Americas hurt Spain's economy. **Inflation,** or an increase in the supply of money, led to a loss of its value, and it cost people a great deal more to buy goods with the devalued money. Additionally, monarchs and the wealthy spent their riches on luxuries, instead of building Spain's industries.

The Spanish conquests had a major impact on the New World. The Spanish introduced new animals to the Americas, such as horses, cattle, sheep, and pigs. However, they destroyed two advanced civilizations, with the Aztecs and Incas losing much of their culture along with their wealth. Many became laborers for the Spanish, and millions died from disease. In Mexico, for example, there were about 25 million native people in 1519, but by 1605, this number had dwindled to one million.

5. Other European Explorations

Spain and Portugal dominated the early years of exploration, but rulers in rival nations wanted their own share of trade and new lands in the Americas. Soon England, France, and the Netherlands all sent expeditions to North America.

Key Explorers Explorers often sailed for any country that would pay for their voyages. The Italian sailor John Cabot made England's first voyage of discovery. Cabot believed he could reach the Indies by sailing northwest across the Atlantic. In 1497, he landed in what is now Canada. Believing he had reached the northeast coast of Asia, he claimed the region for England.

Another Italian, Giovanni da Verrazano, sailed under the French flag. In 1524, Verrazano explored the Atlantic coast from present-day North Carolina to Canada. His voyage gave France its first claims in the Americas. Unfortunately, on a later trip to the West Indies, he was killed by native people.

Francisco Pizarro was able to conquer the Inca Empire after a civil war had left it weakened.

John Cabot hoped to reach Asia by sailing across the Atlantic Ocean, but instead, he reached present-day Canada and claimed it for England.

Henry Hudson made claims for land in North America on behalf of the Dutch and, later, the English.

This illustration shows Henry Hudson being greeted by native people as he lands on Manhattan.

Sailing on behalf of the Netherlands, English explorer Henry Hudson journeyed to North America in 1609. Hudson wanted to find a northwest passage through North America to the Pacific Ocean. Such a water route would allow ships to sail from Europe to Asia without entering waters controlled by Spain.

Hudson did not find a northwest passage, but he did explore what is now called the Hudson River in present-day New York State. His explorations were the basis of the Dutch claim to the area. Dutch settlers established the colony of New Amsterdam on Manhattan in 1625.

In 1610, Hudson again tried to find a northwest passage, this time under the flag of his native England. Searching farther north, he sailed into a large bay in Canada that is now called Hudson Bay. He spent three months looking for an outlet to the Pacific, but there was none.

After a hard winter in the icy bay, some of Hudson's crew rebelled. They set him, his son, and seven loyal followers adrift in a small boat, and Hudson and the other castaways were never seen again. Hudson's voyage, however, laid the basis for later English claims in Canada.

Unlike the conquistadors in the south, northern explorers did not find gold and other treasure. As a result, there was less interest, at first, in starting colonies in that region.

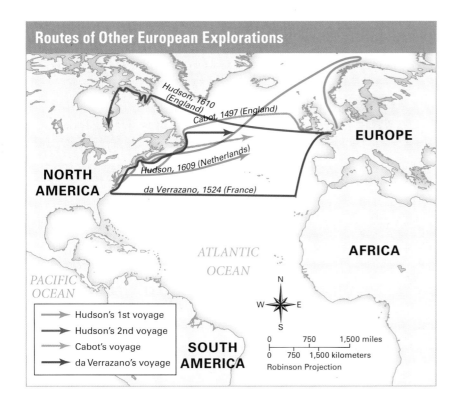

Routes of Other European Explorations

Hudson, 1610 (England)
Cabot, 1497 (England)
Hudson, 1609 (Netherlands)
da Verrazano, 1524 (France)

EUROPE

NORTH AMERICA

AFRICA

ATLANTIC OCEAN

PACIFIC OCEAN

N
W E
S

→ Hudson's 1st voyage
→ Hudson's 2nd voyage
→ Cabot's voyage
→ da Verrazano's voyage

SOUTH AMERICA

0   750   1,500 miles
0   750   1,500 kilometers
Robinson Projection

The English, Dutch, and French also sent out explorers in search of new land claims and new goods to trade. By the early 1600s, Europeans had established a number of trading posts in North America.

Canada's shores did offer rich resources of cod and other fish. A few years after Cabot's 1497 trip, fishing boats regularly visited the region. Europeans were also interested in trading with Native Americans for whale oil and otter, beaver, and fox furs. By the early 1600s, Europeans had set up a number of trading posts in North America.

English exploration also contributed to a war between England and Spain. As English ships roamed the seas, some captains, nicknamed "sea dogs," began raiding Spanish ports and ships to take their gold. Between 1577 and 1580, sea dog Francis Drake sailed around the world. He also claimed part of what is now California for England, ignoring Spain's claims to the area.

The English raids added to other tensions between England and Spain. In 1588, King Philip II of Spain sent an armada, or fleet of ships, to invade England. With 130 heavily armed vessels and about 30,000 men, the Spanish Armada seemed an unbeatable force, but the smaller English fleet was fast and well armed. Their guns had a longer range, so they could attack from a safe distance. After several battles, a number of the armada's ships had been sunk or driven ashore. The rest turned around but faced terrible storms on the way home. Fewer than half of the ships made it back to Spain.

The defeat of the Spanish Armada marked the start of a shift in power in Europe. By 1630, Spain no longer dominated the continent. With Spain's decline, other countries—particularly England and the Netherlands—took a more active role in trade and colonization around the world.

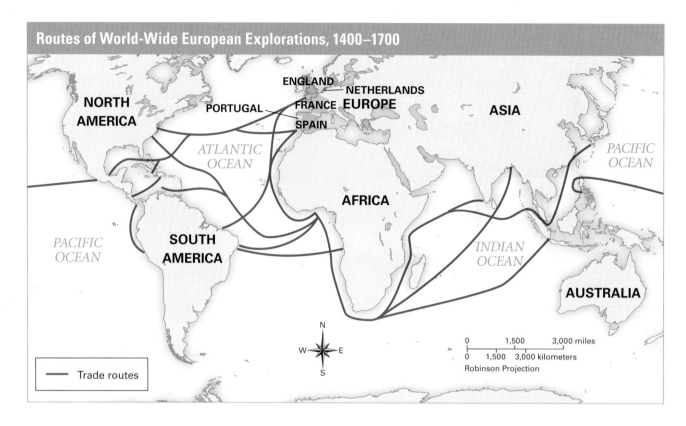

NORTH AMERICA

ATLANTIC OCEAN

ENGLAND
NETHERLANDS
FRANCE EUROPE
PORTUGAL
SPAIN

ASIA

PACIFIC OCEAN

PACIFIC OCEAN

SOUTH AMERICA

AFRICA

INDIAN OCEAN

AUSTRALIA

N
W E
S

0   1,500   3,000 miles
0   1,500   3,000 kilometers
Robinson Projection

—— Trade routes

By the late 1700s, European explorers had voyaged around the world and claimed many lands for their nations.

capitalism an economic system based on investment of money for profit

market economy an economy in which prices are determined by the buying and selling decisions of individuals in the marketplace

cottage industry a small-scale business in which people produce goods at home

mercantilism an economic policy by which nations try to gather wealth by controlling trade and establishing colonies

6. The Impact of Exploration on Europe

The voyages of explorers had a dramatic impact on European commerce and economies. As a result of exploration, more goods, raw materials, and precious metals entered Europe. Mapmakers carefully charted trade routes and the locations of newly discovered lands.

By the 1700s, European ships traveled trade routes that spanned the globe. New centers of commerce developed in the port cities of the Netherlands and England.

Exploration and trade contributed to the growth of capitalism. This economic system is based on investing money for profit. Merchants gained great wealth by trading and selling goods from around the world. Many of them used their profits to finance still more voyages and to start trading companies. Other people began investing money in these companies and shared in the profits, and soon, this type of shared ownership was applied to other kinds of businesses.

Another aspect of the capitalist economy concerned how people exchanged goods and services. Money became more important as precious metals flowed into Europe. Instead of having a fixed price, items were sold for prices set by the open market. This meant that an item's price depended on how much of the item was available and how many people wanted to buy it. Sellers could charge high prices for scarce items that many people wanted. If the supply of an item was large and few people wanted it, sellers lowered the price. This kind of system, based on supply and demand, is called a market economy.

Labor, too, was given a money value. Increasingly, people began working for hire instead of directly providing for their own needs. Merchants hired people to work from their own cottages, turning raw materials from overseas into finished products. This growing cottage industry was especially important in the manufacture of textiles. Often, entire families worked at home, spinning wool into thread or weaving thread into cloth. Cottage industry was a step toward the system of factories operated by capitalists in later centuries.

A final result of exploration was a new economic policy called mercantilism. European rulers believed that building up wealth was the best way to increase a nation's power. For this reason, they tried to reduce the products they bought from other countries and to increase the items they sold.

Having colonies was a key part of this policy. Nations looked to their colonies to supply raw materials for their industries at home. These industries turned the raw materials into finished goods that they could sell back to their colonies, as well as to other countries. To protect this valuable trade with their colonies, rulers often forbade colonists from trading with other nations.

Weaving cloth became a growing cottage industry as families set up looms and workshops in their homes.

Lesson Summary

In this lesson, you learned about the Age of Exploration. Beginning in the 1400s, European explorers went on great voyages of discovery.

The Causes of European Exploration European explorers sought wealth and land for their monarchs, as well as knowledge and adventure for themselves. They also wanted to spread Christianity. A number of advances in knowledge and technology made their journeys possible.

Portugal Begins the Age of Exploration In the early 1400s, under the leadership of Prince Henry the Navigator, the Portuguese became the first to purposefully explore the seas beyond Europe. They explored Africa's coasts, charted a sea route to South Asia, and claimed Brazil for Portugal.

Spain's Explorations The voyages of Christopher Columbus led to Spanish colonization in the Americas. Hernán Cortés and Francisco Pizarro conquered vast areas in Mexico and South America. The Aztec and Incan empires were destroyed. West Africans suffered greatly when they were brought to the Americas as slaves.

Other European Explorations England, France, and the Netherlands sent explorers to North America. The expeditions of Henry Hudson were the basis of Dutch land claims in what is now the Hudson River Valley and English land claims in Canada.

The Impact of Exploration on Europe Exploration vastly increased Europeans' knowledge. New foods led to a population explosion. Investments in expeditions and colonies contributed to the growth of capitalism, a market economy, cottage industries, and mercantilism.

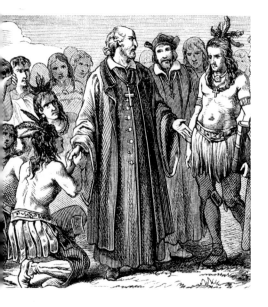

Former conquistador Bartolomé de Las Casas became an early defender of the rights of the native peoples conquered by the Spanish.

Bartolomé de Las Casas: From Conquistador to Protector of the Indians

Bartolomé de Las Casas experienced a remarkable change of heart during his lifetime. At first, he participated in Spain's conquest and settlement of the Americas, but later in life, he criticized and condemned it. For more than 50 years, he fought for the rights of the defeated and enslaved peoples of Latin America. How did this conquistador become known as "the Protector of the Indians"?

Bartolomé de Las Casas (bahr-taw-law-MEY day las KAH-sahs) ran through the streets of Seville, Spain, on March 31, 1493. He was just nine years old and on his way to see Christopher Columbus, who had recently returned from his first voyage to the Americas. Bartolomé wanted to see him and the "Indians," as they were called, as they paraded to the church.

Bartolomé's father and uncles were looking forward to seeing Columbus, as well. Like many Europeans during the late 1400s, they saw the Americas as a place of opportunity and signed up to join Columbus on his second voyage. Two years after that, Bartolomé followed in his father's footsteps and voyaged to the Americas himself. He sailed to the island of Hispaniola, the present-day nations of Haiti and the Dominican Republic.

Las Casas as Conquistador and Priest

One historian wrote that when Las Casas first arrived in the Americas, he was "not much better than the rest of the gentlemen-adventurers who rushed to the New World, bent on speedily acquiring fortunes." He supported the Spanish conquest of the Americas and was a loyal servant of Spain's king and queen, Ferdinand and Isabella.

Las Casas began his experiences in Spanish America on the island of Hispaniola in the Caribbean. There, he managed his family's businesses, which used enslaved Indians as labor.

Once in Hispañiola, Las Casas helped to manage his father's farms and businesses. Enslaved Indians worked in the family's fields and mines.

Spanish conquistadors wanted to gain wealth and glory in the Americas, but they had another goal, as well—to convert Indians to Christianity. Las Casas shared this goal, so the young conquistador went back to Europe to become a priest. Sometime in 1509 or 1510, he returned to Hispañiola, where he started to teach and baptize the Indians. At the same time, he continued to manage Indian slaves.

On a Path to Change

History often seems to be made up of moments when someone has a change of heart. The path that a person has been traveling takes a dramatic turn. It often appears to others that this change is sudden. In reality, a series of events usually causes a person to make the decision to change. One such event happened to Las Casas in 1511.

Roman Catholics in Hispañiola witnessed horrible acts of cruelty and injustice against the native peoples of the West Indies at the hands of the Spanish conquistadors. One of the priests there, Father Antonio de Montesinos, spoke out against the harsh treatment of the Indians in a sermon delivered to a Spanish congregation in Hispañiola in 1511. De Montesinos said:

> *You are in mortal sin . . . for the cruelty and tyranny you use in dealing with these innocent people . . . by what right or justice do you keep these Indians in such a cruel and horrible servitude? . . . Why do you keep them so oppressed? . . . Are not these people also human beings?*

One historian called this sermon "the first cry for justice in America" on behalf of the Indians. Las Casas recorded the sermon in one of his books, *History of the Indies,* although no one is sure if he was present at the sermon or heard about it later. However, one thing seems certain; even though he must have seen some of the same injustices described by de Montesinos, Las Casas continued to support the Spanish conquest and the goals of conquering new lands, earning wealth, and converting Indians to Christianity.

Las Casas sailed with Christopher Columbus on his third voyage in 1498. This image shows Columbus being arrested in 1500 for mismanaging the Spanish colonies in the Indies. Colonists disliked his excessively cruel policies toward native people.

In 1518, Las Casas went before the Holy Roman emperor and ruler of Spain, Charles V, to plead for the rights of the native peoples. Influenced by Las Casas, Charles eventually ended slavery in Spanish America.

However, in 1513, something happened that changed Las Casas's life. He took part in the conquest of Cuba and, as a reward, received more Indian slaves and an *encomienda,* or land grant. But Las Casas also witnessed a massacre when the Spanish killed thousands of innocent Indians, including women and children, who had welcomed the Spanish into their town. In his book *The Devastation of the Indies: A Brief Account,* he wrote, "I saw here cruelty on a scale no living being has ever seen or expects to see."

A Turning Point

The Cuban massacre in 1513 and other scenes of violence against Indians that Las Casas had witnessed finally pushed him to a turning point. He could no longer believe that the Spanish conquest was right. Before, he had thought that only some individuals acted cruelly and inhumanely. Now he saw that the whole Spanish system of conquest brought only death and suffering to the people of the West Indies.

On August 15, 1514, when he was about 30 years old, Las Casas gave a startling sermon. He asked his congregation to free their enslaved Indians and said that they had to return or pay for everything they had taken away from the Indians. He refused to forgive the colonists' sins in confession if they used Indians as forced labor. Then he announced that he would give up his ownership of Indians and the business he had inherited from his father.

Protector of the Indians

For the rest of his life, Las Casas fought for the rights of the Indians in the Americas. He traveled back and forth to Europe working on their behalf. He talked with popes and kings, debated enemies, and wrote letters and books on the subject.

Las Casas influenced both a pope and a king. In 1537, Pope Paul III wrote that Indians were free human beings, not slaves, and that anyone who enslaved them could be thrown out of the Catholic Church. In 1542, Holy Roman emperor Charles V, who ruled Spain, issued the New Laws, banning slavery in Spanish America.

In 1550 and 1551, Las Casas also participated in a famous debate against Juan Ginés Sepúlveda in Spain. Sepúlveda tried to prove that Indians were "natural slaves," a belief shared by many Spaniards, especially those hungry for wealth and glory. Las Casas passionately argued against Sepúlveda with the same message he would repeatedly deliver throughout his life. Las Casas argued that:

- Indians, like all human beings, have rights to life and liberty.
- The Spanish stole Indian land through bloody and unjust wars.
- There is no such thing as a good encomienda.
- Indians have the right to make war against the Spanish.

Las Casas died in 1566. The voices and the deeds of the conquistadors slowly eroded the memory of his words. However, outside Spain, people began to read *The Devastation of the Indies: A Brief Account*. As time passed, more of Las Casas's works were published. In the centuries to follow, fighters for justice took up his name as a symbol for their own struggles for human rights.

This 19th-century painting, which is part of a series of murals in the U.S. Capitol, symbolizes the role of Las Casas as "Protector of the Indians."

The Legacy of Las Casas

Today, historians remember Las Casas as the first person to actively oppose the oppression of Indians and to call for an end to Indian slavery. Later, in the 19th century, Las Casas inspired both Father Hidalgo, the father of Mexican independence, and Simón Bolívar, the liberator of South America.

In the 1960s, Mexican American César Chávez learned about injustice at an early age. His family worked as migrants, moving from place to place to pick crops. With barely an eighth-grade education, Chávez organized workers, formed a union, and won better pay and better working and living conditions. Speaking for the powerless, he rallied people to his side with his cry, "Sí, Se Puede!" ("Yes, We Can!") Just as the name "Chávez" will always be connected to the struggles of the farm workers, the name "Las Casas" will forever be connected to any fight for human rights and dignity for the native people of the Americas.

Lesson 39

The Scientific Revolution

How did the Scientific Revolution change the way people understood the world?

Introduction

Between 1500 and 1700, modern science emerged as a new way of gaining knowledge about the world. This major shift in thinking became known as the Scientific Revolution. Before this time, Europeans relied on two main sources for their understanding of nature. One was the Bible and religious teachings. The other was the work of classical thinkers, especially the philosopher Aristotle.

During the Scientific Revolution, scientists challenged traditional teachings about nature by asking fresh questions and answering them in new ways. Inventions like the telescope exposed a universe no one had imagined before, while careful observation revealed errors in accepted ideas about the physical world.

A good example is Aristotle's description of falling objects. Aristotle had said that heavier objects fall to the ground faster than lighter ones. Although this idea seemed logical, the Italian scientist Galileo Galilei (gal-uh-LEE-oh gal-uh-LAY) questioned it.

According to his first biographer, Galileo performed a demonstration in the city of Pisa, where he was teaching. He dropped two balls of different weights from the city's Leaning Tower. The results shocked the crowd of students and professors since they expected the heavier ball to land first. Instead, the two balls landed at the same time.

Galileo's demonstration is an application of the scientific method. As you will learn, the scientific method uses both logic and observation to help people understand the natural world.

In this lesson, you will learn about the origins of the Scientific Revolution and how it changed the way people understood the world. You will meet some of the key scientists of the period and find out about their major discoveries and inventions.

Social Studies Vocabulary

geocentric theory

gravity

heliocentric theory

hypothesis

mass

rationalism

scientific method

Scientific Revolution

◄ New tools like the telescope helped change how people understood the world.

Humanist ideas and works from the Renaissance influenced later scientific discoveries. Leonardo da Vinci's drawing Vitruvian Man (detail) is a famous study of the human body from this period.

Scientific Revolution a major shift in thinking between 1500 and 1700, in which modern science emerged as a new way of gaining knowledge about the natural world

rationalism a belief in reason and logic as the primary paths to knowledge

1. Roots of the Scientific Revolution

Humans have asked questions about nature since ancient times. What was different about the **Scientific Revolution** of the 16th, 17th, and 18th centuries? What factors helped it arise?

During the Middle Ages, two major sources guided most Europeans' thinking about the natural world. The first was the Bible because, for Christians, the Bible was the word of God. Therefore, whatever the Bible seemed to say about nature must be true.

The second source was the teachings of Aristotle, a Greek philosopher who had written about logic in the 300s B.C.E. In the late Middle Ages, philosophers like Thomas Aquinas combined Aristotle's thinking with Christian faith by arguing that reason, or logical thought, could be used to support Christian beliefs. He held that the existence of God, for example, could be proven by reason.

During the Renaissance, many thinkers began to question the conclusions of earlier thinkers. For example, Renaissance scholars rediscovered the cultures of ancient Greece and Rome. Arab, Christian, and Jewish scholars in the Muslim world translated many classical works and made advances of their own in such fields as medicine, astronomy, and mathematics.

From the works of these scholars, Europeans learned about a greater variety of ideas. Many European philosophers were influenced by Greek **rationalism,** which was the belief that reason, or logical thought, could be used to discover basic truths about the world. Renaissance thinkers also observed nature directly. The Renaissance physician Vesalius dissected corpses to test ancient ideas about the body. Trust in reason and observation became a key part of modern science.

Additionally, the Age of Exploration helped inspire the growth of science. For instance, in the 2nd century C.E., Ptolemy had stated that there were only three continents: Europe, Africa, and Asia. However, explorers who visited the Americas proved him wrong. Such discoveries encouraged Europeans to question existing knowledge.

Gradually, scientists developed a new method for probing nature's mysteries. Their work led to many dramatic discoveries.

2. Copernicus and Kepler: A New View of the Universe

The Scientific Revolution began with the work of the Polish astronomer Nicolaus Copernicus. His work led to a new view of the universe.

For nearly two thousand years, most people considered Earth the center of the universe. According to this **geocentric theory,** the sun, stars, and planets—everything believed to be the universe—traveled around a motionless Earth. Aristotle had taught this theory. The Bible also seemed to support it since, in one Bible story, God stops the sun from moving across the sky. Additionally, the geocentric theory seemed to make obvious sense because the sun and stars do appear to travel around Earth.

Aristotle had also taught that all heavenly bodies move in circles. Unfortunately, this belief made it difficult to explain the observed movements of planets, such as Mars and Jupiter. In the 2nd century C.E., Ptolemy created a complicated theory to account for this.

Both ancient and medieval writers, including Muslim scientists, found problems with Ptolemy's theory. In the early 1500s, Copernicus tackled these issues when he used observations and mathematics to propose a very different idea. According to his **heliocentric theory,** Earth and the other planets travel in orbits around the sun, which is at the center of this solar system. Earth also turns on its own axis every 24 hours, explaining why heavenly objects seem to move around Earth.

Like Ptolemy, Copernicus had trouble predicting the movement of planets with perfect accuracy, but he still believed his theory was simpler and more satisfying than Ptolemy's. In 1543, he described his idea in a published book. However, the book convinced very few people and was even attacked by some Church officials and scientists.

Then, in the early 1600s, German scientist Johannes Kepler expanded on Copernicus's theory. After studying detailed observations, Kepler realized that the orbits of the planets were ovals, not circles. With this insight, he wrote precise mathematical laws describing the planets' movements around the sun.

Kepler's laws coincided beautifully with actual observations, proving that the Copernican theory was correct. Once the theory was accepted, people would never again hold the same view of Earth's place in the universe.

geocentric theory a theory that Earth is the center of the solar system or the universe. Geo is Greek for "earth."

heliocentric theory a theory that places the sun at the center of the solar system with the planets, including Earth, revolving around it. Helio is Greek for "sun."

Copernicus's heliocentric theory put the sun at the center of a solar system. Before his work, most people believed the sun, planets, and universe revolved around Earth.

3. Galileo and the Copernican Theory

Galileo Galilei lived at the same time as Johannes Kepler. Galileo explored many questions, but he was especially interested in problems of motion. As you have read, he disproved Aristotle's theory that heavy objects fall faster than lighter ones. He made other discoveries about motion, as well. For example, he used mathematics to describe the path of a projectile, or something that is thrown or shot.

Galileo's most notable discoveries came when he turned his curiosity toward the sky. What he learned there made him a champion of the Copernican theory.

Galileo's Discoveries In 1609, Galileo heard about an invention from the Netherlands: the **telescope**. A telescope uses glass **lenses** to make distant objects appear much closer.

Galileo decided to build his own telescope, so he learned how telescopes worked and how to grind glass for lenses. Soon he was building more and more powerful telescopes.

Galileo began studying the sky through a telescope and noticed things no one had seen before. He saw that the moon's surface was rough and uneven, and he discovered four of the moons that revolve around the planet Jupiter.

Galileo also observed the planet Venus. To the naked eye, Venus resembles a bright star, but Galileo noticed something new. You know from looking at the moon that it goes through phases. It takes on what appear to be different shapes, from a thin sliver to the full moon. With his telescope, Galileo could see that Venus also passed through phases. Sometimes it was brightly lit, while at other times it was partially dark.

Galileo's work with telescopes helped him discover new information about the planets that supported Copernicus's theories.

Galileo's discoveries contradicted the traditional view of the universe. For example, Aristotle had taught that the moon was perfectly smooth, but Galileo observed that it wasn't. Although Aristotle had said that Earth was the only center of motion in the universe, Galileo saw moons moving around Jupiter. Aristotle believed that Venus and other planets traveled around Earth. However, Galileo realized that the phases of Venus meant that it was traveling around the sun.

Conflict with the Church Galileo's discoveries supported the Copernican heliocentric theory and led him into a bitter conflict with the Catholic Church. Church leaders viewed the Copernican theory as wrong and dangerous because the idea that Earth was at the center of the universe was part of their system of religious belief.

Church officials feared that attacks on the geocentric theory could lead people to become skeptical of the Church's teachings. In 1616, the Catholic Church warned Galileo against teaching the Copernican theory.

Galileo refused to be silenced and, in 1632, he published a book called *Dialogue on the Two Chief World Systems*. The book described an imaginary conversation about the theories of Ptolemy and Copernicus. Although Galileo did not openly take sides, the book was really a clever argument for the Copernican theory. The character who upheld the geocentric theory was portrayed as foolish, while the one who believed the heliocentric theory was logical and convincing.

Galileo's *Dialogue* caused an uproar. In 1633, the pope called Galileo to Rome to face the Catholic court, known as the Inquisition.

At Galileo's trial, Church leaders accused him of heresy and demanded that he confess his error. Initially Galileo resisted, but eventually the court forced him to swear that the geocentric theory was true, and he was forbidden to write again about the Copernican theory.

Galileo's Influence However, the Church's opposition could not stop the spread of Galileo's ideas. Scientists across Europe read his *Dialogue*, which helped convert many to the Copernican theory.

Galileo's studies of motion also advanced the Scientific Revolution. Like Kepler, he used observation and mathematics to solve scientific problems. Galileo's theory of motion describes how objects move on Earth, while Kepler's laws describe the movements of the planets. The next scientist you will meet united these ideas in a single great theory.

Galileo was tried before the Roman Catholic court known as the Inquisition for heresy, or going against Church teaching. Church leaders demanded that he agree that Earth is at the center of the universe.

4. Isaac Newton and the Law of Gravity

Isaac Newton was born in England in 1642, the same year Galileo died. Newton was a brilliant scientist and mathematician whose greatest discovery was the law of **gravity**.

In later life, Newton told a story about his discovery. He was trying to figure out what kept the moon traveling in its orbit around Earth. Since the moon was in motion, why didn't it fly off into space in a straight line? Then Newton saw an apple fall from a tree and hit the ground and realized that when objects fall, they fall toward the center of Earth. He wondered if the same force that pulled the apple to the ground was tugging on the moon. The difference was that the moon was far away, so Newton reasoned that the force was weaker there but still strong enough to bend the moon's motion into an oval orbit around Earth.

This was Newton's great insight. A single force explained a falling apple on Earth, as well as the movements of heavenly bodies. Newton called this force *gravity*.

Newton stated the law of gravity in a simple **formula**. All physical objects, he said, had a force of attraction between them. The strength of the force depended on the masses of the objects and the distance between them. **Mass** is a measure of the amount of matter in an object. For example, the moon and Earth tug on each other. At a certain point in space, these "tugs" cancel each other out. The result is that the moon is trapped in its orbit around Earth. In contrast, an apple has a small mass compared to Earth and is very close to Earth, so gravity pulls it toward Earth's center.

In 1687, Newton published a book known as the *Principia*, or *Principles*, which presented the law of gravity and described three laws of motion. Newton's laws provided an explanation for what earlier scientists had observed. For example, others had shown that the planets moved around the sun, but Newton's laws explained why. Just as gravity kept the moon traveling around Earth, it kept the planets traveling around the sun.

Newton's laws dramatically changed people's view of the universe. Many people began to view the universe as a beautifully designed machine. Some compared it to a well-built clock. People needed only to discover how it worked.

Inspiration for new ideas often comes when the ordinary is seen from a different viewpoint. Isaac Newton gained insight into the laws of nature after observing an apple fall to the ground.

5. The Scientific Method

A key outcome of the Scientific Revolution was the development of the **scientific method**. Two philosophers who influenced this development were Francis Bacon and Rene Descartes (reh-NAY dey-KAHRT).

Francis Bacon was born in England in 1561. Bacon distrusted much of the traditional learning of the Middle Ages and argued that people could gain knowledge only if they rid their minds of false beliefs. He outlined a method of scientific investigation that depended on close observation.

Rene Descartes was born in France in the year 1596. Descartes prized logic and mathematics. To gain knowledge that was certain, he suggested, people should doubt every statement until logic proved it to be true. Descartes also saw the physical universe as obeying universal mathematical laws.

These ideas helped create a new approach to science. Eventually, scientists developed this approach into the scientific method, which combines logic, mathematics, and observation into five basic steps:

1. The scientist states a question or problem.
2. The scientist forms a **hypothesis,** or assumption, that might explain the problem.
3. The scientist designs and conducts an experiment to test the hypothesis.
4. The scientist measures the data, or information, produced by the experiment and records the results.
5. The scientist analyzes the data to determine whether the hypothesis is correct.

Galileo's demonstration with falling objects illustrates how this method works. Galileo wondered whether objects of different weights fall at the same speed. He formed a hypothesis that they did, then designed and conducted an experiment to test it. He dropped a heavy and a light ball together from the same height off a tower and observed that they landed at the same time, which showed that his hypothesis was correct.

Scientists still use this basic method today. An advantage of the scientific method is that any trained scientist can repeat what another has done. In this way, scientists can test each others' ideas.

In one way, the spread of the scientific method marked a separation from the past. Fewer and fewer people looked to traditional authorities for the answers to scientific problems, but that did not mean they discarded all their old beliefs. For example, thinkers such as Descartes and Newton were deeply religious. For many, science was a way to better understand the world God had made.

scientific method a step-by-step method of investigation involving observation and theory to test scientific assumptions

hypothesis an idea or assumption to be tested in an experiment

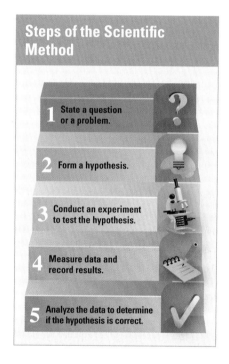

Steps of the Scientific Method

1 State a question or a problem.

2 Form a hypothesis.

3 Conduct an experiment to test the hypothesis.

4 Measure data and record results.

5 Analyze the data to determine if the hypothesis is correct.

The scientific method has five basic steps. Bacon's and Descartes's ideas led to a new approach to science, which eventually developed into this method.

6. Key Inventions

The Scientific Revolution spurred the invention of new tools for studying the world. These tools, such as the telescope, helped scientists discover new facts and measure data more accurately.

Microscope Scientists use **microscopes** to make small objects appear much larger. The microscope was invented by Dutch lens makers in the late 1500s. In the mid-1600s, Dutchman Antonie van Leeuwenhoek (LAY-ven-hook) designed his own powerful microscopes and became the first person to see bacteria. Leeuwenhoek was amazed to find a tiny world of living things and exclaimed, "All the people living in our United Netherlands are not so many as the living animals that I carry in my own mouth this very day!"

Antoine van Leeuwenhoek observed microorganisms through microscopes that he designed (right). A replica of his microscope is shown below. Today's high-powered microscopes are based on the first designs from the 1600s.

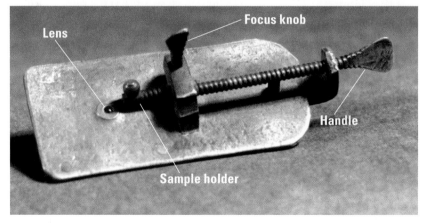

Lens

Focus knob

Handle

Sample holder

Barometer Another important tool developed in this period was the barometer, which measures changes in the pressure of the atmosphere. Evangelista Torricelli (tawr-ih-CHEL-ee) invented the barometer in the 1640s. He filled a glass tube with a liquid metal called mercury, and then placed the tube upside down in a dish.

Over the next few days, Torricelli watched the tube and observed that the height of the mercury did not stay the same. The column of mercury moved up and down vertically as the pressure in the atmosphere changed. The barometer soon proved to be a valuable tool in studying and predicting the weather.

A barometer is used to measure atmospheric pressure. Instead of using mercury, many barometers today have pointers that show changes in pressure.

Thermometer Galileo likely made the first thermometer. In the early 1700s, however, a German scientist, Daniel Gabriel Fahrenheit, made thermometers more accurate. He put mercury in a glass tube, and as the mercury grew warmer, it expanded and rose up the tube. The height of the mercury provided a measure of temperature. Additionally, Fahrenheit designed a new temperature scale. In the United States, we still measure temperature using Fahrenheit degrees.

Lesson Summary

In this lesson, you learned about the Scientific Revolution. This movement marked a major shift in the way people thought about the natural world.

The Roots of the Scientific Revolution Several factors contributed to the birth of the Scientific Revolution. Renaissance thinkers questioned traditional learning and observed nature for themselves. Translations of classical texts and some new thinking exposed scholars to new ideas. Discoveries by explorers showed that accepted ideas could be wrong.

Copernicus, Kepler, and Galileo The Scientific Revolution began when Copernicus proposed the daring idea that Earth and the other planets travel around the sun. Kepler built on this heliocentric theory by correctly describing the planets' orbits. Galileo's discoveries about motion and his observations of the planets supported the Copernican theory, although it brought him into conflict with the Catholic Church.

Newton and the Law of Gravity Newton took all this work a giant step forward. His law of gravity explained why planets orbited the sun. Newton also showed that the same laws applied everywhere in the known universe.

The Scientific Method The ideas of Bacon and Descartes helped to shape the scientific method, which proved to be a powerful way of testing ideas about nature.

Key Inventions New tools, such as the microscope, the barometer, and the thermometer, also aided scientific progress. They helped scientists discover new facts and more accurately measure and collect data.

The Enlightenment

How have the ideas of the Enlightenment influenced modern government?

Introduction

During the late 1600s, a new outlook put great emphasis on reason as the key to human progress. This period of new thinking among many educated Europeans is called the *Enlightenment*, and by the 1700s, it had become widespread throughout Europe.

Enlightenment thinkers were inspired by the example of scientists, such as Galileo, Bacon, and Newton. Scientists used observation and logic to understand the physical world, and their methods rapidly overturned old beliefs. Now, believing a new age of reason was dawning, thinkers wanted to take a similar approach to the problems of human life and forget the teachings of the past. In this new age, governments and social institutions would be based on rational understanding, not on errors and superstitions of earlier times.

A Frenchman, Bernard de Fontenelle, expressed this optimistic faith in reason and progress. In 1702, he wrote that the new century "will become more enlightened day by day, so that all previous centuries will be lost in darkness by comparison."

In France, *philosophes* (philosophers) championed these new ideas. These thinkers often gathered in private homes for informal meetings, called salons, which were often organized by women. There they exchanged and debated ideas and helped shape and spread the ideas of the Enlightenment.

In this lesson, you will learn about the roots of the Enlightenment. You will meet five philosophers whose ideas greatly influenced the Enlightenment and see how their works led to new ideas about government and individual rights. Finally, you will meet several women who played important roles in the Enlightenment.

Social Studies Vocabulary

bill of rights

constitutional monarchy

despotism

Enlightenment

natural rights

religious tolerance

social contract

separation of powers

◀ Eighteenth century French thinkers gather in the salon of Madame Marie Thérèse Rodet Geoffrin to discuss new ideas.

Enlightenment a period from the late 1600s to the late 1700s in Europe, in which people changed their outlook on life by seeing reason as the key to human progress

Desiderius Erasmus was a humanist scholar of the Renaissance who challenged the authority of the Catholic Church and paved the way for Enlightenment thinkers. This is a monument to him in his hometown of Rotterdam, Netherlands.

1. The Roots of the Enlightenment

Enlightenment thinkers wanted to examine human life in the light of reason. Rational understanding, they felt, would lead to great progress in government and society.

These thinkers believed they were making a major break with the past. Like everyone, however, they were influenced by what had come before them. In this section, we will first examine the roots of the Enlightenment and then consider ways in which the new ideas of the Enlightenment clashed with old beliefs.

The Scientific Revolution Enlightenment thinking grew out of the Scientific Revolution. In science, observation and reason were revealing natural laws that applied throughout the physical world. The thinkers of the Enlightenment wanted to apply this approach to human life and experience. They asked questions such as: Are there natural laws that tell us how to live? How well do our current institutions follow natural laws? Do natural laws give all people certain rights? What is the best form of government?

Philosophers did not always agree about the answers to these questions, but they all thought about these questions in a similar way. Like scientists, they placed their trust in reason and observation as the best sources of understanding and progress.

The Renaissance and the Reformation The Enlightenment also had roots in the Renaissance and the Reformation. The humanists of the Renaissance questioned accepted beliefs and celebrated the dignity and worth of the individual. During the Reformation, Protestants rebelled against the Catholic Church by putting individual conscience ahead of religious tradition and authority. Enlightenment thinkers went even further in rejecting authority and upholding the freedom of individuals to think for themselves.

Classical and Christian Influences Like the humanists of the Renaissance, many Enlightenment thinkers were inspired by classical culture. Trust in reason, for example, goes all the way back to the ancient Greeks, as does the idea that people should have a voice in their government. Philosophers who argued for this idea could point to the democracy of ancient Athens or to the republic of ancient Rome.

Christian ideas also influenced Enlightenment thinking. Enlightenment philosophers preferred rational thought to faith based on the Bible, but most of them continued to believe in God. They saw the laws of nature as the work of an intelligent Creator and human progress as a sign of God's goodness. Often, their approach to moral problems reflected Christian values, such as respect for others and for a moral law.

New Ideas Versus Old Beliefs The thinkers of the Enlightenment prized reason over authority; questioned the foundations of religion, morality, and government; and believed that everything must be re-examined in the light of reason. This outlook led to many clashes with accepted beliefs and the ruling powers who upheld them.

Christian faith, for example, was based largely on trust in the Bible as God's word. However, Enlightenment thinkers believed that humans were perfectly capable of discovering truth for themselves. Some even questioned the existence of God, while others sought a "natural religion" based on reason. These thinkers believed the order in the universe was proof enough of an intelligent Creator and that there was no need to base belief in God on revelations in holy books. Similarly, they maintained that ideas about right and wrong should be based on rational **insight,** not on the teachings of religious authorities.

Enlightenment thinkers also criticized accepted ideas about government. Some questioned the long-held belief that God gave monarchs the right to rule, and many insisted that governments must respect individual rights. Toward the end of the 18th century, these ideas played a major role in revolutions in both the American colonies and France.

Ideas from ancient Greek and Rome, such as representative government, inspired Enlightenment philosophers. This painting shows a scene in the Roman senate.

2. Thomas Hobbes: Absolute Rule by Kings

Thomas Hobbes was born in England in 1588. He wrote about many subjects, including politics and government, and tried to give a rational basis for absolute, or unlimited, rule by kings.

The son of a clergyman, Hobbes studied at Oxford University. As an adult, he traveled to other European countries, where he met many writers, scientists, and philosophers. In addition to studying history and government, Hobbes studied mathematics and science, which inspired him to take a scientific approach to problems of human society.

Hobbes's thinking about society was greatly influenced by events in England in the mid-1600s. King Charles I was struggling for power with Parliament, England's lawmaking body, and civil war erupted between the monarch's supporters and Parliament in 1642. Hobbes sided with the king.

In 1649, the king was beheaded. For the next several years, England was ruled by Parliament's House of Commons, but disorder and discontent continued. Finally, in 1660, the monarchy was restored.

The chaos of these years had a powerful impact on Hobbes. What, he asked, is the basis of social order? To answer this question, he tried to reason from his observations of human nature.

In Hobbes's view, human beings were naturally cruel, selfish, and greedy. In 1651, he published a book called *Leviathan*, in which he wrote that people are driven by a restless desire for power. Without laws or other social controls, people would always be in conflict, and in such a "state of nature," life would be "nasty, brutish and short."

Governments, Hobbes believed, were created to protect people from their own selfishness. Because people were selfish by nature, they could not be trusted to make decisions that were good for society as a whole. Only a government that has a ruler with absolute authority could maintain an orderly society.

In his book *Leviathan*, Hobbes argued that people are inherently selfish and that governments are created to make decisions that are best for society as a whole.

Later Enlightenment thinkers came to quite different conclusions about human nature and the best form of government. Hobbes was important, however, because he was one of the first thinkers to apply the tools of the Scientific Revolution to problems of politics. During the Enlightenment and the years that followed, many European countries moved away from absolute monarchy.

3. John Locke: Natural Rights

John Locke was born in England in 1632. His thinking about government and people's rights had a major impact on the Enlightenment.

Whereas Thomas Hobbes had argued that kings should have absolute power, Locke favored **constitutional monarchy**. In this type of government, a basic set of laws limits the ruler's power.

Locke's ideas reflected a tradition of limitations on the English monarchy dating back to 1215, when English nobles forced King John to sign Magna Carta, or the "Great Charter." Magna Carta established the idea that even monarchs had to obey English laws and respect certain individual rights.

Over time, Parliament became the main check on the monarch's power. During the civil war of the 1640s, Locke's father fought on the side of Parliament. The young Locke was greatly influenced by his father's beliefs.

In the 1680s, another crisis developed. The new king, James II, was Catholic. James's enemies in Protestant England feared that he wanted to put Catholics in power and forced him to flee the country in 1688.

In 1689, Parliament gave the crown to James's Protestant daughter Mary and her husband, William. Parliament also passed a **bill of rights**, which strengthened the power of Parliament as the representative of the people. For example, the English Bill of Rights forbade the monarch from keeping a standing army in peacetime or levying taxes without Parliament's consent. It also listed individual rights, including protection in court cases from excessive fines and "cruel and unusual punishment."

constitutional monarchy a form of government in which the monarch's power is limited by a basic set of laws

bill of rights a list of basic human rights that a government must protect

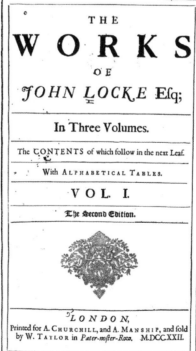

John Locke believed that all people have natural rights, including the rights to life, liberty, and property.

social contract an agreement in which people give power to a government in exchange for its protections

natural rights rights that belong to people "by nature," simply because they are human beings

separation of powers the division of powers among branches of government

despotism rule by a single person with absolute power

Locke approved of these changes in England. In 1690, he published *Two Treatises of Government,* in which he offered a theory of government that justified Parliament's actions.

Locke denied the divine right of monarchs to rule and argued that the true basis of government was a social contract, or agreement, among free people. Under this agreement, the purpose of government was to protect people's natural rights, including the right to life, liberty, and property. The people are the sole source of power and must agree to give power to the government to rule on their **behalf**. Therefore, according to Locke's social contract, a government's authority was based on the consent of the governed. If the government failed to respect people's rights, it broke the contract and could be overthrown.

Locke's view of government had a wide influence. In 1776, his ideas would be echoed in the American Declaration of Independence.

4. Montesquieu: Separation of Powers

Charles-Louis de Secondat was born in France in 1689. He is better known by his title, the Baron de Montesquieu (MON-tuh-skyoo).

In his youth, Montesquieu attended a Catholic school. Later he became a lawyer. When his uncle died in 1716, Montesquieu inherited the title of baron along with his uncle's fortune, and he also became president of the local parliament.

In 1721, Montesquieu achieved fame as a writer with a book called *Persian Letters,* which described French society as seen by fictional travelers from Persia. It used humor to criticize French institutions, including the king's court and the Catholic Church. It quickly became very popular, and Montesquieu became an admired guest in the salons of Paris.

Montesquieu's most famous book was *The Spirit of Laws,* published in 1748. In this book, he described his theory of how governments should be organized.

Like John Locke, Montesquieu was concerned with how to protect political liberty. The best way to do this, he argued, was to divide power among three branches of government. In such a system, the legislative branch made the laws, the executive branch enforced the laws, and the judicial branch interpreted the laws. This concept, which Montesquieu called the separation of powers, would ensure that no one branch would become too powerful.

Montesquieu's theory reflected his admiration for the English government. In England, Parliament made the laws, the monarch enforced them, and courts interpreted them. Each branch of government checked, or limited, the power of the others. When powers were not separated in this way, Montesquieu warned, liberty was soon lost. Too much power in the hands of any one person is called despotism.

Montesquieu was an influential French political thinker who argued that a government's power should be divided among separate branches.

Montesquieu's ideas had a powerful impact on later thinkers, including the men who wrote the U.S. Constitution. They made the separation of powers a key part of the U.S. system of government.

5. Voltaire: Religious Tolerance and Free Speech

Francois-Marie Arouet was born in France in 1694. Under the pen name Voltaire, he became one of the most celebrated writers of the Enlightenment.

As a young man, Voltaire attended a Catholic college in Paris before settling on a career in literature. He soon earned fame as a writer and as a witty participant in Paris salons.

Voltaire believed passionately in reforming society in the name of justice and human happiness. He warned against what he saw as superstition, error, and oppression. With biting humor, he attacked the French court and the power of the Catholic clergy.

Like Montesquieu, Voltaire admired England's constitutional monarchy and separation of powers. In his view, the English were governed by law, not by the **arbitrary** wishes of a single ruler. To be governed by law, he said, was "man's most cherished right."

Voltaire was one of the main thinkers of the Enlightenment. His ideas about tolerance and free speech influenced the writers of the U.S. Bill of Rights.

Voltaire was especially concerned with freedom of thought and expression. He championed **religious tolerance**, or allowing people to practice religion in their own ways. Voltaire thought religious conflict was one of the main sources of evil in the world. He argued that no single religion possessed all the truth but instead held that there was a core of truth in all religions. This core was the "natural religion" that reason made available to everyone.

Voltaire also spoke out for the right of free speech. Once he wrote a letter to a man whose views he strongly opposed and said that he would give his life so that his opponent could continue to write. A later writer expressed Voltaire's feeling in the words, "I disapprove of what you say, but I will defend to the death your right to say it."

Throughout his life, Voltaire criticized intolerance and oppression wherever he saw them. His outspokenness often led to conflicts with authorities, causing him to spend time in prison twice and to flee to another city or country on several occasions.

Voltaire's ideas about religious tolerance and free speech greatly influenced colonial American political thinkers, such as Thomas Jefferson. They demanded that freedom of religion and free speech be included in the U.S. Bill of Rights.

> **religious tolerance** the acceptance of different religious beliefs and customs

6. Cesare Beccaria: The Rights of the Accused

Cesare Beccaria (beck-kah-REE-ah) was born in Milan, Italy, in 1738. He was a pioneer in the field of criminology and his work stressed the rights of accused people to fair treatment.

The son of an aristocrat, Beccaria attended a Catholic school as a boy and received a degree in law from the University of Pavia in 1758. When he finished his studies, he returned to Milan, where he was soon caught up in the intellectual excitement of the Enlightenment.

In 1763, Beccaria began a study of the justice system. He was upset by the harsh practices that were common in his day. Torture was often used to force confessions from accused persons or statements from witnesses to a crime. People might have their thumbs crushed in a device called a thumbscrew or have their bodies stretched on a device called a rack until their joints were pulled apart.

Beccaria objected to other practices, as well. It was not unusual for trials to be held in secret or for judges to be corrupt. People found guilty of crimes were frequently sentenced to death.

Beccaria attacked these practices in a famous book called *On Crimes and Punishments*. He argued that laws exist to preserve security and order and that punishments should be designed to serve this purpose. Like other people, criminals made rational decisions. To stop people from committing crimes, punishment did not have to be brutal. It only had to be certain and severe enough to outweigh the crime's potential benefits.

Cesare Beccaria argued against forms of punishment that had been in use for centuries, such as stretching a person on a rack.

THE RACK.

Beccaria also argued for other specific rights, including the right to a fair and speedy trial for persons accused of a crime and an end to the use of torture. In addition, he felt that it was wrong to punish some people more harshly than others for the same crime and that a punishment should fit the seriousness of the crime. He believed that capital punishment—putting someone to death—should be ended completely.

Beccaria's book encouraged the scientific study of crime. His ideas about rights and punishment influenced reform movements throughout Europe. In the United States, many laws concerning crime and punishment reflect his ideas.

7. The Impact of the Enlightenment on Government

Enlightenment thinkers proposed new ideas about human nature and the best forms of government. Let's take a look at the influence of these ideas in Europe and America.

Enlightened Rule A few European absolute monarchs tried to apply Enlightenment ideas in the 1700s. These rulers, including Frederick the Great of Prussia, Catherine the Great of Russia, and Joseph II of Austria, became known as "enlightened despots" or "benevolent despots." *Benevolent* means "to be kind; to do good for others."

Enlightened monarchs founded universities and scientific societies and introduced reforms, such as greater religious tolerance and an end to torture and capital punishment. However, these rulers pushed change only so far. They wanted to maintain their own power and avoid angering the noble classes, whose support they needed.

The American and French Revolutions The ideas of the Enlightenment greatly influenced leaders of the American Revolution. Many people in the American colonies shared the traditions of Magna Carta and the English Bill of Rights, as John Locke had. When the colonists rebelled in 1775, they pointed to the abuse of their rights by the English king. The Declaration of Independence echoed Locke's ideas on natural rights and the social contract.

The U.S. Constitution also contains ideas from the Enlightenment. The Constitution includes Montesquieu's idea of separation of powers. The Bill of Rights protects the freedoms of religion and speech championed by Voltaire, as well as some of the rights promoted by Beccaria, such as the right to a speedy trial.

In 1789, a revolution broke out in France, and the absolute monarchy there was overthrown. France's National Assembly produced the Declaration of the Rights of Man and of the Citizen, a document that proclaimed liberty and equality. It upheld the rights to own property and to resist oppression and guaranteed freedom of speech and religion. All these ideas grew out of the Enlightenment.

Enlightenment ideas greatly influenced the writing of the U.S. Declaration of Independence. From left to right, Benjamin Franklin, John Adams, and Thomas Jefferson work on drafting the document.

8. Women of the Enlightenment

The women of the 1700s did not enjoy the same rights or status as men, and yet a number of women played an important role in the Enlightenment. Some helped spread Enlightenment thinking through their published writing or by hosting salons. Others extended ideas about rights and equality to women.

Madame Geoffrin One of the most prominent sponsors of salons was Madame Marie Thérèse Rodet Geoffrin (jhef-FRANH). Beginning in the mid-1700s, the brightest minds in Europe met in her home for lively talks about the latest ideas. Madame Geoffrin also gave financial support to the Encyclopedists, a group of men who put together the first encyclopedia.

At Madame Geoffrin's salons, princes and politicians mingled with artists, writers, and philosophers. Geoffrin led these gatherings with a firm hand. She reserved Mondays for artists and Wednesdays for writers and philosophers.

Abigail Adams was an influential and outspoken supporter of equal rights for women during the American Revolution.

Abigail Adams Abigail Adams firmly supported the American colonies' struggle for independence from England. She was married to John Adams, a leader of the American Revolution and the second U.S. president. During the war, she reminded John not to forget women's rights in the new American government. She wrote, "If particular care and attention is not paid to the Ladies, we are determined to foment [start] a Rebellion." Women, she went on, "will not hold ourselves bound by any Laws in which we have no voice." Abigail also spoke out for a woman's right to education.

Olympe de Gouges French Olympe de Gouges was the daughter of a butcher. Despite having little education, she became an important writer and social reformer. In 1791, she published the Declaration of the Rights of Woman and of the Female Citizen, her answer to the National Assembly's Declaration of the Rights of Man and of the Citizen. De Gouges argued for women's equality in every aspect of public and private life. She believed that women should have the right to vote, hold office, own property, and serve in the military and that they should have equal power with men in family life and in the church.

Mary Wollstonecraft English writer Mary Wollstonecraft was another early leader in the struggle to gain equal rights for women. In an essay published in 1792, she argued that women deserve the same rights and opportunities as men. "Let woman share the rights," she wrote, "and she will emulate [imitate] the virtues of men, for she must grow more perfect when emancipated [freed]."

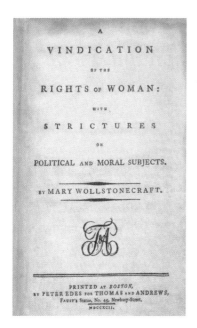

Writer Mary Wollstonecraft was an early reformer in the women's rights movement. She believed that access to education was necessary for women to achieve freedom and equality.

Wollstonecraft believed that education was the key to gaining equality and freedom. She called for reforms to give women the same education as men. In the 19th century, her ideas about equality for women inspired early leaders of the women's rights movement in the United States.

Lesson Summary

In this lesson, you learned about the Enlightenment, a new way of thinking that began in Europe in the late 1600s and became widespread in the 1700s.

The Roots of the Enlightenment The Enlightenment grew out of the Renaissance and the Scientific Revolution. Much Enlightenment thinking challenged accepted beliefs. Enlightenment philosophers wanted to apply the ideas and methods of the Scientific Revolution to problems of government and society.

Enlightenment Thinkers Thomas Hobbes used logic and his observations to reach conclusions about government. John Locke championed the rights to life, liberty, and property. Montesquieu argued for a separation of powers in government. Voltaire championed religious tolerance and free speech. Cesare Beccaria called for reform in criminal law to protect the rights of the accused.

The Impact of the Enlightenment on Government Modern views of government owe a great deal to Enlightenment thinkers. The Enlightenment influenced monarchs in Europe, especially "enlightened despots," and greatly affected revolutions in the American colonies and France.

Women of the Enlightenment Several women, such as Abigail Adams, Olympe de Gouges, and Mary Wollstonecraft, worked to extend ideas of liberty and equality to women.

How Did the Enlightenment Influence the Declaration of Independence?

During the Enlightenment, many educated Europeans emphasized reason to understand how humans can best live together. This new way of thinking spread to Britain's American colonies. You will read four primary sources that reflect this thinking and then write an argument to explain how the Enlightenment influenced the Declaration of Independence in America.

In the late 1600s, the English philosopher John Locke spent years of his life thinking and writing about the role of government and individuals in a peaceful and successful society. One of Locke's most famous works of political philosophy was called *Two Treatises of Government*.

At the time that Locke wrote this work, England's government leaders were arguing about the power of their monarch and the strength of citizen representation within the Parliament. In this excerpt from *Two Treatises of Government*, what rights does Locke suggest mankind naturally has? According to this text, why is it important to understand natural rights? Why would a monarch likely not support these ideas?

Two Treatises of Government

4. To understand political power right, and derive it from its original, we must consider what state all men are naturally in, and that is, a state of perfect freedom to order their actions and dispose of their possessions and persons, as they think fit, within the bounds of the law of nature; without asking leave, or depending upon the will of any other man . . .

6. . . . no one ought to harm another in his life, health, liberty, or possessions: for men being all the workmanship of one omnipotent and infinitely wise Maker . . . ought he, as much as he can, to preserve the rest of mankind, and may not, unless it be to do justice to an offender, take away or impair the life, or what tends to the preservation of life, the liberty, health, limb, or goods of another.

7. And that all men may be restrained from invading others' rights, and from doing hurt to one another, and the law of nature be observed, which willeth the peace and preservation of all mankind, the execution of the law of nature is, in that state, put into every man's hands . . . And if any one in the state of nature may punish another for any evil he has done, every one may do so: for in that state of perfect equality . . . naturally there is no superiority or jurisdiction of one over another . . .

—*John Locke, 1689 or 1690*

About 60 years after Locke wrote his *Two Treatises of Government*, a Frenchman known as the Baron de Montesquieu wrote a famous book about how governments should be organized. Montesquieu's *The Spirit of Laws* was published in 1748 and conveyed his beliefs about limiting political power for any one individual or group in the government. The book details his concept of separation of powers, which became the basis of the three branches of government in the United States. In many European cities, the book received praise, especially by Enlightenment thinkers. In Rome, however, it was placed on a list of "forbidden books" because some felt it threatened the faith or morals of Roman Catholic people.

This excerpt from *The Spirit of Laws* explains Montesquieu's ideas about how laws should be written. How does Montesquieu suggest laws should be worded? Why do you think Montesquieu advises against including too many details in laws? What connections might there be between these ideas and the Declaration of Independence?

The Spirit of Laws

Things to observe in the composition of laws

Those who have a comprehensive enough genius to be able to give laws to their own nation or to another should pay certain attentions to the way they are formed.

Their style should be concise . . .

The style of the laws should be simple; direct expression is always better understood than indirect . . .

It is essential for the words of the laws to awaken the same ideas in all men . . .

When the ideas of things have been well fixed in a law, one must not return to vague expressions . . .

The laws should not be subtle; they are made for people of middling understanding; they are not an art of logic but the simple reasoning of a father of the family.

When exceptions, limitations, modifications, are not necessary in a law, it is much better not to include them in it. Such details plunge one into new details.

One must not make a change in a law without a sufficient reason . . . When one goes so far as to give a reason for a law, this reason must be worthy of it.

—*Montesquieu, 1748*

Montesquieu: The Spirit of Laws (1748)
Edited by David W. Carrithers (Berkeley: University of California Press, 1977)

While Montesquieu wrote about limiting government power and protecting individual liberty, an Italian philosopher, Cesare Beccaria, was writing about power and rights in the criminal justice system. Beccaria was deeply concerned about how punishments for crime should be used for the good of the society. In 1764, Beccaria wrote *An Essay on Crimes and Punishments,* which argued for rights of accused individuals. Many authorities consider this work to be the first and most important systematic statement of principles about the treatment of people accused of crimes.

According to this excerpt from Beccaria's essay, when is punishment unacceptable? Based on this excerpt, what is the purpose of a punishment? What are Beccaria's suggestions about reducing crime and punishments? What does this excerpt have in common with the other two primary sources you read?

An Essay on Crimes and Punishments

Every punishment which does not arise from absolute necessity, says the great Montesquieu, is tyrannical. A proposition which may be made more general thus: every act of authority of one man over another, for which there is not an absolute necessity, is tyrannical. It is upon this then that the sovereign's right to punish crimes is founded; that is upon the necessity of defending the public liberty . . .

The laws only can determine the punishment of crimes . . . No magistrate then, (as he is one of the society,) can, with justice, inflict on any other member of the same society punishment that is not ordained by the laws . . .

It is not only the common interest of mankind that crimes should not be committed, but that crimes of every kind should be less frequent, in proportion to the evil they produce to society. Therefore the means made use of by the legislature to prevent crimes should be more powerful, in proportion as they are destructive to the public safety and happiness, and as the inducements to commit them are stronger. Therefore there ought to be a fixed proportion between crimes and punishments . . .

The end of punishment, therefore, is no other, than to prevent the criminal from doing further injury to society, and to prevent others from committing the like offence. Such punishments, therefore, and such a mode of inflicting them, ought to be chosen, as will make the strongest and most lasting impression on the minds of others, with the least torment on the body of the criminal.

—Cesare Beccaria, 1764

The philosophies of the Enlightenment thinkers spread to North America. By 1775, many colonists were dissatisfied with the way Britain's king was treating them. Colonial leaders agreed with John Locke and others about the natural rights of individuals, such as life and liberty.

With these ideas in mind, Thomas Jefferson drafted the Declaration of Independence, which freed the 13 colonies from Britain's rule and created the United States of America. Here is the beginning section of the Declaration. How has Jefferson constructed the document as a logical argument for separation from Britain?

The Declaration of Independence

When in the Course of human events it becomes necessary for one people to dissolve the political bands which have connected them with another, and to assume among the powers of the earth, the separate and equal station to which the Laws of Nature and of Nature's God entitle them, a decent respect to the opinions of mankind requires that they should declare the causes which impel them to the separation.

We hold these truths to be self-evident, that all men are created equal, that they are endowed by their Creator with certain unalienable Rights, that among these are Life, Liberty and the pursuit of Happiness.—That to secure these rights, Governments are instituted among Men, deriving their just powers from the consent of the governed,—That whenever any Form of Government becomes destructive to these ends, it is the Right of the People to alter or to abolish it, and to institute new Government, laying its foundation on such principles and organizing its powers in such form, as to them shall seem most likely to effect their Safety and Happiness . . . The history of the present King of Great Britain is a history of repeated injuries and usurpations, all having in direct object the establishment of an absolute Tyranny over these States. To prove this, let Facts be submitted to a candid world.

He has refused his Assent to Laws, the most wholesome and necessary for public good . . .

For transporting us beyond Seas to be tried for pretended offences:

For suspending our own Legislatures, and declaring themselves invested with power to legislate for us in all cases whatsoever . . .

—1776

How are the concepts of the first three primary sources visible in the Declaration of Independence? Use your findings to write a claim to explain how Enlightenment thinkers influenced this document.

Europe Enters the Modern Age

1492
Columbus Reaches the Americas
Christopher Columbus sails from Spain and reaches the Americas when he lands in the West Indies.

1519–1532
Spanish Conquer "New Spain"
Spanish conquistadors Cortés, pictured here, and Pizarro conquer the Aztec and Inca empires. Wealth from the Americas helps Spain become one of the world's richest and most powerful countries.

1500s–1700s
Scientific Revolution
New thinking leads to the scientific method and tools such as the microscope that allow rapid advances in understanding nature.

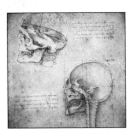

1400	1450	1500	1550	1600

1500s
Asian Trade
Portuguese control of the Indian Ocean breaks the Muslim and Italian hold on Asian trade, lowering the price of goods, such as spices and silk, for Europeans.

1543
Copernicus's Heliocentric Theory
The heliocentric theory of the universe is published by Nicolaus Copernicus, changing scientific opinion about Earth as the center of the universe.

1588
Spanish Armada Defeated
The defeat of the Spanish Armada by England leads to declining Spanish power in Europe and abroad.

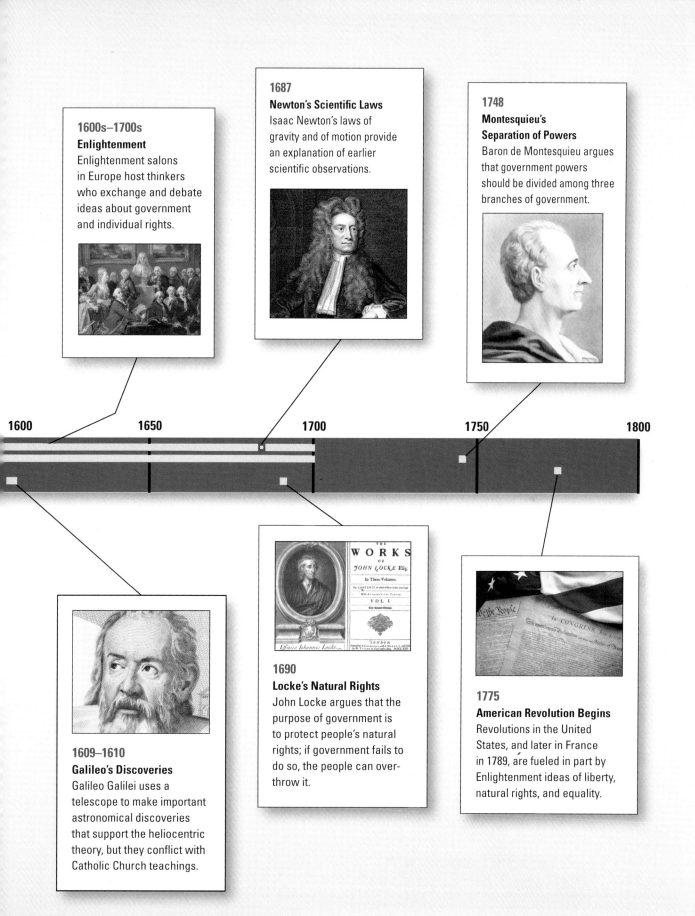

1600s–1700s
Enlightenment
Enlightenment salons in Europe host thinkers who exchange and debate ideas about government and individual rights.

1687
Newton's Scientific Laws
Isaac Newton's laws of gravity and of motion provide an explanation of earlier scientific observations.

1748
Montesquieu's Separation of Powers
Baron de Montesquieu argues that government powers should be divided among three branches of government.

1600   1650   1700   1750   1800

1609–1610
Galileo's Discoveries
Galileo Galilei uses a telescope to make important astronomical discoveries that support the heliocentric theory, but they conflict with Catholic Church teachings.

1690
Locke's Natural Rights
John Locke argues that the purpose of government is to protect people's natural rights; if government fails to do so, the people can overthrow it.

1775
American Revolution Begins
Revolutions in the United States, and later in France in 1789, are fueled in part by Enlightenment ideas of liberty, natural rights, and equality.

Resources

The Strahov Library in Prague, Czech Republic, has thousands of books, prints, and manuscripts that date from the 9th to the 18th century.

Physical Features of the World

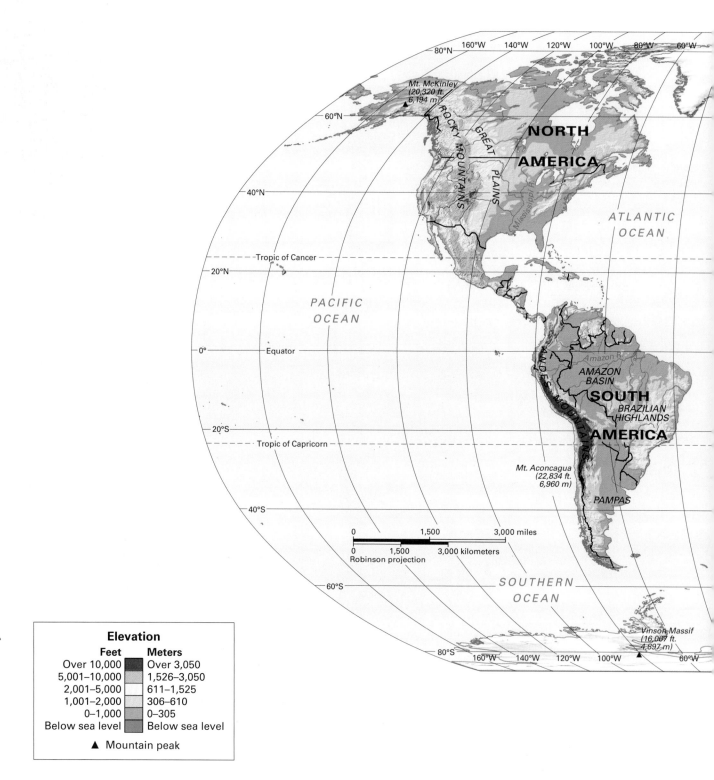

80°N
160°W 140°W 120°W 100°W 80°W 60°W

Mt. McKinley
(20,320 ft.
6,194 m)

60°N

ROCKY MOUNTAINS

GREAT PLAINS

NORTH
AMERICA

Mississippi R.

ATLANTIC
OCEAN

40°N

Tropic of Cancer

20°N

PACIFIC
OCEAN

Equator 0°

Amazon R.

AMAZON
BASIN

ANDES MOUNTAINS

SOUTH
BRAZILIAN
HIGHLANDS

AMERICA

20°S

Tropic of Capricorn

Mt. Aconcagua
(22,834 ft.
6,960 m)

PAMPAS

40°S

0	1,500	3,000 miles

0	1,500	3,000 kilometers

Robinson projection

60°S

SOUTHERN
OCEAN

Vinson Massif
(16,067 ft.
4,897 m)

80°S
160°W 140°W 120°W 100°W 60°W

Elevation

Feet	Meters
Over 10,000	Over 3,050
5,001–10,000	1,526–3,050
2,001–5,000	611–1,525
1,001–2,000	306–610
0–1,000	0–305
Below sea level	Below sea level

▲ Mountain peak

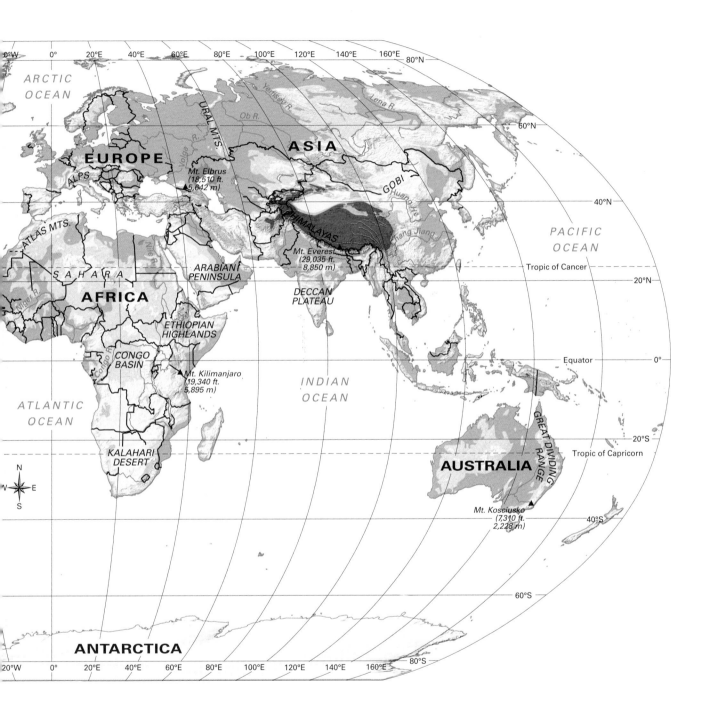

ARCTIC
OCEAN

0°W   0°   20°E   40°E   60°E   80°E   100°E   120°E   140°E   160°E   80°N

60°N

EUROPE   ASIA

ALPS   Mt. Elbrus
            (18,510 ft.
            5,642 m)   GOBI   40°N

URAL MTS.   Huang He

ATLAS MTS.   PACIFIC
                                                        OCEAN

S A H A R A   ARABIAN   HIMALAYAS
                  PENINSULA   Tropic of Cancer

Niger R.   Nile R.   Mt. Everest   20°N
                                   (29,035 ft.
AFRICA   8,850 m)   Chang Jiang

DECCAN
PLATEAU

ETHIOPIAN
HIGHLANDS

CONGO
BASIN   Equator   0°
                  Mt. Kilimanjaro
Congo R.   (19,340 ft.   INDIAN
                  5,895 m)   OCEAN

ATLANTIC
OCEAN   20°S

KALAHARI   GREAT DIVIDING RANGE   Tropic of Capricorn
DESERT
N   AUSTRALIA
W   E

S   Mt. Kosciusko
                                         (7,310 ft.   40°S
                                         2,228 m)

60°S

ANTARCTICA   80°S

20°W   0°   20°E   40°E   60°E   80°E   100°E   120°E   140°E   160°E

Political Boundaries of the World

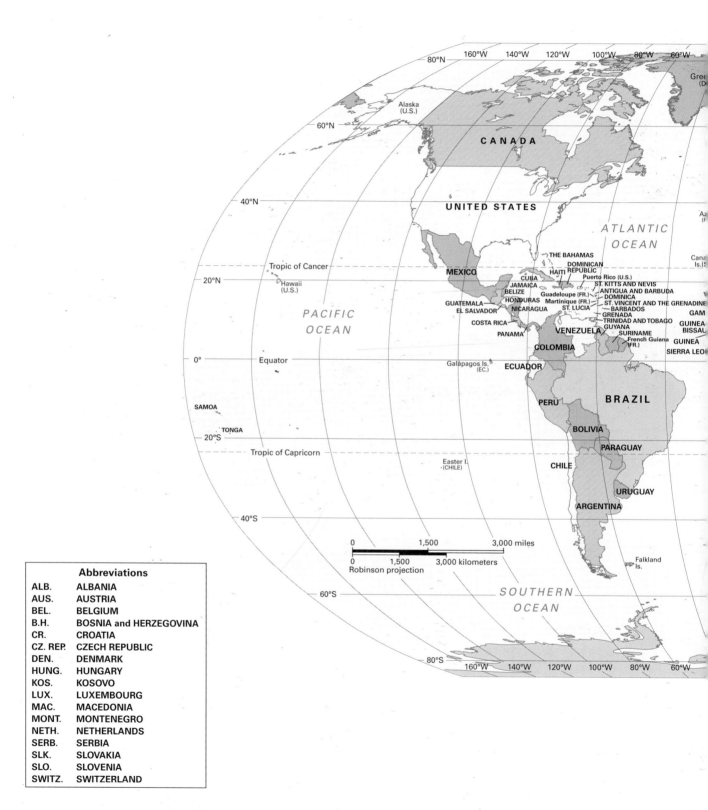

Abbreviations	
ALB.	ALBANIA
AUS.	AUSTRIA
BEL.	BELGIUM
B.H.	BOSNIA and HERZEGOVINA
CR.	CROATIA
CZ. REP.	CZECH REPUBLIC
DEN.	DENMARK
HUNG.	HUNGARY
KOS.	KOSOVO
LUX.	LUXEMBOURG
MAC.	MACEDONIA
MONT.	MONTENEGRO
NETH.	NETHERLANDS
SERB.	SERBIA
SLK.	SLOVAKIA
SLO.	SLOVENIA
SWITZ.	SWITZERLAND

- Independent nations are printed in bold capital letters: **FRANCE**.
- Nations whose independence or governing rule is in dispute are printed in bold type: **Taiwan**.
- Territories, provinces, and the like governed by an independent nation are printed in bold type, with an abbreviation for the ruling nation: **French Guiana (FR.)**.
- Areas whose governing rule is in dispute are printed in nonbold type: Falkland Islands.
- Areas that are part of an independent nation but geographically separated from it are printed in nonbold type, with an abbreviation for the ruling nation: Hawaii (U.S.).

Physical Features of North America

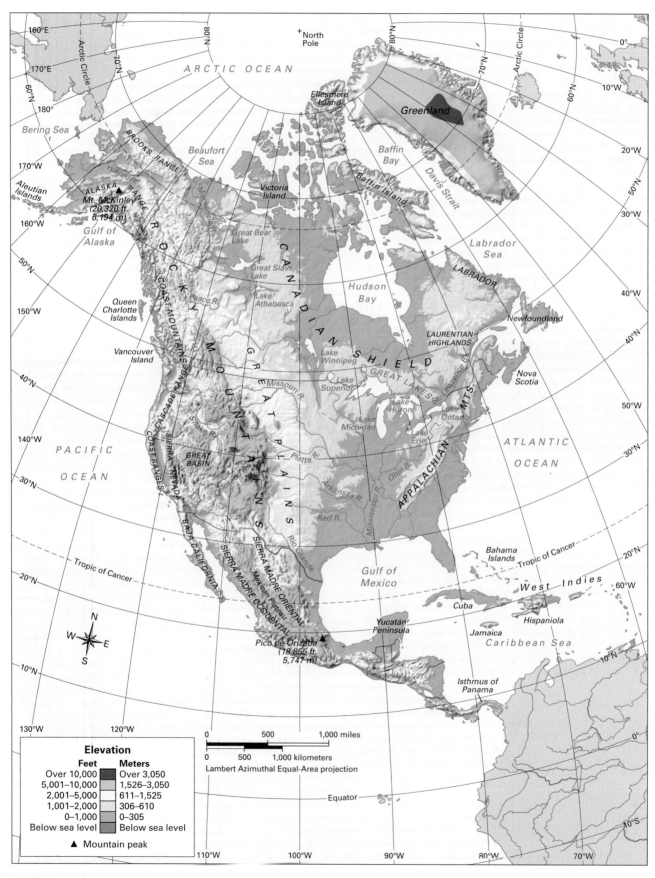

North Pole

ARCTIC OCEAN

Bering Sea

BROOKS RANGE

Beaufort Sea

Ellesmere Island

Greenland

Baffin Bay

Baffin Island

Victoria Island

Davis Strait

Aleutian Islands

ALASKA
Mt. McKinley
(20,320 ft.
6,194 m)

YUKON RANGE

Gulf of Alaska

Mackenzie R.

Great Bear Lake

Labrador Sea

LABRADOR

Queen Charlotte Islands

COAST MOUNTAINS

ROCKY MOUNTAINS

Peace R.

Great Slave Lake

Lake Athabasca

Hudson Bay

CANADIAN SHIELD

LAURENTIAN HIGHLANDS

Newfoundland

Vancouver Island

CASCADE RANGE

COAST RANGES

SIERRA NEVADA

GREAT PLAINS

Lake Winnipeg

Lake Superior

GREAT LAKES

St. Lawrence R.

Nova Scotia

PACIFIC

OCEAN

GREAT BASIN

Snake R.

Missouri R.

Lake Huron

Lake Michigan

Lake Ontario

Lake Erie

APPALACHIAN MTS.

ATLANTIC

OCEAN

Colorado R.

Platte R.

Ohio R.

Arkansas R.

Mississippi R.

Red R.

Rio Grande

SIERRA MADRE OCCIDENTAL

SIERRA MADRE ORIENTAL

Mexican Plateau

BAJA CALIFORNIA

Tropic of Cancer

Bahama Islands

West Indies

Gulf of Mexico

Cuba

Hispaniola

Yucatán Peninsula

Jamaica

Caribbean Sea

Pico de Orizaba
(18,855 ft.
5,747 m)

N
W E
S

Isthmus of Panama

Equator

Elevation

Feet	Meters
Over 10,000	Over 3,050
5,001–10,000	1,526–3,050
2,001–5,000	611–1,525
1,001–2,000	306–610
0–1,000	0–305
Below sea level	Below sea level

▲ Mountain peak

0   500   1,000 miles

0   500   1,000 kilometers

Lambert Azimuthal Equal-Area projection

Political Boundaries of North America

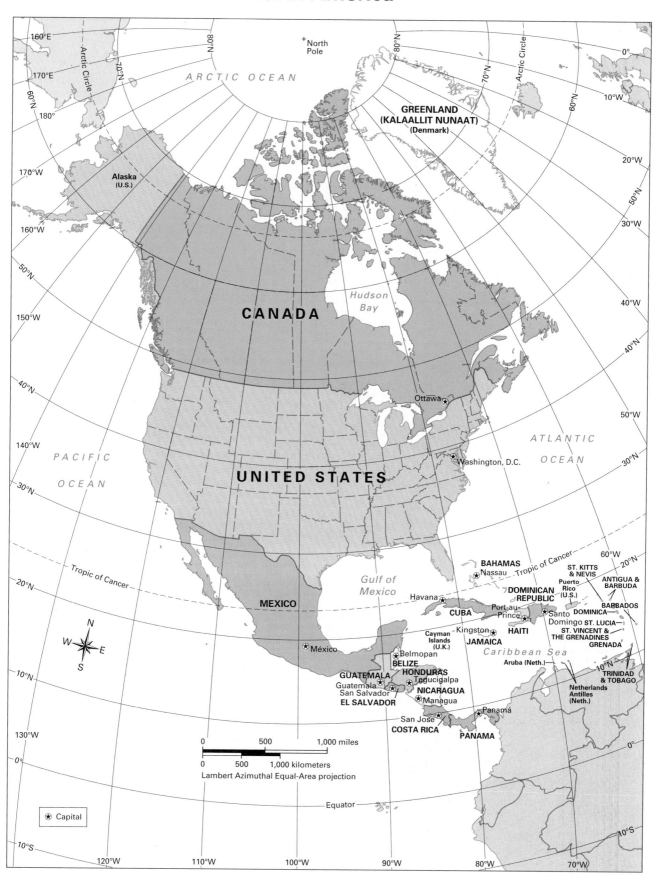

North Pole

ARCTIC OCEAN

GREENLAND
(KALAALLIT NUNAAT)
(Denmark)

Alaska
(U.S.)

CANADA

Hudson
Bay

Ottawa ⊛

PACIFIC

OCEAN

UNITED STATES

Washington, D.C. ⊛

ATLANTIC

OCEAN

Tropic of Cancer

MEXICO

Gulf of
Mexico

BAHAMAS
Nassau ⊛   Tropic of Cancer

ST. KITTS
& NEVIS

ANTIGUA &
BARBUDA

DOMINICAN
REPUBLIC

Puerto
Rico
(U.S.)

BARBADOS

⊛ México

Havana ⊛

CUBA

Port-au-
Prince

Santo
Domingo

DOMINICA

ST. LUCIA

Cayman
Islands
(U.K.)

Kingston ⊛

JAMAICA

HAITI

ST. VINCENT &
THE GRENADINES

GRENADA

Belmopan ⊛
BELIZE

Caribbean Sea

Aruba (Neth.)

GUATEMALA

HONDURAS
Tegucigalpa ⊛

TRINIDAD
& TOBAGO

Guatemala ⊛
San Salvador ⊛
EL SALVADOR

NICARAGUA
Managua ⊛

Netherlands
Antilles
(Neth.)

Panamá ⊛

San José ⊛
COSTA RICA

PANAMA

0   500   1,000 miles

0   500   1,000 kilometers

Lambert Azimuthal Equal-Area projection

Equator

⊛ Capital

Physical Features of South America

Caribbean Sea

ATLANTIC OCEAN

LLANOS

Orinoco R.

GUIANA HIGHLANDS

AMAZON BASIN

Amazon R.

Equator

10°N

0°

10°S

20°S

Tropic of Capricorn

30°S

40°S

50°S

Galápagos Islands

PACIFIC OCEAN

ANDES MOUNTAINS

Lake Titicaca

ATACAMA DESERT

Mt. Aconcagua
(22,835 ft.
6,960 m)

ANDES MOUNTAINS

GRAN CHACO

Paraná R.

Uruguay R.

Iguazú Falls

BRAZILIAN HIGHLANDS

São Francisco R.

PAMPAS

ATLANTIC OCEAN

PATAGONIA

Laguna del Carbón
(-344 ft. -105 m)

Strait of Magellan

Tierra del Fuego

Cape Horn

Falkland Islands

N
W — E
S

0   500   1,000 miles
0   500   1,000 kilometers
Lambert Azimuthal Equal-Area projection

Elevation

Feet	Meters
Over 10,000	Over 3,050
5,001–10,000	1,526–3,050
2,001–5,000	611–1,525
1,001–2,000	306–610
0–1,000	0–305
Below sea level	Below sea level

▲ Mountain peak

Political Boundaries of South America

Physical Features of Europe and Russia

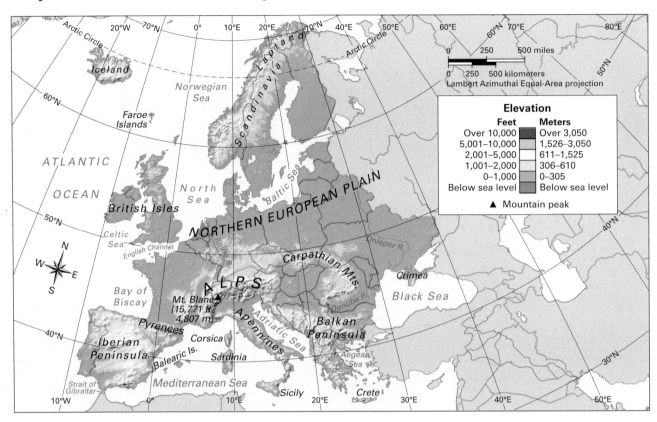

Elevation

Feet	Meters
Over 10,000	Over 3,050
5,001–10,000	1,526–3,050
2,001–5,000	611–1,525
1,001–2,000	306–610
0–1,000	0–305
Below sea level	Below sea level

▲ Mountain peak

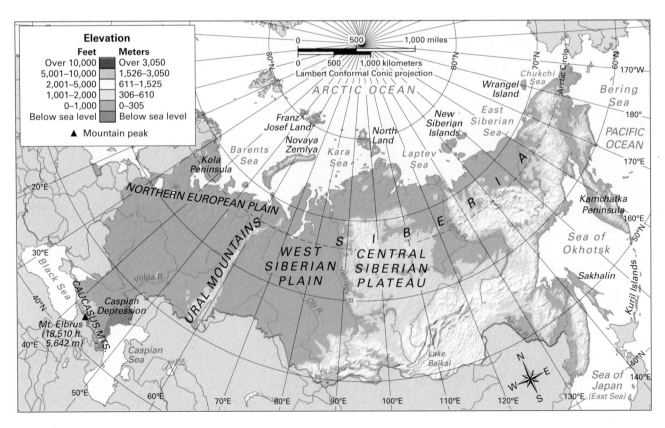

Elevation

Feet	Meters
Over 10,000	Over 3,050
5,001–10,000	1,526–3,050
2,001–5,000	611–1,525
1,001–2,000	306–610
0–1,000	0–305
Below sea level	Below sea level

▲ Mountain peak

Political Boundaries of Europe and Russia

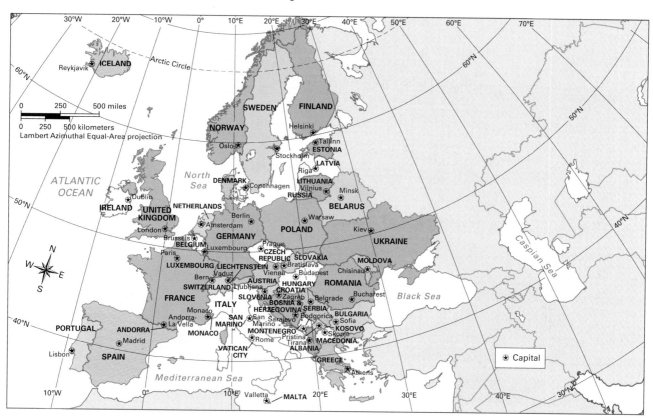

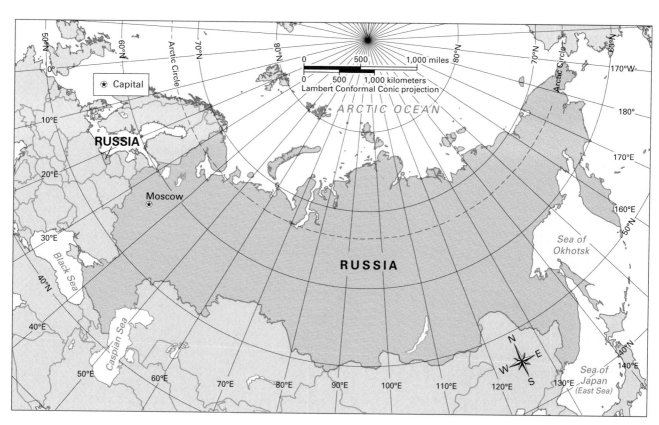

Physical Features of Africa

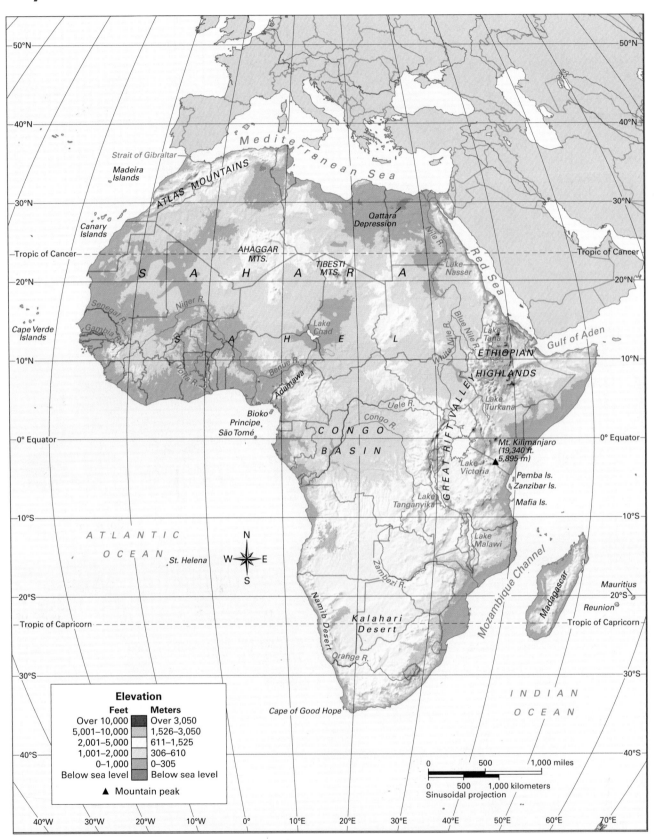

50°N
40°N
30°N
Tropic of Cancer
20°N
10°N
0° Equator
10°S
Tropic of Capricorn
20°S
30°S
40°S

Strait of Gibraltar
Madeira Islands
ATLAS MOUNTAINS
Mediterranean Sea
Qattara Depression
Canary Islands
AHAGGAR MTS.
TIBESTI MTS.
S A H A R A
Nile R.
Lake Nasser
Red Sea
Cape Verde Islands
Senegal R.
Niger R.
Gambia R.
S A H E L
Volta R.
Lake Chad
Benue R.
White Nile R.
Blue Nile R.
Lake Tana
ETHIOPIAN HIGHLANDS
Gulf of Aden
Adamawa
Uele R.
Bioko
Principe
São Tomé
C O N G O
Congo R.
Lake Turkana
B A S I N
Mt. Kilimanjaro (19,340 ft. 5,895 m)
Lake Victoria
GREAT RIFT VALLEY
Lake Tanganyika
Pemba Is.
Zanzibar Is.
Mafia Is.
ATLANTIC
OCEAN
St. Helena
N
W   E
S
Lake Malawi
Zambezi R.
Mozambique Channel
Madagascar
Mauritius
Reunion
Namib Desert
Kalahari Desert
INDIAN
OCEAN
Orange R.
Cape of Good Hope

Tropic of Cancer
20°N
10°N
0° Equator
10°S
Tropic of Capricorn
20°S
30°S
40°S

40°W 30°W 20°W 10°W 0° 10°E 20°E 30°E 40°E 50°E 60°E 70°E

Elevation

Feet	Meters
Over 10,000	Over 3,050
5,001–10,000	1,526–3,050
2,001–5,000	611–1,525
1,001–2,000	306–610
0–1,000	0–305
Below sea level	Below sea level

▲ Mountain peak

0   500   1,000 miles
0   500   1,000 kilometers
Sinusoidal projection

Political Boundaries of Africa

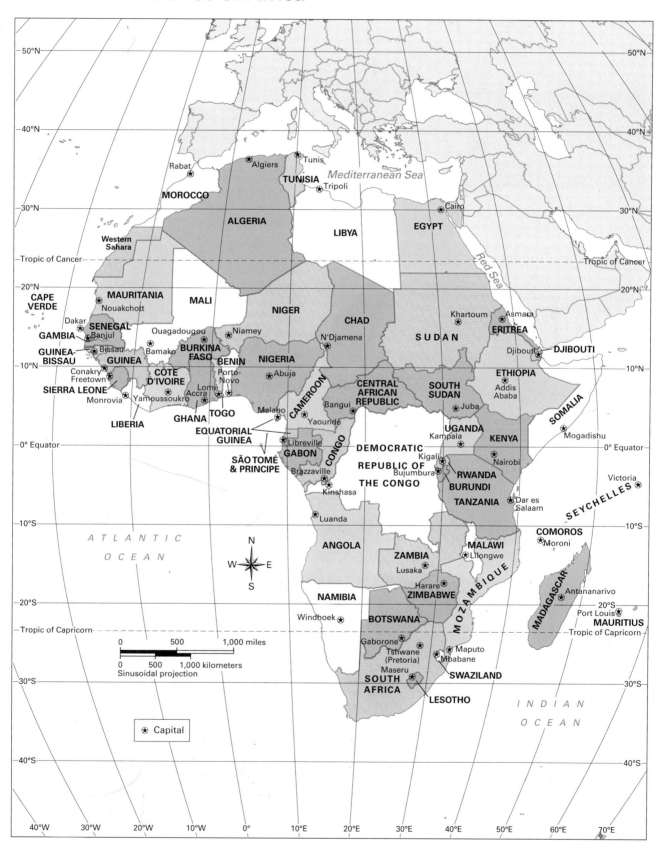

Physical Features of Southwest and Central Asia

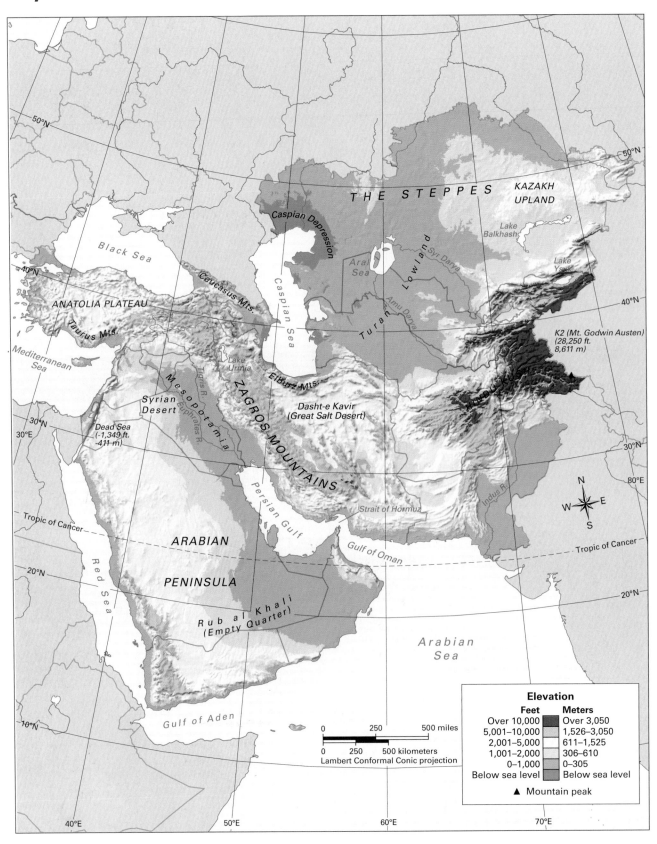

THE STEPPES

KAZAKH UPLAND

Caspian Depression

Lake Balkhash

Black Sea

Aral Sea

Lake Ysyk

Caucasus Mts.

Turan Lowland

Syr Darya

ANATOLIA PLATEAU

Caspian Sea

Amu Darya

K2 (Mt. Godwin Austen)
(28,250 ft.
8,611 m)

Taurus Mts.

Lake Urmia

Elburz Mts.

HINDU KUSH

Mediterranean Sea

Tigris R.

ZAGROS MOUNTAINS

Mesopotamia

Dasht-e Kavir
(Great Salt Desert)

Syrian Desert

Euphrates R.

Dead Sea
(-1,349 ft.
-411 m)

Indus R.

Persian Gulf

Strait of Hormuz

N
W   E
S

Tropic of Cancer

ARABIAN

Gulf of Oman

Tropic of Cancer

Red Sea

20°N

PENINSULA

Rub al Khali
(Empty Quarter)

Arabian Sea

Gulf of Aden

0   250   500 miles

0   250   500 kilometers
Lambert Conformal Conic projection

Elevation

Feet	Meters
Over 10,000	Over 3,050
5,001–10,000	1,526–3,050
2,001–5,000	611–1,525
1,001–2,000	306–610
0–1,000	0–305
Below sea level	Below sea level

▲ Mountain peak

Political Boundaries of Southwest and Central Asia

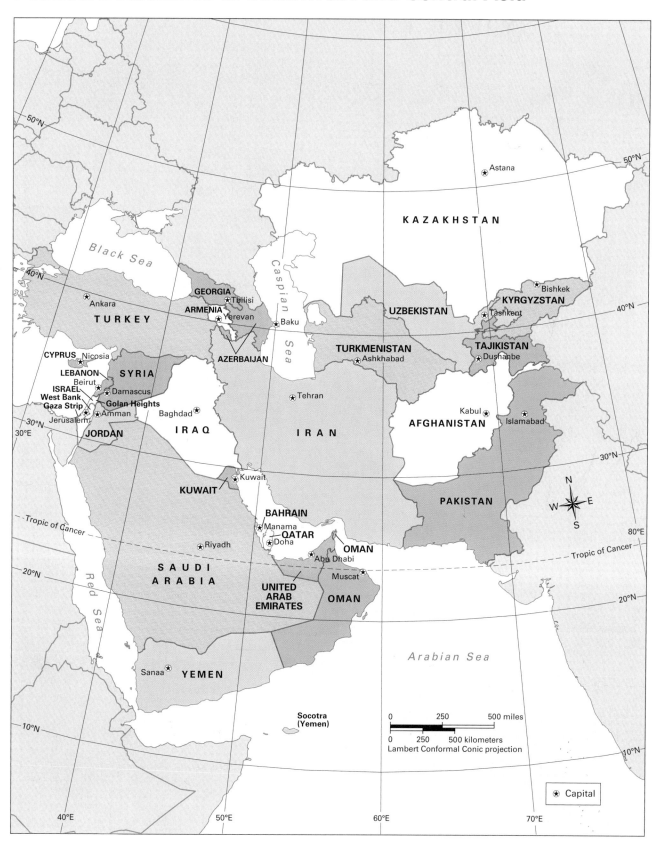

Black Sea

Caspian Sea

Astana

KAZAKHSTAN

GEORGIA
Tbilisi

Ankara

ARMENIA
Yerevan

TURKEY

Baku

UZBEKISTAN

KYRGYZSTAN
Bishkek

Tashkent

CYPRUS   Nicosia

LEBANON
Beirut

SYRIA

AZERBAIJAN

TURKMENISTAN
Ashkhabad

TAJIKISTAN
Dushanbe

ISRAEL
West Bank
Gaza Strip

Damascus

Golan Heights

Tehran

Amman

Baghdad

IRAQ

IRAN

AFGHANISTAN

Kabul

Islamabad

Jerusalem

JORDAN

Kuwait

KUWAIT

BAHRAIN

PAKISTAN

Manama

Tropic of Cancer

Riyadh

QATAR
Doha

Abu Dhabi

OMAN

Muscat

SAUDI
ARABIA

UNITED
ARAB
EMIRATES

OMAN

Tropic of Cancer

Red Sea

Arabian Sea

Sanaa   YEMEN

Socotra
(Yemen)

0   250   500 miles

0   250   500 kilometers
Lambert Conformal Conic projection

⊛ Capital

50°N
40°N
30°N
30°E
40°E
50°E
60°E
70°E
20°N
10°N
80°E
50°N
40°N
30°N
20°N
10°N

Physical Features of South Asia, East Asia, and Southeast Asia

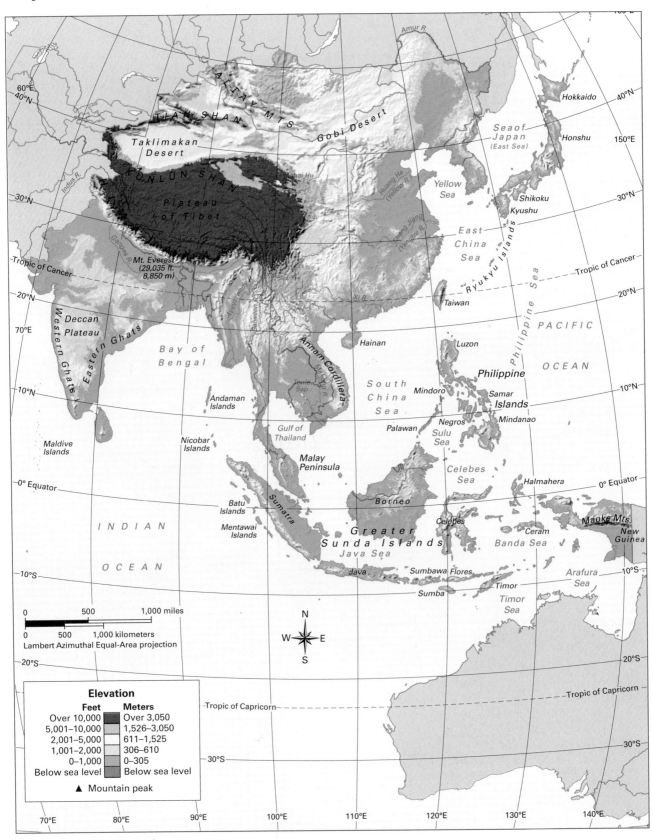

Amur R.

ALTAY MTS.

TIAN SHAN

Taklimakan Desert

Gobi Desert

KUNLUN SHAN

Qinghai Hu

Plateau of Tibet

Huang He (Yellow R.)

Yellow Sea

Chang Jiang (Yangtze R.)

Sea of Japan (East Sea)

Hokkaido

Honshu

Shikoku
Kyushu

East China Sea

Ganges R.

Indus R.

Mt. Everest (29,035 ft. 8,850 m)

Brahmaputra R.

Tropic of Cancer

Deccan Plateau

Western Ghats

Eastern Ghats

Bay of Bengal

Salween R.

Xi R.

Ryukyu Islands

Taiwan

Tropic of Cancer

PACIFIC

Annam Cordillera

Hainan

Luzon

Philippine

OCEAN

Mekong R.

Tonle Sap

Andaman Islands

South China Sea

Mindoro

Samar

Philippine Sea

Islands

Negros

Mindanao

Palawan

Gulf of Thailand

Maldive Islands

Nicobar Islands

Sulu Sea

Malay Peninsula

Celebes Sea

Halmahera

Equator

INDIAN

Batu Islands

Sumatra

Borneo

Celebes

Greater

Ceram

Maoke Mts.

New Guinea

OCEAN

Mentawai Islands

Sunda Islands

Banda Sea

Java Sea

Java

Sumbawa Flores

Arafura Sea

Sumba

Timor

Timor Sea

Scale

0   500   1,000 miles

0   500   1,000 kilometers

Lambert Azimuthal Equal-Area projection

N
W E
S

Tropic of Capricorn

Elevation

Feet		Meters
Over 10,000		Over 3,050
5,001–10,000		1,526–3,050
2,001–5,000		611–1,525
1,001–2,000		306–610
0–1,000		0–305
Below sea level		Below sea level

▲ Mountain peak

Political Boundaries of South Asia, East Asia, and Southeast Asia

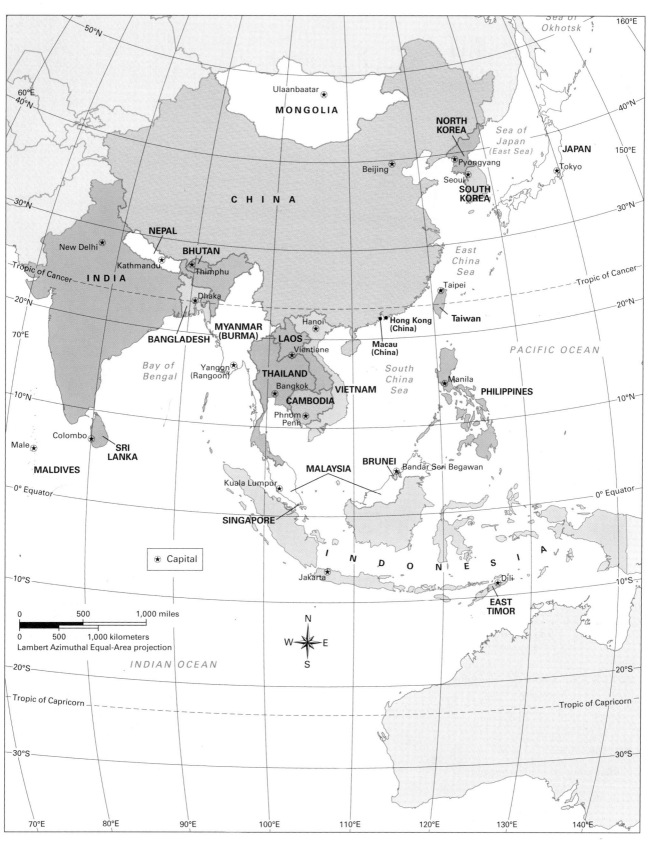

Physical Features of Oceania and Antarctica

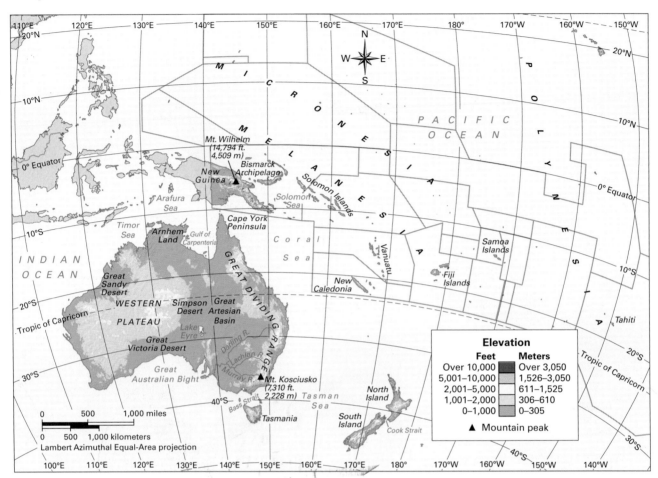

Mt. Wilhelm (14,794 ft. 4,509 m)

Elevation

Feet	Meters
Over 10,000	Over 3,050
5,001–10,000	1,526–3,050
2,001–5,000	611–1,525
1,001–2,000	306–610
0–1,000	0–305

▲ Mountain peak

0   500   1,000 miles
0   500   1,000 kilometers
Lambert Azimuthal Equal-Area projection

Mt. Kosciusko (7,310 ft. 2,228 m)

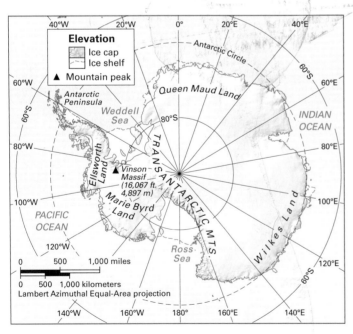

Elevation

Ice cap
Ice shelf
▲ Mountain peak

Vinson Massif (16,067 ft. 4,897 m)

0   500   1,000 miles
0   500   1,000 kilometers
Lambert Azimuthal Equal-Area projection

Political Boundaries of Oceania and Antarctica

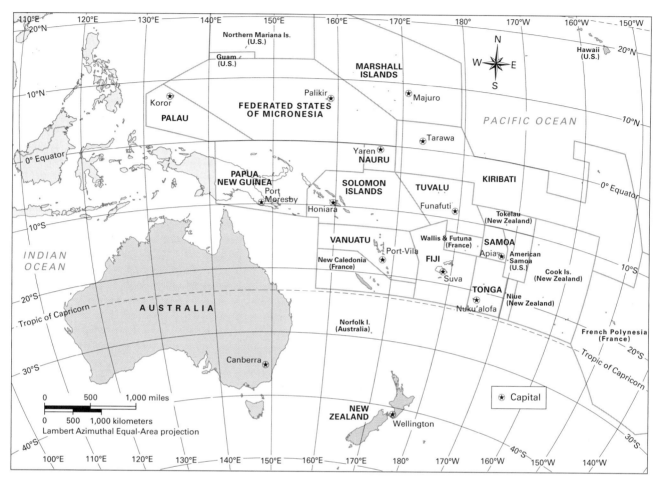

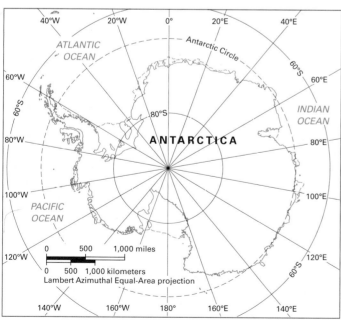

Glossary

Some words in this book have been respelled to help you pronounce them. Respelled words have been adapted from *Merriam-Webster's Collegiate Dictionary, Eleventh Edition; The American Heritage Dictionary of the English Language, Fourth Edition;* and *Random House Dictionary.*

Blue words are defined in the margins.

Black words are Academic Vocabulary terms.

A

abandon to leave something behind

absolute monarchy a monarchy in which the ruler's power is unlimited

abstract existing as an idea without physical form

accumulate to gather something over time, in greater and greater numbers or amount

achievement a positive result gained by hard work

acquire to come into possession of something

adapt to change to fit a new situation

adaptation a change made to an existing object or way of doing things

administer to manage and organize

Age of Exploration a period of European exploration and discovery that lasted from about 1418 to 1620

Alighieri, Dante a great Italian author of the Renaissance who wrote *The Divine Comedy*

alliance a group of countries, city-states, or other entities who agree to work together, usually for common defense or trade

alternative a choice that differs from another option

Amida Buddhism a form of Buddhism founded on the belief that all people can reach paradise by relying on the mercy of Amida Buddha

analyze to examine or think about carefully

Anglicanism a Protestant denomination of Christian faith founded by Henry VIII in England

anti-Semitism hostility or discrimination against Jews

appliqué a technique in which shaped pieces of fabric are attached to a background fabric to form a design or picture

apprentice a person who works for a master in a trade or craft in return for training

approximately a close estimate

aqueduct a pipe or raised channel built to carry water over a long distance

arbitrary based on personal preference instead of reason

aristocracy a ruling class of noble families

aristocrat someone who holds a high social level

artifact an item left by an earlier culture

astronomy the study of the stars and planets

Augustus, Caesar Julius Caesar's grandnephew and adopted son, Octavian; Rome's first emperor

authority the power to influence or command

authorize to give official permission

available ready for use

ayllu an Incan clan (group of related families), the basic unit of Incan society

Aztecs a Mesoamerican people who built an empire in central Mexico that flourished from 1428 to 1519 C.E.

axis a line on which an object spins

B

behalf something that is done for someone else

bill of rights a list of basic human rights that a government must protect

Bhakti movement a movement within Hinduism that emphasized personal devotion and social and religious equality

boycott a refusal to do business with an organization or group

bubonic plague a deadly contagious disease caused by bacteria and spread by fleas; also called the Black Death

bureaucracy a highly complex body of workers with many levels of authority

Bushido a samurai code that called on warriors to be honest, fair, and fearless

Byzantine Empire the name for the eastern Roman Empire, located at the crossroads of Europe and Asia; it lasted from about 500 to 1453 C.E.

C

Caesar, Julius a Roman general who ended the Roman Republic when he seized power and became dictator for life

call-and-response a song style in which a singer or musician leads with a call, and a chorus responds

Calvinism a Protestant denomination of Christian faith founded by John Calvin

capitalism an economic system based on investment of money for profit

capture to take control of a person or thing by force

cartography the science and art of making maps

causeway a solid earthen roadway built across water or low ground

ceremonial center a large plaza in a city center, surrounded by temples and palaces, where religious rituals and other public ceremonies took place

Cervantes, Miguel Spanish Renaissance author of the masterpiece *Don Quixote*

Charlemagne the leader of the Franks from 768 to 814 C.E., who unified most of the Christian lands of Europe into a single empire

Christianity the religion based on the life and teachings of Jesus

charter a written grant of rights and privileges by a ruler or government to a community, class of people, or organization

chivalry the medieval knight's code of ideal behavior, including bravery, loyalty, and respect for women

Christianity the religion based on the life and teachings of Jesus

circulation the passing of something, such as money, from person to person

city-state an independent state consisting of a city and its surrounding territory

civil service examination a test given to qualify candidates for positions in the government

civil war a war between groups in the same country

clarify to make understandable; to make clear

classical art art influenced by the styles and techniques of ancient Greece and Rome

clergy the body of people, such as priests, who perform the sacred functions of a church

collapse to fail suddenly and completely

colony a territory, often very large, under the political and economic control of another country

commerce the buying and selling of goods; business

common law a body of rulings made by judges or very old traditional laws that become part of a nation's legal system

communal shared by a community or group

communicate to exchange or share thoughts, feelings, or information using words, writing, or other methods

conduct a person's behavior, especially in front of other people

conflict a disagreement or fight caused by opposing points of view

conformity uniform behavior according to a set of social or cultural rules or beliefs

consequently as a result of

considerable a large amount

Constantine Roman emperor who, in 330 C.E., moved the capital to Byzantium and later renamed it Constantinople

Constantinople the city on the eastern edge of Europe, which Constantine made the capital of the Roman Empire in 330 C.E.

constitutional monarchy a form of government in which the monarch's power is limited by a basic set of laws

contradict to disagree, especially by saying the opposite

contrast a strong difference between two or more things

convert to change one's belief on something

cooperation the action of working together

corruption a pattern of illegal or immoral activities by government officials

cottage industry a small-scale business in which people produce goods at home

Counter-Reformation a movement of the Catholic Church, in reaction to the Reformation, in which Catholic leaders worked to correct abuses, to clarify and defend Catholic teachings, to condemn what they saw as Protestant errors, and to win back members

courtier a male member of a ruler's court

credibility worthy of being believed

Crusades a series of religious wars launched by European Christians to reclaim Jerusalem and other holy sites from Muslims

cultural diffusion the spread of cultural elements from one society to another

currency the form of money used in a country

D

da Vinci, Leonardo a famous Renaissance artist, scientist, and inventor

daimyo a local lord in Japan in the era of the samurai

decline a slow breakdown or failure

dedicated assigned to a particular purpose

democratic rule by the people; available to the broad mass of people

denomination a particular religious group within a larger faith. For example, Lutheranism is one denomination within Christianity.

despotism rule by a single person with absolute power

detrimental something that does harm or damage

devoted to be completely committed to something; loyal

dialect a regional variety of a language

dictator a ruler with absolute power

disciple a person who helps spread the religious teachings of another

dispute disagreement

distinctive clearly different

distribute to give out or deliver

diverse a group of people or things with obvious differences between one another

divine related to or coming from a god or gods

doctrine a belief or set of beliefs, especially relating to religion

document a written work containing information

dominate to have control or power over something

Donatello a Florentine sculptor who was one of the first to use a realistic, lifelike style

dramatic noticeable and remarkable

drastic extreme or severe

dynasty a line of rulers descended from one family

E

Eastern Orthodox Church a Christian religion that developed out of early Christianity in the Byzantine Empire

economic relating to trade or money

economy a system of managing the wealth and resources of a community or region

edition a version of a printed text

efficient functioning in the best way, with very little or no waste

elaborate detailed and often complicated; carefully planned

elevate to raise

emancipate to free

emerge to appear or arise; to move from a low position to a higher one

emotional related to emotions or feelings

emperor the political leader of a territory containing several countries or groups of people

emphasis special importance

emphasize to call attention to or highlight the importance of something

empire a large territory in which several groups of people are ruled by a single leader or government

Enlightenment a period from the late 1600s to the late 1700s in Europe, in which people changed their outlook on life by seeing reason as the key to human progress

enlightenment the state of gaining spiritual knowledge and finding truth

enormous very large

epidemic an outbreak of a contagious disease that spreads quickly and over a wide geographic area

equation a mathematical statement in which the answer equals the statement

erode to slowly break down or destroy

error something that differs from what is correct

estimate a guess as to the value or size of something

evaporation the process in which a liquid, such as water, turns into a gas

evolution the slow process of change in plants and animals from simpler forms to more complex forms

evolve to slowly change over a long period of time

F

feudalism the economic and political system of medieval Europe in which people exchanged loyalty and labor for a lord's protection

fief land granted by a lord to a vassal in exchange for loyalty and service

Five Pillars of Islam the most basic acts of worship for Muslims: declaration of faith, prayer, charity, fasting, and making a pilgrimage to Mecca

Florence an Italian city-state and leading cultural center during the Renaissance

folktale a story that is passed down orally and becomes part of a culture's tradition

formula a series of numbers or letters that represent a mathematical or scientific rule

foundation the basis from which an idea or situation develops

function the use or purpose of something

fundamental at the most basic level

G

gender roles customs relating to the position of men and women in society

genealogy an account of the line of ancestry within a family

geocentric theory a theory that Earth is the center of the solar system or the universe. *Geo* is Greek for "earth."

geometric one or a number of simple shapes, such as triangles, squares, or circles

Ghana a medieval civilization and empire in Western Africa

glyph a symbol for a word, idea, or sound in a hieroglyphic system of writing

golden age a period in a nation's past during which its culture and society attained the height of achievement and power

Gospel an account of the life and teachings of Jesus; four of them are included in the New Testament of the Christian Bible

gravity the force of attraction between all masses in the universe

griot a talented poet-musician of the Mande people, who tells stories, sings songs, and recites poems to share history

guild an organization of people in the same craft or trade

gunpowder an explosive powder made of saltpeter and other materials

Gutenberg, Johannes a German inventor who, in about 1450, developed the first printing press with movable type in Europe

Gupta Empire the empire covering much of northern India that was ruled by the Guptas from about 320 C.E. to about 550 C.E.

H

habeas corpus the legal concept that an accused person cannot be jailed indefinitely without being charged with a crime

Heian period the cultural flowering in Japan that took place between the late 8th and the late 12th centuries

heliocentric theory a theory that places the sun at the center of the solar system with the planets, including Earth, revolving around it. *Helio* is Greek for "sun."

hereditary passed on from parent to child; inherited

heretic a person who holds beliefs that are contrary to a set of religious teachings

hierarchy a system of organization with lower and higher positions

hieroglyphic writing that uses pictures as symbols

Holy Land the area between Egypt and Syria that was the ancient homeland of Jews and the place where Jesus Christ had lived; also called Palestine

humanism a philosophy that tries to balance religious faith with an emphasis on individual dignity and an interest in nature and human society

humanities collectively, areas of study that focus on human life and culture, such as history, literature, and ethics

Hundred Years' War a series of battles fought by France and England between 1337 and 1453

hypothesis an idea or assumption to be tested in an experiment

I

identify to recognize something for what it is

illuminate to decorate a book with detailed designs and small pictures, especially using gold, silver, or bright colors

immortal able to live forever

imperial belonging or related to an emperor

import to bring in a product from another country to sell it

impressive causing admiration or awe

Incas people of a culture in the Andes Mountains of South America that arose in the 1400s C.E. and lasted until 1532

individualism the belief in the importance of an individual's achievements and dignity

indulgence a grant by the Catholic Church that released a person from punishment for sins

inferior lower in rank or quality

inflation a rise in prices, often due an increase in the supply of money

ingenious especially intelligent, creative, or clever

innovation something new; an improvement

inoculate to protect against disease by transmitting a disease-causing agent to a person, stimulating the body's defensive reactions

Inquisition a judicial body established by the Roman Catholic Church to combat forms of religious error

insight to see the inner nature of a situation; to understand

institution a society or organization founded for a religious, educational, social, or similar purpose

intellectual related to the interest in or study of ideas

intense strong effect or feelings; extreme

irrigation a means of supplying land with water

Islam the religion of Muslims

isolated set apart from other people or things

J

Jenne-jeno an ancient West African city built along the Niger River, which existed for 1600 years

Jesus a man whose life and teachings would later become the foundation of Christianity

jihad an Arabic term that describes the struggle, usually an internal, spiritual one, that Muslims undergo to get closer to God. A small percentage of Muslims interpret jihad to justify acts of violence and terrorism.

K

kente a traditional form of cloth produced in West Africa

Khan the title used by the rulers of Mongol tribes

khagan title in the Mongolian language equal to the status of emperor and used to refer to someone who rules a khanate or empire

khanates a territory led by a khan. The khanates were the four divisions of the empire

kinship family relationship, either by birth, marriage, or adoption

L

lens curved transparent material that, when looked through, changes the appearance of an object, often making it appear larger or smaller. The transparent material is often glass.

logic a way of thinking that uses reason

Luther, Martin a German priest who broke away from the Catholic Church to start his own religion, Lutheranism. His posting of the Ninety-Five Theses started the Reformation.

Lutheranism a Protestant denomination of Christian faith founded by Martin Luther

M

Machiavelli, Niccolò a Renaissance statesman and historian who wrote *The Prince*

Magna Carta a written legal agreement signed in 1215 that limited the English monarch's power

Mahayana Buddhism a branch of Buddhism that became popular in China and focused on salvation through personal faith

magnetic something that acts like a magnet. A magnet attracts iron or some other metals.

maintain to continue in the same way

Mali a West African empire ruled by the Mande that became a major crossroads of the Islamic world

Mansa Musa the first West African ruler to practice Islam devoutly

maritime relating to the sea

market economy an economy in which prices are determined by the buying and selling decisions of individuals in the marketplace

martial arts styles of fighting or self-defense, such as modern-day judo and karate, that began mostly in Asia

mass a measure of the amount of matter in an object

mass-produce to make quantities of an item by using standardized designs and dividing steps of production among the workers

mathematics the study of numbers

matrilineal a family line traced through the mother

Maya the people of an important Mesoamerican civilization that lasted from about 2000 B.C.E. to 1500 C.E.

meditation a spiritual discipline that involves deep relaxation and clearing the mind of distracting thoughts

mercantilism an economic policy by which nations try to gather wealth by controlling trade and establishing colonies

mercenary a professional soldier who is paid to fight for another country or group

meritocracy rule by officials of proven merit

Messiah a savior who many Jews believe had been promised to them by God

Mesoamerica the region extending from modern Mexico through Central America

Michelangelo a Renaissance artist, renowned for his painting and sculpture

microscope an instrument used to make very small objects visible

Ming the dynasty that ruled China after the overthrow of the Yuan

missionary someone who tries to convert others to believe in a particular religion or set of beliefs

Model Parliament a governing body created by King Edward I of England that included some commoners, Church officials, and nobles

momentum a force gathered over time

Mongols foreign rulers of China from Mongolia who established the Yuan dynasty

monotheism the belief in a single God

Moor a name given to Muslims who lived in the Iberian peninsula

mosaic a picture made up of small pieces of tile, glass, or colored stone

mosque a Muslim house of worship

motive something that causes a person or people to act

movable type individual characters made of wood or metal that can be arranged to create a printing job and then be used over again

Muhammad a man born in about 570 C.E. who taught the faith of Islam

Muslim a follower of the Islamic faith

mythical not real; imagined

N

nationalism the identification with, and devotion to, the interests of one's nation

natural law the concept that there is a universal order built into nature that can guide moral thinking

natural rights rights that belong to people "by nature," simply because they are human beings

New World the name given by Europeans to the Americas, which were unknown to most Europeans before the voyages of Christopher Columbus

Niger River the longest river in West Africa, which was a kind of trading highway in ancient times

Nok a people living in West Africa in the 500s B.C.E. who mastered ironworking

O

oracle a person through whom a god or spirit is believed to speak about the future

oral tradition learning and cultural ideas passed down orally, from one generation to the next

orbit to follow a circular path around another object

P

pagoda a tower-shaped structure with several stories and upturned, tiled roofs

parable a simple story that explains a moral or religious lesson

pastoral nomad a person who migrates and depends on the livestock they raise

patriarch in the Eastern Orthodox Church, the bishop of an important city

patrilineal a family line traced through the father

Pax Romana a 200-year period of peace and stability established and maintained by the Roman Empire

persecute to cause a person to suffer because of his or her beliefs

philosopher a scholar, teacher, or thinker who seeks knowledge

philosophy the study of wisdom, knowledge, and the nature of reality

pictograph a drawing that stands for a word, phrase, or name

pilgrimage a journey to a holy site

plaza a public square or open area in a city where people gather

plot a secret plan made for a specific purpose, to bring about a certain outcome

policy an overall plan, especially of a government

polygamy having more than one spouse at one time

polytheism belief in more than one god

portolan charts navigational maps based on compass directions and observations of pilots at sea

predict to say what will happen in the future, based on experience or reason

Prince Shotoku a Japanese ruler who encouraged cultural diffusion from countries on the Asian mainland

process a series of actions that produce a certain result

proclaim to announce publically

prophet a person who speaks or interprets the words of God

proportion the relationship between amounts, numbers, or sizes

prosperity a situation of wealth and success

prosperous wealthy or successful

Protestant a Christian who separated from the Roman Catholic Church during the Reformation; today, any member of a Christian church founded on the principles of the Reformation

proverb a popular saying meant to express something wise or true

province a territory that is part of a country or an empire

Punic Wars a series of wars fought between Rome and Carthage for control of the Mediterranean

Puritans English Protestants who wanted to "purify" the Anglican Church of Catholic elements

Q

Qur'an the holy book of the religion of Islam

R

Ramadan the ninth month of the Islamic calendar, during which Muslims are required to fast

rational using reason and understanding

rationalism a belief in reason and logic as the primary paths to knowledge

rebellious opposing or disobeying authority

reform to make change in order to bring about improvement

Reformation a religious reform movement from the early 1500s to the 1600s that led to the formation of new Christian groups

reign the period of time during which a king or other monarch rules

religion a set of spiritual beliefs, values, and practices

religious order a brotherhood or sisterhood of monks, nuns, or friars

religious tolerance the acceptance of different religious beliefs and customs

Renaissance a great flowering of culture, based on classical Greek and Roman ideas and art, that began in Italy in the Late Middle Ages and spread throughout Europe

republic a form of government in which citizens elect representatives to rule for them

require to have to do something based on a rule or command

resident someone who has lived in a place

response an answer to something that is done or said

restoration the return of a past state, situation, or ruler

restriction a limit or control placed on something

Resurrection in Christian belief, Jesus's rise from the dead

reveal to show or make known something that was hidden or secret

revolt a violent action in opposition to a government or law

ritual a set of actions that is always performed the same way as part of a religious ceremony

Roman Catholic Church the Christian church headed by the pope in Rome

Roman Empire an empire that, at its height, around 200 C.E., spanned the Mediterranean world and most of Europe

rural the countryside, as opposed to a city or town

S

sacrament a sacred rite of the Christian religion

sacrifice a gift of an animal for slaughter to honor the gods

Sahara a large, hot desert in North Africa that covers about 3.5 million square miles

Sahel a zone of semidesert, south of the Sahara, where short grasses, small bushes, and a few trees grow

saint someone officially recognized as holy by the Catholic Church

samurai a member of a powerful warrior class in Japan

savanna a vegetation zone of tall grasses and scattered trees, with a long rainy season

scientific method a step-by-step method of investigation involving observation and theory to test scientific assumptions

Scientific Revolution a major shift in thinking between 1500 and 1700, in which modern science emerged as a new way of gaining knowledge about the natural world

scribe a person trained to write or copy documents by hand

secular relating to earthly life rather than to religious or spiritual matters

segment a part of something that is divided from the whole

segregation the forced separation of one group from the rest of a community

semidivine half-human and half-god

separation of powers the division of powers among branches of government

serf a peasant who could not leave the lord's land on which he or she was born and worked

shah a ruler in certain Middle East lands, especially Persia (modern-day Iran)

Shakespeare, William an English Renaissance poet and playwright whose plays show a deep understanding of human behavior

shamanism Mongol religion characterized by a belief that gods, demons, and ancestral spirits respond to a shaman, a priest

shari'ah the search to understand God's law, which relies heavily on the Qur'an and the Sunnah

Shinto a Japanese religion that expresses love and respect for nature

shogun the head of the military government of Japan in the era of the samurai

sibling a brother or sister

siege a military action in which a place is surrounded and cut off to force those inside to surrender

significant having meaning and importance

simony the selling and buying of positions in the Catholic Church

site of encounter a specific place where people from different cultures meet and exchange products, ideas, and technologies

slash-and-burn agriculture a farming technique in which vegetation is cut away and burned to clear land for growing crops

smelting the process of melting ore to produce iron or other metals from it

social contract an agreement in which people give power to a government in exchange for its protections

social pyramid a social structure in the shape of a pyramid, with layers representing social classes of different rank

solar year the time it takes Earth to travel once around the sun

Songhai a people who broke away from the empire of Mali and eventually built their own vast empire in West Africa

sophisticated having experiences and knowledge, especially with culture and art

starve to suffer or die from lack of food

status the position of a person, either socially or professionally

stele a vertical stone slab or pillar with carvings or inscriptions

stimulate to encourage the growth or activity of something

stress to place importance on something

successor the person who is next in line to hold a position

sultan the supreme ruler of a Muslim state

Sunnah the example that Muhammad set for Muslims about how to live

supreme the highest level

surplus more than is needed or used

survive to continue to exist

suspension bridge a bridge held up by cables anchored at each end

sustain to support or provide nourishment for

T

Tale of Genji a Japanese novel and Heian masterpiece, written by Murasaki Shikibu; considered one of the great works of world literature

technique a specialized method used to achieve a desired result

telescope an instrument used to view distant objects

Tenochtitlán the capital city of the Aztec Empire

terra-cotta a baked clay used to make pottery, tiles, and sculptures

territory a specific area of land

textile a woven cloth

texture the way a surface looks and feels

theocracy a government or state in which God is the supreme ruler, and religious officials govern in God's name

thesis an argument, often written, to support an idea

tolerance to be sympathetic and accepting of what others believe or do, even if those ideas differ from your own

traditional a belief, custom, or way of doing something that has existed for a long time

trans-Saharan trade trade between peoples north and south of the Sahara

transmit to pass something on to someone else

treaty a written agreement between two or more nations

trephination a type of surgery in which a hole is made in the skull

tributary a conquered country or territory that pays tribute to the conqueror

tribute payment made by one ruler or country to another for protection or as a sign of submission

U

unification the process of joining two or more things together

unique one of a kind

urbanization the growth of cities

V

verbal spoken, rather than written

vernacular common language

vision the idea someone has for the way something should be

vital necessary for the existence of something

vocabulary a collection of words that make up a language

W

ward a political unit within a city, often a neighborhood

warlord a military leader operating outside the control of the government

widespread spread out over a large area or among many people

Z

Zen Buddhism a form of Buddhism that stresses self-reliance and achieving enlightenment through meditation

maps of, 221m, 225m

military of, 225, 231

salt trade, 228–229, 231

tax system in, 229

Trans-Saharan trade, 223, **226**–227, 233, 234

gladiators, 23, 27

Globe Theatre (London, England), 496

glyphs, **423,** 425

golden age, 185, **186,** 333

of Japan, *see* Heian period (Japan)

Golden Horde, 440, 444

gold trade in Ghana, 224, 227, 231

Gossamer Years, The (Shonagon), 339

Gothic-style cathedrals, 71

de Gouges, Olympe, 574

government

Absolute Rule, 568

free speech, 571

of Ghana, 224, 231

of Imperial China, 268–269, 273

of Japan, 323, 329

natural rights and, 569–**570**

religious tolerance, **571**

separation of powers, 570–571

in West Africa, 237, 241

Gozen, Tomoe (Japanese woman warrior), 360–363

Granada, Spain, 138, 139, 149, 165

Grand Canal (Imperial China), 279

gravity, **560,** 563

"Great Charter," *see* Magna Carta

Great Learning, The (Confucius), 275

Great Mosque of Samarra, 141

Great Schism, 507

Great Stone Bridge (Imperial China), 289

Great Temple (Aztec Empire), 387, 399, 425

Greco-Roman style, 45

Gregory VII, Pope, 67

Gregory XI, Pope, 507, 509

griots (storytellers), **250**–251

N'Dour, Youssou, 256–259

Guide to Geography (Ptolemy), 537

guilds, **79**

in medieval towns, 79, 84, 85

mystery plays by, 84

gunpowder, **294**

Imperial China, development in, 294

Gupta Empire, 185, **186,** 187m

art, 190–191

literature, 189

metalwork, 192

mathematics, 192-193

rise of, 186

roads, 194–195

universities, 188

Gutenberg, Johannes, **488,** 499, 500–503, 488

H

habeas corpus, **89**

Hagia Sophia (Eastern Orthodox church), 101, 102, 103

Hahua Incas, 412

haiku (poetry), 353

hajj (Fifth Pillar of Islam), 134, 137, 158

halach uinic ("true man"), 374

Han dynasty, 267, 268c, 269

Harris, Joel Chandler, 251

Heian-Jingu Shrine (Kyoto, Japan), 328

Heian-kyo, Japan, 332, 339, 340

Heian period (Japan), 331, **332**

beauty and fashion in, 335, 341

capital of, 332–333, 341

end of, 340, 341

entertainment in, 336, 341

Fujiwara family, 333–334, 341

Japan today, impact on, 341

literature of, 338–339, 341

paintings of, 336, 341

sculpture of, 336, 341

social position in, 334–335, 341

writing during, 338–339, 341

heliocentric theory, **557**

Henry, Prince of Portugal, 538

Henry II, King of England, 88

legal reforms of, 88

Henry IV (Roman Emperor), 67

Henry V, King of England, 92

Henry VIII, King of England, 495, 512–513, 520–521

Herculaneum, Roman city of, 44

hereditary, **392**

heretics, **92**

hieroglyphic, **373**

Hierosolymita (Ekkehard of Aurach), 175

Hinduism, 198–199

universities, 188

law, 189

literature, 189

Hippodrome (Constantinople), 100, 101

Hira Cave, 120

hiragana (Japanese writing style), 338

Hispañiola, 550m, 551

History of the Indies (Las Casas), 551

Hittites, 218

Hobbes, Thomas, 568

Holy Communion, 517

Holy Land, 69, **162,** 163

holy orders, 68c

Horyuji, 328

House of Wisdom (830), 142

huacas (Inca sacred objects/ places), 416

Hudson, Henry, 546

huipiles (Mayan tunics), 423

California's 2016 History-Social Science Framework

TCI's *History Alive!* California Series program was built around the *History–Social Science Framework for California Public Schools.*

New Feature in the Framework	How TCI Was Designed to 100% Meet the Framework
Active Learning and Civic Engagement	• Active learning is at TCI's core. Every lesson utilizes at least one of our six unique, hands-on classroom strategies. • The teacher and student resources are chock-full of places where students interact with the content online and with each other through student-driven debates, response groups, and problem solving groupwork activities. • TCI's Citizenship Toolkit provides students with real-world opportunities to practice citizenship skills.
Student Inquiry	• TCI activities get students excited and asking questions; students are inspired to learn more and conduct purposeful research. • Students build oral and written arguments by sharing claims with evidence. They take informed action where appropriate. • TCI's groundbreaking Interactive Student Notebook (available in print and online) serves as a personal journal for student inquiry.
Literacy and ELA	• Writing assignments are aligned to Common Core to strengthen students' literacy skills and support cross-disciplinary instruction. • High-interest reading extensions provide students with opportunities to analyze expository text and practice key reading and writing skills within the context of history.
ELD Supports	• TCI's activities are carefully designed to spiral in difficulty and reinforce ELD standards. • Integrated reading supports, both print and online—along with a unique narrative that tells history as a story—provide universal access to the text. • Every lesson includes specific differentiation methods and modifications for English Learners.
Primary Sources	• Written and visual primary sources are integrated thoughtfully throughout the Student Text and the activities. • Students build historical empathy by reading various perspectives. • Investigating Primary Sources sections challenge students to carefully analyze historical documents and develop arguments supported by evidence.
Inclusive Curriculum and the FAIR Act	• TCI classroom activities are presented in ways that all students can access content and skills; specific directions are provided to further differentiate instruction. • All legal and statutory requirements are incorporated in a meaningful way, including the specific framework content requirements related to the FAIR Act. • TCI celebrates diversity through visual representation, expository text, and primary sources that showcase a wide-variety of ethnic groups and perspectives.

Every line of content from the 2016 framework was included in our programs. Below is a selected list of content examples found in the new 7th grade framework.

New Feature in the Framework	How TCI Was Designed to 100% Meet the Framework
Additional Content	• Themes of world history • The Americas in 300 C.E., including Mesoamerica and civilizations along the Andean mountain spine • Afroeurasia in 300 C.E., including the Roman Empire, the Sasanian Persian Empire, the Gupta Empire, and China • Migrations and declining empires between 300 and 600 and the rise of new empires as trade and religious ideas spread • Rome and Christendom, 300 to 1200, including the Roman Empire, Pax Romana, government and citizenship, and the fall of Rome • Site of Encounter - Rome (27 B.C.E.–476 C.E.) • Christianity, including its origins, beliefs, spread, treatment of Christians, and the development of Christianity as a unifying state religion • Human-environment interactions in the feudal system and how the manor system allocated ecosystem resources • Site of Encounter - Cairo (1300–1500) • Baghdad under the Abbasids, a site of cultural interaction • Site of Encounter - Norman Sicily (1100-1200) • South Asia, 300 to 1200, including the Gupta Empire in India, the emergence of a common Indic culture, and the development of Hinduism • Site of Encounter - Calicut (1400) • Buddhism and Islam in South Asia • Site of Encounter - Quanzhou (1100-1400) • Cultural Exchanges Between Korea, China, and Japan • Site of Encounter - Tenochtitlan (1428–1600) • The geography of and early societies in West Africa, including Ghana and Mali empires and the gold trade • Site of Encounter - Mali (1300–1400s) • The Mongol Empire's impact on states, empires, trade, travel, and exchange • Increasing interconnectedness of Afroeurasian societies after 1200 • The spread of world religions during the early modern period

California History Social Science Standards, Seventh Grade

TCI's programs are designed to integrate California's History-Social Studies Standards throughout its instructional materials. Here, you can see which lessons meet each standard. For a detailed standards map with links, login to your teachtci account at: **https://subscriptions.teachtci.com/**.

Standards	Where Standards Are Addressed
7.1 Students analyze the causes and effects of the vast expansion and ultimate disintegration of the Roman Empire.	L1 From Republic to Empire L3 The Legacy of the Roman Empire L4 The Development of Feudalism in Western Europe L5 The Roman Catholic Church in Medieval Europe L8 The Byzantine Empire U1 Timeline: Europe During Medieval Times
1. Study the early strengths and lasting contributions of Rome (e.g., significance of Roman citizenship; rights under Roman law; Roman art, architecture, engineering, and philosophy; preservation and transmission of Christianity) and its ultimate internal weaknesses (e.g., rise of autonomous military powers within the empire, undermining of citizenship by the growth of corruption and slavery, lack of education, and distribution of news).	L1 From Republic to Empire L2 The Origins and Spread of Christianity L3 The Legacy of the Roman Empire L8 The Byzantine Empire
2. Discuss the geographic borders of the empire at its height and the factors that threatened its territorial cohesion.	L1 From Republic to Empire L3 The Legacy of the Roman Empire
3. Describe the establishment by Constantine of the new capital in Constantinople and the development of the Byzantine Empire, with an emphasis on the consequences of the development of two distinct European civilizations, Eastern Orthodox and Roman Catholic, and their two distinct views on church-state relations.	L3 The Legacy of the Roman Empire L8 The Byzantine Empire
7.2 Students analyze the geographic, political, economic, religious, and social structures of the civilizations of Islam in the Middle Ages.	U2 Setting the Stage: Islam in Medieval Times L9 The Origins and Spread of Islam L10 Learning About World Religions: Islam L11 Muslim Innovations and Adaptations
1. Identify the physical features and describe the climate of the Arabian peninsula, its relationship to surrounding bodies of land and water, and nomadic and sedentary ways of life.	U2 Setting the Stage: Islam in Medieval Times L9 The Origins and Spread of Islam
2. Trace the origins of Islam and the life and teachings of Muhammad, including Islamic teachings on the connection with Judaism and Christianity.	L9 The Origins and Spread of Islam L10 Learning About World Religions: Islam
3. Explain the significance of the Qur'an and the Sunnah as the primary sources of Islamic beliefs, practice, and law, and their influence in Muslims' daily life.	L10 Learning About World Religions: Islam

Standards	Where Standards Are Addressed
4. Discuss the expansion of Muslim rule through military conquests and treaties, emphasizing the cultural blending within Muslim civilization and the spread and acceptance of Islam and the Arabic language.	L9 The Origins and Spread of Islam L11 Muslim Innovations and Adaptations L17 The Influence of Islam on West Africa
5. Describe the growth of cities and the establishment of trade routes among Asia, Africa, and Europe, the products and inventions that traveled along these routes (e.g., spices, textiles, paper, steel, new crops), and the role of merchants in Arab society.	L6 Life in Medieval Towns L11 Muslim Innovations and Adaptations
6. Understand the intellectual exchanges among Muslim scholars of Eurasia and Africa and the contributions Muslim scholars made to later civilizations in the areas of science, geography, mathematics, philosophy, medicine, art, and literature.	L9 The Origins and Spread of Islam L11 Muslim Innovations and Adaptations U2 Timeline: Islam in Medieval Times
7.3 Students analyze the geographic, political, economic, religious, and social structures of the civilizations of China in the Middle Ages.	U5 Setting the Stage: Imperial China L12 From the Crusades to New Muslim Empires L14 The Evolution of Religion in South Asia L19 The Political Development of Imperial China L20 China Develops a New Economy L22 China's Contacts with the Outside World U5 Timeline: Imperial China
1. Describe the reunification of China under the Tang Dynasty and reasons for the spread of Buddhism in Tang China, Korea, and Japan.	L14 The Evolution of Religion in South Asia L19 The Political Development of Imperial China L20 China Develops a New Economy L22 China's Contacts with the Outside World L23 The Influence of Neighboring Cultures on Japan
2. Describe agricultural, technological, and commercial developments during the Tang and Sung periods.	L20 China Develops a New Economy L21 Chinese Discoveries and Inventions L22 China's Contacts with the Outside World U5 Timeline: Imperial China
3. Analyze the influences of Confucianism and changes in Confucian thought during the Sung and Mongol periods.	L19 The Political Development of Imperial China
4. Understand the importance of both overland trade and maritime expeditions between China and other civilizations in the Mongol Ascendancy and Ming Dynasty.	L19 The Political Development of Imperial China L22 China's Contacts with the Outside World L31 The Mongol Empire
5. Trace the historic influence of such discoveries as tea, the manufacture of paper, woodblock printing, the compass, and gunpowder.	L21 Chinese Discoveries and Inventions
6. Describe the development of the imperial state and the scholar-official class.	L19 The Political Development of Imperial China L22 China's Contacts with the Outside World

Standards	Where Standards Are Addressed
7.4 Students analyze the geographic, political, economic, religious, and social structures of the sub-Saharan civilizations of Ghana and Mali in Medieval Africa.	U4 Setting the Stage: The Culture and Kingdoms of West Africa L15 Early Societies in West Africa L16 Ghana: A West African Trading Empire L17 The Influence of Islam on West Africa U4 Timeline: The Culture and Kingdoms of West Africa
1. Study the Niger River and the relationship of vegetation zones of forest, savannah, and desert to trade in gold, salt, food, and slaves; and the growth of the Ghana and Mali empires.	U4 Setting the Stage: The Culture and Kingdoms of West Africa L15 Early Societies in West Africa L16 Ghana: A West African Trading Empire L17 The Influence of Islam on West Africa
2. Analyze the importance of family, labor specialization, and regional commerce in the development of states and cities in West Africa.	L15 Early Societies in West Africa
3. Describe the role of the trans-Saharan caravan trade in the changing religious and cultural characteristics of West Africa and the influence of Islamic beliefs, ethics, and law.	L16 Ghana: A West African Trading Empire L17 The Influence of Islam on West Africa U4 Timeline: The Culture and Kingdoms of West Africa
4. Trace the growth of the Arabic language in government, trade, and Islamic scholarship in West Africa.	L17 The Influence of Islam on West Africa L18 The Cultural Legacy of West Africa U4 Timeline: The Culture and Kingdoms of West Africa
5. Describe the importance of written and oral traditions in the transmission of African history and culture.	L18 The Cultural Legacy of West Africa
7.5 Students analyze the geographic, political, economic, religious, and social structures of the civilizations of Medieval Japan.	U6 Setting the Stage: Japan During Medieval Times L23 The Influence of Neighboring Cultures on Japan L24 Heian-kyo: The Heart of Japan's Golden Age L25 The Rise of the Warrior Class in Japan
1. Describe the significance of Japan's proximity to China and Korea and the intellectual, linguistic, religious, and philosophical influence of those countries on Japan.	L14 The Evolution of Religion in South Asia L23 The Influence of Neighboring Cultures on Japan L24 Heian-kyo: The Heart of Japan's Golden Age U6 Timeline: Japan During Medieval Times
2. Discuss the reign of Prince Shotoku of Japan and the characteristics of Japanese society and family life during his reign.	L23 The Influence of Neighboring Cultures on Japan
3. Describe the values, social customs, and traditions prescribed by the lord-vassal system consisting of *shogun*, *daimyo*, and *samurai* and the lasting influence of the warrior code in the twentieth century.	L25 The Rise of the Warrior Class in Japan
4. Trace the development of distinctive forms of Japanese Buddhism.	L23 The Influence of Neighboring Cultures on Japan L25 The Rise of the Warrior Class in Japan

Standards	Where Standards Are Addressed
5. Study the ninth and tenth centuries' golden age of literature, art, and drama and its lasting effects on culture today, including Murasaki Shikibu's *Tale of Genji*.	L24 Heian-kyo: The Heart of Japan's Golden Age U6 Timeline: Japan During Medieval Times
6. Analyze the rise of a military society in the late twelfth century and the role of the samurai in that society.	L24 Heian-kyo: The Heart of Japan's Golden Age L25 The Rise of the Warrior Class in Japan
7.6 Students analyze the geographic, political, economic, religious, and social structures of the civilizations of Medieval Europe.	U1 Setting the Stage: Europe During Medieval Times L4 The Development of Feudalism in Western Europe L5 The Roman Catholic Church in Medieval Europe L6 Life in Medieval Towns L7 The Decline of Feudalism L12 From the Crusades to New Muslim Empires U1 Timeline: Europe During Medieval Times
1. Study the geography of the Europe and the Eurasian land mass, including its location, topography, waterways, vegetation, and climate and their relationship to ways of life in Medieval Europe.	U1 Setting the Stage: Europe During Medieval Times L6 Life in Medieval Towns
2. Describe the spread of Christianity north of the Alps and the roles played by the early church and by monasteries in its diffusion after the fall of the western half of the Roman Empire.	L4 The Development of Feudalism in Western Europe L5 The Roman Catholic Church in Medieval Europe
3. Understand the development of feudalism, its role in the medieval European economy, the way in which it was influenced by physical geography (the role of the manor and the growth of towns), and how feudal relationships provided the foundation of political order.	L4 The Development of Feudalism in Western Europe L6 Life in Medieval Towns
4. Demonstrate an understanding of the conflict and co-operation between the Papacy and European monarchs (e.g., Charlemagne, Gregory VII, Emperor Henry IV).	L4 The Development of Feudalism in Western Europe L5 The Roman Catholic Church in Medieval Europe L7 The Decline of Feudalism U1 Timeline: Europe During Medieval Times
5. Know the significance of developments in medieval English legal and constitutional practices and their importance in the rise of modern democratic thought and representative institutions (e.g., Magna Carta, parliament, development of habeas corpus, an independent judiciary in England).	L6 Life in Medieval Towns L7 The Decline of Feudalism L40 The Enlightenment
6. Discuss the causes and course of the religious Crusades and their effects on the Christian, Muslim, and Jewish populations in Europe, with emphasis on the increasing contact by Europeans with cultures of the Eastern Mediterranean world.	L5 The Roman Catholic Church in Medieval Europe L12 From the Crusades to New Muslim Empires U2 Timeline: Islam in Medieval Times

Standards	Where Standards Are Addressed
7. Map the spread of the bubonic plague from Central Asia to China, the Middle East, and Europe and describe its impact on global population.	L6 Life in Medieval Towns L7 The Decline of Feudalism L11 Muslim Innovations and Adaptations
8. Understand the importance of the Catholic church as a political, intellectual, and aesthetic institution (e.g., founding of universities, political and spiritual roles of the clergy, creation of monastic and mendicant religious orders, preservation of the Latin language and religious texts, St. Thomas Aquinas's synthesis of classical philosophy with Christian theology, and the concept of "natural law").	L5 The Roman Catholic Church in Medieval Europe
9. Know the history of the decline of Muslim rule in the Iberian Peninsula that culminated in the Reconquista and the rise of Spanish and Portuguese kingdoms.	L12 From the Crusades to New Muslim Empires
7.7 Students compare and contrast the geographic, political, economic, religious, and social structures of the Meso-American and Andean civilizations.	U7 Setting the Stage: Civilizations of the Americas L28 Daily Life in Tenochtitlán L29 The Incas U7 Timeline: Civilizations of the Americas
1. Study the locations, landforms, and climates of Mexico, Central America, and South America and their effects on Mayan, Aztec, and Incan economies, trade, and development of urban societies.	U7 Setting the Stage: Civilizations of the Americas L26 The Maya L27 The Aztecs L28 Daily Life in Tenochtitlán L29 The Incas U7 Timeline: Civilizations of the Americas
2. Study the roles of people in each society, including class structures, family life, warfare, religious beliefs and practices, and slavery.	L26 The Maya L27 The Aztecs L28 Daily Life in Tenochtitlán L29 The Incas
3. Explain how and where each empire arose and how the Aztec and Incan empires were defeated by the Spanish.	L26 The Maya L27 The Aztecs L29 The Incas L38 The Age of Exploration U7 Timeline: Civilizations of the Americas
4. Describe the artistic and oral traditions and architecture in the three civilizations.	L26 The Maya L27 The Aztecs L28 Daily Life in Tenochtitlán L30 Achievements of the Maya, Aztecs, and Incas U7 Timeline: Civilizations of the Americas
5. Describe the Meso-American achievements in astronomy and mathematics, including the development of the calendar and the Meso-American knowledge of seasonal changes to the civilizations' agricultural systems.	L26 The Maya L27 The Aztecs L28 Daily Life in Tenochtitlán L30 Achievements of the Maya, Aztecs, and Incas U7 Timeline: Civilizations of the Americas

Standards	Where Standards Are Addressed
7.8 Students analyze the origins, accomplishments, and geographic diffusion of the Renaissance.	U9 Setting the Stage: Europe's Renaissance and Reformation L3 The Legacy of the Roman Empire L33 The Renaissance Begins L34 Florence: The Cradle of the Renaissance L35 Leading Figures of the Renaissance U9 Timeline: Europe's Renaissance and Reformation
1. Describe the way in which the revival of classical learning and the arts fostered a new interest in humanism (i.e., a balance between intellect and religious faith).	L33 The Renaissance Begins L34 Florence: The Cradle of the Renaissance U9 Timeline: Europe's Renaissance and Reformation
2. Explain the importance of Florence in the early stages of the Renaissance and the growth of independent trading cities (e.g., Venice), with emphasis on the cities' importance in the spread of Renaissance ideas.	U9 Setting the Stage: Europe's Renaissance and Reformation L33 The Renaissance Begins L34 Florence: The Cradle of the Renaissance L35 Leading Figures of the Renaissance
3. Understand the effects of the reopening of the ancient "Silk Road" between Europe and China, including Marco Polo's travels and the location of his routes.	L31 The Mongol Empire L33 The Renaissance Begins
4. Describe the growth and effects of new ways of disseminating information (e.g., the ability to manufacture paper, translation of the Bible into the vernacular, printing).	L35 Leading Figures of the Renaissance L36 The Reformation Begins L37 The Spread and Impact of the Reformation
5. Detail advances made in literature, the arts, science, mathematics, cartography, engineering, and the understanding of human anatomy and astronomy (e.g., by Dante Alighieri, Leonardo da Vinci, Michelangelo di Buonarroti Simoni, Johann Gutenberg, William Shakespeare).	L33 The Renaissance Begins L34 Florence: The Cradle of the Renaissance L35 Leading Figures of the Renaissance L38 The Age of Exploration U9 Timeline: Europe's Renaissance and Reformation
7.9 Students analyze the historical developments of the Reformation.	U9 Setting the Stage: Europe's Renaissance and Reformation L36 The Reformation Begins L37 The Spread and Impact of the Reformation U9 Timeline: Europe's Renaissance and Reformation
1. List the causes for the internal turmoil in and weakening of the Catholic church (e.g., tax policies, selling of indulgences).	U9 Setting the Stage: Europe's Renaissance and Reformation L36 The Reformation Begins
2. Describe the theological, political, and economic ideas of the major figures during the Reformation (e.g., Desiderius Erasmus, Martin Luther, John Calvin, William Tyndale).	L36 The Reformation Begins L37 The Spread and Impact of the Reformation

Standards	Where Standards Are Addressed
3. Explain Protestants' new practices of church self-government and the influence of those practices on the development of democratic practices and ideas of federalism.	L37 The Spread and Impact of the Reformation
4. Identify and locate the European regions that remained Catholic and those that became Protestant and explain how the division affected the distribution of religions in the New World.	L37 The Spread and Impact of the Reformation
5. Analyze how the Counter-Reformation revitalized the Catholic church and the forces that fostered the movement (e.g., St. Ignatius of Loyola and the Jesuits, the Council of Trent).	L37 The Spread and Impact of the Reformation
6. Understand the institution and impact of missionaries on Christianity and the diffusion of Christianity from Europe to other parts of the world in the medieval and early modern periods; locate missions on a world map.	L37 The Spread and Impact of the Reformation
7. Describe the Golden Age of cooperation between Jews and Muslims in medieval Spain that promoted creativity in art, literature, and science, including how that cooperation was terminated by the religious persecution of individuals and groups (e.g., the Spanish Inquisition and the expulsion of Jews and Muslims from Spain in 1492).	L11 Muslim Innovations and Adaptations L12 From the Crusades to New Muslim Empires L35 Leading Figures of the Renaissance L37 The Spread and Impact of the Reformation
7.10 Students analyze the historical developments of the Scientific Revolution and its lasting effect on religious, political, and cultural institutions.	U10 Setting the Stage: Europe Enters the Modern Age L39 The Scientific Revolution U10 Timeline: Europe Enters the Modern Age
1. Discuss the roots of the Scientific Revolution (e.g., Greek rationalism; Jewish, Christian, and Muslim science; Renaissance humanism; new knowledge from global exploration).	L39 The Scientific Revolution
2. Understand the significance of the new scientific theories (e.g., those of Copernicus, Galileo, Kepler, Newton) and the significance of new inventions (e.g., the telescope, microscope, thermometer, barometer).	U10 Setting the Stage: Europe Enters the Modern Age L34 Florence: The Cradle of the Renaissance L35 Leading Figures of the Renaissance L39 The Scientific Revolution
3. Understand the scientific method advanced by Bacon and Descartes, the influence of new scientific rationalism on the growth of democratic ideas, and the coexistence of science with traditional religious beliefs.	L39 The Scientific Revolution L40 The Enlightenment

Standards	Where Standards Are Addressed
7.11 Students analyze political and economic change in the sixteenth, seventeenth, and eighteenth centuries (the Age of Exploration, the Enlightenment, and the Age of Reason).	U10 Setting the Stage: Europe Enters the Modern Age L35 Leading Figures of the Renaissance L38 The Age of Exploration L40 The Enlightenment
1. Know the great voyages of discovery, the locations of the routes, and the influence of cartography in the development of a new European worldview.	U10 Setting the Stage: Europe Enters the Modern Age L35 Leading Figures of the Renaissance L38 The Age of Exploration
2. Discuss the exchanges of plants, animals, technology, culture, and ideas among Europe, Africa, Asia, and the Americas in the fifteenth and sixteenth centuries and the major economic and social effects on each continent.	U10 Setting the Stage: Europe Enters the Modern Age L35 Leading Figures of the Renaissance L38 The Age of Exploration
3. Examine the origins of modern capitalism; the influence of mercantilism and cottage industry; the elements and importance of a market economy in seventeenth-century Europe; the changing international trading and marketing patterns, including their locations on a world map; and the influence of explorers and map makers.	L38 The Age of Exploration
4. Explain how the main ideas of the Enlightenment can be traced back to such movements as the Renaissance, the Reformation, and the Scientific Revolution and to the Greeks, Romans, and Christianity.	L40 The Enlightenment
5. Describe how democratic thought and institutions were influenced by Enlightenment thinkers (e.g., John Locke, Charles-Louis Montesquieu, American founders).	L40 The Enlightenment
6. Discuss how the principles in the Magna Carta were embodied in such documents as the English Bill of Rights and the American Declaration of Independence.	L40 The Enlightenment

Standards	Where Standards Are Addressed
CHRONOLOGICAL AND SPATIAL THINKING	
1. Students explain how major events are related to one another in time.	U1 Timeline: Europe During Medieval Times L3 The Legacy of the Roman Empire L7 The Decline of Feudalism L8 The Byzantine Empire U2 Timeline: Islam in Medieval Times U3 Timeline: South Asia, 300–1200 U4 Timeline: The Culture and Kingdoms of West Africa U5 Timeline: Imperial China U6 Timeline: Japan During Medieval Times U7 Timeline: Civilizations of the Americas U8 Timeline: The Medieval World, 1200–1490 U9 Timeline: Europe's Renaissance and Reformation U10 Timeline: Europe Enters the Modern Age L39 The Scientific Revolution
2. Students construct various time lines of key events, people, and periods of the historical era they are studying.	U1 Timeline: Europe During Medieval Times L2 The Origins and Spread of Christianity U2 Timeline: Islam in Medieval Times L9 The Origins and Spread of Islam U3 Timeline: South Asia, 300–1200 U4 Timeline: The Culture and Kingdoms of West Africa L17 The Influence of Islam on West Africa U5 Timeline: Imperial China U6 Timeline: Japan During Medieval Times U7 Timeline: Civilizations of the Americas L26 The Maya U8 Timeline: The Medieval World, 1200–1490 U9 Timeline: Europe's Renaissance and Reformation U10 Timeline: Europe Enters the Modern Age
3. Students use a variety of maps and documents to identify physical and cultural features of neighborhoods, cities, states, and countries and to explain the historical migration of people, expansion and disintegration of empires, and the growth of economic systems.	Program Introduction: The World in 300 C.E. U1 Setting the Stage: Europe During Medieval Times L1 From Republic to Empire L6 Life in Medieval Towns L7 The Decline of Feudalism U2 Setting the Stage: Islam in Medieval Times L9 The Origins and Spread of Islam L12 From the Crusades to New Muslim Empires U3 Setting the Stage: South Asia, 300–1200 U4 Setting the Stage: The Culture and Kingdoms of West Africa L15 Early Societies in West Africa U5 Setting the Stage: Imperial China U6 Setting the Stage: Japan During Medieval Times U7 Setting the Stage: Civilizations of the Americas L26 The Maya U8 Setting the Stage: The Medieval World, 1200–1490 U9 Setting the Stage: Europe's Renaissance and Reformation L37 The Spread and Impact of the Reformation U10 Setting the Stage: Europe Enters the Modern Age

Standards	Where Standards Are Addressed
RESEARCH, EVIDENCE, AND POINT OF VIEW	
1. Students frame questions that can be answered by historical study and research.	Program Introduction: The World in 300 C.E. L7 The Decline of Feudalism L10 Learning About World Religions: Islam L12 From the Crusades to New Muslim Empires L14 The Evolution of Religion in South Asia L19 The Political Development of Imperial China L24 Heian-kyo: The Heart of Japan's Golden Age L31 The Mongol Empire
2. Students distinguish fact from opinion in historical narratives and stories.	L3 The Legacy of the Roman Empire L4 The Development of Feudalism in Western Europe L5 The Roman Catholic Church in Medieval Europe L11 Muslim Innovations and Adaptations L13 The Achievements of the Gupta Empire L23 The Influence of Neighboring Cultures on Japan
3. Students distinguish relevant from irrelevant information, essential from incidental information, and verifiable from unverifiable information in historical narratives and stories.	L3 The Legacy of the Roman Empire L4 The Development of Feudalism in Western Europe L6 Life in Medieval Towns L8 The Byzantine Empire L11 Muslim Innovations and Adaptations L13 The Achievements of the Gupta Empire L16 Ghana: A West African Trading Empire L17 The Influence of Islam on West Africa L22 China's Contacts with the Outside World L28 Daily Life in Tenochtitlán
4. Students assess the credibility of primary and secondary sources and draw sound conclusions from them.	L8 The Byzantine Empire L12 From the Crusades to New Muslim Empires L19 The Political Development of Imperial China L24 Heian-kyo: The Heart of Japan's Golden Age L33 The Renaissance Begins L40 The Enlightenment
5. Students detect the different historical points of view on historical events and determine the context in which the historical statements were made (the questions asked, sources used, author's perspectives).	L7 The Decline of Feudalism L12 From the Crusades to New Muslim Empires L26 The Maya L40 The Enlightenment

Standards	Where Standards Are Addressed
HISTORICAL INTERPRETATION	
1. Students explain the central issues and problems from the past, placing people and events in a matrix of time and place.	Program Introduction: The World in 300 C.E. L1 From Republic to Empire L4 The Development of Feudalism in Western Europe L7 The Decline of Feudalism L8 The Byzantine Empire L11 Muslim Innovations and Adaptations L17 The Influence of Islam on West Africa L35 Leading Figures of the Renaissance L40 The Enlightenment
2. Students understand and distinguish cause, effect, sequence, and correlation in historical events, including the long- and short-term causal relations.	L1 From Republic to Empire L2 The Origins and Spread of Christianity L7 The Decline of Feudalism L8 The Byzantine Empire L12 From the Crusades to New Muslim Empires L20 China Develops a New Economy L27 The Aztecs L33 The Renaissance Begins L36 The Reformation Begins L38 The Age of Exploration
3. Students explain the sources of historical continuity and how the combination of ideas and events explains the emergence of new patterns.	L5 The Roman Catholic Church in Medieval Europe L8 The Byzantine Empire L14 The Evolution of Religion in South Asia L18 The Cultural Legacy of West Africa L33 The Renaissance Begins L36 The Reformation Begins L39 The Scientific Revolution L40 The Enlightenment
4. Students recognize the role of chance, oversight, and error in history.	L35 Leading Figures of the Renaissance L38 The Age of Exploration L39 The Scientific Revolution
5. Students recognize that interpretations of history are subject to change as new information is uncovered.	L25 The Rise of the Warrior Class in Japan L28 Daily Life in Tenochtitlán L39 The Scientific Revolution
6. Students interpret basic indicators of economic performance and conduct cost-benefit analyses of economic and political issues.	L1 From Republic to Empire L15 Early Societies in West Africa L16 Ghana: A West African Trading Empire L19 The Political Development of Imperial China L22 China's Contacts with the Outside World L35 Leading Figures of the Renaissance L38 The Age of Exploration

Lesson 1
24: Caesar, Augustus, at www.quotation-books.com.

Lesson 3
41: John Henry Parker, *The Archaeology of Rome,* Vols. 1-3 (Oxford: J. Parker and Co., 1874), at www.books.google.com.

Lesson 4
54: Einhard, *Life of Charlemagne,* trans. Samuel Epes Turner (New York: Harper & Brothers, 1880), at www.books.google.com. Poet, in Robert MacHenry and Philip W. Goetz, eds., *The New Encyclopædia Britannica,* Part 3, Vol. 4 (Chicago: Encyclopædia Britannica, 1983).

Lesson 7
94: Joan of Arc, *Joan of Arc, Self Portrait,* trans. Willard Trask (New York: Stackpole Sons, 1936). 95: Joan of Arc, in Mary Gordon, *Joan of Arc: A Life* (New York: Penguin Books, 2000). 96: Joan of Arc, *Joan of Arc, Self Portrait.* 97: Joan of Arc, *Joan of Arc: In Her Own Words,* trans. Willard Trask (New York: Turtle Point Press, 1996). Bishop Pierre Cauchon, in ibid. Joan of Arc, in ibid. Ibid.

Lesson 8
100: Geoffroi de Villehardouin, in Charles Diehl, *Byzantium: Greatness and Decline,* trans. Naomi Walford (New Brunswick, NJ: Rutgers University Press, 1957). 101: Procopius, *The Secret History,* trans. Richard Atwater (New York: Cosimo, 1927). 107: Oliver J. Thatcher, ed., "The Institutions of Justinian, Book I. Of Persons," in *The Library of Original Sources* (Milwaukee: University Research Extension Co., 1907). 109: Procopius, Procopius, *Literally and Completely Translated From the Greeks for the First Time* (Athens: The Athenian Society's Publications, 1816).

Lesson 11
141: Historian, in Linda S. George, *The Golden Age of Islam* (New York: Benchmark Books, 1998). 142: Muhammad, in ibid. 147: Three lines of verse by Rabi'a from THE ILLUSTRATED WORLD'S RELIGIONS: A GUIDE TO OUR WISDOM TRADITONS BY HUSTON SMITH. Copyright ©1994 by Huston Smith. Reprinted by permission of HarperCollins Publishers. 150: Anonymous, in Charles Perry, "Cooking with the Caliphs," *Saudi Aramco World,* July/Aug. 2006, at www.saudiaramcoworld.com. 157: di Tura, Agnolo in William M. Bowsky, *The Black Death: A Turning Point in History?* (New York: Holt, Rinehart and Winston, 1971) 158: Al-Maqrizi in IM Alazzam, SM Alazzam, and KM Al-Mazyid, "Plagues, epidemics and their social and economic impact on the Egyptian society during the Mameluk Period," in *Asian Culture and History* Vol. 5 No. 2, (Canadian Center of Science and Education, 2013)

Lesson 12
173: Dana Carleton Munro, ed., *Letters of the Crusaders* (Revised Edition), (Philadelphia: The Department of History of the University of Pennsylvania, 1902). 174: August C. Krey, *The First Crusades; The Accounts of Eyewitness and Participants* (Princeton: Princeton University Press, 1921). 175: James Harvey Robinson, *Readings in European History* vol. 1 of *From the Breaking Up of the Roman Empire to the Protestant Revolt* (Boston: Ginn & Company, 1904).

Lesson 16
216: Historian, in A. Adu Boahen and Alvin M. Josephy, *The Horizon History of Africa,* Vol. 1 (New York: American Heritage, 1971).

Lesson 17
235: Al-Umari, in Patricia McKissack and Frederick McKissack, *The Royal Kingdoms of Ghana, Mali and Songhay: Life in Medieval Africa* (New York: Henry Holt, 1995). 237: Ibn Battuta, in Editors of Time-Life Books, *Africa's Glorious Legacy* (Alexandria, VA: Time-Life Books, 1994). 243–245: From: "Travels in Asia and Africa 1325–1354," Ibn Battuta and H.A.R. Gibb (trans.) Copyright © 2005, RoutledgeCurzon. Reproduced by permission of Taylor & Francis Books UK.

Lesson 18
256: J. D. Considine and Michaelangelo Matos, "Biography: Youssou N'Dour," *Rolling Stone,* 2004, at www.rollingstone.com.

Lesson 19
267: Herbert Allen Giles, ed. and trans., *Gems of Chinese Literature* (B. Quaritch, 1884), at www.books.google.com. 274: John Barrow, Travels in China, Containing Descriptions, Observations, and Comparisons, Made and Collected in Course of a Short Residence at the Imperial Palace of Yuen-Min-Yuen, and on a Subsequent Journey Through the Country from Pekin to Canton. (London: A. Strahan, Printers-Street: 1804). 275: O. Shimizu, M. Hirose, and James Legge, trans., The Original Chinese Texts of the Work of Laou-Tsze, The Great Learning, The Doctrine of Man (Hongkong: At the Author's, 1861). 276: A Cultural History of Civil Examinations in Late Imperial China, by Benjamin A. Elman, © 2000 by the Regents of the University of California. Published by the University of California Press.

Lesson 20
279: Marco Polo, *The Travels of Marco Polo, the Venetian* (Adamant Media Corporation, 2005). 284: Marco Polo, in Patricia Buckley Ebrey, *The Cambridge Illustrated History of China* (Cambridge: Cambridge University Press, 1996).

Lesson 22
299: Joanna Waley-Cohen, *The Sextants of Beijing: Global Currents in Chinese History* (New York: W. W. Norton, 1999). 304: Emperor Chengzu, in U.S.-China Peoples Friendship Association, U.S.-China Review, Vol. 28 (U.S.-China People's Friendship Association, 2004). 306: Anonymous, in Laurence Bergreen, *Over the Edge of the World: Magellan's Terrifying Circumnavigation of the Globe* (New York: HarperCollins, 2003). Emperor Chengzu, in Zheng He, "Zheng He's Inscription," at www.hist.umn.edu. 308: Ma Huan, in Gavin Menzies, *1421: The Year China Discovered America* (New York: HarperCollins, 2003 [first printed 2002, by Transword Pub.]). Zheng He, "Zheng He's Inscription," at www.hist.umn.edu. 309: Zheng He, "Zheng He's Inscription," at www.hist.umn.edu.

Lesson 23
323: Prince Shotoku, in Frank Brinkley, *A History of the Japanese People from the Earliest Times to the End of the Meiji Era* (New York: The Encyclopædia Britannica Co., 1915). 325: Japanese emperor (552 A.D.), in W. G. Aston, ed. and trans., *Nihongi: Chronicles of Japan from the Earliest Times to A.D. 697* Vol. 1 (London: Kegan Paul, Trench, Trübner and Co., 1896), at www.books.google.com. 327:

Japanese poet, in Edwin O. Reischauer and Albert M. Craig, *Japan: Tradition and Transformation,* rev. ed. (Cambridge, MA: Harvard University Press, 1989).

Lesson 24
334: Fujiwara Michinaga, in Ivan Morris, *The World of the Shining Prince: Court Life in Ancient Japan* (New York: Kodansha America, Inc., 1994 [originally published in 1964]). **339:** From *The Pillowbook of Sei Shonagon,* by Ivan Morris, trans. and ed. Copyright © 1991 Columbia University Press. Reprinted with permission from the publisher. **342:** Murasaki Shibiku in *A Hundred Verses from Old Japan,* trans. William N. Porter, (Oxford: Clarendon Press, 1909). **343:** "The Diary of Murasaki Shibiku" in *Diaries of Court Ladies of Old Japan,* trans. Annie Shepley Omori and Kochi Doi, ed. Amy Lowell (Boston: Houghton Mifflin Company, 1929). **344:** "The Sharashina Diary" in *Diaries of Court Ladies of Old Japan,* trans. Annie Shepley Omori and Kochi Doi, ed. Amy Lowell (Boston: Houghton Mifflin Company, 1929). **345:** "The Diary of Murasaki Shibiku" in *Diaries of Court Ladies of Old Japan,* trans. Annie Shepley Omori and Kochi Doi, ed. Amy Lowell (Boston: Houghton Mifflin Company, 1929).

Lesson 25
348: Samurai writer, in *Mikiso Hane, Japan: A Historical Survey* (Charles Scribner's Sons, 1972). **353:** From FROM THE COUNTRY OF EIGHT ISLANDS by Hiroaki Sato and Burton Watson, copyright © 1981 by Hiroaki Sato and Burton Watson. Used by permission of Doubleday, a division of Random House, Inc. **360:** Anonymous, in Helen Craig McCullough, trans., *The Tale of the Heike* (Stanford, CA: Stanford University Press, 1988). Ibid. **361:** Ibid. **363:** Anonymous, in Chieko Irie Mulhern, ed., *Heroic with Grace: Legendary Women of Japan* (New York: M.E. Sharpe, 1991).

Lesson 27
383: Diego Durán, *The History of the Indies of New Spain,* trans. Doris Heyden (Norman, OK: University of Oklahoma Press, 1993).

Lesson 30
431: Ephraim George Squier, in John Noble Wilford, "How the Inca Leapt Canyons," *New York Times,* May 8, 2007, at www.nytimes.com. Helaine Silverman, in "Transcripts: Secrets of Lost Empires: Inca," airdate Feb. 11, 1997, at www.pbs.org.

Lesson 32
451: James I of Aragon, in John Forster trans., *The Book of Deeds,* http://libro.uca.edu/chronicleofjames/chronicle.htm

Lesson 33
471: Francesco Petrarch, "Sonnet CXXVI" in *The Sonnets, Triumphs, and Other Poems of Petrarch,* ed. Thomas Campbell (London: George Bell and Sons, 1875). **472:** Francesco Petrarch, "On the Nature of Poetry," *in Petrarch; The First Modern Scholar and Man of Letters,* ed. James Harvey Robinson and Henry Winchester Rolfe (New York: G. P. Putnam's Sons, 1909). **473:** Giovanni Boccacio, "The Plague of Florence," in *The World's Literature Illuminate* vol. 3, ed. J.P. Lamberton (Chicago: The Century Society, 1900).

Lesson 34
479: Giorgio Vasari, in Irene Earls, *Artists of the Renaissance* (New York: Greenwood Press, 2004).

Lesson 35
490: Titian, at www.getty.edu. Charles V, at www.getty.edu. **498:** King Phillip III, in Clifton Fadiman and John S. Major, *The New Lifetime Reading Plan* (New York: HarperCollins, 1997). **503:** Archbishop of Mainz, in Stephan Füssel, *Gutenberg and the Impact of Printing,* trans. Douglas Martin (Burlington, VT: Ashgate Pub., 2003 [first published 1999, by Insel Verlag Frankfurt am Main and Leipzig]).

Lesson 36
509: Martin Luther, in David S. Schaff, *John Huss: His Life, Teachings, and Death, After Five Hundred Years* (New York: Charles Scribner's Sons, 1915).

Lesson 37
516: Martin Luther, in Alister E. McGrath, *Historical Theology: An Introduction to the History of Christian Thought* (Malden, MA: Blackwell Pub., 1998). **518:** Martin Luther, *Luther's Large Catechism,* trans. John Nicholas Lenker (Minneapolis, MN: The Luther Press, 1908).

Lesson 38
535: Antonio Pigafetta, in Laurence Bergreen, *Over the Edge of the World: Magellan's Terrifying Circumnavigation of the Globe* (New York: HarperCollinss, 2003). **540:** Admiral Affonso de Albuquerque, in Craig Lockard, *Southeast Asia in World History* (New York: Oxford University Press, 2009). **550:** Lewis Henke, *The Spanish Struggle for Justice in the Conquest of America* (Dallas, TX: Southern Methodist University Press, 2002). **551:** Antonio de Montesinos, in ibid. Lewis Henke, *The Spanish Struggle for Justice in the Conquest of America.* **552:** Bartolomé de las Casas, in Francis Patrick Sullivan, *Indian Freedom: The Cause of Bartolomé de las Casas, 1484–1566: A Reader* (Kansas City, MO: Sheed and Ward, 1995). **553:** Juan Ginés Sepúlveda, in Rolena Adorno, *The Polemics of Possession in Spanish American Narrative* (New Haven, CT: Yale University Press, 2007).

Lesson 39
562: Antonie van Leeuwenhoek, in Robert Bingham Downs, *Landmarks in Science: Hippocrates to Carson* (Santa Barbara, CA: ABC-CLIO, 1982).

Lesson 40
565: Bernard de Fontenelle, in A. C. Grayling, *Britannica Guide to the Ideas That Made the Modern World* (London: Robinson, 2008). **568:** Thomas Hobbes, *Levianthan,* introduction by C. B. Macpherson (New York: Penguin Books, 1985 [first published 1651]). **571:** Voltaire, in Paul Edwards, ed., *The Encyclopedia of Philosophy,* Vol. 8 (New York: Macmillan, 1972). S. G. Tallentyre, Friends of Voltaire (New York: G. P. Putnam's Sons, 1907). **574:** Abigail Adams, in a letter to John Adams, Mar. 31, 1776, at www.thelizlibrary.org. Mary Wollstonecraft, *A Vindication of the Rights of Woman,* ed. Carol H. Poston (New York: Norton, 1988). **576:** John Locke, "Two Treatises of Government," in *The Works of John Locke* vol. 5 (London, 1823). **577:** Baron de Montesquieu. *Montesquieu: The Spirit of Laws* (1748). Edited by David W. Carrithers (Berkeley: University of California Press, 1977). **578:** Cesare Beccaria, *An Essay on Crimes and Punishments* ed. 2, trans. Edward D. Ingrahm (Philadelphia: Philip H. Nicklin, 1819).

Photographs

Front Cover
Roberto Nencini/Alamy

Title Page
Roberto Nencini/Alamy

Front Matter
v: Thinkstock vii: Wikimedia viii: iStockphoto ix: Yakthai/Dreamstime x: Daniel Gilby/123RF.com xi: Yang Yu/Dreamstime xii: Library of Congress xiii: Tomasz Otap /Shutterstock xiv: Granger, NYC xv: Shutterstock xvi: Wikimedia xix: Wikimedia xxv: Thinkstock

Program Introduction
9: iStockphoto

Unit 1 Opener
10: Getty Images

Lesson 1
14: Mary Evans Picture Library/Alamy 16: INTERFOTO/Alamy 17T: iStockphoto 17B: iStockphoto 18: Rick A Dikeman 20: iStockphoto 22: Ivy Close Images/Alamy 24: Chronicle/Alamy 26: Shutterstock 27: Shutterstock 28: Shutterstock 29: Shutterstock

Lesson 2
30: Shutterstock 33: Shutterstock 34: Pavle Marjanovic/Dreamstime 35: Jozef Sedmak/Dreamstime 36: Shutterstock 37: Shutterstock 38: BaMusee des Beaux-Arts, Marseille, France/The Bridgeman Images

Lesson 3
40: David Soanes Photography/Getty Images 42: North Wind Picture Archives/Alamy 44: Brenda Kean/Alamy 45L: iStockphoto 45R: B Christopher/Alamy 46: iStockphoto 47L: iStockphoto 47R: Corbis 48: Alessandro0770/Alamy 49: Shutterstock 50: Shutterstock 51: Hill Street Studios/Blend Images/Corbis

Lesson 4
54: Scaliger/Dreamstime 55: North Wind Picture Archives/Alamy 56T: North Wind Picture Archives/Alamy 57: Aurelian Images/Alamy 58: Photos.com 59: North Wind Picture Archives/Alamy 60: Gianni Dagli Orti/The Art Archive at Art Resource, NY 61: Photos.com 62: Les Très Riches Heures du duc de Berry, Octobre the Musée Condé, Chantilly/Wikimedia 63: The Pierpont Morgan Library, New York/Art Resource, NY

Lesson 5
64: Philip Chapman/Alamy 66: Craig Lovell/Corbis 67: Wikimedia 68: Kharbine-Tapabor/The Art Archive at Art Resource, NY 69: Thinkstock 70: Malcolm Freeman/Alamy 71B: Robert Harding World Imagery/Shutterstock 71T: Shutterstock 72: Wikimedia 73: North Wind Picture Archives/Alamy 74: Steven Langford/Dreamstime 75: Zvonimir Atletic/Shutterstock

Lesson 6
76: PRISMA ARCHIVO/Alamy 79: Old Images/Alamy 80: The Bridgeman Art Library 81: Osterreichische Nationalbibliothek, Vienna, Austria/Alinari/The Bridgeman Art Library 82: Wikimedia 83: Getty Images 84: adoc-photos/Corbis 85: iStockphoto

Lesson 7
86: Heritage Image Partnership Ltd/Alamy 88: Photos.com 89: Thinkstock 91: The Art Archive at Art Resource, NY 92: Thinkstock 93: Shutterstock 94: Marek Slusarczyk/123RF.com 95B: iStockphoto 95T: iStockphoto 96: iStockphoto 97: Photos.com

Lesson 8
98: PavleMarjanovic/Shutterstock 101: Ivy Close Images/Alamy 102: terry harris just greece photo library/Alamy 103: MFarling/Dreamstime 104: Faraways/Shutterstock 105: Bettmann/Corbis 106: Getty Images 108: North Wind Picture Archives/Alamy

Unit 1 Timeline
110TL: Pavle Marjanovic/123RF.com 110TC: Dha/Wikimedia Commons 110TR: Terry Harris/Alamy 110BL: DeliDumrul/Wikimedia Commons 110BC: B.S.Karan /Shutterstock 110BR: mountainpix/Shutterstock 111TL: stocksnapp /Shutterstock 111TC: Photos.com 111TR: Photos.com 111BL: Library of Congress 111BC: Photos.com 111BR: Roberto Castillo /Shutterstock

Unit 2 Opener
112: Digital Vision/Getty Images

Lesson 9
116: Private Collection/The Stapleton Collection/The Bridgeman Art Library 119: Bird's eye view of Mecca, 1784 (engraving), French School, (18th century)/Collection of Andrew McIntosh Patrick, UK /The Bridgeman Art Library 120: Getty Images 121: iStockphoto 122: Salem Alforaih/Shutterstock 123: The First Four Caliphs, plate 31 from Part III, Volume I of 'The History of the Nations', engraved by V. Raineri (aquatint), Italian School, (19th century)/Private Collection/The Stapleton Collection/The Bridgeman Art Library

Lesson 10
126: Shutterstock 128: Shutterstock 129: Distinctive Images/Alamy 130: ASK Images/Alamy 131: Aleksandar Kamasi/Shutterstock 132: Godong/Alamy 133: iStockphoto 134: iStockphoto 135: Gianni Dagli Orti/The Art Archive at Art Resource, NY 136: Granger, NYC

Lesson 11
138: Shutterstock 141: Yuliang/Dreamstime 142: Gianni Dagli Orti/The Art Archive at Art Resource, NY 143: Francisco Javier Gil Oreja/123RF.com 144: iStockphoto 145: Photos.com 146: Werner Forman Archive/Art Resource, NY 147: Gianni Dagli Orti/The Art Archive at Art Resource, NY 148: Ekin Yalgin/Alamy 149: DAVID HERRAEZ/Alamy 150: Photos.com 151: Courtesy of Museum of Maritimo (Barcelona); Ramon Manent/Corbis 152: dbimages/Alamy 153: Getty Images 154: Rafael Ben-ari/Dreamstime 155: Getty Images 157: Shutterstock 158: Lanmas/Alamy 159: Westend61 GmbH/Alamy

Lesson 12
160: Gianni Dagli Orti/The Art Archive at Art Resource, NY 162: Shutterstock 164: Photos.com 164: Mary Evans Picture Library/Alamy 166: iStockphoto 167: Heritage Image Partnership Ltd/ Alamy 167: iStockphoto 169: Shutterstock 170: Photos.com 172: North Wind Picture Archives/Alamy 176: Shutterstock 177: Shutterstock

Unit 2 Timeline
178TL: ayazad/Shutterstock 178TC: Yamo/Dreamstime 178TR: 123RF.com 178BL: Getty Images 178BC: Salem Alforaih /Shutterstock 179TL: Eric Von Seggern/Shutterstock 179TR: Georgios Kollidas/Dreamstime 179BL: Aramco World 179BC: Photos.com 179BR: Photos.com

Unit 3 Opener
138: Shutterstock

Lesson 13
184: Yakthai/Dreamstime 186: Shutterstock 188: Oleksii Sergieiev/Dreamstime 189: Archivo Iconografico, S.A./Corbis 190: iStockphoto 191L: Thinkstock 191R: Shutterstock 192: National Museum, New Delhi, Delhi, India/ Borromeo/Art Resource, NY 193: Vadim Kulikov/ Dreamstime 195: ephotocorp/Alamy

Lesson 14
196: Shutterstock 198: Shutterstock 199: Shutterstock 200T: Shutterstock 200C: Shutterstock 200B: Shutterstock 201: Shutterstock 202: Shutterstock 203: iStockphoto 204: John Bennet/Alamy 206: Shutterstock 207: Shutterstock

Unit 3 Timeline
208B: 123RF.com 208TR: Wikimedia 208TL: Wikimedia 209BL: Shutterstock 209T: Ivy Close Images/Alamy 209BR: Shutterstock

Unit 4 Opener
210: John Elk III/Alamy

Lesson 15
214: Universal History Archive/UIG/ Bridgeman Images 216: Photolibrary 217: Travelscape Images/Alamy Stock Photo 218: Photos.com 219: National Geographic Creative/Alamy 220: Anthony Asael/World of Stock

Lesson 16
222: Daniel Gilby/123RF.com 224: Private Collection/Photo © Boltin Picture Library/The Bridgeman Art Library 226: Werner Forman/Art Resource, NY 228: iStockphoto 229: Christophe Boisvieux/ Corbis 230: Trevkitt/Dreamstime 231: Socrates/Dreamstime

Lesson 17
232: Donald Nausbaum/Alamy 234: Stephen Sharnoff /National Geographic/ Getty Images 235: John Webb/The Art Archive at Art Resource, NY 236: Paul Almasy/Corbis 237: next24online/ NurPhoto/Corbis 238: Shutterstock 239: Joanne Zh/Dreamstime 240: Images & Stories/Alamy 241: Paul Almasy/Corbis 246: Shutterstock 247: iStockphoto

Lesson 18
248: Margaret Courtney-Clarke/Corbis 250: Michael & Patricia Fogden/Corbis 251: Shutterstock 252: robertharding/ Alamy 253: Fulvio Roiter/Corbis 254: World History Archive/Alamy 255: Chuck Bigger/Alamy 256: NIC BOTHMA/epa/Corbis 257: C Brandon/Redferns/Getty Images 258: MJ Kim/Getty Images 259: YOSHIKAZU TSUNO/ AFP/Getty Images

Unit 4 Timeline
260TL: Kirsz Marcin /Shutterstock 260TR: Will Doherty 260BL: iStockphoto 260BC: Peter Horree/Alamy 260BR: Ramzi Hachicho/Shutterstock 261BL: iStockphoto 261TC: John Webb/ The Art Archive at Art Resource, NY 261TR: 123RF.com 261BC: Jamdotsi/ Dreamstime 261BR: Paco Ayala /123RF. com 261TL: Vorontzoff, Alexis N./ UNESCO

Unit 5 Opener
262: Shutterstock

Lesson 19
266: The Art Archive at Art Resource, NY 269: Corbis 270: Lieska/Dreamstime 271: Burstein Collection/Corbis 273: Bridgeman-Giraudon/Art Resource, NY 277: HIP/Art Resource, NY

Lesson 20
278: The Art Archive at Art Resource, NY 280L: Free Library of Philadelphia/ Giraudon/Bridgeman Art Library 280R: Free Library of Philadelphia/Giraudon/ Bridgeman Art Library 281L: bpk, Berlin/Museum fuer Asiatische Kunst, Staatliche Museen, Berlin, Germany /Jiao Bingzhen/Art Resource, NY 281R: bpk, Berlin/Museum fuer Asiatische Kunst, Staatliche Museen, Berlin, Germany / Jiao Bingzhen/Art Resource, NY 282: V&A Images, London/Art Resource, NY 283: Werner Forman Archive/Bridgeman Images 284: HIP/Art Resource, NY

Lesson 21
286: SuperStock/SuperStock 288: Kellerassel/Wikimedia Commons 289: Croquant/Wikipedia Commons 290: Yang Yu/Dreamstime 291: Victoria and Albert Museum, London/Art Resource, NY 292: DeA Picture Library/Granger, NYC 293: Jorge Royan/World of Stock 294: Science and Society/Science and Society 296: Or 11539 fol.89v Taking a pulse, from an album of scenes of life in China (w/c on paper), Chinese School, (19th century)/British Library, London, UK/Â© British Library Board. All Rights Reserved/The Bridgeman Art Library International

Lesson 22
298: Bertrandb/Dreamstime 301: Granger, NYC 302: National Palace Museum, Taipei, Taiwan, Republic of China/Granger, NYC 305: Kelsen Kong/Dreamstime. 306: Shutterstock 307: Shutterstock 308: iStockphoto 309: Shutterstock 311: Martha Bayona/ Dreamstime 312: Wikipedia 313: Wikimedia

Unit 5 Timeline
314TL: Panorama Media (Beijing) Ltd./ Alamy 314C: 123RF.com 314TR: Shutterstock 314BL: rudolphthered /Big Stock Photo 314BR: Shutterstock 315TL: Parhamr/Wikimedia Commons 315TC: Editor at large/Wikimedia Commons 315TR: yuanann/Shutterstock 315BL: iStockphoto 315BC: Ivy Close Images/ Alamy 315BR: Shutterstock

Unit 6 Opener
316: Photolibrary

Lesson 23
320: Pictures from History/Bridgeman Images 323: Gianni Dagli Orti/The Art Archive at Art Resource, NY 324: 663highland/Wikipedia Commons 325: Jordi Prat Puig/Dreamstime 326: Harvard Art Museum/Art Resource, NY 327T: Peter Horree/Alamy 327C: Tibor Bognar/Alamy 327B: Granger, NYC 328: deepblue photographer/Shutterstock 329: Akiyoko74/Dreamstime

Lesson 24
330: Japan Art Collection (JAC)/Alamy 332T: FG2/Wikimedia Commons 333: Wikimedia 334: RMN-Grand Palais/Art Resource, NY 335: DEA/G. NIMATAL-LAH/Granger, NYC 336: Thinkstock 337: Leigh Anne Meeks/Dreamstime 338: Cowardlion/Dreamstime 339: Library of Congress 340: Jeremy Wee/Dreamstime 342: Digital Image © 2016 Museum Associates/LACMA. Licensed by Art Resource, NY

Lesson 25
346: Library of Congress 348: Cowardlion/Dreamstime 349: Hulton-Deutsch Collection/Corbis 350: Aleksey Baskakov/Dreamstime 351: Lebrecht Music and Arts Photo Library/Alamy 352: Library of Congress 353: Fitzwilliam Museum, University of Cambridge, UK/Bridgeman Art Library 354: Royalty-Free/Corbis 355: iStockphoto 356: mumbojumbo/Shutterstock 357: The Art Archive at Art Resource, NY 358: Photos.com 359: Asia Stock Photos Royalty Free/Fotosearch 360: Wikimedia 361: Library of Congress 362: Library of Congress 363: Siraanamwong/Dreamstime

Unit 6 Timeline
364TL: 123RF.com 364TC: Ixuskmitl/Dreamstime 364TR: Nekosan/Dreamstime 364BL: World History Archive/Alamy 364BC: Shutterstock 364BR: Hannah/Wikimedia Commons 365TL: Cowardlion/Dreamstime 365BL: Shakko/Wikimedia Commons 365TR: LordAmeth/Wikimedia Commons 365BC: Photos.com 365BR: Aleksey Baskakov /123RF.com

Unit 7 Opener
366: Nataliya Hora/Dreamstime

Lesson 26
370: Kaia06/Dreamstime 372: Corbis RF/Alamy 374: Gianni Dagli Orti/Corbis 375: Guillohmz/Dreamstime 376: beatrice preve/Alamy 377: Sabena Jane Blackbird/Alamy 378: Swisshippo/Dreamstime 379: Erich Lessing/Art Resource, NY 380: Markwaters/Dreamstime 381: iStockphoto

Lesson 27
382: Granger, NYC 384: iStockphoto 386: Gianni Dagli Orti/Corbis 387: Ywjelle/Dreamstime 389: World History Archive/Alamy

Lesson 28
390: Schalkwijk/Art Resource, NY 392: Gianni Dagli Orti/Corbis 393: Alexandre Fagundes De Fagundes/Dreamstime 394: Bodleian Libraries/(year) /(shelf mark)/The Art Archive at Art Resource 395: Thinkstock 396: iStockphoto 397: Bridgeman Images 398: Granger, NYC 399: Leszek Wrona/Dreamstime 400: Granger, NYC 401: Granger, NYC 402: Granger, NYC 403: Granger, NYC 404: INTERFOTO/Alamy 405: Wikipedia 406: Internet Archive 407: iStockphoto

Lesson 29
408: Rfoxphoto/Dreamstime 411: Stockimo/Alamy 412: Photos.com 413: New York Public Library 414: Thinkstock 415: Granger, NYC 416: Thinkstock 417: Werner Forman Archive/Bridgeman Images 418: Werner Forman/Art Resource, NY 419: Sean Pavone/Dreamstime

Lesson 30
420: Peter Horree/Alamy 422: blickwinkel/Alamy 423: iStockphoto 424: Tomasz Otap /Shutterstock 425: Grant Faint/Getty Images 426: Photos.com 427: iStockphoto 428: Harald von Radebrecht/imageBROKER/Corbis 429: Eye Ubiquitous/Alamy 430: Glow Images/Superstock 431T: Granger, NYC 431B: Glow Images/Superstock

Unit 7 Timeline
432TL: Shutterstock 432TR: Shutterstock 432BL: Shutterstock 432BC: Shutterstock 432BR: iStockphoto 433TL: Gianni Dagli Orti/Corbis 433TC: Antonella865/Dreamstime 433TR: joseasreyes /123RF.com 433BL: El Comandante-The Field Museum Library/Wikimedia Commons 433BC: Blend Images/Alamy 433BR: iStockphoto

Unit 8 Opener
434: iStockphoto

Lesson 31
438: Wikimedia 440: Granger, NYC 442: Rudra Narayan Mitra/Dreamstime 443: INTERFOTO/Alamy 444: Vera Golovina/Dreamstime 445: Shutterstock

Lesson 32
446: Granger, NYC 448T: iStockphoto 448B: iStockphoto 449: Wikimedia 450: iStockphoto 451: Shutterstock 452: guido nardacci/Alamy 453: iStockphoto

Unit 8 Timeline
454TL: Granger, NYC 454TR: Shutterstock 454B: iStockphoto 455BL: Wikimedia 455T: Wikimedia

Unit 9 Opener
456: Bruce Shippee/123RF.com

Lesson 33
460: B.O'Kane/Alamy 461: Shutterstock 462: Shutterstock 464: Fallostupido/Dreamstime 465: Historical Picture Archive/Corbis 466: Scala/Art Resource, NY 468: Thinkstock 469: Claudio Monni/Dreamstime 470: Peter Barritt/Alamy 471: Granger, NYC 473: Alan King engraving/Alamy

Lesson 34
474: Shutterstock 476: Shutterstock 477: Shutterstock 478: Shutterstock 479: Peter Barritt/Alamy 480R: Image from: www.stpetersbasilica.org 480L: iStockphoto 481: M. Bonotto/Shutterstock 482: Lolloj/Dreamstime 483: Piya Leelaprad/Dreamstime 484: Massimo Listri/Corbis 485: Shutterstock